Acquisition Finance

Tom Speechley

Acquisition Finance

Tom Speechley

written in association with
Macfarlanes, Debt Finance Group

Tottel Publishing Ltd, Maxwelton House, 41–43 Boltro Road, Haywards Heath, West Sussex, RH16 1BJ

© Tottel Publishing Ltd 2008

A CIP Catalogue record for this book is available from the British Library.

ISBN   978 1 84592 017 3

Typeset by Phoenix, Chatham, Kent
Printed by Athenaeum Press Ltd, Gateshead, Tyne & Wear

Preface

The acquisition finance industry has become one of the great success stories of the UK financial services sector. From its focal point in the City of London, some of the world's leading practitioners are at the forefront of an innovative and highly specialized field that is constantly evolving to meet the needs of several financial sectors and ultimately a growing share of UK plc. The United States can certainly lay claim to a larger more developed market but in providing support to the myriad of discrete European M&A and buy-out markets, in addition to the thriving UK market, the UK industry can justifiably reckon itself as having a wider reach and sphere of influence. That breadth of coverage brings with it a vast intellectual infrastructure comprising bankers, accountants, lawyers and other professionals most of whom spend an unhealthy amount of time living and breathing ever more complex financial products, structures and transactions. If we are – or have been – in the golden age of private equity then we have certainly been in the golden age of acquisition finance, although at the time I write this following several months of market turmoil, there are suggestions that the golden age may have passed. Personally, I suspect not.

Acquisition finance has not always been such a big deal of course. For the first part of the 1990s when I first became involved it was certainly not a mainstream activity for finance professionals, although even then those that were involved had a sense of being involved in a relatively glamorous sector. It's all relative of course and as a junior lawyer collecting 'CPs' late into the night (after night) it's easy to lose perspective. I was very fortunate though to have started my legal career in a firm, Norton Rose, that was one of the first to acknowledge that acquisition finance was a specialist field and not merely something that bankers and banking lawyers might turn their hand to occasionally. I was also very fortunate at that time to have been working for a number of partners (Douglas Colliver, Tim Polglase, Philip Whale and Andrew Bamber) who each played a role in developing some of the legal and structuring techniques that are taken for granted now. My interest levels were increased further following a one year secondment to what was then the acquisition finance unit of RBS, lead by Leith Robertson. It was a nine person operation and several of those original members have gone on to play a major role in the development of the market in London in some form or other. It also introduced me to the commercial side of the deal and looking back it was an important turning point in my career. Not only did I know a lot more jargon, the valuable commercial insights learned stayed with me when I returned to the law. Throughout this period of my career it struck me that there was very little written on the subject of acquisition finance although perhaps hardly surprising given the hours the leading practitioners were putting in. So with that in mind I convinced Norton Rose to allow me to take off four weeks unpaid leave in the summer of 1998 to write a practical guide to the subject from a lawyer's perspective. What ultimately came out of that exercise was "Norton Rose on Acquisition Finance" which was published later that year by Butterworths. Although it is – thankfully for reasons I will mention – long out of print I would like to acknowledge the contributions of the editors. In addition to Messrs Polglase, Bamber and Whale, Stuart McAlpine of Cinven and Bruce McLaren of RBS lent their considerable expertise and names. Other contributors to that publication included Jonathan Coppin, Jill Gauntlett, Brian Greenwood, Liz Jones, Stuart Lippiatt, Tracey Paine, Isla Smith, Gilles Thieffry, Tom Vita, Ross Pooley, Katherine Watts and Iain Macdonald.

It wasn't long – a few months no more – before it became apparent that there was another reason no one had written much on the subject; the subject matter changed often and significantly. That is to say, the market and the way it structured deals was evolving noticeably. A further edition was published in 2000 (edited by Philip Whale) but by this time I had long since ventured to New York and had begun working on the sponsor side rather than for banks and in a quite different market, so I more or less forgot about UK acquisition finance. By the time I had returned to the UK in 2001 the market was almost unrecognisable from the one I had tried to summarise just three years previously, especially in terms of deal sizes and complexity but also the documentation and deal processes. On top of this there was significantly more competition across all aspects of the industry. Ultimately, it is this competition – particularly between banks, between private equity sponsors and between investor constituencies – that has driven so much of the change that has since occurred in the market. Higher prices for assets as a result of greater competition between sponsors, in particular, has been the catalyst for greater leverage in structures and the use of new financial products to meet ever more funding gaps. As it turns out the evolution of the market following 2001 has been much more pronounced than anyone would have expected back then adding a number of new aspects to the industry as a whole. And that's really why this book exists. With the earlier publication by now so out of date I certainly had a sense of not wishing to leave it at that and so in late 2003 I began again, essentially with a completely blank sheet of paper. Of course I could not have chosen worse timing and in the period since then the market has moved as much as in any prior period. We have had in effect two entirely new financial instruments take a prominent position in the market, the overhaul of the most relevant legislation, the arrival in practical terms of schemes of arrangement as a takeover tool and the most significant changes in commercial terms since the market began. Having said that, in the last six months at least, there has been a hiatus in the evolution of the market as a result of the aftershocks of the US sub-prime crisis. Even so, I see already that my attempts to summarise the pricing of various instruments don't necessarily take into account the correction that has occurred in that period. But then they are mostly in the footnotes rather than the main text for a reason. Structures too have changed significantly.

Having left the UK, acquisition finance and the law a year and a half back to join Abraaj Capital in Dubai, I have necessarily leant heavily on what resources I could count on to get this project finished and a great debt is due to my former partners and colleagues at Macfarlanes who have helped fundamentally in doing just that. I know from experience that it is an extremely big ask to expect any busy lawyer to contribute valuable time to 'initiatives' such as this but the support of my friends at Macfarlanes – led by Julian Howard and his colleagues in the Debt Finance Group – has been unstinting and invaluable. A number of people deserve specific mention. In addition to Julian Howard, whose experience of the market from a number of angles gave me great comfort, Richard Rogerson has read and commented on the whole whilst completing an avalanche of deals. Valuable contributions to various sections were also made by several of their colleagues including Graham Gibb, David Coleman, Bronwen Jones, Stephen Drewitt, Hugh Arthur, Colin Morgan and Damien Crossley with support provided by Sarah McIvor and Elaine Armour. Additional perspectives were provided by Marcus Dougherty of Latham & Watkins in New York and by John Cutler of DLA Piper in London, both leading players in their respective markets. Finally, from the buy-side market in London Peter Allan (now of Aladdin Capital) was a reliable source of market information. On a personal note, I must thank my wife Kathryn for her incredible patience in sharing pretty much all of our holidays throughout the past three years or more with a draft book on finance (and indeed for her extremely valuable help in getting the manuscripts finalised in the last few weeks).

Working within what is necessarily a dynamic sector, I have tried to provide as up to date a position as possible and, subject as follows, the statements of law and practice included in the various chapters are intended to be accurate as at 1 January, 2008. I must make one obvious caveat to this, however, and that is that pricing and structures have certainly been impacted by the market correction that has happened in the wake of the US sub-prime crisis. I have taken the view that this is temporary rather than structural and that in time both pricing and structures will move back to where they were in 2005 or 2006 even if not early 2007. As a more general matter, the 'market' can look quite different depending on your perspective and whilst I have tried hard not to take sides between capital providers and capital users certain sections may reflect the fact that for many years I approached the market from the side of the acquisition financiers. In any event it is hardly meant to be the last word on any particular topic but rather to indicate the major issues that arise in transactions.

Although I have spent the majority of my career as a lawyer, by no means is this book intended to be a legal guide. It is essentially a commercial perspective that draws upon my experiences as a transactional lawyer, as a temp banker and subsequently as a principal in private equity. I hope it will be of equal use or interest to principals as well as advisers.

Tom Speechley
Dubai
January, 2008

Contents

CHAPTER 6   SECOND LIEN DEBT
Second lien debt   225

CHAPTER 13   MULTI-JURISDICTIONAL BUY-OUTS

Glossary

acquisition financiers	banks, specialist finance houses and other institutional investors that provide senior, second lien, mezzanine, high yield, PIK and other debt based forms of finance used in buy-outs
AIM	alternative investment market of the London Stock Exchange. Originally targeted at smaller growing companies but now many established UK and international public companies' shares also trade on AIM. Unlike the main market there is no requirement for a trading history or financial track record and the regulation is generally lighter than the main market
amortise	repay the principal of a debt instrument over time in scheduled installments, often six monthly. Cf 'bullet' repayment
average life	average amount of time that a debt instrument is scheduled to be outstanding if it is repaid on time. For example a 7 year loan that is repaid in equal installment throughout its life will have an average life of 3.5 years. The same loan repaid in a single 'bullet' at year 7 will have an average life of 7 years
balloon payment	repayment of majority of the principal of a debt instrument towards the end of the term (maturity) of the instrument, usually in the last two years. Cf 'bullet' repayment
basis points or bps	hundredths of a percentage point. 100 basis points is 1%
bid	prospective takeover of a public company. May be by takeover offer or scheme of arrangement
bidco	name given to main acquisition SPV in a public-to-private
bondco	name given to SPV which acts as issuer of high yield debt
bullet	repayment of debt principal in a single amount.
capex	capital expenditure
CBO	collateralised bond obligation. A security issued by a vehicle backed by a pool of bonds including high yield. CBO issuers are a source of liquidity for the bond markets
CDO	collateralised debt obligation. A security issued by a vehicle backed by a pool of loans, bonds and other debt instruments. CDO issuers are a source of liquidity for the acquisition finance markets, particularly for B and C tranches of senior debt and junior debt

certain funds	funding that has no conditions (or substantially reduced conditionality) to drawing once signed. Is a Code requirement in public-to-privates but also used in private buy-outs
CLO	collateralised loan obligation. A security issued by a vehicle backed by a pool of loans. They are a more limited form of CDO (see above)
Code	The City Code on Takeovers and Mergers. Often shortened to the Takeover Code, the Code or the "Blue Book". It provides the main regulatory framework for acquisitions of UK listed companies. Published by the Panel (see below)
Companies House	The central registry for filing of information on UK companies as required by UK companies legislation – in particular the Companies Act 1985 as superseded by Companies Act 2006. It is located in Cardiff, Wales and is overseen by the Registrar of Companies.
condition precedent or CP	condition that must be satisfied before an agreement becomes effective. In acquisition finance context means the detailed schedule of documentary and other conditions that must be satisfied before the financiers are obliged to lend
condition subsequent or CS	condition that must be satisfied after an agreement has become effective or in acquisition finance context after drawdown of the funds
corporate acquisition	acquisition by a corporate sponsor rather than a financial sponsor (private equity house). May be leveraged with debt in a leveraged corporate acquisition
credit support	guarantee, security or a loan granted or made in support of acquisition finance facilities
CREST	the central securities depository and settlement system for the U.K. (and Irish) stock markets. Shares held electronically in CREST are said to be dematerialized although CREST can also physically hold stock certificates on the behalf of customers.
D tranche	second lien debt as used in buy-outs. The second lien forms a separate tranche within the wider senior debt package albeit on a subordinated basis
DDB	deep discount bond. Bonds that are issued at a discount to par. The bonds then accrete capital value (the redemption price increases) until they reach par value at maturity. The capital accretion is in lieu of a yield, which may have tax benefits
dividend recap	recapitalisation of a buy-out funding structure to fund a distribution to the equity investors (possibly through a holdco PIK). See also 'leveraged recap'
drag-along	right of a majority shareholder to 'drag' a minority shareholder into a sale of its stake in the business. Used by institutional equity investor (sponsor) to ensure a 100% sale of a business in an exit. Sponsor will 'drag' the management team's stake into the exit. Cf 'tag along' (which is equivalent right of a minority shareholder)

due diligence	exercise of analysis and verification of legal, financial and commercial status of target business by a prospective buyer
equity	generic term to describe the capital that is provided by equity houses and management teams to fund buy-outs together with acquisition finance. It includes 'true' equity in the form of ordinary share capital and 'quasi-equity' in the form of subordinated loan capital or redeemable preference shares
equity cure	right granted under loan agreement to allow the equity investor to 'cure a breach of a financial covenant by investing further equity in the borrower group
equity house	private equity institution. Also called the 'sponsor' in a buy-out. Most equity houses manage funds raised from institutional wholesale fund managers including pension funds, insurance funds, endowments, foundations and fund of fund investors as well as high net worth individuals and family offices of wealthy family groups
EURIBOR	Euro Interbank Offered Rate. The rate at which euro denominated interbank term deposits within the euro zone are offered by one prime bank to another prime bank
exit	mechanism whereby parties to a buy-out realize their investments. Common exits are flotation/IPO, trade sale, secondary buy-out and leveraged recap
FSA	Financial Services Authority the UK's main regulator of the financial services industry
financial assistance	legal limitation on ability of a company (or its subsidiaries) to give assistance for an acquisition of its shares. In UK can be relaxed for private companies (see 'whitewash') but is an absolute prohibition for public companies. As of 1 October 2008 the financial assistance restriction applicable to private companies is being abolished completely but will remain for public companies (under Companies Act 2006)
financial covenant	borrower's undertaking to maintain a certain level of financial performance or status, usually expressed as a financial ratio. Used extensively in senior and mezzanine loan documents
financial sponsor	another name for an equity house to distinguish it from a corporate sponsor (a trade buyer)
flex	market flex or reverse flex
flotation	listing of a company's shares on a stock market. See also 'IPO'
high yield debt/bonds	debt security that is issued into the debt capital markets (specifically the high yield market) as a source of junior debt in buy-outs. Takes the form of a bond instrument rather than a loan
HMRC	Her Majesty's Revenue & Customs. UK government body that collects taxes
holdco	name commonly given to an SPV that sits above the acquisition SPV (newco or bidco). Where there are several such

	SPVs they will typically be given different names, eg holdco1, holdco2, topco, etc., usually reflecting where they sit in the structure
holdco PIK	public PIK note issued by a holdco on a structurally subordinated basis. The proceeds are commonly used to fund a dividend recap
hybrid instrument	financial instrument that has some features of a debt instrument and some of an equity instrument. May increasingly be used in buy-out funding structures between traditional equity and traditional junior debt instruments. See also 'preferred equity'
incurrence covenant	form of undertaking given by a borrower or bond issuer that is tested only once, at the time the restricted activity is first incurred. An example would be for a restriction on additional indebtedness in a high yield bond deed or indenture; provided that the relevant test (usually financial) is passed at the time of the new borrowing it will be permitted. Cf 'maintenance' covenant
institutional equity investor	equity house providing equity for a buy-out
institutional lender	CDOs (and similar vehicles), hedge funds and other fund type institutions that provide liquidity to the acquisition finance markets. To be distinguished from a bank
IPO	initial public offering. The first time a company offers securities (usually refers to an equity listing but can be debt securities) for sale on a public market. See also 'flotation'
IRR	internal rate of return. The annual return to an investor on its investment expressed as a percentage of the capital invested
irrevocable	shareholder undertaking to accept a bid in public-to-private transaction. There are various levels of irrevocable undertaking. Some are true irrevocable undertakings to sell shares to the bidder once the offer is launched and at the other end of the scale they may only amount to a current intention to accept provided that no higher bid is made
junior debt	acquisition finance that is subordinated to or ranks behind senior debt
LBO	leveraged buy-out. Literally a buy-out financed with debt
leverage	another term for debt (and usually implying a significant amount of debt)
leveraged recap	recapitalisation of a buy-out funding structure involving new debt being raised to fund the return of capital to the equity house. See also 'dividend recap'
leveraged loan	acquisition finance loan facility including senior debt, second lien loans and mezzanine debt. To be contrasted with public debt securities such as high yield
LIBOR	London Interbank Offered Rate. The rate at which banks in the London wholesale money market offer to lend term deposits to each other

loan note/stock	form of debt instrument structured to be like capital or a security
make-whole payment	form of yield protection on high yield bonds. If issuer redeems bonds early (usually in first half of the life of the bonds – the 'non-call period') it must make a payment to the bond holders equal to the total amount of interest the bond holders would have received if the bonds had been repaid at the first opportunity after the non-call period but discounted to reflect the fact that the amount was received earlier than scheduled. See also 'non-call period' and 'yield protection'
maintenance covenant	form of undertaking given by a borrower or issuer, compliance with which must be maintained over a period. Cf 'incurrence' covenant
management team	select senior managers of the business the subject of a buy-out that are to take an equity stake in the capital structure. Will usually be the incumbent management at the time of the buy-out but may also be new management brought in by the financial sponsor (in a 'management buy-in'. See 'MBI')
margin ratchet	mechanism to automatically reduce interest rate margin on a senior debt facility as the borrower's financial status improves
market flex	provision enabling an arranging bank to increase the pricing, alter the structure or otherwise amend the terms of the acquisition finance in order to ensure a successful syndication. See also 'reverse flex'
maturity date	scheduled date on which the principal amount of a debt instrument falls due for final repayment
MBI	management buy-in. A management led buy-out by a new management team
MBO	Management buy-out. A management led buy-out by the existing management team
mezzanine debt	form of junior ranking acquisition finance
mid-market	that part of the market that is below the large cap market and above the smaller deal market. Typically a mid-market deal will have a total funding requirement of between £50m and £500m. Distinction may be drawn between lower mid-market, true mid-market and upper mid-market across this range
MLA	mandated lead arranger. Bank that is awarded an exclusive or joint mandate by the sponsor to arrange and underwrite the acquisition finance package or a particular portion of it
newco	name given to the SPV that makes the acquisition at core of a buy-out. Is usually also the main acquisition finance borrower
non-call period	period during which a financial instrument (eg, high yield bond) can not be repaid or redeemed by the borrower/issuer. Exceptions usually require payment of a penalty (eg, make-whole payment). See also 'prepayment fee' and 'yield protection'

note	another term for a financial instrument evidenced by a certificate but usually reserved for bonds. Also the term is sometimes applied to different tranches of senior debt eg 'A note'
Panel	The Panel on Takeovers and Mergers. The Panel publishes and oversees the Takeover Code and is the body primarily responsible for regulating acquisitions of UK listed companies
PIK	payment in kind. Means the payment of interest or yield other than in cash. The amount of interest or yield is capitalised and added to the principal and thus compounded
PIK note debt	form of deeply subordinated acquisition finance instrument structured with a payment in kind yield (see also 'PIK'). May be issued in 'public' or 'private' form depending on its intended market
PIK toggle	see 'toggle'
PLUS	PLUS Markets is a London stock exchange (previously known as OFEX) with relatively light regulation and targeted at small and mid cap companies. It is similar to AIM
preferred equity	a financial instrument that has the economic features of an equity instrument but which ranks ahead of traditional equity and usually below the most junior form of acquisition finance in a buy-out structure (eg, PIK notes may be used as preferred equity or as deeply subordinated acquisition finance). See also 'hybrid instrument'
prepayment	a repayment of principal before the scheduled date
prepayment fee	fee payable by borrower if it prepays a facility within certain time of utilisation (eg, in first two years after borrowing in case of mezzanine debt). See also 'yield protection' and 'make-whole payment'
private PIK	PIK notes that are not intended for the public debt markets (see 'public PIK') and which are less widely held, perhaps by a single institution
public PIK	PIK notes that are structured and documented for distribution in the public debt markets, essentially because the size of the issue requires a deep and liquid market
public-to-private or PTP	buy-out of a public listed company
quasi-equity	equity that takes the form of subordinated loan capital or preference share capital
ranking	order or priority between two or more layers of finance. See also 'subordination'
reverse flex	market flex that operates in favour of the borrower by reducing the interest rate or improving the structure where primary syndication is materially oversubscribed. See also 'market flex'
Rule 3 adviser	target's independent financial adviser in a public-to-private. Rule 3 of the Code dictates the appointment

scheme of arrangement	court-sanctioned process (Cf takeover offer) to effect a takeover of a public company in a public-to-private
SEC	Securities and Exchange Commission of the United States. Federal body that oversees US securities legislation
second lien debt	form of acquisition finance that ranks immediately behind the senior debt and ahead of any core junior debt (eg, mezzanine)
secondary buy-out or secondary	buy-out of a business that is owned by a financial sponsor (and management team) as a result of a prior buy-out
seller note	deferred sale consideration structured as a form of capital in buy-out funding structure. Often referred to as 'vendor note'
seller protection provision	provisions in an acquisition agreement that reduce ability of buyer to sue seller under warranty and indemnity provisions
senior debt	core acquisition finance product that ranks above all other acquisition finance instruments
SPV	special purpose vehicle. A bankruptcy remote newly formed company that has never traded
subordinated debt	debt that is expressed to rank behind other layers of finance. Another name for junior debt
subordinated loan capital	form of core capital (part of overall equity package) structured as a debt instrument
subordination	mechanism to create order of ranking and priority between two or more layers of finance, especially when borrower/issuer become insolvent. Most common forms are contractual subordination and structural subordination
syndication	distribution of debt underwritten by an arranging and underwriting bank to other lenders so as to reduce its exposure to a single borrower group and to free up its balance sheet to do other deals. Essential part of acquisition finance market dynamics
takeover	acquisition of a public company. May be effected by a takeover offer or a scheme of arrangement. See also 'bid' and 'public-to-private'
takeover offer	mechanism established under Takeover Code for effecting a takeover. Alternative to a scheme of arrangement
Takeover Code	see 'Code'
tag-along	minority shareholder right to 'tag' onto a sale by a majority shareholder of its stake in a business. Management team shareholders look to get this right in buy-out scenario so that they can exit when the equity house exits. Cf 'drag-along' (which is equivalent right of a majority shareholder)
target	the company or business the subject of a buy-out
toggle	option for borrower to choose to pay interest (usually on mezzanine debt) in kind rather than in cash. May be called 'PIK toggle' (see also 'PIK')
topco	uppermost SPV in a buy-out corporate structure. Usually the vehicle into which the true equity is invested by the equity house and the management team. Also normally acts as the

	ultimate management company for the buy-out for governance purposes
trade buyer	corporate buyer (see also 'corporate sponsor') of a business, perhaps one that operates in the same sector (trade) as the target. To be contrasted with financial buyer (sponsor, or equity house) and buy-out transaction
trade sale	sale of business to a trade buyer (corporate sponsor). One of the main exits used for buy-out investors
upstream credit support	credit support (loan, guarantee, security) given by a subsidiary for the benefit of a parent company. Eg, guarantee and security by target for acquisition debt borrowed by newco
venture capital	historic name given to private equity. Now reserved for early stage equity investing in businesses that are not mature enough to support acquisition finance
warrant	form of share option usually issued by the equity vehicle in a buy-out (see 'topco') to mezzanine lenders or PIK investors. Until the early 2000s majority of mezzanine debt had warrants but from mid 2000s relatively rare
warranties and indemnities	form of contractual comfort usually obtained from a seller as to the legal, financial and commercial status of a target business
whitewash	procedure that a private company goes through in order to be able to give financial assistance for the acquisition of its shares or those of its holding company. Being repealed by Companies Act 2006 effective as of 1 October 2008. See also 'financial assistance'
yield protection	provisions in finance documents that protect the yield (interest) to the creditors. In particular, include prepayment fees and make-whole payments. Also include tax indemnities, market-disruption, increased cost provisions

Table of Statutes

CHAPTER 1

Introduction and Overview

BRIEF OVERVIEW

What is an acquisition finance transaction?

1.1   There are various forms of transaction that may be described as acquisition finance transactions. Any acquisition of a business that is financed through funds raised specifically to effect the acquisition can be included. However, amongst the acquisition finance deal-doing community there are really two distinct categories of acquisition finance transaction: those that have a financial sponsor effecting the acquisition and those that have an existing corporate business making the acquisition. There are a plethora of terms that describe different forms of these transactions[1] but in this book the former are generally described as leveraged buy-outs and the latter as leveraged corporate acquisitions. In either case the target company might be a private company or business or it might be a public company whose shares are listed or quoted on an exchange. Both situations are considered, with most of the book devoted to acquisitions of private companies and a separate section – **Chapter 12** – specifically devoted to the acquisition of public companies.

Although the market for each type of acquisition is not static, and in particular there has been steady growth in leveraged corporate acquisitions since the late 1990s, LBOs and other forms of buy-out are the more common form of acquisition finance transaction in the UK. This book is primarily aimed at buy-outs, although many of the principles considered will still be relevant to a leveraged corporate acquisition.

A buy-out transaction is an acquisition of a target company or business by a private equity house together with a management team (usually the existing senior managers of the target) with a view to increasing the value of the business before disposing of it in a few years time at a profit.

The consideration payable by the buyer in respect of such an acquisition will be financed from two principal sources. First, there will be a significant element of private equity to be provided by the equity house and, to a lesser extent, the management team. Additionally, a large part of the required funding will be in

---

1   See para **1.15**.

the form of debt finance raised from banks and specialist finance houses. The debt element of the finance package is called acquisition finance. In the case of a takeover of a public target it is sometimes also called bid finance.

Financing a leveraged buy-out

Acquisition finance and private equity

1.2   As mentioned above, acquisition finance and private equity are the two principal forms of funding that are combined to finance buy-out transactions. Private equity takes the form of share capital and subordinated loan capital and is provided by equity houses: private equity institutions and funds including, in smaller transactions, venture capitalists. Acquisition finance takes the form of medium and long term debt and is provided by acquisition finance banks and other financial institutions.

Debt and equity

1.3   A key distinction to draw between the two elements of funding used to finance buy-outs – acquisition finance and private equity – is in the nature of the instruments used, namely debt versus equity. Acquisition finance comprises the debt component and private equity comprises the equity component. For these purposes equity means true equity in the form of ordinary share capital and quasi-equity in the form of redeemable preference share capital or more usually subordinated loan capital.

Acquisition finance debt comprises many different forms, which are typically divided into senior debt and junior – or subordinated – debt. Senior debt has prior rights to be repaid and as a result gets a lower investment return. Junior debt is subordinated to the senior debt and as a result gets a higher investment return. It may take the form of private bank debt or a public capital markets issue of notes or bonds or a hybrid instrument.

The equity element may also take several forms and typically the true equity element, comprising ordinary share capital, is only a small part of the overall 'equity' package. Typically, the largest part of the equity package is actually in the form of subordinated debt, commonly structured as subordinated loan notes or loan stock.

Together the debt and equity components enable the buyer to fund the acquisition:

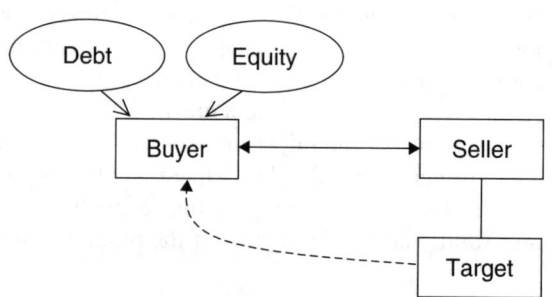

Debt and equity finance the acquisition of the target

What is the process for a buy-out?

1.4   Most buy-out transactions will proceed through a number of common stages.

Initial sale process

1.5   At the outset, in a typical private buy-out (that is, where the acquisition is of a private company), a seller will decide to sell the target business in question; this may be initiated by its management team, the seller or by a prospective buyer. There may be an auction process or the sale may be exclusively negotiated with a single buyer. The buyer and its backers will carry out an initial evaluation of the quality of, and price to be paid for, the target business. In addition, a business plan will be devised, setting down the rationale for making the acquisition and, in particular, the projected performance of the business after completion of the acquisition and the opportunities for realisation of the equity investments in due course.

Finance

1.6   The buyer, as a newly formed SPV (generally called 'newco'), will need to raise finance to fund the acquisition. Some of the finance will be provided as equity by the sponsor (private equity house) and the management team. The remainder will be provided as debt by acquisition finance banks and other institutions. Each of the equity and debt providers will analyse the historical performance of the target, the business plan and other financial information concerning the target, and will devise a financial structure to meet the purchase price, deal costs and any post-acquisition funding requirements.

Due diligence

1.7   Prior to agreeing to provide finance, the equity and debt providers will carry out due diligence. This will typically comprise financial, commercial and legal analyses of the target business and usually analysis and verification of the business plan. The tangible product of this will be a number of due diligence reports provided by accountants, lawyers and other consultants. In addition, the individual members of the management team will be evaluated by the sponsor and the acquisition financiers.

Legal documentation

1.8   Once a commercial 'deal' has been agreed, lawyers acting for the various parties will document the different aspects of the transaction. These principally comprise the acquisition by the buyer, the investments in the buyer by the equity providers, and the provision of debt to the buyer by the acquisition financiers. In order to have the parties commit to the process as early as possible, the documentation process may be split into an initial 'commitment paper' stage to be followed by full documentation at a later stage.

Signing

1.9   The legal agreement of the parties will be established at 'signing', which is also called 'exchange'. At signing there may be some outstanding transaction conditions to be satisfied before the acquisition and its funding occur, which is why 'completion' may be at a later date, although not necessarily.

Completion

1.10   Once documentation is signed and all completion conditions met or waived, the finance can be provided to the buyer and the acquisition completed. Completion may be as much as a number of months after signing if regulatory (eg, merger authority clearance) conditions are to be satisfied.

Syndication

1.11   Having advanced the debt to the buyer, the acquisition financiers will usually establish syndicates by selling the debt into the acquisition finance markets. The syndication process will often be commenced prior to completion, although it is typically completed within a period of months thereafter. In larger transactions, two or three acquisition finance banks may join together to provide the acquisition finance at completion before syndicating more widely after completion.

Exit

1.12   Ultimately, the equity and debt providers will wish to realise their investments in the transaction. In the case of the debt providers, this essentially means repayment of the debt, together with interest, in line with an agreed timeframe. For the equity providers, this means recovering their investment and realising the earnings and capital growth in the underlying business out of the proceeds of a sale of the business or flotation on a stock exchange. (Plus, they may also have received yield distributions prior to full exit.)

Public-to-privates

1.13   Where the target company is a public company that is listed or quoted on the London Stock Exchange or AIM or PLUS, an acquisition of that company will involve a different process. Such a company will be acquired either by way of a takeover offer made by an SPV – which, in this context, is often called 'bidco' or the 'offeror' – to the target's shareholders, or though a court-sanctioned scheme of arrangement under Companies Act 1985, s 425 (and, from 6 April 2008, see Companies Act 2006, Pt 26). In both cases the process involves compliance with the regulatory regimes enshrined in the City Code on Takeovers and Mergers and the Companies Act 1985 (as superseded by the Companies Act 2006) and, to a lesser extent, with various other pieces of applicable legislation. The provision of equity and debt finance for such an acquisition – called a public-to-private or take-private because it involves the target company coming back into private ownership – is also required to be effected in a manner that is consistent with the regulatory regime.

WHAT IS ACQUISITION FINANCE?

Private equity and acquisition finance

1.14   Private equity and acquisition finance are the two principal forms of funding which are combined to finance buy-out transactions and other highly leveraged – or debt funded – acquisition transactions. Private equity takes the form of share capital and subordinated loan capital and is provided by equity houses: private equity institutions and funds and, in smaller transactions, venture capitalists. Acquisition finance takes the form of committed term debt and is provided by acquisition finance banks and other financial institutions.

'Buy-outs' and historical terminology

What are 'buy-outs'?

1.15   'Buy-out' is a generic term used to describe most acquisition transactions sponsored by private equity houses. The traditional, and historically most commonly referred to form of buy-out is the management buy-out or MBO. In these transactions certain members of the incumbent management of a target company or business acquire, using an SPV referred to as newco, the shares, or sometimes assets, of the target from the target's existing owners. Ownership of newco (and, after the acquisition, the target business) by the managers is shared with a private equity house which will have provided a substantial amount of finance for the acquisition in the form of private equity. The remainder of the finance will be acquisition finance provided by one or more banks and other financial institutions.

Similar to a true MBO, which is a buy-out initiated and driven by the existing management team, is a buy-out that is initiated and driven by external, new management, called a management buy-in or MBI. Sometimes, the buy-out will involve both new and existing management and will sometimes be called a buy-in management buy-out or BIMBO. More occasionally, employees of the target are offered a small equity stake in what are called MEBOs (for management and employee buy-out) and similarly BIMEBOs occasionally occur. In the 1990s a further category of MBO emerged, where the process was initiated not by the management team but by the seller itself encouraging the management of the target business to put together a management buy-out. These transactions were historically described as VIMBOs or vendor initiated management buy-outs. Finally, the mid to late 1990s also saw the first secondary buy-outs where one equity house is exiting a buy-out by selling to another equity house. There have also been quite a number of tertiary buy-outs where a target business undergoes a third successive buy-out and even some quaternary buy-outs. Generically secondary, tertiary and quaternary buy-outs are all called 'secondaries'.

Buy-outs that were not traditional MBOs, MBIs or BIMBOs were often called institutional buy-outs to reflect the fact that they were being led and driven by an equity house – an 'institutional' investor – rather than management.

However, since the late 1990s, the terms leveraged buy-out[2] and LBO are used almost exclusively to describe all buy-outs. The terms MBO and MBI are gener-

---

2   Leverage is the term used to describe the fact that an acquisition is financed with a significant amount of debt.

ally reserved now for buy-outs that are truly led by the management team rather than the equity house, which is relatively rare nowadays. Other historically used terms are also only rarely used. Finally, it is common now to refer to a private equity house as a 'financial sponsor'.

A buy-out might be of either a private company or a listed public company. In the UK, buy-outs of public targets are generally referred to as public-to-privates (PTPs for short or take-privates) as they involve the target being taken back into private ownership.

Buy-outs and other acquisition finance transactions

1.16   Although the term buy-out is sometimes used interchangeably with the concept of the leveraged acquisition, the latter encompasses forms of transaction which are not necessarily buy-outs in the traditional sense including, in particular, corporate acquisitions and takeovers financed with debt. Whereas the structures and principles underpinning non-buy-out leveraged acquisitions may have much in common with a buy-out, such transactions are more likely to require consideration on a deal specific basis.

Leveraged corporate acquisitions and takeovers often involve larger amounts of finance than a traditional buy-out and this may result in a greater degree of financial engineering, which in turn might produce a more complicated structure than the basic buy-out structure. Similarly, since the late 1990s there have been an increasing number of jumbo-sized LBOs with multi-layered financial structures that again do not easily compare to typical buy-out structures.

With this in mind, the principles set out in this chapter may be more relevant to a traditional 'buy-out' than a more complicated leveraged acquisition financing.

The basic 'buy-out' structure

1.17   Buy-out structures pivot around an SPV (newco) set up by an equity house – which will often be referred to as the deal 'sponsor' or, to contrast it with the management investors, the 'institutional' equity investor – and the management team, into which they will inject an initial equity investment. Newco enters into an acquisition agreement with the seller to acquire the target. The target may be a discrete corporate entity (or group of companies) or a business owned by the seller without a distinct corporate identity.

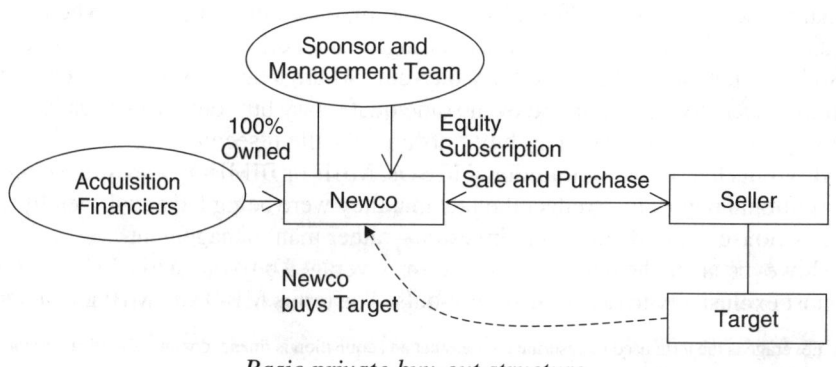

Basic private buy-out structure

The structure shown above assumes that the target is a private company. In the case of a listed public company, the buy-out – in this context, called a public-to-private – will have no seller entity per se and will be structured either as a takeover offer or as a scheme of arrangement under Companies Act 1985, s 425 (and from 6 April 2008 see Companies Act 2006, Pt 26).[3] For example, the diagram below shows a public-to-private by way of takeover offer.

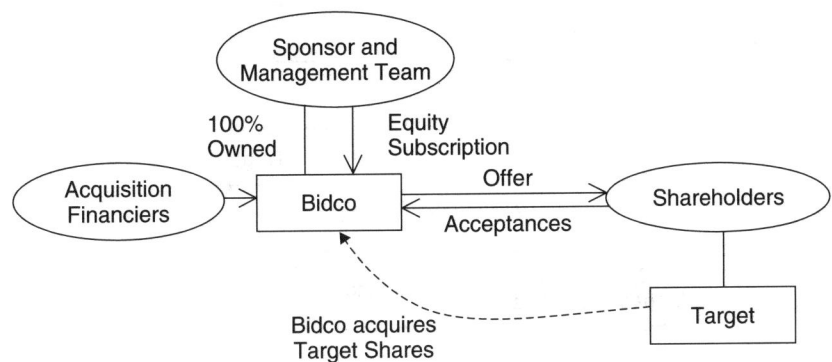

Basic public-to-private buy-out structure

Corporate acquisitions

1.18   Buy-outs are to be contrasted with corporate acquisitions, which are transactions where the target business is acquired from the seller not by a private equity (and management) sponsored SPV but by an existing corporate business. Such a buyer will often be a company operating in the same trading area as the target business and hence such deals are often called 'trade' purchases. It is common, where one or more prospective corporate buyers are, in addition to one or more equity houses, considering a purchase of a target business, for the prospective buy-out parties to be described as 'financial' buyers or bidders to distinguish them from the corporate or trade buyers. For a long time, corporate acquisitions were far more prevalent than buy-outs but with the buy-out boom during the 2000s buy-outs do now account for a significant proportion of all acquisitions in the UK.

As mentioned, acquisition finance may be employed to finance a corporate acquisition, either where the target is a private company or where it is a public company. However, unlike buy-outs, corporate acquisitions are less likely to be financed through dedicated acquisition finance debt than through other sources such as the buyer's balance sheet cash, an equity rights issue or general corporate debt. For this reason specialist acquisition finance is generally not associated with corporate acquisitions in the way that it is with buy-outs. That said, an increase in the number of leveraged corporate acquisitions has been one of the features of the acquisition finance market in the UK since the late 1990s.

---

3   See **Chapter 12** generally on public-to-privates.

The diagram below provides a structural contrast between a corporate acquisition and a buy-out, in each case, of a private target:[4]

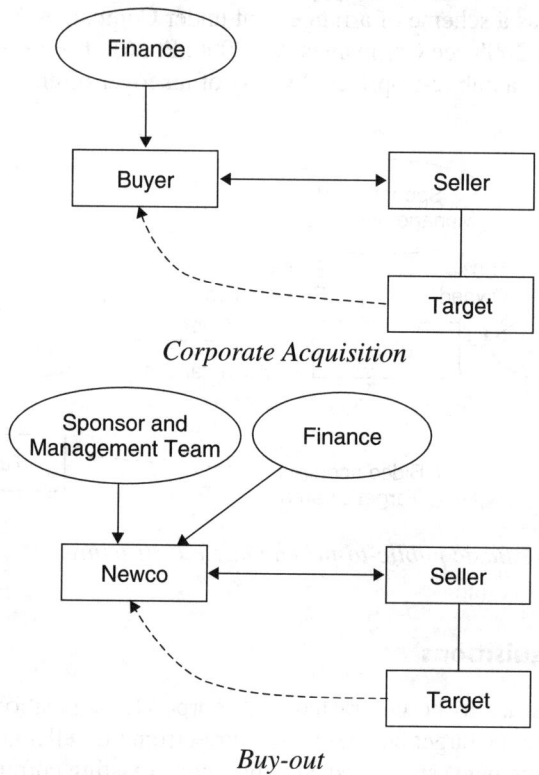

Corporate Acquisition

Buy-out

Note how the real, economic 'buyer' in a buy-out – that is, the equity investors comprising the private equity house together with the management team – does not itself contract with the seller as is the case in a corporate acquisition. Newco does so, on its behalf on a non-recourse basis.

From a finance perspective, the two principal differences between corporate acquisitions and buy-outs are the nature of the finance for the deal and the recourse for any financiers.

Types of finance

1.19   A corporate buyer is a pre-existing business which may have cash reserves which it wishes to use for the acquisition. In addition, it can seek finance in other ways. If it is a private company it may use a further issue of shares to its shareholders to raise additional finance. A public company will have access to public equity and capital markets to secure further finance and most large public and private corporates will have access to the corporate banking market to raise

---

4   The same distinctions arise in a public-to-private transaction.

debt finance which may be used as a full or partial bridge to a rights issue or capital markets issue.

With a buy-out, private equity and specialist acquisition finance debt are the main forms of finance available.

Recourse for the financiers

1.20 The second major distinction relates to the recourse of the financing banks and other financiers and the credit risk taken on the borrowing group. With most corporate acquisitions the corporate sponsor – that is the parent company of the acquiring group – will offer recourse to the acquiring group in addition to the target group upon its acquisition.[5] The credit risk for financing banks therefore encompasses both groups.

In the case of a buy-out, the private equity sponsor will not offer recourse to itself and the only recourse the lenders will have will be to newco as acquirer and the target group itself upon its acquisition. Since newco is only an SPV, in practical terms the credit risk is solely on the target group.

Types of acquisition finance

1.21 To this point the chapter has assumed that the typical buy-out will be funded from a combination of private equity funds (the equity) and acquisition finance facilities (the debt). The following paragraphs differentiate the sub-categories of acquisition finance which are commonly employed.

Senior debt

1.22 The principal category of acquisition finance, which will be used in all buy-outs, is the senior debt provided primarily by acquisition finance banks and also by certain 'institutional' lenders that are described in more detail elsewhere in this book. It will comprise a secured loan to newco to fund part of the acquisition price, a working capital facility and possibly other specific purpose facilities.[6]

Junior debt

1.23 Junior debt is the other major form of acquisition finance used in buy–outs. It is used to increase the total amount of debt available for a buy-out and notionally plugs the funding gap where the senior debt and private equity packages are insufficient to meet the total funding requirement. It is also called subordinated debt and ranks behind the senior debt in terms of priority of repayment and right to receive a yield. Because of its subordinated status the yield payable on the junior debt will be higher than that payable on the senior debt: but not as high as the returns that can be made on the equity component. The principal forms of junior debt used in buy-outs are second lien debt, mezzanine debt, high yield bonds and PIK notes. They are different in various ways, principally because they target a different part of the capital structure of a buy-out, although

---

5   Note also that even with a corporate acquisition an SPV may be used to effect the acquisition.
6   See **Chapter 5** generally for more detail on senior debt facilities.

they are also documented differently from each other. In practice, certain combinations of these instruments may be used together in the same structure. In an evolutionary market, like the UK buy-out market, it remains possible for additional new forms of hybrid instrument to appear as ever more kinds of investor are attracted to buy-outs with different risk and return expectations.

The four types of junior debt currently used in UK buy-outs are considered briefly in the following paragraphs and in more detail in later paragraphs and chapters.

Second lien debt

1.24   Second lien debt is a relatively new product to the UK buy-out market, having been first used in 2003. It has its roots in the US market, although the version used in the UK and the rest of Europe differs in certain key respects from US second lien. In many buy-outs it is used, in relatively small amounts, as a form of stretched senior debt that is sandwiched between the core senior debt and a tranche of core junior debt, either mezzanine or high yield. In others, including refinancings of mature buy-outs (and indeed, when the market is at its most liquid, in buy-out structures generally) and certain leveraged corporate acquisitions, it may be used in place of mezzanine or high yield debt, and in such circumstances is viewed as a cheaper version of mezzanine debt.

This form of debt is arguably not true junior debt but rather senior subordinated debt and is sometimes referred to as such. This is partly because it ranks ahead of any other junior debt – mezzanine or high yield debt – in the same financing structure. In addition, the original US form was aimed at investors that would not invest in true 'subordinated debt'. Moreover, as already mentioned, in first time buy-outs in the UK it is generally documented in the same agreement as the senior debt, as a further tranche of 'senior debt'.

The yield on second lien will be in the form of cash interest at a margin over LIBOR/EURIBOR.

Although it may initially be underwritten by the acquisition finance banking market the targeted end-investors include hedge funds and other institutional investors including leveraged loan funds.

Mezzanine finance

1.25   Despite an exponential increase in the use of second lien debt through the 2000s, increasingly in place of mezzanine debt,[7] mezzanine finance remains arguably the most liquid source of junior debt used in UK and other European buy-outs. It was the first type of junior debt used in Europe, has the most mature market and is also the most flexible. Historically, mezzanine lenders could demand equity options in the form of warrants issued by the equity vehicle, as part of the mezzanine package, but 'warranted' mezzanine is now relatively rare and the vast majority is 'warrantless'. Some of the larger deals have both warranted and warrantless mezzanine tranches, but there are now two discreet mezzanine markets (and products) in Europe; the institutional mezzanine market

---

7   The traditional dominance of mezzanine debt in Europe is under severe threat as senior and second lien only structures become more common.

which provides warrantless mezzanine to mid-market and larger buy-outs and the true mezzanine market which provides warranted mezzanine to lower mid-market and smaller buy-outs.

Mezzanine loans yield interest in cash at a margin over LIBOR/EURIBOR plus a further amount of PIK interest. The PIK element is capitalised and repaid as principal at maturity of the loan. Mezzanine is more expensive than second lien debt.

Mezzanine debt is provided by acquisition finance banks, specialist mezzanine houses and institutional investors such as pension and insurance funds, hedge funds and other dedicated leveraged loan funds.

High yield debt

1.26 High yield debt first appeared in UK buy-outs in the mid to late 1990s, several years after mezzanine debt but before second lien and PIK. It is a public debt security and is structured as an issue of bonds or 'notes'. As with second lien, high yield bonds have their origins in the more mature US market, where initially they were known as 'junk bonds' given their sub-investment grade credit ratings. They have been an integral component of the US acquisition finance market since the late 1980s. In Europe by contrast, the market has proven to be more volatile.

Unlike second lien and mezzanine, high yield is normally priced at an all-in fixed rate, although floating rate notes priced at a margin over underlying cost of funds have become more common in the 2000s.

Because of the historically greater appetite for high yield debt in the US capital markets, in addition to being placed with European investors, a bond issue may also be offered to 'qualified institutional buyers' (generally speaking, large institutional investors) in the US under Rule 144A of the US Securities Act 1933, which exempts the issue from the registration requirements of that Act.[8] Alternatively, where the bond issue is not intended to be marketed in the US at all – although the issue may still be available to US investors that acquire the bonds in primary markets outside the US – it can be structured to fall within the Regulation S exemption of the US Securities Act 1933. As the bonds are issued in a leveraged buy-out context, and there is likely to be a significant tranche of secured senior debt in place to which the high yield debt will be subordinated, the bonds are generally classified below 'investment grade' by the rating agencies.[9] The investors in the bonds will consequently expect a high return because of the high degree of risk associated with those bonds, hence 'high yield'.

High yield debt will not be used in the same deal as mezzanine debt; they are alternatives. High yield is only used in the larger deals, typically in the region of £500 million or more, by total deal size, with a minimum high yield issue of approximately £75m–100m. Mezzanine can also be used in smaller deals and in smaller amounts.

---

8   Absent the exemption the bond issue would need to be registered with the US Securities and Exchange Commission (SEC).

9   That is, they are issued with a rating of lower than Baa (Moody's Investor Service, Inc.) or BBB (Standard & Poor's).

PIK note debt

1.27   PIK notes are the most recent form of junior debt to be used in UK and European buy-outs. The acronym 'PIK' stands for 'payment in kind' or 'paid in kind'. It is a generic term used to describe the payment of yield by capitalising the interest due. In other words, no cash interest payments are made and instead the accrued interest is added to the principal and paid at final maturity of the debt. It tends to be more deeply subordinated than any other form of junior debt and in different structures it may be structured – optically at least – to form part of the equity package rather than the acquisition finance package. Its position in the capital structure will generally be reflected in a higher yield than other forms of junior debt (although some mezzanine-replacing PIK has been issued with a lower yield than mezzanine). Its key advantage is that it can increase the total amount of debt without using up additional cashflow.

There are actually two discrete types of PIK notes used in practice – private PIK and public PIK. Private PIK, which is probably more common in buy-outs (but in smaller amounts), is generally structured as a privately placed issue of subordinated loan capital to one or a small number of investors. It may also take the form of a subordinated loan. Public PIK is structured and documented specifically for the public debt markets and is really akin to an issue of high yield debt with no cash yield. It is commonly subscribed by hedge funds. Public PIK is often used as an equity-replacing instrument in a recapitalisation of a mature business, in particular to fund dividend recaps.[10] In such circumstances, public PIK is often referred to as 'holdco PIK' reflecting the fact that it is generally issued by a new holdco SPV at the top of, or above, the existing group.

Seller finance

1.28   It is possible that the seller itself will provide a source of finance for a buy-out. Typically this will occur where the buyer is not willing to pay the seller's headline price at completion but is willing to pay a higher price in due course if the target business performs to an agreed level over an agreed period after completion. Such 'deferred consideration' is generally structured as a debt owing by newco to the seller – or, equally, a loan from the seller to newco – which is payable as and when the relevant payment conditions are met. The debt is often structured as a subordinated loan note and may be referred to by the parties as the 'seller note'.

THE PARTIES

1.29   The following paragraphs consider who the principal parties to a buy-out are; and briefly touch upon the role played by their major advisers. The principals can be shown in diagrammatic form as follows.

---

10 See **Chapter 9** for more detail on the use of public PIK notes to fund dividend recaps and on PIK notes generally.

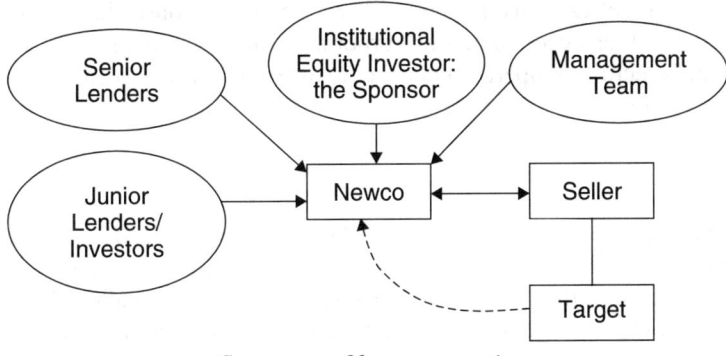

Summary of buy-out parties

Institutional equity investor: the sponsor

1.30   The institutional equity investor – the financial sponsor of the deal – will typically be a specialist private equity institution or a private equity unit or subsidiary of a commercial or investment bank. A number of these 'equity houses' are, or started life as, units within the fund management arms of pension/assurance companies. Most operate as fund managers, investing private equity funds in buy-outs and related transactions either directly for the institution within which they operate or by raising independent, third-party funds from institutions, such as insurance/assurance companies, pension funds and banks and high net worth individuals. Such funds generally take the form of limited partnerships set up in tax-exempt jurisdictions specifically for investment in buy-outs.

Because the most common fund structures used by these institutional investors are limited partnerships, where the fund manager is the general partner and the fund investors the limited partners, the terms 'GP' and 'LP' are often used to describe the equity house (the GP) and their fund investors (the LPs) respectively. The proceeds of successful buy-outs are split between the GP and the LPs on a pre-agreed basis, and the GP will also be paid a fee for managing the fund.[11] Most GPs are corporate entities. Most operating in the UK market are members of the British Venture Capital Association (BVCA) and the European Private Equity and Venture Capital Association (EVCA).[12] Traditionally, the UK buy-out market has been dominated by UK private equity houses, although during the 2000s the leading US houses have played an increasingly significant role, as have, to a lesser extent, a number of continental European institutions.

In very large deals two or perhaps three or even more equity houses may join together prior to completion to provide the institutional equity through a consortium. Alternatively, one house may underwrite the equity – possibly using equity bridge finance – and then syndicate the equity post-completion.

---

11 See **Chapter 4** for further detail.

12 Note that the abbreviated names of these institutions nominally refer to venture capital rather than private equity. This reflects the terminology in use when the BVCA and EVCA were formed. The latter term has taken over since the mid-1990s and 'venture capital' now refers to early stage and start-up equity finance rather than equity finance for real buy-outs.

Most investment executives who work within equity houses have a financial background such as accountancy or corporate finance, although there is also a trend towards recruiting operational executives from industry to compliment the financial expertise.

Key advisers

1.31   The sponsor will be advised by lawyers in respect of three principal areas – the acquisition, the equity investment and the debt finance. Specialists in each of these areas will generally be used. Alternatively, in smaller MBO transactions where the management team are leading the negotiations, the management team may appoint lawyers to act on behalf of both themselves and the institutional equity investor in respect of the acquisition and debt finance aspects of the transaction. In any case, negotiation of the acquisition and the debt finance facilities will be on behalf of newco as the entity which is actually the buyer and the borrower. Here there is a natural alignment of interest for each of the sponsor, the management team and newco. However, in respect of the equity investments to be made in newco and the shareholders agreement between the sponsor and the management team, both the sponsor and the management team will invariably need their own legal advisers.

One set of lawyers – usually those representing the deal sponsor (the institutional equity investor rather than the management team in most cases) – will also carry out the legal due diligence exercise in respect of the target business for the benefit of newco and all of its financial backers.

In addition to lawyers, the sponsor may also be advised by a corporate finance house. This will certainly be the case with a public-to-private and may also be true for a private buy-out that is especially large, complex or involves a regulated sector. Specialist advisers are also hired for the various aspects of the due diligence process. Finally, an increasing trend among certain sponsors is to hire advisers to negotiate the debt finance package with the banks and the growth in 'debt advisery' firms or teams has been a key development in acquisition finance during the 2000s.

Management team

1.32   All but the largest and most institutionally driven buy-outs will have an active ownership and executive role for one or more key managers. This 'management team' may be the incumbent management of the target, a new, external management team or a combination of both. The management team will comprise those of the senior managers of the target (current or prospective) who are either leading the buy-out or who have been identified by the sponsor as key to the delivery of the business plan and who therefore should be incentivised with an equity stake. One of the defining features of successful private equity and buy-outs is that the interests of the senior management team should be economically aligned with those of the sponsor. Ultimately, since the performance of the management team can be influenced by both incentives to perform well and disincentives to perform below par, a carrot and stick approach is often used. This generally means requiring management to invest a reasonably large amount of their own money in the deal, an investment that usually they will either lose altogether or turn into a lot more money.[13] In this way they are said to have 'skin in the game'.

Key advisers

1.33 The management team members will almost certainly have their own legal and financial advisers in relation to the various legal and financial aspects of the deal. A key legal area for a manager involved in the buy-out of a business of which he or she is currently a manager is the implications of progressing an MBO on his or her current employment. The relevant issues stem from the basic conflict of his or her position: acting in the company's best interests and having a personal interest in the MBO. This conflict of interest is underpinned by a number of duties which, as a matter of law, a manager owes to the company of which he or she is a manager. Such duties arise as a result of case law, under statute or regulation and by virtue of specific contractual arrangements between the company and the manager. For instance, most employment contracts of managers require the individual to devote full time and attention to the business, to act in the best interests of the company and to keep information relating to the business confidential. Even if not covered by specific contractual provisions, the common law implies a duty on all directors to act in the best interests of the company. Breach of these duties may render the individual liable to summary dismissal without compensation. For these reasons, it is often the case that managers approach the seller prior to getting very far into the process of an MBO. Often, individual managers leave the seller group in order to progress a buy-out of a business within the group. In any event there will be constraints on the dissemination of confidential information by the managers before and after termination of their employment. This is particularly true with a public company.

The management team's lawyers will also advise them in relation to their equity investments (including the tax treatment), the shareholders' agreement with the sponsor, the terms of their new employment contracts with the target business and possibly in relation to the acquisition itself and the acquisition finance. As previously mentioned, it is common for the sponsor's lawyers to take the lead on behalf of newco in advising and negotiating the terms of the acquisition and the acquisition finance, and most buy-outs are now led by the private equity sponsor.

Individual members of the management team may also have personal financial advisers on hand, perhaps in relation to tax matters to the extent such advice is not being provided by the legal advisers.

Newco

1.34 Newco – the actual buyer – will be an SPV, probably a 'shelf company', which has not previously traded and is therefore 'bankruptcy-remote'. It will be

---

13 Often there is provision for the management team's shareholding to increase with performance, in the form of a 'performance ratchet', or to take it away in extreme circumstances of low performance.

acquired or set up specifically for the acquisition and will remain in its nominee shareholders' names until signing. In practice, in all but the simplest of transactions, there will be more than one SPV used in the acquisition or financing structure.[14]

Key advisers

1.35   Since newco does not actually do anything until the date of signing of the legal documentation, it has no real need for lawyers of its own prior to such time. However, its interests, as the buyer of the target and as borrower of the acquisition finance, will effectively be represented by the lawyers appointed by the sponsor leading the deal. Importantly, the various professionals carrying out due diligence in respect of the buy-out, principally at the request of the sponsor and the acquisition financiers, will be required to extend reliance on their due diligence reports directly to newco as buyer, in addition to its financiers.

Senior lenders

1.36   The senior lenders will generally be providing the majority of the acquisition finance for a buy-out. Many UK and non-UK banks are active in the UK senior debt market. The small deal market – up to £50 million total deal size – and mid-market – £50 million to £500 million total deal size – have traditionally been dominated by the UK clearing banks. Competition has increased as the market has matured, however, and other European and North American banks also play a significant role in arranging and underwriting deals in the mid-market (particularly the upper-end) and larger deals. In mid-market and larger deals the senior debt package will generally be syndicated after completion of the acquisition and one of the lenders – usually the lead arranger (often called the mandated lead arranger or MLA for short) – will act as agent for the syndicate in dealings with the other parties to the buy-out. Although banks dominate in terms of arranging and underwriting senior debt, an increasing amount of the debt is actually provided by another group of lenders, generally referred to as institutional lenders. In this category fall pension and insurance funds, hedge funds and leveraged loan funds, including CDOs and CLOs. Throughout the 2000s the increased liquidity brought about by this expansive category of lender has had a major impact on the senior debt market and buy-outs in general, many of which are considered in further detail later in the book.

In large transactions it is common for two or more banks to co-arrange and underwrite the acquisition finance package between themselves before syndicating more widely after completion. In such cases, each of the lead banks will have MLA or equivalent status,[15] an important feature for deal league table and reputational purposes.

---

14 See para **1.74** below.
15 Such as 'bookrunner', which title is given to the bank or banks that lead the primary syndication process.

Most senior debt providers have specialist units dedicated to acquisition finance, although this may be part of a larger structured or specialised finance department. The individuals within such units will have expertise of all kinds of buy-out. They may be bankers by training or often, as with private equity players, chartered accountants.

Key advisers

1.37 The senior debt MLA will be advised principally by a firm of lawyers with acquisition finance expertise. It will also rely – for due diligence purposes – on the consultants and advisers that perform the due diligence exercise.

Second lien creditors

1.38 Second lien debt is generally underwritten by the senior debt underwriter as part of a single acquisition finance package ie, usually by a senior bank. However, the targeted end-investors may include a significant proportion of US and European institutional investors, including hedge funds and dedicated leveraged loan funds. They will not be involved in the buy-out process itself, however. Where the second lien is documented as a discrete facility with full syndicate voting mechanics,[16] a separate facility agent will be appointed. With second lien in the form of stretched senior debt – ie, no separate facility agreement and reduced syndicate voting rights – the senior debt agent will take on the agency role for the second lien lenders as required.

Key advisers

1.39 In most cases, the second lien lenders will not require a separate set of legal advisers from those advising the core senior debt providers. An exception might be made where a large tranche of second lien debt is being underwritten by a separate institution using a separate document, although, as with mezzanine debt, this should not be necessary where the intercreditor issues[17] are effectively pre-agreed between the principle parties.

Mezzanine lenders

1.40 There are several specialist mezzanine houses or funds active in the UK and European buy-out markets. Hedge funds, leveraged loan funds and other institutional investors also constitute an increasingly large proportion of the end-investors, particularly in larger deals. In addition, most acquisition finance banks have in-house mezzanine debt capacity in support of their senior debt franchises. As with senior debt, mezzanine facilities of a reasonable size will most likely be

16 See **Chapter 6** generally in this regard.
17 That is, issues between different classes of creditor, such as between the senior lenders and the second lien lenders. See **Chapter 10** generally on intercreditor matters.

syndicated after completion and one of the lenders will also act as agent for the syndicate in dealings with the other buy-out parties. By convention, it is common for different institutions to act as senior agent and mezzanine agent, even where the same institution arranges and underwrites both senior and mezzanine debt. The idea ˙ ˌ to avoid a conflict of interest arising for a single institution should the two syndicates take opposing stances on any issue.

Individuals within mezzanine houses or mezzanine teams of other institutions will be very experienced in the buy-out market and will often have previously worked, or currently also work, in senior debt or perhaps private equity.

Key advisers

1.41   The mezzanine lenders will be advised by lawyers with expertise in acquisition finance. It is relatively common for the same firm of lawyers advising the senior lenders to advise the mezzanine lenders in order to keep deal costs down. In most matters at the documentation stage the interests of the senior and mezzanine lenders are aligned – or at least not in conflict – and so no conflict of interest should arise for that firm. The one area where this is not the case is in relation to the intercreditor arrangements between the two sets of lenders and here matters may need to be negotiated directly between the lead senior and mezzanine lenders, respectively. In practice, however, given that the customary senior-mezzanine intercreditor issues are reasonably settled and well rehearsed between the main market participants, the potential for conflicts of interest for the law firm can be managed. In particular, it is common for separate lawyers within the firm to advise the respective parties and for an 'ethical wall' to be established between the advising lawyers.

High yield bondholders

1.42   In a buy-out incorporating high yield debt, the end-investors (bondholders) will principally comprise institutional investors that are active in the high yield markets. This will include insurance funds, pension funds, banks and other financial institutions. However, individual investors will have very little, if any, involvement in the buy-out process. This is because the bonds themselves will not be issued at completion of the buy-out. The timetable for completing a successful issue of high yield bonds is generally not predictable enough for the sponsor to be sure that it will coincide with completion of the acquisition itself.[18] Instead a dedicated bridging loan is used, which can be funded by an underwriting bank with more flexibility and certainty of execution. This is then refinanced with the proceeds of the bond issue within a period of between one and six months after completion.

In practice, the arrangers of the high yield bond or note issue – they are generally called 'managers' – will often be one of the senior debt MLAs and it or they are likely to underwrite the bridging loan. The lead manager will act on behalf of

---

18   This is especially true in Europe where the high yield markets have at times proven to be relatively unreliable sources of capital. See also **Chapter 8** generally.

all of the investors (bondholders) in negotiating the terms of the high yield bonds or notes with the issuer and the other buy-out parties.

Following the launch of an issue of high yield bonds, a further entity will act as 'trustee' on behalf of the bondholders in the on-going relationship with the issuer and any other party in the financing structure.

Key advisers

1.43   The lead manager of the high yield issue will retain its own legal counsel. In the US, it is not uncommon for the same law firm to advise both the senior lenders and the high yield manager. For historical reasons, this is less common in Europe, however. There are really two reasons for this. First, it is only relatively recently that the intercreditor issues between senior lenders and high yield bondholders have becomes settled and separate advisers were traditionally required to ensure a proper arms' length negotiation. Secondly, there has not always been that many legal firms operating out of London that have had sufficient expertise in both senior and high yield debt and the mandates were often split.

PIK noteholders

1.44   There is no discrete market for private PIK note debt per se. The end-investors may be specialist mezzanine houses, hedge funds or certain other institutional investors now active in the European subordinated debt market. In practice it is often underwritten as part of the senior or core junior debt package and then sold on. Public PIK issues tend to be used only in refinancings of mature buy-outs, with the notes sold into the high yield bond markets and to hedge funds.

Key advisers

1.45   As with most other forms of junior debt, whether or not the PIK note debt providers have separate legal advisers from the other parties will usually depend on whether the instrument is being arranged by one of the other principal parties such as the core senior or junior debt arranger. The parties may opt to minimise the number of law firms involved and, as with the mezzanine debt, allow the relevant law firm to put in place internal conflict of interest procedures to avoid any real conflict problems arising on the negotiation of the intercreditor issues.

Target

1.46   The target may be a subsidiary of the seller or a company owned by one or more individuals. It may be a division of the seller business without a separate corporate identity or it may comprise a number of divisions or business units within the seller group. It might be a company or group that has already been the subject of a buy-out and be owned by another financial sponsor and members of its management team. Usually the shares of a single target company are acquired and, indirectly, all of that company's subsidiaries.

Key advisers

1.47   The target will rarely engage its own legal advisers in relation to a buy-out, although a major exception is for public-to-privates where the target is the main counterparty to the buyer. In practice, where a target company is required to execute legal documentation as part of a private buy-out – for example, it will almost certainly be required to provide credit support for the acquisition finance at completion – it can rely on either the seller's advisers (in relation to matters arising pre-completion) or the buyer's advisers (at or post-completion).

Seller

1.48   Sellers range from sole traders to large FTSE 100 corporates and overseas equivalents and increasingly include private equity sponsors exiting from a prior buy-out. In practical terms, sellers play less of a role in a buy-out than many of the other parties. They are really only concerned with the sale itself and not the financing. This may mean that the seller is relatively distant from the acquisition financiers. An exception to this, where the seller will be concerned with the finance arrangements, is where signing and completion are not scheduled to occur simultaneously. In such circumstances, the seller will be acutely concerned as to the extent of the acquisition financiers' conditions to completion and the buyer's ability to satisfy them. This is true even where the buyer does not have a condition in the acquisition agreement that it has finance available (a 'financing out'), as newco will be unable to complete the acquisition without all of the funding being in place.[19] Similarly, when selling through an auction the seller will want to satisfy itself before awarding preferred or winning bidder status to a particular sponsor that the sponsor has the necessary finance in place to complete the buy-out.

In addition, the buyer and seller may occasionally agree to defer some of the purchase price for a period following completion in the form of a seller note. In those circumstances, the terms of the seller note – and, in particular, the terms of its relationship to the core acquisition finance (which is usually one of subordination) – will need to be pre-agreed with the acquisition financiers.

Key advisers

1.49   The seller will inevitably be advised as to all legal matters and the transaction generally by a firm of lawyers. It may also engage financial advisers, particularly where, as is increasingly common, the seller is to conduct an auction process to find its preferred buyer. This role is typically performed by a corporate

---

19 See also **Chapter 11** and the discussion on 'certain funds'.

finance team in a firm of accountants or an investment bank. It is also increasingly common for the seller to engage specialist consultants and advisers to
undertake pre-emptive due diligence in respect of the target in order to facilitate
the deal process.[20] Similarly, the seller may also approach a bank with a view to
obtaining a so-called 'stapled offer' of acquisition finance for the buy-out, again
with a view to streamlining the overall sale process.[21]

THE BUY-OUT PROCESS

1.50   The process for most buy-outs will comprise a number of common
stages. These include the initial sale process, the award of exclusivity to a buyer,
raising finance, due diligence, documentation, signing and finally completion.
Once the buy-out is completed, the financiers may syndicate some of the debt to
reduce their exposure to the target business. In due course, the equity investors
will look to exit their investments and if all goes to plan, realise a significant
return on their investment. The following summary indicates the likely steps
involved in each stage.

Initial sale process

1.51   The precise format of the initial sale process will vary from deal to deal
but a basic differentiation can be drawn between traditional MBOs and other
leveraged buy-outs.

Traditional MBO

1.52   With a traditional MBO, the incumbent management team – either alone
or with an equity house already on side – are likely to initiate the sale process
having determined that an MBO is something which they would wish to and are
able to pursue. The following initial steps will usually be taken:

- The management team initially approaches the seller setting out the case for
  divestiture of the target. Alternatively, the management team may prefer to
  take the following two steps below before approaching the seller with a
  more studied plan for a buy–out.[22]

- The management team will seek preliminary financial and legal advice on
  the proposed buy–out.

- In anticipation of the approaches which will be made to equity houses and
  acquisition finance providers, the management team (and its financial

---

20 See **Chapter 11** in relation to seller due diligence.
21 See para **1.57**.
22 The risks associated with this strategy are discussed in more detail below at para **1.33**. An MBI is more
    likely than an MBO to involve this strategy, where the individual managers' current employment is
    less likely to be jeopardised.

advisers) will produce a detailed business plan for, typically, the next three to five financial years.

- Within the management team a deal leader will be selected for the whole process or for each relevant part of it.

- With an MBO, the management team will be familiar with the target business, so there is unlikely to be much in the way of initial due diligence by them prior to the management team making a formal offer to the seller.

Leveraged buy-out

1.53   Although prospective sellers will often initiate the sale process for an LBO, financial sponsors are adept at finding target businesses to acquire even before the current owners have made a decision to sell. They may, therefore, instigate the seller's decision to sell. In either case, the sale process that follows the initial decision to sell will be similar, including the following steps:

- In order to find a buyer, the seller – usually with the help of its financial adviser – will prepare an information memorandum in relation to the target. This will cover the target's historic financial performance (ideally by reference to the last three years' audited accounts and current year-to-date unaudited management accounts), its financial prospects (which may include a business plan for, typically, the next three to five financial years), and any other information deemed appropriate for what is effectively a sales brochure.

- The seller or its financial adviser will distribute the information memorandum to a number of prospective buyers. This is likely to be the first stage of a formal or informal auction process.

- Alternatively, the seller may approach the target's senior management to suggest they do a buy-out and the transaction may then follow the deal process for a traditional MBO. That said, even with sponsor-led leveraged buy-outs, the target's senior management will typically be brought in to one or more of the competing equity houses' bids.

- If an equity house is interested in acquiring the target then prior to it making an offer or, in the case of an auction, putting in its bid to the seller, it will usually have carried out some initial due diligence including site visits to the target business and meetings with the target's management. It will also have approached prospective acquisition financiers about providing finance for the buy-out.

- Financial sponsors that are interested will line up a management team – either a new team or the existing team – in support of their offer or bid. More than one may line up the incumbent team, who may in effect wait to see who is likely to be successful before declaring too much allegiance to any one sponsor. Trade buyers, by contrast, will not need a 'management team' as such in support of their offer.

Seller initiated buy-outs

1.54 Since the late 1990s, sellers have become much more used to dealing with financial sponsors. Many now construct competitive tender processes, which may or may not be a formal auction, accepting that a financial sponsor will often be the successful bidder. With this in mind sellers will often pre-empt some of the requirements of financial sponsors such as due diligence and committed finance by arranging this themselves. Seller due diligence and 'stapled' offers of finance are considered below.

Buyer exclusivity

1.55 From a buyer's perspective, the most difficult part of the process will often be getting into an exclusive dialogue with the seller. Since the late 1990s, a seller's market has generally prevailed in the UK and most of Europe, in large part on the back of increasing numbers of competing private equity sponsors. As a result, actually getting into exclusive talks with the seller, which either means pre-empting an auction or prevailing in any auction process that the seller conducts, is an increasingly difficult goal to achieve. The ideal route for a buyer is to pre-empt an auction altogether. Not only will this require agreeing an in principle deal with the seller – usually documented under 'heads of terms', a 'memorandum of understanding' or 'letter of intent' – it will also usually mean demonstrating to the seller a significant amount of commitment to and capability of closing the deal. In fact, demonstrating that it is a willing and knowledgeable buyer that has real insights into the target business and the sector in which it operates, together with a successful track record in closing deals, is one of the key competitive advantages any private equity house can have. In any given deal scenario this usually means the buyer must have done a reasonable amount of due diligence into the specific opportunity and possibly have obtained a reasonable level of commitment from a provider of acquisition finance. A seller will generally be reluctant to enter into any level of exclusive talks with a buyer unless it feels that there is a strong chance that the buyer can deliver the deal at the seller's asking price. This often means that any award of exclusivity occurs at a reasonably advanced stage of the entire buy-out process.

In practice, it is more common in Europe nowadays, before awarding exclusivity, for a seller to run an auction of sorts. The aim will be both maximising the sale price and ascertaining which prospective buyer is most committed to and capable of getting the deal done. Auctions are usually conducted in a number of rounds. During each successive round prospective buyers are required to carry out more detailed diligence into the opportunity – for which purposes they will be given greater access to the target business – and to provide a greater level of commitment to completing the deal. This also usually means submitting or reconfirming a bid price and the proposed terms of their bid. At a certain stage the buyer will need to demonstrate that it has concluded much of its due diligence, has the necessary finance available to it (on as unconditional a basis as possible – and usually on a 'certain funds' basis[23]) and that generally its bid is

---

23 See **Chapter 11**.

relatively unconditional – all of this, usually, at the highest price on offer.[24] This means that with auctioned deals, awards of exclusivity happen relatively late in the overall process, perhaps with legal documentation the only major remaining stage. And in some auctions, the sellers will not even award exclusivity until the legal documentation process is essentially completed, effectively running a contract race to the end.

Raising finance

1.56   Once a sponsor has identified that a deal with the seller is in principle possible or, in the case of an auctioned deal, because it is required to by the seller, it will need to find sufficient funding to complete the acquisition and to demonstrate the availability of this to the seller.[25] Greater levels of commitment will need to be shown the further into the process the bidders are.

In practical terms, the following steps will typically be taken by each financial sponsor looking to raise finance for a buy-out.[26]

- In an MBO, if equity funding is not already in place, the management team advised by its financial advisers will first seek to mandate an equity house. The following steps all assume that an equity house is mandated as financial sponsor and is then leading the process.[27]

- The sponsor will distribute the seller's information memorandum (if any) and the management team's business plan to the prospective financiers.

- Subsequently, the sponsor will seek to mandate one or more acquisition financiers to arrange the acquisition finance required.

- Interested acquisition finance providers will submit an indicative offer letter to the sponsor setting out the proposed level of funding and pricing. The initial offer letter will usually be expressly subject to completion of satisfactory due diligence, necessary internal credit approvals, documentation and market and business MAC conditions.[28]

- A finance mandate will usually only be awarded by the sponsor if the relevant finance provider can demonstrate that it has reviewed all the available information on the target business, carried out the requisite level of due diligence and is otherwise committed to and capable of closing the deal within the required timeframe. In practice nowadays the sponsor will generally leave the award of an exclusive mandate to the acquisition financiers until

---

24 Price is not always everything, however, and unconditionality of offer plus proven ability to close deals will also be significant factors for most sellers.

25 Corporate/trade bidders may not need third-party acquisition finance to complete the deal but they will probably still need to demonstrate this to the seller.

26 In a true MBO the management team may lead the process advised by their financial advisers.

27 In most transactions the equity house will take the leading role.

28 'MAC' refers to a 'material adverse change'. Broadly speaking, a market MAC is an event that results in a material adverse change in the debt finance markets and a business MAC is an event that results in a material adverse change in the financial position of the relevant company. In practice, relatively standard definitions exist for each.

relatively late in the process, in order to increase the competitiveness of the terms and amount of funding that the acquisition financiers are willing to provide. It will in effect run an auction for the debt mandate.

- Ultimately, the sponsor will agree a form of mandate letter and detailed term sheet with the winning bank. Increasingly, the form of the mandate letter and term sheet will have been originated by the sponsor itself in an attempt to obtain financing on more favourable terms. At this stage the mandate letter – that is the level of commitment being offered by the bank – should be subject only to documentation, with due diligence, credit committee approval and ideally market and business MAC conditions removed.

- Where the levels of finance required are sufficiently high so that more than one financier is required to underwrite the entire funding package, joint mandates or preferred financier status will be awarded to each co-arranger/underwriter of the relevant finance element.

- With a full funding package available, a sponsor can demonstrate a greater level of commitment to the seller in respect of the acquisition. Ideally the sponsor will look to agree heads of terms with the seller and a period of exclusivity (say, 45 days) within which to carry out full or final confirmatory due diligence, document the deal and complete the acquisition. Where the seller is running an auction process, this will need to be set in the context of that process and the relative merits of each bidding party's offer.

Stapled offers of finance

1.57   During the early 2000s a significant trend began in the UK acquisition finance market whereby sellers that were proposing a disposal through a buy-out would pre-arrange the debt package through what is called a 'stapled' offer of finance.

In practice this means that the seller will approach an acquisition finance bank (probably the target's existing bankers) to agree the terms on which that bank would be willing to provide acquisition finance for the proposed buy-out. These terms are then notionally 'stapled' to the seller's information memorandum to enhance the prospects of a successful disposal.

The acquisition financier providing such terms may have an initial advantage in being mandated by the ultimately successful buyer since it will be further into the process than competing banks. But it is not legally assured of being the successful bank, as it will be up to the ultimate buyer (not the seller) to award the debt mandate. Furthermore, the confidentiality of its initial terms will necessarily be compromised, thus removing some of its competitive advantage of having been given the first opportunity to look at the transaction.

Due diligence

1.58   Unless the buyer is relying solely on seller due diligence,[29] the due diligence and documentation processes will generally overlap substantially. Due diligence will generally be commenced and completed first, however.

---

29 As to which see para **1.59**.

In an auctioned deal the due diligence process will be commenced relatively early in the process, because one of the main purposes of an auction is to identify which prospective buyer is most committed to the deal, which will be based in part on its approach to the due diligence information. An award of exclusivity or preferred bidder status will usually occur at a point at which a significant amount of the due diligence process has been completed. In bi-laterally negotiated deals, by contrast, the buyer may only begin due diligence in earnest once there is agreement in principle with the seller and an award of exclusivity. The due diligence process generally is discussed in more detail in **Chapter 11**.

Seller due diligence

1.59   As indicated above, in some cases – notably auctioned deals – the seller may have already commissioned some due diligence prior to commencing the full sale process. This will usually mean that there are financial and legal due diligence reports available at the minimum. The idea is that this will give the prospective buyer or buyers an initial view on the viability of the project in addition to identifying at the outset any matters of sufficient importance as to merit immediate disclosure. Whether or not a buyer decides to rely solely on such reports or not – and in many cases it will still commission its own due diligence reports, either to update the seller commissioned reports which may have been put together some months back, or because it is not satisfied with the scope of such reports[30] – it will use the reports as one basis for its assessment of the target business.

Legal documentation

1.60   Both the sponsor and the management team will appoint lawyers to advise on the transaction and ultimately to document it legally. This will include advising on and documenting:

- the structuring of the buy-out including finalising both acquisition and funding structures;

- the establishment of one or more SPVs to effect the acquisition and its financing;

- the terms of the acquisition itself;

- the terms of the acquisition finance;

- the terms of the respective equity investments of the sponsor and management team;

- the shareholders agreement between them;

- the management team's individual employment contracts; and

---

30 Including the terms (if any) on which it and its financiers can formally rely on the reports.

- the legal due diligence exercise, subject to any seller due diligence that may have already been carried out.

One set of lawyers – usually those appointed by the sponsor – will also lead on matters on behalf of newco, including the terms of the acquisition and the acquisition finance.

The mandated acquisition financiers will also appoint lawyers to document the acquisition finance terms and advise generally on the buy-out. In practice, lawyers will often have been appointed at an earlier stage, even before any mandates are awarded to the principal parties, in order to provide preliminary advice on basic structural issues and the prospective terms of the acquisition finance to be provided.

The legal documentation process for a buy-out is considered in some detail in **Chapter 11**.

Signing and completion

1.61   Signing and completion refer to the two principal legal steps which occur to give legal effect to the buy-out. Signing means the signing of the acquisition agreement by the buyer and seller creating a legal contract for the acquisition. Signing is sometimes referred to as 'exchange' as the buyer and seller, notionally at least, exchange contracts for the sale and purchase. Completion of the deal is subject, in most cases, to satisfaction of certain conditions precedent such as merger authority clearance. Ideally, signing and completion will be simultaneous but because there may be unsatisfied conditions, and merger authority clearance is a common example, certainly in large deals, completion may not be able to occur for a period after signing. This period may be as little as one or two weeks or it might be as much as three or more months.

At completion of the acquisition, all conditions having been satisfied, the formalities necessary for perfecting the transfer of the shares in the target to the buyer or, in the case of an asset acquisition, the transfer of the assets will be effected.

The formalities and practicalities of signing and completion are also considered in some detail in **Chapter 11**.

Post-completion

Management of the business

1.62   Completion having occurred, the target will be owned by newco and indirectly the sponsor and the management team. At this point, the real challenge begins for the management team as they set out to achieve the objectives of their business plan and to make the buy-out a success, ultimately through an exit.

During the post-completion period the equity and acquisition finance documentation will impose certain obligations and controls on the management and operation of the business. These will dictate that major strategic decisions by the management team beyond those set out in the business plan will generally require the approval of the sponsor and the acquisition financiers. The sponsor will, in most cases, have a controlling equity stake in the business, through which it controls the board, and will also generally participate in the strategic direction of the business at board level; meaning that documentary controls are less important from the sponsor's perspective. For the acquisition financiers, on the other hand, without any board representation or shareholder rights, the 'controls' are purely contractual, as set out in the acquisition finance documentation.

Conditions subsequent

1.63   Often it is not possible to satisfy all of the initial conditions set by the acquisition financiers by the time completion occurs. Those that the bank are willing to defer until after completion are commonly called 'conditions subsequent'.[31] They will typically be required to be fulfilled within a period of up to 90 days after completion. For example, one common condition subsequent is the execution by the borrower of interest rate hedging for the acquisition finance.[32]

Completion accounts

1.64   One important task which may be required after completion – as a requirement of the acquisition agreement – is the preparation and agreement of completion accounts. This involves the seller and newco ascertaining what the balance sheet of target is at completion; effectively to see what newco actually acquired in the target by way of assets and current liabilities. The reason for this is that the quantum of the purchase price is often predicated on the basis of assumed levels of net cash and working capital. In most businesses net cash and working capital will fluctuate on a daily basis. Consequently, it is rarely possible to accurately determine what the levels of those items are at completion unless completion accounts are subsequently prepared. If it transpires that there was a significant difference between the assumed and actual levels of net cash and working capital at completion a further payment between the seller and newco may be required to put them in the financial position they should have been in given the levels assumed in agreeing the price prior to completion.

An alternative to a completion account mechanism, which is gaining in popularity particularly with auctioned deals as it avoids the prospect of protracted negotiation of completion accounts following completion, is for fixed price deals using what is often referred to as a 'locked-box' mechanism. With this approach the buyer and seller agree a fixed price for the target business in advance of signing, usually based on a balance sheet drawn up and agreed between the parties as of a pre-signing particular date (the 'locked-box date'). To compensate the seller for receiving the agreed purchase price after the locked-box date a 'daily earnings amount' reflecting the earnings of the target business between the balance sheet date and completion or alternatively an agreed rate of interest on the agreed

---

31   Although, as with the 'conditions precedent,' they will not amount to conditions that can be used legally to avoid the contract constituted by the finance document.

32   See also **Chapter 5** for more detail on interest rate hedging and other conditions subsequent.

purchase price for that period may be agreed. The seller will give a series of undertakings to the buyer that, from the locked-box date until completion, there has been no cash or value leakage out of the business to the benefit of the seller or its affiliates (eg, dividend payments, management fees or sales of assets at an undervalue). These undertakings will typically be given on a pound for pound indemnity basis so the buyer is compensated if they are breached. It is inherent with this approach that the buyer must be satisfied that the agreed balance sheet is accurate and, in addition to carrying out due diligence, it would be common to receive a seller warranty on the balance sheet to the effect that it has been prepared with reasonable care based on reliable figures and to be able to rely on a due diligence report from an accountancy firm on that balance sheet.

Syndication

1.65   Where the amount of acquisition finance in a transaction is above a certain level, the acquisition financiers who acted as arrangers and underwriters of such debt will seek to syndicate the debt to other acquisition finance banks and institutions. The acquisition finance documentation will contain provisions to facilitate the legal steps required to effect syndication and the consent of or consultation with the borrower may or may not be required.

In practical terms, the arrangers of the debt – with the detailed input of the sponsor and the management team – will put together an information package comprising detailed information on the target business, the business plan and the funding structure (in the form of an information memorandum), the due diligence reports and the legal documentation, all of which will be sent to prospective syndicate members or made available via the internet.

In all but the smallest deals, syndication of the debt will be of key strategic importance to the arrangers, as being left with large amounts of unsyndicated debt may tie up their balance sheets, restricting their ability to arrange and underwrite other deals, and leave them overly exposed to a single borrower group. For this reason, the arrangers will try to ensure at all stages of the process that the deal being done is within the acceptable parameters of the acquisition finance market. Consequently, in structuring a deal and negotiating the legal documentation, issues raised by the sponsor may not be accepted by the arrangers on grounds of 'syndication risk', although in times of exceptional liquidity this argument may be of less persuasion than at other times.

In very large transactions two or perhaps more private equity houses and two or more acquisition finance banks will join together before completion in order to provide the equity and debt finance packages respectively. The acquisition finance banks will each then syndicate their positions following completion.

Exit

1.66   Ultimately, the sponsor and the management team will be aiming to realise their investments in the business. Such realisations are generally described as 'exits'. The principal exits which the parties would pursue are sale of the business, either to a trade buyer or to a new buy-out team in a secondary buy-out, and flotation of the group (in an IPO). The sponsor might also achieve a partial return on its investment (but not a full exit) through a leveraged recapitalisation. For the acquisition financiers, realisation of their investment should simply be repayment of the debt in accordance with, or ahead of, the agreed schedule. Exits are considered in further detail later in this chapter.

All of the various stages of a buy-out are considered in more detail in the other chapters of this book and, in introductory format, in the sections that follow in this chapter.

Public-to-privates

1.67   Where the target is a listed public company, the timetable for the deal, from the time that a takeover offer or scheme of arrangement is announced will necessarily follow the relevant regulatory regime. For a UK target listed on the London Stock Exchange or admitted to AIM or PLUS this timetable is enshrined in the City Code on Takeovers and Mergers and the Companies Act 1985 (as superseded by the Companies Act 2006). Public-to-privates generally are considered in detail in **Chapter 12**.

Summary timetable for private buy-out

1.68   The following table summarises the various stages that are completed in the execution of a standard private buy-out. A more detailed examination of the buy-out process, including suggested timetables, can be found in **Chapter 11**.

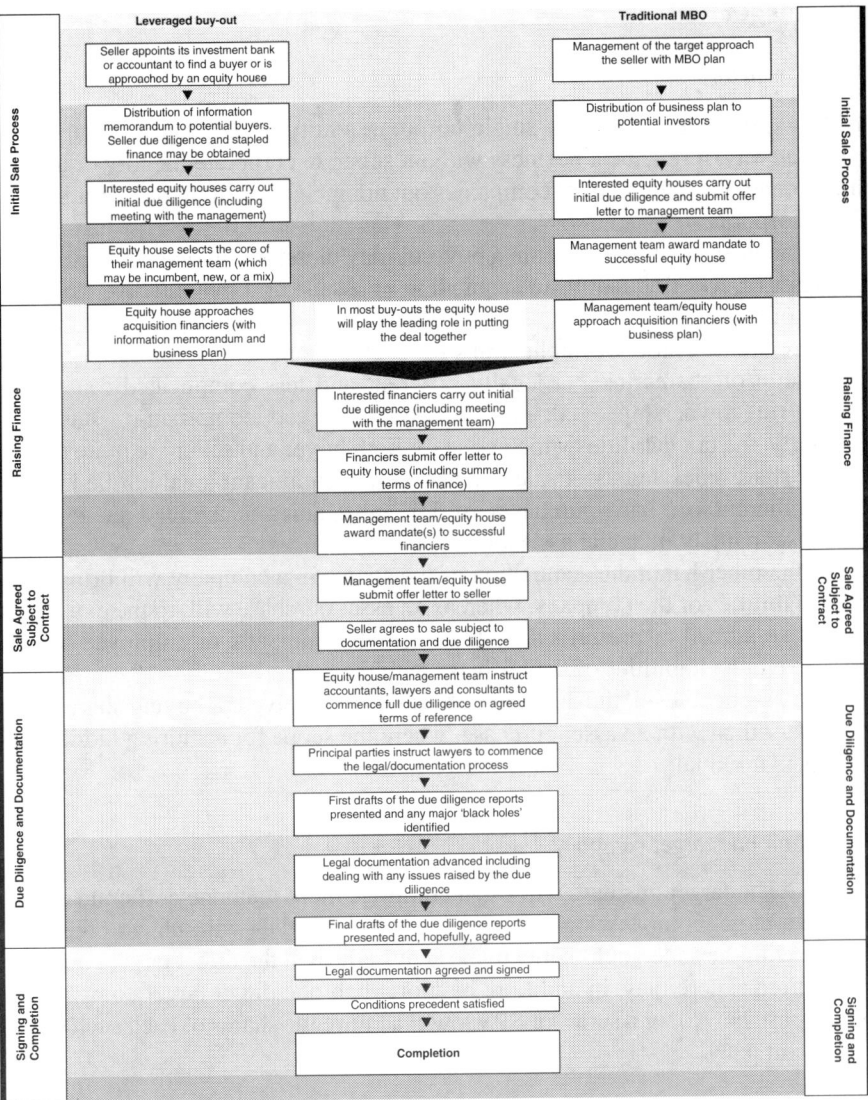

THE ACQUISITION

1.69 At the heart of every buy-out is an acquisition and the structure of the acquisition will reflect a number of the key features of the buy-out.

The precise corporate structure of a buy-out will depend on the nature of the target and the complexity of the financing structure. Thus far in this chapter the 'typical buy-out structure' assumed has been very simple, with a single SPV (newco) acquiring the target from a single seller. In practice this is unlikely other than in the most basic of deals. As considered further below, the reality may involve several SPVs, more than one target in more than one jurisdiction and other variables.

The target

Shares or assets

1.70   The target may be a single corporate entity or a group of companies. Alternatively, it may be a business without separate corporate identity or a division spread over a number of companies but not including all of the operations of those corporates.

The acquisition of the target in a buy-out may therefore involve an acquisition of shares or, less frequently, an acquisition of assets, or it may involve a combination of both.

There are a number of implications for each type of acquisition. Transferring ownership of shares takes a legally different and less complicated route than transferring ownership of all of the individual assets comprising a business. Similarly, the tax liabilities which arise for both buyer and seller are quite different for share sales and asset sales. In addition, a significant legal hurdle historically inherent in share purchases of UK companies is avoided in an asset purchase, namely financial assistance.[33]

On the other hand, the acquisition of the shares in a company will bring with it the liabilities of the company, whereas an asset purchase will, to the extent not otherwise agreed or prescribed by law (eg, environmental or employee liabilities), leave the liabilities of the business with the seller.

On a practical level, the due diligence exercise involved in buying shares may be greater than with an asset purchase, where the scope for acquiring hidden liabilities is minimal.

More than one target company

1.71   The target business will often comprise more than one corporate entity. Where a target company has subsidiaries of its own they will, unless otherwise agreed with the seller, automatically be acquired when the direct target company is acquired. There may, in addition, be more than one direct target company, in which case newco, or a series of SPVs, will acquire the shares of each such direct target company.

Public targets

1.72   If the target is a listed public company a different process is followed. This is because in many jurisdictions, and certainly in the UK, the acquisition of listed public companies is separately regulated. In the UK the City Code on Takeovers and Mergers, which is promulgated and overseen by the Panel on

---

33 In fact, the prohibition on private companies giving financial assistance is to be repealed on 1 October 2008. The prohibition applicable to public companies is to remain under the Companies Act 2006, Pt 18, Ch 2, which is to be brought into force on 1 October 2009.

Takeovers and Mergers, and the Companies Act 1985 (as superseded by the Companies Act 2006) contain the key regulations. The acquisition of UK listed public companies is considered in detail in **Chapter 12**.

Multinational targets

1.73   The target business may comprise companies and assets in more than one jurisdiction, in which case local laws concerning the transfer of ownership of shares and assets will require consideration. In particular, the taxation liabilities arising on transfers of shares and assets respectively may mitigate towards choosing either a share purchase or an asset purchase in any of the relevant jurisdictions.

Acquisition vehicles

1.74   Thus far the chapter has assumed that a single SPV (newco) will itself borrow the acquisition finance, raise private equity finance and make the acquisition.

In practice, in all but the most basic deals, there will be more than one SPV established to raise the necessary finance and effect the acquisition. Typically there will be two or more SPVs established by the deal sponsor, one on top of each other. Where the financing structure comprises several layers of finance a number of SPVs will be formed, into which the respective financial instruments are invested. By having the subordinated and junior ranking debt higher up the structure and further away from the cash generative target group operating companies (opcos), a form of 'structural subordination' is established. In simple terms, the flow of cash up the corporate structure can be siphoned off by the senior creditors before it reaches the SPVs against which the subordinated and junior creditors have recourse.

In addition, by establishing the principal equity investment vehicle in a tax-friendly jurisdiction (perhaps Luxembourg) there may be tax benefits for the private equity investors in a multi-jurisdictional transaction. Similarly, again in a multi-jurisdictional transaction, more than one SPV may be used to acquire different parts of the business in different jurisdictions in the most tax efficient or legally beneficial manner.

The various SPVs in a structure are often given different names reflecting their position in the structure. Thus there may be a 'topco', a 'midco' or 'holdco' and a 'newco' (or 'bidco' in a public-to-private).

Example Structures

1.75

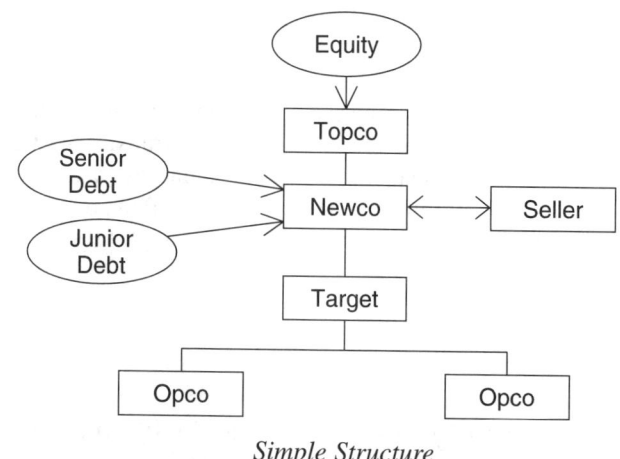

Simple Structure

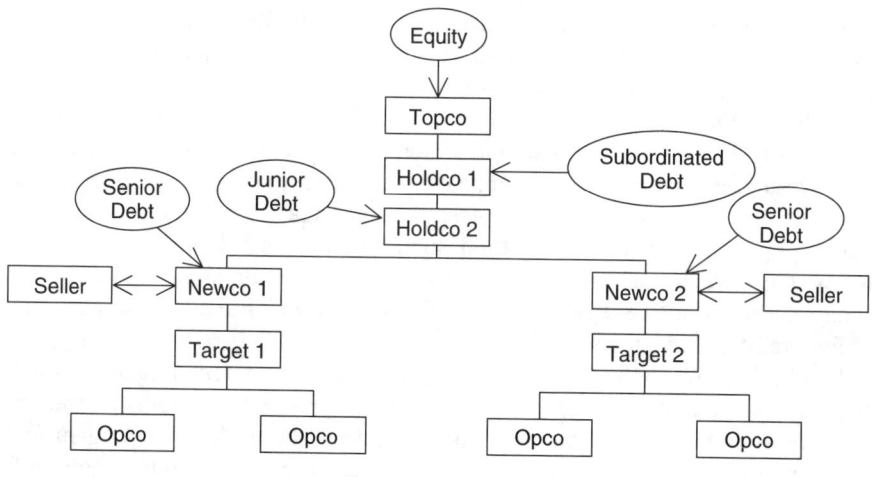

Complex Structure

THE FUNDING STRUCTURE

Determining the funding requirement – the uses of funds

Purchase price and deal costs

1.76   The basic element of the funding requirement for a buy-out will be the purchase price payable to the seller. In addition, the buyer will incur transaction costs, including the fees and external costs of the acquisition financiers and sponsor. For smaller deals these may be as much as 10% of the total funding requirement and will reduce as a percentage the larger the deal is. In very large deals they may still account for say 3% to 5% of the total funding requirement, however.

Refinancing debt

1.77   A further component of the funding requirement, which might be assumed within the price but which, for a number of reasons, will often be identified as a distinct element of the funding requirement, is an amount for the refinancing of the existing debt of the target. In establishing the purchase price for a business it is often assumed that the business is to be bought on a cash and debt free basis. The seller will discharge the debts of the target group at or prior to completion effectively out of the purchase price consideration. However, there may be significant benefits in buying the target with the debt in place (for a reduced price) and refinancing that debt directly from the acquisition finance banks. This is particularly so in multi-jurisdictional buy-outs and UK public -to-privates.[34] Where this is the case the funding requirement will include a separate amount for refinancing existing target debt.

Working capital

1.78   In most cases there will also be a working capital requirement, the size of which will depend on the working capital profile of the business; which will be a function of the periodic and relative movements of the amounts of debtors, stock and creditors in the business.

Capex

1.79   In certain cases, the business plan may involve investment in new fixed assets, such as a production line or a new factory, or in a development project which requires significant capital expenditure. Where this capital expenditure requirement exceeds the surplus cashflow forecast to be generated by the target, it will need to be financed through specific external funding. The senior debt providers may be willing to provide a separate 'capex' facility to meet some or all of this requirement.

Other banking facilities

1.80   In addition, the target business may require discrete tranches of finance leasing, bonding or other trade-related finance or have other specific financial needs which extend the funding requirements beyond the basic components. Such requirements can, for the purposes of this section, be treated in the same way as the working capital requirement, reflecting the fact that they may be provided as part of a working capital facility. It is not proposed that specific consideration be given to such requirements.

---

34 See **Chapters 12** and **13**.

Further acquisition facilities

1.81   Finally, the senior debt providers will occasionally agree to provide a further acquisition facility to enable the buyer to 'bolt-on' a further business after completion of the principal deal. Having once been rare in the UK, these facilities have increased in popularity in the banking market throughout the 2000s, especially in larger deals, but still generally require deal specific consideration. These facilities may be of the committed or uncommitted variety.[35]

Satisfying the funding requirement – the sources of funds

General

1.82   When first considering a sources and uses analysis, it might appear that the natural order of events is to determine the funding requirement and then to obtain sufficient finance to meet the requirement; and on paper this is what appears to have happened when the funding structure of a completed deal is examined. However, the amount which the buyer is able to pay for the target will ultimately be influenced by the amount of finance that the sponsor and acquisition financiers are willing to put into the deal. In practice this means that the purchase price offered by the buyer – and therefore the funding requirement – will often be determined by direct reference to, and at the same time as, the determination of the sources of funding. The link between the amount of debt available to financial sponsors to do buy-outs and the price they are willing to pay is clear. The result, in an extremely competitive market, has been to put acquisition finance at the centre of the buy-out industry and the demand for various forms of acquisition finance has continued to grow. In response and through aggressive financial engineering, the acquisition finance market has consistently developed new funding structures to satisfy the growing demand for leverage.

Since the late 1990s the UK market has seen the debuts of stretched senior debt, alphabet notes, single 'B' note facilities, 'institutional' mezzanine including jumbo-sized tranches, mezzanine notes, senior and junior mezzanine tranches, second lien debt and public and private PIK notes. At the same time as new products are developed new classes of investor are attracted to the market or, in some cases, new products are developed in order to attract new classes of investor.

In particular, the growth in the UK and elsewhere of CDO, CLO and other leveraged loan funds, which invest in specific elements of buy-out funding structures, such as the B and C tranches of senior debt packages[36] or certain junior debt products, has provided arranging banks and sponsors with a source of finance previously not available to them. At the same time as stretching or refining existing and accepted models of funding structures with new products, the traditional products, such as the core A tranche of senior debt, have, where still utilised[37], become commoditised with instantly recognisable features such as pricing, rela-

---

35 See also **Chapter 5** for more detail.

36 B and C tranches of senior debt are considered in further detail in **Chapters 3** and **5**.

37 A development in the latter half of the 2000s has seen senior debt structures with just B and C tranches (or a single B tranche) and no amortising A tranche. See also **Chapters 3** and **5**.

tive size and, to a lesser extent, size as a multiple of earnings and an increasing number of other terms and features. Similarly legal documentation is converging allowing for shorter timeframes to achieve deal completion.

The various sources of funds that may be used to finance a buy-out are set out in the following paragraphs.

Equity

1.83 A core component of newco's financial resources will be the capital contribution of its shareholders – the management team and the sponsor.

Management equity

1.84 Management equity will take the form of ordinary shares funded from the management team's personal resources. Of all the forms of finance in a buy-out it will carry the maximum risk and, together with the institutional equity, the maximum return. The management team may also subscribe for quasi-equity in the form of redeemable preference shares or, more likely, subordinated loan capital. In a secondary buy-out the management are likely to be required – by the sponsor – to roll-over a significant amount of equity from the initial buy-out and this will often take the form of quasi-equity.

Institutional equity

1.85 Institutional equity – subscribed by the sponsor – will take the form of ordinary shares[38] and quasi-equity in the form of redeemable preference shares or subordinated loan capital.[39]

Overall level of equity

1.86 The total amount of equity (including quasi-equity) which the sponsor and the management team will invest as a portion of the total funding requirement is largely a function of the nature of the funding structure and in particular the other forms of finance being used. So, in a structure with equity and senior debt – but no junior debt – the total equity component will often comprise 40 to 50% of the total, although, in practice, structures of this nature are quite rare in all but the smallest buy-outs. Where there is also junior debt in a structure the amount of equity can sometimes be as low as 20% or even less of the total funding requirement. In any given structure, the majority of the equity component will usually comprise institutional quasi-equity subscribed by the sponsor.

The absolute level of equity will be set principally by reference to the return on investment which the sponsor will seek to make assuming the business plan is achieved. The projected total return on investment is determined by reference to

---

38 Often they will be ordinary shares with preferred rights to dividends and returns of capital ahead of the management ordinary shares.

39 Subordinated loan capital is generally a more tax efficient instrument than preference share capital.

the assumed annual yield accruing on the equity (if any) and an exit at an assumed point in the future at an assumed value (normally based on a pre-determined multiple of earnings in the year of exit). This return is commonly expressed as the internal rate of return – the IRR – of an investment.[40]

Senior debt

1.87   Senior debt provided by senior lenders is the main element of all acquisition financings. It will typically take the form of a core floating rate[41] medium term loan for acquisition funding purposes together with other facilities required to meet other specific funding requirements. These may include a loan to finance specific capital expenditure projects, a further acquisition facility and a working capital facility to meet the working capital requirements of the business after completion. The senior debt is usually split into one, two or three separate loans or tranches, called the A note, B note and C note respectively. The A note will generally amortise over seven years, the B note will be repayable in one or two 'bullet' instalments at years 7.5 and 8 and the C note will be repayable in one or two instalments at years 8.5 and 9. In the latter half of the 2000s, the larger deals and some mid-market deals have included only B and C notes (or possibly just a single B note) and no A note.[42] This is partly to satisfy institutional demand for the non-amortising tranches but it also enables higher leverage to be employed given the reduced debt service requirement with no principal falling due. At the other end of the scale, some lower mid-market and smaller deals may only have a single A note tranche forming the core senior debt.[43] The interest rate margin for each of these tranches is set to reflect the respective maturities.[44]

The amount of senior debt which the senior banks[45] are willing to make available will be determined principally on the basis of a credit assessment of the target business, encompassing its sector, the strength of its management and its business prospects generally, and the known element of the finance structure

---

40 How the amount of equity invested affects the IRR of an investment is considered further in **Chapter 3**.
41 That is, the interest rate will be a margin above a variable underlying cost of funds; usually LIBOR or EURIBOR.
42 See para **1.96** for example structures.
43 When they originally appeared in the UK market in the late 1990s the additional (B and C) tranches were referred to as alphabet notes. The word 'note' is often used to describe a particular discrete tranche of a debt package. It is a reference to the US practice of having promissory notes issued to lenders to evidence the loans owing to them.
44 Thus the interest rate margin has traditionally been priced at around 2.25% for an A note, 2.75% for the B note and 3.25% for the C note. In a typical structure with A, B and C notes this provides a blended return (margin) of between 2.75% and 3.00%, depending on the exact split of amounts between the A, B and C tranches and taking into account the amortisation of the A note. That all said, in the mid to late 2000s there has been significant downward pressure on the pricing of senior debt and margins in the region of 2.00%, 2.25% and 2.75% (or lower in some cases) for the A, B and C tranches, respectively, have been seen. Capital expenditure and further acquisition facilities would usually be priced from 2.25% to 2.75%, depending on maturity among other factors, and the working capital facility is normally priced at the same rate as the A note (if any, typically being 2.25% or perhaps 2.00%).
45 In fact, unless the amounts involved are above, say, £200 million, it will often be just a single bank which arranges and underwrites the entire amount of senior debt at completion. However, that bank will probably syndicate the senior debt to other banks and institutions following completion.

– basically, the amount of equity to be invested and an assumed purchase price. The analysis of the target business will specifically include reference to the projected cashflow which the target is forecast to generate in the management team's business plan.[46] It is the cashflow generated over the life of the loans which will be used to repay, and pay interest on, the senior debt, and the banks will lend against those cashflows rather than the underlying asset value of the business.[47]

On a rule of thumb basis only, and noting that each deal will be different, the senior debt figure may account for up to 50 to 60% of the total funding requirement. Where there is also a large tranche of junior debt the amount of senior debt is likely be less.

Funding gap

1.88 Having determined the respective amounts of equity and senior debt available, the total of these amounts will ideally satisfy the funding requirement. If not, the amount of finance available will be insufficient to enable newco to pay the purchase price which the seller is expecting and to meet newco's deal costs. In other words, there will be a 'funding' gap.

The principal way in which the gap is filled is by using junior debt in addition to senior debt. In actual fact, funding gaps are often only notional. It is more often the case that junior debt is used to increase the amount of funding available to newco in advance of determining the funding requirement. Junior debt of one sort or another will be found in a majority of UK and other European buy-outs.

Junior debt

1.89 Junior debt comes in various different forms. The common feature is that it is invariably junior ranking to the senior debt. That is, it is subordinated to the senior debt to a certain extent – and it may also be referred to as subordinated debt. There are four main varietals of junior debt currently used in UK buy-outs, although in such a dynamic and evolving market hybrid instruments and even entirely new forms of debt may appear.

Second lien debt

1.90 Second lien debt is a relative newcomer to the buy-out market, having first appeared in 2003. In traditional buy-out structures – by contrast with refinancings of mature buy-outs and leveraged corporate acquisitions – it is often used in relatively small amounts as a form of stretched senior debt rather than core junior debt; comprising the 'D' tranche of the larger senior debt package. It will still be subordinated (to some extent) to the other senior debt tranches, however. In these structures it is common for there also to be a core tranche of other

---

46 These projections are referred to as the management team's base case or, given that they will be produced in the form of a financial model, the base case model. A key element of the financial due diligence will be verification (and viability) of the base case model.

47 Although some comfort will be obtained from a strong asset base, over which the senior lenders will take security, acquisition finance is cashflow based financing.

junior debt – either mezzanine or high yield debt – which ranks behind the second lien tranche. It is also increasingly used – often in refinancings of mature buy-outs and leveraged corporate deals but also, at times of high market liquidity, in a wide variety of buy-out structures – in larger amounts as an outright alternative to high yield and mezzanine debt.

The stretched senior form of second lien debt is a tool to increase leverage while preserving the other elements of the funding structure. This amounts to fine tuning of the financial structure through an instrument that has intermediate risk and intermediate pricing between traditional senior and junior instruments. As the name suggests it is secured with second-ranking target group security, behind the core senior debt. It is normally priced at an agreed margin above the underlying cost of funds.[48] Where used in the same structure as mezzanine debt or high yield it would rank ahead of these investments. It is sometimes referred to as senior subordinated debt and may be documented as a loan or as an issue of bonds.

Mezzanine finance

1.91 Mezzanine finance remains the most commonly used form of junior debt and has been the traditional answer to a funding gap or notional funding gap since the early 1990s. It will take the form of a floating rate[49] medium term loan repayable shortly – perhaps six months or more usually one year – after the last tranche of senior debt to be repaid.[50] Because it is only repayable after the senior debt it will carry a higher rate of interest to reflect the greater risk of it not being repaid.[51] The mezzanine lender will carry out a substantially similar credit assessment of the target and newco's ability to repay, and pay interest on, the senior debt based on the projected cashflow in the base case model as the senior lenders. In addition, it will need to assess newco's ability to pay interest on the mezzanine debt and, in theory at least, to repay the mezzanine debt after all the senior debt has been repaid.[52]

Until the early 2000s the mezzanine lender would also expect to receive share warrants from newco – or whichever SPV in the structure is the true equity vehicle – in return for taking on this higher risk form of debt. A warrant is an option

---

48 Perhaps in the region of, say, 400-600 basis points above LIBOR/EURIBOR all of which will be payable in cash unlike say European mezzanine debt which also has a significant PIK component to the interest rate. Note that a basis point is 1/100th of a percentage point; so 400 basis points ('bps' for short) is the same as 4%.

49 That is, the interest rate will be a margin above a variable underlying cost of funds; usually LIBOR or EURIBOR.

50 That is, the 'A', 'B', or 'C' tranche (as applicable) or in deals with second lien debt, after that has been repaid too.

51 Interest rate margins will typically be in the region of say 750–1050 basis points (and historically 1000–1200 basis points), of which approximately half will be payable in cash and the remainder will be capitalised as principal; that is, the interest will be paid-in-kind. See **Chapter 7** for more detail, including the use of PIK 'toggle' provisions that allow the borrower to elect to pay interest in cash or in kind.

52 In fact, it is now quite common for the sponsor to seek to recapitalise a transaction in the first two or three years. This will inevitably involve a refinancing of the senior debt and the more expensive mezzanine debt with a new senior and reduced junior debt package that has a lower overall interest cost. For this reason analysis of the cashflows generated in the period after the scheduled repayment of the senior debt is not generally required per se.

to subscribe for ordinary shares in the equity vehicle in certain circumstances, usually where an equity exit is about to occur. Such warrants are by their nature potentially very lucrative – they were historically called the 'equity kicker' – and allow a mezzanine lender to take a different economic view of the transaction to the senior lender.

Since the early 2000s, increasingly fewer mezzanine finance packages include warrants and their use is now generally confined only to smaller deals. This is largely as a result of the advent of a new class of 'institutional' mezzanine provided by institutional investors – particularly leveraged loan funds – that are specifically attracted to long term interest yield and consequently do not require warrants, and because, given the choice, sponsors prefer not to give away equity.

High yield debt

1.92   High yield debt is an alternative form of junior debt to mezzanine used in large transactions. The debt takes the form of bonds – also called notes – issued by an SPV established for this purpose and under common ownership with newco. To be commercially viable, a high yield bond issue relies on very strong and proven cashflow streams from the underlying target business. As a capital market instrument the size of the issue must be sufficient for there to be a 'market' in the bonds, which generally means that the issue must be no less than £75-100 million, and in practice it will usually be substantially more. As a result high yield debt is only appropriate in the larger transactions.

As between high yield debt and mezzanine debt there are sound reasons that favour both forms of junior debt. Traditionally the deciding factor was deal size, with mezzanine debt being the junior debt instrument of choice for medium sized mid-market deals of up to say £250 million total deal size and high yield issues being the staple junior debt product in larger deals. In the 1990s and early 2000s there was insufficient liquidity in the European mezzanine market to fund deals much above this level. That changed in the early 2000s with the arrival of mezzanine hungry CDOs and CLOs, new dedicated mezzanine funds and other institutional buyers of mezzanine debt that were also new to the market in the UK and Europe, such as US pension, insurance and hedge funds. The appearance of these investors effectively resulted in the creation of a new asset class, namely institutional mezzanine, that could be used in significant sums in larger buy-outs than before. The fact that these new mezzanine investors did not require the equity diluting warrants made this form of mezzanine popular with sponsors and put mezzanine on a par with high yield as regards this key feature. Institutional mezzanine thus became a real alternative to high yield in all but the largest multi-billion pound deals.

High yield debt providers will still point to the lower all-in cost of high yield debt in larger deals.[53] They will also refer to the fact that high yield bonds contain

---

53   The deal costs and fees tend to be higher with high yield issues than with mezzanine but the all-in yield or 'coupon' of between say 8 and 10% typically (having moved from nearer 10–12% in the late 1990s and early 2000s), compares very favourably with the floating rate yields of 7.5–10.5% over cost of funds on mezzanine (even taking into account that perhaps half of the mezzanine margin will be payable in kind rather than cash). See **Chapters 3, 7** and **8** generally for more detail on the pricing of these instruments.

looser incurrence tests and no financial covenants by comparison with the more onerous maintenance tests found in mezzanine debt documents. On the other hand, high yield bonds typically contain more extensive 'call protection' provisions than mezzanine debt, meaning that an exit in the early years of a financing structure would be more expensive with high yield than would be the case with mezzanine debt.

There are a number of other competing features of both instruments that may lead to the sponsor favouring one rather than the other[54] but the ultimate deciding factor may still be deal size. High yield debt should still provide the greatest leverage in a deal and thus the greatest buying power for the sponsor.

High yield bridging debt

1.93   By contrast with mezzanine debt, it is usual for high yield to be bridged by a dedicated bridging loan prior to the issue of the bonds some time following completion of the acquisition. This is because the timetable for the marketing and issue of high yield bonds does not conform to the timetable for a conventional UK buy-out and the bond issue must be bridged in order to close the buy-out within the usual timing parameters. The terms of high yield bridging debt have evolved significantly since high yield debt first appeared in the European market. A reason for this has been the relatively hit-and-miss nature of that market for significant periods of the economic cycle and the need for a fall back scenario if the bonds are not ultimately taken up. In practice high yield bridging finance is generally structured as a bridging loan that, if the high yield debt has not been successfully issued after a period of, say, 12 to 18 months, converts into either conventional institutional mezzanine, with pricing that will attract sufficient investor appetite, or another form of debt security that can be successfully sold down, which will often simply amount to increasing (flexing) the coupon on the high yield to a sufficiently high level. The bridge itself will generally be priced to reflect the high yield being bridged. In addition, to incentivise the sponsor to get the issue away, the margin will often be set to increase by say 25 bps[55] every quarter, a so-called 'exploding bridge'.

PIK note debt

1.94   PIK note debt, which like second lien has only been around since the early to mid 2000s, is a further form of junior debt that may be incorporated into a funding structure in addition to the senior and core junior debt. Its purpose is to increase the leverage in a deal without using up any available cashflow generated by the target business. It will invariably be the most junior ranking form of acquisition finance and will be structurally or contractually subordinated to all the other elements. There are really two distinct types of PIK note debt, private PIK and public PIK. Public PIK is structured and documented for issue in the public debt markets. Private PIK is not, and may be structured and documented in vari-

---

54   A more detailed comparison is provided in **Chapter 3**.

55   Bps refers to basis points. There are 100 basis points in each single percentage point; so 25 bps means 0.25%.

ous formats. It is usually subscribed and held by a single investor or a relatively small syndicate of investors.

Private PIK is probably the more common form in buy-outs per se, although it is still relatively infrequently used. It usually takes the form of subordinated loan capital issued either as loan notes or as deep discount bonds (DDBs) or occasionally as a straight subordinated loan.[56] To reflect its higher risk profile subordinated behind all senior and core junior debt, the PIK note investors will receive a relatively high return,[57] which might include warrants as with true mezzanine debt. In fact, it is perhaps useful to think of PIK notes as a form of stretched mezzanine or junior debt. In practice, the PIK note element of the deal might be underwritten by the junior debt underwriter.

Public PIK is essentially a form of high yield debt with a coupon that pays in kind rather than cash. It is not really used in primary buy-outs per se but more often in a refinancing of a mature buy-out and in particular to finance dividend recaps. Public PIK which is used for these purposes is sometimes also referred to as 'holdco PIK'.[58]

In each case, PIK note debt is usually priced to have a yield that reflects its subordinated status. In the case of notes and loan capital this will be an interest rate. In the case of DDBs the bonds are issued at a discount and over time the redemption price increases at the same rate as a compounding interest rate. In either case the principal amount invested grows substantially over time as the initial investment compounds (usually six monthly or annually). Generally the yield is a fixed rate, but floating rate yields are also possible.

Seller finance

1.95   If there is a gap between the headline price which the seller requires for the target and the amount of acquisition finance and equity available, the seller may, assuming that no other prospective buyer is willing to pay its full asking price, agree to defer payment of part of the purchase price. Such deferred consideration will generally be structured as subordinated loan capital issued by newco, or sometimes as a straight loan to newco; it is often referred to as a seller 'note'. In any case, the buyer in effect pays the higher headline price but the seller invests the deferred portion as finance into the buy-out funding structure.

The terms of realisation of the deferred consideration by the seller – that is, the period of deferral and any conditions thereof – will be a function of the precise reason why deferred consideration is required ie, why there is a price gap. If the seller's justification for a higher headline price is that the business is sounder than is suggested by the base case model assumed by the financiers, then the deferral period may be linked to the achievement of performance targets that justify the higher purchase price. Ideally the acquisition financiers would prefer that a seller note would not be redeemable prior to repayment in full of all of the

---

56   See **Chapter 9** for further detail.
57   Yields for PIK note debt might be in the region of 10–20% per annum, which when compounded six-monthly or annually makes the investment very high yielding.
58   See **Chapter 9** generally.

senior and junior debt but in practice this is unlikely to satisfy a seller. A seller on the other hand may insist that the deferral is simply a time deferral and that the seller note is to be treated as cash, payable in instalments after completion. The point at which both can agree usually means that the redemption conditions require a material over-performance against the base case, thus justifying the higher price, and that in any other circumstance, including insolvency, the seller note is fully subordinated to the acquisition finance.

An alternative to deferred consideration for dealing with a price or funding gap, which takes the opposite approach to assuming the higher headline price, is to include a 'non-embarrassment clause' in the acquisition agreement. These clauses provide for an initial assumption of the lower price for which funding is available but on the basis that additional consideration is payable if the target is sold on at a higher price relatively quickly following completion. Such clauses are resisted strongly by sponsors but in special circumstances the seller may be able to require such a provision.

'Sources and uses' tables

1.96   Satisfaction of the funding requirement is often demonstrated by a 'sources and uses' table. The following example tables illustrate this. The structures illustrated are not necessarily all 'on market' as of the date of this book or indeed likely to remain so given the evolutionary nature of the acquisition finance market.

Example 1: Small deal

Use of funds	(£)	Source of funds	(£)
Purchase price	20.0m	Management equity	0.5m
Deal costs	2.0m	Institutional equity	9.5m
		Senior debt (acquisition term loan)	12.0m
Working capital	3.0m	Senior debt (working capital facility)	3.0m
TOTAL	25.0m	TOTAL	25.0m

Example 2: Lower mid-market deal

Use of funds	(£)	Source of funds	(£)
Purchase price	90m	Management equity	1.2m
Deal costs	5m	Institutional equity	28.8m
		Seller note	5m
		Mezzanine loan	15m
		Senior debt (acquisition term loan A)	30m
		Senior debt (acquisition term loan B)	15m
Capex	3m	Senior debt (capex loan)	3m
Working capital	10m	Senior debt (working capital facility)	10m
TOTAL	108m	TOTAL	108m

Example 3: Upper mid-market deal

Use of funds	(£)	Source of funds	(£)
Purchase price	330m	Management equity	5m
Deal costs	10m	Institutional equity	135m
		Mezzanine loan	42m
		Senior debt (acquisition term loan A)[59]	–
		Senior debt (acquisition term loan B)	70m
		Senior debt (acquisition term loan C)	70m
		Second lien debt (acquisition term loan D)	18m
Working capital	20m	Senior debt (working capital facility)	20m
TOTAL	360m	TOTAL	360m

Example 4: Large deal

Use of funds	(£)	Source of funds	(£)
Purchase price	525m	Management equity	5m
Deal costs	25m	Institutional equity	145m
		Mezzanine loan	75m
		PIK note debt	25m
		Senior debt (acquisition term loan A)[60]	100m
		Senior debt (acquisition term loan B)	100m
		Senior debt (acquisition term loan C)	100m
Working capital	30m	Senior debt (working capital facility)	30m
TOTAL	580m	TOTAL	580m

Example 5: Mega deal

Use of funds	(€)	Source of funds	(€)
Purchase price and	3850m	Management equity	10m
deal costs		Institutional equity	690m
		High yield bond	900m
		PIK note debt	250m
		Senior debt (acquisition term loan A)[61]	1000m
		Senior debt (acquisition term loan B)	500m
		Senior debt (acquisition term loan C)	500m
Working capital	425m	Senior debt (working capital facility)	425m
TOTAL	4275m	TOTAL	4275m

59 Note that this structure has no A tranche, which became quite common in the late 2000s. See also **Chapter 5** as regards senior debt structures without A tranches.
60 Note that this structure has A, B and C tranches of equal size, which was common during the mid 2000s in particular. See **Chapter 5**.
61 Note that this structure has a relatively large A tranche by comparison with the B and C tranches (in the ratio of 2:1). This was common during the first half of the 2000s but less common thereafter, when the A tranche was more likely to be downsized or possibly even dispensed with entirely. See **Chapter 5**.

Risk and return

Risk matched with return

1.97   There is a logical balance between the return that each of the parties investing in a buy-out can expect and the risks facing such investments. Simply put, as between the various parties, the greater the potential risk that a party faces in respect of its investment the greater the return that can be expected if the deal is a success.

Ultimately, this is because the required levels of return of the various institutions should, in theory, reflect a statistical analysis of the chances of that return materialising over a portfolio of similar investments together with a premium reflecting the amount of risk taken. In practice, it may be more difficult to link risk and return in any directly quantifiable manner.

Risks

1.98   What is meant by the risk of a financial investment is the ability of the relevant investor or financier to realise the investment made, both in terms of the capital invested and to receive a yield on that investment. Thus the senior banks will have a greater right to the repayment of the senior debt than the junior creditors will to repayment of the junior debt. Similarly, the senior banks have greater rights to receive interest on the senior debt than the junior creditors do on the junior debt. If all goes well all the parties will receive their capital back plus the applicable yield but if it doesn't – and ultimately in insolvency – the agreed order of priorities will apply.

The order of priorities – and thus the relative risk each of the parties faces – is principally effected through the application of so-called 'subordination' principles. There are essentially four subordination principles. First, share capital is subordinated on insolvency to loan capital and other debt. Secondly, certain debt will be secured, whereas some will not. Thirdly, certain debt will be structurally subordinated to other debt through the use of different SPVs as borrowers in the funding structure. Fourthly, and most fundamentally in practice, the parties will agree in an intercreditor or subordination agreement to a pre-determined order of priorities. This agreement will override all other applicable principles. Subordination principles and intercreditor documents are considered in detail in **Chapter 10**.

The subordination arrangements will effectively ensure that the order of priorities and risk in a buy-out funding structure will be as follows:[62]

- least risk, senior debt;

- junior debt;[63]

---

62   The analysis ignores seller finance which may rank between junior debt and institutional quasi-equity but this may only be determined on a deal specific basis. In addition, the ranking of the institutional equity and the management equity will occasionally be pari passu.

63   As considered elsewhere there are a number of forms of junior debt which are treated in different ways for subordination purposes. In some transactions there will be more than one layer of junior debt with further ranking between such layers. See **Chapter 10** generally.

- institutional quasi-equity;[64]

- institutional equity; and

- highest risk, management equity.

Returns

1.99 The returns which can be expected on the respective investments referred to above might be of the following magnitude:[65]

Investment	Return
Senior debt	2.25 to 3.25%[66]
Second lien debt	400-600 bps[67]
True mezzanine debt	14–16% IRR[68]
Institutional mezzanine debt	750–1050 bps[69]
High yield debt	8–10% fixed interest[70]
PIK note debt	10–20% fixed interest[71]
Institutional equity	20-35% IRR[72]
Management equity	£££[73]

64 Where, as is sometimes the case, there is more than one form of institutional quasi-equity there may be further ranking between the various instruments.

65 The figures given are necessarily illustrative. As market conditions change, so typically does the pricing of the various instruments.

66 This is the traditional standard range of interest rate margins, above cost of funds (LIBOR or EURIBOR), for the three tranches of senior debt commonly used in buy-outs. The senior A note facility has traditionally been priced at 2.25% subject to a margin ratchet (see **Chapter 5**), the senior B note at 2.75% and the senior C note at 3.25%. In addition, the B and C notes may be subject to downward flex to 2.50% and 3.00%, respectively, particularly in larger deals. In fact, in the latter half of the 2000s, downward pressure on acquisition finance pricing generally has resulted in margins as low as 2.00%, 2.25% and 2.75% (or lower in some cases) for the A, B and C notes respectively. Senior debt pricing is considered in further detail in **Chapter 5**.

67 This is a typical range of the interest rate margin above cost of funds (LIBOR or EURIBOR). See **Chapter 6** for further detail.

68 Warranted mezzanine is typically quoted on an 'all-in' basis so that the warrant return can be factored in. See **Chapter 7** generally.

69 This is a typical range of the interest rate margin above cost of funds (LIBOR or EURIBOR). See **Chapter 7** for further detail.

70 Although high yield is commonly priced with a fixed yield, issues of floating rate notes (FRNs) priced at a spread (margin) over cost of funds (LIBOR or EURIBOR) have increased during the 2000s.

71 This might be expressed as an IRR but since the interest rate will compound annually or semi-annually the IRR will also closely correlate to this amount. If warrants are included, the IRR may be higher. As with high yield, fixed rate yields are more common but floating rate yields are also possible.

72 This will be the target return on a blended basis combining the quasi-equity and the true equity.

73 The return to the management is not usually expressed as an IRR. It will typically be viewed as an absolute amount that is of sufficient size to properly incentivise the management.

DUE DILIGENCE

1.100 In the case of an acquisition of an asset, a business or a company, due diligence is the exercise which the buyer will carry out prior to contracting to buy the asset, business or company in order to verify the financial, commercial and legal assumptions which it has made in determining the price to be paid and that the acquisition is viable generally. Where the acquirer is a corporate entity a satisfactory due diligence exercise will assist the directors in demonstrating that they exercised their powers in the interests of the company in binding it into the proposed acquisition. Due diligence is equally important to the financiers of an acquisition and will be required by the acquisition financiers in a buy-out.

Due diligence in buy-outs

1.101 The due diligence exercise will comprise two elements. To a certain extent the principal parties will carry out some due diligence matters directly themselves and in addition they will appoint third-party advisers to carry out additional specific due diligence tasks.[74]

Due diligence by the parties

1.102 The direct due diligence really falls into three main categories. First, the buyer and its financiers will wish to review in some detail the financial information relating to the target that has been provided to them by the seller. This will be at the core of the buyer's valuation analysis and the financiers' credit analysis. Secondly, they will wish to visit the main sites where the business operates. This will serve a number of purposes, including, on a simple yet fundamental level, enabling the parties to have a real sense of what they are buying or financing. It will also be an opportunity to meet management. The third major category of direct due diligence will be an assessment of the senior management of the business. The success of most buy-outs places a heavy responsibility on the ability of the management team to deliver the business plan and the principal parties will be keen to assess their abilities carefully.

Third-party due diligence – due diligence reports

1.103 The most extensive element of the due diligence process involve the commissioning of due diligence reports from specialist advisers and consultants. Typically they will cover some or all of the following aspects of the target business.

Accounting and finance

1.104 This is generally the most important area of due diligence. It is intended to verify the financial status and health of the target business. More particularly it is used to identify unusual or non-recurring income and expenditure items in

---

74 Due diligence generally and specific due diligence reports are also considered in **Chapter 11**.

order to verify the reliability of the base earnings of the business as represented in the base case model. It may separately cover pensions and tax or there may be separate reports on these items. It may also look at the target's IT systems and, in particular, any financial reporting systems.

Commercial or market due diligence

1.105   Market consultants will often be commissioned to comment on the commercial environment within which the target business operates. In particular, it may detail the target's actual and potential competitors and the target's market share. The market report should also cover market trends in the relevant business sectors and, ideally, specifically comment on the commercial and market-orientated assumptions underlying the business plan and confirm whether they are achievable. In the larger private equity houses, where there may be sector expertise, much of this work may be done in-house.

Environmental matters

1.106   Depending on the nature of the target business and the properties it owns or occupies, environmental consultants may be instructed to undertake an environmental audit of real estate owned, occupied or used by the target. Usually it is a simple desktop survey of the historic and current use of the relevant sites and the likely environmental risks if any. This is often called a Phase I survey. A Phase II survey, which is rare, unless there are known material concerns, would involve the taking of soil samples and scientific analysis.

Insurance

1.107   There may be a full report by an independent broker of the insurance that is in place, its adequacy for the target business and what further cover might be advisable and at what cost. Alternatively, it is quite common for there to be a relatively simple letter from the target's insurance brokers that the target is insured in accordance with sector and industry standards.

Legal matters

1.108   The legal due diligence report is extremely important for risk mitigation purposes. It should cover the corporate structure of the target group, employment contracts, material supply and sales contracts, current finance arrangements, other material contracts (such as acquisition and disposal agreements), real estate (although there may be separate reports on title and/or valuation/condition reports), regulatory issues (where the target business is in a regulated industry), details of plant and machinery owned or used, intellectual property, litigation and other disputes and the legal aspects of environmental, insurance, planning, pensions and tax issues. The report is generally prepared by the buyer's lawyers but occasionally the seller will commission one as part of a seller due diligence package.[75]

---

75 See para **1.59**.

Pensions matters

1.109   There may be a separate pensions report, or pensions issues may be covered in the accountants' report or the legal due diligence report. The report should include full details of all schemes sponsored by the target group or to which target group companies contribute or are potentially liable to contribute, including confirmation of the actuarial funding level of any defined benefit pension scheme on an on-going basis and on a termination basis and what the on-going funding requirements will be. Defined benefit schemes[76] in particular have become a major issue in UK buy-outs during the 2000s, as many have been found to be in material deficit, leaving target companies with material liabilities to such schemes. Increased powers granted to pension scheme trustees by new legislation – the Pensions Act 2004 in particular – have further raised the stakes for prospective buyers when considering a buy-out of a company with such a scheme because in many cases the trustees may now effectively have a 'seat at the table' in negotiations with the buyer and its financiers. In a number of cases, prospective deals have been aborted as a direct result of the failure of the sponsor or its financiers to reach agreement on all matters with the trustees of the target's pension scheme, such as the basis for on-going contributions to the scheme after completion or the intercreditor status of the scheme's claims against the company *vis-à-vis* those of the acquisition financiers. Consequently, as a practical matter, full due diligence and analysis of the target's pension schemes at the outset of the deal process is vital.[77]

Real estate valuation/condition report

1.110   Depending on the value and importance to the business of any real property owned by the target group, the buyer may commission a valuation report from professional valuers and, sometimes, structural survey reports.

Real estate reports on title

1.111   There will usually also be reports or certificates on title establishing title of the target to the properties owned by it. A report on title is a document more usually used by a solicitor when making a report to its own client on the title to a property prior to completion of a transaction. A certificate of title goes into greater detail and is usually given by the target group's solicitors.

If there are a very large number of properties, such as with a retail or pub chain, then the property due diligence may be limited to a number of key revenue producing properties or be carried out on a random sample basis, to save time and costs in reporting on all of the properties.

Tax

1.112   Of increasing importance, even in purely domestic UK buy-outs, are tax reports. These are usually prepared by the same firm of accountants that prepares

---

76 Defined benefit schemes include final salary schemes and career average schemes.
77 See **Chapter 11** for more detail on pensions generally.

the accountants' report. Because of the complicated legislation that affects the treatment of interest on shareholder debt for tax purposes, the principal parties will wish to obtain comfort that the post-completion tax treatment of the target business in the base case model is correct. The tax report is intended to provide this comfort. Similarly, with multi-jurisdictional buy-outs the assumed level of tax in the base case model will need to be verified by reference to the tax regimes in more than one jurisdiction, and in such deals the tax report is one of the key items of due diligence.

In multi-jurisdictional buy-outs it is common for there to be a tax structuring report or memorandum that, in addition to verifying the tax assumptions in the base case model, includes prescriptive advice as to how the acquisition and its financing should be structured. Tax reports and tax structuring memoranda are considered separately in **Chapter 11**.

Technical report

1.113 For target businesses that operate in technology-dependent areas or that involve specialist or scientific processes, a technical adviser may be appointed to report on the quality and reliability of those processes. The adviser should also be asked to comment on the ability of any technical equipment or machinery to deliver any performance enhancements assumed in the business plan. Even with relatively low-tech industries, where the output is highly dependant on plant and machinery it is good practice to carry out an audit of the condition and working life of the equipment.

Reports generally

1.114 Generally, the report providers will be reporting on material issues which should be brought to the attention of the relevant parties. The level at which materiality is set will usually depend on the size of the deal; so the larger the target business the higher the level at which, in financial terms, materiality will be set. Each issue of concern should be analysed by newco and its financial backers and reduced to a potential financial exposure to the target group and therefore newco and, by extrapolation, its financial backers. The financial exposure may be as a result of a direct liability, cost to remove the issue or the cost of insurance to hedge against crystallisation of the potential liability. Ultimately it may be reflected in a reduced value and creditworthiness of the business.

Ideally, each report should be commissioned in favour of newco as buyer, the sponsor and the acquisition financiers. Resistance may sometimes be encountered from some advisers to their report being relied upon by future syndicatees of the debt. Invariably, the reporting accountants and other advisers will expect to limit the scope of their liability to those relying on their reports.[78]

In a multi-jurisdictional buy-out the analysis carried out for each of the commissioned reports should extend to each jurisdiction in which the target has a material business operation.

---

78 See **Chapter 11**.

Timing of the reports

1.115   The reports will usually be circulated in draft form, enabling the parties to review and comment, including requesting further diligence, before being finalised some time before signing.

Seller due diligence

1.116   An increasing feature in UK buy-outs, particularly alongside competitive tendering processes (auctions) is the use by sellers of due diligence reports commissioned in advance and made available to all potential buyers. This is intended to reduce transaction times, reduce deal costs and to flag material issues to potential buyers early on. In practice, many buyers do not choose to rely solely on seller due diligence, perhaps because it is out of date by the time the deal is signed or perhaps because the scope, or the buyer's ability to rely on the reports, is not sufficient for its purposes. As a result buyers often end up commissioning their own reports in addition but possibly not across all areas.

Dealing with issues

1.117   If a material issue arises during the due diligence process, a number of options will be available to the buy-out parties and their financial backers:

- they could carry out further due diligence into the issue that has arisen;

- they might look to negotiate specific seller warranties, indemnities or undertakings, to provide protection against the issue;

- they might seek a purchase price reduction or insist on a retention of part of the purchase price for a period until the potential issue has safely passed by; or

- finally, they could just 'take a view' or at the other extreme withdraw from deal.

Each of these options, and due diligence generally, is considered in further detail in **Chapter 11**.

LEGAL DOCUMENTATION

Overview

1.118   There are three distinct aspects to a buy-out that require legal documentation. First, the acquisition requires one or more agreements between the buyer and seller. Secondly, the terms of the equity investments and the arrangements between the various equity investors will be set out in a further set of documents.

Finally, the terms of the acquisition finance will be documented in a discrete suite of finance documents. All of these documents are considered in more detail elsewhere in this book but a brief summary is outlined below.

Acquisition

1.119 The core acquisition document in a private acquisition is of course the acquisition agreement, which will often be described as a share purchase agreement or 'SPA' for short. The buyer and seller will be parties and in some cases there will be a guarantor of the seller's, and possibly the buyer's, obligations too. In addition to this main document there is likely to be a disclosure letter and possibly a tax covenant. Acquisition documentation is considered in further detail in **Chapter 2**.

Equity

1.120 Assuming that, as is typical, the equity comprises ordinary share capital (true equity) and subordinated loan capital (quasi-equity) there will typically be three core documents. First, there will be the articles of association of the relevant equity issuing vehicle, which will set out the 'terms and conditions' of the share capital to be issued to the equity investors. The subordinated loan capital will be constituted by a subordinated loan capital instrument, under which certificates or loan notes evidencing ownership of the capital will be issued. Finally, there will be an investment agreement (it is also sometimes called a shareholders agreement), which serves two principal purposes. On the one hand it provides for the commitment of the respective equity investors to subscribe for the equity and quasi-equity. On the other it contains detailed agreements between the institutional equity investor and the management team (respectively) including management warranties relating to the target business, decision-making on material matters and certain matters relating to exits. Equity documentation is considered in further detail in **Chapter 4**.

Senior debt

1.121 The principal senior debt document is the senior facilities agreement under which each of the senior debt facilities is made available. This document typically includes a guarantee to be given by all relevant group companies.

The senior facilities agreement will be supported by a number of additional finance documents. There will be an intercreditor agreement, which will set out the terms upon which the subordinated loan capital and any junior debt are subordinated to the senior debt. If there is seller finance this will usually be subordinated also, although this may be dealt with in a separate 'subordination' agreement. In addition, there will be one or more security documents, the precise nature and number of which will depend on the jurisdictions in which the target group assets are located. There will also be a number of less important ancillary finance documents. Senior debt documentation is considered in further detail in **Chapter 5**.

Junior debt

Second lien debt

1.122   Second lien debt may generally be documented in the same document as the senior debt or it may (less often) be documented under a separate facilities agreement. In traditional buy-out structures second lien debt is often used in relatively small amounts[79] as a form of stretched senior subordinated debt. In these circumstances, where it is in the form of a loan, it will be documented as the 'D' tranche of senior debt in the same agreement as the core senior debt. By contrast, where some or all of the second lien debt is structured as bonds and/or where the second lien debt covenants are structured as incurrence test covenants rather than maintenance test covenants, a separate second lien document will certainly be required. In certain leveraged financings, including refinancings of mature buy-outs and leveraged corporate acquisitions and increasingly (when market liquidity is particularly high) in a wider variety of buy-outs, the second lien tranche may replace a tranche of mezzanine or high yield debt. In these circumstances there may be a discrete second lien debt document although it is quite common even in these circumstances for it to be documented as the D tranche of 'senior' debt. The issue here is essentially a function of the relative size of the second lien tranche and the consequent matter of whether the second lien lenders are to have totally separate rights to determine whether to amend or waive any terms of the second lien debt and to accelerate the second lien debt upon default.

Whether in the same agreement as the senior debt or not, the second lien debt will be expressed to be subordinated (to varying degrees in practice) to the senior debt under the terms of an intercreditor agreement. The extent of the subordination of second lien debt is considered in more detail in **Chapter 10**. Second lien debt is supported by second ranking security documents, although in a UK deal the same set of security documents is likely to be used to secure both the core senior debt and the second lien debt. Second lien debt documentation is considered in more detail in **Chapter 6**.

Mezzanine debt

1.123   Where the finance structure includes mezzanine debt the documentation for this will largely mirror that for the senior debt, with a mezzanine facility agreement setting out the terms of the mezzanine debt. For 'true' mezzanine debt with warrants there will be a warrant instrument to constitute the mezzanine warrants with certificates issued under that document to the mezzanine lenders.

In most transactions – and in a purely UK deal – there is no need for separate mezzanine security documents and subordination documents in addition to those required for the senior debt. This is because one of the senior banks will act as a 'security trustee' on behalf of the senior lenders *and* the mezzanine lenders in respect of a single set of security documents and in respect of the subordination of the more junior ranking layers of finance. The security documents will stipulate that the senior debt is secured in priority to the mezzanine debt; that is, that any proceeds of realisations under the security documents will be applied first to

---

79   Say 5–10% of the total acquisition finance package.

repay the senior debt in full before any are applied against the mezzanine debt. Mezzanine finance documentation is considered in further detail in **Chapter 7**.

High yield debt

1.124 With high yield debt the documentation is quite different. There will be an offering memorandum issued by the bond issuing vehicle to prospective high yield investors which will set out information about the target group itself, the buyer and the issuer of the bonds, together with all of the terms of the bonds to be issued. The bonds are then subsequently issued on the 'impact date' pursuant to a trust deed or, if they are US bonds, a trust indenture which contains all of the terms of the bonds. This will include the form of subsidiary guarantee whereby the bonds obtain upstream credit support from the target group. High yield documentation is considered in further detail in **Chapter 8**.

If, as is typical, the high yield debt is to be bridged from completion with a bridging loan, this loan will either be provided under the senior facilities agreement or, more often, under a separate bridging loan agreement in a similar format.

PIK note debt

1.125 If the funding structure includes PIK note debt there will be further finance documents containing the terms of this instrument. PIK note debt may take the form of private PIK notes or a public issue of PIK notes. Public PIK is often issued as a form of high yield debt and will be documented accordingly, although it may also be documented as a straight loan. Private PIK note debt is generally constituted by a separate subordinated loan capital instrument under which certificates will be issued to the PIK noteholders, in much the same way as for the institutional subordinated loan capital forming the bulk of the equity package. Alternatively, it may be documented as a straight subordinated loan under a loan agreement. PIK note debt documentation is considered in more detail in **Chapter 9**.

EXITS

What is an exit?

1.126 An exit is the circumstance whereby the sponsor, the management team and the acquisition financiers realise their investments in the buy-out.

Successful exits are the reason why equity houses are in the business of buy-outs. They do not invest for long term strategic reasons. The funds managed by them generally require capital gains and this means exits. For the management team, although it is less likely to be as final as it is for the other parties involved, an exit may also be the opportunity to realise a substantial amount of their personal investment in a buy-out. For the acquisition financiers an exit has the least significance in terms of return but it will represent another successful transaction completed. In the case of the senior debt providers it may herald a new relationship with a more mature and robust client than the one which it backed at the outset of the buy-out.

Exit strategy

1.127   The three principal exits which the sponsor and management team will contemplate are flotation, trade sale (corporate sale) and secondary buy-out. In addition, leveraged recapitalisations, where new debt is incurred to finance the redemption of some of the equity and quasi-equity originally invested, are increasingly used.[80] For the acquisition financiers, each of these forms of exit will provide an opportunity to be repaid, although with any form of recapitalisation or refinancing they will often have the opportunity of participating again.

The sponsor will include the exit strategy as a key element of its investment analysis and in many cases sponsors will decline potential investments for the simple reason that no obvious exit exists. For example, in some sectors there may not be an obvious trade buyer. As for flotation, the size of the target, or lack of it, may be critical. Generally, a full listing on the London Stock Exchange is only viable for large businesses. With this in mind, an exit opportunity used with increasing frequency is admission to AIM where the absolute size of the business can be significantly lower. In fact, the lack of trade sales and IPO opportunities in the early 2000s led to the development of a previously unused exit route, the secondary buy-out. Historically, there was considerable reluctance for one equity house to acquire a business from another following an initial buy-out, for reasons considered below, but secondaries are now extremely common.

Most equity houses will not wish to hold an investment for more than five or so years. The longer it is held the greater the capital gain must be to generate the required IRR. In addition the life of many private equity funds may mean that investments made later in a fund's investment period are required to be realised within a short number of years after investment. Purely as a rule of thumb, an exit after say three or four years of investment would generally be preferred.

Types of exit

Flotation

1.128   A flotation is a listing of a company's shares on one or more stock exchanges coupled with an offering for sale of existing shares held by the sponsor and the management team. Usually there will also be an issue of new shares enlarging the capital base of the issuer and reducing its gearing. Acquisition finance will normally be repaid out of a combination of the proceeds of the new issue and the raising of new corporate debt under a post-flotation facility with a lower margin and generally more borrower–friendly terms reflecting the higher creditworthiness of the group at this stage. For a buy-out company this will almost certainly be its initial public offering and such a flotation is generally referred to as an IPO. It is common commercial practice for a company to be listed on an exchange in the principal jurisdiction in which its business operates,

---

80 According to some statistics produced in early 2007, leveraged recapitalisations of one form or another account for something in the region of 20% of all 'buy-outs'.

but possibly in more than one jurisdiction in circumstances where the business is truly international. Investors are more likely to invest in a company operating in their own jurisdiction, where they will have a greater understanding of its markets and greater access to information in respect of the company. For most UK buy-outs, flotation means a listing on the London Stock Exchange or admission to AIM.

Trade sale

1.129   In the business world as a whole, corporate acquisitions are more prevalent than buy-outs and any given buy-out target might in theory have been acquired in a corporate acquisition. So, when exiting a buy-out, a sale to a corporate buyer is an obvious option to consider. In terms of realisation of the various parties' investments it will usually provide a full exit. Such disposals are usually referred to as trade sales since the acquirer usually operates in the same trade sector as the target business.

Secondary buy–out

1.130   An alternative form of sale to the trade sale is the secondary buy-out. Here the sponsor sells to another equity house, either with a new management team or with the existing one rolling over its equity stake. It has become one of the most commonly used exits since the beginning of the 2000s. Traditionally, competition between equity houses made them suspicious of buying from each other. In particular it was also thought unlikely that sufficient further returns could be generated from a business that had already been through a private equity ownership cycle. However, as competition for assets for new funds has increased on the one hand and the existing portfolios of equity houses expanded on the other, creating a need to show returns on existing funds, strategic sales/acquisitions of this type have become justified.

One further inhibiting factor historically is that private equity institutions are unwilling to give typical seller warranties. This is unattractive to a financial buyer. However, the lack of seller warranties can, to some extent, be offset by greater due diligence together with comfort from the fact that the target will have already been the subject of an extensive due diligence exercise at the time of the first buy-out, and subject to the strict regime of private equity controls and an acquisition finance package since then. In addition, the incumbent management team – whether exiting or rolling over – may be required to give seller-style warranties to the new institutional equity investor as a condition of the deal. In any event, the result has been that secondaries have gained general acceptance in the UK market and are now one of the most commonly used forms of exit; there have even been a number of tertiary buy-outs and at least one quaternary buy-out.

Sponsorless secondary buy-out

1.131   A small number of acquisition finance institutions offer a further hybrid form of exit to equity houses. These transactions are really secondary buy-outs without a new sponsor. In place of a new equity house the acquisition financiers

will provide senior debt, mezzanine debt *and* equity to the existing buy-out vehicles and take-out the existing sponsor in full from the existing structure. The
management team will retain or be left with a majority of the equity and the
acquisition financiers will hold the minority stake in the equity.

Leveraged recapitalisation

1.132   Leveraged recapitalisations[81] typically involve a significant portion of
the quasi-equity and, less frequently, the true equity being replaced by new debt
finance. At times when other full exit options are limited, equity houses may be
able to draw upon the liquidity in the acquisition finance markets and aggressive
lending practices of the leading banks and engineer a partial exit through a leveraged recap. In doing so, they will recoup some of their initial investment and
show a partial – which might still be significant – return to their investors. At the
same time, since it is generally quasi-equity that is redeemed, most of the true
equity will be retained in the business and the sponsor can await a potential further realisation from any capital gain in the equity at a subsequent final exit.

Equity returns

1.133   The principal return to the sponsor and the management team in respect
of their equity investments will, in a successful exit, be represented by capital
growth in their equity stakes. This will often occur through an increase in the
enterprise value of the business, since all of that growth will accrue to the
equity.[82] In addition, where leverage – acquisition finance debt – is use to effect
the acquisition, even where the enterprise value of the business does not increase,
the reduction in the amount of the debt over time, as it is repaid by the target
business, will have the effect of increasing the value of the equity.

By way of simple example,[83] the capital growth in a company which was
acquired in a buy-out for £100 – financed by equity of £5, quasi-equity of £35
and senior debt of £60 – which is exited at a value of £150, is £50. All of the £50
will accrue to the equity since the quasi-equity and senior debt will be redeemed
and repaid (respectively) at par. From a pure equity perspective this represents an
eleven times return – £5 invested and £55 returned. Taking into account the
quasi-equity invested as well, the return to the equity investor is still a healthy
2.25 times return – £40 invested and £90 returned.[84] This example assumes that
the principal amount of the senior debt has not been reduced prior to the exit. In
practice the senior debt may have reduced by the time of the exit,[85] in which case
the effective return to the equity investors will be even greater. Thus, using the

---

81 They are also referred to as 'dividend recaps' or just 'recaps'.
82 Where there are warrants in favour of mezzanine lenders or other financiers, exercise of such warrants
    at exit will dilute the returns to the equity investors to a degree.
83 Ignoring, for instance, the transaction costs.
84 In practice, the equity investors – the sponsor at least – will generally have a further return through
    yield accruing on the quasi-equity.
85 Depending on whether the senior debt includes an amortising tranche (the A note).

example above, had £20 of the senior debt already been repaid by the time of the sale or flotation, so that only £40 of the £150 then realised would be applied in repaying the senior debt, the remaining £110 would all go to the equity investor, a return of nearly three times its money invested even on a gain of only £50 above the initial £100 price. This is the rationale of leverage – using debt to finance the acquisition – for private equity sponsors.

In addition to capital growth in the equity, a fixed yield may be payable on the quasi-equity component of the equity package, which further enhances the overall equity return.[86]

Most institutional equity investors are investment funds for which the sponsor acts as the fund manager. On a successful exit the proceeds of the exit over and above the capital initially invested (the gain) will be split between the investors in the fund and the fund manager, typically in the ratio 80:20. The 20% interest of the sponsor as fund manager is called the carried interest. Most private equity funds have 'hurdle rates' which require that the first portion of any gain (usually the first 8 or 10%) is payable to the fund investors alone and not shared with the fund manager but on the basis that thereafter the fund manager 'catches up' to the agreed 80:20 split.[87]

Repayment of the acquisition finance debt

Senior debt

1.134   For the senior lenders an 'exit' will usually signify repayment in full of the senior debt still outstanding.[88] In the case of a flotation, whether or not this triggers a mandatory prepayment in full of the debt – because even if it does the borrower will often require post-flotation facilities – the lead senior lender (especially if it is a clearing bank) may have gained a new listed client.

Junior debt and yield protection

1.135   Although the successful repayment of debt owing to it might seem like a successful exit for a lender, in the case of junior debt, and where this happens relatively soon after completion, this will also be seen as a lost opportunity to receive yield on the investment. It is with this in mind that junior debt instruments usually have some form of yield protection built into them. This may take the form of an early repayment penalty or fee to compensate for the lost yield or there might be a prohibition on early repayment – a 'non-call' provision. The nature of the yield protection – in the case of high yield it is known as 'call protection' – varies from instrument to instrument and may be a key determining factor for a sponsor in choosing one form of junior debt over another.

---

86 See also **Chapter 4**.
87 See also **Chapter 4**.
88 It will usually be a condition of the senior debt documentation that any exit event including a sale or IPO triggers a mandatory repayment of all of the debt. However, for IPOs that do not result in a change of control the senior debt may be reduced by a certain proportion of the proceeds of the IPO but it may be that the remainder will remain outstanding after the partial IPO.

Second lien debt

1.136　The repayment in full of the outstanding principal amount of any second lien debt will almost certainly be required upon the occurrence of an exit event. In the UK, second lien debt may also benefit from yield protection. As a general rule of thumb it will be similar to that applicable to mezzanine debt.[89]

Mezzanine debt

1.137　For mezzanine lenders holding warrants, an exit will have more significance than for the senior lenders. Not only should the occurrence of an exit event require repayment in full of the mezzanine debt but it will also represent the opportunity to exercise their warrants to subscribe for the valuable ordinary shares in the equity vehicle.

Mezzanine debt typically benefits from some yield protection in the form of early prepayment fees such that if it is repaid significantly earlier than scheduled maturity the borrower has to pay an additional fee on the principal amount paid.[90] This prepayment fee should be payable on the occurrence of any prepayment triggered by an IPO, trade sale, secondary buy-out or refinancing subject to two caveats. First, warranted mezzanine debt doesn't usually benefit from a prepayment fee arising on an IPO, trade sale or secondary because in such circumstances the exercise of the warrants should more than compensate the lenders.[91] Secondly, in the case of a prepayment arising from a debt refinancing, lenders that participate in the refinancing are often excluded from the receipt of a prepayment fee on the basis that they are not actually being prepaid and that in any event they will generally receive an up-front fee for participating in the refinancing of a similar magnitude to the prepayment fee.

High yield debt

1.138　Where the buy-out funding structure includes high yield debt there will already be a part listing of the business.[92] On a flotation it is possible that the high yield debt will stay in place[93] since its terms will usually allow for at least a partial IPO[94] without entitling the bondholders to call for redemption of the bonds. Disposal of the target business in a trade sale or secondary buy-out however, is more likely to trigger the bondholders' right to put the bonds back on to the issuer (ie, demand early redemption) and the terms will usually include an economic penalty for the issuer.[95]

89　Say a 1% or 2% prepayment fee in the first one or two years after completion. But see para **1.137** below in relation to mezzanine debt.

90　This will typically be in the region of 2% for a repayment in the first year after initial funding and 1% in the second year (or perhaps 3% in year one tapering to 1% in year two or three).

91　It follows that a distinction can be drawn for warrantless mezzanine.

92　The high yield bonds will be listed (as tradeable securities) on a stock exchange, most probably the Luxembourg Stock Exchange.

93　In fact, there is relatively little precedent for the flotation of a UK company which has high yield debt outstanding.

94　Of typically up to 35% of the equity.

95　See **Chapter 8** for more detail.

There will almost certainly be a material economic penalty if the issuer wishes to redeem the bonds early for other reasons, such as pursuant to a voluntary refinancing. This is because the high yield bond terms are likely to include significant 'call protection' provisions. That is, provisions whereby the company may not prepay the bonds without incurring an economic penalty designed to protect the yield to the bondholders. Call-protection provisions in high yield bonds include a non-call period[96] during which the issuer is prohibited from making voluntary early redemption unless a make-whole payment is made to the bondholders at the time of redemption.[97] The rationale for such extensive call protection provisions is that the high yield bondholders will have committed what is perceived to be relatively cheap money – for a relatively high risk investment – in the initial buy-out on the basis that when the business represents a sounder investment their returns (yield) will remain the same.[98]

PIK notes

1.139 With PIK notes, the yield (interest) is capitalised during the life of the investment and thus repaid as principal upon exit. Given the relatively high rates of interest that accrue on PIK notes and the fact that capitalisation usually occurs on a six-monthly or annual basis, causing the capital growth to compound materially, the principal amount actually due to the PIK note holders at an exit will generally be significantly greater than the initial amount invested. PIK note holders may on occasion also receive warrants as part of their finance package, in which case a successful exit will generate an equity return in addition to the repayment of the principal amount of the PIK notes. Such a combination can make PIK notes a very high yielding instrument, reflecting their high risk profile within the funding structure.

In the case of public PIK notes structured as a form of high yield debt, it might be expected that they would receive the same call protection as high yield with a significant non-call period. However, there have been a number of issues where this has not been the case – principally because they have been issued in the expectation of an IPO exit in a relatively short period thereafter – prompting many commentators to question the attractiveness of such instruments to investors.

Private PIK notes are likely to benefit from some limited call protection in a form similar to that applicable to mezzanine debt.

---

96   By convention the non-call period is the first half of the life of the bonds.

97   Make-whole payments are intended to put the bondholders in the same economic position that they would have been in had the bonds been redeemed at final maturity or the first optional redemption opportunity after the non-call period, and assuming that they had received all scheduled yield payments up to such time, but with a discount for early receipt. The extensive call protection afforded to high yield bondholders is perceived as one of the less attractive features of that form of junior debt when compared to say mezzanine debt.

98   See **Chapter 8** generally for further consideration of the typical call protection provisions.

CHAPTER 2

The Acquisition

ACQUISITION STRUCTURES

2.1   At the core of every buy-out is an acquisition. How that acquisition is structured will have implications for the funding, legal and documentary structures of the transaction. Although there will usually be more than one viable structure, most acquisitions will have an optimal structure that can be determined by reference to certain key factors.

Choosing the right acquisition structure

The nature of the target

2.2   A target business may comprise a single discrete corporate entity, a group of companies, a business without corporate status (eg, a division within a larger business that is being retained by the seller) or a combination of one or more of these. Where there is more than one company comprising the target business those companies will often be owned by a single holding company such that only the shares in that holding company need be acquired to take ownership of the entire target group. Alternatively, and less often, the shares in more than one target company must be directly acquired by the buyer to effect the acquisition of the target business. Other, deal-specific, reasons may also dictate an acquisition structure that does not simply comprise the purchase of a single target's shares. For example, in a multi-jurisdictional acquisition, it might be necessary to effect a target group reorganisation at the time of the acquisition in order to create a more tax efficient group structure for the post-acquisition period when the target group will have large amounts of debt to service.[1]

Shares or assets

2.3   Share purchases are much more common than asset purchases. The main reason for this is the simplicity of acquiring an entire business through the transfer of shares in the target company. Asset purchases are generally only used

---

1   See also para **2.14** below, with respect to the structuring of multi-jurisdictional buy-outs.

in two circumstances. First, by acquiring only the assets comprising the target business the buyer should be able to avoid unknown liabilities otherwise residing in the company that owns the target business. This might be appropriate where the buy-out is of a business owned by a company that has been through an insolvency process or where the target company has been the subject of material litigation or could become the subject of material litigation claims. The second common circumstance is where the target business has no discrete corporate form, eg, it is one division of a larger business owned by a company. In this case, a share purchase may not be possible without the seller first undertaking a group reorganisation, something that it is unlikely to be willing to do in advance of an agreed sale ie, before the deal is signed.

In a multi-jurisdictional buy-out there may be tax advantages or other legal benefits to be gained from acquiring shares in certain jurisdictions and assets in others.

In any given circumstance, these and other factors will usually mitigate towards one structure or another.

Basic buy-out structure

2.4   As discussed above, depending on the nature of the target, the acquisition element of a buy-out may be structured as an acquisition of shares, an acquisition of assets or, occasionally, a combination of both.

Share purchases

2.5   Share purchases are by far the most common form of acquisition structure for the reasons given above. Generally the acquisition will be of shares in a single company which may or may not own shares in other target group companies which are automatically acquired upon its acquisition.

Single Target

2.6

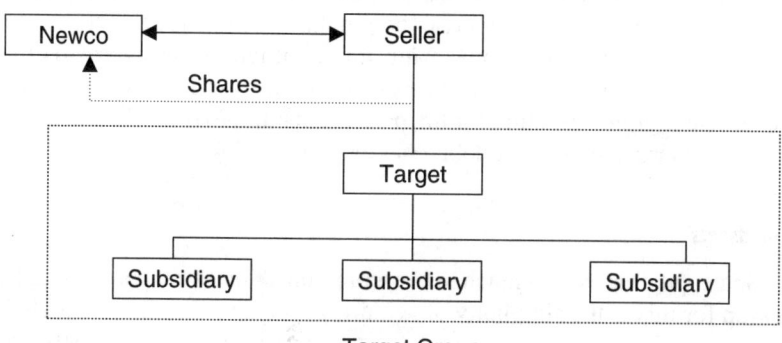

Target Group

Share purchase structure (single target with subsidiaries)

In the above diagram newco acquires the shares in the direct target company from the seller and, since the target has three subsidiaries, they are automatically acquired too. Following the acquisition the group structure will be as follows:

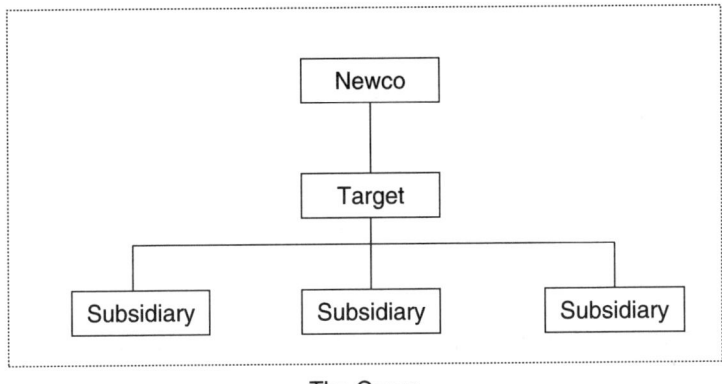

The Group

Post–completion structure (single target with subsidiaries)

Multiple Targets

2.7 If there is more than one direct target company then the structure will look slightly different.

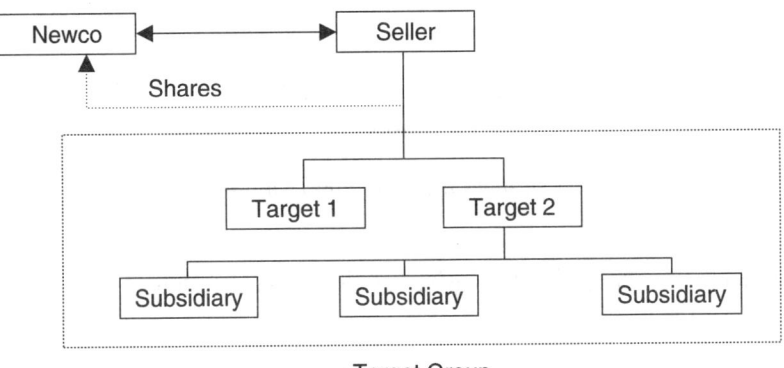

Target Group

Share purchase structure (multiple targets and subsidiaries)

In the above diagram newco acquires the shares in both direct target companies from the seller and, since one target has three subsidiaries, they are automatically acquired. Following the acquisition the group structure will be as follows:

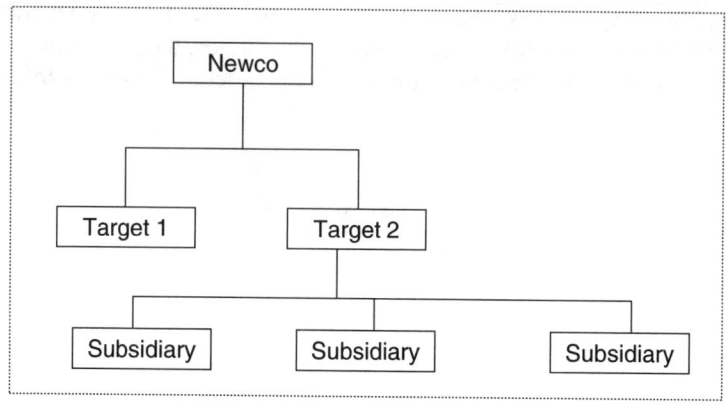

The Group

Post–completion structure (multiple targets and subsidiaries)

Asset purchases

2.8   In the case of an asset purchase, newco will acquire assets from the seller. There are a number of possibilities depending on how the assets are held by the seller and on how newco wishes to acquire the assets.

Simple asset purchase

2.9

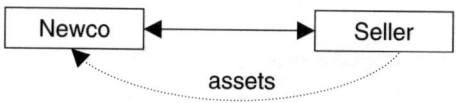

Asset purchase structure (simple)

Following completion the 'group' structure will be as follows:

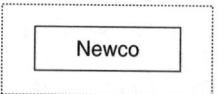

Post completion structure (simple asset purchase)

In fact, in such a transaction it is highly unlikely that a single SPV will be used to effect the acquisition. The acquisition financiers will almost certainly insist that the assets are acquired by one SPV owned by another SPV: a double SPV structure. The reason for this is to facilitate a subsequent enforcement sale of the business by the acquisition financiers since the shares in the acquiring SPV could be sold by its holding company. With a single SPV the acquisition financiers would not normally have share security over the SPV, such shares being owned by the equity investors which very rarely offer any recourse as part of the security for a buy-out. In addition, the sponsor will often wish to simplify its projected exit by being in a position simply to transfer the shares in the acquiring SPV without itself having to directly contract with the prospective buyer. Again, a double or multiple SPV structure will achieve this.[2]

Where the target assets are not held directly by the seller entity, but by one or more members of the seller group, the structure will be slightly different:

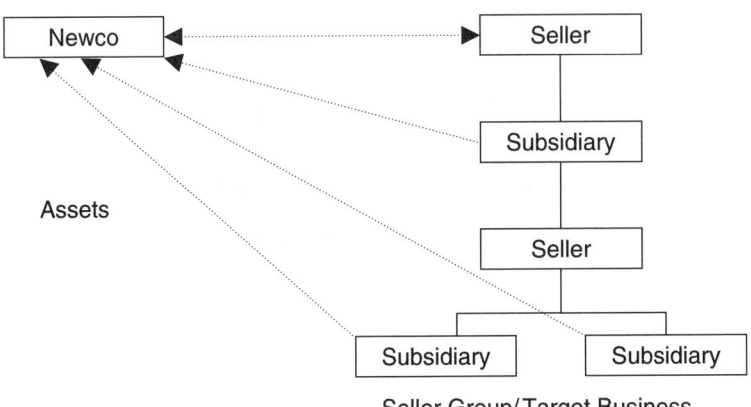

Asset purchase structure (composite)

In the above example newco will contract with the seller and its subsidiaries to acquire some or all of their assets.[3] The subsidiaries themselves remain under the ownership of the seller and may own other businesses as part of the overall seller group. As with a single asset purchase transaction it is more likely that a double SPV structure would be used to effect the acquisition.

Double SPV asset purchase

2.10   An alternative to the single SPV structures above is where two or more SPVs are used in order to make the acquisition; each SPV owned by another with an ultimate SPV (topco) at the top. This is a more favourable structure for the acquisition financiers who as part of their security package will take security over the shares in the acquisition SPV, without need for recourse to the investors. Such a structure enables the acquisition SPV to be sold as a going concern by simple enforcement of the share security, should this become necessary. Similarly, it may also provide a more beneficial exit structure for the investors.

---

2   Double SPV structures are considered in para **2.10** below.
3   Alternatively, newco and the seller alone will contract on the basis that the seller procures the transfer of the assets of each subsidiary.

In such circumstances the acquisition and post–completion structures might (with a double SPV structure) look as follows:

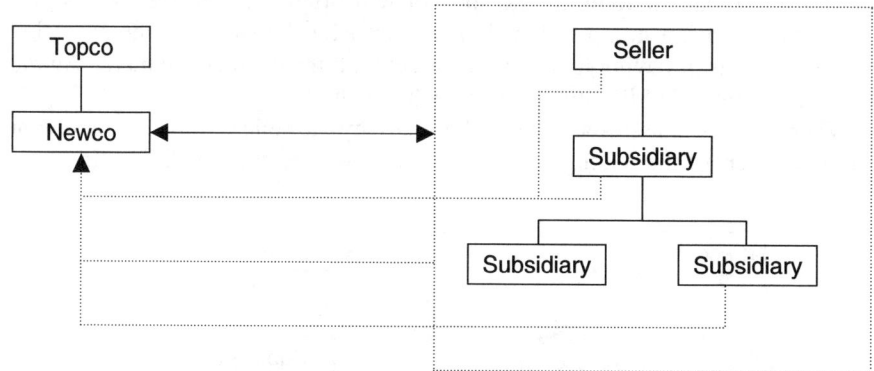

Seller Group/Target Business

Asset purchase structure (by double SPVs)

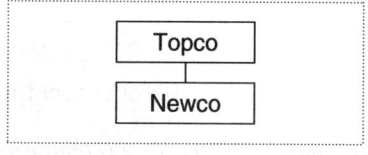

The Group

Post–completion structure (asset purchase by double SPVs)

In practice, the funding structure for any buy-out will almost invariably dictate at least a double SPV structure even for a simple share purchase. There are resultant benefits for the acquisition finance security package for both asset and share purchase structures.[4] Consequently, in determining whether there will be one, two or more SPVs both the acquisition structure and the funding structure must be considered.

Seller hive-up/down

2.11   As a further structural variable, the seller may transfer (hive–up or hive–down) the relevant assets comprising the target business into one or more target companies, which may be incorporated specifically for the purpose, immediately prior to completion with a view to then effecting a share sale of the relevant target companies. In such circumstances, the sale itself will be a simple share sale to newco.

---

4   For example, see paras **2.31** and **2.54** in relation to security over newco's rights under the acquisition documents.

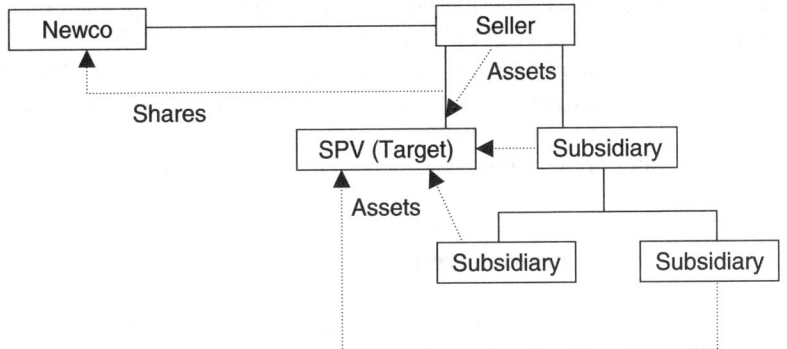

Seller hive–down (single target)

Typical buy-out acquisition structure

2.12 Probably the most common UK buy-out structure involves the purchase of shares in a single target company, together with a number of subsidiaries, by a double or triple SPV structure such as the one shown below.

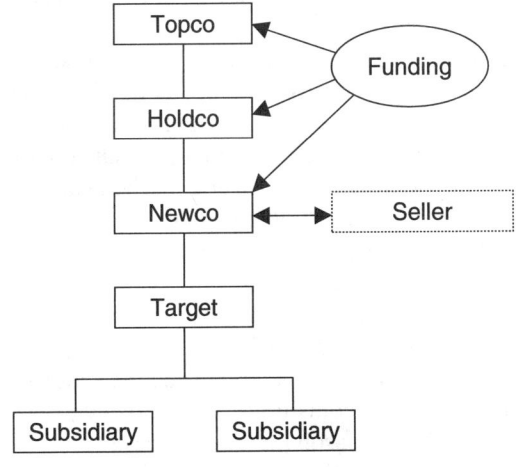

Typical UK buy-out structure

Public-to-private buy-out structure

2.13 A public-to-private buy-out may be effected either by way of a takeover offer in accordance with the City Code on Takeovers and Mergers or by way of a scheme of arrangement under the Companies Act 1985 (and from 6 April 2008, see Pt 26 of the Companies Act 2006). A takeover offer involves the transfer of shares in target plc. A scheme involves either a transfer of shares or, generally in order to save on stamp duty, a cancellation and new issue of shares in target plc.

The 'seller' will be each of the individual shareholders in the public company (target plc) to be acquired. Target plc may have one or more subsidiaries, which will automatically be acquired. With both takeovers and schemes the SPV (often called bidco) which acquires target plc will generally be one of a number of SPVs required by the funding structure as with a private buy-out.

Public-to-privates are considered in more detail in **Chapter 12**.

Multi-jurisdictional buy-out structure

2.14   With a multi-jurisdictional buy–out there will generally be more than one target entity, since there will be more than one jurisdiction in which the target business has substantial operations. The important question is whether there are direct targets in different jurisdictions or whether a single direct target holds other operating entities in different jurisdictions.

Generally, the same structuring principles that apply to domestic UK buy-outs also apply to multi-jurisdictional buy-outs. Thus, share purchases, asset purchases or combinations of both may each provide the optimum structure. The tax regimes in the relevant jurisdictions may, however, suggest a different acquisition structure to that which would be favoured in the UK. Selecting certain jurisdictions for the location of one or more of the SPVs may also assist with the tax structuring.

For instance, given the favourable network of tax treaties that each has and favourable domestic tax provisions relating to holding companies, both the Netherlands and Luxembourg are often selected as the location for one or more SPVs (or as a holding company for a number of subsidiaries) in a European multi-jurisdictional buy–out structure. Invariably the deal sponsor will have tax advisers working on the most favourable structure.

In a multi-jurisdictional buy–out one of the common features is the use of more than one SPV to make acquisitions. That is, the use of multiple SPVs for the purposes of the acquisition itself and not just as part of the funding structure or to improve the sponsor's or acquisition financiers' position in the overall structure.[5] One of the usual reasons for structuring the acquisition in such a manner would be to have discrete acquisitions in certain key jurisdictions, each to an extent separately funded. The reason for this is to have discrete tranches of acquisition debt borrowed in each of the relevant jurisdictions. In this way it may be possible to have interest on that debt directly deductible from the operating profits arising in those jurisdictions and so reduce the tax payable on those operating profits. With certain jurisdictions this can be achieved by having an SPV incorporated in each jurisdiction where an acquisition is to take place and then ensuring that part of the overall finance is provided to each such SPV to enable it to effect the acquisition. However, merely having the debt and the profits in the same jurisdiction might not be enough and the desired tax deductibility might only be achieved by having the debt and profits in the same company, which is usually achieved through a so-called debt 'push-down' following the initial

5   As discussed in **Chapters 3** and **10**, multiple SPVs may be used to impose structural subordination between different layers of finance.

acquisition. Debt push-downs may or may not be legally feasible in the relevant jurisdiction.[6]

The tax deductibility position may also be enhanced by using one or more SPVs that are incorporated in certain, tax favourable, jurisdictions.

Leaving aside the tax benefits for the target business and its new owners, the acquisition financiers will also generally prefer to have acquisition debt lent directly into the jurisdictions where the target business has operations. The idea is to have the debt and the business operations that generate the cash flows to repay the debt as proximate as possible. There are a number of potential benefits in this. For one, the positive cash impact of reducing the group's tax benefit will not only benefit the target business but it will also free up cashflow to service acquisition debt. In addition to this, and of material importance to them, the acquisition financiers will look to obtain a greater degree of credit support (that is, guarantees and security) from the target group operating companies as a result.[7] That said, as with tax deductibility, the benefits to the guarantee and security package of such structuring will often only be achieved if the debt is lent directly into an operating company and this is unlikely to be possible where the debt is being borrowed to acquire that operating company.[8] It may, in some circumstances, however, be possible to overcome this hurdle through a debt push down as part of or, more often, following the acquisition.

ACQUISITION DOCUMENTATION

2.15   The following paragraphs provide a basic guide to the acquisition documentation commonly found in a buy-out. The analysis includes the acquisition financiers' perspective on the documents, such as their concern that newco acquires from the seller exactly what the acquisition financiers are assuming it will acquire, and that, for such purposes, sufficient comfort is obtained from the seller by way of contractual protection.

The first section below details the purpose and principal provisions of the various acquisition documents that would be required in a typical buy-out.[9] The following section provides guidance on what to look for when reviewing acquisition documents on behalf of the acquisition financiers.[10]

The core acquisition documentation will comprise:

- acquisition agreement – either a share purchase agreement (SPA) or business transfer agreement (for asset purchases);

- seller's disclosure letter – making disclosure against the seller's warranties in the acquisition agreement;

6 See **Chapter 13** for further consideration of debt push-downs.
7 See **Chapters 5, 11** and, in particular, **13** as to the reasons why.
8 Usually because of financial assistance laws.
9 **Chapter 12** considers the documentation that would be required for a public-to-private buy-out.
10 A large amount of detail could be included in respect of the drafting and negotiation of acquisition documents. However, these tasks will in practice be carried out by newco's lawyers (and the seller's lawyers) with the acquisition financiers' lawyers essentially only shadowing the negotiation of the acquisition documents and focusing on matters of specific concern to the acquisition financiers. Consequently, given the focus of the book generally, this section is necessarily a relatively basic consideration of the issues which arise in respect of the acquisition documents.

- indemnity undertakings – there may be a stand-alone tax covenant or, less frequently, environmental indemnity undertaking.

Acquisition agreements

2.16   The acquisition agreement is the principal acquisition document, containing the contractual obligation on the seller to sell and on the buyer to buy the target business. In a share sale the buyer will acquire the shares in the direct target companies and in an asset purchase the buyer will acquire the assets and business comprising the target business directly. Naturally there are a number of key differences between a share sale and purchase agreement and a business transfer agreement.

The following paragraphs outline the main provisions commonly included in an acquisition agreement.

Share sale and purchase agreement

2.17   A share sale and purchase agreement (SPA) will typically include the following provisions:

- Agreement to buy and to sell the shares of the target.

- Consideration (the purchase price) – which will usually be a fixed cash sum that may be subject to adjustment by reference to the amount of the target's assumed net asset or current net asset position when compared against the actual position as at completion.[11] As an alternative to the purchase price adjustment mechanism, the buyer and seller may agree a fixed price based on a balance sheet drawn up and agreed as of a date before signing. That price is not then adjusted. The buyer may also agree to pay an amount for the period from that balance sheet date to completion that represents a 'daily earnings amount' for the target business or interest at an agreed rate on the full purchase price. This approach is called a 'locked box' mechanism.

- Conditions precedent to completion (if any) – such as, obtaining of approvals or clearances from domestic, European or other competition authorities, other regulatory approvals or seller shareholder approval.

- Completion mechanics – unless completion of the agreement is subject to the fulfilment of relevant conditions, completion will occur immediately following signing of the sale and purchase agreement. Completion will be effected by delivery of, among other things, stock transfer forms and share certificates in respect of the target shares, statutory books, title deeds to all properties and title documents in respect of the assets held by the target which are not transferable by delivery.

---

11 The actual adjustment mechanism may be set out in the main body of the agreement or in the schedules/appendices. If a purchase price adjustment mechanism is to be used, a completion balance sheet (ie, as at completion) for the target will be drawn up after completion and, to the extent that it shows that the amount of the target's net assets at completion were different from that assumed by the parties for the purposes of determining the headline purchase price, a balancing payment may be required from the seller or buyer as the case may be.

- Continuation of business undertaking – where there is to be split signing and completion the buyer should seek documentary comfort from the seller that it will continue to run the business in a prudent ordinary course manner until completion.

- General post-completion undertakings – these may include matters such as release of guarantees given by the target, the net asset purchase price adjustment mechanic[12] and the processing of insurance claims arising prior to completion.

- Transitional services arrangements – if the target business is not entirely self-supporting (perhaps because it is a division of a larger business for which the seller is retaining all centralised functions[13]) the target may require the continued provision of central functions for a transitional period of a few months until the buyer has put in place new arrangements. If the required services are extensive or specific, or the period lengthy, then a separate transitional services agreement may be required.

- Non-competition and non-solicitation covenants – the buyer will often seek an undertaking from the seller not to compete with the target following completion. This may include a restriction on the seller using the trading names of the target. In addition the provision should prohibit the seller from soliciting customers or employees of the target.

- Seller indemnities – these will be sought in respect of specific liabilities relating to events or matters arising prior to completion but which may affect the target after completion.[14]

- Seller warranties – a schedule will set out a number of detailed warranties in relation to the target and its business.[15]

- Seller protection provisions – these will include limitations on the ability of the buyer to make a claim for breach of warranty.[16]

- Performance guarantee from the seller's parent – this will only be required by the buyer where there is justifiable doubt as to the creditworthiness of the seller itself perhaps because it has no assets other than the target business, and thus concerns about its ability in the future to meet a claim against it by the buyer for breach of warranty or by way of indemnity claim.

Business transfer agreement

2.18   Where the acquisition is of the target business directly, that is the assets constituting the business and not the shares in the company owning the business,

---

12 And see earlier in relation to 'locked box' mechanisms.
13 For example, accounting, IT, human resources and the like. See also para **2.27** below in respect of transitional services arrangements generally.
14 See para **2.19** below in respect of indemnities generally.
15 See para **2.19** below for consideration of the nature of warranties generally.
16 See para **2.40** et seq below for a more detailed consideration of seller protection provisions.

the acquisition agreement[17] will contain detailed provisions dealing with the transfer of all assets comprised within the business. It will also contain provisions dealing with the assumption by the buyer of business-related liabilities since, by contrast to a share purchase, only those liabilities which the buyer contractually agrees to assume or which are transferred by operation of law (such as employee liabilities) will pass to the buyer. The agreement will typically deal with the following:

- Agreement for the sale and purchase of the target business – including detailed descriptions, often by reference to scheduled lists, of the assets being transferred, such as:
  - real property;
  - plant and machinery;
  - intellectual property;
  - goodwill;
  - vehicles;
  - business records;
  - stock
  - contracts
  - book debts;[18]
  - petty cash;
  - any other assets exclusively used in the target business; and
  - the liabilities of the business being assumed by the buyer.

- Excluded assets – if the assets being transferred are described in general terms or part of the business is being retained by the seller it will be important for the seller to specify those assets excluded from the sale.

- Consideration – there will be an overall purchase price figure, which will often be apportioned between the various categories of assets in the agreement or subsequently in completing the relevant form supplied by the Stamp Office.[19]

- Allocation of liabilities and rights between seller and buyer – certain liabil-

---

17 Which may be called a business transfer agreement.
18 However, in order to save stamp duty (payable on a transfer) book debts are often retained by the seller and collected by the buyer as agent for the seller. The buyer will discharge creditors (as liabilities retained by the seller) from the proceeds of the book debts collected and any balance is paid to the seller.
19 Stamp duty liabilities and tax implications (including the availability of capital allowances going forward) will arise in relation to the transfer of the various different categories of assets. The apportionment must be on a bona fide basis having regard to the commercial value of each asset.

ities (such as periodic outgoings) and rights (such as receivables) may be apportioned between the seller and the buyer on a time basis, with the seller being responsible for settling these up to the date of the transfer and the buyer thereafter. On a practical level the seller may require the buyer to assume certain liabilities and obligations since the seller may lack the means for fulfilling them (such as product servicing obligations).

- Conditions precedent to completion (if any) – such as obtaining of approvals or clearances from domestic, European or other competition authorities, other regulatory approvals or seller shareholder approval. With a sale of a business (as opposed to a share sale) there may also be regulatory licences and consents in the name of the company whose business is to be transferred which will need to be obtained in the name of the buyer. Similarly, a key contract of the business may be required to be novated to the buyer as a pre-condition to completion. Additionally, landlord's consent to assignment of leases of key properties may also be required before completion.

- Completion mechanics – unless completion of the agreement is subject to the fulfilment of relevant conditions, completion will occur immediately following signing of the business transfer agreement. Completion in respect of most assets will be effected by exchange of the business transfer agreement together with payment of the purchase price. In respect of certain categories of assets (such as real property and registered trade marks) there may be other necessary formalities or transfer documents to execute and deliver to the buyer.

- Continuation of business undertaking – where there is to be split signing and completion the buyer should seek documentary comfort from the seller that it will continue to run the business in a prudent manner until completion.

- General post-completion obligations – typically, the post-completion obligations will be extensive since there is a greater amount of unravelling to be done between the seller and the buyer in respect of an asset purchase. There is likely to be a need for a specific transitional services undertaking or separate agreement.

- Transitional services arrangements – this may include the supply of components and the supply of assistance and services between the parties for a limited time for purposes such as accounting, IT systems and redirection of customers to the buyer.

- Non-competition and non-solicitation covenants – as with a share purchase, the buyer will often seek an undertaking from the seller not to compete with the target business following completion. This may include a restriction on the seller using the trading names of the target business. In addition the provision should prohibit the seller from soliciting customers or employees of the target business.

- Employees – the employees of the business will, in most cases, be subject to the TUPE regulations,[20] which, in simple terms, operate to transfer all the liabilities of the seller as employer in respect of the employees of the business to the buyer. Such liabilities do not include employees' rights under occupational pension schemes but do include any contractual obligations of the employer, eg, to contribute to an employees' personal pension scheme.

- Seller indemnities – these will be sought in respect of specific liabilities relating to events or matters arising prior to completion but which may affect the target business after completion.[21]

- Seller warranties – these will differ to some extent from those in a share purchase and will be tailored to the specific assets and liabilities being transferred.[22]

- Seller protection provisions – these will include limitations on the ability of the buyer to make a claim for breach of warranty.

- The appendices will typically include detailed lists of all the different categories of assets and liabilities being transferred and retained, the employees, the seller's warranties and provisions relating to the mechanics of transfer of certain types of asset.

Warranties and indemnities

2.19   A key area of an acquisition agreement for newco and each of its financial backers is the warranty and indemnity cover provided by the seller.

A warranty is a statement of fact given by one party to a transaction to another on the understanding that the second party will rely on the statement in relation to the transaction. If the statement proves to be incorrect, and the recipient party incurs a loss under the transaction as a result, then that party may make a claim for such loss against the party giving the warranty. Disclosures of facts may be made against a warranty for the purpose of providing exceptions to the warranty and thus to reduce the circumstances where a claim may be made for breach of warranty.

An indemnity is an undertaking by one party to indemnify another party in respect of a loss occurring to such other party if certain circumstances or eventualities arise. Disclosure will not be a mechanism for reducing the scope for a claim being made under an indemnity. Indeed it is often the case that a buyer will require an indemnity from a seller where the seller has disclosed a matter against a warranty given by it to the buyer, which suggests that the buyer (or the target) is or may become subject to a liability or loss. The indemnity is designed to protect the buyer against such liability or loss.

Seller warranties and indemnities – and the seller protection provisions that limit the right of the buyer to make a claim for breach of warranty or indemnity – are considered in further detail below.

---

20   Transfer of Undertakings (Protection of Employment) Regulations 2006.
21   The scope of such liabilities is likely to be less than with a share purchase, where a corporate entity is acquired, as the liabilities assumed by the buyer will be specified.
22   See para **2.19** below for consideration of the nature of warranties generally.

Disclosure letters

2.20 Next to the acquisition agreement itself, the most important acquisition document is the seller's disclosure letter. A disclosure letter is a letter from the seller to the buyer disclosing to the buyer the existence of certain facts which could render the warranties given by the seller in the acquisition agreement incorrect. For example, a share sale and purchase agreement will usually include a warranty that the target company is not currently involved in any litigation. The disclosure letter will list any exceptions to this statement. The wider the warranties given by the seller, the wider the disclosures are potentially going to be. The disclosure letter is therefore the most important mechanism used by the seller to limit its liability to the buyer under the warranties.

Typically, a disclosure letter will contain general disclosures and specific disclosures. General disclosures include matters which the buyer can discover itself. There will be general disclosure of publicly available information in respect of the target, the due diligence reports commissioned by the buyer or the seller[23] in relation to the target and usually all of the information made available to the buyer by the seller for the due diligence exercise – the transaction data room. Importantly, if the data room is a permitted disclosure the buyer will be forced to review all of its contents as part of the due diligence exercise to avoid being fixed with notice of any adverse matter that it would not otherwise be aware of. Faced with general disclosures of this kind, buyers can try and limit the extent to which the information disclosed does qualify the warranties. For example, they may accept the general disclosure but only to the extent that any information so disclosed has been 'fully and fairly' disclosed.

Specific disclosures will be made in respect of individual warranties and will set out, in as much detail as possible, the nature of the disclosure indicating why the specified warranty is not true.[24]

Indemnity undertakings

2.21 In buy-outs structured as share purchases, a separate indemnity undertaking – called a 'tax covenant' – will often be executed by the seller in favour of the buyer in respect of tax liabilities of the target group.[25] Occasionally a separate indemnity undertaking will also be executed in respect of environmental liabilities but usually only when the target group companies have been engaged in environmentally sensitive activities. Specific indemnity undertakings are required by buyers for two reasons. First, by having an indemnity the buyer does not need to prove damage and mitigate loss to the extent it does with a warranty claim. Secondly, a stand-alone indemnity will be appropriate where the liability the subject of the indemnity might not arise for a considerable period after completion. This is because the seller warranties and general

23 But only to the extent the seller due diligence reports are made available to the buyer. See **Chapter 11** for further consideration of seller due diligence.
24 See also para **2.50** in relation to disclosure letters generally.
25 This will not be required with an asset purchase because tax liabilities attach to the corporate entity, not its assets.

indemnities will be given for a limited period only.[26] In respect of tax liabilities, HMRC may pursue the relevant company – the target or any of its subsidiaries – for up to six years after the end of the accounting period in which the tax liability arose. This means that if a tax liability arose in relation to the target prior to completion, which had not been met by the target and of which the buyer was unaware, HMRC might then pursue the target for the tax liability during this six-year period. The tax covenant is used to claim compensation from the seller for any such tax liabilities. The indemnity will normally be expected to last for a period of seven years after completion to enable any claim to arise and be settled within the period.

Similarly, environmental liabilities may lay dormant within a target company for several years. If a business is particularly environmentally sensitive and the environmental due diligence suggests, perhaps even inconclusively, that hidden liabilities may exist then the seller may agree to provide the buyer with a specific environmental indemnity.

REVIEWING ACQUISITION DOCUMENTS

2.22   The following paragraphs are intended to provide guidance for the review of acquisition documents from the perspective of the acquisition financiers.

The review of the acquisition documents has a number of objectives. To state the obvious, the buyer and its financiers will wish to ensure that newco is acquiring exactly what they have assumed it is acquiring and that the seller is providing sufficient comfort in respect of the transaction through warranties, indemnities and undertakings. There will be a general concern that the acquisition is legally effective and that all other matters relating to the acquisition are documented in accordance with the commercial deal struck.

The primary job of ensuring that these objectives are achieved falls to the sponsor's lawyers and this of itself will give comfort to the acquisition financiers since, in many respects, the interests of the sponsor and the acquisition financiers are aligned in respect of the acquisition.[27] However, although the acquisition financiers will take comfort from the fact that the sponsor's lawyers will be looking to get the best deal they can for the buyer, the different risk sensitivities for the acquisition financiers as lenders and the sponsor as an equity investor will mean that the alignment has its limits. Given the different risk-return profiles of the acquisition finance debt and the equity investments, it is not uncommon for the acquisition financiers to adopt a more conservative risk averse stance on any particular issue. For this reason, the acquisition financiers and their lawyers should also review the acquisition documents from their own perspective.

---

26 Typically this will be two years or less.
27 This will normally be the lawyers appointed by the sponsor, but in a true MBO it may be the lawyers appointed by the management team.

Acquisition agreement

2.23   A general review of the agreement is advised, but the following matters are suggested as the key areas for the acquisition financiers to focus on.

Commercial deal

2.24   The financiers will wish to satisfy themselves that the acquisition agreement reflects the basic commercial agreement between the seller and the buyer. In particular, are the agreements as to price, the post completion net asset adjustment (if any) and the description of the shares or assets to be acquired as agreed?

Completion conditions

2.25   The completion conditions should be reviewed carefully to ascertain what transaction specific conditions or consents are required to be obtained prior to completion of the acquisition. In addition, where there is likely to be a reasonable period between signing and completion – as a result of such conditions – the extent of the buyer's 'outs' will be a key issue. There are two main scenarios where this is the case. The most common is that a regulatory consent – merger authority clearance, in particular – is required and an application for consent will only be made at signing. Secondly, in larger deals the sheer complexity of the legal and commercial planning that is required to complete the deal may dictate a two-stage process. An 'out' is a condition that the buyer can invoke to pull the deal before completion.

Not surprisingly, a seller will want as much certainty as possible that the deal will complete and will wish to limit conditionality to precisely those matters that are delaying completion in the first case (eg, merger clearance). A buyer on the other hand would ideally wish to be able to pull the deal if a material matter adversely affecting the target or the deal occurred between signing and completion; such as a huge litigation claim against the target or the loss of a large revenue contract. Such concerns are often dealt with by the inclusion of a no-material adverse change (MAC) condition. If a MAC event occurs the buyer can elect not to proceed to completion. Similarly, the buyer may attempt to include a specific termination right for circumstances where it can show that any of the material warranties is untrue at completion.

Generally the outcome of these negotiations will reflect the relative bargaining power of the parties. In a seller's market there will be relatively little conditionality. In a buyer's market the opposite could be true. In certain cases the conditions might even extend to a 'financing out' condition whereby the buyer can pull the deal if its funding is not available when it needs to complete. It used to be the case that sellers would commonly rely on the reputational damage that could attach to equity houses and acquisition financiers if they pulled out of a deal, and financing outs were common. But since the early 2000s that is far from a foregone conclusion and any proposal for a financing out will be fiercely resisted by the seller. In the absence of a financing condition, buyers will need to insist that the same limited conditionality incorporated in the acquisition agreement is adopted in the acquisition finance documentation; otherwise if there is more conditionality in the finance documents the buyer could be left without finance when it is required to complete the acquisition. This may mean considerably less conditionality for the acquisition financiers than they might otherwise expect. Indeed in many cases sellers will insist that there is effectively no conditionality in the acquisition agreement between signing and completion other than regulatory (merger authority) approval. It follows, from the buyer's perspective, that there should be no conditionality in the acquisition finance documentation. Newco cannot be obliged to complete the acquisition if its debt funding is not available. This amounts to a 'certain funds' requirement for the lenders.[28]

Business continuity

2.26   Where signing of the acquisition agreement and completion of the acquisition are not simultaneous, the buyer should seek undertakings from the seller that it will continue to manage the business in a prudent ordinary course manner and not in any manner which may be materially adverse to the business or to the buyer. A properly drafted 'conduct of business' undertaking will include express reference to actions that the seller will not take outside the ordinary course of business such as new borrowings, the granting of security, the making of disposals and acquisitions and the settling of disputes.

Transitional services

2.27   Where the seller has previously been providing centralised functions for the target company or business which are not being transferred as part of the acquisition, there will often need to be a requirement for the provision of ongoing business support by the seller during a transitional period. This might cover such matters as IT, accounts and financial reporting, treasury, tax, supply chain controls, human resources, business development and public relations. This will either be dealt with by an undertaking from the seller or, if the required services are extensive, a separate transitional services agreement.

Seller warranties and indemnities

2.28   This section of the agreement – together with the seller protection provisions that limit the ability of the buyer to make any claim under the warranties and indemnities – will generally be the most heavily negotiated between buyer and seller. It is also one area where the interests of the buyer and its financiers are not totally aligned, so a separate review by the financiers is important. Although a buyer will generally have the same interest as its financiers in having as full a set of warranties and indemnities as possible, private equity buyers may make a different risk assessment of any particular issue from the acquisition financiers. The latter will generally be more risk averse, given that they will have less to

---

28   The concept of 'certain funds' is also found in the public-to-private market where it is a requirement of the UK Takeover Code. It has been adopted for standard private buy-outs since the early 2000s. See **Chapter 11** for a more detailed consideration of the concept as applied in private buy-outs and **Chapter 12** for its use in public-to-privates.

gain from the transaction and potentially more to lose as a result of any serious defect that is not picked up by the warranty and indemnity cover. A detailed consideration of the warranty and indemnity section of the acquisition agreement is set out below.

Seller protection provisions

2.29   This section should be read in conjunction with the warranties and indemnities as its principal function is to limit the right of the buyer to make any claim on the seller for breach of warranty or indemnity including the amount of any such claim. Again, given its importance, there is more detailed consideration below.

Seller's status

2.30   The nature of the seller entity that is party to the acquisition agreement will be one of the buyer's major concerns. The key issue is the financial standing of the seller and, in particular, its ability to stand behind all of the warranties and indemnities for the duration of the entire claim period.[29] The issue will be most obvious where the seller is simply a shell company that distributes the sale proceeds to the *real* seller(s) and then has no further assets to meet any claim by the buyer. But given the length of time within which a claim may be made by the buyer, even a real trading company with sound financial standing at the time of the sale may no longer be in a position to meet a claim in two years, say. With this in mind a buyer will often need to seek further comfort in the form of parent company or bank guarantees or a purchase price retention mechanism. These concepts are considered in further detail below.[30]

Assignability

2.31   In a typical UK buy-out the acquisition financiers' security package will extend to all of the assets of the group including newco and the other SPVs. This will include newco's rights under the acquisition documents[31] and the security agreement will expressly include security over such rights. The security is usually taken by way of an assignment and provided that notice of assignment is given to the seller the financiers may be able to make a direct claim against the seller under the acquisition documents in due course. Failure to give notice of the assignment to the seller will leave the financiers with more limited rights to pursue claims against the seller in due course.

During the documentation process the acquisition financiers will wish to confirm that the acquisition agreement and any related documents such as specific indemnity undertakings are capable of being assigned as part of the security package. The preferred position is for the acquisition documents to expressly acknowledge their assignability, although silence on the matter should suffice in

---

29 See para **2.41**.
30 See para **2.47** et seq.
31 Including any specific indemnity undertakings; see para **2.21**.

most circumstances. Ideally, the assignability of the acquisition documents would extend to any assignee or transferee of the acquisition financiers. This would enable the acquisition financiers to pass on the benefit of the acquisition documents to a receiver appointed by them or any third-party buyer from them or the re⸍ ⸍iver. In practice the seller may not accept this.

If the seller resists any granting of security over newco's rights under the acquisition documents, the acquisition financiers should be able to take the benefit of such rights indirectly through the share security granted over newco. In a default scenario this enables the acquisition financiers to enforce the share security and leave newco to pursue any rights against the seller directly. This is one of the benefits of a double or multiple SPV structure.[32]

Seller warranties and indemnities

Warranties and indemnities generally

2.32   The warranties to be included in an acquisition agreement, initially at least, are likely to be based on a relatively standard set covering all common areas of concern. That said, a standard set of warranties for a sale of shares will differ a little from those used for a sale of assets. The latter will exclude warranties relating to purely corporate matters and liabilities which attach to a corporate entity. Equally, the warranties in an asset sale will be more detailed in respect of the title to and condition of the assets being acquired.

Indemnities by contrast will mostly be deal-specific matters relating to actual or potential liabilities thrown up in the due diligence process or resulting from disclosure against the warranties by the seller.

The impact of due diligence

2.33   The warranties and indemnities cannot be negotiated on a purely desktop basis. They can only be finalised – certainly from the buyer's perspective – as the due diligence findings are obtained. In the case of the warranties, the knowledge of the target business that the due diligence exercise provides, enables the buyer to refine the specific warranty statements so that they more accurately reflect the real facts and circumstances of the target business. Standard warranty schedules are deliberately generalist and wide in scope and in theory they can work satisfactorily for any type of business. But in practice, the buyer will prefer to focus certain of the warranties on the areas that it knows are of most concern in the context of the specific business that it is seeking to buy. In other words, in addition to the general warranties that are included as standard, the buyer may include specific warranties concerning particular aspects of the target or target business. For instance, it might wish to include specific statements about certain identified pension schemes that the target operates. There might be specific statements about known litigation claims and so on.

As far as the indemnities are concerned, these are almost entirely deal-specific

---

32 See para **2.10**.

and by definition they can only be drafted with specific issues in mind, usually meaning issues that have been identified during the due diligence exercise. For example, the buyer might seek an indemnity from the seller in respect of a specific defect in the title of the target to one of its material properties that the real estate due diligence uncovered. The drafting and negotiation of the warranties and indemnities is therefore directly dependant on the due diligence exercise and findings.

A further level of inter-relationship between the due diligence exercise and the seller warranties relates to the disclosure process. The materials that the seller discloses to the buyer (the 'data room') will largely comprise the subject matter of the due diligence exercise. With this in mind, the seller will normally seek to formally disclose the contents of the data room by way of general qualification of the warranties. This is done through the seller's disclosure letter. If the contents of the data room are disclosed in this way, the buyer must review all of the information in the data room as part of its due diligence exercise to avoid having the warranties qualified by a fact or circumstance that it is not made aware of. What is more, most sellers will wish to expressly disclose the contents of the due diligence reports themselves by including them as a further general disclosure in the disclosure letter. In practice, buyers are often able to negotiate certain limits to the extent of such general disclosures, including the general data room disclosure, and one common approach is to limit disclosure only to those matters that have been 'fully and fairly' disclosed in the data room or the due diligence reports. But even with those caveats it is vital that the buyer and its financiers do commission due diligence in respect of all information that is disclosed and then take the time to study the due diligence reports that the advisers subsequently produce.[33]

The due diligence exercise generally is considered in further detail in **Chapter 11**.

Standard warranties

2.34   Set out below are some of the standard warranties which would be expected in an acquisition agreement.[34] These examples are short form summaries, for indicative purposes only, providing a basic template for the main areas which the warranties should cover. The actual warranty provisions will run into considerable detail in respect of the various areas covered over many pages. For simplicity, a single list is provided to cover both a share acquisition and an asset acquisition. Many of the warranties will be very similar in both types of agreement.

The warranties will be given at signing but if signing and completion are not simultaneous the buyer should seek repetition of the warranties at completion. If repetition of the warranties is to occur at completion the seller will usually resist the principle that breach of warranty is a ground for not completing the

---

33 See also para **2.50** for further consideration of disclosure letters and how they may be negotiated by the buyer and seller.

34 It is common for the acquisition financiers' lawyers to have a lawyer with corporate M&A experience review the acquisition documents, in order to assess whether the warranties are standard and so on.

acquisition, with the exception perhaps of the most fundamental warranties, such as title to the target shares or for breaches that otherwise constitute a material adverse circumstance.

Short form warranty summary

2.35

- seller (and guarantor, if any) capacity (possibly including as to solvency) and authority to enter into and perform the agreement, and status as solvent entities;

- beneficial ownership of the target shares or the target assets and business free from encumbrances;

- no options exist for the issue of shares or loan capital and the target group companies own no shares other than in the specified subsidiaries;

- no insolvency circumstances exist in respect of the target group;

- compliance with corporate formalities and legal and regulatory requirements and all necessary licences and consents are in place;

- documents of title and records of the business held by the seller are in order;

- accounts are accurate and give a true and fair view of the target group, and there has been no material adverse change since the date of the last set of audited accounts;

- all plant and equipment is in good condition and seller's possession and name;

- all stock is in marketable condition and seller's possession and name;

- no outstanding commitments for capital expenditure;

- no outstanding or unusual obligations outside the ordinary course of trade;

- no borrowings or financial arrangements in place other than as specified;

- no outstanding encumbrances or title retention arrangements over any assets;

- no onerous or unusual agreements and all agreements are on arms length terms;

- the acquisition will not result in a loss of customers or suppliers;

- no outstanding litigation or other legal proceedings and none are pending or threatened, and the list of historic proceedings is accurate and complete;

- no outstanding claims made or threatened by customers, as to product liability or otherwise, and the list of historic claims is accurate and complete;

- appropriate insurance is in place and insurance policy premia are paid up to date and no claims are pending under the policies, and the lists of policies and of historic claims are accurate and complete;

- no disclosure of intellectual property or confidential information or know-how other than in the ordinary course of trade and all intellectual property rights are beneficially owned by the target group with appropriate registrations in place, and there have been no licences granted by the target in respect of any intellectual property rights. No breach of the target group's intellectual property rights or breach by the target group of a third-party's intellectual property rights;

- no outstanding guarantees or indemnities given by or in respect of the target group;

- no outstanding liabilities for tax in respect of the period up to completion other than to the extent a provision has been made in the accounts or tax arising in the ordinary course of business since the date of the last set of audited accounts;

- all relevant employment-related information supplied is accurate and complete, compliance with all employment laws and contractual obligations, no plans for redundancies or alterations of employment terms and conditions, and completion of the acquisition is not likely to cause the termination of employment of any employee;

- the lists (and annexed copy documents) of all relevant pension related information supplied is accurate and complete,[35] no disputes in relation to the pension schemes, compliance with all relevant laws and regulations and all governing documents relating to the pension scheme, the pension funds are fully funded and otherwise in compliance with all appropriate laws and practices, and no plans for establishing, altering the terms of or terminating the scheme;

- beneficial owner of the properties specified, which properties comprise all the properties owned or occupied, free from any encumbrances or third-party rights or interests and the information specified in respect of the properties is accurate and complete;

- no leases of or a licence to assign any leasehold property or a guarantee of the lessee's covenants contained in any such document, in respect of leases prior to 1 January 1996 at no time has a lease been assigned or otherwise disposed of without receiving an indemnity in respect of its liability under such lease, and no claim has been made in respect of any leasehold property formerly held nor is any such claim anticipated; and

- full compliance with all environmental laws, all necessary environmental licences have been obtained, there are no pending environmental claims

---

35 The pension schemes will be either final salary or money purchase and may be taken over in whole or in part. With a final salary scheme there is a concern as to whether the scheme is adequately funded and/or the transfer payment calculated on an appropriate actuarial basis. For a money purchase scheme each member has its own fund so these concerns do not generally arise. Where the whole scheme is being taken over the buyer will want to know everything about the scheme and its related arrangements. Where a transfer payment is being taken, the buyer will generally only be concerned with the benefits of the relevant members and the basis for calculating the transfer payment.

and no use has been made of, nor substances brought on to, the site which may give rise to a claim or adversely affect the value of any property.

With a share acquisition the warranties should be given in respect of each company within the target group, in all applicable jurisdictions. With an asset/business acquisition all areas of the target business, again in all applicable jurisdictions, should be covered.

Management buy-outs

2.36   With a management buy-out, the seller may be less willing to extend full warranty cover to the buyer if the incumbent management of the target is involved in the buy-out, ie, as a shareholder of the buyer. For instance, a seller may resist warranties in respect of current trading performance and day-to-day matters which an incumbent management team should be fully aware of. In extreme circumstances a seller may, at least initially, insist that warranties will only be given in respect of elements of the target business which have been run from the seller's head office (if applicable) or which are of a similar nature; for example, in respect of the accounts, tax, insurance and pensions. Alternatively, the seller may agree to give full warranties but only on the basis that the management provides much of the disclosure materials. In these circumstances the seller would usual require the management team to give a 'reverse' warranty to the seller confirming the accuracy and completeness of the disclosures. Similarly, it might also seek a warranty from newco that newco is not aware of anything that is inconsistent with the warranties. This should be resisted by the buyer since it shifts too much of the burden of proof of a claim onto the buyer.

A more general approach by the seller, one that it will usually seek to apply in any type of buy-out, is to qualify the warranties by reference to its own knowledge. That is, by including a provision in the seller protection provisions that it is only liable for breach of warranty in respect of a matter of which it has actual knowledge. Knowledge qualifiers are considered separately below.[36] The seller may also wish to qualify the warranties by reference to matters of which the management team involved in the buy-out is aware or should have been aware.

Generally, a buyer will prefer to have a full warranty suite from the seller even if the warranties are subject to greater qualifications as to the seller's knowledge than to have limited warranties. This is so even if the gaps in the warranty cover would normally be the subject of management team warranties in favour of the sponsor under the investment agreement. This is because recourse to the seller under the acquisition agreement – assuming a claim can be made – will generally be more fruitful (and less controversial) than claims made against the individual members of the management team under the investment agreement.[37]

A compromise position is to have slightly reduced warranties in respect of matters truly under the control of the existing management team and to qualify the warranties in relation to matters not under their control by the seller's knowl-

---

36 See para **2.44**.
37 The acquisition financiers will usually also insist on this approach not least because they do not benefit from warranties given by the management team in the investment agreement.

edge. From the acquisition financiers' viewpoint this approach will generally be acceptable but without any understanding themselves of what the seller's would and would not have knowledge of it does leave them in a relatively uncertain position regarding the enforceability of the warranties.

Secondary buy-outs

2.37   The scope for obtaining seller warranties and indemnities in a secondary buy-out will be extremely limited by comparison with most other forms of acquisition including first time management buy-outs. The main reason for this is the need for most selling equity houses to achieve a 'clean break' on an exit. Since most equity houses are fund managers they will wish to return realised investment proceeds to the fund investors as soon as an exit occurs. In doing so the IRR on the investment is crystallised at that point.[38] As a result the proceeds will not be retained by the equity house to meet any warranty or indemnity claims and the equity house will not be able to return the proceeds to investors and then claw it back if a warranty or indemnity claim arises. In addition, following a basic principle of private equity, an equity house will not give recourse directly to any other party to a buy-out, including a buyer from it in a secondary buy-out.[39] The practical effect of all this is that the selling equity house will generally only give basic warranties as to title to the target shares and its legal ability to effect the sale. This theoretically leaves a 'warranty' gap for newco as buyer. There are a number of solutions to this, of varying degrees of value to newco.

First, the buyer can require and rely upon warranties and indemnities from the management shareholders of the target business. Where the management are not rolling over their shareholdings into newco and the new buy-out, they may be reluctant to give warranty cover particularly where they are not a central member of that management team or where their cash proceeds are relatively small. Managers that *are* participating in the new buy-out or significant manager shareholders that are cashing out can usually be expected to give standard warranty and indemnity cover, but not without a cap on their liabilities which may in total deal size terms be relatively low. The level of the cap is therefore important. It should be large enough to ensure that the manager warrantors make full disclosure and thus to enable an exhaustive due diligence exercise to be carried out. Moreover, as a general matter, it is better for newco not to compromise on the scope of the warranties and indemnities themselves even where the liability cap is relatively low. Full warranties will elicit a more complete disclosure than partial ones. In addition to warranties in the acquisition agreement relating to the target business, the institutional equity investor will seek warranties from the management in the investment agreement, in particular relating to the business plan and certain personal information.

Where a specific and quantifiable issue is brought to light during the due diligence and disclosure process the exiting equity house may be willing to give a

---

38   The longer an investment is outstanding the greater the return will need to be to generate the same IRR.

39   But note the recent trend in large deals of equity commitments and reverse break fees. See **Chapter 11** for further detail.

specific indemnity subject to a fixed cap on liability. This is to be contrasted with general warranty and indemnity cover. A specific indemnity will often be a straight alternative to a price reduction and the equity house may put aside sale price proceeds to meet any claim under the indemnity.

The selling equity house, along with management, might in any event be willing to put some of the sale proceeds into an escrow account for a limited period of time after the sale, and even for these proceeds to be available to meet claims under warranties given by the selling management shareholders. This appears to be the same as giving the warranties themselves, but the formal distinction is important, given the need not to establish precedent for giving general warranties and indemnities. In addition it avoids distribution and claw-back to the equity fund investors.

A further mechanism that can be used to provide protection to a buyer in a secondary buy-out – as regards financial and accounting matters in particular – is a purchase price adjustment mechanism. Typically the process will involve the production of completion accounts, which are verified by a firm of accountants. Depending on what the accounts show, a payment may be due from the buyer to the seller or vice versa. Most selling equity houses will accept that they have a pro rata obligation to meet this payment even though it departs from the clean break principle. The fact that the payment is an adjustment of the purchase price is an important distinguishing feature from warranty and indemnity cover. These mechanisms are of most use in mitigating risks relating to the financial position of the target business at completion and in particular the existence of financial liabilities or reduced asset amounts – especially stock, cash and receivables – of which the buyer may not be aware at signing or completion. This is in effect an alternative to a warranty on the accounts of the target that were used to determine the purchase price. A more direct mitigant to a warranty gap, which is gaining in popularity, is warranty and indemnity insurance, which is considered separately below.

Finally, a more drastic mitigating approach to a large warranty gap is to structure the deal as an asset purchase. Any hidden liabilities in the target's corporate shell will be left behind.

Warranty and indemnity insurance

2.38   Warranty and indemnity insurance may not be as satisfactory as a full set of warranties and indemnities from a creditworthy seller but it can provide the buyer with a level of comfort not otherwise available in, say, a secondary buy-out. Cover is available to both buyers – in the situation where a matter arises but is not covered by the seller's warranties, generally because the amount of the claim exceeds the cap on warranty liabilities – and sellers – in the situation where a claim is made on the seller. There are significant differences between these two types of policy; for example, a seller policy will be cheaper given that it only pays out if an actual warranty claim is made. At its most effective a buyer policy will enable the buyer to make a claim where it uncovers a liability that would be within the warranties provided by the management but for the fact that the amount exceeds the cap on liability agreed. In fact it can be used to persuade the purchasing equity house to keep the cap on liabilities under the management's warranties relatively low; which will improve alignment between the equity house and management in the new deal. This in turn may persuade the management team to give a full suite of standard warranties. An insurer will normally require that it will not pay out until the claim is above a threshold level that reflects a sufficiently large proportion of the total insured amount. Below that level the warrantors themselves will pay out or if their liability cap is too low the buyer itself will be exposed – self-insurance in effect.

Representations and warranties in the finance documents

2.39   Ultimately how the sponsor negotiates the seller warranties may raise a further direct concern for the acquisition financiers. Newco may attempt to limit the scope of the warranties it is required to give to the acquisition financiers in the finance documents by conforming those warranties to the seller warranties in the acquisition agreement. The theory is that it should only be in breach of the warranties in the finance documents in circumstances where it has a claim against the seller under the acquisition agreement. However, this argument misses the essential difference between seller warranties and borrower representations and warranties. Seller warranties are designed to force the seller to disclose all material information about the target business to the buyer and to provide compensation to a buyer if the disclosure process is flawed or a warranty given is untrue. Borrower representations on the other hand are intended to force the borrower to carry out due diligence into the target business – and to report back on anything that is a material defect – and to provide an acceleration right, as opposed to a claim for compensation, if untrue.[40] Consequently, they tend to have very different levels of materiality, with borrower representations being liberally qualified by materiality and seller warranties much less so. Trying to match them too closely, therefore, is not well conceived. In practice, the acquisition financiers should not accept a reduction of the representations in the finance documents simply because newco has not obtained equivalent warranty protection from the seller.

Seller protection provisions

2.40   The seller will insist on including extensive seller protection provisions in the acquisition agreement in order to limit its exposure to claims for breach of warranty or under the indemnities. The provisions delineate the circumstances in which newco can and cannot make a claim for breach of warranty or indemnity against the seller. In particular, there may be limitations as to the minimum and maximum amounts of claims, the period within which a claim may be made and instances which will prohibit newco from making a claim at all. This is consequently a key area for the acquisition financiers as it will be for newco, the sponsor and the management team. The forms of seller protection set out below are common.

---

40 The borrower representations and warranties may be drafted as such, with a right in theory to sue for breach of warranty if untrue, in practice they are merely used as a ground for acceleration of the debt.

Time periods

2.41   The seller will wish to restrict claims to those which are made within a specified period. Usually the seller and buyer will agree that all claims must be notified to the seller within a fixed period after completion, typically, 18 months to two years.[41] It may also be agreed that after this period expires any disputed claim notified prior to the expiry of the period will be deemed waived if proceedings are not commenced within a further specified period. This period should not be so short as to precipitate litigation, however.

Exceptions to this provision are for certain specific indemnities including any separate indemnity undertakings. Thus, under the tax covenant the period within which a claim may be brought is typically around seven years, reflecting the fact that HMRC may pursue a tax liability for up to six years after the end of the financial year in which the liability arose.

Similarly if there is an environmental indemnity undertaking, the period within which a claim may be brought may be considerably longer than two years, depending on the nature of the claim. For example, for claims arising out of contamination, a typical period would be six years or sometimes much longer, where the buyer's negotiating position is particularly strong, although it is unlikely to be longer than ten years. This is designed to reflect the time period which may elapse before any contamination may come to light. Similar considerations apply in the context of the risks arising from a failure to comply with relevant procedural steps, potential environmental claims from employees and claims by third parties.

Liability cap

2.42   The seller will wish to restrict the aggregate amount of all claims which may be made against it. It is possible that a target business could have liabilities of an amount greater than the purchase price paid for the business.[42] However, it is not uncommon for the seller and the buyer to agree that the aggregate of all claims will not exceed the purchase price payable. In fact, sellers will often attempt to set the limit below the purchase price payable, particularly in larger deals. In a seller's market the cap may end up as low as 25% of the purchase price, although the size of the deal is important in this regard.

De minimis amounts

2.43   The seller will also seek to exclude claims of amounts below a certain de minimis threshold and to only allow claims once the aggregate of all claims exceeds a further threshold limit. In negotiating the de minimis threshold for individual claims, a seller will often seek to exclude such claims from even counting towards the aggregate threshold limit. What is acceptable as the

---

41 The rationale for this is that it will allow the buyer to have at least one full audit of the target business and time to commence claims in respect of defects or other matters becoming apparent from the audit.

42 Where the target is acquired with debt in place and the buyer is to discharge the target's debts after completion, the liability cap should ideally be no less than the aggregate of the purchase price and the debt acquired (the enterprise value).

aggregate threshold for making a claim – that is, when all individual claims are aggregated – will to some extent depend on the purchase price, but generally speaking the purpose of the aggregate limit is simply to eradicate small claims where it would not be economically viable for full proceedings to be commenced. When negotiating this provision, the sponsor should ensure that if a claim is made above the threshold limit the whole amount claimed can be recovered and not just the excess over the limit.

Knowledge qualification

2.44   In a trade purchase, the buyer would rarely accept a qualification that the seller is only liable for breach of warranty in respect of matters of which it is actually aware or should have been aware of. The principal purpose of warranties is to allocate risk between the seller and the buyer for matters which come to light rather than merely identifying the extent of the seller's knowledge. On this basis, the risk of all matters relating to the period prior to completion should be allocated to the seller, whether or not it had or should have known of such matters.

However, in a management buy-out the members of the management team that are involved in the buy-out will have significant knowledge of the target business, if not more knowledge than the seller. For this reason the seller will often seek to limit its liability by excluding claims which are outside its actual knowledge or which are beyond its deemed knowledge based on the functions which the seller performed in relation to the management of the target business.[43] Alternatively, it will seek to exclude claims in respect of matters of which the management team are actually aware or which they should have been aware of. Knowledge qualifications may be incorporated into the seller protection provisions so as to apply generally to the warranties or, more likely, to a selected majority.[44] From the buyer's perspective, a more acceptable alternative to qualifying all or a selected majority of the warranties generally in the seller protection provision, is to incorporate an 'as far as the seller is aware, having made due and careful enquiry' type qualification selectively into the body of the warranty statements themselves.

The starting position for the sponsor will be to argue that *it is* a third-party buyer, as with a trade buyer, and should receive full unqualified warranties irrespective of what its management team or the seller are aware of. It will certainly have a stronger position to resist knowledge qualifiers in respect of any matters for which the seller specifically can be expected to take responsibility. These might include head office functions such as accounting, IT, tax, insurance and pensions. Beyond this, much comes down to detailed negotiation and the relative bargaining power of the parties.

In a true management buy-out, where the management take a controlling interest in newco, it is more difficult for the buyer to resist a general qualification

---

43 In practice even in a trade sale not all of the warranties will be given without qualifications as to the state of the seller's knowledge.

44 Certain warranties should not be qualified at all, such as warranties as to the target's accounts or as to title to the target shares or material assets.

relating to matters of which the management team is actually aware. Other forms of buy-out, on the other hand, where the management team are not taking a controlling stake in the buyer, and possibly do not have a greater knowledge of the target business than the seller, will be more akin to trade purchases for these purposes and knowledge qualifications should be more easily resisted. In any event, knowledge qualifications are not ideal since it is difficult to prove what a party is actually aware of or should have been aware of, leaving uncertainty as to whether a claim may be made for breach of warranty.[45]

Double recovery

2.45   The seller will certainly expect to restrict the buyer's right to claim from the seller where the buyer has recovered from another source in respect of the same matter such as through insurance or because seller deferred consideration is available to meet the claim. Negotiation of this provision often focuses on circumstances where a claim for breach of warranty arises against the seller and the buyer also has a right against a third-party. The buyer may agree that in such circumstances, the seller can take over the claim against the third-party but only so long as the buyer's reputation is not damaged.

Disclosure

2.46   The principal seller protection provision is its ability to make disclosures in respect of the warranties. This is done through a 'disclosure letter'. Disclosure letters are considered in further detail elsewhere in this chapter.[46]

Seller status

2.47   The nature of the seller entity that is party to the acquisition agreement will be of key concern to the buyer. In particular, the buyer will be concerned as to the financial status of the seller and its ability to stand behind all of the warranties and indemnities for the duration of the entire claim period.[47] The issue will be most obvious where the seller is simply an SPV holding company with no on-going business. Assuming that the SPV distributes the sale proceeds on to the real seller – which might be the parent company of the seller group, the seller's shareholders or investors in a private equity fund – the value of the warranty and indemnity cover will be limited to the residual net worth (if any) of the SPV. The buyer really has only two options in these circumstances.

---

45 It should also be noted that where the buyer's knowledge is deemed to include the knowledge of the management team (because they are officers of the buyer, say), it may not be able to rely on a warranty in any event where the management team were aware of the matters giving rise to a breach, whether or not knowledge qualifiers are included. This is because the courts may not allow a party to rely on a warranty which it actually knows to be incorrect at the time the warranty is given.

46 See paras **2.20** and **2.50**.

47 See para **2.41**.

Parent company or bank guarantee

2.48   First, if the seller has a creditworthy parent company then a parent guarantee of the seller's liabilities under the warranties and indemnities should be sought. The parent may instead prefer to arrange for a guarantee to be provided by an acceptable bank.[48] In most cases a buyer will prefer a bank guarantee to a parent company guarantee given that an acceptable bank is more likely to retain its financial status for the entire period within which a claim may be made under the warranties and indemnities.

Purchase price retention

2.49   If a parent guarantee or bank guarantee is not available, or even if it is and the buyer requires further comfort from the seller, the buyer should insist on a purchase price retention mechanism. Typically this means having a portion of the purchase price – of an amount that, logically, should be equal to the maximum amount claimable by the buyer under the warranties and indemnities – held in an escrow account for the duration of the warranty and indemnity claim period. Usually the escrow account will be held with a third-party that both buyer and seller are happy with, such as a bank. The escrow 'agent' will agree to act in accordance with the pre-agreed instructions given to it by the buyer and the seller in an 'escrow letter' or 'escrow agreement'. This will include agreeing to disburse the escrow amount either to the buyer to meet claims or to the seller at the end of the escrow period.

     As indicated above, escrow accounts are not only used where the seller entity is a shell company such as an SPV holding company. Because the potential claim period for the warranties and indemnities may be two years or more, the buyer may insist that a certain portion of the sale proceeds be held in escrow irrespective of the financial status of the seller at the time of the sale. Much can change over time and there will be no guarantee that the seller will be able to meet a claim made by the buyer in, say, two years time.

     Where the maximum claimable amount under the warranties and indemnities is a significant proportion of the sale price, it is unlikely that the seller will agree to have that entire amount held in escrow. This leaves a potential shortfall for any claims that may be made and, irrespective of what the actual warranty and indemnity cover provided by the seller was, means a de facto 'warranty gap'. In these circumstances the buyer might seek to use warranty and indemnity insurance, which is being used with increased frequency in the UK market.[49]

Disclosure letters

2.50   The review of the seller disclosure letter is a key task for the acquisition financiers. The specific disclosures made in it will directly limit the recourse of

---

48 Perhaps determined by reference to its credit rating.
49 See para **2.38**.

newco to the seller under the warranties and by their nature will be deal-specific matters of major interest to a buyer and its financial backers. Consequently, the specific disclosures should be reviewed by both the acquisition financiers and their lawyers with a view to identifying and quantifying actual and potential liabilities and in particular in order to differentiate material from non-material liabilities. With this in mind the acquisition financiers should determine at the outset what level of financial exposure for the target group will be deemed to be material.

The general disclosures included in a disclosure letter are also very important. Typically a seller will make a general disclosure of anything that the buyer could have discovered for itself. This will include matters that are in the public domain, including matters on public registers, such as real estate title and land charges registers and the Companies House registry. This will force the buyer to make all necessary searches of applicable registers.

In addition, the seller will usually include all information that is included in the transaction 'data room' within this general category. In this way, the contents of the data room will be deemed to have been disclosed against all of the warranties. Ideally the buyer should try and resist this level of general disclosure as much as possible but in practice it may have little option. One relatively standard approach is for the buyer to accept the disclosure of information in the data room only to the extent that it amounts to a 'full and fair disclosure' of the relevant information; that is, only information that is fully and fairly disclosed in the data room is deemed disclosed against the warranties. It would be usual to define 'full and fair' disclosure to mean that the disclosure is sufficiently clear that it would enable a reasonable buyer to make an informed and accurate assessment of the relevant matter disclosed.

In addition to disclosing the data room in this way the seller will generally wish to make a general disclosure of anything contained in the due diligence reports that the buyer (or seller) commission. In this circumstance, the buyer should also attempt to apply the full and fair disclosure principle. It might also try and limit the disclosure to matters of fact only (and not of speculation) and perhaps only to matters of fact that are set out in the executive summaries of such reports.

Indemnity undertakings

2.51   The following paragraphs deal only with tax and environmental indemnity undertakings. These are the two forms of separate indemnity undertaking most frequently provided in a buy-out scenario, although discrete environmental indemnity undertakings are rarely given in practice. Other indemnities may be provided in the acquisition agreement for specific liabilities and should be reviewed carefully as part of the general review of that document.

Tax covenant

2.52   A tax covenant – that is a separate tax indemnity undertaking – will only be relevant if, as is common, the acquisition structure includes a share purchase.

The relevant tax liabilities will only attach to a corporate entity and not a business or assets. As with the acquisition agreement, newco has primary responsibility for ensuring the tax covenant is satisfactory from a buyer's perspective. There will usually be little for the acquisition financiers to add, although they will certainly need to review and be happy with the cover provided. The scope of the tax covenant will normally be limited to liabilities arising prior to completion. Even though tax may be payable on a consolidated basis at target level, the tax covenant should cover the direct target and any other company within the target group being acquired.

Environmental indemnity

2.53 Since environmental liability may attach to the present owner or occupier of a piece of real estate, an environmental indemnity may be required with either a share acquisition or an asset acquisition. Environmental indemnities are usually only conceded by sellers with considerable reluctance. A seller will not be keen to take on any long term exposure to the buyer in respect of environmental liabilities.[50] A specific indemnity is most likely to be negotiated with the seller where the target business operates in a particularly environmentally sensitive sector or where the initial environmental due diligence suggests that latent environmental liabilities may exist in the real estate or any of the companies being acquired.

The acquisition financiers will want their lawyers to review the environmental indemnity to ensure that it is satisfactory for their purposes. They will have particular concerns in relation to any real estate falling within their security package on the basis that, as secured lenders, they may in certain circumstances become subject to environmental liabilities arising from the real estate in question.[51] For example, a party which enforces security over real estate which is contaminated may in certain circumstances be found liable for clean up costs in respect of the contamination by virtue of being in occupation. In any event, the mere fact that that real estate is contaminated will reduce its value. If the real estate in question comprises a substantial part of the security package the overall credit assessment of the target business may need to be revised.

Even without enforcement of security over contaminated real estate and irrespective of the effect of the contamination on the value of the real estate, a party which exerts sufficient control over an owner or occupier of contaminated land, effectively managing or participating in the management of the business, may be held to be liable for clean up costs in respect of such contamination. Such liability is not confined to the problems that may arise from the contamination of land. It can, in addition, extend to and affect the value of the business in the context of third-party claims for environmental damage caused off-site, for example

---

50 There will in any event be environmental warranties, which newco may enforce against the seller. However, these will usually be limited in time to the relevant claim period, which may be two years or less.

51 For example, under Part IIA of the Environmental Protection Act 1990 which deals with liabilities for contaminated land.

polluted ground, water or toxic air emissions. Such liability may also extend to the plant operated as part of the business which may require environmental improvement, usually at some considerable cost, failing which the plant could face the threat of shut-down by the environmental regulator. Although the level of control exerted by acquisition financiers under the acquisition finance documentation should not trigger these concerns, these types of liability are another reason why the acquisition financiers will be keen to see a sufficient indemnity from the seller in favour of newco.

As far as the terms of the various environmental indemnities contained in the indemnity undertaking are concerned, these will need to be sufficiently widely drafted to cover all categories of liability which may accrue to newco or any of the persons relying on the indemnity. Such indemnities will typically be limited to matters arising prior to completion. It is also important to check that any indemnity undertaking is given in respect of each company within the target group and not just the direct target.

Given the concerns about incurring direct liability, the acquisition financiers would prefer that they, any receiver appointed by them and ideally any buyer of the business on enforcement, could benefit from the indemnity, although in practice, the issue of assignability of the environmental indemnity will usually be keenly negotiated by the seller.

Security over indemnity undertakings

2.54   The acquisition finance security package should include all newco's rights under the acquisition documents, including any separate indemnity undertakings. This can either be achieved through direct security from newco or indirect security through a share charge over newco itself, allowing newco to continue to pursue such rights directly. If the indemnity undertakings are given in favour of target companies, in addition to newco, the same principles apply to target group security.

In respect of any environmental indemnity, the acquisition financiers should if possible ensure that the benefit of the indemnity can be assigned both to them and to any receiver appointed by them, although this may be very difficult to agree with the seller in practice. As a general rule a receiver will be reluctant to accept instructions in relation to any real estate, or any facility located on any real estate, that is potentially the subject of environmental liabilities.[52]

In any event, taking security over the shares in newco, in addition to direct security from newco over its rights under the acquisition documents, will invariably give the acquisition financiers the most flexibility. In practice, since double or multiple SPV structures are used in most buy-outs, this is a standard approach.[53]

---

52 In such circumstances, the acquisition financiers might provide an indemnity for the receiver or, if they unwilling to do so, environmental insurance may be an option.
53 See also **Chapter 3** in relation to double and multiple SPV structures.

Raising acquisition financier issues

2.55 The primary negotiation of the acquisition documents will be between the sponsor and the seller. However, the acquisition financiers should be copied in on all drafts with sufficient opportunity to make appropriate comments. All comments on behalf of the acquisition financiers should be passed to the sponsor rather than the seller so that all the 'buy-side' comments are consolidated. That said, it is occasionally a useful tactic for the sponsor, in its negotiations with the seller, to be able to state that the acquisition financiers do not agree with a particular concession being requested of the sponsor. However, if the seller is particularly sensitive to the fact that the sale is to be treated in the same way as a trade sale (and in seller's markets generally), this approach may not be well received. Depending on the current economic cycle and other market dynamics, sellers may have a sufficiently strong position to be able to require the sponsor to negotiate the acquisition documents with very little input from its financiers.

As far as the acquisition financiers are concerned, the review carried out by their lawyers should ideally include a general commentary on the overall favourability or otherwise of the acquisition agreement and, in particular, the strength of the warranty and indemnity protection. The sponsor's lawyers will usually be in a position, and open, to discuss with the acquisition financiers' lawyers why particular provisions have or have not been included since they, unlike the acquisition financiers' lawyers, will be privy to the detailed negotiations with the seller's lawyers. Establishing an open channel for discussion in this regard at an early stage will be in the interests of the acquisition financiers.

CHAPTER 3

Financing the Acquisition

INTRODUCTION

3.1   Buy-outs and other leveraged acquisitions distinguish themselves from other forms of acquisition through the way they are financed. Indeed the most rapidly evolving aspect of the UK buy-out market, certainly during the 2000s, has been in the nature of the funding structures used. In particular, the level of financial engineering employed in transactions has increased significantly, with innovative financial instruments and even new markets combining to create greater flexibility for the financing of buy-outs. In practice, this means that the key variable component of a buy-out is generally the funding structure.

THE TYPES OF FINANCE AVAILABLE

3.2   Buy-out finance broadly falls into two categories, equity and debt. Equity is provided by private equity institutions and funds and is called 'private equity'. In practice, it is not all true 'equity' and usually includes a significant element of debt in the form of subordinated loan capital, which is sometimes referred to as the 'quasi-equity'. Debt is provided by banks and other financial institutions or entities under the broad categorisation 'acquisition finance' and there are various types of acquisition finance available to fund buy-outs, as detailed below. The following sections contain introductory descriptions of all of these forms of finance and more detailed analyses are included in later chapters.

Hybrid instruments with debt and equity features, such as convertability options, are also used in some structures between the equity and debt but at the time of writing this was rare and deal-specific and they are not specifically considered.

Equity

Institutional equity and management equity

3.3   Equity is one of the two core forms of finance used in buy-outs. It is provided by the sponsor – the private equity house sponsoring the buy-out – and, in most buy-outs but typically in substantially smaller amounts, the management team that the sponsor is backing. The following paragraphs give an overview of the nature of private equity. Its various forms and typical terms, and how it is documented, are considered in more detail in **Chapter 4**.

Equity and quasi–equity

3.4   Despite its name, the equity investment will not entirely comprise true equity share capital. In fact the vast majority of it will comprise quasi-equity in the form of redeemable preference shares or more often subordinated loan notes, deep discount bonds, PIK notes or other subordinated loan capital. Only a relatively small element will comprise true equity in the form of ordinary share capital. In most structures, the equity invested by the sponsor – the institutional equity – will largely comprise subordinated loan capital, whereas the equity invested by the management team will often comprise a greater proportion (but still only a minority) of the true equity. Generally, the term 'equity' is used in the wider sense to mean both true equity and quasi-equity.

Since it is subordinated behind the acquisition finance debt, and effectively locked into the company until such debt is repaid, subordinated loan capital is treated by the acquisition financiers as equity even though it is actually debt (ie, it is treated as equity, on a financial, but not necessarily legal, analysis). Redeemable preference share capital is a further alternative form of 'quasi-equity' to subordinated loan capital but this does not currently have the same tax benefits as subordinated debt (ie, interest deductibility) and is now rarely used.

The quasi-equity will generally be expressed to have a yield. This will be interest in the case of subordinated loan capital, a fixed dividend in the case of preference shares or an increasing redemption price in the case of deep discount bonds. The terms of the acquisition finance will generally dictate that the yield on the quasi-equity is not actually payable in cash on a current basis. In the case of interest this means that it will be capitalised and compound, usually six- or twelve-monthly. It will only be realised when the principal is redeemed at exit or on fixed dates after a number of years if no exit has occurred by then.[1]

Senior debt

3.5   Senior debt is the core element of any acquisition finance package. It is the cheapest and most plentiful source of debt available to a sponsor.

Senior debt market

3.6   Senior debt is sourced from dedicated acquisition finance teams within banks and other financial institutions and funds. The European senior debt market is very deep with hundreds of banks, institutions and funds focused on providing senior debt packages for sponsors. The huge liquidity of the market generally has meant that deal sponsors can create aggressive structures to finance

---

1   The requirement of a current cash paying yield on the quasi–equity will vary from sponsor to sponsor and on the cashflow capacity of the relevant target business. The various funds or investors whose funds or investments are actually being invested in the deals by the deal sponsor may have different priorities for achieving the desired IRRs as between current yield and exit value. In any case a current yield will normally need to be negotiated with the acquisition financiers. In many cases the sponsor's desire to receive a cash yield will conflict directly with the acquisition financiers' insistence that any excess cashflow after payment of all other on-going finance costs is applied in prepaying the acquisition finance debt.

buy-outs, often with less equity required from them than they would ultimately be willing to invest. For most prospective transactions there will be at least one bank willing to provide the requisite senior debt. In many there will be several banks chasing the arranging mandate.

What does the senior debt comprise?

Acquisition facility

3.7　　The core element of a senior debt package will comprise one or more medium term acquisition loans, with maturities of between five and nine years. These loans will be made available to newco for funding the acquisition of the target and for paying the buyer's fees and costs in respect of the transaction. They may also be made available to certain members of the target group to enable them to repay any existing debt. In many cases there will be significant advantages in using senior debt to repay a target group's indebtedness rather than buying the business on a debt-free basis. This is particularly true in both multi-jurisdictional deals and UK public-to-privates.

Working capital facility

3.8　　In addition to the acquisition term loans, the target business will generally have a need for a working capital facility. This will be provided by the senior lenders and comprise part of the senior debt package. The amount of the working capital facility will reflect the working capital requirement of the business determined as part of the uses of funds analysis.[2]

　　The working capital facility will typically comprise a committed revolving credit facility together with ancillary facilities including an overdraft and other ancillary working capital requirements, such as guarantees, bonding, letters of credit and foreign exchange.

Capex facility

3.9　　Where a specific capital expenditure funding requirement is included in the business plan and the uses of funds analysis, this may be provided by the senior lenders as part of the senior debt package.

Further acquisition facilities

3.10　　Additional acquisition facilities, which allow the sponsor to make one or more further 'bolt-on' acquisitions using the existing buy-out group as a platform are increasingly common.

Second lien debt

3.11　　Second lien debt is a form of junior – or subordinated – debt that may be used in conjunction with senior debt, and other forms of junior debt, to increase the amount of leverage available to the sponsor.

2　See also para **3.28**.

The second lien debt market

3.12   Second lien debt, which is also sometimes called senior subordinated debt, was originally an import from the US market. It was initially used as a means of attracting certain US institutional investors, particularly hedge funds into European buy-outs. As the acquisition finance market has developed, second lien has been used in buy-outs in two different ways. One use, which is arguably more common in true buy-outs, is as a form of stretched (but to some extent subordinated) senior debt. It is generally documented as the D note in a senior facilities agreement and this form of second lien debt has commonly been used in structures that also incorporate a large tranche of core junior debt, whether mezzanine or high yield. The other way second lien may be used, which was initially more frequent in the leveraged corporate market or in recapitalisations of mature buy-outs, is as a replacement of mezzanine or high yield in the capital structure. Such senior–second lien only structures (sometimes with a PIK note in addition) are a natural result of excess liquidity in the acquisition finance market and at times of reduced liquidity the more traditional structures with senior, second lien and mezzanine may be more common.

As already indicated, the use of second lien debt in European buy-outs can be traced to a desire to attract US institutional investors and hedge funds in particular, to the European market. Consequently, when it first appeared in Europe it was generally only offered – that is arranged and underwritten as part of an acquisition finance package – by financial institutions with a distribution capability and track record in the United States institutional investor market. For this reason US investment banks and international commercial banks with US operations were the key players. As second lien became more widely recognised by the leveraged finance market generally, the major European banks also realised the opportunity it offered for fine tuning structures and accessing a new investor market. It is now offered by most of the major European and US arranging banks.

Ultimately, following completion of the transaction most or all of the second lien debt will be sold to the end investors in both the US and Europe. In addition to hedge funds the target investor base now includes other institutional investors such as insurance companies, mutual funds, CDOs and CLOs. US institutions still make up a significant proportion of the 'market'. A number of European-based leveraged loan funds will take second lien paper, although those set up to invest primarily in mezzanine products may find the second lien yields too low to fit within the fund's investment profile.

What form does the second lien debt take?

3.13   Second lien debt takes the form of loans or bonds that are secured with second ranking security immediately behind the core senior debt – in this context, often referred to as the 'priority' senior debt. It is also sometimes called senior subordinated debt and in buy-outs is often structured to rank ahead of the core subordinated debt, whether mezzanine or high yield. Unlike mezzanine debt, where some of the interest capitalises and is paid in kind (PIK), all the interest on second lien debt is payable in cash.

In structures with mezzanine debt the second lien will be documented in the form of a second lien loan. Where the structure has high yield bonds it will either be a loan or an issue of notes (bonds), or even a combination. This is part a documentary issue and part market driven.

In either case the second lien debt matures immediately after the core senior debt, usually at year 9.5, which will be six months before the mezzanine or high yield tranche. When structured as a loan the second lien has traditionally been documented as the D tranche of senior debt in the senior facilities agreement. This reflects its status as a form of stretched senior debt rather than core junior debt.[3]

The terms on which second lien debt is subordinated to the core senior debt are considered in **Chapter 10**.

Mezzanine debt

3.14   Mezzanine debt is a further type of junior debt used in buy-outs. Despite the increased used of second lien debt, during the mid-2000s, mezzanine has by and large remained the most widely used form of junior debt across the entire acquisition finance market.[4]

The mezzanine finance market

3.15   Mezzanine finance is provided by acquisition finance banks, specialist mezzanine houses, other financial institutions and specialised funds set up to invest in leveraged finance products such as mezzanine debt. In actual fact there are now two discrete mezzanine markets operating in Europe. For lower mid-market and smaller deals there is the 'true' mezzanine market where the features of the mezzanine debt are those that have characterised the mezzanine market since the early 1990s. The key defining characteristic is that this mezzanine debt will be warranted. That is, the mezzanine lenders will receive equity warrants as part of the overall finance package. Many of the original specialist mezzanine houses still play a prominent role in this market, as do a number of banks. The other market is the institutional mezzanine market which deploys mezzanine debt in upper mid-market and larger transactions. Here the mezzanine debt is warrantless and provided in very large syndicated tranches of debt. This market is dominated by the leading banks but much of the liquidity is provided by funds and other institutional investors. As a result of the emergence of institutional mezzanine since the early 2000s, the potential size of a mezzanine loan has increased significantly. During the 1990s a mezzanine loan would rarely have exceeded £50m whereas mezzanine loans in excess of £500m are now possible. There are a number of reasons for this development. One is the sporadic lack of liquidity in the European high yield debt market, which has created demand for large tranches of junior debt. Arguably more important has been the increasing number of institutions willing and able to invest in mezzanine debt products, including CDOs, hedge funds and a significant number of specially formed

---

3   However, as previously mentioned, second lien debt can also be used as core junior debt in place of, say, mezzanine. This was originally less common in true buy-outs and was more a feature of the leveraged corporate market or in recapitalisations of mature buy-outs. However, in times of excess liquidity, this form of second lien may also be used in a wide variety of buy-out structures.

4   In fact when the European high yield market is open it can provide greater liquidity and larger tranche sizes.

mezzanine funds raised by financial institutions, particularly US institutional investors. The effect of this has been to elevate institutional mezzanine finance to be a competitive product to high yield debt in all but the largest deals.

What form does mezzanine finance take?

Mezzanine and junior mezzanine

3.16   A mezzanine finance package will typically comprise a single term loan repayable in one bullet amount 12 months after the final instalment of senior debt, or in structures with second lien debt six months after the second lien debt matures. Thus if the senior debt includes A, B and C tranches repayable over seven, eight and nine years respectively, the mezzanine loan will be repayable ten years after completion.[5] Second lien debt would usually mature at year 9.5 in that same structure. Interest on mezzanine debt is payable in a combination of cash and PIK, and in certain cases the borrower can select the proportions that are payable in cash and PIK.

In certain circumstances, usually only in the larger deals in the institutional mezzanine market, the mezzanine debt may be structured as two tranches in order to increase the overall amount of mezzanine debt. In doing so it is likely that the mezzanine arranger would have a 'junior' mezzanine loan in addition to the conventional mezzanine loan. The junior mezzanine loan would be repayable after the core mezzanine loan, and in most cases would actually be subordinated in right of payment behind the mezzanine loan. Junior mezzanine tranches may be warranted, a feature they have in common with true mezzanine debt.

All mezzanine debt in a structure will be subordinated to the senior debt and any second lien debt. The terms of its subordination are considered in **Chapter 10**.

High yield debt

3.17   In transactions above, say, £500m total deal size, high yield debt is an alternative source of junior debt to mezzanine debt. In mega-deals above, say, £2,000m total deal size, it may be the only viable option for the required junior debt layer.

The high yield debt market

3.18   The European high yield market was established in the second half of the 1990s to provide subordinated debt for the largest buy-outs. Since that time it has been instrumental in financing some landmark buy-outs that would not have happened without access to that market. Equally it has proved to be relatively unpredictable at times, prone to bouts of reduced liquidity, often as a result of factors not directly related to the buy-out market.[6]

---

5   It is a fundamental characteristic of junior debt that it is only repayable after all of the senior debt has been repaid in full.
6   For instance, TMT market weakness in the early 2000s caused a significant loss of appetite for high yield amongst investors across all sectors.

Fundamentally it is an extremely deep market with greater capacity even than the European mezzanine market. This is largely because there are huge numbers of US institutional investors that are willing to take positions in high yield bond issuances. Depending on the prevailing market conditions, it can provide large tranches of junior debt for the largest buy-outs and increasingly large numbers of European banks are able to offer a high yield debt product. This has enabled those banks to compete with the US investment banks that have traditionally dominated this end of the buy-out market. As an aside, it is worth noting that high yield debt is rarely referred to as junior debt. Its US heritage means that it is more commonly referred to as subordinated debt.[7]

The bonds themselves will be subscribed by institutional investors from around the world, and in particular Europe and North America.[8]

What form does the high yield debt take?

3.19 High yield debt takes the form of an issue of bonds into the public debt markets.[9] Unlike most other forms of junior debt they are rated by the rating agencies. The bonds, which are also called 'notes', carry an interest coupon. The interest rate is usually fixed, but floating rate notes are also possible and issues of floating rate notes (FRNs) have increased in recent times. High yield bonds differ from their main competitor product mezzanine debt in a number of significant aspects and certain transaction structures and proposals tend to favour bond issues where others would be better suited to mezzanine debt. One key factor is size. The minimum size for a high yield bond issue is probably in the region of £75m whereas mezzanine debt can be used in much smaller amounts. All of the interest on a high yield bond is payable in cash at six-monthly intervals. There is no PIK element, as there is with mezzanine. High yield bonds have traditionally had a maturity of ten years, which means that they mature after all of the prior ranking debt. However, eight year tenors are also possible, which either means that the maturity of the C tranche of senior debt is truncated at eight years or there is a theoretical refinancing risk for the senior lenders at year eight when the high yield bond matures.[10] As with all other junior debt, high yield will be subordinated to the senior debt and any second lien debt and the terms of its subordination are considered in **Chapter 10**.[11]

PIK note debt

3.20 In certain cases the demand for debt in a structure will be sufficiently great that even the use of B and C tranches of core senior debt, a second lien (or

---

7 Although, particularly in the US, it is also possible to have unsubordinated senior ranking high yield bonds, usually in structures without core senior bank debt.

8 See also Chapter 8 in respect of high yield generally.

9 In fact, they are often privately placed initially before becoming more widely traded in the capital markets generally.

10 This is more theoretical than real since the debt structure can usually be refinanced after much shorter a time than eight years.

11 Note that in some structures it is possible to have an issue of high yield debt without any prior ranking senior bank debt. Such 'senior notes' might even be secured in the same way as conventional senior bank debt, in which case they would be 'senior secured notes'. Senior notes and senior secured notes remain rare in the European acquisition finance market, however.

D) tranche and a large tranche of mezzanine or high yield debt is still not sufficient to meet the total funding requirement. In such circumstances the acquisition
financiers might consider that a PIK note is a viable addition to the structure.

The advantage of PIK note debt is that the yield accruing is all paid-in-kind.
There is no current cash element. This means that total leverage can be increased
without using up any further cashflow.

The PIK note debt market

3.21   As with second lien debt, PIK notes may take the form of a private market instrument or a public market instrument. Private PIK is structured as subordinated loan capital, direct loans or deep discount bonds and is arranged and
underwritten by senior banks and mezzanine houses. It is then distributed to
institutional investors with appetite for higher risk, higher yielding leveraged
loan paper. The banks themselves will not usually hold this type of paper. Public
PIK is structured as a capital markets bond issue. It can perhaps best be viewed
as a form of non-cash pay structurally subordinated high yield debt. Because of
its structural status it is often referred to as 'holdco PIK'. To date hedge funds
have been the most active buyers of this form of PIK notes. They tend to have
less strict investment criteria than most other types of financier and are often
attracted to hybrid instruments such as this.

Both forms are relatively rare in buy-outs and public PIK in particular is more
often used as an equity replacing instrument as part of a recapitalisation of a
mature buy-out. Generally, it may be instructive to view PIK notes as a form of
stretched junior debt or even senior equity.

What form does the PIK note debt take?

3.22   As discussed above, PIK notes are a debt instrument which will either
take the form of private subordinated loan capital, loans or DDBs or an issue of
bonds (or a loan) in the public debt markets. Much depends on the purpose of the
financing and the nature of the other instruments in the funding structure. So, for
example, in a buy-out that also includes mezzanine debt it will often be in the
form of private subordinated loan capital or DDBs. In structures with high yield
debt it might also be in the form of a capital markets bond issue but public PIK
issuances are more often found in recapitalisations of late stage buy-out businesses, perhaps in advance of a full IPO.

Warrants may be issued to the PIK note holders as part of the agreed deal for
investing in this high risk asset class. As far as maturity is concerned, the PIK
notes will be due for redemption (repayment) after all the senior and all other
junior debt has been repaid, which is likely to be at the end of years 10, 11 or 12
following completion depending on the precise nature of the core junior debt.
PIK notes are subordinated to all other forms of acquisition finance and the
extent and terms of the subordination are considered in **Chapter 10**.

Seller capital

3.23   In addition to the standard equity and debt components provided by the
sponsor, management team and acquisition financiers, there may be circum-

stances when the capital structure also includes an investment by the seller, although this is relatively uncommon. Seller finance is mostly structured in the form of a subordinated loan. It is generally referred to as a seller (or vendor) 'note'.

A seller note will generally be used where there is a gap between the price that the seller expects for the target business and that which the deal sponsor is willing to pay, perhaps as a result of matters arising during the due diligence process. A seller note is one solution for filling the price gap. A more detailed consideration of seller notes is set out in **Chapter 4**.

By contrast, where the seller is seeking to participate in the future growth in the business, rather than receiving deferred consideration, true equity would be the appropriate instrument. This is called an earn-out. Earn-outs are considered briefly in **Chapter 4**.

STRUCTURING TECHNIQUES

Sources and uses analyses

3.24   As obvious as it sounds, at the outset of the structuring process for a particular transaction the parties will need to determine the total amount of finance that is required. They will then match this need with the various types of finance considered above. One of the tools commonly used to do this is a sources and uses analysis. The 'uses' will represent the purposes for which funding is required; principally the purchase price for the target – and the 'sources' will detail the types of finance that will be raised and applied to meet those requirements.

Uses of funds

3.25   Initially the parties will make relatively broad assumptions about the amount of finance required. As the funding structure is finalised these assumptions will be verified and the numbers crystallised.

A simple uses of funds analysis might look as follows:

Uses of funds	(£)
Purchase price	●
Deal costs	●
Working capital	●
Total	●

Typical uses of funds analysis

Purchase price and deal costs

3.26   The funding requirement will principally comprise the purchase price for the target and an assumed figure for the deal costs. The deal costs will include the fees payable to the various financiers for providing each element of the funding structure and to each adviser involved in putting the deal together including the lawyers, accountants and other professional advisers.

In addition to these core items the funding requirement may also include a separate requirement for refinancing the target group's existing debt, a working capital requirement and possibly other deal-specific, debt-based financial needs such as a capital expenditure (capex) facility, a guarantee facility or a bonding facility[12].

Refinancing existing debt

3.27   Where the target business has third-party borrowings, the seller may use part of the overall purchase price consideration to repay the existing debt on the basis that the target is then acquired on a debt free basis. Alternatively, there are usually good reasons why the buyer would prefer to acquire the target with its debt in place – but for a commensurately reduced purchase price. In particular, by leaving the target's existing debt in place at the time of the acquisition and having the acquisition financiers lend directly to the target to enable it to repay such debt immediately upon completion of its acquisition, rather than lending to newco the equivalent amount to acquire target free of that debt, the acquisition financiers are likely to achieve a number of benefits. This is particularly so in a multi-jurisdictional buy-out where the consequent benefit of having debt and operating profits located in the same corporate entities may enable interest deductibility for tax purposes and the obtaining of target group asset security.[13] Similarly, in a public-to-private, where the obtaining of target group security is subject to specific timing constraints as a result of financial assistance laws the ability to lend directly into the target group will enhance the acquisition financiers' initial security position materially.[14]

Working capital

3.28   A working capital requirement is, in simple terms, the cashflow requirement that arises by virtue of the fact that a business generally has to expend funds in advance in order to generate income. Since most businesses do not meet accounts payable immediately – they will typically benefit from deferred payment terms agreed with suppliers of anywhere between 30 and 90 days – or expect accounts receivable to be paid immediately (and again the deferred terms will be negotiated with customers), the working capital profile of a business will be highly dependant on the payment terms which the business has with suppliers and customers. The ideal scenario is for accounts receivable to be met in a shorter time frame than accounts payable, which should mean that there is no working capital requirement. Supermarkets may be an extreme example of this type of business provided that stock/inventory is sold sufficiently quickly so that it becomes cash before the accounts payable are due. At the other extreme are seasonal businesses, where revenue is only generated at a particular time of year. For instance, manufacturers that sell their products to seasonally dependent

---

12 In practice, some of these specific facilities may fall within the overall working capital requirement of the business and therefore be provided as part of a working capital facility.

13 See **Chapter 13** for further detail.

14 See **Chapter 12** for further detail.

retailers may find that their own income is similarly seasonal. In the off-season they will usually still produce and carry stock/inventory and meet all of their overheads but they may not generate significant revenue. In such businesses the working capital requirement is less a function of the payment terms that can be negotiated with suppliers and customers and more a simple feature of the seasonality of sales. In accounting terms analysing a working capital requirement will involve assessing the rate of churn (ie, the incidence, reduction and replacement) of the ongoing balances of the creditor, debtor and stock/inventory items in the balance sheet of the business.

Sources of funds

3.29   In order to meet the assumed funding requirement, the parties will consider various combinations of the sources of finance considered above. The core sources are equity (true equity and quasi-equity) provided principally by the institutional equity investor sponsoring the acquisition but also by the management team, and senior debt provided by one or more senior lenders.[15] These two components alone might satisfy the funding requirement.

With many buy-outs, however, when the available amounts of equity and senior debt are added together, there is a shortfall of funds. This shortfall is sometimes called the 'funding gap' between the overall funding requirement and the amount of funding available. If structuring refinements cannot fill the gap, other sources of funds will be necessary.

Where the gap is relatively small the senior lender may be willing to provide an additional tranche of senior debt. This is sometimes called 'stretched' senior debt and is provided in the form of a second tranche called a 'B' tranche (or adopting US terminology, a B 'note'[16]) which is repayable after the main 'A' tranche. The purpose of creating a separate tranche rather than merely increasing the amount of the A note, is really two-fold. First, by having a second tranche that is repayable as a bullet after all of the A note, the amount of amortising debt is not increased, leaving more cashflow available to meet the inherent interest costs. Secondly, the use of a B note means the overall financial shape and profile of the A note is preserved, in particular its size as a multiple of the target's earnings. This enables it to be priced in line with market norms for syndication purposes.[17] If the A note were materially increased in size the banks would wish to re-price it to reflect the greater leverage. Instead they create a whole new tranche with higher pricing (the B note). The fact that the B note is repayable after the A note, which will be the case so that the A note retains the first call on the target's cashflows during the life of the financing, means that it has a higher risk profile. This is why the B note will

---

15 The working capital requirement will be satisfied by a dedicated facility within the overall senior debt package.

16 The term 'note' is borrowed from the US market, where different tranches of debt are represented by separate promissory notes issued to the lenders.

17 For many years this was absolutely true with standard A note pricing invariably meaning a margin of 2.25% over LIBOR/EURIBOR. However, during the latter half of the 2000s the vast amount of liquidity in the senior debt market eventually resulted in lower pricing for senior debt generally and eventually the A note margin could be reduced to around 2.00% instead. See **Chapter 5** for further discussion of this trend.

attract a higher interest rate margin than the A note. Where the additional funding requirement is sufficiently large there may be need for a 'C' tranche in addition to A and B notes. The C note would be repayable after the B note and would attract a higher margin still.

In practice, since the late 1990s, as banks have become willing to structure deals with more and more debt in them at greater leverage multiples, these so-called 'alphabet notes' (that is, B and C notes) are automatically used in most deals and considered to be core senior debt. In actual fact, in the latter half of the 2000s, larger deals – and some mid-market deals – are more likely to be structured with only B and C tranches (or just a single B tranche) and no A tranche.[18] By contrast, the smallest deals may not have B and C notes at all and have only an A tranche; usually because the acquisition financiers do not feel comfortable increasing the leverage multiples to such high levels for what are often less mature and stable businesses.

In liquid markets with senior debt effectively already stretched, any notional funding gap will need to be filled with an entirely separate layer of finance. This means using what is called junior or subordinated debt in the form of one or more of second lien debt, mezzanine debt, high yield debt and PIK note debt. Junior debt is considered further in the following sections.

The sources of funds will only be finalised when the assumptions underlining the funding requirement are finalised but it will inevitably comprise the core elements of equity and senior debt and, in most structures, one or more layers of junior debt.

A simple sources of funds analysis might look as follows:

Sources of funds	(£)
Management equity	•
Institutional equity	•
Institutional quasi–equity	•
Junior debt	•
Senior debt	•
Senior debt (working capital facility)	•
Total	•

Typical sources of funds analysis

As to the question of how much equity, senior debt and junior debt is available, the respective parties providing those layers of finance will apply certain financial criteria to the prospective investments which must be met if the level of finance required of them is to be viable. The investment criteria will initially relate to purely financial and structural matters rather than to the target business itself. This is on the basis that if those fundamentals are not met, the deal will not go ahead with the specified financial structure, even if the target business is fundamentally sound, its management impressive and the business plan viable.

---

18 This trend has been fuelled by the exceptional liquidity in the institutional senior debt market and, in particular, from leveraged loan funds. This segment of the market is attracted to the higher yielding and non-amortising tranches (B and C) rather than the lower yielding amortising tranche (A). In addition, by reducing the amount of amortising debt, sponsors and acquisition financiers can increase the total amount of debt that a particular business can support by reducing the debt service requirements during the life of the loan. See also para **3.49** and **Chapter 5** generally.

The principal tool used by the parties and their financial advisers to determine if their respective financial criteria may be met is the financial model.

Financial modelling

3.30   Financial models are used to assist the sponsor and acquisition financiers and, to a lesser extent, the management team in determining what level of investment is viable for them in a proposed buy-out.

A financial model is an electronic spreadsheet based on a set of trading assumptions relating to the target business onto which each of the potential investors and financiers overlay possible funding structures. In doing so and by changing the inputs they are able to assess the viability of the transaction and, in particular, the level of their potential investment. For equity providers the key element of their assessment will be the IRR shown in the model, which will be a function of both the projected current yield on their investments[19] and the projected earnings and capital growth of the business.[20] For the debt providers the key element will be the ability of the group to service the assumed level of debt, which will essentially be a function of the cashflow projected to be generated by the group and the on-going financing costs.

Building a reliable and achievable set of financial projections upon defensible assumptions is the key to determining the cashflow capacity of a business, which in turn helps to set the debt and equity structure. The core assumptions regarding the target business, which will provide the basic framework for the model, will be the projected balance sheet, profit and loss account and cashflow statement of the target business for each financial year from (and including) the last complete financial year to, probably, the next five or more financial years thereafter. The financial model is therefore essentially the numerical heart of the business plan produced by the management team – that is, the projected trading figures for the business. The finally agreed model – including trading projections that the parties accept as achievable – will be called the base case model since it represents the agreed 'base case'.[21]

Other assumptions that are needed to derive the final profit and loss and cashflow statements will also be input. These will include the corporation tax rate, currency exchange rates[22] and underlying interest rates and the like.

The model will display the financial position of the group at the end of each financial year – and typically each month or quarter within each year – following the assumed acquisition completion date. It will show, for instance, if sufficient cash is generated to meet the scheduled payments in respect of the debt. By

---

19 The quasi-equity in particular may be expressed to carry a running yield, in the form of interest. Often the payment of such yield is conditional upon the financial performance of the business. If it is not paid in cash it will be capitalised and realised when the principal amount invested is realised on a successful exit. This will be shown in the model.

20 This will indicate the exit value of the business.

21 In practice there will generally be more than one version of the model. The management team, sponsoring equity house and acquisition financiers will each have their own versions with slightly adjusted assumptions. For instance, the financiers' case may be more conservative in terms of trading projections than the management team's.

22 In a multi-jurisdictional deal all of the various revenues and related cashflows will be converted into a single currency, say Euro, for the purposes of the model.

varying the amount of debt and the rate at which it is repaid (the amortisation schedule) it is possible to ascertain what amount of debt and rate of amortisation can be sustained by the cashflows which the target business is projected to produce.[23] Equally, varying the trading assumptions will affect what cashflow is projected. In practice the funding and trading assumptions may change as the results of the due diligence process are obtained and will be factored into the financial model. Each time the assumptions are changed the model will automatically output the revised picture. The financial model can thus determine what level of debt, rates of repayment and rates of interest will be sustainable. By extrapolation it will also show what level of earnings and capital growth and thus value enhancement should be achievable for the equity investors. All of this is on the basis of a given set of trading projections and financial assumptions. Bearing in mind that the various investors and financiers have certain key requirements and principles relating to the financial variables, it can be seen that different trading projections and financial assumptions will lead to different funding solutions. Sometimes the financial nature of the target business will mean that there is no viable financial structure for a buy-out.

At this point, it is worth noting that, although the prospective equity and debt financiers, in determining the funding structure, assume that the projections in the base case financial model will be met, this assumption is not a blind leap of faith. Extensive financial due diligence into the target business together with market due diligence in respect of the target's markets will be carried out for precisely the purpose of verifying the business plan projections; and to the extent that this due diligence does not support the base case model then the deal will not be done without an alteration to the business plan and hence the trading assumptions, the financial structure or the purchase price.

The model will also be used to ascertain the effects of certain downside scenarios, such as lower than expected sales as a result of, say, recession in the relevant market. This is called a sensitivity analysis and is effected by altering the trading assumptions used in the model.

Each of the prospective investors and financiers will have its own model, but by the end of the deal process there should be a single agreed base case model which will be used by all the parties for certain purposes. Chief among these will be determining the levels at which the financial covenants to be included within the acquisition finance documentation should be set.[24] This is done by ensuring that they are breached only when the business has underperformed by an agreed amount. Since the principal purpose of the financial covenants is to act as an early warning of significant underperformance, if the covenants are set to trip at the right level, a review of the funding structure or other steps may be taken following a breach of the covenants before the position has deteriorated too far. It follows that in determining the amount, types and amortisation of the finance for a particular structure by reference to the financial model the principals will allow for some underperformance before the group actually defaults in meeting payments due to the financiers. This 'headroom' will need to be sufficiently large so

---

23 Note that by removing the amortising A tranche altogether, leverage can be maximised (see para **3.49**).

24 See **Chapter 5** for a more detailed consideration of the use of financial covenants in acquisition finance.

that the financial covenants are not breached by a slight downturn in performance but not so great that they are breached only when the business is about to have a full scale payment default or insolvency event. Thus the level of financial covenant breach might be set at, say, 20%[25] of underperformance against the base case model with actual payment default requiring even greater underperformance. It follows that the principals will not provide as much finance as the base case model would theoretically allow but an amount that can still be serviced even with some underperformance.

Ultimately, the financial model will form a key element of an institution's internal credit approval submission.

Two example transactions, Project Alpha and Project Bravo, will be used to demonstrate how a funding structure can be created. Project Alpha is of typical lower mid-market size and Project Bravo is a relatively large deal. In many cases, however, the principles applied will be equally relevant to most other sizes of transaction although perhaps not very large and mega transactions above, say, £1,000m, where different dynamics may apply.

Example transactions

Project Alpha

3.31   The uses of funds analysis for Project Alpha is as follows:

Uses of funds	(£m)
Purchase price	65.0
Deal costs	3.0
Working capital	5.0
Total	73.0

Project Alpha: uses of funds

Project Bravo

3.32   The uses of funds analysis for Project Bravo is as follows:

Uses of funds	(£m)
Purchase price	500.0
Refinancing target debt	175.0
Deal costs	25.0
Working capital	50.0
Total	750.0

Project Bravo: uses of funds

---

25 In practice, headroom of as much a 25% or 30% is not unknown for senior financial covenants with potentially a further 10% being allowed for mezzanine covenants.

CREATING A FUNDING STRUCTURE

3.33   Having determined, initially at least, the funding required (the uses of funds), the principals will need to analyse the available sources and come up with a viable funding structure. The following paragraphs consider the available sources of finance that may be utilised to satisfy the funding requirement.

Equity

3.34   In most buy-outs – true management buy-outs being one possible exception and very small deals being another – the vast bulk of the overall equity package will be put up by the equity house leading the deal (the sponsor). The proportion put up by the management team will not be determinative of the total amount of equity made available. It will amount to fine-tuning of the structure. Consequently, in order to assess how much equity will be available for a particular transaction, it is necessary to focus on the institutional equity.

How much institutional equity is invested, and indeed how it is split between true equity and quasi-equity, will in large part be driven by the targeted internal rate of return (IRR) of the sponsor.

An IRR is a mathematical expression of the return on an investment made by an investor over the lifetime of its investment. Basically, it reflects the amount of money received by the relevant investor by way of yield and capital gain, expressed as a percentage of the initial investment and on an annual, usually compound, basis. In an extremely simple example, an investment of £100 which is realised for £144 after two years will reflect an IRR of 20% to the investor.[26]

In applying a target IRR to a particular transaction the sponsor will make assumptions not only about the performance of the underlying business, which will be reflected in the base case model, but also as to when its investment would be realised and at what level. Often it will assume that the exit price is determined by reference to the same multiple of earnings as the purchase price. This will be a common assumption for base case purposes. In practice, however, depending on the nature of the target business the sponsor may see an opportunity to try and increase the multiple that is applicable at exit. This might be possible with improvements to the business or increased scale, each of which may take the business to a higher level within its peer group and enable it to attract a premium valuation. Another possibility is to target an exit via an IPO where a higher multiple may be possible than with a trade sale or secondary. In any event, as mentioned above, assuming that the exit multiple matches the entry multiple will be a common assumption for the base case. This leaves the exit timing as the only real variable. Here too the sponsor will make an assumption, often by targeting an exit after say three or four years, these being reasonably common holding periods. The holding period of an investment is fundamental to an IRR – that is, the IRR is very

---

26   A return of £44 after two years represents a 20% annual return on capital of £100 (on a compounded basis, so that the second year is 20% of £120). In practice, the use of leverage in a transaction can significantly increase the IRR on the equity investment because the buying power of the debt enables the equity investor to acquire a larger business than it could otherwise have done with the equity alone and all of the capital growth (less the cost of servicing the debt) accrues to the equity rather than the debt.

sensitive to the length of time an investment is held – because the longer the investment is held the greater the return must be to generate the same IRR. This means that an ideal holding period from a pure IRR perspective might be only two years, say, provided that sufficient improvements can be made to the business – and its profitability in particular – in that period. Much depends on the nature of the target business, the return drivers in the business plan and the likely exit the sponsor has identified.

One technique that some sponsors use to counteract the dilutive effect of time and to enhance the IRR is the use of yield bearing quasi-equity. In particular, by taking cash payments of interest on the subordinated loan capital provided by the sponsor – and thus receiving a return on the investment throughout the life of the investment and not just at exit – the IRR of the investment is increased. This is true even if the absolute quantum of all receipts on the investment is not greater, or indeed it might even be less. This is also the thinking behind leveraged recapitalisations. The sponsor brings forward a major proportion of its return through a dividend or redemption of quasi-equity (financed with a new debt package) in advance of a full exit.

In summary, when the sponsor is structuring the equity package it will use the base case, incorporating all the aspects of the funding structure, and apply its assumptions concerning exit to model the projected return on the equity investment. The less equity that is included the higher the potential IRR will be. On the other hand, by including more debt the structure becomes more susceptible to any underperformance by the business. The sponsor can also fine-tune the equity component by varying the amounts and split of the true equity versus quasi-equity and possibly having some cash yield.

The targeted IRRs of private equity institutions have in practice reduced as the UK private equity market has matured.[27] This is largely as a result of the significantly greater competition to acquire businesses and the higher prices that sponsors must pay as a result. In addition, finding the business that could benefit most from a buy-out has become more difficult in absolute terms, as more and more buyouts are completed. For a management team the buy-out is likely to be its only opportunity to make a significant equity return. This, together with the relatively lower quantum of their actual equity investment, will mean they will look for a much greater return on their capital, although it is not usual to assess a management team's prospective return in IRR terms but rather in absolute quantum terms.

The different return expectations for the sponsor and the management team basically require that most of the management team's investment goes into true equity (which produces higher returns) and most of the sponsor's investment goes into quasi-equity. This is not to say that the management team will take a majority of the ordinary shares. Indeed, since these shares will carry all the

---

27 Historically, equity houses might have sought to obtain an average IRR on their investments of between 30 and 40% say. Some investments will have higher targeted returns than others and usually this correlates with risk. Thus, the higher the perceived risk the higher the required IRR the investors will expect for taking the risk. In fact, since most private equity institutions are private equity fund managers they will take a portfolio approach over the entire fund rather than a purely investment-by-investment approach. They will look to achieve the target IRRs for each fund that they manage as a whole. In recent times return expectations may have reduced for many houses largely as a result of the greater competition for deals which has lead to sellers looking for higher prices.

shareholder voting rights, the split between the management ordinary shares and the institutional ordinary shares determines the ultimate management control of the business. Other than in true MBOs, the sponsor will wish to have the ultimate control over the business and will take more than 50% of the ordinary shares.

The chief factor in determining how much management equity will be invested is often how much the sponsor determines the individual members of the management team can afford and, when the performance ratchet (if any) is taken into account,[28] what level will truly incentivise them to perform well. It is acknowledged that a high level of personal investment (possibly through the use of a bank loan secured on a home) as well as the large potential return on a successful transaction will act as an incentive to achieve the business plan. As between the individual members of the management team, the general rule is the more senior and/or key to the business an individual is, the greater the equity stake he or she takes.

All of these factors generally mean that the equity will be made up of a smaller amount of true equity – which may be as low as, say, only 2% of the entire equity or as high as 30% or more, depending on the economics, and in particular the total size, of the deal – and a larger amount of quasi–equity, with the management team taking a share of the true equity but probably a relatively small fraction (if any at all) of the quasi–equity.

Example structures

3.35   Turning to Projects Alpha and Bravo, the equity structures are as follows:

Equity structure	(£m)
Management ordinary shares	1.2
Institutional ordinary shares	8.4
Institutional loan notes	22.4
Total equity	32.0

Project Alpha: equity structure

Equity structure	(£m)
Management ordinary shares	10.0
Institutional ordinary shares	40.0
Institutional loan notes	250.0
Total equity	300.0

Project Bravo: equity structure

Senior debt

3.36   The overall amount of senior debt which the senior lenders are willing to provide will be determined principally on the basis of a detailed credit analysis of the target business and a structural analysis using a financial model. At the

28 See **Chapter 4**.

outset of the structuring process the deal sponsor will usually make an assumption about the total amount of acquisition debt required. This may be a simple function of deducting the assumed level of equity from the total funding requirement. The bank arranging the senior debt will then be set the task of confirming that it is willing to provide that amount of debt.[29]

In order to assess how much it is willing to lend, a bank will input the assumed level for the acquisition debt into the financial model along with all of the other deal specific and general assumptions, including the proposed level of equity. The model will show whether the cashflow forecast to be generated by the group after completion will be sufficient to enable all finance costs to be paid as scheduled including the payments of principal and interest on all of the acquisition finance. As with the deal sponsor, the senior lenders will also run sensitivity analyses to see what effect adverse changes in the trading environment, interest rates and other variables have on the ability of newco to service the assumed level of senior debt and any other acquisition finance to be employed. The senior lenders will usually provide for a certain amount of headroom in performance below the agreed base case so that the senior debt is not in jeopardy immediately a performance downturn occurs.

By adjusting the repayment profile of the senior acquisition debt[30] and, if necessary, the overall amount of the senior debt a deal specific structure will be developed which will indicate how much senior debt the arranging bank believes to be viable. Hopefully, this will coincide with the amount which the sponsor (and management team) are expecting. If not, further structural changes or, possibly, changes to the trading projections – but only in line with supporting financial due diligence – will be needed if the deal is to be done at the assumed price.

The amount of the working capital facility will be set by reference to the agreed working capital requirement determined as part of the overall funding requirement (uses of funds).

In addition to the analysis of the financial model and a credit analysis of the target business, the senior lenders will also consider a number of other indicators of the viability of the senior debt figure. One of the most important will be the ratio of debt to EBITDA in the proposed structure.[31] Taking into account the sector in which the business operates and the general economic climate and market dynamics, certain multiples are deemed acceptable at different times. In other words there are market benchmarks that the financiers can compare the proposed structure to. The importance of this benchmarking is that in order to successfully syndicate a large debt package the structure will need to fall within recognisable

29 In actual fact it is more common for the sponsor to approach a number of banks to get them to compete for the senior debt mandate. This often assists banks in going that little bit further with their calculations.

30 The average life of the debt, however, will be a key element of the assessment of a financial structure. See **Chapter 5**.

31 In fact, two ratios will often be considered. First, the ratio of the total amount of senior debt (usually net of cash balances) to earnings (profit) before interest, tax, depreciation and amortisation (EBITDA) for the last complete, or current projected, financial year of the target group. This is often called the senior leverage ratio and is expressed as a 'multiple' of one. In addition, a total leverage ratio will also be considered whereby the senior net debt figure is replaced with a total net debt figure including certain other debt that the group will have at completion including any junior debt.

parameters, one of which will be the applicable leverage ratio (debt to EBITDA).[32]

If the level of senior debt together with the equity is insufficient to satisfy the funding requirement, a number of further options should still be available to enable the deal to go ahead. Usually this will mean incorporating a whole new layer of finance into the structure.

Usually, the sponsor will be as aware as the senior banks of the need for junior debt in a given structure, since they are likely to be using very similar assumptions in their own financial model to those used by the competing senior banks. Aside from including junior debt in a structure, banks use a variety of financial engineering skills to increase the overall amount of debt available, such as allocating more debt to non-amortising tranches to free up cash flow.[33]

Example structures

3.37   Turning again to Projects Alpha and Bravo, the senior debt structure for each is as follows:

Senior debt structure	(£m)
Acquisition loan A	24.0
Acquisition loan B	12.0
Working capital facility	5.0
Total senior debt	41.0m

Project Alpha: senior debt structure

Senior debt structure	(£m)
Acquisition loan A	100.0
Acquisition loan B	100.0
Acquisition loan C	100.0
Working capital facility	50.0
Total senior debt	350.0

Project Bravo: senior debt structure

Funding gaps: the need for junior debt

Example structures

3.38   The sources and uses analysis for Project Alpha shows that there is no need for a further layer of finance. This is unlikely in all but the smaller and lower mid-market deals where the overall multiple of debt to EBITDA is likely

---

32 Successful syndication is vital for arranging banks since, in simple terms, most will be unable to continue to do further deals if they tie up their balance sheets with a number of very large loans to individual borrowers. Diversification of risk is also of key importance to them. See also **Chapter 11**.

33 See para **3.49** below and **Chapter 5** generally.

to be less and thus the need for junior debt – or indeed B and C notes as part of the senior debt – consequently lower. Mid-market, large and mega deals almost invariably require junior debt in addition to a full senior debt package of A, B and C notes.[34]

The Project Alpha senior debt structure has a B note but no C note.

Uses of funds	(£m)	Sources of funds	(£m)
Purchase price	65.0	Management equity	1.2
Deal costs	3.0	Institutional equity (and quasi–equity)	30.8
		Senior debt (tranche A)	24.0
		Senior debt (tranche B)	12.0
Working capital	5.0	Senior debt (working capital facility)	5.0
Total	73.0	Total	73.0

Project Alpha: sources and uses

For Project Bravo the initial sources and uses analysis showed that there was a funding gap and thus a need for a junior debt tranche in addition to a full senior debt package of A, B and C notes.[35] In this instance, given the size of the funding gap, the additional layer of junior debt is deemed to be institutional mezzanine debt reflecting the more common form of junior debt for transactions of this size.[36]

Uses of funds	(£m)	Sources of funds	(£m)
Purchase price	500.0	Management equity	10.0
Refinancing target group debt	175.0	Institutional equity (and quasi–equity)	290.0
Deal costs	25.0	Mezzanine debt	100.0
		Senior debt (tranche A)	100.0
		Senior debt (tranche B)	100.0
		Senior debt (tranche C)	100.0
Working capital	50.0	Senior debt (working capital facility)	50.0
Total	750.0	Total	750.0

Project Bravo: sources and uses

It should be emphasised that in practice the order of events might not be quite

34 In fact, in the latter half of the 2000s structures with no A note and just B and C notes (or perhaps just a single B note) have become popular. See also para **3.49**.

35 The senior debt structure for Project Bravo, with equal sized A, B and C notes, was common during the mid-2000s. In the late 2000s the size of the A note might be reduced below that of the B and C notes and perhaps even dispensed with altogether; see also para **3.49**.

36 In practice both second lien and PIK note debt could also be used together with mezzanine debt in the same structure. High yield is also a possibility but it is more often used in larger deals. These options are considered below.

as it appears from this analysis, with junior debt an afterthought if the equity and senior debt are insufficient. When putting the deal together in the first instance, the sponsor will usually be able to identify whether or not a strip of junior debt is required. Where it is they will approach banks on the basis that they are to provide both senior and junior debt or they will approach senior banks and specialist junior debt providers at the same time. A structure will then evolve following input from all parties. It is arguably more common, given that most arranging banks in the senior debt market can now offer to arrange and underwrite junior debt[37] in addition to senior debt, for the prospective senior debt arranger to be asked to arrange a full acquisition finance package including junior debt if necessary. In such circumstances, senior banks might still approach junior debt arrangers with which they have good relations to co-arrange the full acquisition finance package.

Filling the funding gap

3.39   Until the early 2000s the only options that the parties had to fill a funding gap were mezzanine debt and high yield debt. Mezzanine tended to be used in mid market and smaller deals and, sporadically, in some larger deals when high yield debt was unavailable. High yield would be used in large deals. Since that time, with the evolution of the institutional mezzanine market, there is significantly greater liquidity – and larger tranche sizes – available to mezzanine underwriters, thus enabling them to compete with the high yield market in many large deals. But since 2003 mezzanine itself has also been forced to live with a new competitor product, in the form of second lien debt. Initially, in true buy-outs at least, second lien tended to be used much more frequently as a form of stretched senior debt sandwiched between the senior debt and a larger tranche of mezzanine or high yield debt. In that sense it was complimentary to mezzanine debt and high yield. It can also be used, however, in place of mezzanine debt effectively as a form of 'cheap mezzanine'. Such senior – second lien only structures were originally reserved for refinancings of mature buy-outs and in leveraged corporate acquisitions but they have also been used in some first time buy-outs. Finally, in addition to these products, there has been increasing use of PIK notes to further enhance buy-out funding structures and it will often be used – generally in relatively small amounts (although jumbo PIK tranches have also been used) – in combination with each of the other products.

Although it might appear that all four junior debt products can be used interchangeably, in practice the current state of the market at any given time tends to dictate that certain structures and combinations of products are more in vogue than others. Looking back over the evolution of the acquisition finance market and more than one full economic cycle the most commonly used products are clearly mezzanine and high yield debt with second lien in particular and PIK notes to a lesser extent appearing later in the current cycle as the market has heated up to record levels. With this in mind mezzanine and high yield are considered in a little more detail before second lien and PIK notes.

---

37 Mezzanine and second lien at least but perhaps not high yield, or all types of PIK note debt.

Mezzanine debt

3.40 Once it is established in principle that mezzanine debt will be required in a structure, the arranging bank or mezzanine house will need to establish how much debt it is prepared to underwrite. In practice, the precise amount can only be determined at the same time that the total amount of the debt and the overall funding structure are finalised. As with the senior banks, mezzanine underwriters will use a financial model to satisfy themselves that newco will have sufficient cashflow to pay principal and interest not only of the senior debt but also the mezzanine.[38] Equally, a detailed credit analysis of the target business will also be a key factor in assessing how much junior debt may be made available. Assuming that the financial model shows sufficient cashflow to meet the cash interest payments due on the proposed amount of mezzanine debt and the funding requirement is thus met, the parties will be close to having finalised the structure. When analysing mezzanine debt, however, the sponsor will not only be concerned with the cash interest payable out of the cashflows generated by the business. It will also consider the impact of the PIK element of the mezzanine interest on its IRR. Before the equity can be realised, all prior ranking debt will need to be paid off and this will include PIK interest that has capitalised and compounded during the life of the mezzanine debt. Again, the financial model will provide the necessary analysis.

If the input amounts of equity, senior debt and mezzanine debt provide sufficient funding and a viable structure, the transaction should be financeable.

High yield debt

3.41 As is the case with the amount of a mezzanine loan, although again this is more theoretical than in practice, the amount of the high yield debt will principally be determined on the basis of the funding gap remaining where the combination of equity and senior debt alone does not meet the total funding requirement. In addition, to be commercially viable a high yield bond issue will usually need to exceed £75million. As a result high yield debt is not appropriate for a significant number of financing structures.

As a capital markets instrument, high yield is entirely distribution dependent: that is, the success of an issue is inherently susceptible to market forces and more so than with other forms of acquisition finance. For this reason, its structuring and pricing must conform to the prevailing market requirements. Specialist high yield desks within the banks arranging the overall acquisition finance package will therefore be closely involved in the entire structuring process.

---

38 Note, however, that because the principal amount of the mezzanine loan and a portion of the interest (the PIK element) will only be payable after year 8, 9 or 10, the cashflow requirements for mezzanine debt are different from those for the senior debt. In practice therefore, the mezzanine lenders will need to be satisfied that there will be sufficient cash generated by the business to meet all of the senior debt service requirements as well as the interest component of the mezzanine.

Example structure

3.42   The following structure for Project Charlie demonstrates the use of high yield debt in practice.[39]

Uses of funds	(€m)	Sources of funds	(€m)
Purchase price	460.0	Management equity	5.0
Refinancing target group debt	150.0	Institutional equity (and quasi–equity)	270.0
Deal costs	35.0	High yield debt	190.0
		Senior debt (tranche A)	60.0
		Senior debt (tranche B)	60.0
		Senior debt (tranche C)	60.0
Working capital	55.0	Senior debt (working capital facility)	55.0
Total	700.0	Total	700.0

Project Charlie: sources and uses

Additional sources of junior debt

3.43   Since the early 2000s at least two further forms of junior debt have been successfully used in UK and European buy-outs: second lien debt and PIK notes. In true buy-outs, by contrast with certain other leveraged structures, second lien and PIK notes have tended to be used in the same structure as one of the staple junior debt products, mezzanine and high yield. This is not an absolute rule though and second lien debt can also be used as an outright alternative to mezzanine or high yield and PIK can be paired with senior only or more often senior and second lien.

Second lien debt

3.44   In traditional buy-out structures, by contrast with refinancings of mature buy-outs and leveraged corporate acquisitions in particular, second lien debt will often be structured as a form of stretched senior debt rather than true junior debt.[40] It will be positioned in the capital structure above the main tranche of junior debt and just below the core senior debt. In fact, in UK and European buy-out structures it is commonly documented as the 'D' tranche of senior debt in the same document as the core senior debt (tranches A, B and C). In these circumstances, a second lien tranche will usually form only a relatively small part of the capital structure, perhaps as little as 5% of the total acquisition finance package and rarely more than 15%.

---

39 But see also fn **35** above in relation to the senior debt structure.
40 Indeed it is often referred to as senior subordinated debt.

Example structure

3.45 The following structure, for Project Delta, demonstrates the use of second lien debt in practice. Note that there is no A tranche of senior debt, a feature of many deals in the latter half of the 2000s.[41]

Uses of funds	(£m)	Sources of funds	(£m)
Purchase price	285.0	Management equity	20.0
Refinancing target group debt	50.0	Institutional equity (and quasi–equity)	100.0
Deal costs	15.0	Mezzanine debt	60.0
		Senior debt (tranche A)	–
		Senior debt (tranche B)	75.0
		Senior debt (tranche C)	75.0
		Second lien debt (tranche D)	20.0
Working capital	15.0	Senior debt (working capital facility)	15.0
Total	365.0	Total	365.0

Project Delta: sources and uses

Senior-second lien structures

3.45A As already mentioned above, second lien debt may also be used – at times of high liquidity in particular – as an outright and cheaper alternative to mezzanine debt. In that case it will replace the mezzanine (or high yield) debt in the structure altogether.

PIK note debt

3.46 PIK notes generally comprise the final element of an acquisition finance package and, in practice, this form of debt remains relatively rarely used compared to other junior debt products. Generally it may be useful to view PIK notes as a form of stretched mezzanine or high yield debt or even senior equity, sitting in the capital structure above all of the institutional equity and quasi-equity but below conventional mezzanine or high yield debt. Consequently, as a non core element of the funding structure it usually contributes only a relatively small amount to the overall source of funds.[42]

The following structure, for Project Echo, demonstrates the use of private PIK notes in a structure that also incorporates second lien and mezzanine debt. It is also possible to find private PIK notes used in less structured mid-market buyouts. Public PIK notes will generally only be used in vary large transactions where

41 See also para **3.49** in relation to this trend.
42 PIK notes might account for, say, only 5% or so of the overall funding requirement. That said, there have been a small number of jumbo size public PIK issuances where it forms a core strip of junior debt.

the dynamics of the public debt markets are more appropriate and typically only in recapitalisations of mature buy-outs as opposed to first time buy-outs.

Example structure

3.47

Uses of funds	(£m)	Sources of funds	(£m)
Purchase price	1,000.0	Management equity	50.0
Refinancing target group debt	305.0	Institutional equity (and quasi–equity)	350.0
Deal costs	50.0	PIK notes	70.0
		Mezzanine debt	230.0
		Senior debt (tranche A)	185.0
		Senior debt (tranche B)	200.0
		Senior debt (tranche C)	200.0
		Second lien debt (tranche D)	70.0
Working capital	30.0	Senior debt (working capital facility)	30.0
Total	1,385.0	Total	1,385.0

Project Echo: sources and uses

HOW STRUCTURES HAVE EVOLVED

3.47A   It is evident from the various structures shown in the preceding sections that the UK acquisition finance market has evolved significantly since the late 1980s and indeed that the rate of development has if anything accelerated through the 2000s, particularly for larger deals. The following table illustrates the evolution of the market over this period by showing what might be seen as typical market structures at different times[43]; it also shows in relative terms how deal sizes and leverage have increased over the entire period. The structures shown are indicative only and the relative amounts of each layer of finance are necessarily approximate. At the beginning of 2008 there is some uncertainty as to where the market will go in light of the 're-setting' of the market since the summer of 2007 in response to the US sub-prime triggered liquidity crisis.

---

43 Necessarily it does not show every type of structure that has been used. For example it doesn't show a classic leverage recap structure with a significant public PIK element.

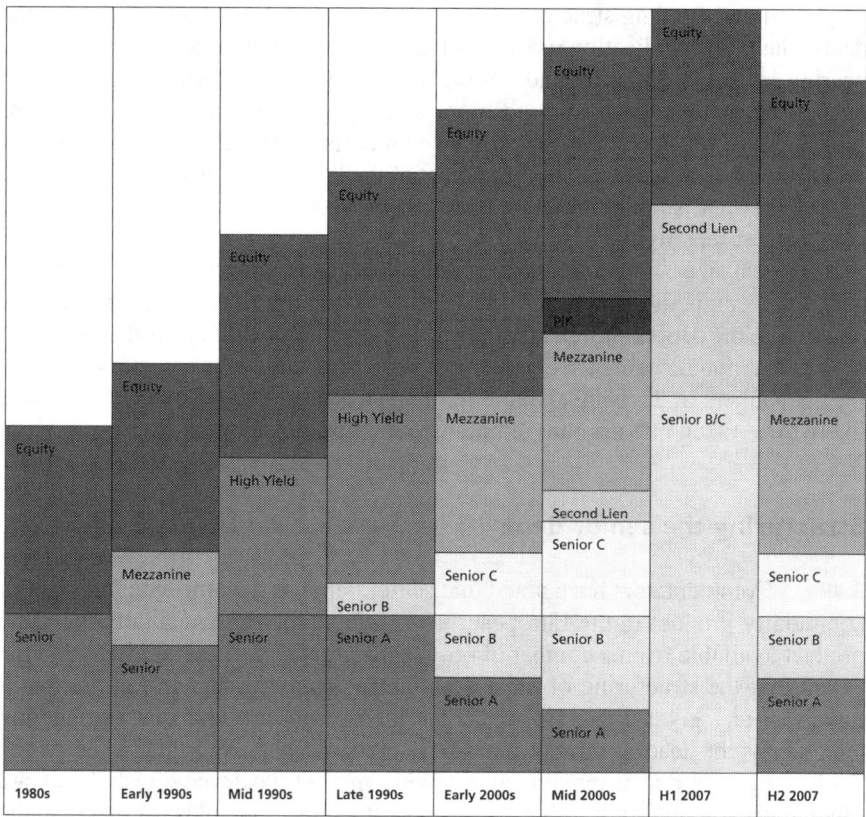

The evolution of acquisition finance structures

CHOOSING THE OPTIMUM FUNDING STRUCTURE

3.48 A considerable amount of effort and skill goes into the formation of a viable funding structure. Each instrument will have features that are not necessarily attractive to the providers of the other instruments and the balancing of competing interests between the various layers of finance requires experience and, in particular, a deep understanding of the markets for the various forms of debt used in buy-outs. Not only must deal doers have their funding structures approved by a rigorous internal credit or investment authorisation process, but, in the case of large deals in particular, a great deal hangs on whether the 'market' approves of the chosen structure or not.

If an arranging bank cannot syndicate the deal it has underwritten it will be faced with significant exposure to a single business and materially reduced balance sheet availability to do other deals. Perhaps even more critically, its credibility in the market and to sponsors may be severely damaged.

Larger deals usually have greater levels of financial engineering than mid-market and smaller deals partly because they tend to be more highly leveraged and partly because of the greater number of possible instruments that can be employed and funding structures that can be devised. In addition, these are the deals where the syndication risk is most acute. Whilst there is less financial engineering in the mid-market and below, the assessment of credit risk for target businesses in this space may be more acute given the less mature nature or robustness of businesses of that size by comparison with the usually very well established businesses that are the subject of the larger buy-outs. This means that mid-market and smaller structures need to be very carefully analysed from an independent sensitivity analysis.

In all deal sizes, but particularly in large deals and increasingly in mid-market deals, the competition between the leading acquisition finance institutions to underwrite the debt is sufficiently intense to cause significant upward pressure on total debt amounts being used in buy-out structures. This in turn raises the stakes for the bankers in devising a viable funding structure. The following factors are likely to be taken into account in finding the optimum solution.

Structuring the senior debt

3.49   Commentators have noted that senior debt has to some extent become a commodity product in the European buy-out market, with essentially the same product available from a number of possible sources. This is certainly true to the extent that the structuring of most deals means applying market familiar parameters at any given time. However, the innovation and financial engineering applied by the leading arranging banks, particularly in the latter half of the 2000s, suggests that it remains an evolving market where new techniques are often applied in addition to historic market-standard principles. In practice, the main reason why the market has continued to evolve and develop new techniques has been the need to create structures with ever greater leverage multiples. This has been the challenge for the leading arranging banks for most of the 2000s.

In most cases arranging banks can still apply a number of basic principles established over the evolution of the market. Additional leverage, for example, will usually be applied to B and C notes.[44] This explains why the relative amounts of the A, B and C notes in any given structure have changed over time. For a long time the A note was often set at twice the size of each of B and C (i.e. in the ratio 2:1:1). Subsequently, A, B and C would be of equal sizes and eventually A notes began to disappear altogether in some deals; leaving just B and C notes or even just a single B note.[45] The effect of reducing the relative amount of amortising debt in the structure is to leave as much of the cashflow as possible available to meet interest payments on the debt. In other words, this enables the overall debt package to be increased.[46]

Although leverage multiples have increased steadily through the 2000s, the pricing of European senior debt has remained relatively stable.[47] In other words,

---

44 And ultimately a D note, in the form of second lien debt.
45 See also para **3.29** above.
46 The trend is also driven by exceptional liquidity in the institutional lender market – from leveraged loan funds in particular, which target the higher yielding non-amortising tranches (B and C).
47 But see **Chapter 5** generally on senior debt pricing.

the key variable has been the amount of leverage that banks are willing to apply to transactions rather than the pricing of the debt.[48] Ultimately, the amount of leverage that the banks are able to provide is largely a function of the ability of the underlying business to service that debt; hence the moves to reduce the amortising portion of the debt mentioned in the preceding paragraph. In practice this should mean that the core skill for European senior debt arrangers remains the ability to structure a deal based on their credit assessment of the underlying business and its cashflows. Indeed, certainly in the UK, credit driven banks have historically proved the most market resilient participants.

Structuring the junior debt

3.50   As indicated earlier, for first time buy-outs the main junior debt products are probably still mezzanine and high yield debt. Both products have been through the full economic cycle and remain used in substantial volumes and numbers of deals. Second lien has also made a huge impact on the acquisition finance market in the 2000s, taking market share from mezzanine debt in particular, although many commentators believe this to be a reflection of the heat and liquidity of the market during this period rather than a structural change. In any event, it has proven to be extremely popular with deal sponsors and debt underwriters and may be used either as a form of stretched senior debt, contributing a relatively small amount to the overall funding structure, or as core junior debt in place of mezzanine or high yield. Because it is materially cheaper than mezzanine debt there is really no structuring choice to be made between these products per se. If second lien debt is available as a replacement for mezzanine then generally speaking it will be used. The question as to whether it is available or not may or may not prove to be a function of market conditions.

So, for the purpose of this section, leaving aside second lien debt as a structuring choice, the key question in structuring many first time buy-outs, will be whether to use mezzanine or high yield debt for the core junior debt. The following paragraphs consider some of the respective advantages and disadvantages of mezzanine debt versus high yield debt. A subsequent paragraph then considers the structuring implications of using second lien debt in the same structure as mezzanine or high yield and the final paragraph considers how PIK note debt may be used in a buy-out structure.

Advantages of mezzanine debt over high yield

Documentation process and execution formalities

3.51   Documenting mezzanine debt is inherently more straightforward in a buy-out than documenting high yield debt. This is primarily because the mezza-

---

48   This is a notable difference from the US acquisition finance market where pricing is more flexible and more credit, as well as leverage, driven.

nine debt documents are substantially the same as those used for the senior debt. Not only does this streamline the process greatly, it also means that the mezzanine debt can sign and fund at the same time as the senior debt. A high yield debt issue, by contrast, requires an entirely separate set of documents and because of the more onerous public bond issuance process it must be bridged for a period following completion of the acquisition.

In addition, the information package that is used to attract senior lenders can also be used to attract mezzanine lenders. This is not so with high yield debt.

Nature of documentation

3.52   Mezzanine documentation has certain inherent advantages over high yield documentation:

- Substantially similar covenant package – as indicated above, the mezzanine documents have essentially the same level of restrictions as in senior documentation. The borrower need not be concerned with an additional layer of restrictions.

- Financial reporting – in particular, there are none of the stringent regulatory reporting requirements that a high yield issuance dictates.

- Ease of modification – see the following paragraph.

Ease of modification

3.53   Given the fact that mezzanine debt is not publicly traded in the way that high yield debt is and the fact that the documentation provides for a relatively straightforward amendment or waiver process, the obtaining of modifications and waivers is notably easier for mezzanine debt. This reflects the difference between the private and public debt markets. It is logistically difficult to arrange bondholder meetings in particular.[49]

Limited call protection

3.54   A key feature of mezzanine debt is the limited period within which a prepayment of the debt will trigger any penalty or premium for the borrower, and even within this period the premium is likely to be relatively small.[50] The early redemption of high yield bonds is materially more costly by comparison with the early prepayment of mezzanine debt. It is standard for high yield bonds to be non-redeemable at the option of the issuer for a minimum of half the life of the

---

49 Though the trustee of the issue will often be given power under the terms and conditions of the bonds to grant waivers of defaults, the exercise of such power is limited by a proviso to the effect that the giving of such waivers is 'not materially prejudicial to the interests of the bondholders' and trustees are often not willing to exercise such a discretion without seeking directions from the bondholder base.

50 There might even be no yield protection in some deals.

bonds unless a significant premium or, more often, 'make-whole' amount[51] is paid to the bondholders.[52]

Minimal execution risk

3.55 Because the European mezzanine market is relatively predictable and stable, a sponsor and underwriting acquisition financier can structure a deal with mezzanine debt and be relatively confident that the deal will proceed with the mezzanine layer as structured. The same cannot always be said of high yield debt and the bridging requirement becomes higher risk as a result.

Lack of credit rating requirement

3.56 Because mezzanine debt has traditionally been structured and sold without the need for a credit rating, the deal doers need be less concerned with the amount of leverage in the structure. High yield debt does require a credit rating as part of the issuance process.

Senior banks prefer mezzanine

3.57 European acquisition finance banks have traditionally favoured mezzanine debt over high yield debt. Historically this may have been because of their own lack of a high yield structuring or distribution capability or because of perceived weaknesses in the high yield market. This has become less of an issue as the market has matured.

Restructuring support

3.58 High yield bond investors have historically taken more aggressive stances in work-out and recovery/refinancing situations than mezzanine lenders. This may be due to vulture fund investors[53] buying bonds, at below par, and attempting to force a settlement with the senior lenders and institutional equity. Typically, only 25% of the high yield investors, by value of the bonds held by them, are required to accelerate the entire amount of the bonds whereas 66 2/3% is typically required with mezzanine debt. With the advent of institutional mezzanine, however, and the wider investor base that this entails this may no longer hold true.

---

51 See **Chapter 8**.
52 In fact, a common exception to this allows for up to 35% of the bonds to be redeemed at the issuer's option from the proceeds of an IPO within the first two or three years. Such a redemption would also be subject to a significant premium, however, usually as much as the annual coupon on the notes. See also **Chapter 8** for further detail.
53 'Vulture funds' are funds established to invest in businesses that have a failed to some extent or are otherwise in a distressed state.

Currency liquidity

3.59   Unless a significant appetite among European investors for the issue is forecast, it may be necessary for the issue to be denominated in US dollars, in order to make it more marketable in the US capital markets. If the target business does not have substantial US dollar income streams it will need to enter into hedging arrangements in order to convert its non-US dollar income into US dollars for the purposes of making payments on the high yield bonds. This will increase the costs of the transaction to the issuer.

Advantages of high yield debt over mezzanine debt

Covenant flexibility

3.60   High yield debt documentation provides far greater flexibility than does mezzanine documentation. A typical mezzanine debt covenant package, including all positive and negative undertakings, is inherently more restrictive than a typical high yield debt package. This manifests itself in at least two ways:

- Mezzanine documents contain 'maintenance' style covenants, compliance with which must be satisfied on an all-times basis.[54] High yield covenants are largely of the 'incurrence' style which means that compliance is only required at the time of the proposed transaction – such as the incurrence of debt or making of a dividend – and not thereafter. Consequently, with high yield debt, there will typically be significantly greater flexibility for the borrower to carry out material transactions, such as future acquisitions of businesses during the life of the deal, than with mezzanine debt.

- Mezzanine debt documents include a suite of financial covenants, whilst high yield debt documents do not. Although these are typically set at a lower default threshold than those in the senior debt documents,[55] they do still prescribe a level of financial performance for the target business that is not mirrored in high yield documents.

In addition, high yield bonds are not usually repayable at the request of the holders upon a flotation of the group, unless a full change of control occurs. Mezzanine debt has traditionally not had this flexibility although that may be changing.

Pricing

3.61   High yield is a cheaper all-in product than mezzanine; although the initial issuance costs are higher which means the comparative economics are more attractive the larger the issue. However, given the PIK element of mezzanine debt, there is not a significant difference in cost to the borrower on a current cash basis.

---

54 Although there have been mezzanine deals done with 'covenant-lite' documentation (see **Chapter 5** in relation to covenant-lite senior debt structures) this is extremely rare.
55 Often with about 10% more headroom than the senior covenants.

Hedging

3.62   High yield is traditionally a fixed rate product providing a long-term predictable cost without the need for interest rate hedging. Mezzanine debt by contrast is a floating rate product which needs to be subject to interest rate hedging to cap the overall cost.

Larger potential investor base

3.63   The high yield market is ultimately deeper than the European mezzanine market. This means it is a better source of finance for mega deals, with the largest high yield tranches much bigger than the largest mezzanine tranches.

Greater leverage

3.64   The use of high yield bonds may increase the amount of leverage that is possible in a given structure more than mezzanine can.

Public market exposure

3.65   Having gone through a public offering of debt, a target business may be better placed to achieve an exit through an equity IPO.

Using second lien debt

3.66   Second lien is either used in buy-outs to stretch the senior debt or alternatively as core junior debt in place of mezzanine or high yield. Combining second lien with mezzanine or high yield in this way will influence the way the second lien is structured. For example, when used with mezzanine debt it will be structured in the form of a second lien loan rather than notes so that it sits most cleanly between the senior and mezzanine loans.

In structures with high yield bonds on the other hand, the second lien can be structured as a loan or an issue of bonds or both. A determining factor will be the investor base to which the second lien debt is aimed, reflecting the greater expected appetite for the underlying credit. Where both loans and bonds are used in the same structure in this way, the parties will need to carefully consider the interaction between the two instruments given that the standard documentation for each is different. In particular, there will be a need to match default triggers, acceleration and enforcement rights and credit support notwithstanding the different forms of documentation.

Using PIK note debt

3.67   PIK note debt will often be seen as the last piece of the structure to be put in place. It provides the ultimate tool for increasing leverage without using up cashflow. It should not be viewed as an afterthought, however, and in many transactions PIK notes form an integral part of the structuring process. This may be because none of the other core financiers are willing to occupy that part of the capital structure that the PIK note return and credit risk reflect. Using a PIK note may be the only way that the transaction can be successfully financed.

As previously mentioned PIK note debt may take the form of a public issue of bonds, in which case it is really a form of non-cash coupon high yield debt which is often structurally subordinated at holding company level. That form of PIK is generally not used in first time buy-outs; more often it is used in recapitalisations of mature buy-outs or other leveraged structures, where the proceeds are used to return capital to the equity investors. More often in buy-outs PIK is used in a different way and structured as private subordinated loan capital.

OPCO-PROPCO STRUCTURES

Why use an opco-propco structure?

3.68   If the business being acquired includes significant real estate, a further option for the sponsor to consider may be opco-propco financing. In essence, this involves transferring the properties of the business from the trading companies (opcos) to specially created property companies (propcos), and leasing the properties back to the opcos. The acquisition of the properties by the propcos, which have no resources of their own, is funded using property finance.

The primary rationale for using the structure is to take advantage of the different attitudes of acquisition financiers (who look to the underlying cashflow generation of the business) and property financiers (who look to the underlying property values) and arbitrage the resultant difference in debt pricing. From a acquisition financier's perspective, properties embedded in a trading group and used by that trading group are usually non cash generative, and so do not contribute to the underlying EBITDA of the business upon which the agreed multiple of leverage debt will be based. From a property financier's viewpoint, properties leased on market terms to the opcos are valuable assets, and they will lend on an asset value multiple, usually at interest rates lower than the interest rates required by acquisition financiers for senior debt.

Opco-propco debt

3.69   Opco-propco financing is usually medium term, perhaps seven to ten years in maturity, pays interest on a current cash basis, and may amortise very slightly over the life of the loan or be repaid as a bullet payment at maturity. Aside from the basic lending, repayment and interest payment terms, the finance documents will include covenants designed to preserve the value of the properties and restrict amendments to the lease terms. Given that this is essentially asset financing, this 'asset preservation' approach is to be expected.

The financing will also include covenants dealing with substitutions of properties, whereby one property in the propco's portfolio can be swapped for another, and property disposals, where a single property may be permitted to be sold, usually resulting in a partial repayment of the property finance loan.

Security will be required to be granted by the propcos over the properties and their other assets, and in the case of several propcos they may cross-guarantee each other. There will, however, be no recourse to the opcos, other than under the lease terms for rental and other lease payments. Conversely, the opco financing will have no recourse to the propcos or their assets.

As mentioned, the propcos will be specially formed for the opco-propco transaction. At least initially, the propcos are usually entities within the same group as the newly acquired business. In the longer term, the propcos, including their embedded properties, could be sold to one or more third parties, so as to take advantage of capital appreciation. The leases to the opcos would survive any such sale, although any outstanding property finance may require prepayment or refinancing.

Opco-propco lease terms

3.70 The initial valuation of the properties will be determined, in part, by the terms of the leases put in place between the propcos and the opcos. A lease which is significantly off-market will probably result in a lower valuation, and to a lower amount of debt which can be borrowed against that property.

Leases tend to be long – often 25 to 35 years, with a tenant's option to renew at the end of that period in many cases. Rental levels will clearly need to be sufficient to support the debt service obligations of the propcos, but will also be subject to periodic review and increase. Whilst uncapped upwards rental increases may be desirable from the propcos', and the propcos' financiers', perspective, as this will maximise property valuations, for the opcos potentially unlimited increases are unattractive. Often a compromise is reached whereby rental increases are capped (eg, capped at the higher of the retail prices index and an agreed percentage).

Other key lease terms relate to property insurance and how any insurance proceeds will be dealt with, change of control of the opcos, lease assignments, use of the properties and alterations.

Implementing an opco-propco structure

3.71 In the short time frames in which leveraged acquisitions now tend to occur, there is normally not enough time to carry out the necessary property valuations and implement the property sales and leasebacks in time for closing of the acquisition. Real estate, unlike may other assets, cannot be dealt with 'en masse' but must be dealt with by individual property title numbers, and consequently this is often a significant and time-consuming exercise for a portfolio of tens, or sometimes hundreds, of properties.

It is therefore quite common for short-term bridge financing to be used initially, to be replaced in due course by the longer term opco-propco financing. The bridge finance, along with all the other acquisition debt and equity, is borrowed by the acquiring SPV and used to complete the acquisition.

Post completion, the properties are evaluated for suitability in a propco structure, the leases negotiated, any necessary landlords' consent obtained and the independent valuations obtained. The property finance, which may have been committed but not fully documented at the acquisition closing, will be documented, including all necessary mortgages and other security documents.

The propcos will then simultaneously borrow the property finance and use the proceeds to purchase the properties. The opcos will use the property sale proceeds received from the propcos to repay the bridge debt.

Example structure

3.72

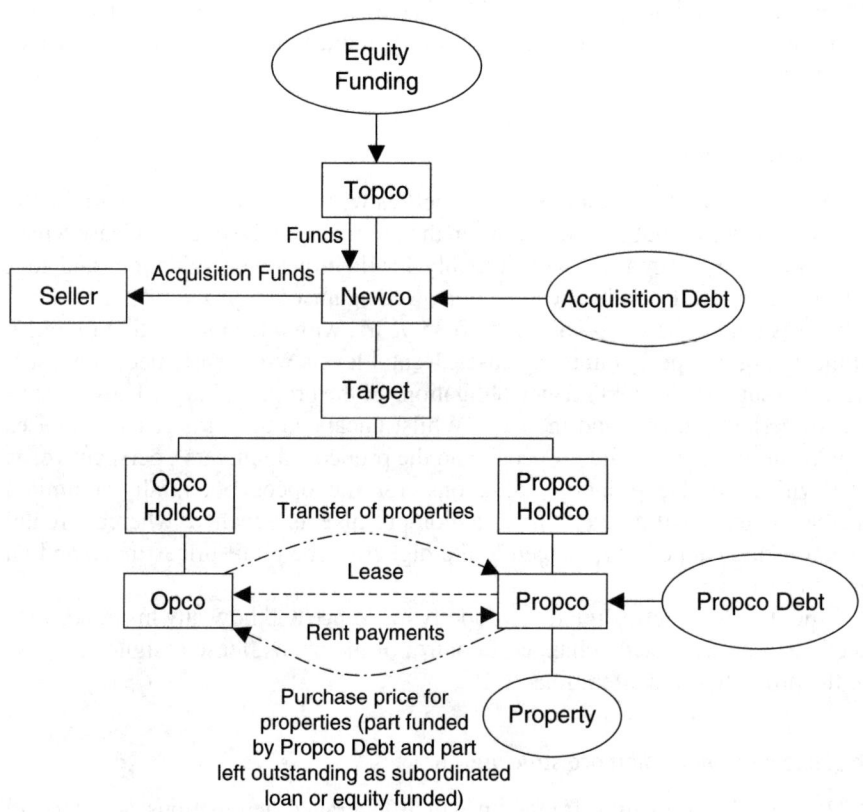

CHAPTER 4

The Equity Investment

PRIVATE EQUITY

4.1   A fundamental component of every buy-out funding structure is the private equity investment made by the deal sponsor – the institutional equity investor – and usually, but to a lesser extent, the management team. Maximising the return to the private equity investors – by improving the performance, and thus value, of the underlying business – is the principal commercial rationale for buy-outs in the first place. It follows that private equity is the most lucrative form of investment used to fund buy-outs. Equally it bears the highest risk if the business underperforms.

Evolution of the UK private equity industry

4.2   The UK private equity industry can be traced back to the 1940s. Two new institutions – Finance Corporation for Industry[1] and Industrial and Commercial Finance Corporation[2] – were established in 1945 to help develop key industrial sectors in the UK economy by providing a new source of capital to small and medium-sized enterprises. But the real growth of a dedicated buy-out industry began in the 1980s. At this stage of the market's evolution most buy-outs still involved backing management teams in early stage businesses in what was really 'venture capital' rather than the private equity we know today. The term 'private equity' did not really take hold until the 1990s and when the industry's trade association was formed in 1983 by the main players in the UK it was called the British Venture Capital Association (BVCA[3]).

The growth of the industry since the early 1980s has been remarkable. For example, in 1984 some 479 investments totalling £190 million were made by the BVCA's membership of less than 50 houses. In 2000, 150 members invested

---

1 FCI was set-up with the backing of institutions from the City of London, including insurance funds.
2 ICFC was established by the UK's clearing banks and the Bank of England. It was the forerunner of Investors in Industry, which is now 3i plc.
3 Although still known as the BVCA, this now refers to the British Venture Capital and Private Equity Association. The same is true of the European equivalent, the EVCA, which was also formed in 1983.

some £6.2 billion in 1,597 companies (£4.8 billion in 1,307 UK companies).[4] As these figures also show, however, the bifurcation in the industry between venture capital and private equity had become clearly demarcated, with different houses operating in one arena or the other. Of the investments made by BVCA members in 2000, some 56% were of less than £1 million. Venture capital remains a related but quite discrete industry in the UK. One of the key distinctions is the fact that venture capital does not attract acquisition finance. Companies that need venture capital can rarely support borrowings, either because all cashflow that is generated is needed to fund rapid expansion and so is not available to service debt, or because banks are generally unwilling to lend to a business at such a formative stage of its life cycle. Many such businesses are, in effect, start-ups. Private equity by contrast really means buy-outs with total funding requirements in excess of £10 million – and usually much more.

The private equity industry as it is seen today really developed during the 1990s, largely in parallel with the senior debt market, and important relationships were established between the leading players in these complementary markets. Over time, different houses began to operate in different segments of the market doing different sized deals, and a large cap market developed as distinct from the 'mid-market'. The first institutions to establish strong track records in the early 1990s were more easily able to raise larger funds and to move into the large deal space, and to this day many of those houses still dominate in that market (some operating under different names from their original). They have been joined by the large US private equity houses and some pan-European funds and many of the deals that these houses pursue are of significant multi-jurisdictional businesses in transactions that look as much like large scale merger and acquisition deals as they do buy-outs. As deal sizes have grown so has the perception of what is a 'big deal'. Whereas for much of the 1990s the mid-market probably meant deals of anywhere between £10 million and £50 million (total funding requirement), by the mid-2000s the limit for 'upper mid-market' deals was probably seen as £500 million. Above this, mega buy-outs with deal sizes in the £billion plus range are now relatively commonplace.

The UK private equity industry is comfortably the largest in Europe. Historically, the value of transactions completed in the United Kingdom has been over twice that recorded in any other European country, and in 2005, for example, it accounted for 51% of total European private equity investment.[5] It remains second only to the United States in terms of size. Between 1984 and 2005, according to the BVCA, the UK private equity industry had invested over £80 billion in around 29,000 companies worldwide (£60 billion in 24,000 UK companies). Similarly, its significance to the UK economy cannot be underestimated, and, while precise numbers vary from source to source, it is estimated that some 19% of the UK private sector workforce is employed by companies that have received private equity backing.[6] Private equity owned enterprises typically create employment, and again, although the studies vary on the precise numbers, it

4   Source: British Venture Capital Association.
5   Source: British Venture Capital Association.
6   Source: Financial Services Authority, *Private Equity – A Discussion of Risk and Regulatory Engagement*, (November 2006).

has been estimated that, in the five years following a buy-out, employment with a company rises by an average of 26%.[7] On top of this, the contribution by the industry itself to the financial services sector of the UK economy is enormous. In addition to the 5000+ people working for private equity firms in the United Kingdom there are significant numbers of professional advisers that support the industry. In 2005 over £3 billion of revenues were generated in fees for accountants, lawyers, bankers and other professional advisers through the industry's fund raising, investment and divestment activities.[8]

Private equity structures

4.3 A typical structure, incorporating institutional and management equity, can be shown in diagrammatic form as follows:

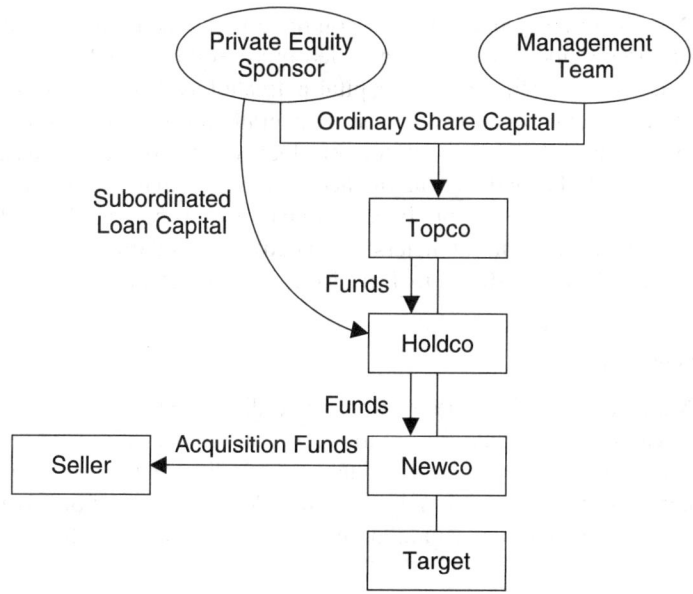

Typical Equity Structure

Who provides the equity?

4.4 Equity is provided by institutional private equity investors and senior members of the management of the target business, either new or incumbent. Occasionally a seller may invest quasi-equity as a form of deferred consideration or true equity as an earn-out.[9]

---

7 Source: Centre for Management Buy-out Research.
8 Source: BVCA report, *Private Equity's Impact as a UK Financial Service*.
9 See para **4.12**.

Most institutions which invest in private equity do so on behalf of funds which they manage or for affiliated entities within their overall institutional group. In other words, the actual equity is invested not by the equity house itself but by one or more funds which are raised and managed by that house or in the case of captive investors, by one or more other entities within the same institutional group.[10] Further, in particularly large transactions, more than one institution may sponsor the transaction and provide the institutional equity. The institutional equity investor will commonly be paid an up–front fee by newco for sponsoring the deal and providing the institutional equity. This is usually defined as a percentage of the total amount of institutional equity provided.[11]

What does the equity comprise?

Equity and quasi–equity

4.5   A typical equity package will comprise both true equity, usually ordinary share capital, and what is often called quasi-equity, usually subordinated loan capital. The subordinated loan capital is treated as if it were equity by the acquisition financiers – and thus part of the overall equity package – because of the way it is subordinated. It is effectively locked into the capital base of the group until all of the acquisition finance has been repaid. This particularly applies in an insolvency situation. In economic terms it is made to look like share capital from the acquisition financiers' perspective, even though it is debt.[12] The institutional equity will differ in its form from the management equity.

Management equity

4.6   Management equity often comprises ordinary share capital only. These shares will carry voting rights, a right to receive an ordinary dividend and a right to participate in any distribution of capital on a winding up of the company. The management equity may occasionally also include an element of quasi–equity in the form of subordinated loan capital or, in theory, redeemable preference shares.

---

10 On a successful exit the proceeds in excess of the initial investment – the gain or profit – will be split between the fund investors and the equity house as fund manager, typically in the ratio 80:20. The 20% of the gain retained by the equity house is called the 'carried interest' or 'carry' and it is common for some of the carry to be payable to executives in the equity house, particularly those that worked on the deal. It is usual for a carry to be payable to the equity house only once the gain reaches a certain threshold called a 'hurdle rate'. Typically this is in the region of 8% or so determined as an annual return on the equity invested by the fund. Once the 8% return threshold is reached the equity house 'catches up' to its 20% share, by being entitled to gain above the 8% until the 80:20 split is reflected. In addition to the carried interest, the equity house receives an annual management fee, payable by the fund, usually in the range of 1.5% to 2% of the total amount of the fund. Other fees such as transaction success fees or portfolio management and monitoring fees may also be payable to the equity house in respect of each transaction or investment.

11 This may be in the region of 1% to 3%.

12 Redeemable preference share capital is a further alternative form of quasi-equity to subordinated loan capital but this does not currently have the tax benefits of subordinated debt – ie, deductability of interest – and is now rarely used. See also para **4.9**.

Institutional equity

4.7   Institutional equity will comprise both true equity in the form of ordinary shares and quasi–equity in the form of subordinated loan capital.

True equity

4.8   The institutional ordinary shares will often be preferred ordinary shares carrying voting rights, a right in preference to the management ordinary shares to receive an ordinary dividend, and a right in preference to the management ordinary shares to participate in any distribution on a winding up of the company.

The ordinary (and preferred ordinary) shares, as the true equity in the business, carry the real value of the business which will be realised upon exit.[13]

Quasi–equity – subordinated loan capital

4.9   The institutional quasi–equity will comprise subordinated loan stock or notes or other subordinated loan capital such as PIK notes or deep discount bonds (DDBs). PIK notes are loan notes that have a capitalising and periodically compounding interest yield. All the interest is said to be 'paid-in-kind' by the issue of further loan notes representing the capitalised interest. Those additional PIK notes are then redeemed at final maturity together with the principal amount originally invested. The term PIK note is actually applied to a number of different types of instrument in buy-out terminology but each is based on this basic premise.

Unlike other subordinated loan capital, DDBs do not bear interest. Instead they are initially issued at a discount to par and then accrete capital value at a rate equivalent to a notional rate of interest by virtue of being redeemable at a periodically increasing price that reflects that notional rate. There are tax advantages for the equity investors in using DDBs as opposed to other subordinated loan capital; although the late payment of interest rules promulgated under the Finance (No 2) Act 2005 have made DDBs less attractive – by denying a deduction for the discount until redemption – particularly when compared with PIK notes which avoid the late payment of interest rules (and which, if listed on a recognised exchange, can also avoid withholding issues). Historically, redeemable preference shares were a viable alternative to subordinated loan capital for UK transactions but since the late 1990s subordinated loan capital is almost invariably used.[14]

The quasi-equity will generally be expressed to have a yield. This will be interest in the case of loan notes or stock, a fixed dividend in the case of preference shares or an increasing redemption price in the case of deep discount bonds. However, that is not to say that the yield is actually payable in cash on a current basis. In most cases, the equity will actually be structured on the basis that there

---

13 This is because all other elements of the capital structure will be redeemable at par plus an agreed fixed yield.
14 That is because subordinated loan capital is more tax efficient than preference shares. The interest accruing on it may be tax deductible.

is no cash yield. Instead, as with PIK notes, it will be capitalised and compounded, usually six or twelve monthly. This is only realised when the principal is redeemed at exit or on fixed dates after a number of years if no exit has occurred by then. Having a cash yield is in principle attractive to sponsors, mainly because, if structured properly, the effect will be to enhance the equity IRR.[15] The return of cash on an investment before exit reduces the average time that the investment is outstanding and this increases the IRR (being an annual or other periodic measure of return). As indicated above, however, in practice the sponsor may elect to structure the equity investment so that there is no cash yield. There are really two connected reasons for this. The main reason is that sponsors generally prefer to allocate the cashflow that would otherwise be available to pay an equity yield to increasing the amount of acquisition finance in the structure. This will also have the effect of enhancing the equity IRR and generally to a greater extent because, in simple terms, acquisition finance is a cheaper form of finance than equity. In other words, if a sponsor wishes to increase the leverage on a deal beyond a certain level it will need to forego any cash yield on the equity. The target group's cashflows will all be allocated to servicing the acquisition finance. The second, related, reason is that acquisition finance banks are generally resistant to cash being returned to the equity investors before all of the debt has been paid down.[16] This is particularly the case in highly leveraged structures.

Ultimately, equity structuring techniques also vary from sponsor to sponsor. Different institutions may have different priorities for achieving the desired IRRs as between current yield and exit value, which may be a function of the types of investors in their funds.

On top of the restriction on payments of yield, it would be extremely rare for a redemption of quasi-equity *principal* to be scheduled to occur before all of the acquisition finance has been repaid. In fact, even if it were scheduled to be redeemed prior to the scheduled repayment dates of the acquisition finance, typically at the end of year 8, 9 or 10 after completion, the terms of the subordination arrangements that the acquisition financiers will require to be put in place will provide that no such redemption could occur until all of the acquisition finance has been repaid in full. The express provisions of the equity documents would be overridden by the subordination arrangements.

There are other differences, apart from those mentioned above, between the rights attaching to the institutional equity and the management equity, reflecting the different nature of these two types of investor and their investments. For instance, the management equity will usually represent a minority equity stake and consequently the management shareholders will require minority shareholder protection rights such as a tag-along right.[17] Another difference will relate to the applicable transfer rights of the different classes of shares. Thus, the spon-

---

15 See also **Chapter 3** on equity structuring.
16 There are of course exceptions to this. In particular, dividend recaps have become a feature of the market in the mid to late 2000s as a way of returning money early to the equity investors. See also para **1.132**.
17 See para **4.23**.

sor will normally be permitted to transfer some of its investment to other entities within its own corporate or fund structure, whereas the transfer restrictions applicable to the management equity will be more onerous.[18] Other restrictions simply reflect the greater bargaining power of the sponsor.

Alignment of management team and equity house

4.10 One of the most important principles of private equity is the alignment of the economic interests of the management team with the sponsor backing them. This is the reasoning behind giving the management team an equity stake. The incentive of a substantial capital gain at exit will be a prime motivating factor for the management team in delivering the business plan. In addition, because the management equity will be structured as paid-in capital, rather than equity options, the management team will be required to commit their own financial resources to the deal. The amount of their personal commitment will often be set at a level that does cause some financial pain if the buy-out is not a success. Economic alignment thus has both 'carrot and stick' aspects.

In some instances the amount of equity being committed by the management team does not of itself provide sufficient potential upside to fully incentivise them. This is usually as a result of it constituting a relatively small amount of the entire equity share capital when the institutional equity is factored in. In this circumstance a performance ratchet may be used to provide additional upside to the management team upon a successful exit. Performance ratchets are considered below.

Alignment is maintained through the life of a buy-out through two contractual mechanisms. First, the management team will be prohibited from transferring their shares – which usually also means a prohibition on charging them – until the eventual exit. Secondly, the management equity will be made subject to a compulsory transfer mechanism which applies to any manager that leaves the management team. Depending on the circumstances of the departure, a leaver will be denominated either as a 'good leaver' or as a 'bad leaver'. The consideration payable to the leaver for his or her equity will reflect the type of leaver that the manager is. So, it is not uncommon for a good leaver to receive the higher of par (or subscription cost) and market value and for a bad leaver to receive the lower of par (or subscription cost) and market value.[19]

Alignment is more difficult to achieve in a secondary buy-out where the management team from the original buy-out are participating in the secondary. Where the management are taking substantial cash off the table following the successful 'exit' of the original buy-out they will have less incentive to make the secondary a success. The equity house will therefore push for the cash consideration to be minimised and for the bulk of the management's return from the original buy-out to be rolled over into the new buy-out. Often this will structured as

---

18 This is to ensure the continued economic alignment of the management team with the equity house throughout the life of a buy-out. Alignment is considered in the following paragraph.

19 Good leaver and bad leaver provisions are considered further in para **4.19**.

deferred consideration in the form of a seller loan note that is redeemable on a deferred basis, perhaps only at a subsequent exit of the secondary buy-out. In practice a balance will need to be struck and in auction situations the management team may be able to strike a better bargain than would otherwise be the case by playing competing equity houses off against each other with respect to this feature of the deal.

The compulsory transfer or 'leaver' provisions are also complicated in a secondary buy-out. The management team will quite often feel that the returns generated by the original buy-out have fully vested even though they are rolling a significant proportion of the proceeds over into the new deal. They will therefore not want to lose that equity if they subsequently become a 'leaver'. A private equity house, by contrast, will be extremely keen to avoid the management team having any 'vested equity'. If a manager with vested equity subsequently leaves in acrimonious circumstances the presence of a dissenting shareholder in topco could be damaging for the prospects for the business. Even if there is no direct negative consequence, however, the fact that a leaving manager continues to benefit from the hard work of the remaining management will be a cause for resentment.

Ultimately, each deal will be different but the most common approach in a secondary buy-out is for the selling management to roll-over a reasonable percentage of their proceeds (up to 50% would be normal) into a strip of loan notes and equity with the balance. Typically the loan notes would have the same economic terms as the institutional subordinated loan capital, including as to yield and repayment. In addition, the management will be re-incentivised with additional equity in the new deal, the amount of which may be determined along similar lines as for a primary buy-out. This equity would in most cases be subject to the usual compulsory transfer provisions for leavers. How exactly the deal with management is cut, however, is less important to the deal sponsor than the overriding interest in ensuring that economic alignment is achieved.

Performance ratchets

4.11   Given the relatively limited personal resources which the management team may have at their disposal, they may not have the financial capability to purchase sufficient equity in order to achieve the levels of return which are deemed appropriate for incentivisation purposes. In response, the private equity market has developed a mechanism whereby the returns to the management team can be enhanced upon a successful exit. Adequately incentivising the management team is equally important for the sponsor itself, which will be relying on high levels of performance within the business to achieve its target IRR. This is the underlying purpose of economic alignment discussed above. Ratchets take more than one form but nearly all have the aim of increasing the management's share of the equity upon a successful exit. The most common form of ratchet is one which converts an agreed proportion of the sponsor's equity into deferred shares just before exit. Deferred shares have terms that render them economically worthless. The conversion would be expressed to be conditional upon the achievement by the business of certain levels of performance within specified time frames, as reflected in the exit price. The ratchet may be stepped such that, as each level of performance is reached, which will usually be measured upon realisation of the equity at exit, the management team's share of the equity increases another step.

Although rarely used in the United Kingdom, there are also reverse ratchets which operate in a negative direction as well as positively for the management team. Here, if the business underperforms, the management team's share of the equity will be diminished.

Seller capital

4.12   In addition to the equity invested by the management team and the sponsor there may be circumstances when the capital structure includes an investment by the seller, although this is relatively rare.[20] The most common form of seller capital is a subordinated loan representing deferred purchase price consideration. It is generally referred to as a seller 'note' (or vendor note).

The principal circumstance when a seller note is used is where there is a notional gap between the price the seller expects for the target business and that which the deal sponsor is willing to pay, perhaps as a result of matters arising during the due diligence process. The solution is to have the parties agree the higher price requested by the seller but to have the seller re-invest the incremental amount back into the capital structure, thus reducing the funding required by the amount of the seller's investment. The amount invested can only be redeemed in due course if certain agreed criteria are satisfied. It is usual for the criteria to be financial performance targets that support the seller's rationale for a higher purchase price. The key condition might be a minimum EBITDA level for the target business for instance. As indicated, the seller's investment will usually be structured as a loan. The acquisition financiers will generally view a seller note as part of the equity package and for such purposes they will require it to be subordinated in a similar way to the subordinated loan capital invested by the sponsor.

Occasionally a seller note may be structured so that it ranks ahead of the institutional loan capital. This may mean that it is secured in order to take priority over the trade creditors of the group but this would be unusual because the principal rationale of most seller notes is that they are structured to reward a strong financial performance and not as a defensive instrument for underperformance.

Where the seller is seeking to participate in the future growth in the business rather than receive deferred consideration, it will look for an 'earn-out'. Earn-outs are often used where the seller wishes to benefit from capital growth resulting from capital investment made by it prior to the acquisition which is not reflected in the purchase price. Seller equity of this kind may also be used for

---

20 In this section the term seller is not intended to include a management seller that is rolling over his or her interests into a secondary buy-out. So although such a manager will often be taking deferred consideration in the form of loan notes (see para **4.10**) such loan notes are not considered further in this section. This section is concerned with a conventional seller that is exiting from the buy-out and not participating in the management of the business going forward.

political purposes, such as in a privatisation where the business is sold on relatively quickly for a large profit. In order to receive an earn-out the seller will take a small proportion of the true equity in the capital structure (ordinary shares), which on a subsequent exit will reflect the capital growth in the business. Earn-outs are rare.

How much equity will the parties invest?

4.13   The total amount of equity to be invested in a buy-out can be anywhere from as little as 10% of the total funding required to 50% or more. Typically it is in the 25 to 45% range and the larger the deal the more likely the number will be towards the lower end of the range.

In determining the quantum of equity to be invested, the deal sponsor will principally be concerned with its target IRR from the deal. Thus the amount will be set on the basis of an assumed exit at a certain point in the future, usually at the same multiple to earnings as at the investment date and on the basis that earnings have grown in accordance with the base case. This will suggest the basic IRR that the base case projects. In addition, the total IRR projected will take into account any accrued yield on the investment up to the point of exit.

The sheer quantum of the equity available for investment by the sponsor by contrast with the management team will invariably mean that institutional equity will largely comprise subordinated loan capital. Since the capital growth accrues to the true equity it will be allocated precisely between the sponsor and each member of the management team. The sponsor will wish to take more than 50% in any event, so that it retains ultimate management control of the business through the voting rights attached to the ordinary shares. Only in a true MBO would the management take the majority. The precise split of the types of equity invested by the institution and the management team will be set to reflect their expected returns based on the projected performance and the assumed absolute returns at exit of the different equity instruments. In the case of the sponsor the assumed return will be expressed in terms of the annual IRR. For the management team it may simply be considered in absolute terms.

In a secondary buy-out the amount and types of equity to be invested by a management team that were shareholders in the original buy-out is subject to further considerations. These are considered in the section on 'Alignment' above.[21]

A more detailed discussion of the relevant factors taken into account in determining the amounts to be invested is set out in **Chapter 3**.

DOCUMENTING THE EQUITY INVESTMENTS

4.14   The following paragraphs detail the purposes and key provisions of the documents that give legal effect to the equity investments. A subsequent section provides guidance on what to look for when reviewing equity documents on behalf of the acquisition financiers.

21 See para **4.10**.

Equity documents

4.15   In a UK buy-out the equity documentation will comprise the following core documents:

- investment agreement;[22]

- topco articles of association;

- loan capital instrument;[23]

- downstream funding loan agreement;[24] and

- management team service contracts.

In addition to these core documents there will generally be a number of subsidiary documents. These include a management questionnaire that the equity house will require individual managers to complete in relation to certain personal matters such as their creditworthiness, health and legal/professional good standing. The responses to the questionnaire will be warranted by the managers. There will also often be a management disclosure letter which includes details of the disclosures the management wish to make against any of their warranties in the investment agreement. Where the managers are required by the equity house to provide joint warranties they may insist that a deed of contribution is entered into. This will provide that, where only one manager warrantor is sued, the other manager warrantors will also be required to contribute to any successful claim, usually by reference to the amount of equity that each manager invests in the deal.

Side letters might also be used to document any deal specific issues that do not fit neatly into any of the main documents.

There may on occasion also be an equity commitment letter. These began appearing in the mid-2000s, often in secondary buy-outs. An equity commitment is effectively a direct undertaking by the sponsor to the seller to invest the equity into the buyer. The precise terms may vary but equity commitments represent a further step towards unconditionality – or certain funds – in relation to buy-outs where signing and completion are not simultaneous. This is a significant development and marks a departure from the principle in a buy-out that the equity

---

22 This will often be called the shareholders agreement or subscription and shareholders' agreement.

23 The quasi-equity almost invariably takes the form of subordinated loan capital for the reasons explained in para **4.9**. If it takes the form of redeemable preference share capital the terms of such share capital will be incorporated within the topco articles and there will be no requirement for a further instrument. Subordinated loan capital will variously be described as loan stock, loan notes, PIK notes or deep discount bonds. If there is more than one type of loan capital being invested each will have its own instrument.

24 In a UK buy-out topco will on-lend the proceeds of the equity investments to newco for the purposes of meeting the acquisition consideration and costs. In a structure with several SPVs there will be more than one such loan to downstream the proceeds to the ultimate acquisition vehicle. Each such loan might be documented separately. In non-UK buy-outs there might be a requirement, under thin capitalisation regulations, for some of the proceeds to be downstreamed by way of subscription of share capital.

house will not provide direct contractual recourse to a third-party, such as a seller. In fact, a further development has seen equity houses being asked by sellers to agree – again by a direct contractual obligation – to 'reverse break fees' in the event that the equity house pulls out of a transaction in certain circumstances.

Investment agreement

4.16   The investment agreement is the document which contains the formal obligation on the sponsor and the management team to make their respective equity subscriptions in topco and to invest the agreed amounts of quasi-equity in topco or certain other SPVs as dictated by the funding structure.[25] It will also contain the terms of the agreement between the shareholders of topco – the sponsor and the management team – relating to the management and control of topco and the group. An investment agreement will usually contain warranties from the management team to the sponsor with regard to their knowledge of the target and one or two other matters relating to the management team's involvement in the buy-out.[26]

In summary form, the key provisions usually included in an investment agreement are as follows:

- Agreement by the sponsor and the management team to make the equity investments in topco and any other relevant newco, including the amounts and types of equity to be subscribed by each party.

- The up-front and on-going fees payable to the sponsor in respect of its investments.

- Completion conditions – that is, conditions precedent to the equity investments by the respective parties.

- Undertakings by topco and the management team in relation to the target business and its management. The sponsor will typically require that certain management decisions require their prior approval – either through a special director nominated by them or by their approval as shareholder. These are often called reserved matters and relate both to corporate matters (eg, not changing topco's constitution) and operational matters (eg, not entering into material transactions and the like). There will also be positive undertakings. Typically these include a requirement to produce and deliver financial information to the sponsor and to manage the business in a prudent manner, to maintain appropriate insurance and the like. There may also be covenants by an incumbent management team with respect to the conduct of the target business between signing and completion, if not simultaneous.

---

25 In a triple SPV structure it is common for the subordinated loan capital to be invested in the middle SPV so that it is structurally subordinated to the acquisition finance advanced to the bottom SPV. Structuring in this way is considered further in **Chapter 11**.

26 For example, a warranty as to certain personal circumstances and the absence of any exit or inducement payments from the seller to them.

- Management veto rights for the management team. The sponsor may concede rights to the management team over a small number of fundamental matters such as change of business, amending the constitution to the detriment of the management team and transactions with related parties not on arm's length terms. However, such veto rights if granted are likely to be subject to an override in situations where the sponsor would need the flexibility to take key decisions quickly (eg, if it were necessary to amend the constitution in order to refinance the business in an urgent restructuring situation).

- Anti-dilution of the management's equity. This is usually expressed as a 'put-up or shut-up' pre-emption right whereby if new equity is to be raised the management team can participate pro rata but if they don't their equity stake is diluted.[27]

- The appointment of an observer director or one or more non-executive directors (with voting powers) to the board of topco by the sponsor and any fees payable to such directors.[28]

- Non-compete, confidentiality and non-solicitation undertakings from management. These will be expressed to extend for a period after any manager has ceased employment with topco, usually for between one and three years.[29]

- Warranties by the management team to the sponsor and provisions relating to the circumstances when claims may be made against the management team for breach of such warranties.[30]

- Subordination override clause as required by the acquisition financiers.[31]

Management warranties

4.17   The inclusion of management warranties is not designed to give the sponsor real financial recourse in the event they are incorrect. The purpose is to force disclosure by the management team of matters that might not have surfaced during the due diligence process. This is normally achieved by including warranties as to the accuracy and completeness of the due diligence reports themselves and to the effect that the managers are not aware of any material issue that has not been disclosed. The warranties would usually be given subject to a knowledge qualifier – perhaps 'to the best of the knowledge and belief of the management having made due and careful enquiry'. In addition, the management

---

27 Where the equity being raised includes subordinated loan capital – which it typically would – the management would be required to participate pro-rata in this too in order not to be diluted.
28 Typically an equity house will have one or more non-executive director seats on the board of topco for which director fees will be payable by topco.
29 Even though the sponsor will insist on including an equivalent provision in the employment contracts of the management team, such provisions should also be included in the investment agreement where the enforceability – especially as to duration – is likely to be legally more robust.
30 These are considered separately in para **4.17**.
31 See para **4.41**.

may be asked to confirm that the information in the business plan is accurate and that the projections used in the business plan were arrived at after careful consideration on the basis of assumptions that the management team reasonably believed to be true at the time. Each manager is normally asked to complete a manager questionnaire relating to his or her personal circumstances including employment history, credit status or net asset position, health, and that they have no criminal record and have not been disciplined by any professional body etc. This will also be warranted.

Breach of the warranties would usually be expressed to be subject to a maximum claim amount set either by reference to the amount of each member of the management team's equity stake or perhaps annual salary or small multiple thereof.[32] The equity house will generally insist that the management warranties are given on a joint and several basis. In such circumstances the managers may agree to sign up to a deed of contribution that ensures that if any warranty claim is made they each suffer any loss on a proportionate basis, usually by reference to the amounts of their respective equity stakes in topco.

In order to limit the potential for any breach of warranty in the first case the management team will insist on producing a management disclosure letter setting out disclosure of any matter which would render their warranties untrue.

Given the fact that a selling equity house will not agree to give customary seller warranties in a secondary buy-out, management warranties take on more significance for a purchasing equity house in such deals. **Chapter 2** considers management warranties in this context.

Topco articles of association

4.18   The articles of association of a company govern the internal affairs of the company and the relationship between the company and its shareholders. Topco's articles will be quite different from standard form company articles of association – certainly those used for intermediate holding companies and possibly many operating company subsidiaries. This is because topco will be both an investment vehicle and a management company. As a result its articles will contain a number of deal-specific provisions relating to the nature of the investments in it and the management of the company and its subsidiaries. Usual provisions in topco's articles will cover:

- The composition of the share capital of the company.

- The rights attaching to the various classes of shares comprising the share capital of the company.[33]

- The management powers of the board of directors. Such powers will typically be subject to a requirement for sponsor approval in relation to major matters.[34]

---

32 Capping liability at between one and three times annual salary is not unusual.
33 Including rights in respect of dividends, returns of capital or assets and voting.
34 These will mirror or cross-refer to the 'reserved matters' that will be included in the investment agreement. See para **4.16**.

- Proceedings of shareholder and director meetings.

- The transfer and transmission of shares. The sponsor will usually insist that the management shares are not transferable at all (other than on a compulsory basis by a member of the management team that leaves the business[35]). A possible exception to this is for immediate family members, subject always to the compulsory transfer provisions if the manager leaves. Even transfers within the management team are normally prohibited in order to preserve the spread of incentives.

- Compulsory transfer 'leaver' provisions – these are considered separately below.

- Exit provisions – these are considered separately below.

- Performance ratchet.[36]

- Subordination override clause as requested by the acquisition financiers.[37]

A relatively recent development applicable to buy-outs of larger, more mature businesses has seen deal sponsors requiring the topco articles to be more akin to public company articles or at least to adopt certain corporate governance features of public company articles, such as audit and remuneration committees and having a number of third-party non-executive directors on the board of directors.

As part of a buy-out transaction, topco will adopt its buy-out specific articles at completion replacing those adopted by it when first formed as a shelf company.

Compulsory transfer 'leaver' provisions

4.19   As previously mentioned in this chapter, one of the fundamental structuring principles applied in buy-outs is the economic alignment of the management team with the sponsor. This involves requiring the management team to take an equity stake in the business. The incentive to perform and deliver the business plan is driven by both upside – the very significant gains that can be made on a successful exit – and downside – the loss of the invested capital in an unsuccessful 'exit' – consequences. It follows that if any member of the management team leaves the employment of the business the alignment will be lost. For this reason the equity held by any 'leaver' will be subject to compulsory transfer provisions, requiring the equity to be transferred to the sponsor or its nominee; which may be a replacement manager. Each leaving manager will be designated as either a 'good leaver' or a 'bad leaver'. The denomination is principally concerned with the amount of consideration that the leaver receives for the equity that is transferred by it.

A 'bad leaver' will be a manager shareholder who leaves under certain negative circumstances – usually following a dismissal with cause or by resignation.

---

35 See para **4.19** in relation to 'leaver' provisions.
36 See para **4.11** in relation to performance ratchets.
37 See para **4.41**.

A 'good leaver' will often simply be designated as a leaver who is not a bad leaver. Management team members who leave by virtue of incapacity/permanent illness, retirement at the normal age or death are sometimes expressly set out as good leavers. There may on occasion be a third category of leaver to deal with managers who are asked to leave for reasons that don't amount to gross misconduct.

As mentioned, the denomination of an employee or member of the management team who is leaving the business as a good leaver or a bad leaver most importantly determines the price which the good leaver or bad leaver receives for his or her shares. Thus a good leaver can normally expect to receive the higher of market value at the time and the amount he or she paid for the shares initially. A bad leaver will normally get the lesser of market value and the amount he or she paid for the shares initially. In addition to these basic principles the consideration receivable by a good leaver might also depend on how long the individual concerned had been a manager shareholder before leaving. So perhaps for the first three years or so there may be a sliding scale that allocates market value to an increasing proportion of the shares to be transferred and a decreasing remainder subject to transfer at cost.

With a secondary buy-out the issue of alignment with a management team that is both exiting the original buy-out and participating in the secondary is complicated. To some extent the management team will not wish any equity that is rolled over from one deal to the next to be subject to the compulsory transfer provisions. They will argue that it has already 'vested'. In practice, alignment in a secondary is usually achieved by allowing management to take some cash out at the time of the secondary and for a large part of the original exit proceeds to be re-invested in loan capital alongside the institutional loan capital. A further amount is then invested in new equity in the deal, on the basis that it *is* subject to the customary 'leaver' provisions.

Good leaver/bad leaver provisions could theoretically be incorporated into the investment agreement but in the UK it is more common for them to be in the topco articles.

Exit provisions

4.20   The exit provisions are designed to facilitate an exit for the sponsor and, to a lesser extent, the management team. They fall into the three main categories set out below.

Management team co-operation

4.21   The management team will be required to co-operate with the sponsor in achieving an exit. This will include meeting with prospective buyers or prospective investors in an IPO or prospective lenders in a leveraged recapitalisation. The management team will generally also be expected to agree to give customary warranties in respect of the business on any exit, although this may be a heavily negotiated provision.

The sponsor, by contrast, will want it expressly recorded that it will not give seller warranties other than as to title to its shares.

Drag-along rights

4.22 'Drag-along' rights are used to compel a minority shareholder to sell its shares if a specified number of ordinary shareholders – usually a simple majority by shares held – wish to accept an offer for the purchase of all the ordinary shares of topco. A qualifying offer would normally need to be a genuine arm's length offer for which the minority shareholder is getting the same price per share as the recipient majority shareholder.[38] In a buy-out the sponsor will use the drag-along provision to compel the management team and any other minority shareholders to sell their shares into an exit. A buyer will usually only be concerned with an acquisition of 100% of the equity of a business so the equity house needs to be able to deliver this.

Tag-along rights

4.23 A 'tag-along' right is the equivalent right of a minority shareholder to compel a majority shareholder that receives a qualifying offer to procure that the offer is extended to the shares held by the minority. So, in simple terms, even if an equity house received an offer for less than 100% of the equity it could not simply exit leaving the management team behind.

Drag and tag rights could theoretically be incorporated into the investment agreement but in the UK it is more common for them to be in the topco articles.

Loan capital instrument

4.24 A loan capital instrument is used to constitute the subordinated loan capital comprising the bulk of the equity package. Subordinated loan capital typically takes the form of loan stock, loan notes, PIK notes or deep discount bonds. The funding structure may include more than one form of subordinated loan capital, each with its own instrument and there may be more than one issuer as a result. Each SPV that is issuing subordinated loan capital will execute a loan capital instrument.

In addition to forming the largest part of the sponsor's equity investment, subordinated loan capital is the most common form of seller capital where seller deferred consideration is part of the overall funding structure.[39]

Since the acquisition financiers will wish to treat the sponsor's loan capital as part of the 'equity' structure, it will be subordinated to the acquisition finance debt in accordance with the requisite subordination arrangements.

Occasionally the loan capital provided by the sponsor, although subordinated, is actually secured in order to rank ahead of the target group's trade creditors. In practice this is generally rare as it is not popular with acquisition financiers.

Loan capital instruments usually contain the following principal provisions:

- the principal amount to be issued;

---

38 The consideration receivable by the majority shareholder might in theory not be all cash in which case the provision will stipulate whether the minority shareholder is to receive non-cash consideration too.

39 See also para **4.12**.

- interest rate or redemption price schedule in the case of deep discount bonds;[40]

- principal redemption dates;

- circumstances, usually in the form of limited events of default, when the loan capital can be redeemed early;

- basic representations by the issuer as to its ability to issue the loan capital;

- meetings and decision making of loan capital holders;

- transfer provisions; and

- a subordination override provision as required by the acquisition financiers.[41]

Loan capital instruments do not usually contain any undertakings on behalf of the issuer with regard to the target group business. In practice there will be no need for such undertakings since the sponsor will exercise the agreed level of control through its shareholding and directorships and through the reserved matters set out in the investment agreement.[42]

Downstream funding loan agreement

4.25   Where, as with most buy-out structures, there are two or more vehicles used to establish the funding structure, the funding invested in the higher vehicles will need to be downstreamed to where it is to be applied, usually by the acquisition vehicle, newco. This is usually done by way of intercompany loans between the respective vehicles.[43] The acquisition financiers will usually wish to have these intercompany loans documented so that their terms, including in particular what and how payments may be made back under them, are clear. They will also take structural security over such loans and ensure that they are subordinated to the acquisition finance as part of the intercreditor arrangements.[44]

The agreement will be in very simple form setting out the headline terms of the loan. The amount will reflect the amount of equity funding to be downstreamed. The interest rate will usually be set to mirror the yield payable on the equity that is being downstreamed; and will only be payable when that yield is payable. This is because payment of interest on the downstream funding loans – and repayment of the principal – will be the most efficient method by which funds are subsequently up-streamed from the target group operating companies

---

40 See para **4.9**.

41 See para **4.41**.

42 See para **4.16**.

43 In multi-jurisdictional buy-outs, thin capitalisation rules in certain jurisdictions may require that each SPV be capitalised with a minimum amount of share capital as a proportion of its total capital base including shareholder loans. This may mean that funding proceeds are downstreamed by a mixture of loans and share capital.

44 See **Chapter 10**.

to meet yield payments and redemption of the principal amount of the subordinated loan capital at exit in due course.

The acquisition financiers will normally require that the loan agreement acknowledges the subordination of the loans thereunder to the acquisition finance debt. Where there are three or more vehicles in the SPV group more than one loan agreement may be used to document each loan to be made between the vehicles or a composite loan agreement may be used. With multiple vehicles the parties will usually ensure that the loans are made vehicle by vehicle and not, in a triple SPV structure from topco to the acquisition vehicle missing out the intermediate SPV. There are typically structural benefits, especially for the acquisition financiers, relating to the funding structure in doing so. The principal benefit is that it enables security over an SPV's shares to be enforced and the shares sold with the benefit of the shareholder debt owing by the SPV. A sale leaving a debt owing to a company higher up the group would compromise the viability of the sale.

Finally, the loan agreement(s) should be expressed to be assignable so that they can be part of the security package taken by the acquisition financiers. As mentioned above, the taking of security over such loans is an essential part of the acquisition finance security package since it enables proper enforcement of share security in the SPV structure.

Management team service contracts

4.26 As part of a buy-out it would be common for the senior management to enter into new service contracts with topco. Although not strictly 'equity' documents, they will often be drafted and negotiated together with the core equity documents. It is the service contracts which reflect the extent of the sponsor's desire to have the members of the management team contracted as employees of the business and the terms of such employment. The form of the employment contracts will not be particularly unusual for executive directors of a business but may be carefully negotiated between each manager and the sponsor to the extent that they are personal to the managers.

The principal provisions of the service contracts will be the headline terms of employment, including title, salary, work description and duties, emoluments, and notice period. A fundamental provision that the acquisition financiers may wish to check will be the undertaking and restrictive covenants requiring the relevant individual to devote all of his or her time to the management of the business, not to compete with the business and, following the cessation of employment with the business, not to set up in competition with the business, or solicit customers or employees of the business, for a fixed period thereafter.[45]

45 The length of this non-compete period will typically vary between 6 months and 12 months, or occasionally more, based on the negotiations between the sponsor and the management team. Non-compete clauses of employment contracts are subject to legal limitations and may not be enforceable if deemed to be unreasonable in terms of their geographical scope, activities which are restricted, or duration. It is for this reason that an equivalent provision should also be included in the investment agreement where it should be more easily enforced legally and where, in particular, a period of between one and three years may be enforceable.

Other equity documents

Bonus scheme documentation

4.27   In circumstances where certain managers are not investing equity in topco, or very little, a bonus scheme may need to be put in place. This is much less preferable for the sponsor who wants to see management have something to lose as well as to gain as part of the incentivisation concept. It is more likely to be used for less important management and senior employees if at all. The scheme may take the form of a cash payment linked to the exit realisation value of the ordinary shares of topco.

Equity security documents

4.28   On a rare number of occasions the subordinated loan capital invested by the sponsor or possibly the seller may be guaranteed and secured by members of the target group. Having the loan capital secured is of benefit to the sponsor or seller in an insolvency situation arising in the target group, in particular where it leads to a receivership or winding–up. As a secured creditor the sponsor or seller would rank ahead of most of the unsecured creditors of the target group including the trade creditors. From another perspective, however, taking security might be seen as disadvantageous to the stakeholders in the business. The concern is that if the business were to get into difficulties the all important trade creditors would be less likely to continue to provide trade credit to the group or to extend the terms of the trade credit to the group and generally to be amenable to any work-out scenario knowing that even the subordinated loan capital would rank ahead of them if the business went into insolvent liquidation or receivership.

Acquisition financiers will usually strongly resist any equity or seller security on the basis that it does not leave them in the structurally superior position that they can normally expect to be in with respect to the equity and that it complicates the intercreditor arrangements between the debt and equity investors. Where there is unsecured junior debt in the structure, securing the equity will not be an option given the agreed ranking of junior debt ahead of any equity.

In the limited situations where any subordinated loan capital is secured, topco (possibly), newco and the target group will be required to give guarantees and grant security to the relevant subordinated loan capital holders. Such security will typically be documented on the same terms as the security package for the acquisition financiers.[46]

Importantly, the equity or seller security will be expressed to rank behind the acquisition finance security as either second, third or, in multi-layered structures, fourth ranking security and it should not in any circumstances be enforceable until all of the acquisition finance has been repaid. Even where there is equity security, it would be very unusual for a senior lender to agree to act as security

---

46   In practice the security documents will often mirror the acquisition financiers' security documents so that the documentation process is streamlined. There will be a small number of necessary differences and in particular the equity (or seller) security will be expected to rank behind the acquisition finance security as second or third ranking security etc.

trustee for the sponsor or seller, such as it would under a common trustee arrangement as used for the acquisition finance debt.[47]

With a seller note, even if target group security is not on offer the seller may wish to get into a structurally superior position to the core equity investors. This may be achieved either by conventional structuring of the relevant investee vehicles or by the use of structural security in the form of share security in the SPV group. Structural security would be more acceptable to the acquisition financiers than target group security.

REVIEWING EQUITY DOCUMENTS

Overview

4.29 On a general level, the acquisition financiers need not be too concerned with the contents of the equity documents. This is because their key concerns in respect of the equity invested by the sponsor and the management team will be dealt with in the acquisition finance documents themselves, and where necessary those documents will be expressed to override the equity documents. Thus, it will be a condition of the first drawing under the acquisition finance agreements that the requisite total amount of equity has been invested. Further, the intercreditor agreement will effectively ensure that the equity is subordinated behind the acquisition finance. In any event, even though the contents of the acquisition finance documents will be drafted so as to override the equity documents, it is clearly preferable to ensure that the two sets of documents are as consistent on their face as possible. In addition, there are a number of detailed matters relating to the various documents – and not necessarily relating to subordination matters – which the acquisition financiers will be concerned to have sight of and approve. These matters are set out below.

Investment agreement

4.30 The following items are a suggested list of matters to consider when reviewing an investment agreement from the standpoint of the acquisition financiers.

- *Subscription amounts* The total amount of equity to be subscribed should be at the agreed level. Such amounts should be required to be fully paid up in cash at completion.

- *Transfer provisions* To the extent that the investment agreement regulates the transfer of any of the equity, the provisions should stipulate that any transferee of the equity must adhere to the subordination arrangements.

---

47 See paras **7.36** and **10.30**.

- *Security (if any)* To the extent that any of the subordinated loan capital is to be secured and the investment agreement contains provisions relating to such security, reference should be made, where appropriate, to the fact that the equity investors' security is subject to the subordination arrangements and ranks behind the acquisition financiers' security.

- *Fees* The acquisition financiers will usually wish to confirm that the fees payable to the sponsor in respect of its equity investment and the non-executive director(s) are at acceptable levels and cannot be subsequently increased.[48] The amount of the up-front fee payable to the sponsor should also be set out in the summary of deal costs delivered to the acquisition financiers as a condition precedent to funding.

- *Management warranties* Although the warranties are likely to be generic in nature, the acquisition financiers will wish to check that suitable warranties are included. The extent of the warranties will be greater for an incumbent management team that has been running the target business entirely. They may be particularly important in a secondary buy-out, where the scope of the selling sponsor's warranties in the acquisition agreement is likely to be extremely limited.[49] The inclusion of warranties is of no direct benefit to the acquisition financiers, as they are only given in favour of the sponsor. However, the fact that management are willing to give the warranties at all will be of indirect comfort to the financiers. Where the management produce a disclosure letter to qualify the warranties, the financiers will need to review this to ensure that nothing of material concern to them is disclosed in it.

- *Acquisition finance override provision* The acquisition financiers should require the inclusion of an override clause in the event of any inconsistency with the acquisition finance documents and specifically to acknowledge the subordination arrangements applicable to all of the equity investments.[50] In fact, in the case of the investment agreement this is not always absolutely necessary since it does not usually create any payment obligations on topco which need to be subordinated. The key documents to include it in are the topco articles and the subordinated loan capital documents.

- *General consistency with the acquisition finance documents* For example, the cross–references to the acquisition finance documents, acquisition finance facilities and the acquisition financiers themselves should be accurate.

- *Warrant holder concerns* If the acquisition finance includes true mezzanine debt, or perhaps PIK note debt, with the benefit of warrants, a number of warrant specific issues will need consideration. These are set out below.

---

48 Equity fees and director fees – possibly with the exception of the initial deal fees – should be subject to payment conditions under the subordination and intercreditor arrangements as with other payments to the equity investors. In any event, the amounts and timing of the fees are important and should not represent a form of real yield to the investors.

49 See also para **4.17** in relation to management warranties and **Chapter 2** and para **2.37** in particular, in relation to warranty cover in secondary buy-outs.

50 See para **4.41** for an example of an override provision.

Specific issues for warrant holders

4.31 Where the equity documents deal with the mechanics of an exit, including, in particular, provisions relating to the conversion of ordinary shares prior to an exit or drag-along and tag-along rights, the relevant provisions should contemplate the fact that warrant holders will also wish to be in a position to participate in the relevant exit. Thus, the drag-along and, more importantly, tag-along rights should also extend to the warrant holders. This can be achieved through the use of third-party rights or by having the warrant holders as direct parties to the relevant agreement. In practice, the tag-along rights are typically dealt with in the topco articles which the warrant holders cannot be party to or take the benefit of. However, even in that circumstance, a contractual right to benefit from such rights could be incorporated into the investment agreement rather than the topco articles so that the sponsor is bound directly by them.

The warrant holders will, however, be concerned that certain provisions of the investment agreement, such as transfer restrictions, do not apply to them. For this reason it is generally better to use third-party rights to take the benefit of only those provisions of which the warrant holders require the benefit. One particular concern will be the scope of any performance ratchet which may operate to convert certain classes of shares held by the sponsor into management shares prior to exit. Care should be taken to ensure that this does not catch the warrant shares unintentionally. In most cases though, the performance ratchet is contained in the topco articles rather than the investment agreement.

Additionally the definitions used for 'sale', 'flotation' and the like should be consistent with the equivalent definitions in the warrant instrument or, more likely, vice versa.

Management disclosure letters

4.32 As indicated above, where there is a management disclosure letter, for the purposes of qualifying the warranties given by the management team in the investment agreement, the acquisition financiers and their lawyers will wish to review this in case it reveals important information regarding the target business or the management team.

Topco articles

4.33 As with the investment agreement, the review of the topco articles of association will have both a general aim of ensuring consistency with the assumed financial structure and a number of specific aims relating to provisions which are typically required by the acquisition financiers.

The following matters are suggested points to look for.

- *Share capital* The descriptions and amounts of the various classes of shares should be consistent with the assumed financial structure.

- *Dividends* The terms of the dividends payable in respect of the ordinary shares should be in accordance with the assumed financial structure and should be subject to the subordination arrangements with the acquisition financiers. In the vast majority of cases no dividend will be payable until all of the acquisition finance has been repaid, in which case any statement in the articles that a dividend is payable will need to be expressly overridden by the acquisition finance documents and the subordination arrangements in particular.

- *Redemptions* As a general rule, none of the share capital will be redeemable prior to the repayment of all of the acquisition finance. Any scheduled redemption would need to be subject to the acquisition finance override and this will be achieved by the standard provision referred to below.

- *Share transfers* If the intercreditor agreement includes topco's shareholders as parties, which may or may not be the case, any transferee of shares in topco should agree to adhere to the intercreditor agreement.

- *Acquisition finance override provision* The acquisition finance documents should be expressed to override the topco articles in case of any inconsistencies and the articles should specifically acknowledge the subordination arrangements applicable to all of the equity instruments.[51]

- *Warrant holder concerns* If the acquisition finance includes mezzanine debt, or perhaps PIK note debt, with the benefit of warrants a number of warrant specific issues will need consideration. These are set out below.

Specific issues for warrant holders

4.34   One obvious concern will be that the authorised share capital contemplates the shares to be issued upon exercise of the warrants. In particular, the warrant holders will be concerned to check that they are getting the right class of shares issued to them under the warrants. For example, it is important to ensure that the rights attaching to the shares to be subscribed by the warrant holders have the same rights – but not necessarily the same obligations – as the ordinary shares held by the sponsor or that such shares are the same class of shares as the ordinary shares held by the sponsor. For the warrant holders the preferred position has three aspects. First, they will generally wish to have shares with effectively the same rights as the sponsor's shares as these should reflect an institutional shareholding. They will not want shares of the same class as the management team's ordinary shares as these are likely to have certain unattractive features such as restricted transfer rights. Secondly, the warrant holders will wish to reduce the cost of exercising the warrants by having shares for which the subscription price is low. This is to ensure that the subscription cost does not dilute the value of the warrants and thus conflict with the assumed IRR calculation carried out to establish the number of warrants to be issued in the first place – such calculation will often not take into account the subscription cost. In other words, since shares may not be issued at a discount, the shares into which the warrants are exercised should have as low a par value as possible. Typically, one

---

51 See para **4.41** for an example override provision.

penny shares rather than one pound shares would be preferable. This would reduce the subscription costs arising upon exercise of the warrants by a factor of 100. Finally, the warrant holders will not want the warrant shares to be subject to any management performance ratchet. Their shares once issued should not be subject to dilution based on the management team's performance.

The warrant holders will also be concerned that the tag-along rights granted to minority shareholders are extended to the warrant shares and warrant holders. At the time the warrant holders would want to exercise tag-along rights – for example, where a third-party has made an offer to the sponsor to buy the business – they are unlikely to have exercised the warrants and become shareholders as this normally only occurs just before an exit. Therefore, at the time they would want to be able to exercise a tag-along right the warrant holders would not be 'party' to the articles and able to exercise such right. Consequently, a contractual obligation needs to be created to allow the warrant holders to exercise tag-along rights prior to exercise of the warrants. This may be achieved through the investment agreement (and third-party rights).[52]

Drag-along rights, by contrast with tag-along rights, are less relevant to warrant holders as they would not hold enough warrants to benefit from such rights. The warrant shares would normally be expected to be caught by a drag-along right, however, and the relevant provision may be constructed accordingly.

Additionally the definitions used for 'sale', 'flotation' and the like should be consistent with the equivalent definitions in the warrant instrument or vice versa.

Loan capital instruments

4.35 Subordinated loan capital will comprise the majority of the overall equity investment in a buy-out and the review of the instrument(s) governing its terms is an important task for the acquisition financiers' lawyers. The key matters to look out for should include the following:

- *Memorandum on front page* Although not necessary per se, it is good practice for the acquisition financiers to require that a note be inserted on the front page of the instrument acknowledging that the notes are subordinated under and subject to the intercreditor agreement (or other subordination agreement).

- *Amount* The amount of the loan capital to be constituted should be consistent with the agreed level to be invested by the sponsor and possibly the management team.

- *Payment of yield* The accrual and payment of interest on the loan capital or, in the case of deep discount bonds, the increase in the redemption price and the terms of redemption should be subject to the agreed subordination arrangements with the acquisition financiers. This will involve inclusion of an acquisition finance override provision as referred to below.

---

52 See para **4.31**.

- *Redemption of the loan capital* The redemption of the loan capital will, in most circumstances, be deferred until all of the acquisition finance facilities have been repaid, but in any event the redemption provisions should be expressed to be subject to the subordination arrangements with the acquisition financiers, again through the override provision.

- *Events of default* There may be limited events of default (as early redemption triggers) covering major events such as payment default, insolvency and the like. Their inclusion is usually acceptable provided that the acquisition finance override clause effectively disarms the provision until repayment of the acquisition finance debt.

- *Rights to subscribe for additional loan capital* If there is a provision relating to the subscription for further loan capital and this is not contemplated by the funding structure, an explanation should be requested. Any new loan capital should be on the same terms as, and subject to the subordination arrangements in the same manner as, the initial loan capital.

- *Transfer of loan capital* Any transferee of the loan capital should be required to adhere to the subordination arrangements as a condition of such transfer.[53]

- *Undertakings* Usually the loan capital instrument will not contain any undertakings relating to the operation of the target business. Such management controls are to be found in the investment agreement. If included an explanation should normally be sought.

- *Acquisition finance override provision* The acquisition finance documents should override the loan capital instrument and the loan note instrument should specifically acknowledge the subordination arrangements applicable to all of the equity instruments.[54]

- *General consistency with the acquisition finance documents* The cross—references to the acquisition finance documents, acquisition finance facilities and the acquisition financiers themselves should be accurate.

Downstream funding loan agreement

4.36   There are usually three main issues for the acquisition financiers to consider with regard to the downstream funding loan agreement. First, the loans to be made under it should reflect all of the equity funding required to be downstreamed from topco, or any intermediate SPV that issues subordinated loan capital as part of the equity structure, to newco. In addition, any such funding should pass through any intermediate vehicles in the funding structure. Secondly, there should be an acknowledgement that the loans are subject to the acquisition finance subordination arrangements. This may be in the form of a simple

53 In practice this will mean adhering to the intercreditor agreement with the acquisition financiers.
54 See para **4.41** for an example override provision.

acknowledgement somewhere in the agreement or a full override provision. Finally, the loan agreement and the rights of the lender under it should be expressly assignable by way of security as part of the acquisition financiers' security package. In addition, the agreement should be reviewed for general consistency with the agreed buy-out structure and documentation.

Management team service contracts

4.37 In a true management buy-out the acquisition financiers will usually wish to review the service contracts of the members of the management team themselves to ensure that the management are bound in as employees of the business to the extent deemed desirable – for instance with a long notice period and non-compete covenants – and to check the headline terms of their employment. In legal terms, there is very little for the acquisition financiers' lawyers to review. The task of negotiating the service contracts with the members of the management team on behalf of topco will fall to the sponsor's lawyers and it will be their primary task to ensure that the provisions of such contracts are legally enforceable. In this regard, there may be a question mark over the enforceability of the non–compete covenants if they are too restrictive.[55] In larger buy-outs the management as individuals may be less important in the overall scheme of things and the precise terms of their contracts may be less crucial to the acquisition financiers.

Bonus scheme documentation

4.38 It is rare for there to be separate management bonus scheme documentation, and if there is the acquisition financiers often have no real need to review it since their investments will usually be unaffected by the contents. However, to the extent that topco may be liable to pay material amounts under the scheme, and not just issue shares, prior to an exit, the headline terms of such bonuses should be reviewed and approved.

In addition, warrant holders will be particularly concerned with material payments leaving the group as part of an exit as this may dilute the value of the warrants.

Equity security documents

4.39 The following items are some suggested points to look out for when reviewing security documents given in favour of the sponsor or the seller.

---

55 Either geographically, in terms of restricted activities, or regarding the duration of the covenants (6 to 12 months may be seen as the standard period which is usually enforceable). Non-compete provisions should also be included within the investment agreement, however, where they are likely to be more enforceable and for a longer period. See also para **4.16**.

- *Ranking* The acquisition financiers' security will always rank in priority to the sponsor's or seller's security and the security documents should acknowledge this on their face.

- *Scope* The equity security documents should not be wider in scope than the acquisition financiers' security documents so that, for instance, security is not granted over assets which are excluded from the security in favour of the acquisition financiers.[56]

- *Inconsistency with the acquisition financiers' security* The security documents will contain positive and negative covenants by the companies creating the security and it is important that they do not covenant in favour of the sponsor or the seller in terms which are inconsistent with or tighter than the equivalent covenants in favour of the acquisition financiers.[57]

- *Enforcement provisions* The acquisition financiers will take first (and possibly second and third) ranking security in priority to the equity security, which means that the sponsor or the seller will not be able to enforce their security over the same assets without regard to the acquisition financiers' security. This does not, however, provide sufficient comfort on enforcement matters. In essence, enforcement action of any kind must be prohibited until the acquisition finance has been repaid. Consequently, it is common practice for the provisions relating to enforcement and the application of proceeds of enforcement to be expressly stated as being subject to the acquisition finance documents, including the prior ranking security documents and the subordination arrangements.

- *Subordination arrangements generally* The security documents should contain a full override clause specifying that the acquisition financiers' security documents override the equity security documents to the extent of any inconsistency and that all the terms of such equity security documents are subject to the acquisition finance documents including the intercreditor agreement.[58]

Subordination arrangements

4.40   The key element of the review of the equity documents from the acquisition financiers' perspective is the issue of subordination. A fundamental principle of a typical buy–out structure will be that the principal amount of

---

56 The most efficient approach is to have security documents that, subject to a number of exceptions, mirror the acquisition financiers' security documents. This speeds up the review process and ensures as much consistency as possible.

57 Again, using the acquisition finance security documents as a template should remove most inconsistencies. However, certain undertakings in the acquisition financiers' security documents will not be appropriate for second, third or fourth ranking security. For instance, the undertaking to collect debts and pay them into an account with the secured party. A common sense review should pick up similar provisions.

58 See para **4.41** for an example override clause.

equity invested in topco and any other SPVs will not be redeemed until all the acquisition finance debt has been repaid whether in the ordinary course of the passage of time or in an insolvency situation.[59] In addition, the payment of any yield in respect of the equity will be subject to strict conditions relating to the ability of the target business to continue to meet all of its prior ranking financial obligations in addition to all of its trading obligations. Together, such concepts constitute the principles underlying the acquisition financiers' subordination arrangements in respect of the equity. **Chapter 10** considers in detail how such subordination may be effected.

Acquisition finance override provision

4.41   When applying the subordination arrangements to the equity documents one of the main tools of the acquisition financiers will be an override provision. Its purpose is to ensure that no matter what the equity documents themselves provide the acquisition finance documents, including the intercreditor agreement, will be determinative on any areas of inconsistency. The following clause is an example form of override provision. It should be included in the topco articles of association and each loan capital instrument[60] as a separate article or clause.

> **'Override**
>
> Notwithstanding anything else in these [articles/conditions[61]], the [articles conditions] are all subject to the provisions of the [intercreditor agreement/finance documents[62]] which will override these [articles/conditions] to the extent that there is any inconsistency and, in particular, but without limitation, the payment of any [dividend/interest] and any payment in respect of the [redemption or purchase/repayment] by the company of [any class of shares/any loan capital/any [deep discount] bonds] shall not be made except to the extent permitted by the [intercreditor agreement/finance document(s)].'

The override provision could go on to expressly state that any payment which is blocked by the operation of the override provision would not be a debt due to the equity investors, irrespective of whether such amounts are payable. The implications of this are two-fold. First, the equity documents commonly provide that default interest will accrue in respect of any unpaid equity payments. This means that to the extent that an equity payment is blocked by the operation of the override provision, when the override provision subsequently permits such payment to be made, an additional payment will also be due from topco (or other equity vehicle) in respect of default interest. This has a financial implication for

---

59 An exception to this might be where the acquisition financiers expressly agree to a capital redemption, perhaps as part of a leveraged recapitalisation some time after completion.

60 And if, as is occasionally the case, the investment agreement includes provision for any payments to the equity providers, the investment agreement should also contain an override provision.

61 In a loan capital instrument there will usually be a separate schedule of 'conditions' which is the usual location for the override clause.

62 Finance documents will be defined to mean the relevant acquisition finance document(s) including the intercreditor agreement, and this wider definition may be used to pick up any relevant provisions not contained in the intercreditor agreement itself.

the group and, especially if such default interest would be payable at a time before the acquisition finance debt is repaid, the acquisition financiers will prefer the override provision to specify that no default interest would accrue in such circumstances. As a general matter, the acquisition financiers may wish to ensure that the rate of default interest payable in respect of unpaid amounts of equity will be no greater than the default interest payable in respect of unpaid amounts of acquisition finance debt.

Secondly, if the unpaid amounts are debts due, even if not then payable, then there will be adverse implications for the net asset position – and therefore solvency – of the group, which might in theory trigger a default under another financial obligation of the group and thus precipitate a financial crisis.

From the sponsor's perspective, they will be keen to ensure that unpaid equity payments are debts due so that they rank as creditors if the relevant equity vehicle is to be wound up. From the acquisition financiers' perspective, it would be preferable for the unpaid amounts not to be debts due for the reasons set out above. One compromise is to stipulate that such amounts do not become debts due until such time as the acquisition finance debt has been repaid in full. In practice, the matter is open to negotiation.

Raising acquisition financier issues

4.42   The equity documents will primarily be negotiated between the management team and the sponsor. Most of this will be in relation to the investment agreement and the topco articles where the interests of the different classes of investor and shareholder are not completely aligned. In addition and to the extent previously noted in this chapter, the acquisition financiers will require the equity documents to be in a form acceptable to them. In practical terms, all of the drafts of the equity documents should be circulated to the acquisition financiers and their lawyers and any comments should be passed directly to the relevant lawyers drafting such documents.

It is good practice to have the acquisition financiers themselves at the very least confirm the basic headline numbers set out in the equity documents: namely, the amounts and types of equity and the terms of any payments in respect of the equity during the life of the acquisition finance facilities. Otherwise most of the provisions of the equity documents can be reviewed principally by the lawyers advising the acquisition financiers who will report to their client as appropriate.

Generally the equity documents will be produced and negotiated over the same period as the acquisition finance documentation, although they are typically subject to less negotiation and as a result will go through fewer drafts before being finalised.

CHAPTER 5

Senior debt

SENIOR DEBT

5.1   Senior debt is synonymous with the acquisition finance market. It forms the largest single layer of finance in most buy-outs and has proven to be the most liquid and flexible product used in buy-out funding structures. Buy-outs are still completed with just senior debt and equity in the funding structure, although most often only at the lower end of the market. Mid-market and larger buy-outs will generally also include at least one tranche of junior debt but even in those structures senior debt is generally the largest single component.[1]

Evolution of the senior debt market

5.2   Over the years the senior debt market has expanded significantly. For much of the 1990s it was dominated by the UK's commercial banks together with a small number of international commercial and investment banks from Europe and the United States. Some commentators point to the willingness of the UK's leading bankers to support the buy-out industry during the mid-1990s as one of the reasons why the UK market grew so significantly by comparison with the markets in other European economies and why it easily remains the largest market in Europe today. Significant franchises were established by the leading banks and relationships with all of the main private equity sponsors have proved enduring. This has allowed banks and sponsors to navigate the full economic cycle without serious disruption to the availability and use of senior debt; at least until Summer 2007 when the US sub-prime mortgage crisis induced a global tightening of liquidity for senior debt (and other leveraged loan products).

Until the early 2000s senior debt was largely provided by banks. Not only were many of the largest arranging houses commercial banks with big balance sheets and a lending – and not just an arranging – mentality, but most syndicates were completed by a growing number of European banks with an increasing appetite for acquisition finance opportunities. A significant change has occurred since the

---

1   For much of the 1990s the 'mid-market' encapsulated buy-outs with a deal size (total funding requirement) of less than £50m-100m. Anything greater was deemed to be a large deal. Since the early 2000s this has changed significantly and many industry professionals now consider the mid-market to extend from £50m-500m. Generally the mid-market is now split into the lower, mid and upper mid-markets.

early 2000s, however. In particular, the vast amount of effectively new 'institutional' money that has been raised for acquisition finance transactions in Europe has changed the make-up of many senior debt syndicates. In this context institutional money means finance other than bank debt, raised from pension and insurance funds, hedge funds and other leveraged loan funds, such as CLOs and CDOs. Industry statistics suggest that by the mid 2000s senior debt syndicates would be made up of as much as 50% institutional money, most of it entirely new to European senior debt during the 2000s. A significant portion of this new money has been raised in North America from institutional investors keen to expand their portfolios into European deals, often because the yields in their home territories were less attractive. The increase in liquidity that this 'boom' has caused has fuelled many of the developments in the European acquisition finance market during the 2000s.[2]

The dynamic of the senior debt market over the years has also been affected by the increasing numbers of banks competing for the arranging mandates. In the 1990s there were very few banks with strong track records in successfully arranging acquisition finance packages and almost as few leading individual bankers. This kept the market surprisingly small in sheer numbers of participants. However, as the numbers of individuals with track records proliferated and dispersed the numbers of credible participants has also grown significantly. A key effect of this has been to remove much of the 'club' mentality that at one time existed in the market, although this still exists in lower mid-market and smaller deals to an extent. The knock-on effect has been to commoditise senior debt to a large degree. Important relationships still exist between sponsors and banks but increasingly these are characterised by the greater choices that the sponsors have within the senior debt market, choices that are often brought to bear in the relatively one-sided negotiations of senior debt arranging mandates. This has also been exacerbated by the fact that there is more competition than ever between sponsors to complete deals, often in the immediate format of an auction. In an attempt to gain an edge sponsors are far more likely to drive a harder bargain with the banks, which has resulted in less genuine negotiation of arranging mandates.

Senior debt structures

5.3   A structure incorporating senior debt and equity can be represented in the diagrammatic form shown on the next page. The senior debt will be made available to the acquisition vehicle to finance the acquisition and often to the target to refinance its existing debt and for working capital purposes. The use of two (or more) SPVs is common as it enables the senior banks to structurally subordinate the loan capital provided by the equity investors to the senior debt. It also means that share security can be taken over the shares in the senior debt borrower, which may have benefits for the senior banks.[3]

---

2   Such as increasing B and C tranche sizes, where much of the institutional money is invested, and the rise of second lien debt and institutional mezzanine debt. The increase in total leverage multiples can also be attributed to the additional liquidity provided by the institutional debt market.

3   Such as enabling the banks to take the benefit of newco's rights under the acquisition documents without an assignment of such rights (see paras **2.31** and **2.54**) and any tax losses in newco.

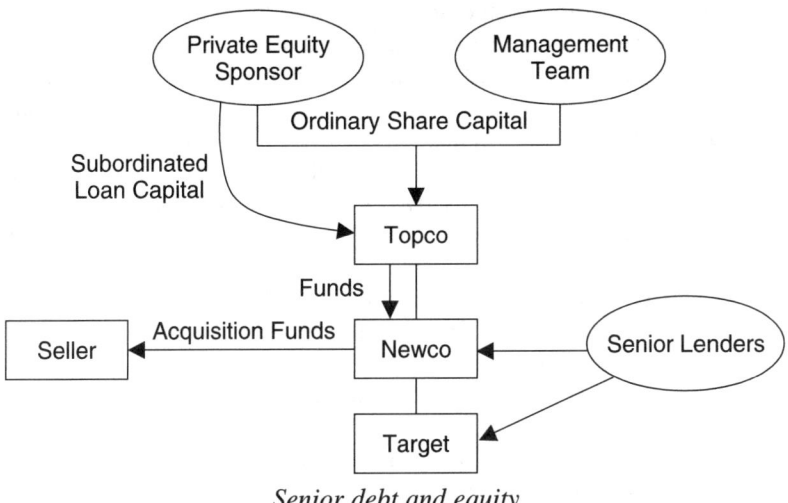

Senior debt and equity

A more common structure than the one above, which incorporates junior debt, can be represented in diagrammatic form as follows. Depending on which type of junior debt it is, the junior creditors may share the borrower with the senior lenders or an additional SPV may be required.

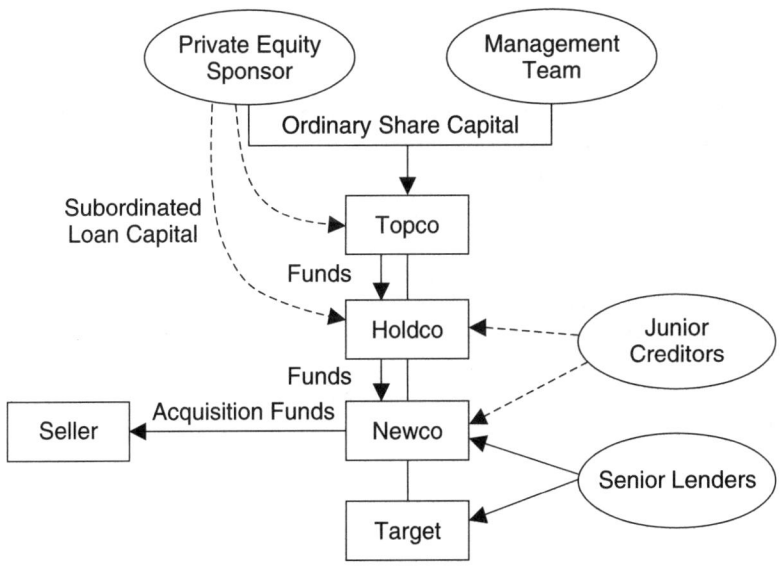

Senior, junior and equity

Who provides the senior debt?

5.4 Senior debt is provided by acquisition finance banks, other financial institutions and dedicated leveraged loan funds including CDOs and CLOs. The bank that is mandated to arrange and underwrite the senior debt is generally referred to as the arranging bank or the mandated lead arranger (MLA for short). Where the senior debt is of a certain size[4] the MLA will syndicate most of the senior debt to one or more other lenders who, together with itself, will form the senior lender syndicate. This syndication usually occurs only once the deal has been completed. In most cases the MLA will also act as the agent and security trustee for the syndicate. Sometimes, two or three banks will be jointly mandated prior to signing and completion and then fund the deal together. If it is a small deal they may then choose not to syndicate the debt. In large transactions two or three banks may be needed to underwrite the acquisition finance on the basis that it is too large for any single bank. In that situation the joint-MLAs will then syndicate the debt in a coordinated manner following completion.

In return for arranging and underwriting the senior debt package, MLAs get an up-front arrangement/underwriting fee payable by the borrower on completion. The amount of the fee is generally equal to a percentage of the total amount of the senior debt.[5] On syndication a portion of the up-front fee will be paid by the MLA or joint-MLAs to the syndicate banks as an incentive to come into the deal. The up-front fee is an important source of revenue for banks and is used as one measure of annual activity and ultimately of the incomes of the deal-doing bankers.

What does the senior debt comprise?

Acquisition facility

5.5   The core element of the senior debt package for a buy-out will be the acquisition facility. This usually comprises one, two or three medium-term loans repayable over seven, eight and nine years respectively. The A tranche or 'note' of seven years' maturity will typically amortise over that period with an average life[6] in the region of four to five years. The B note is generally repayable in two equal instalments at years 7.5 and 8 and C notes are usually repayable in equal instalments at years 8.5 and 9.[7]

Each tranche will carry an interest rate margin over the senior lenders' cost of funds.[8] The pricing of senior debt in the United Kingdom has followed a very stable model for a number of years and is not dependent in any direct way on the underlying borrower group. The amount of leverage that will be made available

---

4   Different banks have different thresholds at which they would need to syndicate the debt but as an approximate rule of thumb any deal with more than £30m of debt would usually be syndicated. Typically the minimum amount that would be syndicated to any single lender would be in the £5m-10m range.

5   This would usually be in the region of say 1.75% to 2% or more, depending on market conditions.

6   The average life of a loan is the average amount of time that the loan will be outstanding if it is repaid in full in accordance with the agreed schedule. It reflects the rate of amortisation of the loan.

7   See also para **5.11** in relation to 'alphabet' notes.

8   For banks funding in the UK this will usually be the European Interbank Offered Rate (EURIBOR) for amounts lent in euros or the London Interbank Offered Rate (LIBOR) for amounts lent in sterling and other currencies, together in each case with applicable banking regulatory costs.

will generally vary depending on the strength of the borrower group, but the senior debt pricing will remain broadly the same for all borrowers.[9] Thus the interest rate margin for the core acquisition debt was, for many years, including most of the 2000s, 2.25% for the A note, 2.75% for the B note and 3.25% for the C note. In fact, the market developed two notable concepts that operated to reduce the headline figure in practice.

First, it is common for this headline margin figure to be subject to a so-called 'ratchet' which operates to automatically reduce the margin – usually in three or four steps of 25 basis points per step, so an A note could theoretically ratchet down to 1.50% or 1.25% – if the company meets certain financial performance criteria.[10] For a long time ratchets only applied to the A note. B and C notes, which were targeted at the institutional investor market,[11] were exempt. Over time this changed, with first B notes and then ultimately C notes being subject to the ratchet mechanism in addition to the A note.

Secondly, there is the concept of pricing 'flex'. Flex provisions operate to adjust the headline pricing by reference to the demand of the senior debt market for the facilities in primary syndication. Originally flex provisions only operated in an upward direction, enabling underwriting banks to increase pricing in order to avoid an otherwise unsuccessful syndication. However, at some point in the mid-2000s, 'reverse flex' provisions also began being used by the leading sponsors to bring down their borrowing costs in response to oversubscribed syndications. Commonly this will mean reducing the C and, possibly, B tranches by up to 25 basis points provided that, in doing so, in simple terms,[12] the successful syndication of those tranches is not affected. The development of reverse flex has largely been a product of the increased liquidity in the institutional debt markets, particularly due to the explosive growth of leveraged loan funds and other institutional – non-bank – investors. Institutional money now constitutes a significant proportion of the money that takes up B and C tranches and, given that institutional lenders are often able to raise funds at a relatively low cost, together with their strong appetite for investments generally, a reduction of 25 bps in the margin on these tranches will often not deter the investors from participating in the syndication.

In actual fact in the latter half of the 2000s the market underwent a step change in the headline pricing of senior debt. In some deals, rather than the traditional 2.25/2.75/3.25 pricing, came 2.00/2.25/2.75 for the A, B and C notes respectively, although the 2007/2008 liquidity crisis has reversed that trend.

The acquisition loan will generally be made available to newco for funding the acquisition of the target and for paying newco's fees and expenses in respect of

---

9   This is a notable departure from the US market where pricing is more flexible and deal-specific. But see also the discussion on 'reverse flex' later on which has the effect of introducing deal-specific pricing into UK deals.

10 The most common financial test is a leverage ratio test. Margin ratchets are considered in more detail later in this Chapter. See para **5.39**.

11 See earlier. Institutional investors, including leveraged loan funds in particular, are substantial investors in B and C note senior debt. Historically they have proved less flexible on interest rate ratchets than have banks.

12 See paras **11.104** and **11.105** for more detail on flex and reverse flex provisions.

the transaction. It may also be made available to certain members of the target group to enable them to repay any existing debt.[13]

The currency of the acquisition term loan will reflect its purposes. Thus, the main element will be in the currency of the purchase price. The borrower needs it in that currency to pay the seller. There are also occasions, however, where the borrower will not wish to borrow in the same currency as the purchase price. This is because its overriding aim will be to have borrowings denominated in the same currency or currencies as its cashflows. In this way currency exchange rate movements will not affect its ability to service those borrowings. This is most likely to arise in a multi-jurisdictional buy-out since the seller may insist on the purchase price being payable in one particular currency, even though the operating cashflows of the target business may include significant amounts in other currencies. The buyer will usually prefer to borrow some of the acquisition finance in the same currency, and approximately the same proportion to the overall position, as such cashflows. At first glance the requirements of the seller and the buyer appear to be at odds, but both can be achieved by newco borrowing the acquisition debt in the currency of the target group cashflows and exchanging it for the currency of the purchase price on the day of completion to pay the seller. The seller gets the purchase price in its desired currency and the borrower has the acquisition debt outstanding in the same currency as the target group's cashflows.

In a typical private buy–out the acquisition loan will be drawn down, and its proceeds applied, in full at completion. Similarly, a public-to-private structured as a scheme of arrangement will be funded in one amount at completion. With a public-to-private structured as a takeover offer, however, the acquisition loan will be drawn in stages as batches of acceptances fall due for payment.[14]

Working capital facility

5.6   In addition to the acquisition facility, the target business will generally have a need for a working capital facility. This will be provided by the senior lenders and form part of the senior debt.

The working capital facility will typically comprise a revolving credit facility, which may be utilised by way of cash advances or guarantees and letters of credit, together with ancillary facilities including an overdraft.[15] It is common for the ancillary facilities to be provided by a single bank in the senior debt syndicate, usually the MLA if it is a clearing bank.

The facility is typically available for utilisation by newco and the target group until the senior acquisition A note (if any[16]) has been repaid at year 7 if not before,

---

13 There are usually a number of potential advantages in allowing the target to repay its own debt from the proceeds of the new senior debt facilities rather than having the seller discharge it at completion (in return for a higher price). These are considered in para **3.27**.

14 See **Chapter 12** generally, in relation to public-to-private transactions.

15 The ancillary facilities may also include bonding, guarantees and foreign exchange.

16 See para **5.11**.

although the overdraft and ancillary facilities may be made available on an on-demand basis. The working capital facility may be a multi–currency facility, depending on the group's needs.

The facility will usually carry an interest margin equal to that applicable to the senior acquisition A note. In addition there will be a non–utilisation fee payable on the undrawn portion of the facility from time to time.[17]

Capex facility

5.7   Where a specific capital expenditure funding requirement is included in the business plan, perhaps to fund the installation of a new production line for a manufacturing business, this may be provided by the senior lenders as part of the senior debt package. The terms of capex facilities are often agreed on a deal specific basis. That said they tend to be in the form of a term loan facility, rather than a revolving credit facility, which may be borrowed in a number of sub-loans, usually for an initial 'availability period' of say two or three years. A capex loan might be repayable by a single 'bullet' payment at the same time as the final repayment instalment of the core senior acquisition loan (the A note) or it may amortise in line with the A note following the end of the availability period. The interest rate margin on a capex facility is not as standard as with the acquisition facility and will generally be separately negotiated. However, it will be no less than the A note and generally not subject to any margin ratchet.[18] As with the working capital facility, a non–utilisation fee will be payable on the undrawn portion of the facility during the period it is available for drawing.

Further acquisition facilities

5.8   In certain transactions the business plan contemplates the target business being consolidated with other businesses in the same sector. This is often described as a 'buy and build' strategy. In order to avoid negotiating debt funding every time a further acquisition is to be made, as part of such a strategy deal sponsors often prefer to have committed funding in place from the outset. This means a dedicated further acquisition facility. Not all banks are happy to provide further acquisition facilities since they are in effect agreeing to fund the acquisition of businesses as yet unidentified. In order to meet some of their concerns the

---

17 This fee, which is also called a commitment fee, is intended to compensate the senior lenders for having a facility committed for utilisation by the group and therefore unable to be advanced to other borrowers in other transactions. It will usually be in the region of 75 basis points or perhaps be set at 50% of the margin, so that it reduces in line with the margin ratchet (see para **5.39**).

18 As a general rule of thumb a capex loan would typically be priced at between 2.25% p.a. and 2.75% p.a. depending on its maturity and any amortisation, or possibly as low as 2.00% if set to match an A note priced at that level. So, if it is repayable in a bullet at the end of year seven or eight it is likely to be priced at the same level as a B note, traditionally with a margin of 2.75% but possibly as low as 2.25%. If – as is more often the case – it amortises, it is more likely to be priced like the A note, at 2.25% (or perhaps less). See para **5.5**, generally, on the pricing of senior debt.

drawdown conditions for these facilities usually include requirements as to the financial status of any further business to be acquired and as to the level of due diligence that the company must carry out before making the acquisition.

An alternative approach, perhaps where the additional acquisitions are less certain, is to have a fully documented but uncommitted further acquisition facility. This means that if and when the sponsor wants to make an acquisition it only needs to find lenders prepared to provide the facility – it does not need to seek permissions from the existing lenders or to incur the costs of waivers and amendments to the documentation. Also, by not committing the facility at the outset it can save arrangement and commitment fees, if not entirely, then at least until it needs the new facility.[19]

Other specific funding requirements

5.9   In theory, other transaction-specific facilities can be included within the senior debt package, perhaps a dedicated equipment finance facility, a real estate bridge facility and so on.

How much senior debt will be made available?

5.10   The overall amount of senior debt which the senior lenders are willing to provide will be determined principally on the basis of a detailed credit analysis of the target business and a structural analysis using a financial model. There will also be market forces dictating how much debt would be acceptable for syndication purposes. In practice, the amount of the working capital facility will be set by reference to the agreed working capital requirement determined as part of the overall funding requirement – the uses of funds – and not usually by reference to market dynamics. A detailed consideration of the relevant factors used to determine the total amount of the senior debt package is included in **Chapter 3**.

If the level of senior debt that the banks are willing to provide, together with the equity, is insufficient to satisfy the funding requirement, further sources of funding must be considered. In practice this generally means one or more layers of junior debt.

However, the provision of a further layer of finance may not necessarily be needed where the funding gap is relatively small and more than one senior lender is competing for the mandate to arrange the senior debt. In such circumstances, the deal sponsor may be relying on one bank taking a particularly aggressive view to get the mandate, possibly offering a slightly larger senior debt package than it might in normal circumstances. Over the years banks have developed various financial engineering techniques to increase the total amount of senior debt that can be made available. Given the intense competition between banks many of these are now used routinely to ensure that as full a package as possible is offered to the deal sponsor in order to win the senior debt mandate.

---

19 See para **5.25** for further detail.

Stretched senior debt and alphabet notes

5.11   One of the first techniques used by senior lenders to extend the senior debt package beyond the standard without the requirement for a further layer of finance was to 'stretch' the senior debt.

This was done by extending the maturity of the senior debt from the conventional seven years to eight or nine. This allowed more debt to be included without imposing a greater annual repayment obligation on the borrower, although the total interest burden would inevitably increase. This method became popular for a time in the latter half of the 1990s prior to the development by the leading banks of more structured methods of meeting the funding gap. It is now very rarely used.

As previously indicated, senior debt packages are now commonly structured through the use of 'alphabet notes'.[20] This is where the senior lender includes a second and often third discrete tranche of senior debt, called the 'B' note and 'C' note respectively, in addition to the main tranche of senior debt (the 'A' note). In most deals with a total funding requirement above say £50m, a B and possibly a C note will generally be included. For deals of say £150m or more B and C notes – or possibly, as mentioned below, a single B note with a blended B/C profile in place of A, B and C notes[21] – will be used as a matter of course within the senior debt structure. The main reason for this is not so much absolute quantum of the debt used but the applicable leverage multiples, that is, the ratio of debt to EBITDA. It follows that the greater the leverage there is the less cashflow (which is largely a derivative of EBITDA) there is available to service the debt. This necessarily means having a greater proportion of the debt in the non-amortising tranches, which by definition have no principal repayment requirements until final maturity. Thus, as the leverage multiple increases so the proportion of the debt made available under the A note must decrease. In addition, by using B and C notes the standard profile and pricing of the A note can remain within market acceptable parameters. The B and C notes will be priced at higher levels to reflect their longer maturities.[22]

In actual fact, in the latter half of the 2000s debt packages have been structured without an amortising A note at all, just B and C notes. In some cases the senior debt will even be structured with just a single B note of eight years' maturity priced at a blended margin reflecting a B and C note structure.[23] These developments take the logic mentioned above to its natural conclusion. For completeness, however, and to demonstrate how the senior debt market has evolved – the following paragraphs assume that the structure follows the more traditional model with A, B and C notes.

---

20 The concept of a 'note' in this context is a colloquial reference to a promissory note that in certain jurisdictions (including the United States) is issued by the borrower to the lenders of a particular tranche of debt to evidence the debt owing. A reference to a 'note' can be used to mean the particular tranche of debt evidenced by it.

21 See following sections of para **5.11**.

22 See para **5.5** as regards pricing of senior debt.

23 This, like so many developments in the European market, mirrors US senior debt structuring practice.

For a period in the 2000s senior debt packages in most mid-market and larger transactions became sufficiently commoditised for the relative amounts and principal terms of the A, B and C notes to have become similarly standardised. Thus the allocation of the amount of total senior debt between the A, B and C notes was for a number of years almost fixed at 50%, 25% and 25% respectively. During the mid 2000s this began to change, however, with the total senior acquisition facility being evenly spread across the A, B and C notes (that is, one-third to each) or perhaps with more allocated to each of B and C than to A. Indeed, as mentioned above, more recent structures have no A note at all.[24] As indicated, the main reason for this development has been to accommodate greater leverage multiples in any given transaction. There is, however, a further contributing factor that must be considered.

By allocating more debt to B and C notes, the institutional lender market[25] can be further utilised to ease syndication concerns. This is because the institutional market is more attracted to the B and C notes, with their higher pricing and no amortisation, than to the A note.[26] This in turn creates downward pressure on the pricing of the B and C notes, which is a further attraction of the trend for deal sponsors.[27]

DOCUMENTING THE SENIOR DEBT

5.12   The following paragraphs consider in some detail the nature of the principal documents which are used to document the senior debt facilities.

Senior debt documents

5.13   In a UK buy-out the senior debt documentation will comprise the following core documents:

- senior facilities agreement;

- ancillary facilities letter;

- intercreditor agreement;

- security agreement; and

- hedging documents.

---

24 See an earlier part of para **5.11**.

25 See para **5.2**.

26 This is partly also because participants in the A note are also usually required to participate in the working capital facility and institutional lenders – many of which are leveraged loan funds – tend to be unable to provide revolving credit debt.

27 The downward pricing pressure manifests itself in the use of margin ratchets on B notes and C notes (see para **5.39**), and also through the application of reverse-flex provisions by deal sponsors (see para **11.105**). In the latter half of the 2000s it has also resulted in lower headline pricing of the B and C notes (see para **5.5**).

In addition to these main documents there will be various supporting documents including fee letters and other side letters. These are all considered in the documentation section of **Chapter 11**.

Commitment papers

5.14   There is a further category of senior debt documentation not listed above that has become of increasing importance in the execution of buy-outs – commitment papers. Commitment papers document the terms of the debt and its availability before execution of the full documentation suite. They are generally used by sponsors to obtain an initial commitment from the senior debt arranger to provide the finance at the outset of the buy-out process often before the sponsor undertakes full due diligence or makes an initial bid in an auction process. In return banks use them to gain exclusivity for the role of MLA, which is why they are also often called 'mandate letters'.

There are various levels of commitment letter, with varying degrees of commitment offered under them. At their weakest they may only express confidence in their ability and willingness to arrange and underwrite the debt facilities (often referred to as 'highly confident' letters) or they may go further and offer to do so, subject to a number of conditions including general due diligence, credit committee approval, full documentation and perhaps specific issues for the bank to obtain comfort on. Letters offering to arrange and underwrite facilities, even though conditional, will generally attach a detailed term sheet setting out the proposed terms of the full documentation. These types of 'commitment' letter will expressly state that they do not constitute an offer or commitment to provide the debt and the sponsor will merely have the reputation of the relevant bank as comfort that the debt will ever be forthcoming.

At the other end of the spectrum are full legally binding commitments, under which the bank can be required to actually advance the funds without any further documentation being required. This form is a relatively new concept that has been used more extensively in the 2000s to enable sponsors to launch offers (including public-to-privates) at very short notice without waiting for full documentation to be negotiated. In order to be legally enforceable to this extent, the letter and attached term sheet must provide certainty as to the terms on which the debt is made available, which in turn means the term sheet must be sufficiently detailed to be without ambiguity and to include actual mechanics for drawdown.

In practice, it is still rare for funding to take place under a commitment letter itself without a more formal loan agreement being documented – either the ultimate facility agreement or perhaps in the form of a short term bridge document, often referred to as an interim loan agreement.[28] In that sense the commitment letter does not advance the documentation process. However, there are other advantages with the stronger varietals of commitment letter. In particular, commitment letters are used by sponsors to demonstrate the strength of their bid in a competitive tender process. By demonstrating to the seller that they have

---

28 See para **5.15**.

committed finance – particularly with no due diligence or credit committee conditionality – the seller will take their offer that much more seriously.[29] The same applies in fully negotiated rather than auctioned buy-outs. The sooner in the process that the sponsor can show the seller that it has committed funds, the more seriously the seller will take the sponsor. This may result in the sponsor being awarded exclusivity by the seller to complete the buy-out.

During the early to mid-2000s certain sponsors began taking a more active role in negotiating the terms of the debt that MLAs would provide in commitment papers by insisting on producing the commitment letter and term sheet themselves. Inevitably this resulted in the documents being much more pro-sponsor, at least at the outset. By combining their own commitment papers with competitive tendering for the debt mandates, sponsors are able to drive a harder bargain on the terms of the acquisition finance that they are able to obtain. Banks are faced with the choice of potentially losing a mandate or playing ball. Whilst this does not always happen – much depends on the sponsor and its initial bargaining power with the banks – it is one of the necessary effects of the increased competition for debt mandates that the leading banks have faced during the 2000s.

Interim loan documents

5.15   As with sponsor-driven commitment letters, interim loan documents and short term facilities have become a feature of deal execution in the 2000s. The idea is to truncate the full documentation process through the use of an interim loan agreement that is quicker to document because it doesn't include all of the representations, covenants, events of default and other heavily negotiated sections of a full facility agreement. An interim loan agreement would typically only be 20 or 30 pages long. Funds made available under it will be repayable a short time after drawing, probably 20 or 30 business days; though in the case of a public deal, because of 'certain funds' issues, this period is likely to be six months after signing. The facilities to be provided will include the full-term loans required for the acquisition, plus any working capital which the target group may need during the period of the interim facility. It would not usually include any further acquisition or capex facilities. As for covenants, as indicated above, these will not include all of the covenants seen in a full facility agreement. Indeed they will only usually apply to the SPV group and not the target group. Similarly, the only security for the interim loan tends to be security from the SPV group and not from the target group, not least because any grace period for putting target security in place is likely to be longer than the maturity of the facility itself. It is accepted that this is not a perfect position for the lenders, as they have no contractual protection against the target group weakening its financial position during the term of the interim financing, but, given the short period of time the loans are outstanding, market practice indicates that banks can get com-

---

29   See also the concept of 'certain funds' in private buy-outs in **Chapters 2** and **11**.

fortable with this; and in any event both lender and borrower have a powerful incentive to agree full form documentation as neither want to see a default on the repayment date and enforcement.

Interim loan facilities are of particular use in auctions where a tactical advantage can be obtained by having the debt available at short notice to enable a bidder to complete an acquisition as soon as preferred bidder status is awarded. In addition to the basic security from the SPVs the acquisition financiers might also require a simple intercreditor or subordination agreement to be executed by the SPVs in order to subordinate any claims under shareholder loans/funding loans arising in relation to the equity proceeds to the interim loans provided by the acquisition financiers.[30]

Senior facilities agreement

5.16　The senior facilities agreement is the principal senior debt document. It contains the terms and conditions of the senior debt facilities.[31]

Typically, the senior facilities agreement will take the form of a multi-option syndicated credit agreement tailored for an acquisition finance transaction. This section looks in detail at some of the specific provisions which are commonly required in an acquisition financing. For completeness, but in summary form only, the standard provisions to be found in syndicated credit agreements generally are also considered. Most are based on the Senior Multicurrency Term and Revolving Facilities Agreement template published by the Loan Market Association (often simply referred to as the 'LMA' template).

Basic structure

5.17　A standard senior facilities agreement used in a typical UK buy-out should contain the following provisions (with highlighted provisions considered in further detail below).

- Parties – this will be newco as principal borrower, possibly one or more target group companies as borrowers under working capital and other facilities, topco as parent company of the group, each member of the group as guarantors and the senior lenders.[32]

- Interpretation – definitions and construction of certain terms.

- **Conditions precedent** – the conditions of the first drawing under the facilities.

- Drawdown conditions – the basic conditions of all drawings.

30　See also para **11.116** in relation to short term facilities.
31　In practice, a separate ancillary facilities letter will often be used to document ancillary working capital facilities.
32　Unless the senior debt is being provided by a 'club' of two or three lenders, at completion only a single underwriting bank as mandated lead arranger – or, in larger transactions, two or more joint MLAs – will be party. Assuming that the senior debt is to be syndicated, the other syndicate banks will join in by way of novation after completion. The lead senior lender (the MLA) will be party in various capacities in addition to as a lender, typically being agent, arranger, security trustee, hedging counterparty and possibly ancillary facilities lender – all of which are discussed later in this chapter.

- **Facilities** – the mechanical provisions and principal commercial terms of the various facilities including, amounts, drawdown administration requirements, repayment, interest, fees and expenses.

- Yield protection and indemnities – 'boilerplate' provisions in respect of market disruption, taxes, increased costs and certain indemnities.

- Guarantee.

- **Representations.**

- **Information undertakings.**

- **Financial covenants.**

- **General undertakings.**

- **Events of default.**

- **Transfer provisions.**

- Boilerplate provisions – including in respect of administration of the facilities, matters concerning the finance parties including appointment of the senior agent, **decision making**, notices and governing law.

- Schedules/Exhibits – including lists of **documentary CPs**, details of the group companies, forms of drawdown request, mandatory cost formulae, form of transfer certificate used to effect transfers by the lenders and possibly certain other agreed form documents, such as an ancillary facilities letter.

Conditions precedent

5.18   The conditions precedent are intended to ensure that prior to the drawing of any of the senior debt and, in particular, the acquisition facility to fund the acquisition, all of the legal and commercial assumptions on which the senior debt arranger and underwriter had based its decision to provide the senior debt are satisfied. They will mostly comprise documentary conditions precedent – considered briefly below – in addition to certain other event-based factual conditions precedent, all of which are considered in further detail in **Chapter 11**.

Documentary CPs

5.19   The borrower will be required to deliver copies and in some cases originals of the following documents, duly executed by all parties in the case of legal documents.[33]

- all other senior debt documents including:
  - security documents (together with related title documents including target share certificates and stock transfer forms or an undertaking to produce them[34]);

---

33 See also **Chapter 11** for more detail on many of the CPs.

34 The transfer of the target shares to newco may be subject to stamp duty adjudication. This will mean that the required stock transfer forms and share certificates in the name of newco will not be available at completion.

- – intercreditor (and subordination) agreement(s);[35]
- – ancillary facilities letter; and
- – hedging document;[36]

● junior debt documents;

● confirmation from the junior creditor that the junior debt is unconditionally available to newco – subject to any conditions relating to unconditionality of the acquisition and the senior debt – or other evidence that the junior debt has been made available;

● equity documents;

● confirmation from newco that it has received the subscription moneys in respect of the institutional and management equity or other evidence that the total amount of equity required has been invested in topco and holdco if applicable, and the proceeds downstreamed to newco;

● seller finance documents if applicable;[37]

● acquisition documents;

● confirmation that the acquisition documents are unconditional;

● other transaction documents such as an upstream intra-group loan agreement;

● corporate authorities of each group company that is entering into the finance documentation including:

- – board resolutions and shareholder resolutions approving execution of all documents by the respective companies;
- – copies of memoranda and articles of association of the respective companies; and
- – specimen signatures of authorised signatories referred to in the board minutes;

● *financial assistance whitewash documents in respect of each company giving financial assistance, including:*

- – *statutory declarations by all of the directors of each company giving financial assistance in respect of all relevant companies;*
- – *auditors' statutory report in respect of each statutory declaration;*
- – *special resolutions of each relevant company which is not wholly-owned; and*

35 See para **5.80** and **Chapter 10** generally. There may be a single composite intercreditor agreement or possibly more than one providing for subordination of different elements of the funding structure. Seller finance, for instance, will often be subordinated separately in a shorter form agreement.

36 In practice this may be a condition subsequent to be fulfilled within a period (say, one month) after completion. In its place the borrower and MLA will execute a hedging strategy letter (see **Chapter 11**).

37 See **Chapters 2** and **3** in relation to seller finance.

- *auditors' net asset letter in respect of each respective company giving financial assistance;*[38]

- due diligence reports and reliance letters in respect of the following areas and others as required:[39]

  - financial (accounting);

  - environmental;

  - insurance;

  - legal;

  - market/commercial;

  - pensions;

  - real estate;

  - tax; and

  - technical;

- tax structuring report;[40]

- historical financial statements in respect of:

  - last one, two or three financial years – audited accounts; and

  - current year to date – management accounts;

- management team's business plan and the agreed form base case financial model;

- (in a true MBO) references on the management team;

- group structure chart including the target group;

- auditor confirmation in respect of financial covenant compliance certificates;[41]

- landlord consent to charge and/or assignment of leasehold properties;[42]

- real estate search results;

- insurance broker's letter confirming that adequate insurance is in place;[43]

---

38 After years of legal debate about the financial assistance provisions of the Companies Act 1985, legislation to be enacted pursuant to the Companies Act 2006 is set to repeal the financial assistance prohibition applicable to private companies, and with it the whitewash procedure. This will be effective from 1 October 2008. The prohibition applicable to public companies will remain under Chapter 2 of Part 18 of the 2006 Act which will come into force on 1 October 2009.

39 See **Chapter 11** in respect of due diligence and due diligence reports.

40 See **Chapter 11** for further detail on tax structuring reports.

41 This may be a condition subsequent.

42 Leases of property will generally have covenants against charging or assigning the lease without the landlord's consent. This consent will be required for security to be taken over the lease and for a transfer of the lease in a business sale.

43 This may be covered in an insurance due diligence report.

- evidence that there is no external indebtedness in the target group, usually in the form of a director/secretary certification or confirmation in the financial and legal due diligence reports,

- evidence that there is no security over any target group assets, usually in the form of director/secretary certifications and/or company search results together with release documentation where appropriate;

- legal opinion(s) in all relevant jurisdictions;

- fee letters setting out the up-front arrangement and underwriting fees[44] and the annual agency or monitoring fee payable by newco to the lead senior lender(s);[45]

- confirmation that all requisite regulatory approvals have been obtained; and

- any other deal specific matters on which the senior agent requires comfort prior to lending any money.

Facilities

5.20   The principal facility will be the acquisition facility, which is typically made available in two or three tranches of term loan debt generally called the A note, B note and, as required, C note.[46] In the senior facilities agreement itself, these tranches are often referred to as facility A, facility B and facility C. The principal documentary provisions dealing with the drawdown mechanics, amounts, currency, scheduled repayments, prepayments and the rate of interest and commitment commission of the acquisition facilities are relatively straightforward to document and do not merit detailed explanation here. However, certain provisions – particularly those specific to buy-outs – are discussed further below.

Working capital facilities – ancillary facilities

5.21   Most working capital facilities comprise a revolving credit facility for substantial cash advances and an ancillary working capital facility that includes commercial banking facilities such as overdrafts, guarantees and letters of credit. Borrowers use the two elements to meet both large long-term working capital requirements and more short-term ad hoc requirements respectively.

Where the debt package is to be syndicated a practical issue arises in relation to the ancillary element. A revolving credit facility can easily be syndicated; each bank provides its pro rata share of each cash advance borrowed. With ancillary facilities syndication is less straightforward. In particular, many types of ancillary working capital facility cannot be directly syndicated. An overdraft, for example, will not work on a syndicated basis. In practice therefore, the senior

---

44 What the up-front fees are called and cover exactly varies from institution to institution and to some extent deal size.

45 The details of these fees are generally set out in separate fee letters, certainly for syndicated deals, so that the syndicate banks do not see precisely what the level of the fees payable to the MLA(s) are.

46 The commercial terms of the acquisition facilities are considered in some detail earlier in this chapter.

facilities agreement will provide for a specified bank to provide those ancillary facilities which cannot be made available on a truly syndicated basis. This will require a bank, usually the MLA where it is a commercial bank or, if not, a commercial bank in the syndicate, to agree to act as the ancillary facilities lender.

In fact, of the ancillary facilities mentioned, guarantees and letters of credit are often made available as part of the main revolving credit facility in addition to or instead of in the ancillary facilities letter. In this case an 'issuing bank', in addition to the ancillary facilities lender, will agree to provide the guarantee and letter of credit facility for the syndicate. The issuing bank will issue the guarantee or letter of credit and each syndicate bank will provide the issuing bank with a back-to-back indemnity for that proportion of the guarantee/letter of credit that represents its commitment to the working capital facility.

Ancillary facilities letter

5.22   In terms of documenting ancillary working capital facilities, there are a number of factors which may mitigate towards having a separate document, in the form of a facility letter.

The principal reason is that many of the main terms of the ancillary facilities – including mechanics, pricing and the incorporation of standard business terms – are quite different from the terms of the other senior facilities. It is practically easier therefore to set them out in a separate document. In addition, there is no need, per se, to have the ancillary facilities documented in the senior facilities agreement itself. The parties to an ancillary working capital facility usually comprise only one of the senior banks and one or more borrowers; so there is no need to have all of the parties to the senior facilities agreement (eg, other banks, the agent, arranger and hedging bank) as party to the ancillary working capital facility document. Further, ancillary facilities are generally made available on an on-demand basis, reflecting standard banking terms and the need for such facilities to be withdrawn at short notice if a business becomes insolvent and the bank wishes to withdraw support. This means that there is no need to incorporate default triggers, such as the covenants and events of default used in the senior facilities agreement, into the terms of such facilities. As a result it is not necessary to have the ancillary facilities documented in the senior facilities agreement in order for the same covenants and events of default to apply.

The terms of the ancillary facilities will usually reflect standard banking terms as provided by the ancillary facilities lender to its corporate customers. Consequently, the form of the ancillary facilities letter will often be based on a standard bank in-house document. As a senior debt document, however, it will need to be in a form acceptable to all of the senior debt syndicate and may be scheduled to the senior facilities agreement in an agreed form.

Given that the amount of the ancillary facilities drawn may change on a daily basis it is usual for a fixed portion of the working capital facility to be carved out and allocated to ancillary facilities.

Syndicate lender participation in the ancillary facilities

5.23   Even though only one bank may provide the ancillary facilities, the other syndicate lenders may still participate in such facilities, and the nature of their participation has an important economic impact on the spread of credit risk amongst the syndicate and also the investment returns. There are essentially three alternative approaches. First, if the syndicate lenders do not participate at all then only the ancillary facilities lender takes the economic exposure in the ancillary facilities and, similarly, the return. Secondly, if the syndicate lenders do participate, through the use of a fronting bank structure[47], they take a share of the economic exposure in such facilities – through an 'exposure-sharing' or 'loss-sharing' mechanism – and also a share in the economic return. Finally there is a hybrid structure whereby the exposure to the borrower under the ancillary facilities is to some extent spread between all the lenders using a 'loss-sharing' mechanism but the return is retained by the ancillary facilities lender. There are key differences between these three alternative structures, as summarised in the following table.

Structure	Loss Sharing	Yield Sharing
1. Ancillary facilities provided bilaterally by a senior bank for its own account completely separately from the other senior facilities.	No. If the ancillary facilities are drawn to a greater extent than the revolving capital facility at acceleration point the ancillary facilities lender faces greater exposure.	No. The ancillary facilities lender keeps all of the interest and non-utilisation and other fees on all ancillary facilities provided by it.
2. Ancillary facilities provided as part of the senior facilities by a fronting bank on behalf of the entire working capital facility syndicate. The ancillary facilities lenders itself takes no credit risk and receives no yield.	Yes. Each senior lender in the working capital facility syndicate indemnifies the fronting bank for its pro rata share of any credit exposure (unpaid amount) sufferedby the fronting bank. The fronting bank has an exposure to the senior lenders that are indemnifying it for which it charges the borrower a 'fronting fee'.[48]	Yes, the fronting bank passes the interest margin and non-utilisation fees to the senior lenders in the working capital facility. It retains the 'fronting fee' and any other administration fees that it charges to the borrower for providing the ancillary facilities.
3. Ancillary facilities provided as part of the senior facilities but bilaterally by a senior lender for its own account in place of some or all of its participation in the revolving credit facility.	Yes. At the time of an acceleration the exposure of each senior lender in the working capital facility including the ancillary facilities lender under the ancillary facilities are re-allocated among the lenders pro rata to their participation in the working capital facility.	No. The ancillary facilities lender keeps all yield and other payments under the ancillary facilities. The senior lenders under the revolving credit facility keep all interest under that part of the working capital facility.

Structure 1 is a purely bilateral ancillary facilities structure provided separately from the core senior facilities. Both risks and return are taken by the ancillary facilities lender alone. Structure 2 is the extreme alternative with a fully syndicated ancillary facilities structure as part of the core senior facilities. Risks and return are taken by all of the syndicate lenders. The ancillary facilities lender

---

47 Where one lender fronts the facilities for all of the syndicate lenders.
48 Usually in the region of 12.5 bps.

takes no risk or return other than the risk on the syndicate lenders not paying it under the relevant indemnity, for which it receives a fronting bank fee.

Structure 3 acknowledges that the ancillary facilities are really part of the core senior facilities package but the ancillary facilities lender acts less as a fronting bank for the syndicate and more simply as one of the syndicate lenders which happens to be providing part of its overall participation in the working capital facility by way of ancillary facilities.

Which structure is used in practice will depend on the preferred approach of the senior debt MLA that is responsible for the senior debt documentation. Structure 3 is the most common and is the approach adopted in the LMA[49] leveraged loan precedent.

Capex facilities

5.24   Capex facilities are of more than one type but typically will comprise a multi-advance term loan, which may be drawn down for specific capital expenditure purposes during a specified drawdown availability period of say two or three years. It will often be repayable in one or two instalments after the acquisition facility or, alternatively, it may be structured to amortise in line with the acquisition facility.[50] The senior lenders will generally wish to have greater control over the utilisation of a capex facility than the core senior facilities. This is because, in broad terms, capex facilities are commonly made available to finance future cashflow generation by the company, of which the banks will have less visibility than the existing cashflows supporting all of the core senior debt. In practice, specific conditions will often apply to the drawing of capex advances.

They fall into two main types. There are those that are designed to ensure that the additional debt is only used for the specified purposes agreed with the lenders. Secondly, there are conditions that only allow drawings if the target business is continuing to perform in line with the business plan. So for instance, they might include the following:

- the drawing must be for specified capital expenditure which has previously been approved by the senior lenders and which was not budgeted to be funded from cashflow;

- the amount drawn down will be applied for the specified purpose within a specified number of days or months of drawing;

- only a specified percentage of the proposed capital expenditure can be funded from drawings under the facility;

- the proposed capital expenditure has been approved unanimously by the board of directors of the borrower; and

- drawings may only be made if certain financial criteria are met – possibly that the target's performance is in line with or ahead of the agreed base case model .

49 Loan Market Association.
50 But see para **5.11**, in relation to senior debt structures that have no amortising debt. In that case a capex facility is more likely to be structured with a bullet repayment.

Further acquisition facilities

5.25   As with capex facilities the precise terms of a further acquisition facility are less standardised than the main acquisition facility. Usually they take the form of a multi-advance term facility that is available to finance permitted acquisitions during a specified availability period after completion of the initial acquisition. Once drawn outstanding advances will usually amortise in line with the core acquisition facility A note.[51]

Further acquisition facilities are typically subject to extensive drawdown controls. This reflects the concern of lenders that, inherently, the facility will be used to acquire companies or businesses of which the lender may be previously unaware. At one extreme a further acquisition facility may be subject to the same sort of conditionality, including extensive documentary CPs, as the core acquisition facility. From the borrower's perspective, however, it is really looking for committed funds that can be borrowed to finance an acquisition without the need for any approval of the debt syndicate. In practice, the drawdown conditions should strike a balance between the legitimate concerns of the lenders that the business to be acquired is sufficiently financially sound and the borrower's need for committed funds to effect its acquisition strategy. Typically the borrower will be required to provide due diligence materials to the lenders in respect of any business to be acquired and if the business is sufficiently large a revised business plan in respect of the enlarged group.

In addition, it is usual for there to be conditions relating to the financial status of the borrowing group when the acquisition is made, perhaps that current trading is in line with the business plan. As regards the additional business to be acquired, this must usually have positive EBITDA. In addition, it is a common requirement that following the identified acquisition and the borrowing made to fund it, the financial position of the enlarged group satisfies benchmark financial criteria. This will normally mean that the leverage ratio[52] is no greater than a pre-agreed level, which will either be the level required by the financial covenants or perhaps even a more stringent test. In practice it is common for a specific condition to be included that all of the financial covenants would be satisfied on a pro forma basis (assuming that the acquisition goes ahead) looking back over the last 12 months – the usual period for the testing of financial covenants – taking into account the EBITDA of the acquired business and the debt that would be incurred to acquire it.

In actual fact, where a further acquisition facility is to be included, the financial covenants should be documented from the outset so that they can adjust to take account of any additional business acquired. This will happen automatically to some extent under standard financial definitions because most financial covenant definitions operate on a consolidated basis taking into account all members of the group from time to time. Where this does not work is with the leverage test where the debt that is drawn to fund a further acquisition will be taken into account in full immediately but the benefit of the EBITDA of the acquired business will only begin to be included on a prospective basis. To deal with this

---

51 Although see para **5.11** in relation to senior debt structures that have no amortising facility. In that situation the further acquisition facility might be structured as a bullet facility.
52 The ratio of total debt (usually on a net basis) to EBITDA.

the EBITDA definition used in the covenants is adjusted artificially to incorporate the EBITDA of the acquired business from the period before it was acquired. This is often referred to as 'Pro forma EBITDA'.

An alternative to a further acquisition facility that is fully committed at the outset – usually for situations where the proposed acquisition is not certain to be completed or at this stage is merely speculative – is to have the facility fully documented but not committed. At the time the borrower wishes to utilise the facility it must obtain commitments from either the existing debt syndicate or (if negotiated with the MLA) third party lenders. Although this leaves the sponsor without the facility committed it means that the up-front fees can be deferred until the time when the commitments are actually required and should avoid the need for non-utilisation/commitment fees to accrue in the interim period, although that has not always been the case in practice. It also means that there are no waiver and amendment fees for subsequently putting the facility in place.

Clean-down clauses

5.26   A clean-down clause is typically included within a working capital facility. They are favoured by certain lenders as a mechanism to ensure that the working capital facility is used for working capital purposes only and not as long term capital.

Clean-down clauses operate by ensuring that the working capital facility is undrawn for one or more periods in each financial year. The periods most commonly used are of the order of 5 or 10 consecutive days in each half year or year. In practice, rather than require that the facility is undrawn during the clean-down period the provision may require that the average *net* working capital position is zero during such a period.[53] The length of the periods should, in theory at least, reflect the working capital profile of the business but more often than not they are determined on a simple negotiated basis.

The borrower will sometimes argue that clean-down clauses are impracticable given the unpredictability of working capital ebbs and flows, and cite the difficulty of agreeing in advance not to utilise the working capital facility at all for fixed periods during the financial year. The counter arguments advanced are that the business plan will be predicated on the basis that the business is cash generative, thus creating a cash buffer against an unpredictable working capital cycle, and only a lack of cash generation will require utilisation of the working capital facility at all times. It is for precisely this reason that such clauses are used, as they are intended to prevent utilisations of the working capital facility for the purposes of meeting payments of principal or interest on the core acquisition facilities or capital expenditure that should be being financed from the business itself. In addition, a working capital cycle would need to be particularly erratic for the borrower to be required to draw under the working capital facility during every period of 5 or 10 consecutive days during a financial year. The accountants' report will cover in some detail the working capital cycle and, in addition to the base case model, may be used to dispel arguments to the contrary.

---

53 That is, the amount of the working capital facility utilised at any time net of cash balances at such time is zero. Cash standing to the credit of a cash collateral account the proceeds of which are allocated to some purpose other than working capital, such as acquisition facilities prepayment, should not be taken into account.

Optional prepayment of the facilities

5.27 Optional prepayment clauses fall into two categories:

5.28 *Optional prepayment of one or more senior debt facilities* It is common for the agreement to provide that the borrower can prepay the facilities (pro rata each lender) in advance of the scheduled repayment dates subject to certain conditions, such as:

- prior notice – perhaps of 10, 20 or 30 days – is given to the lenders;

- prepayment must be on an interest payment date to avoid broken funding costs for the lenders – or on any other date together with broken funding costs;

- prepayment will be limited to a minimum amount and integral numbers above this amount;

- any prepayment will reduce all of the subsequent scheduled repayment instalments in a pre-agreed manner.[54]

5.29 *Optional prepayment of a single lender* Syndicated facilities agreements also provide that the borrower can prepay any *lender* – typically only on the basis that all amounts owing to the lender are prepaid – to which that borrower has become obliged to pay increased amounts under certain provisions of the agreement.[55] A trend in the London market during the mid 2000s has also been to include so-called 'yank-a-bank' clauses that allow a borrower to prepay or replace a lender that has not voted in favour of unanimous amendment or waiver requests from the borrower that the majority of lenders have voted for.

Mandatory prepayment of the facilities

5.30 There are a number of commonly used mandatory prepayment mechanisms that may be incorporated into the senior facilities agreement. The key ones are set out below.

Occurrence of a specified 'exit event'

5.31 Flotation, sale of the business and other changes of control are the most common exit events. If one of these circumstances occurs all facilities must be immediately prepaid in full.

In fact since the mid-2000s this has not necessarily been the case with respect to flotations. In some transactions, generally the larger ones, a flotation may not give rise to a mandatory prepayment event in respect of all of the facilities if there is no change of control as a result of the flotation. In other words a partial

---

54 See para **5.36**.
55 This will usually be due to any of: (i) the imposition of new or increased regulatory costs on the lender which it passes on to the borrower; (ii) because the lender can no longer receive interest from the borrower on a gross basis (typically due to the imposition of a withholding tax) so that a grossing-up payment needs to be made by the borrower; or possibly (but this tends to be negotiable) (iii) because a number of banks cannot fund themselves at the agreed underlying interest rate (LIBOR or EURIBOR typically), a so-called 'market disruption' event.

IPO may be permitted. Typically the proceeds of the partial IPO must still be applied in prepaying senior debt but there is no requirement to prepay *all* the facilities. In fact the provision will often be drafted so that only a proportion of the partial IPO proceeds is required to pay down debt and the borrower can keep some for its own general corporate purposes. This may operate like the excess cash sweep[56] so that as the total leverage ratio[57] of the group reduces to certain pre-agreed levels, so the proportion required to be applied in prepayment also reduces. So, for example, there may be two steps down from 50% to zero, in each case as the leverage ratio hits the pre-agreed levels.

Disposals of assets

5.32   Where assets of a certain minimum value are disposed of and the proceeds are not reapplied in the business within a certain period the unapplied proceeds must be used to pay down the facilities. There will be negotiated exceptions including as to types of assets and de minimis and threshold amounts.

Proceeds of claims

5.33   It is also standard for the senior facilities agreement to include a provision requiring the prepayment of the facilities from the proceeds of claims against the seller under the acquisition documents,[58] claims against professionals for inaccurate or flawed due diligence reports or professional advice and insurance claims. The clause will usually allow the proceeds of such claims to be used first in reducing the relevant liability, reinstating the relevant loss or replacing the relevant asset, or whatever gave rise to the relevant claim, before requiring the excess (if any) to be applied in prepaying the facilities.

Excess cash sweep

5.34–5.35   A cash sweep clause requires that a proportion of any surplus cash at the end of each financial year – determined by reference to the total cash inflow and total cash outflow during the financial year – will be applied in prepayment of the facilities. Typically, the amount of surplus cash at the end of the financial year will be certified by the auditors on the basis of the annual accounts. The proportion of surplus cash that must be applied in prepayment varies from 100% down to 25% and may reduce during the life of the facilities (ultimately to zero) often by reference to a reducing leverage multiple.[59] A threshold level may also apply such that a fixed amount of the surplus cash each year is retained in the business as a cash buffer.

Application of prepayments

5.36   How amounts required to be applied in prepayment are actually allocated to the outstanding senior debt will need to be carefully considered and standard market approaches have developed and continue to evolve.

56 See para **5.34**.
57 Total net debt to EBITDA.
58 Warranties, indemnities and the post-completion net asset adjustment are all possible sources.
59 Typically the ratio of total net debt to EBITDA.

As a general rule borrowers will prefer to pay down the most expensive debt first. Thus they might wish to repay junior debt before senior debt and the C note before the A note. This does not accord with the pre-agreed order of ranking of the facilities, however, and indeed is a key determinant of the pricing of the various layers and tranches of debt. So no amounts can be allocated to junior debt until all senior debt has been repaid. As between the various senior facilities themselves, the standard approach is for the acquisition facility to be repaid first and then the working capital facility. Within the acquisition facility A, B and C notes are often prepaid pro rata so that they reduce proportionately. Similarly the repayment instalments under the A note will often be reduced on a pro rata basis.[60]

The market continues to evolve in this regard, however, and sponsors may insist in having greater flexibility in how they apply prepayment amounts. This is especially the case in respect of voluntary prepayments where they may require the ability to apply prepayment amounts to the different facilities and instalments in whatever order they suggest. The position with mandatory prepayments tends to be less flexible.

Where the senior debt includes a B note and C note, and those tranches are syndicated to institutional investors in addition to acquisition finance banks, the prepayment provisions may give the tranche B and C lenders the right to refuse to be prepaid – other than a prepayment of all the facilities in full. This is so that the B and C lenders can continue to receive the full yield (interest) on tranches B and C in line with their investment criteria for longer term and stable 'cash generating' investments. Where that right is exercisable any amounts that would have gone to pay down facilities B and C would then normally go to prepay facility A or possibly to those B and C lenders that do accept the prepayment or even back to the borrower to be used in the business.

Where there are further acquisition or capex facilities the lenders may insist that these are prepaid before the core acquisition and working capital facilities or at least on a pro rata basis.

Cancellation

5.37   Cancellation as a concept only applies to facilities which have not been fully drawn down and remain available for further drawing. Thus, undrawn amounts under a working capital facility or a capex facility may be cancelled. Cancellation reduces the available amount of a facility and is done by borrowers to avoid paying non-utilisation fees on the undrawn amounts of the facility.[61] Similar administrative conditions will apply to cancellations as apply to optional prepayments of facilities, including as to notice and minimum amounts. Cancellation is permanent and facilities that are cancelled cannot be reinstated.

---

60 Prepayments could be applied in order of maturity (the next instalments first), in inverse order of maturity (the last instalment first) or pro rata (equally across all instalments). Lenders prefer inverse order of maturity since this shortens the overall maturity of the debt. Borrowers prefer order of maturity so that their immediate debt service obligations are reduced. But in practice the most commonly used approach has for years been the pro rata approach.
61 Non-utilisation fees are typically set at 50 or 75 bps or sometimes half the margin on the facility.

Margin ratchets

Margin

5.38   The return which the senior lenders make in respect of the senior debt package is represented by the margin over the underlying interest rate or, in the case of a guarantee/letter of credit facility, the guarantee fee. The size of the margin/guarantee fee is intended to reflect the credit risk associated with the business and in particular the nature of the facility.[62]

Margin ratchets

5.39   A standard requirement of borrowers is that if its financial status moves to a more favourable level during the life of the facilities – so that the credit risk for the lenders is deemed to be lower than it was at completion – then the margin will reduce to a lower level too. The mechanism which effects the change in the margin is called a margin ratchet.

For many years the margin ratchet only applied to the core acquisition loan (the A note) and the working capital facility. Institutional investors – who commonly make up a significant proportion of the B and C note syndicates – were initially very resistant to margin ratchets on those tranches, unlike the more flexible banking market. However, as the market has evolved and become both more sponsor (borrower) driven and more liquid – the vast liquidity in the institutional investor market in particular having a downward effect on pricing generally – so it has become quite standard for the ratchet to apply first also to the B note and then also to the C note, in addition to the A note and working capital facility. Margin ratchets typically provide for the margin to reduce, usually in two or more stages, to successively lower levels upon the group achieving successively better financial positions. However, margin ratchets also operate in both directions so that if the improved financial status is not maintained the margin will step back up.

The most common form of margin ratchet operates by reference to a leverage test.[63]

Margin levels

5.40   Typically, the margin ratchet has two or three stages below the headline margin applicable at completion. The reductions in the margin will usually be in the order of 0.25% per stage.[64]

---

62   In particular its maturity. See para **5.5** for a consideration of the typical margins applicable in a buy-out.

63   Usually total net debt to EBITDA, with EBITDA being for the most recent 12 months for which financial statements have been produced and total net debt being determined at the end of that period of 12 months.

64   So, for instance, where the headline margin for the A tranche of acquisition debt and the working capital facility are each set at 2.25%, the margin ratchet may operate to reduce the margin to 2.00% and then 1.75% and then possibly 1.50% or even 1.25%.

Ratchet conditions

5.41   The basic ratchet condition will be a measure of financial performance or financial status. As mentioned above, the most commonly used ratchet test is the ratio of total net debt to EBITDA ('total leverage').[65] Thus as total leverage decreases by certain agreed quanta so the margin steps down. The exact threshold level for the relevant ratio will usually be set by reference to market standard benchmarks which should also reflect a level of performance ahead of, or in line with, the business plan financial projections enshrined in the base case model.

In addition to the financial ratio itself there will almost invariably be further conditions that must be satisfied before the margin can reduce. In particular, it is typical for there to be a requirement that no default exists under the agreement at the time of any reduction. It is also standard that the first reduction is only made on the basis of a determination of the relevant ratio by reference to the group's first full annual *audited* accounts following completion. Historically the ratchet would only operate in a downward direction – that is, to reduce the margin – one step at a time, that is, one step per time the ratchet is tested.

Testing and applying the ratchet

5.42   The financial ratio at the core of the ratchet will be tested by reference to the consolidated accounts of the group. Often, as mentioned above, the first reduction in the margin must be tested by reference to the audited accounts for the first full year following completion. Subsequent reductions may be triggered from unaudited annual or, more often, quarterly management accounts.

Given that the key variable test is a financial ratio, the ratchet is effectively tested by delivery of the group's accounts to the senior lenders. However, the lenders will usually require that the change is only effected from the beginning of an interest period commencing after delivery. In this way, the margin will remain the same throughout whole interest periods relieving the senior agent of the task of calculating different interest rates during single interest periods. Alternatively – and this is now more common – the new interest rate simply takes effect a set number of days after receipt of the relevant accounts.[66]

Clawback

5.43   A margin ratchet may contain a clawback provision. This will provide that if the margin is reduced on the basis of unaudited management accounts and the subsequent annual audited accounts demonstrate that the management accounts were inaccurate and that the margin would not have been reduced had the audited accounts been used to test the relevant conditions, then the borrower has to pay to the lenders the difference between the amount of interest actually paid and the amount that should have been paid. By historical convention, and because the borrower is ultimately responsible for producing accurate accounts, such a provision would only be provided in favour of the lenders and not, where

---

65 Senior leverage (excluding any junior debt from 'total' debt) may also be used.
66 This might be of the order of five business days to allow the interest rate change to be notified to all the lenders before it takes effect.

the unaudited management accounts were too conservative and the margin should have reduced earlier, in favour of the borrower. Over time this approach has evolved, with clawbacks operating in both directions; although any payments due to the borrower are often netted off future interest payments rather than being rebated immediately.

Representations

5.44   The representations commonly found in a senior facilities agreement used in a buy-out will be more extensive than in a normal corporate facility agreement, although the two principal aims will be the same. First, representations are used to obtain information about the group, by making benchmark assumptions about the group that force the disclosure of material matters that do not conform to the assumptions. At the same time they allocate responsibility for the risk of adverse matters arising that do not conform to the assumptions and which were unknown at completion. Secondly, they can ultimately be used to obtain protection for the lenders by enabling the facilities to be accelerated if the assumptions prove to have been incorrect at the outset or, in some cases, subsequently. The assumptions relate to both the legal and factual status of the group, including the target business. In particular, the assumptions – in the form of representations – will confirm the legal, regulatory and commercial basis of the lenders' credit assessment of the transaction. Thus, there will be extensive representations relating to financial information, the business plan, the details of the target group and certain matters in respect of the acquisition.

Many of the representations are used to allocate risks in respect of defects, particularly hidden defects in the target group. This is done by having extensive representations in relation to the legal and commercial position of the target group, which will effectively oblige newco to carry out due diligence in relation to the target group so that it is able to make the representations. This principle also entrenches the basic assumption that the primary due diligence exercise is being carried out by newco rather than the acquisition financiers. It is common practice to qualify many of the warranties – particularly those that relate to the target business – with materiality thresholds so that only significant matters cause breach. Often this is done with a general 'material adverse effect' qualifier.[67]

Negotiation of the representations tends to centre around the qualifications rather than the representations themselves, which are now quite standard.[68] Much of this will relate to materiality, that is, what level of departure from the absolute representation would be permitted. From a lender's perspective the representations need to be tight enough so that they do in effect oblige the borrower to consider if it can give each of the representations as is; in other words, they must ensure that the borrower carries out the due diligence and reviews the due diligence reports in order to be able to confirm that there are no matters that would amount to a breach of the representations. With this in mind it is crucial that the representations apply to the target group.

67 That is, no breach will occur unless the effect is to have a 'material adverse effect' for the lenders. There are standard definitions for MAE (and material adverse change – MAC).

68 The Loan Market Association (LMA) leveraged loan precedent includes arguably the most market standard set of representations.

A distinction can be drawn between repeating representations and non-repeating representations. Repeating representations are made on the date of signing, on each utilisation request date, on each utilisation date and on every loan rollover date[69] during the life of the facilities and in some cases on certain other specific dates.[70] These representations tend to reflect core legal assumptions about the obligors and the finance documents. They are statements that should remain true throughout the life of the facilities and so can be assumed to be correct when repeated.

Non-repeating representations deal with matters that are required to be true initially but which might change over time. They tend to be factual in nature and form the core assumptions about the business that the lenders rely upon to make the facilities available. They dovetail with the ongoing undertakings given by the obligors in that the undertakings, which may have a lower default threshold reflecting the organic nature of businesses, are designed to ensure that the initial base assumptions about the business reflected in the representations remain true during the life of the facilities. The non-repeating representations dovetail further with the events of default, which provide the mechanism for the lenders to take remedial action if the assumed circumstances either prove to have been incorrect at the outset (breach of representation) or change by a material adverse degree during the life of the facilities (breach of undertaking).

The following list is illustrative of the representations which may be incorporated into the agreement. Heading–style summaries only are given in the majority of cases. An asterisk indicates a representation which will generally only be appropriate in a transaction with a non-UK dimension, including multi-jurisdictional buy-outs.

Repeating representations

5.45

- each group company is duly incorporated;

- corporate power and authority to execute and perform finance documents;

- obligations under finance documents legally binding;

- execution and performance of finance documents do not conflict with other obligations or constitutional documents;

- all authorisations required for performance of finance documents and their admissibility in court and for the conduct of the target business obtained and in full force and effect;

- no registration, notarial or filing fees, etc are payable in respect of any finance documents;

- choice of law in finance documents is valid and judgements enforceable in relevant jurisdictions;

---

69 That is, on the last day of each interest period of the loans, when the underlying cost of funds (LIBOR/EURIBOR) is re-set.

70 For instance, there might be repetition of certain information representations on the date on which primary syndication is completed, when the initial syndicate banks participate in the debt.

- no group company has immunity from legal proceeding;

- no insolvency proceedings commenced against any group company; and

- latest audited financial statements of the group true and accurate and possibly no material adverse change since such statements.

Non–repeating representations

5.46

- historic financial statements of the target group true and accurate and no material adverse change since such statements;

- in relation to the business plan, the various due diligence reports and the syndication information memorandum:[71]

  - full disclosure was made to the relevant consultants by the management team;

  - so far as the management team are aware, the facts contained in such information package are true, complete and accurate; and

  - all forecasts and projections contained in the business plan were arrived at after due and careful consideration and based on assumptions believed to be true;

- copies of all corporate and transaction documents provided – as conditions precedent – are true, complete and accurate;

- the seller's warranties in the acquisition agreement and the management team's warranties in the investment agreement (respectively) are true and accurate in all material respects and, possibly, that nothing material has been disclosed against them;[72]

- the given details of the SPV group and the target group are true and accurate;

- none of the SPVs has traded or incurred liabilities or owns any assets;

- none of the target companies has any financial indebtedness;

---

71 These documents will be particularly important for syndication and the representation is usually repeated on the syndication date. It is important for the MLA that the information memorandum is formally approved by the group, who must stand behind statements in it.

72 Borrowers often insist that the seller's acquisition disclosures (or the management's disclosures) can be disclosed against this representation. This should be resisted by the lenders. From a lenders' perspective, one of the key reasons for having this representation is that it forces the borrower (the sponsor and the management team) to review all of the seller's disclosures, ascertain what is material – particularly, in light of their greater knowledge of the business – and then disclose any specific matters that are not consistent with the representations. This reflects the principle that the burden of identifying material defects, and the risk of not identifying them, falls primarily on the borrower and not the lenders. The lenders will receive the due diligence reports and may even have access to the seller's data room but this should not override this principle. Therefore, specific disclosure should be accepted but general disclosures should not. See also para **5.47** regarding disclosure.

- none of the target companies has any security over its assets;

- there are no option agreements or restrictions on transfer in respect of the shares of any company;

- no withholding taxes are payable on amounts under the finance documents;*

- no litigation exists or is pending in respect of any group companies;

- intellectual property matters;

- environmental matters;

- pension matters, including that there are no defined benefit pension schemes and all schemes are fully funded;

- each group company has good title to the assets used in the business and legal and beneficial ownership of assets given as security;

- security given is first ranking;

- all outstanding taxes have been paid;

- no breach of laws by group companies;

- specifying the accounting reference date for all group companies;

- Centre of main interest (COMI) representation for purposes of applicable EU Council Regulation;*

- not necessary for the finance parties to be licensed to carry on business in any specific jurisdiction;*

- all UK and all material non-UK group companies are guarantors, subject to guarantor coverage test;[73] and

- there is no outstanding default under the finance documents or any material adverse effect.

Disclosure

5.47   To the extent that the borrower is unable to give any of the representations in their absolute terms, it may make disclosure against those representations either in a disclosure letter or, more commonly, by amending the relevant representation/warranty itself. Where the representations are qualified by materiality, however, it necessarily follows that significant matters only would need to be disclosed. With this in mind, the acquisition financiers should not accept general disclosures against the representations. Only very specific disclosures against specific representations would normally be acceptable. In this regard, it is not uncommon for borrowers to propose disclosing the contents of certain of

---

73 A guarantor coverage test requires that companies with a certain percentage of the group's assets, EBITDA and/or turnover are at all times guarantors. Typical percentages are between 70 and 90%. See also **Chapter 13**.

the due diligence reports against the representations on the basis that the reports will have been made available to the lenders. However, where the representations are qualified by materiality, disclosure of the entire contents of a report should be resisted by the financiers on the basis that the borrower should be forced to state precisely what is contained in the reports that amounts to a materially adverse matter. In other words, the responsibility for interpreting the due diligence – and assessing potential defects – is placed on the borrower (the sponsor and the management team). The financiers will argue that the borrower – and in particular the management team – will be in a much better position to do this given its greater knowledge of the business. Ultimately, the lenders should be able to assume that there is nothing in the due diligence that constitutes a material defect[74] unless it is expressly brought to their attention.

Information undertakings

5.48   One of the most important provisions for acquisition financiers is the clause requiring the supply of financial and other information to the lenders. This enables the lenders to monitor the ongoing financial performance of the business and in particular its performance against the business plan and base case model. In particular, the clause will require the regular delivery of financial statements, which are used to determine compliance with the financial covenants.[75]

Typically, a senior facilities agreement will contain the information undertakings set out below.

Preparation of financial statements

5.49   The borrower will be required to prepare consolidated financial statements for the group[76] and possibly divisional accounts for discrete divisions within the business or perhaps on some other sub-consolidated basis. The statements provided will include:

- annual audited financial statements; and
- unaudited management accounts for each month and usually each quarter.

Each set of statements or accounts should comprise:

- cashflow statement, profit and loss account and balance sheet;
- comparison against the budget and the corresponding period in previous years;
- possibly a cashflow forecast for the next three or six months;[77] and
- any other financial information which the lenders will specifically require.

---

74 Particularly if, as is common, the materiality qualifier is set at a standard 'material adverse effect' threshold.
75 See para **5.52** below.
76 For these purposes, the 'group' means the entire credit group including the acquired group and all SPV obligors.
77 This will be required, for instance, where the equity yield payment conditions (if applicable) include a look-forward test (see **Chapter 10**).

Delivery of financial information

5.50   The group's obligation to provide financial information to the lenders should include the following items:

- the annual audited statements will typically be required to be delivered no later than 120 days after the end of the financial year to which they relate;

- the management accounts will typically be required to be delivered within 30 days (for monthly accounts) or 45 days (for quarterly accounts) after the end of the relevant month or quarter;

- in respect of each quarter at the end of which the financial covenants are to be tested, the lenders will require topco to provide a director's compliance certificate confirming that the group is in compliance with the financial covenants;

- at the time of delivery of the annual audited financial statements the lenders will require that the group's auditors provide a form of confirmation that the group is in compliance with the financial covenants or, at the least, a confirmation that the numbers used in the director's covenant compliance certificate have been extracted properly from the accounts and the calculation performed correctly;

- an annual budget will be required, usually no later than a month before the beginning of each financial year although this may be negotiated to say 30 days *after* the start of the financial year;

- where the acquisition agreement includes a purchase price adjustment mechanism – usually based on the net assets at completion – newco will need to supply the completion accounts; and

- it is also usual to require the delivery of any other information or reports and notices issued by the group to its shareholders and creditors generally.

Delivery of further information

5.51   In addition to the financial information specified above it is also standard to require the group to provide the following additional information:

- notice of defaults or material adverse events;

- notice of any litigation, environmental claims and disputes under the transaction documents; and

- any information required for the lenders' know-your-customer purposes

Financial covenants

5.52   Acquisition financiers – and senior debt providers in particular – place particular importance on financial covenants. They operate as an obligation on the group to maintain certain financial performance ratios throughout the life of the facilities; failure to meet the required ratios gives rise to a default. The principal aim of the financial covenants is to enable the lenders to monitor the performance of the target business against the business plan and base case projections and to bring the borrower back to the table to restructure the deal if there is significant underperformance against plan. Ultimately the lenders can accelerate the facilities if the business deteriorates sufficiently and they do not believe that a consensual restructuring will provide a solution.

Given that the financial covenants are used to benchmark the financial performance of the group against the business plan, they are drafted to reflect the construction of the underlying base case model. In other words, when a particular financial term is referenced – such as EBITDA – the defined term used in the financial ratios should mirror the construction of that item in the model.

Typical covenant package

5.53   The most commonly used suite of financial covenants in a buy-out transaction will be financial ratios in respect of interest cover, leverage, cash cover[78] and a limit on capital expenditure. These ratios, and certain less frequently used ones, are considered in the following paragraphs.

Interest cover

5.54   An interest cover covenant will usually be expressed as an undertaking to maintain a minimum ratio of earnings before interest, tax, depreciation and amortisation (EBITDA) to interest costs. EBITDA will usually be defined to exclude non-recurring items, including exceptional and extraordinary items that arise under UK GAAP.[79] The interest costs component will principally comprise the interest payable in respect of the acquisition finance facilities, adjusted to take into account any payments required to be made pursuant to any interest rate hedging agreements taken out. It will also include the 'interest' element of finance leases, since finance leases are generally treated as senior debt for the purposes of the financial ratios. The PIK element of any junior debt may be excluded but this is a function of how the base case model is constructed. Similarly, whether or not the interest costs figure is net of interest receivable by the group (on cash balances) depends on how the ratio is expressed in the base case. Interest should be determined on an accruals basis rather than a cash basis. In other words, interest accruing over the relevant period – provided that it is actually payable – is determined, not interest actually *paid* in the period. This is because a flat 12-month figure is required, whereas the actual interest payment dates can be varied by the borrower resulting in a significant interest payment falling outside the 12-month period. This could distort the intended level of compliance.

Compliance with the covenant will require the maintenance of a specified minimum ratio of EBITDA to interest costs that will increase over time in line with the projected EBITDA increase in the base case and the interest cost reduction as debt is repaid. The covenant will be tested on a 12-month basis looking backwards from the relevant test dates,[80] usually at quarterly periods starting per-

---

78   The cash coverage ratio is also called the 'fixed charge' or 'debt service' cover ratio.
79   UK GAAP will generally be defined to reference International Financial Reporting Standards (IFRS).
80   Also called a 'last twelve months' (LTM) basis

haps six or nine months after completion. The first periods – each starting on the completion date, when the target is acquired – will be for less than 12 months, and in seasonal businesses this may produce a distorted ratio.[81] Once a full 12-month period has passed after completion the covenants will each be tested for the full 12-month period, thus removing the impact of any seasonality. The covenant is tested on each quarter date by reference to the financial statements delivered in respect of the period up to such quarter date.

Interest cover covenants are perceived as a reliable indicator of current financial performance and an early warning sign of a downturn in the business. Part of the reason for this is that they are difficult to manipulate by the group. The required ratio levels will be set to provide an agreed amount of 'headroom' against the agreed base case model.[82] This allows for a certain amount of under-performance before breach, but not so much that by the time the covenant is breached it is too late for the lenders to undertake a financial restructuring and avert a complete financial meltdown.

Where there are different layers of acquisition finance the interest cover covenant may be subdivided into a senior interest cover covenant and a total interest cover covenant. The senior interest cover covenant would incorporate interest on the senior debt and the interest element of finance leases, being the priority interest obligations of the business. Total interest cover would also include the cash-pay element of any junior debt. One rationale of having two measures of interest cover is to have a bottom-line indicator of financial performance in the circumstances where only the senior interest is payable as a result of the operation of payment blockage mechanisms in respect of the junior debt.[83] It also enables the financial performance to be benchmarked against standard senior-only interest cover ratios.

Leverage covenant

5.55   The leverage covenant is typically expressed as a requirement to maintain the ratio of debt to EBITDA below a pre-agreed level, which will reduce over time, as earnings in the group are projected to increase and debt is repaid.

As with interest cover, the leverage covenant will be tested on a historic rolling 12-month basis at quarterly intervals following completion. The debt component is determined on the last day of each relevant 12-month period for which EBITDA is determined. A slight difference from interest cover results from the fact that the debt component of the leverage ratio is not a periodic variable but a snap shot amount taken on a particular date, the last day of the period being tested. This means that until at least 12 months have passed from completion the ratio will compare the full amount of debt against EBITDA for a period

81 See para **5.55** below for adjustments that may be made to covenants in the case of seasonal businesses.

82 Headroom was historically in the range of 10–20%, although as the acquisition finance market has heated up during the 2000s as much as 25–30% can be agreed, with 25% being common, at least prior to the 2007/2008 liquidity crisis. See also the discussion on 'covenant-lite' documentation in para **5.64** and financial covenant headroom as applied in mezzanine loan agreements in **Chapter 7**.

83 The intercreditor arrangements between the senior lenders and junior creditors will include a provision enabling the senior lenders to block payments of junior debt interest in certain circumstances; including in particular, where there is a financial default. See **Chapter 10**.

of less than 12 months.[84] This can produce a leverage ratio that is *apparently* very high when compared with industry benchmarks based on a full 12-month period for EBITDA and optically the parties may prefer to present the test – the required ratio for the initial period of less than 12 months – as falling within market norms. This is most often effected by annualising the EBITDA number. In non-seasonal businesses this can be done on a simple 'straight-line' basis but with seasonal businesses it may be necessary to add specific EBITDA amounts, perhaps taken from the period before completion, to the post-completion numbers.

If both components of a financial ratio are periodic, as with the interest cover and cash cover ratios, a testing period of less than 12 months will only produce a distorted result in a truly seasonal business, where a full 12-month period will be required to mitigate the effect of seasonal EBITDA. In non-seasonal businesses the ratio can remain properly calibrated with market norms, even for periods of less than one year. For seasonal businesses it is common to adjust the EBITDA for the initial periods of less than 12 months by adding pre-completion EBITDA numbers and annualising the ratio.

In common with interest cover, leverage will often be subdivided into total leverage and senior leverage. Senior debt will comprise the senior debt package and possibly also the capital element of finance leases used by the business, as these will be viewed as priority or core finance of the business. The total debt element of total leverage will also include the junior debt and any other long-term debt in the business, usually with the exception of the subordinated loan capital provided as part of the equity package. Debt that forms part of the 'equity' package is not included on the basis of its deep subordination to the acquisition finance. Similarly, PIK notes may not be included in total debt on the basis that there are no debt service requirements during the life of the core acquisition finance.[85] The PIK element of any mezzanine debt may also be excluded on the same basis.[86]

The debt element of a leverage covenant, whether senior or total debt, is generally determined on a *net* basis. That is, the credit balances of the group with banks will be netted off the total or senior debt figure for the purposes of determining covenant compliance. The rationale here is that cash balances are ultimately available to repay debt and it is only a timing issue – of cash being built up during the business cycle before being applied in meeting scheduled repayments of debt usually every six months – that has not registered the reduction in debt already. It follows therefore that only cash that is freely available to repay debt should be taken into account. The provision may also be drafted so that only net balances held by obligors with syndicate banks are taken into account on the

---

84 As mentioned earlier, financial ratios generally only use figures from the date of completion of the acquisition and not before.

85 And also, for optical reasons, by excluding this category of debt from the covenant calculations the actual covenant numbers will be lower. This may have benefits in syndication since the overall leverage can then – apparently – remain within market acceptable parameters for structures without PIK note debt. In any event, the covenant should reflect the manner in which the ratio is determined under the base case model.

86 Note that with mezzanine debt, it is quite common for the sponsor to seek a 'toggle' feature that can enable the borrower to switch between cash and PIK interest. See para **7.4**.

basis that this cash will be part of the security package and thus directly available to pay down debt in all circumstances.

Leverage ratio covenants are good indicators of the general creditworthiness of a buy-out business at a particular moment in time. They are particularly liked by lenders because the leverage multiple is one of the benchmark financial criteria that lenders – and financial sponsors – look at when assessing how much debt can be incorporated into a funding structure in the first place. As such, it is an important part of the jargon and currency of buy-out structuring analysis. By having a covenant that shows a reducing leverage multiple following completion, the acquisition financiers and financial sponsor can directly monitor this key criterion throughout the life of the buy-out. The amount of headroom to the base case will be set at a similar level to that used for interest cover.[87]

Leverage ratios are also commonly used as the trigger-point test for margin reductions pursuant to a margin ratchet,[88] for reduction of the applicable percentage of prepayment from surplus cash used in excess cash sweep provisions,[89] possibly the applicable percentage of prepayment from partial IPO proceeds[90] and possibly to allow payments to the equity investors. Their importance to senior debt documentation generally is significant.

Cashflow cover covenant

5.56 The cashflow or fixed charge cover covenant will be expressed as a requirement that the ratio of operating cash inflow to financing cash outflow – or fixed charges[91] – is not less than a certain multiple of one. In practice it is usually set as a ratio of not less than one to one.[92] Operating cash inflow will principally comprise EBITDA but will also take into account working capital movements and capital expenditure and certain other adjustments. Collectively, the adjustments to EBITDA have the effect of converting the accounting concept of earnings – EBITDA – into the actual cash concept of cashflow. Financing cash outflow or fixed charges will comprise total interest cost, determined on the same basis as for the total interest cover covenant,[93] the principal amounts of the acquisition finance repaid or prepaid, any equity payments made (if any) and any other financing costs not otherwise included – including the capital element of finance leases.

The other principal cash outflow items of a business, its supplier costs and other business expenses and its capital expenditure are incorporated, as deductions, into the operating cash inflow calculation either in determining EBITDA in the first place or as a deduction to derive cashflow.

This covenant is used to ensure that the cash generated by the business is sufficient to meet the financing costs inherent in the funding structure and any other fixed charges of the business such as finance lease costs.

---

87 See para **5.54** and fn **82**.
88 See para **5.41**.
89 See para **5.34**.
90 See para **5.31**.
91 Fixed changes may also be expressed as 'debt service'.
92 Although the covenant is typically set at a level of one to one there may be deal specific circumstances where the test is set at a slightly lower level for specific periods or even at a higher level to ensure that a positive performance buffer is maintained.
93 See para **5.54**.

As with the interest cover and leverage covenants, the cashflow cover covenant will most likely be tested quarterly on a historic rolling 12–month basis.

Capital expenditure

5.57   The capital expenditure covenant is an obligation, applicable to the group, not to incur capital expenditure in any financial year in excess of the budgeted figure or within an agreed percentage above the budgeted figure. Headroom of, say, 10–15% is not uncommon. The budgeted number for each year may be pre-agreed at the outset or less frequently the lenders may permit the borrower to set it each year. In deals that contemplate further acquisitions – such as with a 'buy and build' business plan – the budget for capital expenditure may be automatically scaleable as acquisitions are made so that amendments are not required to the covenant.

Generally, the capital expenditure covenant will permit unused budgeted capital expenditure from one financial year to be carried over to the next financial year, but possibly not to a subsequent year, usually with a limit of, say, 25% or 50% to be carried over in any one year. This has also evolved, in some cases, to allow the group to use up a portion of the following year's capital expenditure budget in the current year. The rationale for allowing unused capex budget to be rolled from one year to the next is to accommodate timing movements for significant capital expenditure items, and it would be rare for this to be necessary for more than one year.

As far as testing is concerned, the capital expenditure covenant will typically be tested annually, on the basis of the accounts for each financial year.

Other financial covenants

5.58   The preceding covenants make up the covenant package used in most buy-outs. The following covenants may also be used but less frequently.

Net worth covenant

5.59   Typically this will be a requirement that the consolidated tangible net worth of the group is no less than a specified amount during specified periods going forward from completion.[94]

Tangible net worth[95] is essentially a balance sheet covenant which will be determined by reference to the capital base of topco on a consolidated basis so that it represents the entire group.

The tangible net worth covenant is nominally an 'all–times' test, in that it will apply at all times during the given period. However, it will only be tested upon the delivery of relevant financial statements usually on a quarterly or possibly monthly basis.

Net worth covenants are used as a backstop test against a material loss in value of the group. Having been popular in the early 1990s they are now rarely used in buy-outs.

---

94   On an increasing basis to reflect the growth projected in the business plan.
95   The covenant may also be referred to as an adjusted net worth covenant.

Gearing covenant

5.60　A gearing covenant is a measure of the total borrowings of the group to the tangible net worth of the group and, as with the net worth covenant, is nominally measured on an all–times basis but usually tested quarterly or possibly monthly.

Gearing covenants are not commonly used in acquisition finance documentation and the leverage ratio covenant is seen as a better benchmark test in respect of the borrowing levels of a group.

Loan to value covenant

5.61　Where the target business is a property development or investment business whose principal assets are real property it is common to include a loan to value (LTV) covenant as one of the key financial covenants. This covenant measures the ratio of total debt to the value of the property portfolio and will typically require that the value of the properties exceeds total debt by a pre-agreed amount of headroom.

With such a covenant the senior lenders should require that the properties are revalued by an independent valuer on a regular basis or upon the reasonable request of the senior lenders.

Compliance certificates

5.62　In order to test the financial covenants, the lenders will require delivery of the financial statements for the relevant accounting period.[96] In addition, with each set of quarterly management accounts, topco will be required to provide a certification by the finance director, or other suitably authorised director, that the group is in compliance with the financial covenants. The certificate will set out the various components of each of the covenants, together with the relevant figures extracted from the financial statements and demonstrate compliance with the required ratio or test. Once the annual accounts have been audited the lenders will require that the auditors deliver to them an auditors' report confirming that the year-end directors' compliance certificate for that financial year was correct or, as an alternative that the auditors may insist on, that the relevant financial figures have been properly extracted from the annual accounts and the calculations performed correctly.

Equity cure rights

5.63　The effect of a breach of financial covenant is the occurrence of an event of default. This entitles the senior lenders to accelerate the facilities and enforce the security. Whilst no grace period typically applies to a breach of financial covenant, two market developments in the mid-2000s have weakened the lender's ability to trigger an immediate event of default upon a breach of financial covenant occurring. The most significant of these is a provision that enables the sponsor to put additional equity – including subordinated shareholder loans – into the capital structure in order to cure a financial covenant breach that has occurred or would otherwise occur. These provisions are called equity cure

---

96　These will typically be unaudited quarterly management accounts, although the audited annual accounts will also be used to re-test the covenants at the end of each financial year for the full financial year.

rights. By paying in more equity, the equity investor is providing a cash injection to counter a financial early warning sign.

The precise scope of the right to cure financial covenant breach in this way is usually subject to detailed negotiation. In particular, depending on which financial covenant is breached, the treatment of that cash injection needs careful consideration. A breach of the interest cover covenant generally requires the cash injection to be counted as EBITDA. The alternative to increasing EBITDA – reducing interest cost through a retrospective repayment of debt – is less direct and would require a greater cash injection to effect the necessary remedy. The sponsor and lenders can simply take polar opposite views on this but the increase to EBITDA is arguably more proportionate for the breach, given the significantly greater cash injection required to reduce interest cost than to increase EBITDA. A breach of the cash cover covenant is relatively straightforward in that the cash injection can simply be counted as additional cashflow in order to cure the breach. Since the test is usually a 1:1 ratio the amount of cash injected has a direct and proportionate effect on the calculation. Leverage covenants are less straightforward. The lenders will argue that, logically, a leverage covenant breach must be cured by paying down debt. The sponsor on the other hand will say that the cash shortfall that led to the breach was in the generation of EBITDA and if that can be plugged the covenant is cured. This is of significant practical importance give the multiplier effect of applying the cash injection to the EBITDA side of the ratio rather than the debt side. A further area for discussion arises where, as is commonly the case, the leverage test is a *net* test. Technically, the additional equity need only hit the balance sheet to reduce the net debt position; it doesn't need to be actually applied in repaying debt.

Whatever is agreed on the mechanics of the cure provision, the sponsor does not usually have an unlimited right to invoke an equity cure provision. For instance, it is not uncommon for the right to be exercisable, say, only once in every four successive tests (ie, once in every four quarters) or perhaps less frequently, such as not more than twice in the life of the facilities. There may also be a time limit within which the additional equity must be injected after breach occurs, although most clauses will also allow the additional equity to be injected before the breach occurs. Some narrower versions of the provision may even insist that the additional equity comes in before the breach occurs. Lenders will also usually insist that the equity invested to cure the breach can not subsequently be extracted until the business has moved to a significantly healthier footing or perhaps not at all until the debt has been repaid.

A further development which is less popular with lenders is a so-called 'mulligan' clause.[97] Under this provision the first financial covenant breach does not give rise to an event of default and only a subsequent breach – or in more extreme versions only a second successive breach at any time – would give rise to an event of default.

In addition to these provisions, it is common for the loan documentation to stipulate that if a particular financial covenant is breached on one test date and the same covenant is subsequently passed on the following test date the initial breach is deemed cured.

---

97 Named after the colloquial golfing term!

'Covenant-lite' documentation

5.64 As should be relatively evident from other paragraphs in this section, many of the developments in senior debt documentation during the 2000s have been borrower – or sponsor – driven. Many are attempts to introduce increasing amounts of flexibility or 'wriggle room' into the documentation – basically to reduce the scope for defaults arising during the life of the facilities. Nearly all are a direct result of the increased liquidity available in the debt markets which has given sponsors much more leeway to insist on borrower-friendly provisions. Without doubt the most significant development of this kind, which started appearing in the second half of the 2000s, is the use of so-called 'covenant-lite' documentation which, like many of the European market's developments, originated in the United States. In a fundamental move away from one of the core provisions of standard acquisition finance documentation, true covenant-lite documents do not incorporate any financial covenants at all. In addition, they include incurrence-based negative covenants[98] which seek to control the borrower and any 'restricted subsidiary' activity and will only bite when certain corporate actions are undertaken, such as when debt is incurred or dividends paid. In the European market, true covenant-lite deals are relatively rare; the European model tends to be 'semi-lite' or 'hybrid covenant-lite' or 'covenant-loose' in that these deals preserve maintenance covenants[99] but retain only one financial covenant, in the form of a leverage ratio.[100]

Some commentators have conjectured that covenant-lite documentation is not a permanent development but merely reflects prevailing market conditions. This suggests that as the debt markets cool down it will prove to be the high water mark of sponsor superiority.[101]

General undertakings

5.65 The general undertakings in a senior facilities agreement will be more extensive than those used in a normal corporate loan agreement and will reflect the greater control which the senior lenders will wish to have in respect of the group given the highly leveraged nature of buy–out funding structures. The main aim of the general undertakings is to ensure that the business remains on the same or no worse a legal and commercial footing as it was on at completion, as confirmed by the documentary conditions precedent delivered prior to completion and the initial representations considered above. In other words the undertakings attempt to preserve the initial creditworthiness of the business as originally assumed by the lenders.

The general undertakings will take the form of positive and negative undertakings that apply to each member of the group or at least each material company in the group. Compliance with the undertakings will need to be maintained at all times. Indeed they are often described as 'maintenance covenants' to differentiate them

---

98 See para **3.60**.
99 See para **3.60**.
100 See para **5.55**.
101 Indeed the global liquidity crisis that began in summer 2007 has had the effect of removing covenant-lite documentation from the market. At the time of writing it remains to be seen if it will return in 2008 or 2009.

from 'incurrence covenants' as would be found in a high yield bond indenture.[102] The positive undertakings oblige the group companies to positively take action to maintain the creditworthiness of the business. The negative undertakings oblige the companies not to do certain things for these reasons. There will also be a small number of one-off undertakings to perform after completion, generally referred to as conditions subsequent. The conditions subsequent are usually matters relating to the completion of the buy-out and its funding which were not able to be done prior to completion.

Undertakings

5.66   The following list is illustrative of the general undertakings which may be incorporated in to the agreement.[103] The LMA leveraged loan precedent also includes a market standard suite of general undertakings. As a general rule, matters that are adequately covered by a repeating representation need not also be the subject of an undertaking.

In each case the undertakings will be subject to a certain amount of negotiation. Typically there are three main areas of negotiation: materiality – that is, the degree of non-compliance required for breach; applicability to non-material companies; and, in respect of the negative undertakings in particular, permitted exceptions.

Positive undertakings

5.67

- compliance with laws;
- filing and payment of taxes;
- maintain pensions on fully funded basis;
- maintain adequate insurance;
- comply with environmental laws and regulations;
- maintain intellectual property and not infringe third-party rights;
- maintain proper accounts and records;
- grant access to books and records to the lenders and their agents;
- pari passu ranking;
- SPVs not to trade or own assets or incur liabilities;
- maintain all bank accounts with the lenders or acceptable third party banks;
- cash management to ensure cash remains with obligors;
- perform, not waive/amend, to enforce and take action under the transaction documents including the acquisition agreement;
- perform, not waive/amend, to enforce and take action under all material contracts;
- replace leaving senior management and enforce service contracts;
- guarantor coverage;

---

102 See **Chapter 8** in relation to high yield bond covenants.
103 Heading summaries only are given in most cases. The full provision will be extensive in each case.

- security granted in accordance with the agreed security principles; and
- further assurance.

Negative undertakings

5.68

- security interests (negative pledge);
- sale and leasebacks or other recourse sale;
- financial indebtedness;
- guarantees;
- treasury transactions and hedging;
- loans or credit;
- other banking transactions;
- disposals;
- transactions with affiliates;
- mergers;
- joint ventures;
- acquisitions and investments;
- increase in capital;
- reduction of capital;
- distributions;
- payments under junior debt and equity instruments;
- payments of director and similar fees;
- amendments or waivers under transaction documents;
- amendment of constitutional documents;
- changes to accounting policies, accounting reference date or auditors;
- change in business; and
- possibly specific ring-fencing undertaking.

A number of the negative undertakings are used to 'ring-fence' the group's valuable assets within the obligors, since these are the companies against whom the lenders have direct recourse. For instance, there will be restrictions on the making of loans or granting of guarantees or the disposal of assets by obligors to non-obligors. Alternatively, or in addition, a specific 'ring-fence' covenant may be included for the same purposes.

Conditions subsequent

5.69   The conditions subsequent are important conditions of the acquisition finance which either cannot be satisfied prior to completion, usually because there is not enough time, or which by convention are to be satisfied within a period after completion. The items that commonly fall within this category include those in the following paragraphs.

Keyman insurance

5.70 Where the success of the target business is particularly dependant on its management,[104] the acquisition financiers will often require that keyman insurance is put in place in respect of the most important members of the management team. Keyman insurance provides the company with a fixed sum of money with which to find a suitable replacement should a specified member of the management team die or be incapacitated. The condition subsequent will normally be that the keyman insurance policy is in place within a fixed number of days following completion.[105]

Hedging

5.71 The acquisition financiers will almost invariably require that interest payments due on some or all of the core acquisition finance debt – that is the senior debt and any second lien and mezzanine debt[106] – are hedged, usually by means of an interest rate swap. The requirement to hedge interest payments on the core term debt may be for a period of, say, three, four, or five years following completion and will typically apply to a specified percentage of the core term debt, such as two-thirds or 75%. Different requirements may be imposed in respect of the senior debt and any second lien and mezzanine debt. It is common for the headline terms of the hedging to be agreed in a side letter at completion – a hedging strategy letter – but for the actual hedging documentation to be agreed and executed as a condition subsequent within, say, 30, 60 or 90 days after completion.[107] Sponsors will often require that any hedging proposal put forward by the lead arranger of the senior debt – which will be in pole position to take on the hedging counterparty role, given that the hedging strategy will be agreed before syndication of the debt – must be benchmarked to market before formally awarding the hedging mandate, and a provision to this effect may be included in the hedging strategy letter.

Assistance with syndication

5.72 Where the senior debt is to be syndicated, the senior facilities agreement will include as standard a requirement that topco assists with the syndication process. Two specific tasks are often expressly referred to. First, topco will agreeto give a representation in the information memorandum that the information in it is accurate and complete and the projections based on reasonable

---

104 Which is generally only the case in true MBOs of businesses that may not have reached full maturity.
105 This would normally be no more than 30 days.
106 High yield debt typically carries a fixed coupon so no interest rate hedging is required for that form of junior debt. PIK note debt has no cash element so there are no payments to hedge.
107 The fact that hedging documentation is standardised, in the form of ISDA standard form documents, assists this process and effectively removes any risk of disagreement over the legal terms of the hedging.

assumptions.[108] Secondly, topco will agree that the management team will make themselves available for the purposes of presentations to potential syndicate members as part of the syndication process.

Auditors

5.73   Topco may not have appointed new auditors for the group by completion, on the basis that it is asking several firms of accountants to bid for the audit work. If so it will be a requirement that the auditors are appointed within a fixed period of, say, 30 days, following completion.

Deal specific conditions

5.74   In any given buy-out further conditions may be imposed by the acquisition financiers as a result of the due diligence process. These may include a requirement to have a further (Phase II) environmental audit carried out, a requirement to have a new IT system put in place and so on. Such items are generally dealt with by way of conditions subsequent.

From the outset of the UK buy-out market one fundamental requirement of acquisition financiers has been that target group guarantees and security are provided as a condition precedent to funding.[109] Nonetheless, deal sponsors eager to get a competitive advantage with sellers by agreeing to very short timeframes within which to complete an acquisition often request that the acquisition financiers defer the taking of security for a period after completion. Traditionally acquisition financiers have strongly resisted this approach. Deals have been known to turn sour quite quickly following completion and if the security is not in place and insolvency occurs soon after completion the senior lenders may find themselves unsecured, structurally subordinated to the trade and other creditors in the target group and unable to take enforceable guarantees and security because of the insolvency of the group. With the rise of auctions and shorter documentation timetables during the 2000s, however, lenders have been forced to accept that target group security may only be granted as a condition subsequent rather than a condition precedent to funding.

Events of default

5.75   The events of default in the senior facilities agreement will be more extensive than would be found in a corporate loan agreement, reflecting the highly levered nature of buy-outs and thus the greater need for tight controls on the activities of the group.

The followings events of default may typically be included in a senior facilities agreement.[110] The LMA leveraged loan precedent also includes a market standard set of events of default.

---

108 The precise form of the representation is likely to mirror the representation in the senior facilities agreement itself, which confirms the accuracy and completeness of the information package to be given to prospective syndicate banks and the reasonableness of the assumptions underlying the business plan. See para **5.46** above.

109 There is an exception to this rule for public-to-privates, where this may not be legally possible. See **Chapter 12**.

110 Again heading-style summaries only are given. The actual provisions will be detailed.

- non–payment;

- breach of material undertakings – such as financial covenants, failure to deliver financial statements, restrictions on equity payments and other specified breaches;

- breach of any other undertakings or obligations;

- breach of representation;

- cross–default;[111]

- insolvency and insolvency events – insolvency, administration, compositions and schemes of arrangement, receivership, enforcement of security, winding up and dissolution;[112]

- creditors' process;

- cessation of business;

- change of ownership of obligors;

- seizure or nationalisation of business;

- unlawfulness or invalidity in respect of the acquisition finance documents;

- repudiation of the acquisition finance documents;

- qualification of the accounts;

- loss of members of the management team;

- material adverse change;

- pensions event;

- occurrence of material environmental matter;

- occurrence of material litigation;

- loss of material contracts; and

- other deal-specific matters.

Many of the events of default specified above will be subject to some level of negotiation, including the length of any grace periods that are to apply, materiality and other conditions which must be satisfied before the basic circumstance becomes a full event of default and whether the insolvency events apply to more than just obligors.

---

111 Much is made of cross-default events of default in bank loan agreements generally. However, in the context of an acquisition finance transaction where the control on external borrowings is very tight there may well not be external borrowings which can be in default to trigger an event of default under the cross-default provision.

112 Where the business has operations outside the United Kingdom, an 'analogous proceedings' provision will be included to extend the categories of insolvency event to non-UK equivalents.

Clean-up period

5.76   With public-to-private transactions, the opportunity for newco to carry out full due diligence into the target business will be more limited than it would be for a private buy-out.[113] Newco will have concerns that there may be hidden matters that might result in a breach of the representations and undertakings and give rise to an event of default. With this in mind acquisition financiers generally agree to give newco a clean-up period after completion to carry out full due diligence on the target and ensure that any hidden problems are dealt with. During the clean-up period many of the representations, undertakings and events of default are disapplied in respect of the target group, subject to certain conditions. Typically the conditions require that the relevant matter that would otherwise give rise to a breach or event of default is not too material, is capable of remedy and was not procured by newco. It is also a matter of negotiation as to which representations, undertakings and events of default continue to apply to the target group during the clean-up period. At the end of the clean-up period all of the representations, undertakings and events of default will apply to the target group so that any problems will need to have been remedied.

During the mid-2000s deal sponsors started asking for clean-up periods even on private buy-outs. Their principal argument being that the aggressive completion time frames set by sellers did not allow for sufficiently detailed due diligence to be carried out on all aspects of the target business. They also point to the fact that in many large multi-jurisdictional buy-outs the level of control exercised by senior management over certain group companies may be limited, meaning that the management involved in doing the deal would not be able to sign-off on all required representations and undertakings for every target company.

Transfer provisions

5.77   The starting point for any acquisition financier is that it will want as much flexibility as possible to transfer its participation in the senior debt. This means being able to freely transfer the debt to any other bank, financial institution or other entity engaged in or established for the purpose of investing in loans and financial assets. The reference to other entities and not just banks and financial institutions is necessary so that the debt can be transferred to institutional investment vehicles such as CLOs and other leveraged loan funds. Since the mid-2000s such institutional investors have accounted for an increasingly large share of both the primary and secondary leveraged loan markets.

Deal sponsors on the other hand have become increasingly concerned as to who owns the debt on their deals. There is a fear that hedge funds and vulture funds[114] might be less supportive in a restructuring scenario than the traditional banking market. Sponsors also like to maintain relationships with a number of banks and to invite them into their deals as part of the syndication process. For primary syndication it is customary for the deal sponsor and the MLA to agree a syndication strategy. This often includes agreeing a prospective list of syndicate

---

113 See **Chapter 12** generally on public-to-privates.
114 A vulture fund is a fund established with the primary objective of investing in distressed businesses.

banks and institutional debt investors. This should provide the sponsor with sufficient input in, if not full control over, the primary syndication process.

As for secondary loan trading the respective concerns of the senior debt market on the one hand and deal sponsors on the other are less easily reconciled. Even the strongest sponsors are unlikely to be able to get a full veto over who the debt is transferred to as a matter of course. Some may get a consent right, subject to such consent not being unreasonably withheld. Equally the banking market will not often achieve total flexibility. A standard position is for there to be a requirement of consultation with topco by the transferring bank before any transfer of the debt is effected. This may be couched so that topco's failure to object to a proposed transfer within a number of days of being notified is sufficient to permit the transfer. Any objection would then require consultation, but, as indicated above, would rarely amount to an absolute veto.

Where there is a requirement for consultation or even consent prior to a transfer being effected there will usually be exceptions where no consultation or consent is required. Exempt transfers will generally include those to existing lenders or their affiliates and related funds and also transfers at any time when an event of default exists. The latter exception is noteworthy since it is precisely when an event of default exists that hedge funds and vulture funds in particular may well acquire the debt.

Finally, sponsors may wish to include a provision that allows them to request details from the agent bank of all syndicate lenders at any given time. This will at least allow them to monitor how the debt is held.

Most transfer provisions will also deal with (ie, regulate) assignment in addition to full novation.[115] Lenders sometimes use sub-participation arrangements to get round overly restrictive transfer provisions and senior facilities agreements do not always expressly regulate these arrangements. From the sponsor's viewpoint, sub-participations that effectively assign voting rights to the sub-participant should generally be treated in the same way as outright transfers.

Syndicate decision-making provisions

5.78   Syndicated loan agreements follow an age-old principle that any decisions and actions that may be made or taken by the lenders under the loan agreement can only be made or taken by a specified majority.[116] A 'majority' is usually defined as 66⅔% of the syndicate by value of the outstanding facility amounts.[117]

---

115   Under English law an assignment is used to transfer rights only and not obligations, whereas a novation is a transfer of rights and obligations. The only material 'obligation' of a lender under a loan agreement is to lend, which will only be relevant where there are facilities that are not all drawn in full at completion, such as a working capital facility.

116   In fact, one customary exception to this, taken from the corporate syndicated debt market, that may be, but is not always, disapplied in practice, is the principle that a single bank can always sue the borrower for repayment of that part of the debt owing to that bank that has fallen due for payment and remains unpaid. That does not mean that the bank can accelerate all of its own portion of the loan; rather it can claim for any amount that remains due, owing and outstanding. Some leveraged loan documents disapply this principle, although even where they do not, in practice it would be extremely rare for a lender to take this step unilaterally without the support of the syndicate.

117   For junior debt this number will often be different. For example, mezzanine debt may occasionally have a 50.1% majority threshold, at least for certain decisions, and high yield debt decisions can generally be taken by 25% of the noteholders by value.

Whereas most decisions, including waivers and consents, can be taken by an affirmative majority decision, certain matters can only be determined by all of the lenders unanimously. The unanimous matters list has evolved over time into a standard list and includes material matters on which *all* lenders should have an approval right, such as the reduction of any amount due to the lenders, the extension of any date for payments under the facilities, a change in the currency of any payment, the voluntary release of security for the facilities and any increase in the amount of the facilities.

In most cases the fact that every lender must consent to these matters appears entirely reasonable. However, in certain circumstances the standard position arguably provides minority lenders with a disproportionate veto power. One of the common circumstances where this arises is where short-term additional working capital is required in a default or financial work-out situation. Even though an individual lender cannot be forced to put in more money, the standard provision gives each lender a right of veto over *any* increase in the facilities at all. The second common circumstance is where the borrower wishes to make a bolt-on acquisition and to use additional debt from the syndicate to finance the acquisition. Permitting the acquisition itself would be a pure majority lender issue under most loan documents, but increasing the facilities would be a unanimous issue, again even if individual lenders are not required to participate.

In response to these concerns, some sponsors have been able to insist on changes to the standard approach to unanimous voting on such matters. A number of formulations may be used. One approach is to have a sub-category of 'super-majority' voting for certain matters that would otherwise require unanimity, which could include an increase in the facilities; in this context the super-majority threshold would commonly be set in the region of 80 to 90% of the syndicate by value of amounts outstanding. Depending on how much of the facilities individual lenders will hold, the threshold should ideally leave enough leeway to enable a decision to be taken without the support of any two recalcitrant institutions. A more flexible provision that may be agreed would enable an increase in the facility amounts with only the consent of those lenders that are increasing their commitments plus the standard majority of the syndicate. An even more aggressive version requires only those lenders that are increasing their commitments to give their consent, but such provisions are relatively rare. It is worth mentioning here that standard intercreditor provisions do also give junior creditors an effective right of veto over additional senior ranking debt, although there will generally be a minimum of 10% headroom built in, certainly in the case of mezzanine debt and possibly more with other junior debt.[118]

In support of these developments away from entrenched minority lender rights, the senior debt market has also developed two other related provisions. One – call the 'yank-a-bank' provision – enables a borrower to mandatorily prepay a lender (a 'non-consenting lender') that has voted against any requested consent that was supported by a majority or perhaps super-majority of the syndicate. This may be seen by some minority lenders as a satisfactory result, notwithstanding the likely loss of market reputation that is likely to follow for it. The

---

118 **Chapter 10** considers the rights of different categories of junior creditor to veto additional prior-ranking debt.

second provision is a deemed consent provision. They have been around for years but have been in the spotlight in the 2000s given the other developments discussed above and have now been given the colloquial term 'snooze-and-lose' provisions. They operate by deeming a lender that does not respond to a consent request within a certain amount of time to have voted in accordance with the wishes of the majority that do respond.

Ancillary facilities letter

5.79   The form of the ancillary facilities letter will often simply reflect the standard banking terms of the bank acting as ancillary facilities lender and, indeed, may be a standard form document produced by that bank. Key terms will include the scope and amounts of the ancillary facilities made available, their pricing and the circumstances when the facilities can be terminated.

Typically overdraft and guarantee facilities will be priced at the same level as the margin on the core revolving credit component of the working capital facility. Other facilities (if any) will usually be priced in accordance with the bank's market rates. If the facilities are on-demand the borrower might argue that no non-utilisation fee should be payable.

It is common for ancillary facilities to be made available on an on-demand basis and reviewed on an annual basis. Alternatively the ancillary facilities letter will provide that the facilities can only be terminated and accelerated upon the occurrence of an event of default under the senior facilities agreement. In either case, there should be no need to include specific events of default in the letter itself.

Where the ancillary facilities are made available on a net basis, the ancillary facilities lender will wish to include a set-off provision in the letter enabling it to set-off credit balances held by it against amounts owing under the ancillary facilities if a default arises. Where there are two or more borrowers a cross-guarantee mechanism will also need to be included so that the set-off can be applied on a joint basis.

If the ancillary facilities are being made available on a fronted basis,[119] it would be customary for the bank to charge a fronting fee, usually in the region of 12.5 basis points, which the bank retains for its own account to compensate it for taking a credit risk on the syndicate banks.

Intercreditor agreement

5.80   An intercreditor agreement will be required in order to set out the subordination arrangements applicable to any junior debt in the structure. The principal purpose of the document is to prioritise the rights of the various layers of finance to receive payments and otherwise realise their investments. In addition this document will be used by the senior lenders and junior creditors to appoint the security trustee or agent on their behalf and to set out the terms of the security trust or other basis on which the security is to be held for the secured acquisition financiers.

---

119 See para **5.23**.

It is common for the same intercreditor agreement to contain the subordination arrangements applicable to the equity investments in addition to the junior debt. A separate subordination agreement is sometimes used to subordinate seller deferred consideration, however. Sellers are often reluctant to negotiate and sign up to a typical full intercreditor agreement to which all of the buy-out investors are party. They tend to prefer short form subordination agreements.[120]

Intercreditor agreements are considered in some detail in **Chapter 10**.

Security documents

What will the security package comprise?

5.81   The senior debt security package should include full asset security from each company in the group, including each SPV and each company in the target group. The only common exception to this approach will be for dormant companies in the target group that have no material assets.

In addition, a UK target group company with no net assets will potentially be unable to give security since it would be unable to go through the financial assistance whitewash procedure that is necessary where UK target companies are giving upstream credit support for acquisition debt.[121] That said, the lenders might in any event require that any such company that has material assets be recapitalised, so that it also has net assets and can go through the whitewash. Alternatively, if it has no material assets it may be exempted from the requirement to give security.

With multi-jurisdictional buy-outs, especially where there are many companies in the target group, the deal sponsor will often argue that the requirement to get credit support from the target group – in the form of guarantees and security – be limited to material companies only. One of the main reasons cited will often be that in many jurisdictions the taking of guarantees and asset security from each and every company may not be legally feasible, is practically very difficult or subject to material costs. In many continental European jurisdictions for instance the corporate benefit and financial assistance laws are more onerous than in the UK. In some jurisdictions there are material notarial or registration costs to meet when security is taken. The compromise position often agreed is that guarantees will be taken from companies together holding a specified percentage of the assets of the entire target group or generating that percentage of the revenues or EBITDA of the group.[122]

Each of the guarantors, in addition to the borrowers, will be required to give asset security to the extent legally feasible, practicable and cost effective. There will usually be a relatively detailed formulation of what is legally feasible,

---

120 This approach also facilitates the process of making any subsequent amendments of the intercreditor agreement or seller subordination agreement.
121 See Companies Act 1985, s 155(2). However, note that the financial assistance prohibition applicable to private companies – and with it the related whitewash procedure – is to be repealed on 1 October 2008. See also fn **38** and **Chapter 11** for more detail.
122 This is often called the guarantor coverage test. A level of between 75% and 95% is common. Guarantor coverage tests are considered further in **Chapter 13**.

practicable and cost effective. A short-form version would exempt a company in circumstances where the granting of the guarantee or security would:

- be unavoidably unlawful;

- result in a material restructuring of the group or material tax consequences for the group

- be prohibited by statute or beyond the corporate power of the company (if such corporate power could not be amended); or

- where, in the reasonable opinion of the MLA, the benefit to the lenders is disproportionately minor by comparison with the cost to the group.

Longer form formulations of such 'agreed security principles' are often scheduled to the senior facilities agreement and go into some detail as to the principles governing the taking of guarantees and security including the types of security that can be taken, relevant provisions to include in the security documents and other related matters.[123]

These principles should not apply to a domestic UK buy-out, however, since the additional burden of having each company in the group give guarantees and security is minimal and there being relatively few legal restrictions that cannot be overcome.[124] In fact, the 'ring-fencing' undertakings in the acquisition finance documentation[125] may mean that it is beneficial to the group for a group company to give a guarantee and security in support of the senior debt and thus fall within the ring fencing.[126]

The security obtained from the target group will include security over operating assets. This will include fixed assets, such as real property, plant and machinery, intellectual property rights including in particular trade names, shares in subsidiaries, minority holdings and joint ventures, intangible assets such as rights under contracts, the revenues generated in the form of trade receivables, cash and bank account credits and the stock and raw materials held by the group.[127]

The security obtained from the SPV group will be of a more limited nature given that the SPVs will be non-trading newly formed companies with no tangible assets. They do, however, hold important assets that the senior lenders will insist on being part of the security package. Chief amongst these will be the shares in the target company held by the acquiring vehicle.

In most security enforcement scenarios the senior lenders' preferred method of realising value from such enforcement would be by selling the business as a going concern to a third-party purchaser. This would be legally effected by a

---

123 See **Chapter 13** for further consideration of these issues.

124 That said, with some long-form security principle formulations some of the principles may also apply to security generally and not just non-English security; such as circumstances when notices of assignment may or may not be sent for the purposes of perfecting the security.

125 See para **5.68**.

126 For instance, an obligor will be able to receive financial support from other companies within the ring-fence.

127 In respect of raw materials and even some produced stock, retention of title provisions in supply agreements with trade suppliers may assert ownership over such raw materials or stock until the supplier is paid. If upheld, such provisions would take such assets out of the security 'net'.

simple transfer of the shares in the target or possibly newco itself.[128] The alternative to the going-concern sale approach would involve enforcing security over individual target group assets in order to realise value. Such an enforcement would usually be materially more complicated legally, costly and time consuming. It would also be perceived as a less satisfactory exit for the buy-out parties and the markets in which they operate. This is why the share security granted by the SPV group is a fundamental part of the overall security package. In public-to-private buy-outs it may even be the only security available to the senior lenders for the first few months after completion.[129]

In addition to shares, the members of the SPV group do have other intangible assets, principally comprising rights under the various transaction documents and, in particular, the acquisition documents. The security package should extend to these assets too. Where the funding structure includes different forms of finance being invested into different vehicles, the proceeds of those investments will be downstreamed to the acquisition vehicle newco where they will largely be applied to meet the acquisition consideration and costs. In a UK buy-out the funds will be downstreamed by way of loan and the senior lenders should take security over such funding loans in support of the share security taken in the SPV group.[130]

The security agreement and its parties

5.82 Only one document is usually required under English law to create effective security over all classes of asset located in England and Wales.[131] Because it creates fixed and floating security over all asset classes, that document is often referred to as a debenture or, where more than one company is party to it as a security grantor, a composite debenture. It is common practice to have all those companies in the group that are giving security to be party to a single agreement.

Companies that are not borrowers will be required to give a guarantee of the principal debt so that in granting security they are securing their own liabilities under the guarantee, rather than those of a third-party.[132] The guarantee itself will either be incorporated within the senior facilities agreement or less commonly in a stand-alone guarantee document or the security agreement itself.

---

128 Given that newco may still have the benefit of rights under the acquisition documents and possibly accumulated tax losses, additional value may be realised by selling the shares in newco which owns all the shares in the target rather than the shares in the target directly. This is one reason why multiple SPV structures are generally preferable to single SPV structures even in simple share acquisition buy-outs. See also **Chapters 2** and **11**.

129 See **Chapter 12**.

130 As a general – and important – rule, when taking share security the security should extend to all shareholder loans made by the security provider to its subsidiary so that the shares can be sold free from or with the benefit of the claims arising under those loans.

131 Whilst it is true that a single security document can be used to create security over any category of asset in England and Wales, with certain assets a separate document may be used out of common practice or perhaps to simplify the perfection procedure (usually registration) for the relevant security agreement. For example, separate security assignments in respect of certain material contracts, insurance policies or trade marks are occasionally used in addition to a full debenture.

132 English law does recognise third-party security but it is a less reliable method of achieving the same result as having a secured guarantee.

Aside from the companies giving security, the other party to the security agreement will be the security trustee on behalf of all secured acquisition financiers. The security trustee is sometimes also called the security agent. This is partly a matter of convention for the relevant financial institution that acts in that capacity[133] but also is more common in multi-jurisdictional buy-outs where a security 'trust' may not be used to establish security in favour of the relevant creditors. In certain European jurisdictions that do not recognise the concept of a security trust a 'parallel debt' mechanism is often used. This mechanism enables the security agent to execute and be party to each of the security documents without the need for all of the secured creditors also to be party.[134]

Certain provisions

5.83   Typically, a security agreement for use in a buy–out will include the following provisions.[135]

Key defined terms

'Secured Liabilities'

5.84   This definition should be wide enough to cover all acquisition finance being secured, including under all supporting finance documents such as ancillary facility letters and hedging agreements etc. It is possible to have the security agreement as an 'all moneys' security agreement so that the secured liabilities include all liabilities owing to the acquisition financiers by members of the group under any agreement – ie, not just under the specified acquisition finance documents. This has the theoretical advantage that any subsequent amendment to the acquisition finance package, including the making available of entirely new facilities, will not require an amendment to the security agreement and hence a re–registration etc. In practice, however, even security agreements that are not 'all monies' are drafted so that the 'secured liabilities' include any amendment to the acquisition finance package and 'all monies' security agreements are relatively rare in buy-outs.

'Secured Parties'

5.85   The secured parties definition identifies the persons that the security is given in favour of. It should refer to each 'finance party'[136] in each of their various capacities including the security trustee itself.

---

133   US banks tend to use the term security agent reflecting the fact that in the United States the role is an agency role rather than a trustee role.

134   This would be particularly cumbersome given the often great number of individual security documents used in a multi-jurisdictional buy-out and the fact that the group of creditors may change frequently as the secured debt is syndicated or otherwise traded.

135   The list of specified provisions is necessarily only a summary of certain key provisions which should be included in an English law security agreement as used in a buy-out. Security documents are essentially functional in nature and this section does not deal with all of the mechanical and boilerplate provisions to be found in a typical English law debenture (or guarantee) generally.

136   The 'finance parties' will be each lender, hedging counterparty, the agent, the arranger, the issuing bank (for guarantees/letters of credit), the ancillary facilities lender, the security trustee and any other secured finance party.

Charging clause

5.86   The charging clause sets out the categories of assets that are to be given as security. It should purport to create first fixed charges over real property, plant and machinery, securities, receivables, bank accounts, insurances,[137] goodwill and uncalled capital, intellectual property rights, pension fund interests and rights under contracts (including under the acquisition agreement and seller indemnities and under due diligence reports[138]). The charging clause should also create a floating charge over all assets not covered by the fixed charge.[139]

In practice, although the charging clause will purport to create fixed charges over all main categories of assets this is unlikely to be achieved as a matter of law. In particular, it is unlikely that a fixed charge will be created over stock, receivables and bank accounts. This is because the legal requirement of control that the secured parties must exercise over such assets is unlikely to be established where the target business is to operate in the normal course. Instead the secured parties will obtain only a floating charge over those assets. In fact it is beyond the scope of this book to detail the circumstances where fixed or floating security will be obtained or the precise benefit to the secured parties of obtaining fixed security.[140]

Security over shares

5.87   A fixed charge will be taken over the shares in each SPV in the SPV group other than topco.[141] Security will also be taken over the target shares and the shares in the target subsidiaries. This is extremely important security for the acquisition financiers as it allows them to sell the business as a going concern upon enforcement. In the case of UK companies the fixed charge can either take the form of a legal mortgage or an equitable mortgage or charge. In the case of a legal mortgage the security trustee or its nominee is actually registered as the shareholder of the relevant companies. In the case of an equitable mortgage or charge the creation of the security should be accompanied by delivery to the security trustee of blank executed stock transfer forms and share certificates in

137   Including an assignment by way of security of any keyman insurance policies.
138   Security over such rights may be effected as an assignment by way of security or a fixed charge. In either case, notice of the charge or assignment should be given to the relevant counterparty (ie, seller or consultant) and, ideally, an acknowledgement obtained.
139   Note that security over leasehold property may result in a breach of the lease if landlord consent is not obtained first. This may mean excluding leasehold property from the fixed charge where such consent is not obtained at completion. When obtained in due course, a supplemental deed will be required to perfect a fixed charge over such leasehold interests. Prior to the taking of a fixed charge once landlord consent is obtained it is common practice for the leasehold property to be subject to the floating charge. Whilst this might cause a technical default under the terms of the lease, purchasers (and landlords) tend to take a more relaxed approach and agree to the floating charge covering the leases.
140   In brief, the principal disadvantages of floating charge security are that, unlike fixed charge security, it will rank behind certain categories of unsecured but 'preferred' creditors settled by statute. It may also be defeated in terms of priority by a subsequent fixed charge over the same asset.
141   Topco's shares will be held by the equity investors who under UK buy-out market practice will not be required to give them as security. However, they carry no material intrinsic value in excess of the value of the shares that topco holds in the acquisition vehicle newco (or any intermediate vehicle), which *will* be given as security.

respect of the relevant shares[142] so that the security trustee or its nominee or a third-party purchaser can be registered as the shareholders without any further recourse to the companies being required. This is to enable the security to be enforced as easily as with a perfected legal mortgage.

There are a number of pros and cons as between legal mortgages and equitable mortgages and charges. In simple terms, the most comprehensive form of security over shares is a legal mortgage but for a number of reasons the parties, including the acquisition financiers, through the security trustee, may not wish the security trustee or its nominee to be actually registered as the shareholder and will usually prefer the equitable mortgage/charge together with delivery of stock transfer forms and share certificates.

Security over acquisition rights

5.88   Newco's rights against the seller under the acquisition documents will include potentially material claims. In particular, it may have warranty and indemnity claims of material value. It is therefore common practice for such rights to be given as security to the acquisition financiers. In order to achieve this the acquisition documents should be expressed to be chargeable or assignable by way of security.[143] Notice of the security must be given to the seller since failure to do so may weaken the secured party's rights against the seller upon enforcement. Ideally an acknowledgement of the notice should be obtained from the seller.

Often a seller will insist that the only permitted beneficiary of the security is the security trustee in respect of the acquisition finance – and possibly a receiver appointed by it – and not a third-party transferee such as a purchaser from the security trustee on enforcement. This does reduce the value of the security to some extent but, depending on how the security package is enforced by the security trustee, this may not be a problem in practice. This is one of the reasons why acquisition financiers prefer double SPV structures. Their security package can then include security over the shares in newco, which will enable newco to be sold on enforcement with all of its rights intact.

In addition to rights under the principal acquisition agreement, the security should extend to newco's, and the target group's, rights under any specific indemnity undertakings, such as a tax covenant or environmental indemnity undertaking, and the same analysis applies concerning assignability as for the acquisition agreement.

Finally, newco's rights against its advisers, and in particular the providers of the various due diligence reports should also form part of the security package.

In a public-to-private the security should also extend to newco's rights under the offer and scheme documents including the receiving bankers' agreement.[144]

---

142 In the case of the shares in the direct target company, the transfer of these pursuant to the acquisition may well be subject to stamp duty adjudication, in which case the share certificates – that is, the new share certificates in the name of newco – and stock transfer forms in respect of them may only be delivered at some point after completion.

143 Silence on the matter may be sufficient but the documents would normally be expected to be non-assignable unless an exception is made.

144 See **Chapter 12** in relation to public-to-privates generally.

Security over funding loans

5.89   In structures with more than one SPV the funding invested in the higher level SPVs will need to be downstreamed to the acquisition vehicle newco to meet the acquisition costs. In the United Kingdom[145] this is typically done by intercompany loans, which are often called funding loans or structural loans.[146] These loans are also the conduit for repaying and servicing the funding so invested.

As part of the subordination arrangements applicable to the various layers of junior debt and equity the acquisition financiers will wish to subordinate these loans to the acquisition finance. In particular the intercreditor agreement will regulate payments under these loans so that they are subject to the same conditions and payment blockage mechanics as the junior debt and equity that will be serviced by such payments. So a funding loan that downstreams junior debt will be subject to the same payment conditions and payment block mechanics as the junior debt. In addition the claim of the lender under such funding loan will be subordinated to the claims of the acquisition financiers against the borrower under the funding loan.[147]

In addition to subordinating the funding loans, the acquisition financiers should take security over them and there are two principal benefits in doing this. First, taking security – a charge or assignment – over intercompany debt owing by a subsidiary to its direct holding company is an essential supplementary step to taking share security from the holding company over that subsidiary. In order to transfer the equity in a company to a purchaser at its full realisable value any shareholder loans made to that company must also be transferred. Absent this the purchaser acquires a company with potentially significant liabilities in place to its former shareholder.

The second related reason is that part of the subordination arrangements for certain forms of junior debt[148] or subordinated loan capital[149] involves the use of 'isolating' security over funding loans, and shares, between the SPVs. The idea is that, by taking security over funding loans made to the senior debt borrower by the SPVs used to invest structurally subordinated junior debt and subordinated loan capital, the senior lenders can crystallise the subordination. This is done by enforcing the security over the funding loans and taking away any rights of the higher SPVs to pursue claims against the senior debt borrower.

In actual fact contractual subordination of the funding loans should in theory be able to achieve the same level of protection required by the senior lenders as isolating security. One important caveat to this generalisation is that in some jurisdictions the laws relating to the enforcement of contractual subordination provisions have not been fully tested in court. In theory contractual subordination provisions may not be as enforceable as the senior lenders would hope. In

---

145   In the United Kingdom, unlike certain other jurisdictions, there are no prescribed capitalisation ratios, although the level of share capital as a proportion of a company's overall capital may have an effect on the availability of tax deductions for the interest on shareholder debt.

146   Funding loans are also considered briefly in **Chapter 4**.

147   Refer to **Chapter 10** generally for a consideration of the applicable subordination arrangements.

148   PIK notes in particular but also, historically at least, high yield debt when it was subject to structural subordination – as to which see **Chapters 8** and **10**.

149   That is, quasi-equity invested by the sponsor, management team or seller.

those circumstances isolating security over shares and funding loans could play an important role.

Hedging documents

5.90   The senior lenders will almost certainly require that the interest exposure of the borrowers in respect of the acquisition finance debt is hedged. Typically this is done through an interest rate swap with one of the lenders acting as swap counterparty.[150] The senior debt MLA will normally wish to act as swap counterparty in order to receive the associated fee or revenue income, which can be quite significant. Sponsors will generally attempt to get a competitive price from the MLA, however, and will often mandate the MLA as swap counterparty on the basis that its quote is competitive with other lenders. Only lenders within the senior debt syndicate would qualify for the role. This is because the swap counterparty will insist on having the swap liabilities secured to avoid being subordinated to all of the secured acquisition finance and the benefit of the security documents would rarely be extended to non-syndicate lenders.

The interest rate swap will be documented in a standard form ISDA master agreement[151] between the borrowers and the relevant lender as swap counterparty. The ISDA master agreement has appended to it a schedule containing any changes to the master agreement and various elections made as to the applicability of certain provisions in the master agreement. The actual terms of the swap are set out in a transaction 'confirmation' which determines the commercial details, including the amount of debt, relevant floating rate of interest being swapped and fixed rate into which the floating rate is swapped, the period for which the swap is to be effected and the dates on which payments under the swap will be made by the borrowers to the swap counterparty or vice versa, depending on how the interest rates have moved since the swap was effected. It is common for the interest rate swap document to be completed by the internal personnel of the bank acting as swap counterparty.

As a creditor under the swap documents, the bank that is appointed swap counterparty will be required to be party to the intercreditor agreement as such. In doing so it will take the benefit of the security granted by the obligors.[152]

In addition, it will agree to a number of provisions regulating its activities as swap counterparty. For instance, the swap counterparty will usually be prohibited from closing out the swap and enforcing its rights unless there has been a declared event of default under the senior facilities agreement. There will also be a restriction on amendments that may be made to the terms of the swap. Certain elections that are to be made under the ISDA master agreement will also be specified.

---

150   In simple terms, the swap counterparty will agree to pay the floating rate of interest applicable to the borrower's core debt in return for receiving a fixed rate from the borrower.
151   The International Swaps and Derivatives Association, Inc produce industry-standard documentation for various forms of hedging contract.
152   Assuming that it is the intercreditor agreement that sets out the terms of the security trust or agency arrangements.

The requirement to enter into the interest rate swap will be contained in the senior facilities agreement, either directly or indirectly by reference to a hedging strategy letter. This side letter will stipulate the amount of debt to be hedged and the period for which the swap is to last. It is not unusual for the swap to be required to cover say 70% of the senior, second lien and mezzanine debt – that is, all the floating rate acquisition finance facilities – for a period of three years. The borrower is usually given 30, 60 or 90 days to put the swap in place following completion.

In addition to interest rate exposure it is possible that the borrowers will have foreign exchange exposure in respect of their cashflows and debt service obligations. This could also be hedged. However, it is more usual that a natural hedge is put in place. This involves the acquisition finance being drawn down in currencies that reflect the underlying cashflows of the business. So a business with cashflows (revenues) split 50:50 between sterling and euro would have debt split between those two currencies in the same proportions. Where there are multiple borrowers care must be taken to ensure that each borrower that is to have a debt obligation in any given currency also has access to the right amount of cashflows in that currency.

CHAPTER 6

Second Lien Debt

SECOND LIEN DEBT

European second lien debt

6.1   In late 2003 the UK and European buy-out markets once again demonstrated their evolutionary nature with the first use of second lien debt finance. Second lien debt is an import from the US market where it was originally developed for use in complex restructurings. As the name suggests,[1] it is debt that is secured to rank immediately behind the first ranking senior debt in the capital structure and thus ahead of any other junior or 'subordinated' debt. In the United States it is often referred to as senior subordinated debt to reflect its position in the capital structure but also so that it can be sold to investors whose investment criteria would rule out taking positions in conventional subordinated debt. In UK and European buy-out structures it often forms a relatively thin layer between the core senior and junior debt packages. It has proved most popular in structures with mezzanine debt but is also used where the core junior debt is an issue of high yield bonds. It may also be used, in larger quantities, in place of the core junior debt layer.

In fact, there are arguably two variants of second lien debt used in Europe. One is essentially a form of stretched senior debt that sits between the core 'priority' senior debt and the core junior debt, either mezzanine or high yield. This is the form of second lien debt that has overall been more common in traditional buy-out funding structures. It will typically be documented as the 'D' tranche of senior debt in the senior facilities agreement although it may also take the form of an issue of second lien notes. The other, where the second lien comprises the core junior debt in place of mezzanine debt or high yield bonds, was originally confined to corporate borrowers and issuers, or perhaps to refinancings of mature buy-outs, rather than in primary buy-out structures. This has changed as the market has evolved and become more liquid, however, and in the latter half of the 2000s second lien has increasingly been used as a cheaper alternative to mezzanine debt in a wider variety of buy-out structures. That said this chapter is mainly

---

1   'Lien' is a US legal term used to describe a consensual security interest. It is not to be confused with the English legal term "lien" which has a narrower scope and describes just one specific type of security interest.

concerned with second lien debt in the stretched senior debt form. In its 'mezzanine replacing' form aside from cheaper pricing (and certain intercreditor differences[2]) it may not differ all that much from mezzanine debt itself.

Before moving on to look at European second lien debt, and given its origins in the US market, it is worthwhile briefly examining the nature of the US product and the extent to which the European market has followed the precedent.

US second lien debt

6.2   As a preliminary matter it is useful to note that in analysing the viability of debt financings, the more mature US market tends to consider underlying asset values and enterprise values in addition to the cash generating potential of a borrower, whereas in European acquisition financings the focus is much more on the underlying cash flows. In the United States, second lien debt is specifically intended to benefit from the underlying security provided by businesses with the requisite asset or enterprise value. That level of analysis has not really been followed in Europe.[3]

In fact, although it is effectively an import from the United States, the US second lien market generally provides little by way of indicative principles for the European form. In one or two important aspects European second lien debt is structured quite differently.

For one thing, US second lien is rarely structured as stretched senior debt in the form of an additional tranche of senior debt documented in the senior credit agreement. Generally, it will comprise a more significant element of the capital structure than is the case with D note second lien as used in European buy-outs. Indeed, it will generally be documented in a stand-alone credit agreement.[4] This approach has largely not been followed in Europe, even in structures where the second lien effectively replaces mezzanine debt in the structure.

A further, perhaps more fundamental, difference to note is that traditional US second lien debt ranks pari passu with the core senior debt; it is neither contractually nor structurally subordinated and the extent of its 'subordination' is limited to a second right to receive the proceeds of enforcement of the security package. One of the consequences of this is that if there is insufficient security to discharge the senior debt, that part of the senior debt that is unsecured ranks pari passu with the second lien debt, which will all be unsecured in that scenario. There are no payment blocks and no turnover provisions.

As far as enforcement of the security is concerned, the senior lenders control the process. The second lien tranche operates either as a 'silent second' or as

---

2   See **Chapter 10** generally.

3   Indeed, in multi-jurisdictional European buy-outs, the second lien debt may in practice be relatively undersecured as a result of the difficulty in obtaining target group security in a number of European jurisdictions. See **Chapter 13**.

4   Although there are also specific, US bankruptcy law reasons that influence this in addition to any commercial considerations.

'quiet second'. Silent second is where the second lien lenders have no rights to enforce the security and only the senior lenders can take such action; second lien notes, by contrast with loans, are more likely to take this form. Quiet second is where the second lien lenders do have a right to compel enforcement by the senior lenders but that right is subject to a standstill period following default.

As considered in the following paragraphs, some of these intercreditor features of US second lien debt have also not been replicated in Europe.

Evolution of a European second lien debt market

6.3   A number of factors have influenced the evolution of a European second lien market. One key catalyst for the use of second lien debt in buy-out funding structures has been the lure of increasing leverage multiples without further extending the size of the core senior debt and without having to use additional amounts of more expensive mezzanine debt.[5] Added to the fact that until the second half of the 2000s debt arrangers had not on the whole seen second lien debt as an outright replacement for mezzanine debt in traditional buy-out structures,[6] this explains why second lien is often structured as a relatively small layer between the core senior and mezzanine tranches. Indeed, the introduction and use of second lien loans in European buy-outs can to some extent be likened to the development of alphabet notes ('B' and 'C' tranches of senior debt) as a form of stretched senior debt in the late 1990s and early 2000s. Hence the fact that, in buy-out structures, second lien loans are widely documented as the 'D' tranche of senior debt in the senior facilities agreement together with the core senior debt, albeit on a (to some extent) subordinated basis to the A, B and C notes. Generally speaking, analysing second lien debt as a form of stretched senior debt rather than as a form of true junior debt is helpful in understanding some of its key features, certainly where used in traditional buy-out funding structures, such as its relatively small size, cheaper pricing and limited separate voting rights.

Second lien debt structures

6.4   A typical buy-out structure incorporating second lien debt in addition to senior and mezzanine debt can be represented in diagrammatic form as follows.[7]

---

5   Second lien is certainly cheap by comparison with mezzanine debt, which is typically priced in the range of say 750–1050 bps over cost of funds. Second lien debt is generally priced at between say 400–600 bps over cost of funds. However, the current cashflow cost of second lien debt is similar to that of mezzanine, given that approximately half of the margin on mezzanine debt (the PIK element) will be capitalised.

6   During 2006 and 2007, in particular, an increasing number of deals were being structured with senior and second lien debt only rather than the more common senior, second lien and mezzanine structure.

7   See **Chapter 3** on structuring generally.

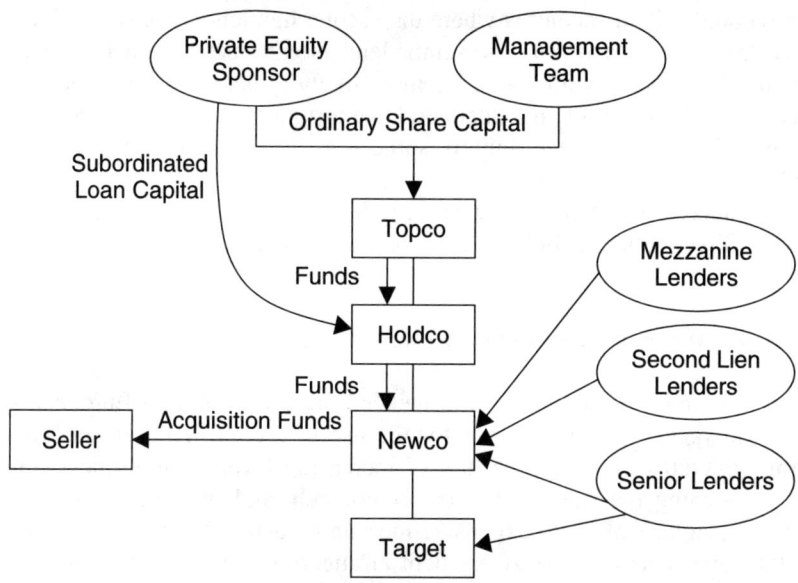

Senior, second lien and mezzanine

Second lien can also be used in conjunction with senior and high yield debt, in which case the structure would typically be as follows:

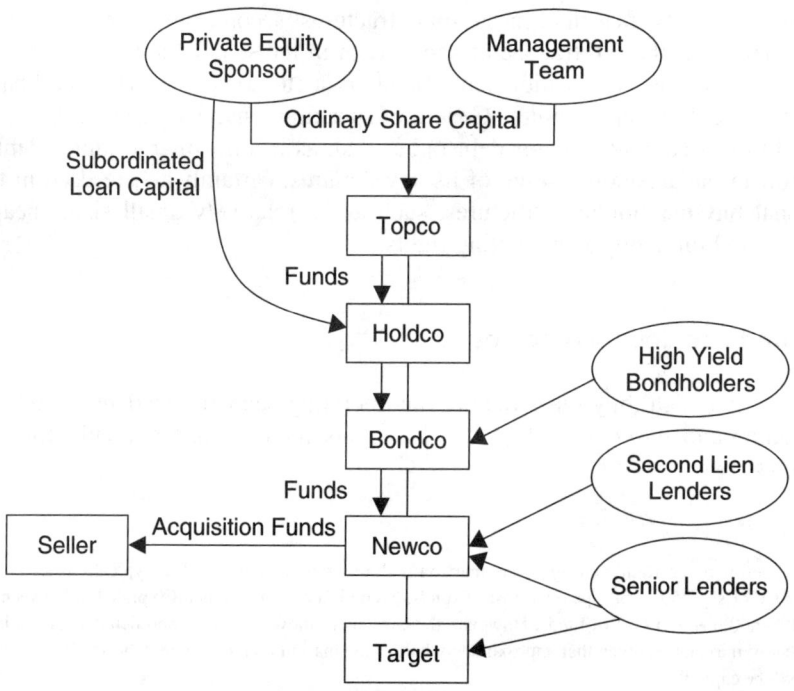

Senior, second lien and high yield

As can be seen in the diagrams on the preceding page, second lien debt benefits from the same structural status as the core senior debt. That is, the second lien creditors will usually share the same borrower (possibly with the exception of the target[8]) and have the same guarantee and security package from the target group as the core senior lenders.

Who provides the second lien debt?

6.5   In addition to the rationale of increasing leverage as mentioned above, a key factor in the evolution of a European second lien market has been that in structuring deals with a second lien loan tranche, sponsors and debt arrangers have effectively been able to tap a new source of investor for the buy-out market, namely hedge funds. Second lien debt has proven particularly attractive to this expansive class of investor who tend to have relatively few investment restrictions unlike some dedicated leveraged loan funds for example for which the investment criteria may preclude or limit the amount of second lien debt.[9]

Even though hedge funds, CDOs, CLOs and some other leveraged loan funds are big end-buyers of second lien paper, in practice, certainly in the buy-out market, much second lien debt is arranged and underwritten by the leading acquisition finance banks as part of an integrated debt package. Such banks may, if necessary to ensure a successful syndication, retain a small amount of the second lien tranche after primary syndication. The syndicated banking market may also be required to buy a portion of a second lien tranche when buying into the core senior debt tranches but usually only where the MLAs are concerned that the debt will not sell otherwise.

Where the second lien tranche is an issue of notes it will be sold to hedge funds and also to the bond markets including some CBOs and CDOs.

Second lien debt is used much more frequently in syndicated facilities – that is in mid-market and larger deals – than in bi-lateral facilities found in the smaller deal market. However, where, as is generally the case in traditional buy-out structures, it is used as a tranche of stretched senior debt, the second lien syndicate will not operate as discretely as would eg, a senior or mezzanine debt syndicate. This is largely because the second lien lender syndicate will usually have limited discrete voting rights.[10] Consequently, the typical agency function of the lead lender in a debt syndicate is less important and the documentation will not always provide for a separate second lien agent at the outset. In practice, an agent may only be appointed if the second lien lenders are faced with an issue that requires their separate vote in due course. Until that time the core senior debt agent will effectively act as agent for the second lien lenders too. When the second lien debt replaces mezzanine in a structure there may (but not necessarily) be a separate second lien syndicate – although certain lenders may opt to be in both syndicates – and, if so, one lender will act as the agent from the outset in the usual way.

---

8 For which there may be adverse consequences for the second lien lenders in a multi-jurisdictional buy-out. See **Chapter 13**.

9 For example a CDO or CLO might have a cap on second lien loans of say 10-20% of the entire fund portfolio.

10 See para **6.12** and **Chapter 10**.

An up-front arrangement and underwriting fee will be payable to the arranger and underwriter as with other forms of debt. However, in buy-outs at least, it is common for a single fee to be payable in respect of the entire senior and second lien package.[11] Whether or not a portion of this fee is passed on to the syndicate lenders generally depends on whether they are banks, who will generally want to take a portion of the fee, or institutional investors, who may forego a fee or take a reduced fee.

In the case of an underwritten issue of second lien notes an underwriting fee will be payable to the managers of the issue. Such fees may be similar in quantum terms to the fees payable for high yield bond issuances.[12]

What does the second lien debt comprise?

Second lien loans and notes

6.6   A second lien debt package will typically comprise a single term loan repayable in one 'bullet' six or, less often, twelve months after the final instalment of core senior debt and before any core junior debt in the structure. In a buy-out this will usually mean scheduled repayment at year 9.5.[13] Second lien debt may also be structured as an issue of notes to be sold into the public debt market. In some larger deals there may be separate tranches comprising a loan and notes.

In economic terms, second lien loans are priced at a margin above cost of funds that reflects their position in the capital structure, after the most expensive tranche of core senior debt – usually the C note – and ahead of the core junior debt.[14] Second lien notes may be priced either with a fixed rate or as floating rate notes. Although the entire interest rate is payable in cash, the pricing of second lien debt remains significantly lower than the all-in cost of traditional mezzanine debt pricing, although there has been some convergence since second lien first appeared, as mezzanine pricing has reduced. In addition, the actual cash cost of second lien debt on a current basis, ignoring the PIK element of mezzanine debt, is not dissimilar to that of mezzanine debt.

Second lien debt will generally only be made available to newco for funding the acquisition of the target business and meeting deal costs,[15] and, if in the form of a loan, will be drawn in full at completion of the acquisition at the same time as the core senior acquisition loan. It will almost invariably be denominated in the same currency as the core senior acquisition debt. If used to finance an acquisition, second lien notes will generally need to be bridged in the same way that high yield is.[16]

---

11 Either a flat percentage is payable on the entire package or sometimes a higher percentage will be payable on the second lien tranche.

12 See **Chapter 8**. It is common for the fee to be structured as a discount on the notes underwritten (see para **8.7**).

13 In some structures, perhaps in a leveraged corporate deal, there might be two instalments – a so-called 'soft' or 'semi' bullet – at years 9.5 and 10.

14 The margin is usually in the range of say 400-600 bps.

15 Which is why, in multi-jurisdictional deals, it may end up being relatively undersecured. See **Chapter 13**.

16 See **Chapter 8**.

Amount of second lien tranche

6.7   The addition of a second lien tranche to a buy-out funding structure is often for the purpose of stretching the core senior debt.[17] Therefore, the precise amount will often be determined by reference to the amount of the core senior debt. It will often form a relatively thin layer sandwiched between the core senior debt and a larger layer of core mezzanine or high yield debt and, in such circumstances, is likely to constitute between 5 and 10% of the overall acquisition financing requirement. Where it is used in place of mezzanine or high yield debt, it may constitute a more significant portion of the overall funding structure.

With an issue of second lien notes the absolute size of the issue is also important since any issue of tradable public debt needs to be sufficiently large to justify a public issuance and to create a market for the notes. In any event second lien notes will only be used in the larger transactions often together with a core high yield bond issue.

DOCUMENTING THE SECOND LIEN DEBT

6.8   The following paragraphs consider the nature of the principal documents which are used to document second lien debt. As previously mentioned, second lien debt may be documented either as a loan or, less often, as an issue of notes (bonds).

Second lien loans and notes

6.9   The form second lien debt takes is dictated by a number of factors. One determining factor is the nature of the core junior debt, if any, which is to sit below the second lien strip in the funding structure. If it is mezzanine debt then the second lien will almost certainly take the form of a loan. In such structures the debt arranger will typically focus on the loan markets for all the layers of acquisition finance. The second lien strip will often be a relatively thin layer in such structures, which is more suited to loans than an issue of notes. Additionally, because mezzanine debt will generally have a materially tighter covenant package than an issue of notes, it is likely to be viewed as inconsistent with the overall ranking of the layers of finance if the mezzanine debt is to sit behind an issue of notes. This will be of particular concern if, as with most debt capital markets issues, including high yield bonds, the second lien notes are to have incurrence style covenants rather than the maintenance style found in leveraged loan documentation.[18]

Where the core junior debt is a high yield issue the second lien tranche may well comprise or include an issue of notes. Such a structure is more likely to be used in the largest transactions, where the dynamics of the capital markets suit issuers and debt quanta of a certain minimum size.

17 But see also para **6.1** in relation to second lien debt that is used as core junior debt in place of mezzanine or high yield.

18 See para **3.60** for a comparison of incurrence and maintenance covenants.

A further determining factor is the investor base that the second lien debt is to be aimed at for syndication purposes. In brief, if the second lien debt is to be aimed at institutions that are more familiar with high yield debt it will be structured as an issue of notes. If the target investors are institutions looking for leveraged loans it will take the form of a loan.

In practice, these factors mean that in a structure that includes senior, second lien and high yield debt, the second lien will either be structured as an issue of notes or as a loan or possibly a combination of both, with tranches of each. In a structure with senior, second lien and mezzanine debt the second lien will almost certainly take the form of a loan.

Second lien documents

6.10   In either case, whether documented as an issue of notes or a loan, the form of the documentation will be largely a derivate of the documentation for the other instruments in the funding structure. Thus, where documented as a loan the second lien document will substantially mirror the senior facilities agreement. In fact, as mentioned already, in a buy-out structure, where the second lien is being used as a form of stretched senior debt, the second lien is likely to be documented *in* the senior facilities agreement.[19] Similarly, where documented as an issue of notes the second lien debt documentation will largely mirror the more junior high yield debt.[20] As a result, second lien covenants may either be bond-style incurrence covenants, in the case of most issues of second lien notes, or the more extensive loan-style maintenance covenants, in the case of second lien loans. Hybrid covenant packages are possible, particularly if there are both second lien loans and notes in the same structure.

Second lien loans

6.11   In a UK buy-out second lien loan documentation will comprise the following core documents:

- facility agreement;[21]
- intercreditor agreement;
- security agreement;[22] and
- hedging agreement.[23]

---

19 **Chapter 5** considers the basic provisions of a senior facilities agreement as used in a typical buy-out.
20 **Chapter 8** includes an analysis of a typical high yield debt documentation suite.
21 See para **6.12**.
22 With UK security a single security agreement will be used to create security for the senior, second lien and mezzanine debt. The security agreement will be executed in favour of a security trustee who holds the benefit of the security on trust for all of the secured lenders.
23 In practice, there is unlikely to be separate hedging documentation for the second lien debt; rather, a single set will document the hedging for all of senior, second lien and mezzanine debt.

Second lien facility agreement

6.12   As mentioned, where the second lien debt is to be documented as a loan it will most likely be documented in the senior facilities agreement itself; reflecting the fact that it is really a form of stretched senior debt. Less frequently it may be documented in a separate facility agreement but this is rare in true buy-outs.

In the latter case the form of that facilities agreement should be substantially similar to the senior facilities agreement. The most efficient and logical approach is that used for mezzanine debt – duplicating the senior facilities agreement and only making the necessary changes to reflect the different commercial terms.

In a traditional buy-out structure, where the second lien is incorporated into the same document as the priority senior debt, the second lien debt will, in theory at least, benefit from the same default triggers as the A, B and C tranches. However, even though the second lien debt may have the same default triggers as the senior debt, the second lien lenders may not be permitted to exercise any rights in respect of them until the core senior debt has been paid off or reduced significantly. This is because the decision-making procedure included in the senior facilities agreement is unlikely to recognise the second lien lenders as a separate class of lenders for most issues that would otherwise require a class decision.

A variety of different scenarios are theoretically possible. At one extreme the second lien lenders could form a separate voting class of lenders who on default could decide to accelerate their debt. At the other extreme they could be denied any voting rights at all. In practice the position is likely to be in between. As the second lien market has developed for UK and European buy-outs some consistency of approach has appeared, with separate decision making by the second lien lenders being permitted for acceleration in circumstances of payment default, cross-acceleration[24] with the core senior debt and insolvency of the second lien borrower or a guarantor. In addition, matters requiring a unanimous decision of all senior lenders will often also require the second lien lenders to give the requisite consent.

In practice, the larger the second lien debt layer as a proportion of the entire funding structure the more likely it is that the second lien lenders would demand – and receive – separate voting rights and possibly even a separate facilities agreement too (as is the case with US second lien). This scenario is (at the time of writing at least) less likely to apply to a traditional European buy-out structure, however, where the second lien tranche is commonly used in small quantities as a form of stretched senior debt.

Absent separate voting rights on issues the second lien lenders are likely to be left with *pari passu* voting rights, such that they can vote their debt as part of the entire senior and second lien debt package. As a general rule this will leave them with a minority say in matters such as acceleration, enforcement and waivers and

---

24 Cross-acceleration means that one facility – here the second lien facility – can be accelerated by its lenders by virtue of another facility – such as the core senior facility – having been accelerated by its lenders.

amendments to the document, subject to the typical exceptions requiring unanimity or, possibly, a super-majority vote.[25]

This means that as the A tranche amortises over time, the proportion of the
voting rights held by the second lien lenders will increase. But whether this is
significant enough to give them a casting vote would depend on the deal specifics
and, in particular, the split of debt between the A, B, C and D tranches.[26]

Not all deals even have pari passu voting, however, and deals have been done
where the second lien lenders have more limited voting rights still. This might
mean that they have no voting rights at all; other than where, as mentioned
above, they can accelerate the second lien debt in certain important circumstances, such as payment default, cross-acceleration and insolvency as mentioned above. In all cases second lien lenders should in any event have the right
to vote on fundamental matters relating to their debt such as would require a
unanimous decision of the senior lenders in respect of the senior debt.[27]

As previously indicated, second lien debt is attractive to deal sponsors because
by comparison with other forms of junior debt it is relatively cheap. One of its
other features that is attractive for deal sponsors is that it does not benefit from
extensive call protection provisions. Second lien debt will usually have only a
relatively modest period (one or two years) where its prepayment would attract a
1 or 2% premium. This is one of several features it shares with mezzanine debt
and which differentiates it from high yield debt. Consequently, second lien and
mezzanine combinations have proved popular with sponsors keen to exit or perhaps refinance in the relative short term after completion of the buy-out.

Second lien notes

6.13   In a UK buy-out second lien note documentation will comprise the following core documents:

- lead manager engagement letter;

- offering memorandum;

- trust indenture or trust deed;[28]

- purchase agreement;

- paying agency agreement;

---

25 Although, as mentioned in the prior paragraph, it is common in practice for 'D tranche' second lien
    lenders to have discrete rights to accelerate in the case of payment default, cross-acceleration and
    insolvency. See also **Chapter 10** generally.
26 Typically a senior debt syndicate will have a decision making threshold of 66⅔%. This means that to
    exercise a casting vote, in terms of their ability to block a decision but not to force one, the second lien
    lenders would need more than 33⅓% of the votes ie, more than one third of the principal amount of the
    senior and second lien debt.
27 Unanimous lender decisions are usually required for issues such as changing the pricing or maturity
    of any debt, increasing the amount of the debt and releasing security.
28 English law issues are usually documented under a trust deed. Trust indentures are used for US issues
    or issues sold into the US market.

- if the notes are to be subject to a full US public offering as opposed to a private placement, a registration rights agreement;

- intercreditor agreement;

- guarantee;

- security agreement;[29] and

- hedging agreement.[30]

These documents will largely take the form of the documentation used for a high yield bond issue, possibly with the exception of the covenant package, which might reflect maintenance-style covenants as used in the senior debt documentation or a hybrid with both maintenance and incurrence covenants.[31] In addition, as far as security is concerned, high yield debt does not typically benefit from target group security, whereas second lien notes would. High yield debt documentation is considered in further detail in **Chapter 8**.

Intercreditor, security and hedging documents

Intercreditor agreement

6.14   There will invariably be an intercreditor agreement between the senior lenders, the second lien lenders and the other acquisition debt providers for the purposes of establishing the ranking of the various layers of debt. It is usual for the same agreement to be used to prioritise all of the layers of acquisition finance, the equity loan capital and the group's intercompany debt.

Aside from the principal economic terms of this form of acquisition finance, the most keenly observed feature of European second lien debt has been its intercreditor status, and in particular the terms of its subordination behind the core senior debt. This is the area where European second lien debt departs most significantly from its US counterpart. A more detailed consideration of the issues is set out in **Chapter 10** but in short the senior debt market has by and large insisted that second lien debt be subject to intercreditor controls similar to those applied to mezzanine debt. These include payment blockage and turnover provisions, enforcement standstills and in some cases (but by no means universally) contractual subordination on insolvency.

However, there is one major area of departure from the intercreditor regime applicable to mezzanine debt; namely in respect of voting rights. As indicated previously, in this regard the second lien investors will generally have very limited rights. So much so that, unless the second lien tranche is a relatively material part of the capital structure (particularly where the second lien debt effectively

---

29 But see para **6.16**. In practice, the second lien lenders would share security documents with the senior debt.

30 Second lien notes may have a fixed coupon, in which case no interest rate hedging would be required. For floating rate notes any required hedging would most probably be documented in the same agreement as for the senior debt.

31 A hybrid package is more likely where there are both second lien loans and notes in the same structure.

replaces the mezzanine or high yield), the second lien lenders typically have no separate voting pool and decision making powers other than in exceptional circumstances. The exceptions are typically where there is a payment default on the second lien debt, cross-acceleration with the core senior debt or an insolvency event has occurred. This means that in many buy-out structures, subject to the exceptions just mentioned, they will vote on matters only as a minority part of the aggregated senior and second lien debt package. In this respect, the second lien lenders are in a weaker position than mezzanine lenders would be in structures without second lien debt.

The intercreditor agreement will usually also contain the appointment of the security trustee or agent on behalf of the senior lenders and second lien lenders (and any other secured acquisition financiers) and set out the terms of the security trust or other basis on which the security is to be held for the two, or perhaps three, sets of secured creditors.[32]

The form of the intercreditor agreement and the subordination arrangements applicable to second lien debt generally are considered in further detail in **Chapter 10**.

Comparison with US second lien subordination

6.15 Before leaving subordination, it is worth briefly exploring how and why the intercreditor status of European second lien debt has not conformed to its US counterpart. One of the reasons often cited is the different insolvency regimes. Under US bankruptcy law, Chapter 11 proceedings[33] provide for a moratorium on payments by the company in order to preserve cash in the business in a 'bankruptcy' situation. A Chapter 11 filing also restricts any enforcement action by the creditors. By contrast, European jurisdictions on the whole do not have equivalent concepts and contractual payment blockages and enforcement standstills are used instead. Another reason is the traditional dominance, in Europe, of the senior debt banking market and the fact that junior debt packages, certainly in the case of mezzanine debt, are often arranged by the same institution that is arranging the senior debt. Consequently, when structuring the senior and junior debt, the arranger will impose its preferred subordination terms on the junior debt. This has led to relatively pro-senior intercreditor positions for most forms of junior debt becoming market standard.

Although at the time of writing there was relatively little evidence in Europe to support the theory, one conceivable attraction of second lien debt in its US form might be that it can be used in refinancings where an existing high yield bond benefits from an anti-layering provision that would prohibit other forms of

---

32 With multi-jurisdictional buy-outs a security 'trust' may not always be applicable. See para **6.16** and **Chapter 13**.

33 The so-called 'Chapter 11' provisions are found in Title 11 of the United States Code sections 101 et seq.

junior debt from being included in the refinanced capital structure.[34] Specifically, this would be where the anti-layering provision prohibits debt that is subordinated in right of payment; which would not catch US-style second lien but would catch other types of subordinated debt. An anti-layering provision that prohibits debt that is subordinated *to any extent* would catch US second lien too.

Security documents

6.16 Second lien debt by definition benefits from second priority security. The security package will be precisely the same as that securing the core senior debt and, as with mezzanine debt, a single layer of first ranking security will be granted for the senior and second lien debt (and any other secured junior debt in the structure).[35] This layer of security will be held by the security trustee or agent for all the relevant secured creditors and the proceeds of enforcement will be applied in the agreed order of priority: first for the 'priority' senior debt, next for the second lien debt and then for any secured core junior debt. With a multi-jurisdictional buy-out there may be jurisdictions involved that do not recognise the concept of a security trust. In those circumstances the security may be held by the relevant senior creditor as a security agent, perhaps with alternative legal mechanisms in place to regulate how the security granted in those jurisdictions is held by the security agent; such as a parallel debt arrangement.[36]

The terms of the security agreement that would be used in a UK deal or in respect of UK assets in a multi-jurisdictional deal are considered briefly in **Chapter 5**.

Hedging agreement

6.17 As with the core senior debt, and any other floating rate acquisition finance, the debt arranger will generally oblige the borrowers to hedge their interest rate exposure in respect of the second lien debt, usually by way of an interest rate swap. In practice, the interest rate swap in respect of the second lien debt will most likely be documented in the same hedging agreement as the core senior debt swap, with the same institution – one of the senior lenders – as swap counterparty. Certain of the terms applicable to the interest rate swap are considered in **Chapter 5**.

---

34 Anti-layering provisions are used in high yield bonds to prevent an additional layer of debt being inserted into the capital structure between the core senior debt and the high yield bonds. They are considered further in **Chapters 8** and **10**.

35 Certainly this will be the case for UK security. The laws of other jurisdictions may require separate layers of security to be created.

36 See **Chapter 13**.

CHAPTER 7

Mezzanine Debt

MEZZANINE DEBT

The European mezzanine debt market

7.1   Mezzanine debt was the first type of junior debt used in UK buy-outs and since 2000, when it overtook the high yield market, it has remained the most widely used junior debt product in the market by volume.[1] It has been around in the United Kingdom since the late 1980s and has evolved markedly, especially in the 2000s. This has partly been in response to the initially stuttering development of the European high yield market, but also as a result of a surge in institutional investor appetite for European mezzanine paper.

The key development has been the creation of a new 'institutional' mezzanine product for use in upper mid-market and larger deals. Institutional mezzanine does not carry warrants and is principally sourced from institutional investors, including pension funds, hedge funds, CDOs, CLOs and other leveraged loan funds. A significant amount of this money is North American and the volume available for European transactions has grown hugely since the beginning of the 2000s. This has significantly increased the amount of mezzanine that may be available for a single transaction. In the 1990s a mezzanine tranche would rarely have exceeded £50 million. In the 2000s tranches of £500 million and more are feasible.

Aside from the huge increase in liquidity in the mezzanine market generally, the other key development that has fuelled the evolution of a separate institutional mezzanine market for larger deals has been the occasional instability in the European high yield debt market. In the late 1990s high yield debt was viewed as the natural product for larger deals in place of mezzanine and in 1998 and 1999 new high yield issuance volumes exceeded those of mezzanine. However, by the early 2000s the European high yield market began faltering, largely in response to the weakness of TMT sector issuers.[2] As a result, deal sponsors and debt

---

1   That said, since the mid-2000s second lien has been gaining market share largely at the expense of mezzanine.
2   The technology, media and telecoms sector had a number of defaulting issuers around this time.

arrangers were finding new high yield issuances for buy-outs more difficult to get away. One of their responses was to revisit the way in which high yield bridging loans were structured. Traditionally the bond bridge would be structured with a rapidly increasing interest rate, a so-called 'exploding' bridge. This would force the issuer to refinance the bridge if the bond issue was not successfully achieved within the bridge period (usually 12 months). Some time during 2000 or 2001 the practice changed so that instead of having an untenable interest rate after 12 months if the bond was not issued, the bridging loan would convert into a layer of mezzanine debt with 8, 9 or 10-year maturity. The mezzanine lenders would receive warrants on the conversion date to complete the new financing structure. At around this time institutional investors that had not previously figured in the mezzanine market became interested in participating in larger mezzanine tranches, such as the ones being created by failed bond bridges, and eventually some started underwriting mezzanine debt as an alternative to bond bridges. Once deal sponsors found that the new class of institutional investor was more interested in the predictable longer term interest rates that mezzanine could deliver, but not necessarily the potential equity upside of warrants, a new warrantless mezzanine product was formed.

One important effect of this has been to elevate mezzanine finance to be a competitive product to high yield debt in all but the largest deals. Traditional or 'true' mezzanine debt with warrants is still used but in smaller volumes.[3] Its use is now generally restricted to lower mid-market and smaller transactions.

From the mid-2000s both second lien debt and PIK notes had begun to be a competitor product to mezzanine in certain structures. Initially this included mostly refinancings of mature buy-outs and leveraged corporate structures but by the latter half of the 2000s second lien in particular was replacing mezzanine in buy-outs more generally. In this sense it is used as a cheap form of mezzanine. In many other buy-out structures, however, the two sit together in the same structure and mezzanine debt will comprise a significantly larger portion of the capital structure than the second lien layer.

Mezzanine debt structures

7.2   A structure incorporating mezzanine debt can be represented in diagrammatic form as follows.[4]

---

3   By one recent statistic, by the second half of the 2000s, it will have accounted for less than 10% by
    volume of all mezzanine debt issued in Europe.
4   See **Chapter 3** on structuring generally.

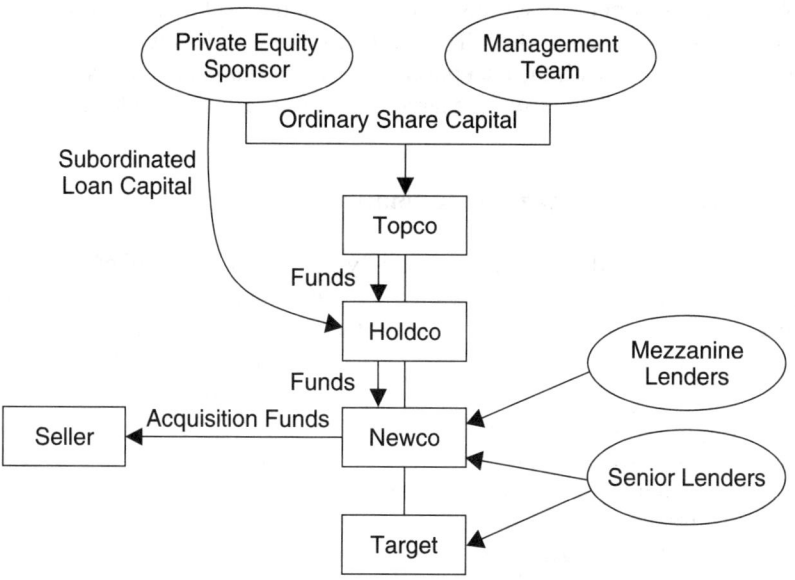

Senior, second lien and mezzanine

As indicated above, mezzanine debt may also be used in a structure with second lien debt, in which case the structure would typically be as follows.

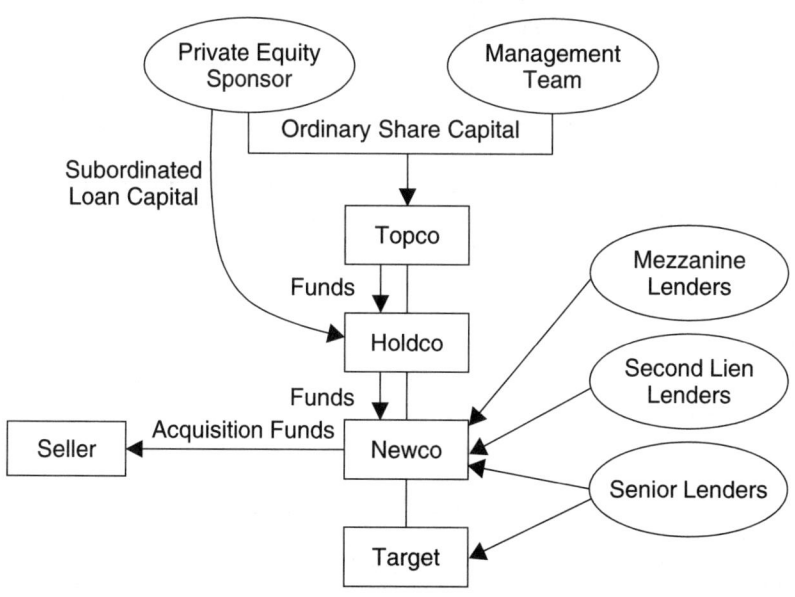

Senior, second lien and mezzanine

As can be seen in the diagrams above, mezzanine debt benefits from the same structural status as senior debt. That is, mezzanine lenders will share the same borrower (possibly with the exception of the target[5]) and have the same guarantee and security package from the target group as the senior lenders.

Who provides the mezzanine finance?

7.3   As indicated above, there are really two mezzanine markets operating in Europe: the warranted or true mezzanine market, and the warrantless or institutional mezzanine market. Whilst it is still the acquisition finance banks and specialist mezzanine houses that are largely arranging and underwriting the finance in each of these markets, the syndication strategies and distribution channels are very different. True mezzanine tranches rarely exceed £25 million and consequently do not need to be syndicated as widely as institutional mezzanine tranches which may be 10 to 20 times that size. So whilst much of an institutional mezzanine tranche will be syndicated to institutional investors, a significant proportion of all true mezzanine paper is still held by banks and specialist mezzanine houses. Aside from the obvious need to syndicate larger tranches more widely, there are two further observations that can be made. First, many institutional investors have limited personnel resources dedicated to finding prospective investments. This naturally means that they tend to focus on transactions where they can make larger investments. Secondly, institutional investors are less interested in warranted mezzanine that characterises the true mezzanine market than warrantless mezzanine that characterises the institutional mezzanine market. Warrantless mezzanine often has a higher interest rate (the 'contracted' return) than warranted mezzanine and the contracted return is the key investment criterion for most institutional investors.

So in most cases – perhaps excluding smaller deals with tranche sizes of £15 million or less – mezzanine debt will be syndicated. The arranger and underwriter will typically retain a portion of the mezzanine debt and in most cases will also act as the agent for the syndicate.

The arranger and underwriter will receive an up-front arrangement and underwriting fee payable by newco on completion. The fee will be of an amount equal to a percentage of the total amount of the mezzanine debt.[6] Customarily a portion of such fee would be paid by the arranger to the syndicate lenders. However, many institutional investors may not demand any, or a significant part, of the up-front fee in return for their investment leaving more for the mezzanine debt arranger. One obvious effect of this has been to reduce the average up-front fee payable for institutional mezzanine debt, although not by as much as the reduction in fees required by the institutional market.

5   For which there may be adverse consequences for the mezzanine lenders in a multi-jurisdictional buy-out. See **Chapter 13**.
6   The amount of this fee will often be higher than the up-front fee payable to the senior debt arranger, perhaps in the region of 2.0 to 2.5% (and historically materially higher). Alternatively, where the entire senior and mezzanine debt package is being arranged and underwritten together by one or more MLAs, the up-front fee may be of an agreed percentage flat on both the senior and mezzanine debt. This might be in the region of say 1.75% to 2.25%.

What does mezzanine finance comprise?

Mezzanine loans

7.4   In all but the largest transactions, the mezzanine finance package will typically comprise a single term loan repayable in one 'bullet' amount 12 months after the final instalment of senior and second lien debt. So if the senior debt includes A, B and C tranches repayable over seven, eight and nine years respectively, the mezzanine loan will be repayable 10 years after completion.[7] In a transaction with second lien debt, which usually matures at year 9.5, the mezzanine will similarly be repayable at year 10. Since the mezzanine loan is subordinated behind the senior debt – it may only be repaid after all of the senior and any second lien debt has been repaid in full, including upon any insolvency and winding up of the borrower – it will have a higher risk profile. Consequently, the interest rate margin over the underlying cost of funds[8] will be much higher than for the senior debt.[9] The margin and thus all-in interest rate (in this context often referred to as the 'contracted' or 'contractual' return) is usually set higher for warrantless mezzanine since there is no potential return under warrants. Of the headline margin figure approximately half, or perhaps a little more than half in the case of warrantless mezzanine, would not actually be payable in cash on a current basis during the life of the loan – rather, on the date that it would otherwise be paid, it will be capitalised and added to the existing principal amount of the loan, and so accrues compound interest. That part of the margin that is capitalised in this way is said to be 'paid in kind'. It is thus referred to as the 'PIK' element of the interest payable. Since it becomes principal, the PIK element is only paid once the principal amount of the mezzanine loan is repaid at final maturity after, say, 10 years.

As with the equity sponsor, mezzanine lenders traditionally benchmarked their prospective returns in terms of a target 'IRR'. This was because of the warrant component of the package. With warrantless mezzanine an IRR is not necessary as the entire return is contracted at the outset. However, for 'true' mezzanine with warrants an IRR is still used so that the warrant can be priced in. The IRR will generally be quoted inclusive of the underlying interest rate,[10] which suggests that the actual IRR sought will be different for loans in different currencies, reflecting the fact that the underlying interest rate will be higher for some currencies than others. Given the rise and widespread use of warrantless mezzanine in place of warranted mezzanine, however, the more common way of referencing the target pricing is to quote it as a margin over 'cost of funds'. This appears to eliminate the effect of differential cost of funds for different currencies, although, of course, for borrowers they will be obliged to pay the all-in cost and bear whatever the underlying interest rate is in the relevant currency. It is worth further noting that whereas senior debt includes a significant proportion provided

---

7   It is a fundamental characteristic of junior debt that it is only repayable after all of the senior debt has been repaid in full.

8   LIBOR or EURIBOR.

9   See fn **12** below.

10   EURIBOR for euros and LIBOR for sterling and other currencies.

by banks that do actually fund themselves through interbank borrowings,[11] such that quoting returns purely on a margin over cost of funds is an appropriate measure of return, mezzanine debt is often provided by non-bank institutional investors. As a result, for many mezzanine investors that do not actually fund their investments through bank or interbank borrowings, an 'all-in' quote including the underlying cost of funds would generally be a more useful measure of their target return than a margin over cost of funds. In any event, the latter approach is still prevalent. In terms of the target returns of mezzanine lenders, this is largely a function of a supply and demand dynamic and mezzanine pricing has generally proven to be more flexible than eg, senior debt. In particular, as the supply of institutional investors willing to invest in this part of the funding structure increased during the 2000s – and with the advent of second lien debt as a viable, cheaper, alternative product – so mezzanine returns reduced.[12]

The mezzanine loan will generally only be made available to newco for funding the acquisition of the target business and meeting deal costs,[13] and it will be drawn in full at completion of the acquisition at the same time as the senior acquisition loan.[14] Typically therefore, it will be borrowed in the currency in which the acquisition purchase price is payable.

In certain circumstances, usually only in the larger deals, the mezzanine debt may be structured in two tranches. This is usually for the purpose of increasing the overall amount of mezzanine debt. In doing so it is likely that the mezzanine arranger would have a 'senior' mezzanine loan and a 'junior' mezzanine loan with the latter being subordinated in right of payment to the former. The junior mezzanine loan will typically have higher pricing to reflect its subordination and the greater risk of not ultimately being repaid. Higher pricing will be reflected in the interest rate margin and possibly also by having warrants – even in the case of institutional mezzanine, where the main mezzanine tranche will be warrantless – or, if the senior mezzanine loan *is* warranted, more warrants than the senior mezzanine loan.

The junior mezzanine tranche might also be structured and documented with fewer protections than the senior mezzanine tranche. For instance it might be structured as a 'pay-if-you-can' (PIYC) or 'pay-if-you-want' (PIYW) mezzanine

---

11 Although the increase in institutional senior debt raised from non-bank institutional investors has been one of the key features of the senior debt market in the 2000s.

12 Until summer 2007 target returns for mezzanine investors had reduced to relatively low levels, in the region of, for warrantless mezzanine, a margin of 750–1050 basis points over cost of funds (historically a range of 800–1200 basis points was common). Based on approximate average interest rates in 2006 and 2007, for euro loans this reflects an all-in return of between 11% and 13% and for sterling loans between 13% and 15%. For warranted mezzanine the target IRRs tend to be higher, say, in the range 14-16% with the differential effect of the underlying cost of funds (i.e. the currency of the debt in particular) not being accredited quite the same relevance. These IRR targets typically exclude the up-front fees payable to the arranger/underwriter.

13 Which is why, in multi-jurisdictional deals, it might end up being relatively undersecured. See **Chapter 13**.

14 In a public to private buy–out structured as a takeover offer, where the acquisition debt is only needed in stages, the mezzanine loan will be drawn down in full at the same time as the first tranche of the senior acquisition loan is drawn down and the equity is invested. This will be when the first batch of acceptances are due for settlement (payment) following the offer being declared unconditional in all respects.

loan. With PIYC mezzanine the cash pay element of the interest rate will be automatically converted into PIK interest if certain financial performance criteria are not met or if such criteria would not be met if the relevant interest payment were made. It is common for the financial performance criteria to be set by reference to the financial covenants in the senior facilities agreement. Importantly, if the cash interest is stopped in this way, the junior mezzanine lenders would not have any acceleration rights in respect of the non-payment as the mezzanine facility agreement would be drafted to provide that no event of default would arise in that circumstance. The effect is therefore that the financing structure effectively self-adjusts upon a downturn in the financial performance of the target business. As less cash is produced so the cash required to meet junior mezzanine interest payments is also automatically reduced. With PIYC mezzanine, dis-application of the non-payment event of default might be for a limited time period only. So in effect the PIYC mezzanine loan reverts to a conventional mezzanine loan after that period.[15]

PIYW mezzanine is very similar to PIYC mezzanine except that the trigger for the cash pay interest to convert to PIK interest is not failure to meet objective financial performance criteria but the borrower's own assessment of the need to defer a cash payment – in other words, it is left to the borrower's discretion whether or not to pay the mezzanine interest in cash or in kind. The ability to switch the cash pay element of the interest to PIK in this way is often described as the PIK or junior interest 'toggle'. A differential margin might be payable for this option; so perhaps an additional 50 basis points would be added to the margin if the cash interest were 'toggled off' (ie, switched to PIK).

As the market for leverage has heated up – with more debt investors willing to provide more debt for acquisition finance structures – both PIYC mezzanine and mezzanine incorporating a PIK toggle (PIYW mezzanine) have become more common and in some cases the entire mezzanine loan (and not just a junior strip) may be structured in that way. This tends to be more common in the larger deals.

Amount of mezzanine loan

7.5   Once it is established in principle that mezzanine debt will be required or used in a structure, the precise amount of the debt will be determined as the total amount of the debt and the overall funding structure are finalised. Although mezzanine debt – or indeed any other junior debt – may appear to be used simply to plug a funding gap, it would be wrong to suggest that this is its only function. Mezzanine debt plays a fundamental role in developing the appropriate structure for many acquisition finance structures and in particular in increasing the total amount of debt available for an acquisition.

As with the senior lenders and senior debt, the mezzanine lenders will use a financial model to satisfy themselves that newco will have sufficient cashflow to pay scheduled principal and interest in respect of all the acquisition finance

---

15 Note, however, that even a conventional mezzanine loan cannot be immediately accelerated upon a
    payment default. Usually a 90-day standstill period applies following a payment default. See **Chapter
    10**.

including the mezzanine loan.[16] In addition, a detailed credit analysis of the target business will be a key factor in assessing how much debt may be made available.

As previously noted, since the early 2000s the potential size of a mezzanine loan has increased significantly. During the 1990s a mezzanine loan would rarely have exceeded £50 million, whereas mezzanine loans of 10 times that or more are feasible since the evolution of institutional mezzanine debt in the 2000s.

Warrants

7.6   Given that the mezzanine loan is a relatively high risk form of debt, sitting behind a large tranche of senior debt and possibly a tranche of second lien debt, mezzanine lenders were historically able to negotiate share options (warrants) from topco[17] to enhance their return on the mezzanine loan. However during the 2000s, for reasons outlined above,[18] a new category of warrantless mezzanine debt emerged (institutional mezzanine) which has firmly established itself as the product of choice in most buy-outs, with the exception of lower mid-market and smaller deals. Financial sponsors prefer warrantless mezzanine since it avoids the dilutive effects of a warrant on the equity upon exit. As a result, other than as indicated, mezzanine warrants have become relatively rare; although on some larger deals junior mezzanine loans may still attract warrants.[19]

The following paragraphs consider the key features of mezzanine warrants.

As indicated, a warrant is a form of share option. In the context of mezzanine finance, a warrant will grant to the holder the right to subscribe for shares in the ordinary share capital of the equity investment vehicle, usually at the top of the acquisition structure – topco. The number of shares that may be subscribed for will either be a fixed number or it will be a fixed percentage of the share capital in issue at the relevant time. From the mezzanine lenders' perspective the latter is generally preferable to the former, since it automatically protects the warrant holder from the dilutive effects of share issues in the period between the date of issue of the warrant and the date on which the warrant is exercised. The number or percentage will be set at that level which, based on agreed assumptions as to the exit price and timing – usually assuming performance of the target business in line with the base case model (ideally from the mezzanine lender's perspective using the more conservative financing case rather than the management team's base case because this will generally lead to more warrants being issued so as to meet the target IRR of the mezzanine lenders) and taking into account the yield on the mezzanine loan (both cash and PIK) – yields the desired IRR for the mezzanine lenders. This might mean that the warrant will be in respect of, say, 3 or

---

16 Note that because the principal amount of the mezzanine loan and a portion of the interest (the PIK element) will only be payable after year 10, say, the cashflow requirements for mezzanine debt are different from those for the senior debt. In any event, the mezzanine lenders still need to be satisfied that there will be sufficient cash to meet all of the senior debt service requirements as well as the mezzanine debt, as the senior debt is payable in priority to the mezzanine debt.

17 Topco is the name often given to the highest SPV in the corporate structure which issues the management and institutional equity (ordinary shares).

18 See para **7.1**.

19 See para **7.4**.

4% of the ordinary share capital ie, either the number of shares representing this percentage at completion or that percentage of the issued share capital outstanding upon exercise. Warrants are exercisable by their holders, the mezzanine lenders, upon the occurrence of certain events, usually limited to pre-agreed exits in respect of the institutional and management equity.[20]

In practical terms, the mezzanine lenders will exercise their warrants immediately prior to a flotation or sale so that the shares issued to them upon such exercise are also subject to the flotation or sale.[21] The capital growth and value of the target business is largely locked into the ordinary share capital of the equity investment vehicle (topco) and this is the class of shares into which the mezzanine warrants will be exercisable.

Because warrants provide the potential economic upside of the equity element of a funding structure they were originally referred to as the 'equity kicker'.

Warrants are structured in the form of transferable 'warrants' rather than a simple share option agreement in order to enable easy transfer, essentially for the purposes of syndication of the mezzanine finance. In documentation terms, a number of individual warrants, each in respect of a fraction of the overall number of warrants to be issued, are constituted by a single warrant instrument executed by topco which sets out all the rights attaching to the warrants. The warrants are then issued to the mezzanine lenders who each get a certificate evidencing its warrants. Warrant certificates are akin to share certificates in that whilst they evidence ownership it is a separate register that formally determines ownership. Warrants are also usually transferred using a stock transfer form in the same way as shares.

DOCUMENTING THE MEZZANINE DEBT

7.7   The following paragraphs consider the nature of the principal documents which are used to document the mezzanine debt.

Mezzanine debt documents

7.8   In a UK buy-out the mezzanine debt documentation will comprise the following core documents:

- mezzanine facility agreement;

- possibly a warrant instrument;

- intercreditor agreement;

---

20 Essentially, flotation or sale, but see para **7.20** for more detail.
21 In practice, at the time of the flotation or sale the mezzanine lenders will often not actually have shares issued to them. Rather, they will simply receive the cash consideration due to them from the sale or flotation, as if they had actually had the shares issued to them, and the warrants are cancelled.

- security agreement;[22] and

- hedging agreement.[23]

Each of these documents is considered in the following paragraphs.

Mezzanine facility agreement

7.9   The provisions contained in the mezzanine facility agreement will substantially mirror those in the senior facilities agreement.[24] Indeed, it is common practice for the mezzanine facility agreement to be duplicated from the senior facilities agreement after much of the negotiation on that document has occurred. Changes are then made only to those provisions which are specific to the mezzanine finance structure. The following section outlines some of the more important provisions of the document which will usually require amendment from the senior template.[25]

Memorandum on front page and intercreditor override

7.10   Often, the senior banks will require the front cover of the mezzanine facility agreement to be endorsed with a memorandum recording that the mezzanine debt is subordinated to the senior debt under the terms of the intercreditor agreement.

In addition, the operative provisions of the document will also usually be expressed to be subject to the intercreditor agreement.

The facility

7.11   Typically a senior debt package will comprise a number of facilities, including up to three or more tranches of acquisition debt. A mezzanine finance package, by contrast, will commonly comprise a single term loan facility although this may be split into two tranches.[26]

Interest

7.12   The interest rate margin applicable to mezzanine debt will incorporate a cash-pay element and a non-cash-pay (PIK) element, whereas the senior interest will be all cash. The interest payment provision should specify that on each

---

22 With UK security a single security agreement will be used to create security for the senior, second lien (if any) *and* mezzanine debt. The security agreement will be executed in favour of a security trustee who holds the benefit of the security on trust for all of the secured lenders.

23 In practice, there is unlikely to be separate hedging documentation for the mezzanine debt; rather a single set will document the hedging for all of senior, second lien (if any) and mezzanine debt.

24 See **Chapter 5**.

25 This section focuses on the principal differences from a senior facilities agreement and **Chapter 5** should be referred to for all other provisions, as they would appear in a senior facilities agreement. In addition to the specific provisions referred to in this section there will necessarily be several consequential drafting changes that the mezzanine lenders' lawyers will need to make.

26 The use of 'senior' and 'junior' mezzanine tranches is quite common. The junior tranche will usually be subordinated in right of payment – and possibly on insolvency and security enforcement – to the senior tranche.

interest payment date the borrower will pay interest to the mezzanine lenders at the rate of the underlying cost of funds (LIBOR/EURIBOR), plus any mandatory costs, plus the cash pay margin.

The provision should also state that a further amount of interest accrues at a rate equal to the PIK element of the margin (sometimes also called the 'capitalised rate'). On each interest payment date the PIK interest is not paid to the mezzanine lenders but is capitalised as principal and added to the existing principal amount of the mezzanine debt. This part of the interest will therefore compound on each interest payment date.

At the insistence of the senior lenders, as part of the mezzanine interest payment conditions in the intercreditor agreement, the interest payment dates will usually be set at fixed three, or more often six, monthly intervals during the life of the loan. Each will be set to fall a short period after a senior financial covenant test date.[27]

With mezzanine that has a PIK toggle[28] the borrower can elect to pay interest either in cash or in kind on the relevant interest payment date and the interest payment clause must be drafted accordingly. Similarly, the interest component of PIYC mezzanine[29] may automatically switch cash pay interest to PIK interest if the relevant financial criteria are not met at the time of payment.

There will be no ratchet applicable to the interest rate margin as there is with the senior margin.

Prepayment

7.13   Although the mezzanine facility agreement will incorporate the same voluntary and mandatory prepayment provisions as the senior facilities agreement, any prepayments should be expressed to be subject to the prior repayment in full of the senior and second lien debt, if any. This may also be achieved by referring to the intercreditor agreement, which will enshrine this principle.

Yield protection

7.14   In addition to standard market disruption, tax gross-up and indemnity and increased cost provisions, in the same form as the equivalent senior provisions, mezzanine debt will traditionally benefit from yield protection in the form of early prepayment premia. This will be structured as a fee that is payable on principal amounts of the mezzanine debt prepaid in the first two or three years following completion.[30] The quantum of the prepayment fee will usually be stepped such that a prepayment in the first year after completion triggers a fee of

---

27 See **Chapter 10**. This period should be long enough to enable the financial covenants to be tested plus a few further days for the senior lenders to assess the covenant compliance and if necessary issue a payment blockage notice to stop the interest being paid. Payment blockage provisions are also considered in **Chapter 10**.

28 See para **7.4**.

29 See para **7.4**.

30 In practice, this will almost certainly mean a repayment of all of the mezzanine debt, rather than a part repayment, arising on a refinancing of the entire debt structure. Mezzanine debt is unlikely to be prepaid in part (rather than in full) because of the restrictions on payments of principal prior to the senior ranking debt.

say 2%, and in year 2, 1%.[31] A lender that is prepaid from the proceeds of a refinancing in which it participates would usually not qualify for a prepayment fee on the basis that by going into the new facility the lender is not losing yield. In addition, such a lender might also receive an upfront fee for recommitting to the new facility.

A prepayment from the proceeds of an equity exit – sale or flotation – will not generally trigger a prepayment fee with warranted mezzanine on the basis that the warrants themselves should generate an equity return for the mezzanine lenders to compensate for the early repayment of the debt and consequent loss of future interest yield. That rationale, however, does not apply to warrantless mezzanine debt and early repayment fees should also apply on an equity exit.

Unlike high yield debt, mezzanine would rarely benefit from a non-call provision prohibiting voluntary prepayment for a period following completion.

Topco board director or observer

7.15   In some cases, the lead mezzanine lender will require an undertaking enabling it to nominate a director to the board of topco either as an observer or, but this is rare, with voting powers. There are two circumstances where this is common. First, with warranted mezzanine it is customary for the mezzanine lender to be permitted to nominate an observer who can attend, but not participate or vote in, board meetings of topco. The rationale is to allow the lender, in its capacity as warrant holder, and thus with an equity interest in the business, to monitor the strategic management of the business. Secondly, certain institutional investors that are directly or indirectly investing US pension fund money generally require that the fund be granted certain management rights in order to qualify as a venture capital operating company (VCOC) for the purposes of the investment. To meet such requirements it is usual for topco to issue to the fund a side letter or to enter into a management rights agreement (commonly known as a VCOC letter) whereby the fund is granted among other things a right to appoint a person to the board of topco or a set of rights to receive information and to consult with management – which might include the right to appoint a non-voting board observer.

Financial covenants

7.16   As a general principle the representations, undertakings, and events of default in the senior facilities agreement will all be mirrored in the mezzanine facility agreement. This includes the financial covenants. Two exceptions to this approach are commonly adopted, however. First, the financial covenants in the mezzanine facility agreement will often be set with greater headroom against the base case model than the financial covenants in the senior facilities agreement.[32] The purpose of this is to avoid a mezzanine default occurring at the same time

---

31 The actual quantum is negotiable but the numbers given are not uncommon.

32 It is not uncommon for there to be 10% more headroom than for the senior financial covenants. This allows for that amount of additional financial under-performance by the target business before breach of the mezzanine financial covenants occurs after breach of the senior financial covenants. The cash-flow/fixed charge cover and capex covenants are not always subject to this approach, however, and they may be set to breach as the same point in both senior and mezzanine facility agreements.

that breach of the senior financial covenants occurs. In this way, any waiver of the breach would only need the support of the senior lenders, and not the mezzanine lenders. Equally, any initial discussions as to refining the funding structure to reflect the financial underperformance would not *need* to involve the mezzanine lenders. This will also deny the mezzanine lenders the opportunity to commence a standstill period as a first step towards acceleration of the mezzanine facility and enforcement of the security given by the group. The senior lenders, on the other hand, will have the option of waiving the breach, blocking the mezzanine interest or accelerating the senior facilities.

If the mezzanine covenants are to be set at a different threshold in this way the cross-default event of default in the mezzanine facility agreement must be drafted so that it is not triggered by breach of the senior financial covenants.

Warrants

7.17 With warranted mezzanine, execution of the warrant instrument and delivery of warrant certificates (and a copy of the warrant register) will be additional CPs.

Warrant instrument

7.18 Traditionally a key commercial element of mezzanine finance has been the granting to the mezzanine lenders of warrants issued by the equity vehicle. However, since the early to mid-2000s warranted mezzanine has largely been confined to the lower mid-market and smaller deals as the vast majority of mid-market and larger deals – the institutional mezzanine market – rarely feature mezzanine with warrants.[33]

Warrants are documented by way of a warrant instrument executed by topco.[34] It is this instrument which constitutes the warrants. Individual warrants are evidenced by warrant certificates and ultimately by entries on a register of warrant holders. It is the register, as with registered shares, which is usually conclusive as to ownership rather than a certificate. The use of a warrant instrument executed as an English law deed poll means that the mezzanine lenders themselves are not party to the instrument although they will receive warrant certificates executed in their names. This facilitates transfers of the warrants as subsequent holders do not need to accede to the instrument; they simply take a transfer of warrants.

The following paragraphs consider a number of the key provisions commonly found in warrant instruments.

Basic structure

7.19 A warrant instrument will typically contain the following provisions, with highlighted areas discussed in more detail below:

● Constitution of the warrants – creation of the rights to subscribe for shares in topco.

33 An exception to this may be with junior mezzanine loans. See para **7.4**.
34 The warrants should be issued by whichever company is the investment vehicle for the true equity.

- Notification of a pending exit event – topco is obliged to inform the warrant holders of those events which would entitle the warrant holders to exercise the warrants.

- **Exercise of warrants**.

- Completion of the subscription for the warrant shares – the issue to the warrant holders of the shares subscribed for upon payment in full of the subscription moneys.

- **Undertakings by topco including anti-dilution provisions**.

- Distribution to the warrant holders on a winding up of topco – this provision deems a solvent winding-up to have been an exit and the warrant holders to have exercised their warrants. It is included for completeness because the warrant holders will not be 'party' to topco's articles of association prior to the exercise of the warrants.[35]

- **Transfer of warrants**.

- Meetings of warrant holders – there will be provisions, similar to those applicable to shareholder meetings in articles of association, dealing with meetings and resolutions of warrant holders.

- Boilerplate clauses – including notices, governing law, resolution of disputes and replacement of lost or defaced warrant certificates.

- Schedules will contain agreed forms of exercise notification and warrant certificate and boilerplate provisions in respect of meetings and decisions of the warrant holders, the transfer and registration of warrants and such like.

Exercise of the warrants

Exit events

7.20   The warrants will be exercisable in respect of certain specified events, usually described as 'exit events' because they reflect economic exit opportunities for the equity investors in a buy-out.[36] In practical terms, *topco* will trigger the exercise process by delivery to the warrant holders of notification that an exit is to occur.[37]

The typical exit events will be:

- IPO (or 'flotation' of shares) by a member of the group; and

- sale of the target business including through a secondary buy-out.

In addition, the instrument may be drafted to allow the holders to exercise their warrants in order to participate in capital events such as a distribution or

---

35 It is theoretically possible that the proceeds of an exit could be distributed by a solvent winding-up of topco but extremely unlikely in practice.

36 Exits are considered generally in **Chapter 1**.

37 Typically, the exit notification must be delivered at least 21 days before the exit is to occur.

redemption of equity. Capital events are considered below under anti-dilution provisions.

In practice, the definitions of 'IPO' or 'flotation' and 'sale' should mirror the equivalent definitions in the equity documents. This will ensure a consistent approach to the relevant exit provisions in the equity documents and, in particular, from the warrant holders' perspective, the application of tag-along rights.[38]

Class of warrant shares

7.21   In most cases the warrants will exercise into their own class of 'warrant shares'. An alternative is for them to exercise into the same class as the sponsor's ordinary shares, although as considered below this is generally less preferable. The warrant shares should be a different class of ordinary shares to the management team's, which will be subject to various rights and restrictions that should not apply to warrant shares.[39]

One determining factor is often the par value of the institutional ordinary shares, which may be £1. For reasons discussed below, the warrant holders will generally prefer one penny shares, or another de minimis par value. In addition, certain rights that may attach to the institutional ordinary shares would not be appropriate for warrant shares; such as the right to appoint one or more full directors to the board of topco or enhanced voting rights in certain circumstances. Where there is a management performance ratchet this may operate by converting institutional ordinary shares to worthless deferred shares or into the management ordinary shares and the warrant holders should not be subject to such a mechanism.

Aside from the matters referred to above, the warrant shares should essentially have the same rights as the institutional ordinary shares. Whatever class of shares is allocated to the warrant holders, the articles of association of topco should provide that a sufficient amount of share capital is authorised to enable the exercise of the warrants in full and the issue of the full amount of warrant shares to the warrant holders at exit.

Given their economic interest in the equity of the group, the warrant holders will have a number of concerns in respect of the equity documents themselves. These are considered briefly in **Chapter 4**.

Number of warrant shares

7.22   Warrant instruments either provide that the number of shares to be issued on exercise of the warrants is a stated number agreed at signing or that it

---

38 However, whilst adopting this general approach is preferable, care must be taken to ensure that the definitions used in the equity documents do pick up every circumstance when an economic exit for the warrant holders should occur. For example, the definition of 'sale' in the equity documents might be expressed to exclude a transfer of equity to a related private equity fund. This is designed to allow the sponsor to place the equity in different funds managed by it. But the definition should not exclude a sale to an entirely different private equity fund, as in a secondary buy-out, as this should be an exit for the warrant holders. The same definitions should also be used in the mandatory prepayment events set out in the senior facilities agreement and the mezzanine facilities agreement.

39 For instance, there will be transfer restrictions, possibly a performance ratchet that will change the number of ordinary shares at exit and usually limited rights to participate in distributions.

is a fixed percentage of the diluted ordinary share capital at the time of the relevant exit.

The warrant holders will prefer to use the percentage approach since their rights will be less vulnerable to dilution by interim issues of shares than is the case with warrants to subscribe for a stated number of shares. This approach also more accurately reflects the commercial purpose of the warrants.[40] Conversely, topco and the equity investors will often prefer the stated number of shares approach. The determination of the number of warrant shares – by percentage or fixed number – that the warrant holders will be allocated will usually be made on the basis of an assumed exit at a valuation determined on the basis that the business performs in line with the base case model[41] and at the same multiple of EBITDA (the exit multiple) as the original purchase price (the entry multiple).

Where the percentage approach is used the number of shares to be issued will be x% of the equity share capital of topco at exit, after taking into account the exercise of any share options and warrants issued by topco, including the mezzanine warrants, and the operation of any management performance ratchet.[42] With the fixed number of shares approach the warrant holders just get that number of shares no matter what the equity share capital of topco is at exit and any interim issue of shares, other than for full market value in cash, will have a dilutive effect on the warrants.

Consequently, where the fixed number approach is used, anti–dilution undertakings should be required by the warrant holders to protect the value of their warrants. Conversely, where the percentage approach is used, which in practice is more common, the sponsor should insist on reverse anti-dilution rights so that the warrant holders do not take the benefit of an interim issue of shares at full market value without participating in that issue and paying in their share of the subscription cost.

Subscription price of the warrant shares

7.23   The warrant holders will wish to be able to exercise the warrants at as low a subscription price as possible. Indeed, in determining the number or percentage of shares they are allocated, by reference to a target IRR, no account may be taken of the subscription price for the warrant shares; that is, the calculations may assume it to be zero. If this is the case the subscription price should in fact be de minimis to ensure consistency with the initial valuation of the warrants.

Since the shares may not be issued at a discount, this means having as low a par value as possible. Thus one penny per share is not uncommon. The par value of topco's other ordinary shares, by contrast, is likely to be £1. As discussed above, this is one reason why the warrant holders might wish to have their own class of ordinary shares.

---

40   In that the mezzanine lenders will assume that they will receive a certain percentage of the exit proceeds in due course and that there will be no interim issues of shares.

41   When determining the relevant percentage (x), the prospective warrant holders may prefer to use their own, more conservative, base case model rather than the 'equity case', on the basis that a greater percentage of the equity would be needed to reach their target IRR; ie, x must be greater.

42   See **Chapter 4** for a brief consideration of management performance ratchets.

Anti–dilution rights

7.24   Where the fixed number of warrant shares approach is taken, the warrant holders should require undertakings from topco in terms which prevent the warrant shares being diluted by further issues of shares. In addition, it is usual to have anti–dilution undertakings which prevent *economic* dilution other than through the issue of further shares and these undertakings should also be included in the warrant instrument *whichever approach is taken.*

Dilution from further share issues

7.25   The principal anti-dilution undertaking to be incorporated, where the fixed number of warrant shares approach is taken, will usually be drafted as a right of the warrant holders to participate in any further issue of ordinary shares – by topco – following completion. The clause will give the warrant holders the right to subscribe for that number of shares that is proportionate to their existing entitlement under the warrants – and thereby maintain the same overall percentage interest in the equity. If the warrant holders do not wish to participate in the further issue then they will be diluted to the extent of the new issue.[43]

An alternative to that form of anti-dilution provision is where the warrant holders are issued with further warrants that give additional subscription rights pro rata to the original entitlements. In that way the warrant holders would not be required to subscribe for their part of the new issue until exit. This approach is arguably more consistent with the general purpose of warrants than the 'put up or shut up' approach referred to in the preceding paragraph.

Where the warrant instrument is drafted using the percentage approach, this form of anti-dilution provision is not necessary because the warrant holders' subscription rights automatically increase proportionately if there is an interim issue of shares prior to exercise. However, the sponsor will usually ask for protection against the warrant holders abusing their non-dilutable position through a reverse anti-dilution provision.

A capitalisation issue, where the company's profits or reserves are capitalised, may also have a dilutive effect on the warrants in the same way that a dividend in specie would and the warrant holders should require that such issues are prohibited or also subject to a participation right in their favour.

Reverse anti–dilution rights

7.26   A warrant that can never be diluted as to the proportion of shares to be subscribed at exit, using the percentage rather than fixed number of shares approach, is called an 'evergreen' warrant. Such warrants are rare in the buy-out market because financial sponsors do not like to give the warrant holders a free ride on any new issues at market value. An issue of new shares at market value will increase the aggregate value of the equity in topco and the increase will not simply be limited to the shares subscribed, it will be spread proportionately over all of the equity share capital, including the warrant shares. So unless the warrant

---

43 Such clauses are often colloquially referred to as 'put up or shut up' clauses because the warrant holders must either subscribe for their share of the new issue or be diluted by it.

holders participate in the new share issue and contribute their proportionate share of the subscription cost, the investors in the new share capital issued will, in effect, have subsidised the value increase to the warrants. Reverse anti-dilution provisions are designed to avoid this.

In its usual form, a reverse anti-dilution clause will state that an issue at market value[44] *will* dilute the warrants unless the warrant holders participate in the new issue at the issue price; it is a form of 'put-up or shut-up'. With a warrant for a fixed number of shares, reverse anti-dilution is not required since *all* issues will dilute the warrants unless the warrant holders participate and subscribe.

Economic dilution

7.27   Although the most obvious cause of dilution of the warrants – that is, the company issuing more shares – is avoided if the percentage approach is used, the making of distributions to shareholders – and not the warrant holders – will also reduce the economic value of the warrants.

The making of a distribution of cash or assets represents value going out of the group and, other than for equity holders that participate in the distribution, will reduce the value of the equity in topco. Warrant holders should therefore insist on a dividend block or dividend sharing provision being included in the warrant instrument. In the case of a dividend sharing provision the preferable form from the warrant holders' perspective will oblige topco to make a payment to the warrant holders of an amount equal to the amount of the dividend, or other distribution, that the warrant holders would have been entitled to had they exercised their warrants and been shareholders on the record date for payment of the dividend. The sponsor may alternatively prefer a provision whereby the warrant holders would have the opportunity to exercise their warrants in order to then participate in the dividend as a shareholder.

In practice, the acquisition finance documentation – the subordination arrangements, in particular – will often restrict the payment of dividends at least until the acquisition finance debt has been repaid and a dividend block may thus apply. In these circumstances and given that in theory, but unlikely in practice since the mezzanine debt is usually repaid out of an exit, the warrants may still remain unexercised even after the acquisition finance has been repaid (and thus no longer have the benefit of provisions in the main acquisition finance documentation), a dividend block should also be included in the warrant instrument.

Capital redemptions are also usually prohibited. Finally, warrant holders should consider the economic effect of the yield on any quasi-equity on the value of their warrant equity; although their model should take this into account in the first place.

Arm's length transactions

7.28   A more general anti-dilution provision that should be included in the warrant instrument is an undertaking by topco not to permit the group to enter

---

44   The 'market value' will often be required to be certified by the board of topco or less often through a third-party valuation.

into transactions other than on a commercial arms' length basis. This undertaking, whilst not onerous on topco, provides a general level of protection for the warrant holders against any other economic dilution to the value of the target business.

Other undertakings

7.29   Warrant instruments will also commonly contain the following undertakings by topco.

Financial information

7.30   The warrant instrument should include an undertaking to provide the warrant holders with financial and other information. The precise scope will be negotiable but from the warrant holders' perspective it should allow them to receive most, if not all, of the information that lenders are entitled to receive under the mezzanine facility agreement.

Authorised share capital

7.31   Topco should undertake that at all times it maintains sufficient authorised and unissued share capital of the same class as the warrant shares to enable full exercise of the warrants and the issue of all the warrant shares to the warrant holders without any further corporate steps being required.

Amendments to constitutional documents

7.32   The warrant holders will also wish to include an undertaking from topco not to amend its memorandum or articles of association so as to prejudice the warrant holders (as prospective shareholders).[45]

Transfer of warrants

7.33   The warrants should be expressed to be freely transferable or at least transferable to anyone that the mezzanine debt can be transferred to. This is necessary to enable the syndication of the mezzanine debt to include the transfer of warrants to the participating mezzanine lenders.

In drafting the transfer provision care must be taken to ensure that the warrants are not expressed to be transferable only with a pro rata proportion of the mezzanine debt itself – so-called 'stapled' warrants – as this could in theory give rise to adverse tax treatment of the mezzanine debt.

Consistency with equity documents

7.34   When drafting and negotiating a warrant instrument the lawyers for the mezzanine lenders will also need to carefully review the equity documents and, in particular, the topco articles and investment agreement. Certain provisions of

---

45   In fact, such an undertaking – by topco – may be unenforceable under English law, even though they are commonly included in warrant instruments.

those documents impact directly on the position of the warrant holders, including, in particular, the rights attaching to the warrant shares and the applicability to the warrants of the drag-along and tag-along rights. Such matters are considered in further detail in **Chapter 4**.

Intercreditor, security and hedging documents

Intercreditor agreement

7.35   There will invariably be an intercreditor agreement between the senior lenders, any second lien lenders and the mezzanine lenders for the purposes of subordinating the mezzanine debt to the prior-ranking debt. It is usual for the same agreement to be used to prioritise all of the layers of the acquisition finance, the equity loan capital and the group's intercompany debt. In addition to the contractual subordination provisions, the intercreditor agreement will include the appointment of a security trustee to hold the benefit of the security on trust for all secured acquisition financiers including the mezzanine lenders.[46] The form of the intercreditor agreement and the subordination agreements generally applicable to mezzanine debt are considered in some detail in **Chapter 10**.

Security documents

7.36   The mezzanine lenders should expect to get precisely the same security package as the senior lenders but on a second 'priority' basis. Historically, there would be a second set of security documents in favour of the mezzanine lenders each expressed to create second ranking security. That practice has now been replaced by the more efficient process of having a single set of security documents for all secured acquisition finance debt.[47] With this approach there is no second ranking security per se and the security package secures all of the debt on a first ranking basis. The intercreditor agreement will then provide that the proceeds of enforcement will be applied first to meet the outstanding senior debt, then any second lien debt and then the mezzanine debt.

A single security trustee, usually the senior debt MLA, will act as trustee for the secured acquisition financiers holding the benefit of the security package on trust and to be applied in the agreed order of priority. With a multi-jurisdictional buy-out there may be jurisdictions involved that do not recognise the concept of a security trust. In those circumstances the security may be held by the relevant senior creditor as a security agent, perhaps with alternative legal mechanisms in place to regulate how the security granted in those jurisdictions is held by the security agent, such as a parallel debt arrangement.[48]

---

46   With multi-jurisdictional buy-outs a security 'trust' may not always be applicable. See para **7.36** and **Chapter 13**.
47   Certainly this will be the case for UK security. The laws of other jurisdictions may require separate layers of security to be created.
48   See **Chapter 13**.

The terms of the security agreement that would be used in a UK deal or in respect of UK assets in a multi-jurisdictional deal are considered briefly in **Chapter 5**.

Hedging agreement

7.37   In most cases it will be a requirement of both the senior facilities agreement and the mezzanine facility agreement that at least an agreed amount of the interest payable under the mezzanine facility is hedged, usually by way of an interest rate swap. However, a separate hedging document should not be required and the interest rate swap in respect of the mezzanine facility will commonly be documented in the same agreement as the senior debt swap, with the same institution – one of the senior lenders – as swap counterparty. Hedging documents are considered briefly in **Chapter 5**.

CHAPTER 8

High Yield Debt

HIGH YIELD DEBT

8.1   In larger transactions with a total funding requirement of, say, £500m or more, high yield debt is an alternative to mezzanine debt. In mega-deals with a total funding requirement of, say, £2,000m it may be the only viable junior debt option.

The European high yield debt market

8.2   High yield bonds, or 'junk' bonds as they were then called, first came to prominence in the United States in the early 1980s. Initially, they were bonds that had begun life with investment grade ratings but had subsequently been downgraded, thereafter trading in the secondary market below par. By the mid-1980s, a public market specifically for debt securities with an original issue rating lower than investment grade had sprung up. The market was dominated by Drexel Burnham Lambert, which for two or three years in the mid to late 1980s underwrote more than 60% of the new issues in the market. Issuers were a mixed bag and included corporations in ailing industry sectors (steel, utilities, airlines), growth companies which could not access bank financing (cable television, telecoms and casinos), and leveraged acquisition funds.

The European high yield market developed much later. Although the use of high yield debt was not entirely new to the European market, with several Swiss issues appearing in the late 1980s and early 1990s, these were not in buy-out structures and it was not until the second half of the 1990s that high yield debt issuances became a relatively common feature in European buy-outs. The appeal of high yield in financing acquisitions rested principally on their cheaper all-in cost and greater covenant flexibility when compared to mezzanine debt. However, high yield also provided a deeper pool of potential investors that allowed larger transactions to be financed with higher multiples.

Since then, the development of the European high yield debt market has been anything but smooth. After the initial enthusiasm of the late 1990s, the European market experienced a turbulent year in 2001, with default rates rising to 9% – a disturbingly high level for a market barely five years in the making. This was largely as a result of weakness in the TMT sector, however, which had been responsible for a significant number of high yield issues, rather than a structural defect in the high yield product or its availability for European buy-outs. A period of recovery occurred in 2002 and 2003 with investor appetite in Europe for high yield paper increasing enormously, but this proved relatively short-lived and in early 2004 a further withdrawal of liquidity occurred as a result of a combination of oversupply, concerns over interest rate movements and the behaviour of certain market participants, principally the hedge funds.

The US market, although also suffering over the same period, has proved rather more stable, no doubt because it is a rather more mature market. In contrast, the European high yield market still has something of a reputation for being very fickle – it is either open for anything or nothing works; there is very little in between. The mezzanine market by contrast is less volatile. On the other hand, when the high yield market is open it can provide finance for larger deals that is cheaper than mezzanine and more flexible for the borrower/issuer in terms of covenant restrictions and the like.

It is interesting to note that in relation to two of the factors that support the health and consistency of the high yield market in the United States (which were noticeably absent in the formative days of the European market) – a stable relationship between the senior secured bank lenders and the subordinated high yield investors and a uniform insolvency regime – progress has certainly been made in Europe in relation to the former, in the context of subordination, where the greatest disconnect had traditionally existed and there is an increasing understanding of the issues raised by the latter. Ultimately, high yield certainly remains a viable financing tool for buy-outs, particularly at the larger end of the deal spectrum.

A new form of high yield debt was introduced to the European buy-out market in 2003. The bonds, called 'mezzanine notes', are a form of high yield debt but with certain features taken from mezzanine debt. Mezzanine notes were introduced in order to address the major concern of the high yield market at the time, that in most structures they were structurally subordinated to the senior debt. In return for allowing the high yield bondholders to receive the benefit of upstream credit support from the target group, and thus removing the structural subordination, the notes were subject to certain pro-senior debt features not present in conventional high yield debt.

In fact, mezzanine notes have been used only on a smaller number of specific occasions[1] and for the purposes of this analysis can be viewed simply as a form of high yield debt with certain documentary differences.

High yield as an alternative to mezzanine debt

8.3   When it was first introduced high yield debt was seen as a direct threat to the use of mezzanine finance in UK buy-outs. Certainly in the larger deals – in fact, a large deal at that time would only equate to a mid-market deal in the size spectrum of the 2000s – high yield debt was seen as the future. For a number of reasons, however, and in particular both the development of the institutional

---

1   Mezzanine notes were introduced to the market specifically to tackle one concern of the high yield debt market in Europe, namely structural subordination. Soon after the first mezzanine note issues the structural subordination debate had moved on and mezzanine notes were no longer necessary. See also **Chapter 10** on subordination of high yield generally.

mezzanine market in the early 2000s and the failure of the high yield market to develop as originally imagined, mezzanine has proven to be the more flexible and consistently liquid instrument. In any event, in deals of a certain size – say above, £500 million but less than £5,000 million – sponsors often face a real choice between the two products.

The use of high yield debt in buy-out funding structures and the pros and cons by comparison with mezzanine debt are considered in further detail in **Chapter 3**.

High yield debt structures

8.4   A number of different structures have been used for European high yield debt and these are considered in further detail in **Chapter 10**.[2] The most commonly used structure for UK buy-outs incorporating high yield debt since the mid-2000s can be shown in diagrammatic form as follows:[3]

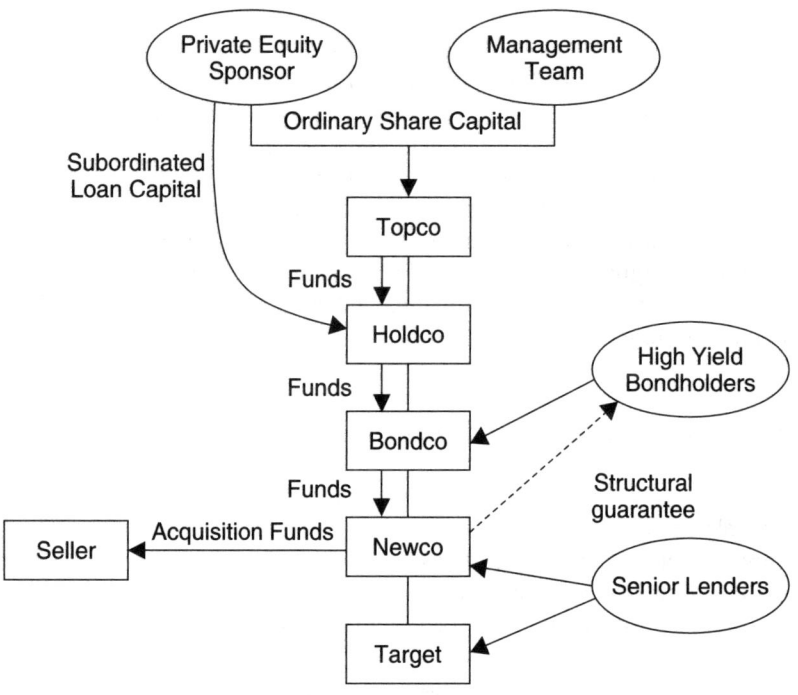

Senior and high yield

This is not the only type of structure that can be used for a buy-out involving high yield debt, although it is probably the one most commonly used in the UK and Europe. As can be seen from the diagram above, high yield debt will generally benefit from structural parity in the SPV group, through the inclusion of a structural guarantee from the senior debt borrower. In addition, the high yield

2   See also **Chapter 3** on structuring generally.
3   Second lien loans or notes might also be incorporated into a structure including high yield debt.

bondholders will typically receive guarantees from the same target group companies as the senior lenders.[4] The key difference in the structural status of high yield debt will be that the target group guarantees are generally unsecured.[5]

Senior notes and senior secured notes

8.5   In the US market it is quite common for high yield bonds to be issued as 'senior notes' and rather than being subordinated to any senior debt, they typically replace conventional senior secured bank debt in the structure. Where this happens the bonds might in theory benefit from the same full security package that conventional senior lenders would expect, including target group asset security.[6] Such bonds would constitute 'senior secured notes'. Both senior notes and senior secured notes can also be found in Europe, although at the time of writing they were relatively uncommon.

PIK notes

8.6   There is a form of high yield debt which has no cash yield at all.[7] High yield debt of this kind can either be structured as a discount note or as a true PIK note. Discount notes are a public form of DDB[8] – they are issued at a discount to par and accrete capital value (back to par at maturity) rather than having any coupon per se. PIK notes do have a coupon but instead of cash it is payable 'in kind' – new notes are issued in place of cash and then redeemed at final maturity along with the original notes. High yield bonds of this kind may also be used in buy-out funding structures, including recapitalisations, and are considered in further detail in **Chapter 9**.

Who provides the high yield debt?

8.7   High yield debt finance is obtained through the issue of high yield bonds by a vehicle company incorporated for this purpose and forming part of the SPV structure, which is often referred to as bondco. The issuer is often an intermediate holding company sitting immediately above the SPV that borrows the senior debt, as shown in the diagram on the previous page. Alternatively, it might be a

---

4   This represents a significant shift in the structural status of high yield bonds since they first appeared in Europe. Until the early 2000s high yield debt would generally be structurally subordinated to the senior debt. Not only would it not have any recourse under a guarantee to the senior debt borrower or any of the target group companies, the senior lenders would take isolating security from the high yield issuer to ensure that in a default scenario they could prevent the high yield bondholders influencing restructuring negotiations at all. See also **Chapter 10**.

5   **Chapter 10** consider the structural status of high yield debt in further detail.

6   In fact, many senior note issuers will prefer to keep the bonds unsecured and to retain the flexibility to bring in secured bank debt subsequently. Consequently, senior secured notes remain relatively rare other than in certain deal specific circumstances.

7   Bonds, including sovereign and municipal government issued bonds, that have no cash yield are sometimes also called 'zero coupon' bonds.

8   Deep discount bonds may also be the chosen form of subordinated loan capital instrument that forms the bulk of the equity package for a buy-out (see **Chapter 4**) or for private PIK notes (see **Chapter 9**).

sister company of newco under the common ownership of an intermediate holding company. It would be unusual for the issuer to be the same vehicle as the senior debt borrower, although that is quite common in the United States.

The issuer will appoint a lead manager – usually an investment bank or international commercial bank – to co-ordinate the entire issue process. The lead manager's role includes providing the issuer with advice as to the type of instrument to be issued, how it should be priced, and in what currency, and when and where the issue should take place. The lead manager may also, in conjunction with the co-managers (see below), underwrite the issue, to provide certainty to the issuer that it will be able to sell the bonds even if an insufficient number of investors buy them.

The issuer will also appoint a financial institution to act as the 'listing agent' for the purposes of listing the bonds on a public stock exchange. The listing agent's roles include providing advice to the issuer regarding the steps to be undertaken prior to the issue and ensuring compliance with the requirements of the relevant regulatory regime.

The culmination of the lead manager's or listing agent's work is the preparation, working together with the issuer, of the offering memorandum which sets out the terms and structure of the issue for potential subscribers to review. In most high yield bond issues, however, a final draft of the offering memorandum (known as a 'red herring') is prepared and used for the purposes of marketing the bonds to potential investors, in conjunction with presentations to investors by the lead manager and the management of the issuer. These presentations are often colloquially referred to as 'roadshows'. The red herring offering memorandum will not contain details of the price of the bonds, or possibly even of the size of the issue, because these will be fixed in response to investor appetite following the red herring and the roadshows.

A trustee will be appointed in respect of the issue and will enter into a trust deed with the issuer. The trust deed (or trust indenture in US parlance) constitutes the high yield bonds themselves. The trustee – usually a financial institution or specific trust company – will act for the benefit of the bondholders under the terms of the trust deed and will owe them a duty of care. As the representative of the bondholders, the trustee will be responsible for bringing claims against the issuer on their behalf. Under the terms of the trust deed and the bonds, the trustee will usually have powers to monitor the issuer to ensure, among other things, compliance with the covenants given by the issuer and will often also have authority to waive certain technical events of default. The appointment of a trustee to act on behalf of all of the high yield bondholders also enables the issuer, and third parties, to deal with the trustee rather than the bondholders individually, thereby avoiding the need to address a diverse group of bondholders with disparate views.

Finally, the issuer will appoint a 'paying agent' for the purpose, once it has been put in funds by the issuer, of paying interest on the bonds and repaying the principal at the end of the term of the issue. Because bondholders may be in a number of countries, there may be additional paying agents in those other countries.

The bonds themselves will be subscribed by institutional investors from around the world, but in particular North America, Europe and to a lesser extent

Asia. These investors tend to be pension and insurance companies and funds and CDOs and other such funds established to invest in the high yield asset class.

Each of the parties that acts as manager, listing agent, paying agent or trustee will charge a fee to the issuer. These are likely to equal a nominal percentage of the overall principal amount of the issue. In an underwritten issue the initial purchasers of the notes, the underwriters – which will commonly be the managers of the issue – will purchase the notes at a nominal discount and then sell the notes on at par to the bondholders. This has the effect of providing the managers with their underwriting fee at the outset, although the issuer effectively only pays at final maturity when the par value of the bonds is payable. The traditional high yield spread was 3% but this has crept down through the 2000s to 2.25% or 2.00% depending on the credit. The closer the issue gets to an investment grade credit rating[9] the smaller the spread.

US Securities Laws

8.8   US securities laws play an important role in the high yield debt market, even for purely European buy-outs. The key reason for this is the need to make the high yield debt marketable to US institutions. The liquidity of the European high yield market, excluding US investors, remains insufficient or at least sufficiently unpredictable such that a US marketing initiative will be necessary in many cases. The US statute book includes significant pieces of legislation directly relevant to high yield debt securities. These acts – the US Securities Act of 1933, the US Securities Exchange Act of 1934, the Trust Indenture Act of 1939 – are far reaching and apply not only to bond issues by US institutions but they may also apply to high yield bond issues by companies outside the United States that are marketed in the United States or to US investors.

In particular, unless the bonds are registered with the SEC[10] under the US Securities Act of 1933 pursuant to a full registration rights offer, the bonds cannot be offered or sold within the United States or to US persons (even outside the United States) except pursuant to one of the registration exemptions. The two main exemptions are:

- under **Rule 144A** of the Securities Act (the private placement exemption), which applies to bonds offered or sold to US persons who are 'qualified institutional buyers'; or

- under **Regulation S** of the Securities Act in relation to offers and sales that occur outside the United States.

What does the high yield debt comprise?

High yield debt

8.9   High yield debt consists of bonds – although they are also widely referred to as 'notes' – issued by bondco at an issue price determined on the

---

9 Investment grade ratings start at BBB (Standard & Poors) and Baa3 (Moodys).
10 The US Securities and Exchange Commission, a Federal body that oversees US securities laws.

advice of the lead manager, by, among other things, the amount of investor interest in the issue. The issue price may be at par (face value) or a premium to par depending on how much demand there is for them at the time of issue and how much finance is required. The bondholders will be entitled to interest accruing on the bonds, usually six-monthly, and the principal value of the bonds on their redemption at the end of the term of the issue, which is typically seven or ten years.

In theory, the high yield bondholders will claim interest on the bonds by submitting coupons attached to the bonds to a paying agent who will then make the payment. In practice, the bonds will generally be represented by one or more global bonds, representing all the individual bonds, which are deposited with a common depository.[11]

The payment obligations of the issuer, following receipt of the proceeds of the issue, will be limited to meeting the periodic interest payments and repaying the principal in one 'bullet' at final maturity.

The 'coupon' attaching to an issue of high yield bonds, that is the interest rate, will generally be a fixed rate, although not invariably.[12]

As with mezzanine debt, high yield will be subordinated to the senior debt and the terms of the subordination are considered in more detail later in **Chapter 10**.[13]

Amount of high yield debt

8.10 As is the case with the amount of a mezzanine loan, although it is even more theoretical than actual with high yield debt, the amount of the high yield debt will principally be determined on the basis of the funding gap remaining where the senior debt and equity do not satisfy the funding requirement.[14] In actual fact, using high yield debt in a structure will invariably have the effect of changing the amounts of the other core elements in the structure – equity and senior debt – generally quite significantly. Structures with high yield debt tend to be more leveraged than structures without it. So, for example, if at a certain point in the economic cycle a benchmark structure with just senior debt and equity has a gearing ratio of 60:40 (debt, equity), one with senior, mezzanine and equity might have a gearing ratio of 65:35 or 70:30 and a structure with senior, high yield and equity might be geared at 80:20.

11 See para **8.38**.
12 High yield bonds, unlike European senior debt, and to a certain extent mezzanine debt, are typically priced to reflect the credit rating of the individual issuer as well as the prevailing market conditions. Prior to summer 2007 the prevailing market interest rates for European high yield debt ranged anywhere from 8% or less to, say, 10%, depending on rating, market appetite and risk factors. Going back several years towards the start of the European market, coupons could be much higher, in the c.12% range say, but this can in part be attributable to the fact that early issues of high yield bonds were structurally subordinated. Floating rate notes (FRNs) had also started appearing in the European high yield bond market in the mid 2000s with all-in coupons at the lower end of the current range but by definition with the possibility of increasing as interest rate yields increase.
13 As will be seen the subordination of high yield debt has been one of the major areas of debate in the European acquisition finance market.
14 See **Chapter 3** generally in relation to the structuring of the debt package.

In any event, to be commercially viable a high yield bond issue will usually need to exceed £75 million or £100 million, and as a result high yield debt is not appropriate for many financing structures. Because of the ready availability of institutional mezzanine in Europe since the early 2000s high yield tends to be used more selectively, usually only in large and mega buy-outs with deal sizes ranging from £500 million to £multi-billion.

DOCUMENTING THE HIGH YIELD DEBT

8.11   The following paragraphs consider in some detail the nature of the principal documents which are used to document high yield debt issuances.

High yield debt documents

8.12

- Lead manager engagement letter.

- Offering memorandum.

- Trust indenture or trust deed.[15]

- Purchase agreement.

- Paying agency agreement.

- If the notes are to be subject to a full US public offering as opposed to a private placement, a registration rights agreement.

- Intercreditor agreement.

- Guarantee.

- Security documents.[16]

Each of these documents is considered in the following paragraphs.

Lead manager's engagement letter

8.13   The lead manager is appointed pursuant to a mandate letter confirming the terms and scope of its appointment. The mandate letter also grants the lead

---

15 English law issues are usually documented under a trust deed. Trust indentures are the US equivalent.
16 Despite a significant move, in the early 2000s, towards giving high yield bondholders the benefit of target group credit support, security from the target group in addition to upstream guarantees remains rare; security is, however, commonly provided over the shares in newco and over the funding loan pursuant to which the proceeds of the issue are lent to newco. See para **8.41** and **Chapter 10**.

manager authority to approach other financial institutions, inviting them to subscribe as co-managers for the bonds being issued and, if applicable, to provide an underwriting commitment. The managers formally agree with the issuer to subscribe or underwrite bonds in a purchase agreement that sets out their respective obligations. The lead manager and each co-manager will then find purchasers for the majority of the high yield bonds for which it has subscribed, usually prior to the issue itself, and sell on the high yield bonds.

Offering memorandum

General

8.14   The offering memorandum is a prospectus or disclosure document prepared by the issuer with substantial assistance from the lead manager. It sets out the terms and structure of the high yield issue, together with detailed business and financial information concerning the issuer and target group. It is sent to prospective high yield investors.

It is usual for a final draft of the offering memorandum – known as a 'red herring' – to be prepared without details of the price of the bonds or sometimes even the size of the proposed issue. The red herring is then used to market the issue in conjunction with presentations by the lead manager and senior management of the issuer to potential investors – known as 'roadshows'. Pricing of the issue and, if necessary, its size will then be finalised in response to investor appetite following the red herring and roadshow.

As a result of the heightened credit risk involved in high yield issues compared to traditional investment grade eurobond issues, higher disclosure standards are applied to high yield issues than those normally expected in relation to investment grade issues, even where the issue is not to be sold into the United States. This standard of disclosure means that significant management resources need to be allocated to the preparation of the offering memorandum and the associated due diligence exercise. This also inevitably involves increased deal costs. If the issue is to be sold into the United States (which many are, given the depth of the US investor base), whether by way of a private placement or a full public offer, where the courts have imposed more rigorous disclosure standards for the protection of securities investors, intensive due diligence is necessary to a degree which may be unfamiliar to European issuers and management.

The offering memorandum will contain financial information on the target group for the previous three financial years and, where the notes are to be sold in the United States, will also set out a detailed description of where the accounting principles adopted in preparing those financials differ from US GAAP.

In addition to a very full description of the business of the target covering an industry overview as well as the position enjoyed by the target operations within that industry, the offering memorandum will also contain Management's Discussion and Analysis of the target group's financial condition and results of operations – the MD&As. These MD&As are a far more detailed description of the factors that have affected the operating business than would normally be disclosed in European jurisdictions, including under the UK listing regime.

Extensive disclosures are also made in the offering memorandum to describe not only those risk factors relating specifically to the business of the target group itself, but also there will be notes on the following:

- *Substantial leverage* The issuer and target group will have substantial leverage and the significant amount of debt upon completion of the transaction may adversely affect their financial health and ability to meet their obligations under the high yield bonds.

- *Corporate structure* The impact upon the high yield bondholders of the finance structure used, particularly given that the issuer will be an SPV holding company only and the fact that some level of structural subordination may apply, with the issuer dependent upon dividends and other distributions from its subsidiaries. Further, the payment of these dividends will be subject to the controls in the intercreditor agreement.

- *Other restrictions* The restrictions placed upon the group by the senior facilities agreement and the effect these could have on the group's ability to finance future operations or engage in certain business activities.

- *Insolvency laws* Of particular importance where the issue is to be sold to US investors who are accustomed to the protections afforded to the issuer by the US Bankruptcy Code,[17] is the difference between any applicable insolvency regime(s) and US insolvency law. Thus, for example, there should be a disclosure to the effect that the provisions of English insolvency law are more favourable to secured creditors than comparable provisions of US law and that a debtor and its unsecured creditors (ie, the issuer and high yield bondholders, depending upon the finance structure adopted[18]) will have only limited protection from the rights of the secured creditors and will be unable to prevent them enforcing their security.

An important aspect of this increased level of due diligence required where an issue is to be sold into the United States, is the 10b-5 opinion letter. This is named after Rule 10b-5, promulgated under the US Securities Exchange Act 1934, which provides for liability for material omissions and misstatements in offering documents and disclosures subject to US securities laws. If securities are sold under an offer document that contains material omissions or misstatements and there is a finding of 'scienter' (generally recklessness or intent) on the part of the defendant, both the issuer and underwriters of the issue can be held

---

17 In particular, by Chapter 11, Title 11, United States Code, which contains the relevant part of the Bankruptcy Code and is commonly simply referred to as 'Chapter 11'.

18 In fact, in structurally subordinated issues the key creditor of the senior debt borrower (to which the analysis is most important) is the bond issuer itself. This is as a result of the issuer downstreaming the proceeds of the bond issue to the senior debt borrower and acquisition vehicle – which will use the proceeds to meet the purchase price – by way of a loan. However, since the early 2000s, full structural subordination is unusual. More common is a hybrid structure where the bonds are supported by a guarantee directly from the senior debt borrower. In that case, the bondholders themselves are creditors of the senior debt borrower, which will necessitate the use of an intercreditor agreement to subordinate their claims to those of the senior lenders. See **Chapter 10** for further detail.

liable. In order to address this risk the issuer will make a 10b-5 representation in the subscription/purchase agreement that the offering memorandum does not contain any material misstatement or omission and the lawyers to both the issuer and lead manager will be required to issue a 10b-5 opinion. In their opinions the lawyers will state that in the course of discussions, in connection with drafting the offering memorandum, with the issuer, the investment bankers, other counsel involved in the issue and the accountants, nothing came to the lawyers' attention that gives them any reason to believe that the offering memorandum contains a material misstatement or omission. The 10b-5 opinion will not however extend to cover financial statements and other data in the offering memorandum.

Principal terms and conditions

Overview

8.15   Whilst the high yield notes are formally constituted under the trust indenture, or trust deed,[19] the offering memorandum contains a detailed description of the notes and sets out the principal terms and conditions.

The terms of most high yield issues are fairly standard. Even in the case of an issue which is to be sold predominantly into the European market and lacks any significant US element, the terms of the notes and their style of drafting reflect the origins of the high yield market in the United States and the involvement of US investment banks in the development of the European market. An exception to this standard approach would be for mezzanine notes where certain key provisions were amended to have a more 'mezzanine flavour'. The differences between true high yield terms and mezzanine notes, in particular in the context of their subordination, are considered in **Chapter 10**. For the purposes of the following paragraphs standard high yield terms are considered.[20]

The terms and conditions set out in the offering memorandum will cover the following.[21]

- Issuer.

- Currency – will in all likelihood be euro or dollar[22] – and principal amount.

- **Maturity date**.

- **Optional and mandatory redemption**.

- Interest – will usually be a fixed rate payable twice yearly.[23] The rate will be

---

19 This section will assume a US-style trust indenture is used, reflecting the fact that this has traditionally been more common, with most high yield issues being sold into the US market.

20 Note that at the time of writing there had only been three issues of mezzanine notes, all in the first half of the 2000s.

21 Provisions highlighted in bold are considered in detail in the following subsections.

22 Sterling issues are uncommon because many businesses of the size required to justify a high yield bond issue in the structure tend to have pan-European revenues rather than UK only revenues and the currency of an issue will as often as possible be documented to match the underlying cash flows of the business, so as to reduce currency exchange rate exposure. Euros and dollars are also much more liquid currencies in the bond markets.

23 Floating rate notes have also made a re-appearance in the high yield market since the mid-2000s

set at a spread above the appropriate benchmark, which in the United Kingdom will be the gilt which has the nearest maturity to that of the bond.[24]

- **Covenant package** – more extensive than conventional investment grade eurobond issues but less extensive than, and different in concept to, the package contained in a senior or mezzanine debt agreement.

- **Events of default**.

- **Credit support, if any, and ranking/subordination**.

- Form of the notes – usually they will be issued in the form of global notes[25] and will be deposited and registered in the name of a nominee for a common depositary with ownership interests in the notes being handled through Euroclear or Clearstream.[26]

- Transfer restrictions – if the notes are sold into the United States in a private placement under Rule 144A of the US Securities Act rather than a public offering or an offering outside the United States in reliance on Regulation S of that Act, then certain restrictions on subsequent transfers of the notes will apply.

- Governing law.

- Listing – a UK issuer will seek to ensure that the notes are listed on a recognised investment exchange to take advantage of the 'quoted eurobond' UK withholding tax exemption under the Income and Corporation Taxes Act 1988.[27] The exchange usually chosen is Luxembourg which has reasonably 'light' regulatory requirements.

- Other miscellaneous provisions dealing with the absence of personal liability of directors and other persons, legal and covenant defeasance – a process by which the covenants contained within the notes, or at least certain of them, can be released – amendments, waivers and notices.

Maturity date

8.16   High yield notes are non-amortising, with principal repayment being required in a bullet at the maturity of the notes. Maturities vary from issue to issue and the market has seen a range from 5 to 12 years, although 7 and 10 years are the most common and 10 years is typical. One of the principal factors determining the maturity of the high yield will be the term of the senior debt; all of which must mature before the high yield notes.

---

24 The spread will reflect the credit rating of the issuer and prevailing market conditions. See also fn 12 above.

25 A global note is a single note that represents the entire bond issue; it replaces individual notes for each bondholder.

26 Euroclear and Clearstream are two European finance houses that provide custody, clearing and settlement services for securities and securities transactions. They are widely used for European high yield issues.

27 See s 349(3)(c).

The terms of the notes will contain a prohibition on early redemptions by the issuer prior to the expiry of a fixed period – the 'non-call' period. By convention the non-call period is half the life of the bonds; 5 years for 10-year bonds and 4 years for 7 year bonds. The provision is designed to protect the yield to the investors that they were expecting over the life of the notes. There are standard exceptions to the basic non-call provision (as set out below) and even at the end of the non-call period the issuer must compensate the holders for some loss of yield. The issuer will also remain able to purchase notes in the open market, during the life of the notes.[28]

Redemption at option of issuer

Optional redemption after the expiry of the 'non-call period'

8.17   The issuer will have the option to redeem the notes in whole at any time after expiration of the non-call period subject to payment of a redemption premium. The redemption premium will operate on a sliding scale, typically starting at par plus 50% of the annual coupon on the notes for a redemption in the 12 months after the non-call period, then par plus 33 1/3% in the next 12 months, then par plus 16 2/3% in the next 12 months, and finally at par thereafter.

Optional redemption within the non-call period

8.18   As indicated above, a key feature of high yield bonds is that they are non-callable for the first half of their term. In fact, it is likely that this is not an absolute prohibition and there are three common exceptions.

Redemption subject to a 'make-whole' payment

8.19   The notes may be redeemable at the issuer's option subject to payment of a make-whole amount. This amount is designed to put the holders in the same economic position they would have been in had they received the benefit of the yield on the notes through the non-call period, and then redeemed them at the redemption price then applicable under the optional redemption provision referred to above. Thus the make-whole amount is derived by reference to the remaining yield receivable in the non-call period plus the first optional redemption price applicable thereafter. That amount is discounted to give the net present value of those yield and redemption payments to reflect the fact that the cash was received in advance and would be available to be re-invested typically by reference to government bonds. The discount rate applied is commonly the annual rate equal to the yield to maturity of a comparable issue of government bonds (US government for US dollars and a major government within the Euro zone for euros) plus a spread of 0.50%.

Redemption from the proceeds of an IPO

8.20   If there is an equity public offering the issuer will have the ability, normally limited to a two to three-year period following the date of issue of the

---

28 Although with a successfully performing business the cost of such a purchase will be above par at a price reflecting, among other things, the prospective yield on the bonds, which potentially makes market purchases expensive.

notes, to redeem a certain proportion – usually 35% – of the notes, subject to payment of a premium. The premium will commonly be equal to the annual coupon on the notes. The terms and conditions will normally provide that a minimum percentage of the original aggregate principal amount of the issue, plus any additional notes issued prior to redemption, remains outstanding following such redemption. This will typically be 65%.

Redemption following tax gross up

8.21   In common with standard eurobond terms, the issuer will also be given the ability to redeem all the notes if it becomes obliged to gross-up payments as a result of the imposition of withholding taxes and such gross-up obligation cannot be avoided. In these circumstances it is usual that the notes are redeemable at par.

Redemption at option of holders

8.22   There are two standard redemption events exercisable by the holders. They are mandatory from the issuer's perspective:

- *Change of control* Where a change of control has occurred each holder of notes will have the right to require the issuer to make a 'change of control offer' to each noteholder and if required by any noteholder, repurchase all or a part of its notes, typically at a 1% premium.

- *Asset sales* The covenant package will typically include a limitation on asset sales.[29] If the proceeds of any permitted asset sale are not reinvested in the business, used to make further permitted acquisitions or applied in repayment of the senior debt, typically within 360 days of receipt of such proceeds, the issuer must make an 'asset sale offer' to each noteholder to redeem *at par* as many of the notes as it is able to with those proceeds, subject usually to a de minimis threshold. Noteholders can elect not to accept the offer.

Covenant package

8.23   The aims of the high yield covenant package are to preserve the credit quality of the issuer group, to ensure unencumbered cashflow (a vital ingredient) and, in order to ensure that value does not pass to the equity holders, to ensure arm's length dealings with affiliates.

The form of covenant adopted in high yield bond documents differs from the form used in leveraged loan documents in a number of key respects. The most notable of these is that high yield covenants apply an 'incurrence' test rather than a 'maintenance' test. Whilst senior and mezzanine debt covenants are ongoing in nature and require regular monitoring and testing and can be breached by ongoing changes in business performance (ie, compliance must be 'maintained'), most high yield covenants will be tested only when the issuer wishes to do something that would otherwise be restricted under a covenant. Provided that the rel-

---

29 See para **8.27** below.

evant test is satisfied at the time of the issuer's restricted action, the covenant is relaxed and requires no further testing or monitoring. High yield covenants therefore only restrict voluntary actions at the time of 'incurrence'.

High yield covenants commonly incorporate the concept of 'restricted' and 'unrestricted' subsidiaries. The majority of restrictions in the covenants will only affect the issuer and its restricted subsidiaries. The unrestricted subsidiaries will, for all intents and purposes, be treated as unrelated third parties to which most of the high yield covenants will not apply and with which the issuer and restricted subsidiaries are required to deal at arm's length. The basic premise is that all subsidiaries of the issuer are classified as restricted subsidiaries unless designated otherwise by the issuer.

The test which must be satisfied for the issuer to be able to designate a subsidiary as 'unrestricted' is typically a complex one and includes the group being deemed to have made an investment reducing the amount of permitted investments under the high yield covenants to the extent of an amount equal to the market value of the designated subsidiary. This ability to designate unrestricted subsidiaries distinguishes the concept from the 'material subsidiary' concept often found in senior and mezzanine debt covenants where a group company's status as a 'material subsidiary' is determined by an automatic test, commonly on the basis of asset value or cash flow.

A standard covenant package will contain the following restrictions, with their scope and any exceptions the subject of negotiation on a deal by deal basis.

Limitation on incurrence of indebtedness

8.24   No debt may be incurred by the issuer, and its restricted subsidiaries, other than permitted indebtedness, unless a specified financial ratio – eg, a fixed charge coverage ratio or a leverage ratio – tested on a pro forma basis including the debt to be incurred, is satisfied.

Permitted indebtedness which may be incurred without applying the incurrence test generally includes: existing indebtedness including the senior debt; refinancing of existing senior debt; finance leases; intra-group indebtedness (between the issuer and restricted subsidiaries only); subordinated debt; and other debt not exceeding a specified amount in aggregate at any time.

Anti-layering covenants

8.25   The 'anti-layering' provision is intended to prohibit the high yield issuer incurring a tranche of debt that ranks between the senior debt and the high yield debt, even where there would be no breach of the overall limit on debt ranking senior to the high yield bonds. Whilst the origins of these clauses may simply trace back to a marketing push for 'senior subordinated' notes that are the most senior ranking subordinated debt issued by a company, their effect is to prevent a separate class of senior ranking creditors in the funding structure having a discrete set of concerns and priorities different from those of the senior lenders. This might be of particular concern in a restructuring or work-out scenario for a group in financial difficulties. Anti-layering covenants may also amount to a back-door mechanism to limit leverage since any additional debt would need to rank pari passu with the existing senior debt, which might not be acceptable to the other parties.

No merger or consolidation

8.26   This covenant is usually subject to a number of relaxations, including in respect of a merger involving the issuer where the merged entity has assumed of all the issuer's obligations under the notes and the trust indenture.

Limitation on asset sales

8.27   This covenant limits the ability of the issuer and its restricted subsidiaries to make any significant asset sales and requires any assets which are disposed of to be disposed of at fair market value and with a negotiated percentage – 75% is common – of the consideration payable in cash or cash equivalents. As discussed above,[30] if the proceeds are not reinvested in the business or applied in prepaying the senior debt within a set period of time, the issuer is usually required to offer to redeem the notes.

Limitation on restricted payments

8.28   This covenant is designed to limit the ability of the issuer and its restricted subsidiaries to pay dividends or make other distributions of cash or property to shareholders, make payments in respect of debt that is subordinated to the notes and make loans or other acquisitions or investments, other than specifically permitted investments. Certain payments will be exempted from this restriction, usually allowing certain amounts to be passed up the corporate chain to pay fees and expenses incurred elsewhere in the wider group, and provided the financial ratio test applicable to the incurrence of indebtedness (see above) is satisfied, a certain amount of the consolidated net income of the group will be available to fund such payments.

Limitation on liens[31]

8.29   This covenant is usually significantly less strict than the senior debt negative pledge and, in common with standard capital market instruments, typically prevents the issuer and its restricted subsidiaries from granting security over their assets to secure other debt unless the high yield bonds are equally and rateably secured.

Limitation on dividend and other payment restrictions affecting subsidiaries

8.30   This covenant prohibits the issuer and its restricted subsidiaries from agreeing to limitations on the payment of dividends, the repayment of intra-group debt and other restrictions on asset transfers. Its purpose is to prevent fetters on the flow of cash up to the issuer to enable it to meet yield payments and ultimately principal on the notes. The covenant is commonly subject to a wide range of exceptions, however, that permit restrictions in existing financing arrangements or arrangements falling within permitted indebtedness. These

---

30 See para **8.22** above
31 A 'lien' includes any consensual security interest in the United States, by contrast with its more limited meaning under English law.

exceptions significantly weaken the position of the high yield *vis-à-vis* the senior banks, since the senior banks will insist on payment blockage mechanics as part of the subordination arrangements.[32]

Limitation on transactions with related persons

8.31 This covenant prohibits the entry into of transactions with affiliates by the issuer and its restricted subsidiaries other than on arm's length terms, subject to certain exceptions. Transactions over a threshold amount will commonly also require the approval of a majority of independent directors and, over a larger threshold, the delivery to the trustee of a fairness opinion from a qualified third-party, eg, an investment bank.

Suspension of covenants

8.32 It is also relatively standard now for certain of the above covenants to be suspended if the notes attain investment grade status (Baa3 or better by Moody's; BBB- or better by Standard & Poor's); should the rating then decline, the covenants will be reinstated.

Reporting covenants

8.33 In addition to the restrictive covenants referred to above, the covenant package will also include certain reporting obligations; the issuer will conventionally be required to provide audited financials and quarterly financial statements together with detailed MD&A's every quarter.

Events of default

8.34 In comparison to the events of default commonly included in the senior facilities agreement or a mezzanine facility agreement, the high yield events of default are limited.

The following events of default will typically be included:

- non-payment – often with a 30-day remedy period in the case of an interest payment default;

- breach of certain principal covenants – such as those relating to change of control and asset sale offers and the restriction on mergers;

- breach of any other obligations – subject to a remedy period (often of 60 days);

- cross-acceleration[33] to other indebtedness of the issuer or any restricted subsidiary – this will be subject to a threshold amount; and

- insolvency events affecting the issuer or any restricted subsidiary.

---

32 See **Chapter 10**.

33 Note that cross-acceleration is different from cross-default. It requires that an acceleration notice has actually been served in another finance agreement not merely that a default has occurred in that finance agreement.

Either the trustee or the holders of at least 25% of the principal amount of the notes may declare all the notes to be due and payable upon the occurrence of an event of default which is continuing.[34] Acceleration is commonly automatic upon the occurrence of certain insolvency events.

Ranking and payment blockage

8.35   The offering memorandum will include a description of the ranking of the notes, the precise details of which will depend upon the structure of the transaction and any subordination provisions (such as payment blockages and enforcement standstills) in the trust indenture or intercreditor agreement (see below).

Trust indenture or trust deed

8.36   This document will constitute the high yield bonds themselves and will be entered into by the issuer and the trustee. The document will also set out all the relevant administrative provisions and the actual form of the notes. In a US transaction the indenture will also contain the subordination provision, but in a European deal these will be contained in an intercreditor agreement – see below.

The trustee acts for the benefit of the bondholders and owes them a duty of care. As their representative it is responsible for bringing claims against the issuer on their behalf and has powers to monitor the issuer to ensure covenant compliance. It will often also have authority to waive certain technical events of default. The appointment of a trustee to act on behalf of the high yield bondholders has the further advantage of enabling the issuer – and third parties, including the senior lenders – to deal with the trustee rather than each individual bondholder.

If the notes are to be subject to a US SEC registration, as opposed to a Rule 144A private placement or Regulation S issue,[35] then certain mandatory provisions of the US Trust Indenture Act of 1939 will be deemed to be part of the trust indenture, whether or not expressly set out in that document. This can be significant because the US Trust Indenture Act requires that any modification to the fundamental payment terms of the notes must be approved by *each* bondholder and cannot be imposed by a majority. This contrasts with the conventional English trust deed which would provide that an extraordinary resolution of a two-thirds or three-quarters majority in value of those voting at a meeting with a requisite quorum could amend even such fundamental terms as those relating to payment. It also impacts the subordination provisions that might be applied to the bonds.[36]

---

34 One of the features of mezzanine notes (see para **8.2**) was that the acceleration voting threshold was increased to more than 50%. This feature has not been adopted by the high yield market, however, except in the very rare cases where the bonds are 'senior secured notes' that share security with other senior debt providers.

35 See para **8.8**.

36 In particular, enforcement standstill provisions are thought to contravene the Trust Indenture Act. See also para **8.40**.

To take advantage of both European and US liquidity it is common for European issuers to structure multiple tranches of bonds, with US dollar denominated bonds sold into the United States under a US trust indenture subject to the 1939 Act and sterling or euro denominated bonds sold outside the United States under an English law trust deed.

Purchase agreement

8.37   This agreement will be between the issuer and the initial purchaser of the notes who will act as the arranger or underwriter of the issue. The agreement will contain the obligation to purchase – conventionally at a discount – and various warranty and indemnity provisions. The notes will then be sold on by the initial purchasers at par (or a small premium to par) in reliance on relevant exemptions from US, UK and other relevant securities laws (ie, under Rule 144A/Reg S of the US Securities Act and under exemptions to the Prospectus Rules published by the UK FSA[37]). The difference between the discount and par reflects the commission payable to the initial purchaser for underwriting the issue.

Paying agency agreement

8.38   This agreement is purely mechanical and deals with the appointment, duties and function of the paying agents, registrar and transfer agents. The paying agents arrange for payments of interest and principal to be made on the notes, the registrar will maintain a register for any notes which are exchanged from bearer form to registered form – which can occur in limited circumstances – and the transfer agent will deal with the transfer of any registered notes. The paying agency agreement will also usually deal with the delivery of the notes to the relevant depositary.

As mentioned previously, the notes will generally be represented by one or more global notes. Each series of notes sold outside the US pursuant to Regulation S of the US Securities Act will initially be represented by one global note, and each series of notes sold within the US to qualified institutional buyers pursuant to Rule 144A of the US Securities Act will be represented by a separate global note. Any global note representing euro notes will be deposited with a common depositary for the accounts of Euroclear and Clearstream; any global note representing dollar notes will be deposited with the trustee as custodian for The Depositary Trust Company (DTC) and registered in the name of Cede & Co, as nominee of DTC.

Ownership of interests in global notes will be limited to persons that have accounts with DTC, Euroclear and/or Clearstream or persons that may hold interests through such participants. These 'book-entry interests' will be shown on, and transfers thereof will be effected only through, records maintained in book-entry form by DTC, Euroclear and Clearstream and their participants.

---

37 The Financial Services Authority, which regulates much of the financial services industry in the United Kingdom.

Registration rights agreement

8.39   If a full US public offering is to be undertaken, this agreement will deal with the issuer's commitment to file a registration statement with the SEC and, once that is effective, the mechanics of an 'exchange offer' pursuant to which the unregistered notes are exchanged for registered ones. The registered notes will have identical terms and evidence the same continuing indebtedness as the unregistered notes, except that the registered notes will not be subject to transfer restrictions.

Intercreditor, guarantee and security documents

Intercreditor agreement

8.40   High yield bonds, like most other forms of junior or subordinated debt will be required to be subordinated to the higher ranking debt under the terms of an intercreditor agreement. However, to understand fully the nature of the subordination of high yield debt it is necessary to consider the history of the European high yield market in some detail. Originally, high yield bonds were fully structurally subordinated to the senior debt. They were issued by a structurally inferior SPV and the bondholders had no direct recourse to either the senior debt borrower or any member of the target group. Over time this has changed and, although still issued by an SPV further up the group than the senior debt borrower (newco), a structural guarantee from newco plus guarantees from target group companies are now standard. In practical terms therefore, the bonds are no longer structurally subordinated. This has placed the emphasis of the subordination onto contractual subordination and the terms of the intercreditor agreement.[38]

The intercreditor agreement will be concerned with two types of liability owing in respect of the high yield debt. First, there are liabilities owing directly to the bondholders, including by the issuer under the bonds themselves, by other SPVs under structural guarantees and by members of the target group under subsidiary guarantees. Of these, the subordination of claims under the bonds themselves, against the bond issuer, is arguably less important than the subordination of claims under the guarantees since the claims under the bonds are only against an SPV at least one level removed from the senior debt borrower and ultimately the target group. The claims against the senior debt borrower (newco) and the claims against target group companies compete more directly with the interests of the senior lenders. That all said, it is still common to include claims under the bonds themselves within the scope of the intercreditor agreement, if just as an added level of protection for the senior lenders. The senior lenders do, after all, have valid concerns that the bondholders do not have competing claims at any point in the group structure, including against the bond issuer from whom the senior lenders will take a guarantee and security.

---

38 See **Chapter 10** generally in relation to subordination and for a more detailed consideration of the evolution of the European approach to the subordination of high yield debt.

Secondly, since the bonds will in practice be issued by an SPV above newco, the intercreditor agreement should also subordinate the indirect liabilities owing by newco to the bond issuer under the funding loan pursuant to which the bond proceeds are advanced to newco. Absent that additional layer of subordination, the bondholders might be able to pursue competing claims against newco indirectly through the funding loan. This might be achieved by causing an insolvency event in respect of the bond issuer – by claiming under the bonds[39] – which then in turn (possibly through an insolvency appointee) would make a claim on newco under the funding loan in order to monetise its assets.[40]

Because of the influence of the US high yield market on the European market and in particular because European issuers do frequently utilise the US bond market, it is worth briefly noting how contractual subordination of US bonds differs from the European approach. In particular, for high yield bonds that are subject to US securities laws,[41] the contractual subordination arrangements will be different in one significant substantive manner. This is as a result of the applicability of the US Trust Indenture Act of 1939 to such bond issues, which in broad terms provides that the bonds cannot be made subject to a typical European-style enforcement standstill provision.[42] A second major difference between the two markets is that US bonds are subordinated through provisions included in the terms of the bonds themselves – in the trust indenture – rather than in a separate intercreditor agreement, as is the case with European issues.[43]

Guarantees and security

8.41   A guarantee of the high yield bonds will be required in any structure where the bonds are not intended to be fully structurally subordinated, which, as indicated above, is now extremely rare.[44] The guarantee is the instrument that typically circumvents the structural subordination. This is primarily through a structural guarantee from newco, as the senior debt borrower, supplemented by subsidiary guarantees from the target group.[45] The form of guarantee is commonly scheduled to the trust indenture or trust deed and, being of the garden variety, does not merit any separate discussion.

---

39 They might not necessarily be able to do this in practice, however, if the bonds themselves are subject to the full provisions of the intercreditor agreement, including an enforcement standstill, but since intercreditor agreements tend to cover all angles where possible the extra layer of subordination will generally be taken notwithstanding. Note also that for bonds that are subject to US securities laws an enforcement standstill in respect of the bonds themselves would not be permitted under the US Trust Indenture Act 1939 (see also para **8.36** and the remainder of para **8.40**).

40 Of course, this all assumes that the bonds and the funding loan are in default.

41 As to which see para **8.8**.

42 See also **Chapter 10**, which examines standstill provisions – and high yield debt subordination generally – in some detail.

43 A further structural difference is that US bonds tend to be issued by an SPV that is also a senior debt borrower, not a dedicated SPV higher up the group as in the typical European structure.

44 In fact, high yield debt in the form of holdco PIK notes will be structurally subordinated still. See **Chapter 9** for more detail.

45 As noted previously, this was not always the case and for some years at the outset of the European market high yield bonds remained fully structurally subordinated as well as contractually subordinated. See **Chapter 10** for more detail on the evolution of the market in this regard.

The structural claims against bondco as issuer and newco as guarantor will generally be further supported by subordinated structural security over the shares in newco and security over the funding loan from bondco to newco.[46] In addition, in some transactions bondholders receive security over the shares in a holdco which sits higher up in the structure, often just below the vehicle in which the equity sits. This level of security is generally fiercely resisted by equity providers but in theory would allow bondholders to enforce higher up in the structure irrespective of whether the senior debt providers are enforcing and thereby enable bondholders to deliver control of the group to a third-party following a bond default. This would allow bondholders to realise the residual 'equity value' in the transaction at a time when the senior debt remains in place. That said, upon enforcement of such security, a change of control prepayment event or cross-default event of default will inevitably be triggered at the senior debt level, resulting in an immediate mandatory prepayment event or acceleration for all of the senior debt. The issue is therefore only of practical relevance once the senior debt has been taken out.

Leaving aside any structural security in the SPV group, 'real' security from the target group remains very rare for high yield debt.[47]

In terms of documentation, to the extent the high yield is to be granted any security, the same set of security documents used to secure the senior debt could be used with a security trustee holding the benefit of the security on trust for both the senior lenders and the high yield investors.[48] Alternatively there may be a second set of second-ranking high yield security documents held by a trustee for the high yield investors, in which case they should mirror the senior security documents as far as possible.

In summary, therefore, high yield bondholders in European issues can expect to receive the following credit support for the bonds:

- a direct senior claim against the bond issuer;

- a subordinated structural guarantee from newco (the main senior debt borrower);

- subordinated guarantees from the other guarantors of the senior debt; and

---

46 The security over the funding loan might be first-ranking or exclusive to the bondholders or it might be second-ranking as with the other structural security for the bonds.

47 An exception to this principle is for an issue of 'senior secured notes', where the high yield debt in effect replaces the conventional senior secured bank debt in the structure. At the time of writing, however, such issues were rare in practice.

48 There may be advantages for the senior lenders in doing this with respect to target group security, on the very rare occasions it is provided. First, the senior creditors would have greater direct control over all the security since the security trustee would be their appointee. Secondly, under the current administrative receiver regime under UK insolvency law they might be able to take advantage of the 'capital markets' exception in the Insolvency Act 1986 (as amended by the Enterprise Act 2002) and still be able to appoint an administrative receiver as an enforcement option. In these circumstances, the necessary voting threshold required to enforce the shared security comes sharply into focus. High yield bondholders would prefer the standard 25% threshold for their vote but senior lenders will often insist on a higher threshold of say 50.1%.

- second-ranking structural security over the shares in newco (and possibly other SPVs) and security over the funding loan pursuant to which the proceeds of the high yield issue are lent to newco.[49]

High yield bridge finance

8.42 Conventionally, high yield debt is not issued at the time of completion of the buy-out. Instead a temporary loan will be put in place at completion – called a 'bridge' facility – with the high yield debt being issued a few months after completion, at which point the proceeds of the high yield issue are used to repay the bridge. The reason for the split timing is principally a function of the complexities of co-ordinating the timing of the bond issue process with that of the underlying acquisition transaction (though it has been done). The bridge will enable the bond portion of the funding structure to be financed at completion without delaying it.

The bridging loan will usually be provided under a separate bridging loan agreement but in a similar format to the senior facilities agreement. The terms of the bridging debt will often reflect the hybrid nature of high yield bridge finance – it is documented as a loan akin to the senior debt but theoretically reflects the economic terms of a note issue – with several features mirroring the terms of the senior debt and others reflecting standard high yield terms. The maturity is likely to be one year only[50] and the interest rate margin will be priced to reflect the ultimate high yield debt to be issued. In fact, one key feature of many high yield bridges is that the interest rate applicable to the bridging loan will be structured to increase quarterly[51] in order to incentivise the borrower/issuer to refinance the loan with the bonds as quickly as possible. In addition, the terms of the bridging loan will usually include an automatic subordinated debt conversion mechanism. Under this, if the high yield bonds have not been issued by the time the bridge loan matures, the loan will automatically convert into longer term subordinated debt. This might take the form of institutional mezzanine debt – priced to attract sufficient investor interest – or another form of debt security that can be successfully sold into the public debt market; in practice this may just mean high yield with a higher than originally intended coupon.

---

49 See fn **46**.
50 Or perhaps 15 or 18 months.
51 Consequently, the bridge will be called an 'exploding bridge'.

CHAPTER 9

PIK Notes

PIK NOTE DEBT

9.1 In certain cases the demand for debt in a structure will be sufficiently great that even the use of B and C tranches of senior debt, a layer of second lien debt and a large tranche or mezzanine debt or high yield debt is not sufficient to meet the funding requirements for the buy-out.[1] In such circumstances the acquisition financiers might consider that a PIK note is a viable addition to the structure. Dedicated PIK note facilities have been used in UK buy-outs since the early to mid 2000s, mostly provided by hedge funds and other leveraged loan and quasi-equity funds with flexible investment criteria.

The advantage of PIK note debt in deal structuring is that the yield accruing on the principal amount of the debt is, as the name suggests, all paid-in-kind. In other words there is no requirement to pay yield on a current cash basis. Instead the yield is capitalised as principal. The fact that the PIK note does not use up any target business cashflow during the lifetime of the investment means that it is relatively easy to introduce it into a structure without affecting the acquisition financiers' analysis of the cashflows required to service the main acquisition finance. Because the yield on PIK notes, which is relatively high in any event,[2] compounds every six or twelve months, the principal amount of the PIK note debt increases significantly during the life of the investment, so that even though no current yield is payable during the lifetime of the investment the ultimate return is very high. Sponsors are attracted to this form of debt, despite the potentially large pay-out to the holders of the PIK notes at final maturity, because of its non-cash effect and also because the call protection applicable to PIK notes is often quite limited. This facilitates an early exit without the diluting effect of the compounding roll-up or a significant early redemption penalty. In fact, given that PIK notes generally form a relatively small layer of the total capital structure,[3] the dilutive effect of an exit even after a number of years is not necessarily punitive from the sponsor's perspective.

---

1 See **Chapter 3** generally as to funding structures.
2 Perhaps anywhere from 10 to 20% p.a. (including, in the case of floating rate PIK notes, the underlying cost of funds).
3 In practice, perhaps only 5% or so.

The PIK referred to above has traditionally been provided by hedge funds and other leveraged loan funds with flexible investment criteria either on a bi-lateral basis or through limited syndicates. However, PIK note debt has also been structured and documented as a public market instrument and issued into the high yield markets. This might be to provide additional leverage in a buy-out structure that already has a high yield bond in the structure or it might specifically be to finance a dividend recap in a mature buy-out.[4] Dividend recaps are used by sponsors to return some of their equity in advance of a full exit. PIK notes used to finance dividend recaps are generally referred to as 'holdco PIKs' and, together with other types of PIK notes issued into the high yield markets, are described in this chapter as 'public' PIK to distinguish them from the quite different 'private' PIK notes that are issued bi-laterally or to syndicates of investors outside of the public markets.

PIK note debt structures

Private PIK

9.2   A typical buy-out structure incorporating private PIK note debt in addition to senior, second lien and mezzanine debt can be represented in diagrammatic form as shown on the next page. This structure shows the PIK notes being issued by an SPV between the borrower of the senior, second lien and mezzanine debt – all of which will in a structurally superior position – and the issuer of the subordinated loan capital subscribed by the equity investors, which the PIK note holders will wish to structurally subordinate to the PIK notes. In some structures the PIK note debt may be issued by an SPV further up the SPV structure, perhaps sharing an issuer with the equity investor debt (the subordinated loan capital in the diagram). Much depends on the intended structural status of the PIK notes and the various other instruments and vehicles being used. In most cases the prior ranking creditors will wish to ensure that the PIK notes are structurally subordinated to their instruments. The issuer will be a vehicle above the main borrower without the benefit of structural guarantees or other credit support from that borrower or from the target group.[5] In other cases the PIK notes will benefit from credit support from the target group, in which case the structural position of the PIK note issuer is moot.[6]

The PIK note holders will generally wish to rank ahead of the equity investor debt and to do this they will look to take structural security in the SPV group – usually in the form of a guarantee given by the SPV that owns the PIK note issuer secured by share security over the PIK note issuer – and in addition may use a structurally superior SPV as the issuer.

---

4   See also para **9.3**.
5   But perhaps with share security higher up the SPV structure.
6   See **Chapter 10** generally on structuring in the context of subordination.

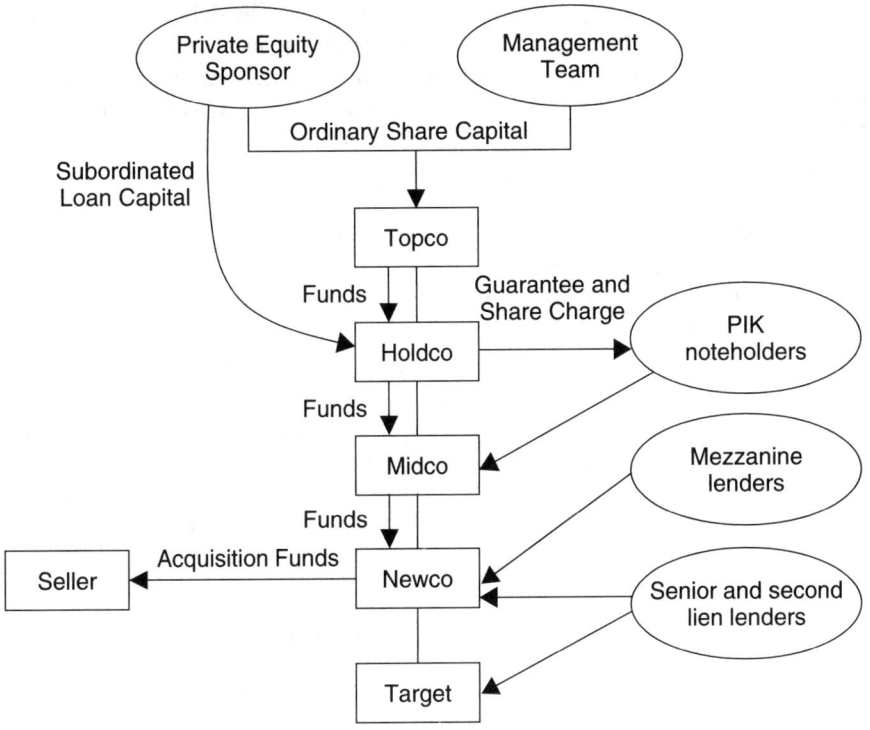

Senior, second lien, mezzanine and 'private' PIK

The structure above shows PIK in a structure with senior, second lien and mezzanine debt. It can also be used in senior – second lien only structures or given the inherently bespoke nature of this instrument, even in conjunction with senior alone.

Public PIK

9.3   The PIK notes in the structure above represent private PIK notes issued to finance a buy-out. A structure incorporating a public PIK issuance may be more complex since public PIK notes are often issued in the most highly structured forms of buy-out. With holdco PIKs used to finance a dividend recap – that is, a payment to the equity sponsor to redeem part of the equity (usually the subordinated shareholder debt) – the PIK notes must be structured into a pre-existing buy-out. Indeed, it is often necessary to ensure that the incorporation of the PIK notes into the structure does not require the consent of the existing acquisition financiers. Such a consent would not necessarily be forthcoming or might require a consent 'fee' to be paid. In practice, consent under the existing acquisition finance documents would be required if the PIK notes breached the covenants restricting the incurrence of debt or the making of payments to the equity investors, or if they triggered the change of control provisions. In the case of change of control, the relevant provisions typically only apply to a change of control measured by reference to shareholdings and management control and would not therefore be triggered by the PIK issuance. The debt and equity payment restrictions may be avoided by the PIK debt being incurred above the existing 'group' as defined for the purposes of the existing debt covenants. Furthermore, since PIK notes do not require any cash flow to service them there is no requirement to access target group cash flows, which the acquisition financiers could also block. Consequently, holdco PIKs will be structured so that they are issued at the very top of the group often just below the equity vehicle.[7] The proceeds of the issuance will then be distributed by way of dividend or lent up to the equity vehicle or directly to the equity investors.

Public PIK notes that are not being used to finance a dividend recap – but as part of an entire buy-out financing package – will also be issued by an SPV towards the top of the group, primarily to ensure that they are structurally subordinated to the higher ranking instruments in the structure.

A 'typical' holdco PIK structure can be shown in diagrammatic form as follows. If topco is an obligor and part of the acquisition financiers' 'group' then a further holding company SPV ('holdco') might need to be inserted above topco to avoid the restrictions in the acquisition finance documentation.

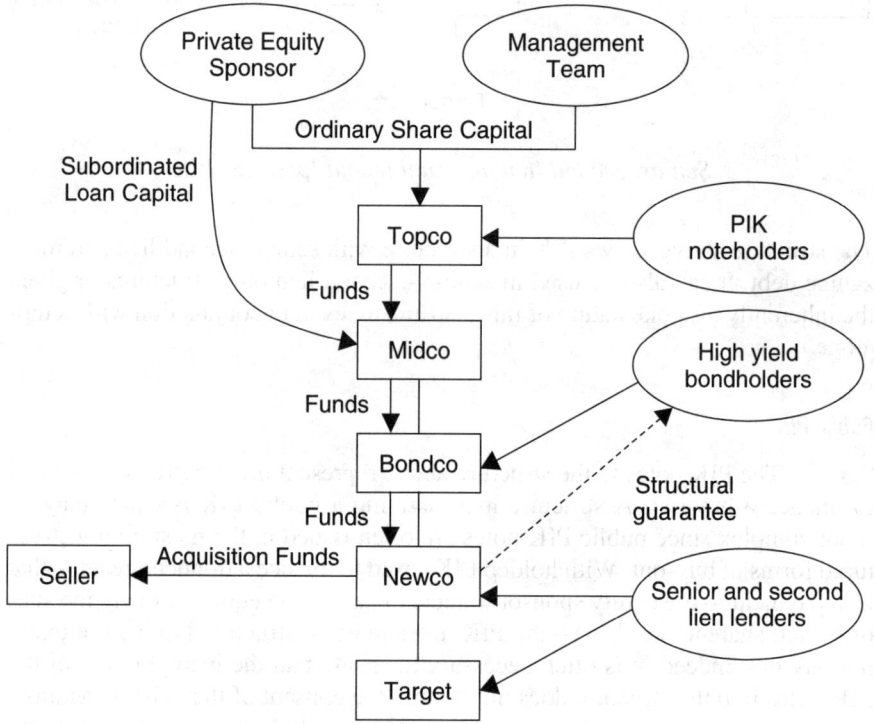

Senior, second lien, high yield and 'holdco' PIK

---

7   There may need to be a new equity vehicle incorporated into the structure for the purpose of effecting the recap, as the existing equity vehicle may be part of the 'group' under the existing acquisition finance documentation.

Who provides the PIK note debt?

9.4   As indicated above, there are really two discrete markets for PIK notes: the public market, and a private market. Each of these markets has its own form of PIK notes. Public PIK is a similar product to high yield debt in that it tends to be structured as an issue of bonds that is sold to investors in the high yield debt markets.[8] This form of PIK notes is only really used in very large transactions, typically as part of a recapitalisation rather than as part of the initial buy-out. Such a product is essentially distribution driven as with high yield bonds and generally it is sold to a niche corner of the market where hedge funds, in particular, have been dominant players.

Private PIK is not issued into public markets. It is structured and held privately, although again hedge funds are significant investors. Because of their position in a financing structure, as the most junior element of an acquisition finance package (or the most senior element of an equity package), PIK notes will appeal to investors that can invest in instruments with that risk profile. This might include leveraged loan funds, CDOs, specialist mezzanine houses and, as mentioned, hedge funds.

What does PIK note debt comprise?

Public and 'holdco' PIK

9.5   As mentioned above, public PIK generally takes the form of a high yield bond issue and the instrument and its issuance formalities will in most cases follow that of high yield debt.[9] There is one significant difference from high yield bonds of course, in that high yield bonds pay cash interest, usually every six months, whereas PIK notes do not. As an alternative to a high yield bond issue, public PIK notes have in certain cases also been structured as loans. This is often driven by the fact that the PIK note market remains relatively niche, and thus less liquid than the conventional high yield market. Indeed much of the paper is acquired by hedge funds that may not be as interested in significant secondary trading. One advantage of using a loan structure is that there is much less disclosure and marketing required, which in any event is not as necessary when there are limited end-users. Hedge fund investors may also prefer loans since the 'price' of the debt is more stable when it does come to secondary trading purposes. Public PIK, particularly where it is used to finance a dividend recap, is often referred to as 'holdco PIK' reflecting its position in the capital structure.

---

8   In fact, public PIK may also be structured in the form of a loan, particularly when it is targeted at hedge funds, who may be less concerned with meeting the documentation conventions of the high yield market.
9   See also fn **15** in relation to 'zero coupon' bonds.

Private PIK

9.6   In true buy-out structures PIK note debt will more often be in the form of private PIK. Private PIK note debt is quite different from the typical public PIK note instrument. It is generally structured as subordinated loan capital in the form of subordinated loan notes or an issue of privately held deep discount bonds (DDBs[10]). This form of instrument most easily lends itself to the deeper level of subordination and reduced creditor rights that will be required in respect of the PIK notes. As a final alternative, private PIK also be structured as a straight loan.

Tax

9.7   Tax considerations may also dictate the precise form of a PIK note instrument. In actual fact tax lawyers often apply a very precise meaning to the term 'PIK note'. They often use this term to refer to the certificates issued by the PIK note issuer to the PIK note investors on each interest 'payment' date to represent the capitalised yield in place of a cash payment, whereas, in practice, a PIK note debt instrument may not include a requirement to issue such certificates.

PIK note terms

9.8   Whatever the precise form of instrument used, the rights of the PIK note investors will be relatively limited by comparison with other forms of acquisition finance. This reflects their position in the capital structure, being subordinated behind all other acquisition finance. In particular the PIK note investors will have limited default triggers and will be subject to extensive subordination provisions.[11]

As far as other commercial terms are concerned, given that PIK notes are the least commoditised acquisition finance product used in buy-outs, there is less standardisation of terms and documentation than with other products. Economically, PIK notes are relatively highly priced compared to other forms of junior debt with an interest rate or, in the case of DDBs, capital accretion rate, reflecting the position of the instrument in the overall funding structure.[12] The yield will often be a fixed rate but floating rate PIK is also possible.

Private PIK note investors may on occasion also receive warrants in order to sweeten their returns – assuming the deal goes well – and to reflect the higher risk associated with the instrument.

As far as maturity is concerned, the PIK notes will be expressed to be redeemable after all the senior and core junior debt has been repaid, which is

10 DDBs are structured to have no yield at all on their face. They generate a yield in economic terms by being issued at a discount to par and having an increasing redemption price over time that reflects a notional yield. At final maturity the redemption price would be the par value of the bonds.

11 See **Chapter 10** for a detailed consideration of the issues.

12 At the time of writing PIK notes might be priced with an annual yield of anywhere from 10 to 20%, which may be a fixed or floating rate (as a margin over LIBOR/EURIBOR). In fact this may mean that PIK is cheaper than mezzanine in some cases and it has been used as an alternative to mezzanine in some structures. In the case of PIK with warrants they may be priced with an IRR in the region of say 15–20%, which will be met through a combination of the yield and warrants. In any case, the pricing should reflect the credit analysis of the PIK note and in particular the amount of debt that ranks ahead of it versus the amount of equity that ranks behind it.

likely to be at the end of years 10, 11 or 12 following completion, depending on the precise nature of the funding structure.

From these various features PIK notes might be viewed as a form of stretched junior debt. Equally, given its position in the capital structure, PIK note debt could otherwise be described as a form of preferred equity or 'senior' equity. In fact, a layer of PIK note debt may theoretically be provided by the equity house sponsoring the deal as part of a larger equity package rather than as part of the acquisition finance package.

Amount of PIK note debt

9.9   PIK notes generally comprise the final element of the finance structure to be determined. In practice, until the mid-2000s at least, when leverage started to increase to levels not seen since the late 1980s, they remained relatively infrequently used. Since then their use has certainly increased but they remain non-core to true buy-outs and as such they typically contribute only a relatively small amount to the overall source of funds for buy-outs.[13]

DOCUMENTING PIK NOTES

9.10   The following paragraphs consider the nature of the principal documents which are used to document PIK note debt. For these purposes it is important to distinguish public PIK from private PIK. Public PIK notes are likely to take the form of a capital markets bond issue, using the conventional documentation forms used for such issues, although straight loans are also possible. Private PIK notes on the other hand are not destined for any 'market' as such and so the form of the documentation is usually negotiated on a deal-by-deal basis. By convention it will often be documented as subordinated loan capital, although, as with public PIK, straight loans are also possible.

Public PIK

9.11   As indicated, public PIK will, in most cases, be documented as a capital markets bond issue.[14] This form of PIK is really only used in the larger transactions, often as part of a refinancing or to finance a dividend recapitalisation. It is rarely used in true buy-outs. As far as documentation is concerned it will substantially follow that applicable to an issue of high yield bonds subject to a number of key differences.

First, and most obviously, the coupon will be non-cash. All of the interest will be payable in kind by the issue of further notes representing principal.[15] And whilst most conventional high yield debt is still fixed rate, the coupon on a public

13 PIK notes might account for say, only 5% or so of the overall funding requirement.
14 Public PIK may also be documented as a loan, however. See para **9.5**.
15 In fact, some forms of 'zero coupon' bonds are structured as discount notes or deep discount bonds (DDBs) that accrete capital value over time from their discount value at the issue date until they reach par value at maturity.

PIK note is quite often a floating rate of a margin over cost of funds.[16] A further difference will be that public PIK, unlike high yield, will not have the benefit of upstream credit support from the operating companies in the underlying business. In fact, it will almost certainly be fully structurally subordinated to any other form of acquisition finance in the structure, often because it is imposed on an existing structure, at the ultimate holdco level,[17] specifically with the intention of not interfering with the existing structure.[18] Another potential departure from high yield bonds might be the lack of extensive call protection. High yield bonds will often be non-callable at the option of the issuer for four or five years unless an extensive make-whole payment is made to the bondholders. This ensures a minimum yield on the bonds for a reasonable investment period. PIK notes, however, particularly those that are being used as a form of pre-exit recapitalisation for the equity investors (as is the case with many holdco PIKs), often do not have the benefit of such extensive protection. There may be no early redemption protection or it may be limited to a relatively short period of, say, six months or one year. Further, in place of a make-whole payment the protection may be limited to a premium of just 1% or 2% of the principal amount redeemed for a period of one or two years after funding.[19] Longer term public PIK finance on the other hand – that is not used for a pre-IPO distribution or other accelerated partial exit – may expect to receive call-protection similar to that applicable to conventional high yield debt.

Public PIK, although often structured to reflect a high yield bond issue in terms of documentation style, may occasionally be documented in hybrid form, with high yield style incurrence covenants set in a facility agreement. This might be appropriate or preferred where the PIK notes are to be privately placed with a small number of institutions, often including hedge funds, which typically take a flexible approach to documentation. The main rationale for this is to benefit from the reduced documentation formalities required for a private loan agreement as compared to a high yield bond offering memorandum and related documentation.

The remainder of this section is dedicated to private PIK which is the more common form used in conventional primary buy-out structures.

Private PIK

9.12   Private PIK will either be documented as a straight loan or, more commonly, as subordinated loan capital, such as loan notes or deep discount bonds. The form that the PIK notes take will to some extent be a function of the underwriter's stylistic preference, and the type of investor that will be holding the PIK notes. Acquisition finance banks and other institutions more used to loan documentation may prefer that form of instrument (although PIK is not typically structured with the banking market in mind), whereas other investors may be ambivalent. In practice, given that PIK notes generally benefit from quite limited

---

16 This might be in the region of anywhere between 5 and 12% over LIBOR/EURIBOR, or even greater for the most deeply subordinated instruments.

17 Which is why it is generally referred to as 'holdco PIK'.

18 See para **9.3**.

19 Such call-protection is more akin to that used for mezzanine debt rather than high yield debt. In practice no one model has been adopted for PIK notes.

covenants and events of default, a loan capital instrument will often be more appropriate than a loan agreement.

PIK note loans

9.13 If documented as a loan, the documentation will largely follow that used for senior and mezzanine debt amended to reflect the commercial terms applicable to the PIK notes, which will usually mean a reduced covenant and event of default package.[20] For instance the PIK notes may not receive the benefit of any financial covenants. However, if there are to be some, they would typically be looser than those in the senior and mezzanine documents, so that if a financial covenant breach were to occur the senior lenders could commence restructuring negotiations with the company without the need to involve the PIK note holders.

PIK note loan capital

9.14 More often the PIK notes will be documented as a form of subordinated loan capital such as loan notes or deep discount bonds, and the following paragraphs consider in some detail this form of PIK note documentation.

PIK note loan capital documentation

9.15

- PIK note instrument (and the PIK notes issued thereunder);[21]

- subscription agreement;

- possibly a warrant instrument;[22]

- intercreditor agreement; and

- possibly a security agreement.[23]

These are considered in turn in the following paragraphs.

PIK note instrument

9.16 As with issues of subordinated loan capital to the sponsor, management team and possibly the seller as part of the equity package, PIK notes in this form (including deep discount bonds) will be constituted by an instrument executed by the issuer of the PIK notes. The issuer will execute the instrument as a deed poll to facilitate transfers of the PIK notes, so that holders need not actually become party to the instrument itself. Instead they will hold a note or certificate evidencing their entitlement and be entered in the register of holders.

Typical provisions included in the instrument will include the following.

---

20 See also para **9.19** and **Chapter 10** in relation to the subordination of PIK notes.
21 This may or may not include a guarantee. As to which see under 'Guarantee' below.
22 The PIK note package may include an issue of warrants as with true mezzanine debt.
23 PIK notes may benefit from some level of credit support. Typically this will only be structural within the SPV group but on rare occasions it might include target group guarantees and security. See **Chapter 10** for a more detailed discussion.

Memorandum on front page

9.17   Usually the senior banks will require the front cover of the instrument to be endorsed with a memorandum recording that the PIK notes have been subordinated to the prior ranking acquisition finance under the terms of the intercreditor agreement.

Constitution of the notes

9.18   The instrument will constitute a certain number of notes of specified par value, with a fixed final redemption date, and specify the form of the notes to be issued in a schedule to the instrument. All of the main commercial terms of the notes (interest, redemptions, etc) will be stipulated in the 'Conditions' which will be set out in the form of the notes actually issued to the holders, which will be scheduled to the instrument.

Covenants/undertakings

9.19   The instrument will include the agreed covenant package of positive and negative undertakings, which in practice may be set out in a schedule. As mentioned above the extent of the covenant package will largely depend on how subordinated the PIK notes are to be. This itself is largely a function of who is providing them and whether the PIK notes are part of the acquisition finance package or really part of the equity package. In the case of PIK notes provided by the sponsor as part of the equity package, a full covenant package regulating what the target business can and cannot do is not necessary. This is because the sponsor will control the management of the whole group in any event through its shareholding in and directorship(s) of topco, together with its arrangements with the management team under the investment agreement. Third-party PIK note holders on the other hand would not have any such controls and would prefer to have their own covenant package in order to exercise some level of credit preservation.

Where there are third-party PIK notes, one of the major issues for both prior ranking acquisition financiers and the controlling shareholders will be the extent to which the PIK note holders have any independent rights to restrict the activities of the target business. In particular, no matter what the covenant package for the PIK notes comprises, the other parties will be concerned at how the associated rights for breach can be exercised, that is, what default triggers the PIK note holders have. The other parties will also be concerned as to what rights the PIK note holders have to restrict amendments to the covenant package that the other parties have agreed to.

As far as exercising rights upon breach are concerned, this really goes to the extent to which the PIK notes are to be subordinated. There are really two options: either the PIK notes are 'silent' or they are 'quiet'. If the PIK notes are silent then the holders will have no rights to exercise default triggers upon breach. In fact, it will never be quite that clear cut and even silent PIK will have rights to accelerate the PIK notes in the most extreme circumstances. Usually they will be entitled to accelerate the PIK notes if the core acquisition financiers have accelerated their facilities or if there is an insolvency event in respect of the

PIK note issuer (or one of its guarantors, if applicable). Quiet PIK will have an additional set of default triggers, whereby a breach of most, if not all, of the covenants will entitle the PIK note holders to exercise some acceleration and enforcement rights subject to a standstill mechanism. These matters are considered in more detail in **Chapter 10**.

As regards the right of the PIK note holders to veto amendments to, and waivers of breaches of, the senior and mezzanine covenant package, this is again a question of how deeply the PIK notes are to be subordinated. The preferred position for the core acquisition financiers and the sponsor/management team will be for the PIK notes to be subject to an override provision. Such a provision operates to automatically effect amendments and waivers of the PIK note covenant package to the extent that an equivalent amendment or waiver is made under the senior (or mezzanine) debt covenant package. There will be exceptions to the basic override principle, often called 'entrenched rights,' that will relate to the fundamental commercial terms of the PIK notes. For instance, the senior lenders should not be permitted, through the override provision, to effect a waiver of an insolvency event in respect of an obligor under the PIK notes[24] or change the pricing or repayment dates of the PIK notes.[25]

In order to delineate the rights of the PIK note holders, and in particular the extent of their covenant package and the circumstances when they can take action upon breach, both of the subordination issues described above (default triggers and override provisions) need to be considered to ensure consistency of approach. For instance, the operation of an override by the senior lenders will have the effect of removing a default trigger from the rights of the PIK note holders in respect of the breach of covenant concerned. Additionally, by removing the PIK note holders' default triggers (as with silent PIK) there may be less need for an override provision because the covenant package is effectively 'toothless' in any event.

Another factor that may dictate the extent of the PIK note covenant package will be what other instruments make up the acquisition finance, and in particular junior debt, package. If there are second lien or mezzanine loans, those instruments will have full maintenance covenant packages.[26] A similar covenant package for the PIK note holders would not necessarily be inconsistent with this. However, where the structure includes second lien notes and high yield bonds, because those instruments will have incurrence test covenants,[27] it would be inconsistent for the PIK note holders in such a structure to have a tighter maintenance covenant package.

In summary, in determining what covenant package the PIK note holders can benefit from, the following factors will need to be considered:

- Is the PIK provided by equity investors with management control of the group? If so there is no need for a covenant package at all. Only third-party investors need credit preservation rights in the PIK notes.

---

24 Although this is unlikely to happen in practice.
25 Override provisions are considered further in **Chapter 10**.
26 See **Chapters 6** and **7** respectively.
27 Or possibly a hybrid package, in the case of second lien notes. See **Chapters 6** and **8** respectively.

- What covenant packages do the prior ranking junior debt instruments benefit from? The PIK investors should have no tighter a covenant package than the prior ranking junior debt providers. In practice the PIK note covenant package will often mirror the prior ranking covenant packages to some extent – so long as its rights on default are subject to override and/or otherwise limited as below. In any event, the PIK would not normally include any financial covenants – these are generally deemed inappropriate for such a junior ranking instrument.

- Will the PIK be subject to an override provision in the intercreditor agreement? This is a question of subordination and is considered in some detail in **Chapter 10**. If there is an override provision, then the extent of the covenant package is less important.

- Do the PIK note holders have any default triggers? Is the PIK 'silent' or 'quiet'? Again, this is a question of subordination. If the PIK is 'silent' then the extent of the covenant package is less important.

Conditions of the notes

9.20   Not to be confused with the conditions precedent applicable to the issue of the notes, which will usually be set out in the subscription agreement, the conditions comprise the principal commercial terms of the notes. These will include:

- description of the notes – registered, par value, secured or unsecured;

- yield – that is, the rate and payment mechanics of interest on the loan capital.[28] In practice, the intercreditor agreement will override this provision and impose its own conditions on when any yield is payable;

- principal – that is, the date(s) (often it will be a single date at final maturity) and payment mechanics for the scheduled redemption of the notes. In addition to the scheduled redemption there will be provisions relating to redemption in other circumstances. These will generally include both voluntary redemption and mandatory redemption provisions. Mandatory redemption provisions will often follow the equivalent provisions in the prior ranking acquisition finance instruments. In the case of DDBs, there will be an annexed table setting out the redemption price on six- or twelve-month intervals after the issue of the notes until final maturity. Again, the intercreditor agreement will restrict the circumstances where the notes may actually be redeemed prior to final maturity. This will almost invariably mean deferring redemption until after the date on which all the core acquisition finance has been repaid in full;

- yield protection – in addition to 'boilerplate' provisions relating to tax gross-up and indemnities and increased costs there may be some more sub-

---

28 This will not apply to DDBs, when there is no yield per se. A notional yield accrues to the DDBs through the increasing redemption price.

stantial yield protection in the form of a non-call period[29] and early redemption premia;[30]

- events of default – the actual list of events of default may be contained in the instrument itself but there will be at least a cross-reference to them and stipulation of the holder's rights on an event of default (the default triggers);

- transfers – the scope of any restrictions on the ability of the PIK note holders to transfer the notes will be specified. These should include a requirement that the transferee adheres to the intercreditor agreement;

- subordination override – the conditions should include a provision that acknowledges the fact that the notes are subordinated pursuant to the intercreditor agreement. The prior ranking acquisition financiers will typically stipulate a form of wording for this provision; and

- 'boilerplate' provisions – there will be the usual raft of standard provisions dealing with payment mechanics, notices, governing law and so on.

Guarantee

9.21   Whether or not the PIK notes are guaranteed will depend on what level of subordination there is and, in particular, what credit support is to be provided. If there is to be either structural security or target group security[31] then a guarantee will be required from those companies granting security. The guarantee, if any, will commonly be documented in the instrument itself but a stand-alone guarantee is also possible.

Events of default

9.22   The list of events of default will be very similar in broad terms to the lists used in the core acquisition finance documentation, with notable exceptions. There is unlikely to be a full cross-default provision that is triggered upon a breach of the core acquisition finance documents, as the effect of this is to import in full the entire covenant package included in those documents.

In place of a cross-default clause the core acquisition financiers and equity investors are likely to insist on no more than a cross-acceleration clause which enables the PIK note holders to accelerate the PIK notes following acceleration of the other acquisition finance facilities.

In any event, the events of default will only provide the PIK note holders with active default triggers to the extent that the agreed subordination arrangements do not provide otherwise.[32]

---

29 That is, a period during which the PIK notes may not be redeemed voluntarily.
30 That is, a fee perhaps in the region of 2% in year 1 and 1% in year 2, that is payable to the holders upon an early redemption.
31 As to which see **Chapter 10**.
32 See para **9.19** and **Chapter 10**.

Topco board directorship

9.23   As with true warranted mezzanine, a third-party PIK note provider might – although this remains quite rare – be able to negotiate a seat on the board of topco. This to some extent reflects the fact that the risk profile of the PIK notes may be nearer to equity than to acquisition finance debt. In addition, certain PIK note investors may need VCOC rights, which may include a right to appoint a board member, but such rights will typically be dealt with separately in a side letter.[33]

Subordination override

9.24   The instrument will include a standard provision acknowledging the overriding subordination arrangements in the intercreditor agreement. The core acquisition financiers will usually dictate the form of this provision.[34]

Boilerplate provisions

9.25   The instrument will also contain a number of standard provisions relating to, among other things, contractual interpretation, the appointment and role of an agent for the PIK note holders and, if relevant, a security trustee for the PIK note security, amendments and waivers, the register of note holders, decision-making by the holders, governing law and the like.

Subscription agreement

9.26   The subscription agreement will be between the PIK note issuer and the initial holders as subscribers. The arranger and underwriter of the PIK notes will normally be the only initial holder at funding. Syndication if any will occur after funding. Unlike the instrument and the notes themselves it does not create any legal relations between the issuer and the note holders generally. Consequently, it will include matters that relate only to the issuer and initial subscriber, such as up-front fees. As with the PIK note instrument it will have a standard form look and feel to it and will usually include the following provisions.

Memorandum on front page

9.27   As with the PIK note instrument, the core acquisition financiers will often require an acknowledgement of the subordination of the PIK notes on the front page of the subscription agreement. The function of this is simply to put the initial subscribers on notice that the notes are subordinated. It is not strictly required in a legal sense since the actual subordination of the notes will be dealt with elsewhere.

---

33 Venture capital operating company (VCOC) rights are required by fund investors who have US pension funds within their investor base. The right to appoint a member of the board is required as a qualification for VCOC status for US regulatory purposes.

34 A sample version is provided in **Chapter 4**.

Agreement to subscribe

9.28 The initial subscriber of the PIK notes will undertake to subscribe for all the notes subject to the terms of the agreement.

Conditions precedent

9.29 The CPs will usually be substantially the same as the CPs for the other elements of the acquisition finance package. They need to include any additional requirements of the PIK note holders, such as any warrants that are to be issued to them.

Drawdown mechanics and purpose

9.30 Typically, the purpose of the notes will simply be acquisition consideration and costs. The issuer will downstream the proceeds of the notes issued to the acquisition vehicle under a funding loan.

Initial representations

9.31 The subscription agreement will include a suite of standard document execution representations by the issuer. It may also include more extensive transaction and due diligence style representations relating to the target business and the acquisition of the sort that would be included in the core acquisition finance documentation.

Fees

9.32 The amounts and timing of the up-front and any on-going agency or monitoring fees payable to the initial subscriber will often be set out in a separate side letter but the subscription agreement will create the obligation on the issuer to pay them.[35]

In addition, there may be a commitment or non-utilisation fee payable from the signing of the subscription agreement until completion and funding.[36]

Subordination override

9.33 Unless the document contains ongoing payment obligations from the issuer to the initial subscriber, a subordination override provision is not strictly necessary. The PIK note instrument and the notes themselves will contain the main on-going financial obligations of the issuer and those documents should always be subject to a subordination override clause. Where there are annual or other ongoing fees payable under the subscription agreement, then, for completeness, an override provision should be included.

---

35 The amounts of these fees is largely negotiable. An up-front underwriting fee of between 2 and 3% of the total amount of the notes issued would not be unusual. Annual agency fees are likely to be relatively de minimis if any are payable at all. Alternatively, an annual monitoring fee may be payable of an amount to be negotiated.

36 The commitment fee might be in the region of 0.50% to 1% per annum (but calculated on a daily basis).

Boilerplate provisions

9.34   The agreement will include a number of standard documentary provisions dealing with notices, the initial subscriber's costs and expenses, governing law and the like.

Warrant instrument

9.35   On the occasions where the PIK note finance package is to include warrants, these will be constituted by a warrant instrument. The form of a PIK note warrant instrument should be substantially the same as that used for warranted mezzanine debt. Mezzanine warrant instruments are considered in more detail in **Chapter 7**.

Intercreditor and security documents

Intercreditor agreement

9.36   There will invariably be an intercreditor agreement between the PIK note holders and the prior ranking creditors for the purposes of subordinating the PIK notes to the core acquisition finance. It is usual for the same agreement to be used to prioritise all of the layers of acquisition finance, the equity loan capital and the group's intercompany debt.

If the PIK notes are being provided as part of the acquisition finance package and are to benefit from the same security package as the other secured acquisition finance,[37] the PIK note holders may be direct beneficiaries under the same security documents as the other acquisition financiers.[38] In this case the intercreditor agreement is likely to contain the appointment of the security trustee or agent on behalf of the core acquisition financiers *and* PIK note holders and set out the terms of the security trust or other basis on which the security is to be held for such parties.

The form of the intercreditor agreement and the subordination arrangements generally applicable to PIK note debt are considered in some detail in **Chapter 10**.

Security documents

9.37   Public PIK will almost certainly not benefit from any guarantees or security. It is typically fully structurally subordinated to all other elements of the capital structure save for the equity. Private PIK note debt, however, may benefit from some level of security. This may be limited to structural security in the SPV group – in order to enable the note holders to protect their position in the structure (ie, ahead of the equity) in a default scenario – or on occasion it may extend to upstream credit support from the target group.[39] Structural security

---

37 As to which see **Chapter 10**.
38 See para **9.37**.
39 See **Chapter 10** for a consideration of the relevant issues.

given in the SPV group will generally take the form of a share charge over the PIK note issuer or another vehicle in the SPV group so that the PIK note holders can step in ahead of the equity investors in a default scenario. Such a share charge will usually secure a guarantee of the PIK notes from the chargor and will also incorporate a charge or assignment of shareholder loans owing to the chargor.

If the PIK notes are to benefit from upstream credit support from the target group the form of the guarantee and security package is likely to mirror that for the senior debt.

If the PIK note debt is being arranged by the senior or mezzanine debt MLA – and being secured – then it will almost certainly be secured under the same security documents as the other acquisition finance and no further documentation will be required. The intercreditor agreement would then include the PIK note holders as beneficiaries under the security trust or other such arrangement if necessary.[40]

If the PIK notes are being provided by a third-party investor – and being secured – then a separate set of second, or possibly third,[41] ranking security documents is possible.[42] The form of such documents should largely mirror the core acquisition finance security documents subject to any necessary consequential amendments. The benefit of such documents would normally be held by a security trustee or agent appointed by the PIK note holders, either in the PIK note instrument itself or in a separate security trust or agency agreement. If a separate PIK security trust or agency arrangement is established, the PIK note holders will not be party to the security trust or agency arrangements in the intercreditor agreement, although they will still be party for subordination purposes.

Where the PIK notes *are* to benefit from any target group security, each party that grants security, other than the issuer itself, should provide a guarantee of the PIK note debt. The guarantee would usually be contained in the PIK note instrument itself. Alternatively it could be contained in a stand-alone guarantee document or in the relevant security document. In any case, all such guarantees would need to be subordinated under the intercreditor agreement.

40 Multi-jurisdictional deals may include jurisdictions that do not recognise the concept of a security trust and may require, for instance, a parallel debt mechanism.
41 This will depend on what other prior ranking layers of secured finance there are in the structure with their own set of security documents. Senior, second lien and mezzanine debt will usually be secured under a single set of first ranking security documents; albeit with first, second and third ranking rights to benefit from such security.
42 Acquisition finance houses generally will not hold security for third-party syndicates that they have not themselves arranged and participated in. They would rarely agree to hold security for equity investors providing secured subordinated loan capital, for instance.

CHAPTER 10

Ranking the Layers of Finance

WHAT IS RANKING?

10.1   As between each of the various layers and sub-layers of investment and finance in a buy-out a specific order of 'ranking' is assumed.

Ranking and priority

10.2   The 'ranking' reflects the agreed order of priority for realising the various investments that make up the overall funding structure. Highest priority goes to those investors that have the least to gain. They take the least risk with their investment. On the other hand, the investors with the highest potential return on their investment take the most risk in realising their investment. In reality return follows risk, not the other way round, but it is two sides of the same equation.

Taking this approach, the principal and capital invested in a buy-out should be repayable or realised in the following order:

- senior debt; then
- junior debt; then
- equity.

In addition to prioritising the order of return of principal or capital invested, the right to receive a yield on the various investments during their life will be prioritised in the same order.

Risk and return

10.3   The concept of 'risk' in terms of prioritising the various layers of finance is used in a purely relative sense to mean the rights of the investors to receive the agreed or projected return and realise their investments relative to the other investments made by other investors in the transaction. Absolute measurements of risk are theoretically possible on a statistical basis but such analysis is beyond the scope of this book.

A more complete risk-return analysis for buy-out investments would also include the various sub-categories of finance that may be utilised in a funding structure, as shown below with some indicative returns. The pricing of the instruments used in acquisition finance are essentially market driven and as market conditions change typical pricing may also change.[1] The figures given should therefore be treated as illustrative only.

- senior debt – 2.25 to 3.25% per annum.[2]

- second lien debt – 4.00 to 6.00% per annum margin.

- mezzanine debt[3] – 7.50–10.50% margin for warrantless or 14–16% blended IRR for warranted.

- High yield debt – 8–10% fixed (or occasionally all-in floating) coupon.

- PIK notes – 10–20% fixed (or all-in floating) coupon.

- institutional subordinated loan capital – 10–20% fixed coupon.[4]

- institutional equity – 20–35% blended IRR including subordinated loan capital return.

- management equity – not usually expressed as target IRR but will be significant.

In addition, seller deferred capital could rank where PIK notes or institutional subordinated loan capital are shown, depending on its nature and purpose.[5]

SUBORDINATION

10.4   In order to effect the agreed order of ranking, the acquisition financiers and other investors will rely on the principle of 'subordination', whereby lower ranking investments are subordinated to higher ones. The concept and techniques used to effect subordination are considered in the following paragraphs.

1   For example the liquidity crisis triggered by the US sub-prime market turmoil in the summer of 2007 caused pricing to be reset to the pricing levels seen in the first half of the 2000s and in some cases higher (see fn **2**).
2   This was for many years in the 2000s the standard range of interest rate margins, above cost of funds (LIBOR or EURIBOR), for the three tranches of senior debt commonly used in buy-outs. The senior A note facility was traditionally priced at 2.25% subject to a margin ratchet (see **Chapter 5**), the senior B note at 2.75% and the senior C note at 3.25%. In addition, the B and C notes may be subject to downward flex to 2.50% and 3.00%, respectively, particularly in larger deals. In fact, in the latter half of the 2000s, downward pressure on acquisition finance pricing generally resulted in margins as low as 2.00%, 2.25% and 2.75% (or sometimes lower) for the A, B and C notes respectively, although the liquidity squeeze mentioned in fn **1** had the effect of reversing this trend, perhaps even to 2.50%, 3.00% and 3.50% respectively. Senior debt pricing is considered in further detail in **Chapter 5**.
3   Mezzanine debt and high yield debt (listed here below mezzanine debt) are in practice alternatives that would not usually be found in the same structure.
4   The coupon on the institutional loan capital will be set at a level that is consistent with the overall equity return target. It should not be viewed on an entirely stand-alone basis for these purposes.
5   See **Chapter 3**.

Share capital versus debt

10.5   There is a fundamental difference between share capital and debt for subordination purposes. Under the laws of most jurisdictions, restrictions apply to payments in respect of share capital, including preference shares, which do not apply in respect of debt.

Under English law, a company's share capital may only be reduced by a purchase or redemption of shares out of distributable profits or the proceeds of a fresh issue of shares or, in the case of a private company, out of capital itself.[6] Similarly, income distributions (dividends) in respect of share capital may only be made out of distributable profits.[7]

In the insolvent winding-up of a company where there are no distributable profits, the practical effect of the legal restrictions on payments in respect of share capital is to lock-in share capital in the company until all of the creditors of the company have been paid off – in other words, to subordinate the share capital of a company to its debts.[8]

This means that, for the purposes of ranking investments in a buy-out on the insolvency of a company, share capital is automatically subordinated to debt. However, since the ranking principal will also need to apply *prior* to the onset of insolvency, further steps will be taken to ensure that the share capital invested in a buy-out is subordinated to the debt finance at all times.

Thus, the acquisition financiers will impose contractual restrictions on the return of capital to shareholders at any time while there is acquisition finance outstanding. Similarly, contractual restrictions will be imposed on the payment of dividends to the equity investors and the making of other distributions.

In the case of dividends, it is interesting to note that, to the extent that a dividend has been declared – and, if a final dividend, this dividend is made in general meeting through the approval of the shareholders – or is otherwise expressed to be payable in the articles of association on certain dates without the need for a specific declaration[9], it will itself be a debt due and owing by the relevant company to the relevant shareholders.[10] Any such dividend will be an actionable debt whether or not the articles of association specify that the debt can be sued upon, although practice varies as to whether this is expressed to be the case. This means

---

6   See Companies Act 1985, s 171 (and from 1 October 2009 see Ch 5, Pt 18 of the Companies Act 2006).

7   See Companies Act 1985, s 263 (and from 6 April 2008 see Pt 23 of the Companies Act 2006).

8   See also Companies Act 1985, s 178(6) (and from 1 October 2009 see s 735 (in Pt 18) of the Companies Act 2006) which has the effect of expressly subordinating the claims of holders of redeemable shares to have their shares redeemed in a winding up of the company behind the claims of the company's creditors.

9   This would almost always be the case with the fixed dividend payable in respect of preference shares forming part of a buy-out equity funding structure. Since the late 1990s, however, this has become rare in buy-outs, with subordinated loan capital being used instead of redeemable preference share capital, on grounds of more favourable tax treatment.

10   By contrast, where the directors *resolve* to pay a dividend but the dividend is not yet *declared*, most legal commentators would suggest that this does not create a debt as the directors could still resolve not to pay it or to defer the payment.

that the unpaid but prospective recipient of a declared dividend or fixed dividend which has fallen due may be a creditor of the relevant company.

Essentially, therefore, for the purposes of ranking the layers of finance, although share capital will to some extent be automatically subordinated to the acquisition finance debt – ie, when the relevant company is insolvent and ultimately upon a winding-up – further steps will need to be taken to provide for full subordination.

Structural subordination

10.6   Structural subordination is used in buy-outs to subordinate certain lower ranking debt instruments to prior ranking debt. It is most often used to subordinate loan capital subscribed by the equity investors and PIK note investors to the core acquisition finance.

Structural subordination operates by having different investments made in different companies in a group structure. Investments in the companies that are nearer in the chain of ownership to the cash generating assets have superior rights to access the cash generated. Consequently, the investments in the companies that are further away from the assets are structurally subordinated in terms of their rights to access cash.

This can be shown in diagrammatic form as follows:

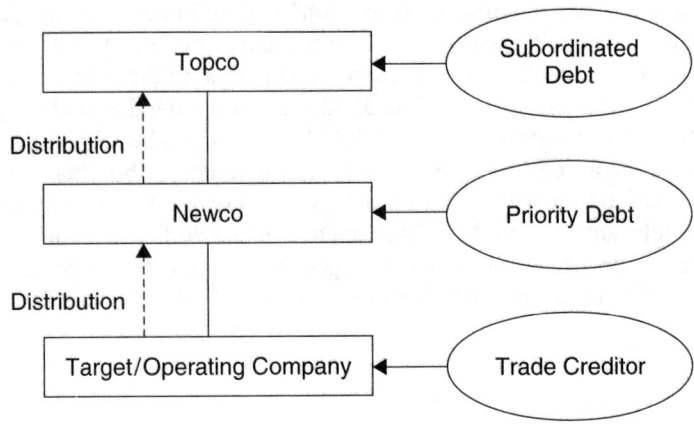

Structural Subordination

In this structure cash is generated by the operating company. In order to service the debts in newco and topco, cash will be upstreamed by the operating company first to newco and then on to topco,[11] in each case when payments are required on the debts. Assuming that there is always sufficient cash to meet all the debts then there is no problem. If there is insufficient cash at any point then

---

11   The operating company could lend the money directly to topco but in practice contractual restrictions will ensure that this is not permitted.

the structural status of the various creditors to access that cash will become relevant. Because of the structure, topco's creditors will be last in line to access any cash. Operating company cash will be used first by the operating company to pay its creditors. Only then, if there is any surplus operating company cash, will it be available to newco, and similarly newco must meet all of its liabilities before upstreaming any surplus to topco.

When the group is in sufficient financial difficulty, such that an insolvency event occurs and the companies are to be wound up, the order of priority crystallises and topco's creditors will only be entitled to access cash that is dividended to topco by the liquidator of newco; ie, once all of newco's creditors have been paid off. In such circumstances newco will not be permitted to lend the money to topco and dividends will be subject to the rules mentioned previously.

In fact, in the structure on the previous page the priority creditor is itself subordinated to the operating company's trade creditors in the same way. Only if the operating company has sufficient assets to pay off all of its creditors can a dividend be paid to newco. Indeed, it is precisely to avoid the structural subordination of their debt to trade creditors that acquisition financiers seek guarantees from the operating companies in a business that they are financing. Guarantees will provide the acquisition financiers with direct claims against the operating companies which will result in the acquisition financiers ranking *pari passu* with the trade creditors. In addition, they will usually try to go one step further and take security for the guarantee obligations so that in fact they rank *ahead* of the trade creditors. This can be shown in simple diagrammatic form as follows.

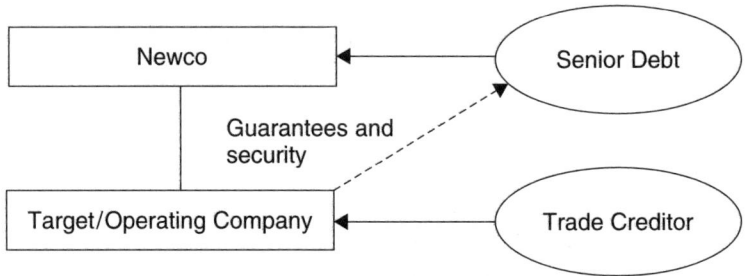

Target group credit support

Indeed, it is not just in respect of trade creditors that acquisition financers use guarantees to ensure structural parity or priority. In more complex transaction structures guarantees will also be used to ensure parity of guarantees at a certain level in the structure where structural subordination would otherwise arise. This may be the case, for instance, where a high yield bond is issued by a company that is not the senior debt borrower but there is no intention for the high yield bond to be structurally subordinated to the senior debt. By having the senior debt borrower guarantee the high yield debt, structural subordination in the SPV group is avoided. This can be shown in the context of a full buy-out structure in the following diagram.

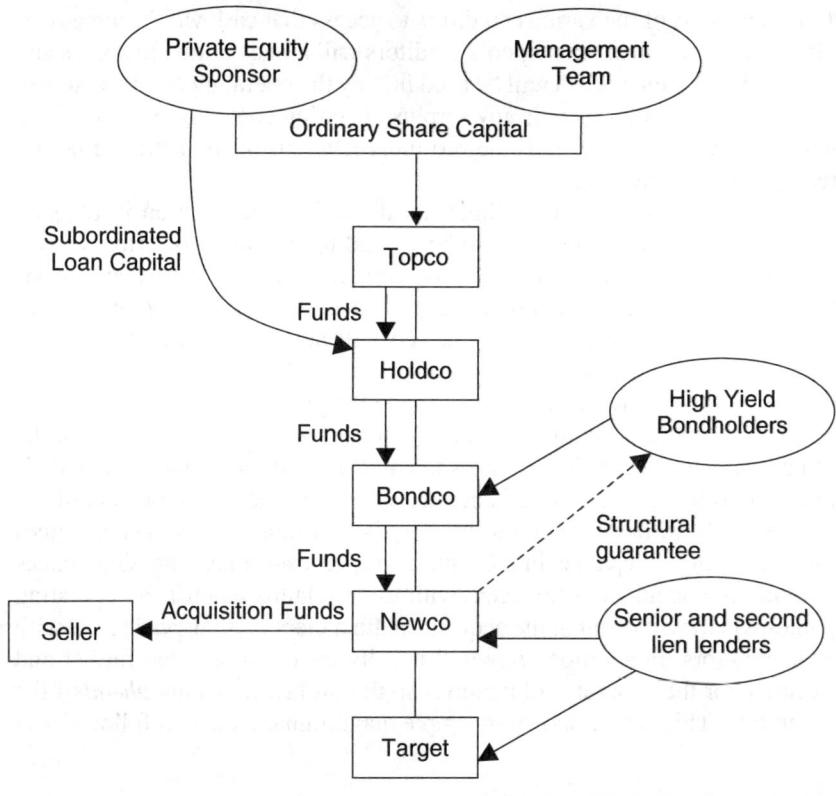

Senior, second lien and high yield

Security

10.7   A third method of effecting ranking of debts is for the prior ranking debt providers to take asset security for the principal or guarantee obligations of a company. Depending on the precise nature of the security taken,[12] a secured creditor will be able to enforce the security and have its debts paid out of the proceeds of that enforcement in priority to the unsecured creditors of the company granting the security.[13]

If guarantees and asset security from operating companies in the target group are not available and the acquisition financers are relying only on share security over the target group they are in effect structurally subordinated to the trade and other creditors of the target group. If the target group were to be liquidated, all of the trade and other creditors of the target group companies would be paid out before any amount of the acquisition finance. In order to avoid that scenario in an

---

12 Under English law, for instance, the difference between fixed and floating security in particular has a material effect on the precise priority of the debt secured.

13 There are exceptions to this general principle. In particular, the UK's insolvency legislation (see, in particular, Insolvency Act 1986, ss 175 and 176A and Sch 6) provides that certain 'preferential' debts and an amount of a company's unsecured debts will rank ahead of the claims of a creditor relying on floating charge security. In addition, any assets supplied to a company under a supply agreement that incorporates an enforceable retention of title provision may be claimed by the supplier in priority to a secured creditor.

enforcement situation the acquisition financiers would need to find a way of mitigating the risk of the trade and other creditors making claims on the target group companies. In practical terms this means that they would need to sell the business as a *going concern*, using their share security over the target group as the means to effect a transfer of the business.

In certain jurisdictions, including the United Kingdom, it is possible to have more than one layer of security over the same assets, which would be ranked either as a matter of law or by contract. In addition, it may be possible, as it is in the United Kingdom, to have more than one layer of creditor secured by a single layer of security. Thus, in a UK buy-out, a single layer of first ranking security will usually secure *all* of the core senior debt, second lien debt and mezzanine debt. As between the respective senior, second lien and mezzanine creditors they will agree *as a matter of contract* that the proceeds of enforcement are applied first to the senior creditors, next the second lien creditors and next to the mezzanine creditors.

Contractual subordination

10.8   Contractual agreement as to the order of ranking will invariably be required with any buy-out structure. The three techniques considered above are not sufficient to establish the ranking of the various layers of a buy-out funding structure to the extent required by the higher ranking financiers. Only the agreement of the parties can effectively achieve that. The automatic subordination of share capital only applies in the extreme circumstance of insolvency and even then it cannot effect an order of priority between two layers of debt. Giving one category of debt security and leaving another unsecured will not be sufficient to the extent of any shortfall in the value of the security. Even structural subordination requires some agreement between the parties to complete the subordination, because, in practice, the proceeds of the structurally subordinated debt will generally be downstreamed by way of loan to the borrower of the senior ranking debt, thus creating a competing creditor at the level of that borrower. So invariably there must also be contractual subordination arrangements.

Full contractual subordination requires the agreement of both creditors, priority and subordinated, and the debtor. The arrangements must not only deal with the ranking between the debts upon insolvency – ultimately as to the distribution of the proceeds of a winding-up of the debtor – but also ensure that the pre-agreed order of ranking is observed during the normal lifetime of the financing. Ranking applies not just to the right to realise the principal but also the right to receive the agreed yield on that principal and one of the main functions of the contractual arrangements will be to delineate all of the circumstances when the investors in the various layers of finance are entitled to receive their yield.

The document that contains most of the contractual subordination arrangements is the intercreditor agreement. It is usual practice for there to be a single intercreditor agreement to contain the contractual subordination arrangements applicable to all the layers of finance. One common exception to this is in relation to seller subordinated loan capital. Sellers will often prefer not to be involved in the negotiation of a full composite intercreditor agreement but instead to have a separate 'subordination agreement' for the seller capital. This also avoids the need to include the seller in any subsequent amendments to the main intercreditor agreement.

The primary tasks therefore of the intercreditor and subordination agreements are to establish ranking between the layers of finance upon a winding-up and to preserve the agreed ranking of rights to realise both principal and yield on the respective investments during the life of the investments. As will be seen in the following sections, this is achieved through a wide variety of contractual provisions.

Summary of subordination techniques

10.9   Any layer of buy-out finance can be subordinated to any other layer using the following techniques and principles.[14]

- Structural arrangements – to create prior rights to access cash flows and assets including through the use of guarantees.

- Contractual arrangements – through the core components of an intercreditor or subordination agreement.

- Security – can be used to establish the priority of one debt to another.

- Share capital – is subordinated to debt upon insolvency as a matter of law.

INTERCREDITOR AND SUBORDINATION AGREEMENTS

10.10   Intercreditor and subordination agreements are perhaps not as standardized as other finance document. At the time of writing there was no LMA precedent form, for example. In any event the following section is an attempt to distil the essential components of an intercreditor agreement. Together with the other principles referred to above, these core components may be applied to subordinate any form of financing used in a buy-out.

Anatomy of an intercreditor agreement

Overall ranking of the investments

10.11   It is usual and good practice at the beginning of an intercreditor agreement to recite the agreed order of ranking or priority of the various investments. This is intended to avoid any doubt as to the overall intentions of the parties.

Ranking of security

10.12   Where there is more than one layer of security the intercreditor agreement should also stipulate the order of priority between the layers. In practice there will often just be one layer of security, which is held on trust[15] for all the secured acquisition financers subject to an agreed order of priority as to the application of the

---

14 Except that debt cannot be fully subordinated to share capital, which is in any event never required.

15 Since trusts are not recognised in all jurisdictions, in a multi-jurisdictional buy-out alternative legal mechanisms may be required to enable the security to be granted for the benefit of a syndicate of lenders. See also **Chapter 13**.

proceeds on enforcement of the security. The agreed order of application of enforcement proceeds is often referred to as the payment 'cascade' or 'waterfall'.

Subordination upon insolvency

10.13 This clause is at the heart of the intercreditor agreement. The key element is an agreement by the subordinated creditor and the debtor, in favour of the prior ranking creditor, that upon any winding-up of the debtor[16] the prior ranking creditor's claim takes priority. There are two ways of establishing this priority. The first has the subordinated creditor agreeing not to prove for its claim until the priority creditor has been paid in full. Such clauses are enforceable under English law[17] but this version is not the most efficient way of ensuring a full return for the priority creditor. A more effective provision has the subordinated creditor proving for its claim in the winding up of the debtor and then turning over the recovered proceeds to the priority creditor.[18]

Permitted payments to the subordinated creditor

Permitted payments

10.14 The intercreditor agreement will include provisions establishing what payments a subordinated creditor is entitled to receive in respect of its investment. All other payments to the subordinated creditor will be expressly prohibited. For instance, a mezzanine lender will be entitled to receive interest at the agreed rate but it will not be entitled to receive any principal until the senior debt and any second lien debt have been repaid in full. The section will set out in some detail the conditions to any permitted payment.

Permitted payment conditions

10.15 The extent of the payment conditions will generally reflect how deeply subordinated the relevant instrument is. Thus, the payment conditions for permitted payments of interest, if any,[19] on subordinated loan capital invested by the equity investors will be more extensive than the conditions applicable to payments of mezzanine interest.

One of the conditions that typically applies to permitted payments on both junior debt and subordinated loan capital is that there is no current or anticipated breach of any of the financial covenants under the senior facilities agreement. This is a key condition of the senior lenders since the financial covenants are used

---

16 Meaning any insolvency proceedings whereby the company's debts are to be settled.

17 In fact, there has been considerable legal debate about the enforceability of such provisions under English law, in particular because they amount to an agreement to contract out of the mandatory insolvency rules applicable in the United Kingdom that establish the *pari passu* ranking of all creditor's claims in a debtor's winding-up. It wasn't until 1994 that the courts first upheld such provisions. In other jurisdictions such provisions remain untested in court, which leaves legal risk for the senior creditors in those jurisdictions.

18 Turn-over provisions of this kind have also been the subject of legal debate, in particular, as to whether or not they create a *registerable* charge. In brief, the answer appears to be that, if properly drafted, they do not (so no registration is required). See also para **10.17** and fn **25**.

19 Quite often no cash payments of interest are permitted at all on the quasi-equity.

as early warning indicators of financial underperformance by the business, precisely the time when the senior lenders may wish to stop cash going out of the business to meet junior debt interest or, even more so, quasi-equity interest.

This is also why the senior lenders will often insist that the payment dates for permitted interest payments are set by reference to the testing of the senior debt financial covenants. Since the financial covenants will be tested quarterly by reference to the delivery of financial information, including the group's management accounts and a covenant compliance certificate from the borrower, the payment dates should be set to fall a short period (say, 15 days) after receipt by the senior lenders of that financial information.[20] They can then assess the information and if it shows that a financial covenant breach has occurred or is anticipated to occur they can serve a payment blockage notice on the debtor before the payment of interest on the junior debt or equity investor debt, as applicable, is actually made.[21] In practice, the senior lenders will often insist that mezzanine interest payments are only made twice per annum at fixed six-monthly intervals coinciding with the financial covenant tests that arise at the end of the corresponding periods.

With interest payments on quasi-equity there may only be one payment permitted each year and, rather than having the payment conditions tested by reference to management accounts, the senior lenders may insist on using the audited annual accounts and auditor's covenant compliance report as the basis for that single payment. Thus the payment date would be fixed to fall a number of days after receipt of the audited financial information.

Other conditions will apply to payments on junior debt and quasi-equity. For example, payments can usually be blocked if any event of default or, more commonly, any material event of default has occurred under the senior facilities agreement, which has not been remedied or waived.

Quasi-equity payments will generally be subject to more extensive conditions than junior debt payments. For instance, it might be a requirement that the business has performed in line with or ahead of the business plan. Bearing in mind that the senior debt financial covenants will usually be set to allow for between 15 and 20%[22] underperformance to the business plan as represented by the base case model, such a condition may mean calculating the financial covenants without the headroom and determining if there is compliance at the higher level or performance or not. Only if the higher level of financial performance is achieved will the payment be permitted. The recalculation of the covenants in this way may be on a historic, current or look forward basis, depending on which testing periods are to be used. Any test that includes a look forward component requires the borrower to provide a cash flow forecast, which is then used as the basis of a *pro forma* testing of the covenant. In each case, whether or not enhanced compliance with the covenant is required (ie without headroom and possibly with a higher test level), it is usual to include the proposed payment in the calculation to see if the effect of making the payment would have caused, or would cause, the test not to be passed.

---

20 In addition to the quarterly compliance certificate from the borrower there will also be an obligation to provide an auditor compliance 'report' with the annual audited financial statements. See **Chapter 5** in relation to financial covenants and how they are tested including the use of compliance certificates.

21 Payment blockage notices are considered in para **10.16**.

22 This is the level of headroom that would be most typical over a full cycle of the market. However, in times of excess market liquidity some sponsors have been able to push this to as far as 30%.

Payment block

10.16 A further provision in the intercreditor agreement will set out the mechanics of how payments, which would otherwise be permitted, may be blocked if the relevant payment conditions are not met.

A distinction must be drawn between automatic payment blocks and manual payment blocks. The latter require active steps to be taken to effect the payment block, usually the service of a payment blockage notice to the debtor and subordinated creditor by the prior ranking creditor. The payment block mechanism operates in conjunction with the permitted payment conditions and in practical terms will often be in the same clause.

Automatic payment blocks are a powerful tool, especially when, as is usual, a turn-over provision is also included in the agreement. Under the turn-over provision the senior creditors are able to retrospectively challenge payments that were made to the junior creditors or equity investor creditors but which, as a result of contractual restrictions, should not have been paid, and to require the amounts to be paid – or 'turned-over' – to the senior creditors. This is why automatic payment blocks are unpopular with junior creditors and equity investors. This is particularly so for fund investors who may distribute the proceeds of a permitted payment to their participant investors as soon as the payment is received. In practice, two compromises are often considered. With the first the junior creditor or equity investor is entitled to give notice to the borrower and the acquisition financiers of the pending permitted payment and, in effect, a reminder that this is subject to conditions. If no payment blockage notice is then issued in respect of the payment the amount can be paid and distributed to the third-party investors without any obligation to claw back if in fact the relevant conditions were not met. The other is to apply an amount equal to the amount that would otherwise be required to be clawed back as a deduction against the next permitted payment. Not surprisingly both suggestions are strongly resisted by senior lenders. Their argument is that the risk of a hidden payment condition breach arising is slim and that they, as senior creditors, should not take the risk of one arising.

Manual payment block provisions, by contrast, do require the senior creditors to actively make an assessment as to whether the payment conditions are satisfied at the time of the permitted payment. If the senior creditors fail to serve a payment blockage notice in any given circumstance they will have missed their chance to block the relevant payment even if it turns out that it should have been blocked.

Automatic blocks apply only to the most serious circumstances, such as the existence of a payment default on the prior ranking debt or where the prior ranking debt has been accelerated.[23] In those circumstances the payment block is indefinite for so long as the payment condition remains unsatisfied. With most categories of junior and subordinated debt this means that an outstanding payment default on the senior debt will act as an indefinite payment block until that payment default is remedied.

Manual payment blocks apply to less serious circumstances such as the occurrence of a financial covenant breach or other event of default under the prior

---

23 Note that the absence of both of those circumstances will normally be identified as separate payment conditions.

ranking debt.[24] In this case it is up to the prior ranking creditor to determine whether or not to block a payment on the junior ranking debt. Manual payment blocks are for limited periods only, usually long enough to enable the next interest payment on the junior or subordinated debt to be blocked.

Generally a payment block mechanism will allow the making of a payment that would otherwise not be permitted if, by reducing the amount of the payment, the payment conditions would then be satisfied.

It is also common for an intercreditor agreement to allow for the 'catch-up' of previously blocked payments as soon as the payment block falls away provided that the payment conditions can then be met.

'Turn-over'

10.17   A 'turn-over' or 'claw-back' provision is used in conjunction with the permitted payment and payment block provisions so that the prior ranking creditor can claim directly against the subordinated creditor if a payment is made contrary to the permitted payment conditions or payment block mechanism. In fact, the turn-over provision will usually have general effect in the agreement and apply to any payment made contrary to any provision of the agreement including, for instance, the subordination on insolvency provision.

In practice the prior ranking creditors will insist on having all of the subordinated creditors party to the intercreditor agreement so that if necessary they have a direct contractual claim against them under the turn-over clause. In addition, the turn-over clause will often purport to create a trust in respect of any moneys received by a subordinated creditor contrary to the intercreditor agreement. The rationale for this is to give the prior ranking creditors a proprietary claim in the payment proceeds themselves, rather than a mere contractual claim against the subordinated creditor. If the proprietary right were upheld it would defeat the unsecured creditors of the subordinated creditor which wrongfully received the payment in insolvency proceedings relating to it. Whether or not such a turn-over trust is enforceable under English law has been subject to legal debate.[25]

Acceleration and enforcement rights

Default triggers

10.18   A subordinated creditor will be restricted from taking action against the debtor to recover its investment, including acceleration of any principal amounts outstanding, other than in very limited circumstances.

---

24   The absence of a financial covenant breach will be identified as a separate payment condition as may 'any other event of default has arisen and is outstanding under the senior facilities agreement'; although this second condition may be limited to other 'material' or 'financial' events of default. It depends on the extent of the subordination. See for example para **10.69** in relation to mezzanine debt and para **10.121** in relation to equity investor debt.

25   In addition, such turn-over trusts are thought by some to create a security interest which must be registered against the relevant subordinated creditor in order to be enforceable in all circumstances. The precise legal status depends on the drafting of the clause and it is possible to avoid the clause having the effect of a charge (and thus to avoid the need for its registration to be effective in all circumstances). A useful analysis of the issues is provided in *Re SSSL Realisations* (2002) Ltd [2006] EWCA Civ 7, CA (Civ Div). This case also provides authority for the enforceability of subordination on insolvency clauses.

Additionally, the terms of the subordinated debt itself may be expressly limited so that a default trigger – usually described as an event of default or right of early redemption – does not arise in the first place. For instance, certain forms of junior debt – such as PIK notes – may not include any financial covenants thus reducing the circumstances when a default can arise under the terms of the debt. Generally, the more junior the instrument the less default triggers there will be. However, even where default triggers do exist in the subordinated debt documentation the intercreditor agreement will override those triggers other than in agreed exceptional circumstances.

There are essentially three levels of restriction that can apply to enforcement action that could otherwise be taken by a subordinated creditor. A total restriction may apply to certain default triggers, for example, breach of a non-material provision in a subordinated debt instrument may not, under the terms of the intercreditor agreement, entitle the subordinated creditor to take any action. The second level of restriction is where certain default triggers are actionable but the action that may be taken is limited. For example, the onset of an insolvency event in respect of a debtor may entitle the subordinated creditor to take action against that debtor only, although usually not in competition with the prior ranking creditor. Similarly, the acceleration of prior ranking debt may entitle a subordinated creditor to take action but the action may be limited to merely accelerating the subordinated debt. Thirdly, certain default triggers will entitle the subordinated creditor to take whatever action it wants to but only after a specified enforcement 'standstill period'.

It would be extremely unusual for there to be no restriction whatsoever on the right of a subordinated creditor to take action under default triggers. The issue is at the core of subordination itself.

Enforcement standstills

10.19   An example of an enforcement standstill provision in practice would be, in relation to mezzanine debt, where the mezzanine creditor is entitled to take action against a debtor in respect of a payment default on the mezzanine debt but only after the expiry of a 90-day standstill period. The standstill period commences either on the date of default – or more specifically on the date the restricted action could have been taken by the mezzanine creditor as a result of the default[26] – or, more usually, the date on which the mezzanine creditor serves notice of the default on the senior creditors.

Enforcement standstill provisions are one of the major tools used in UK buyouts to subordinate junior debt. They operate to give the senior creditor and the debtor – and, in practice, the subordinated creditor – a period of time within which to come up with a detailed proposal to restructure the finance and, if that fails, to allow the senior creditor to take enforcement action on its own terms. If at the end of the standstill period no restructuring plan has been agreed that is acceptable to the subordinated creditor, and the senior creditor has taken no enforcement action, the subordinated creditor is entitled to take action. In such circumstances, however, the proceeds of any action taken by the subordinated creditor would still have to be applied in paying down the senior debt before any of the subordinated debt. In effect, therefore, the end of the standstill period really only signifies the

26 Certain defaults are subject to grace periods.

right of the subordinated creditor to direct the enforcement action to be taken against the debtor but not otherwise to alter the ranking of the debts.

'Deemed consent' or 'override' provisions

10.20   Total restrictions on enforcement action being taken on the occurrence of a *non-material* default under the terms of the subordinated debt may be effected through the use of a 'deemed consent' or 'override' provision. Such a clause will provide that where an amendment, waiver or consent is made under the terms of the prior ranking debt, and an equivalent amendment, waiver or consent is required under the terms of the subordinated debt in order to avoid a default trigger arising thereunder, then that amendment, waiver or consent shall be deemed to have been made. This effectively removes the veto rights of the subordinated creditor in respect of matters agreed between the prior ranking creditor and the debtor and prevents the subordinated creditor using this as a default trigger. In practice, deemed consent provisions should only apply to the less material matters and, to ensure this, a typical deemed consent or override provision will be subject to exceptions, often referred to as the 'entrenched rights' of the subordinated creditor, that cannot be overridden. These would include fundamental matters such as the right to sue for payment if a payment is missed and amendments that alter the pricing and terms of payment or repayment of the subordinated debt and other material provisions.

In fact, although deemed consent provisions were once widely used in respect of junior debt – mezzanine debt in particular – they are now generally only used in respect of more deeply subordinated debt such as equity investor subordinated loan capital and some PIK note debt. Non-material defaults under core junior debt instruments are now dealt with through long standstill periods (typically 150 days in the case of mezzanine and 179 days in the case of high yield debt).

Provisions protecting the position of the subordinated creditor in the capital structure

10.21   The intercreditor agreement will include provisions that restrict certain actions that a senior ranking creditor and/or the debtor can do following funding of the investments that would be adversely prejudicial to the subordinated creditor.

Restricting additional prior ranking debt

10.22   The principle restriction is a limit on the amount of additional debt (after the initial investment) that ranks ahead of the subordinated debt. In simple terms the more debt that ranks ahead of an investment the greater the risk there is of the investor not realising that investment. Typically, subordinated creditors will agree to a level of 'headroom' above the initial amount of prior ranking debt representing the amount by which the prior ranking debt can subsequently be increased without their consent. For example, as between senior and mezzanine debt, headroom of around 10% or more is typically permitted to be added to the amount of senior debt without the need to obtain the mezzanine lender's consent.[27]

---

27   The mezzanine lenders will argue that only 10% of the *amortised* amount of senior debt can be added – that is, having deducted any repayments made to date – rather than 10% of the initial amount of senior debt.

With high yield debt the restriction on additional prior ranking debt is usually delineated in a different manner that does not refer to headroom above the original amount of senior debt. Instead, the amount of prior ranking debt will be limited by reference to a financial ratio – such as the ratio of total debt of the group to the group's most recent annualised earnings (EBITDA) – at the time the new debt is incurred and the condition will only apply at that time, not on an ongoing basis.[28] Such a provision will by custom usually be included in the terms of the bonds themselves but, as with other forms of junior debt, may also be mirrored or referred to in the intercreditor agreement in order to bind the senior creditors directly too.

Equity investors typically do not receive the same protections that a junior creditor does. This reflects the deeper subordination of the equity and quasi-equity in particular, but also the fact that the equity investors can protect their own position through their management control of the group.

Anti-layering clauses

10.23 A specific type of subordinated creditor protection that is used in high yield bonds is the 'anti-layering' clause. These clauses prohibit the creation of an additional layer of debt between the high yield debt and the existing prior ranking debt (the senior debt). So even if the quantum of additional debt to be invested would of itself be permitted (as senior debt), the new debt would not be permitted if it formed its own sub-layer. When these clauses first appeared they were used to justify the marketability of 'senior subordinated' notes by ensuring that the notes remained the most senior ranking form of subordinated debt in the capital structure. However, the effect and rationale for such provisions now is that they prevent an additional set of creditor class rights sitting above the high yield bondholders. This could be prejudicial to the bondholders' negotiating position in a restructuring or work-out situation with a defaulting issuer. The clause may also amount to a back-door way of controlling leverage by forcing any additional indebtedness to rank *pari passu* with the existing debt, which of itself may not be acceptable to the senior creditors. In addition, the ability to include a further layer of debt would create a 'moral hazard' of sorts for the senior lenders. Whilst a senior lender might be more than willing to permit new junior ranking debt in any given scenario – because in essence it provides a further cushion for the senior debt – the additional debt might not make sense for the other financiers and the subordinated bondholders in particular.

Anti-layering provisions operate by restricting the ability of the debtor to incur debt that ranks both ahead of the subordinated debt *and* behind the existing prior ranking (senior) debt. They may prevent debt that is subordinated to the senior debt in terms of *right to payment* only or debt that is subordinated to the senior debt to *any* extent. This distinction may be important where second lien debt is concerned as US second lien debt at least may not be subordinated in right of payment.[29] It may therefore be permitted by the narrower form of anti-layering provision but not by the wider form.

---

28 Conditions that apply in this way are called 'incurrence' covenants and are to be contrasted with 'maintenance' covenants where compliance is required on an ongoing basis not just at the time the relevant transaction occurs (eg, when the debt is incurred).

29 See paras **6.2** and **6.15**.

For high yield bonds, as with the restriction on the overall quantum of prior rank-ing debt, the anti-layering provision will be set out in the terms of the bonds (the trust deed or indenture) instead of, or in addition to, in the intercreditor agreement.

Restricting other amendments to the terms of the prior ranking debt

10.24   A subordinated creditor is concerned not only with the amount of any prior ranking debt but also the terms of that debt. For instance, the rate of inter-est accruing on it and the frequency and amount of repayments of principal of the prior ranking debt each affect the ability of the debtor to meet payments of yield on, and, ultimately, the repayment of the principal amount of, the subordinated debt. The subordinated creditors will have modelled the group's ability to service and repay the prior-ranking debt in the initial funding structure and will be rely-ing on the headline terms of the acquisition finance remaining the same as in the model. For this reason, the subordinated creditors will normally have the right, through the intercreditor agreement, to veto any changes to such headline terms or, sometimes, to veto changes beyond pre-agreed limits.

Subordinated creditor's right to acquire prior ranking debt

10.25   A further provision that may be included for the protection of the subor-dinated creditor is a right, exercisable in a default scenario, to acquire all, and not part only, of the prior ranking debt at full value. By doing so the subordinated cred-itor takes over the rights of the prior ranking creditor to enforce security and other-wise control the taking of enforcement action against the debtor. In theory this will be used to ensure a greater return to the subordinated creditor out of the proceeds of enforcement.[30] From the prior ranking creditor's perspective such a clause would normally be acceptable but the detail must be carefully considered to ensure that there is a clean break for the prior ranking creditor; such that all of its prior ranking debt, together with any outstanding costs, are included in the price that the subordinated creditor must pay it. The prior ranking creditor must be particularly wary of, and in most cases reject, any warranty that it is asked to provide to the sub-ordinated creditor as to its title to the prior ranking debt or otherwise.

The equity investors may be less content for such a provision to be included since by allowing the subordinated creditor to take over all of the debt, effective control of a group that is in default may pass to a single subordinated creditor; perhaps one whose motives and approach to restructuring the funding structure may be much less attractive to the equity investors than other traditional acquisi-tion finance institutions.

Restrictions on amending the terms of the subordinated debt

10.26   The intercreditor agreement will also include a provision restricting amendments to the terms of the subordinated debt that the subordinated creditor can agree with the debtor. This provision will often be drafted so as to mirror the restriction on amendments to the prior ranking debt, which is preferable from the subordinated creditors' perspective; ie, there is a restriction on amendments to

---

30 In fact, under English law, a prior ranking secured creditor is in any event obliged, in foreclosing on its security, to obtain the best price reasonably obtainable in the circumstances.

certain provisions but not a general restriction. This approach also provides for consistency where there are at least three layers of debt and both prior ranking and subordinated creditors are concerned about amendments to the middle-ranking debt. Alternatively, and less favourably for the subordinated creditors, it is drafted the other way around so that it prohibits *all* amendments to the terms of the subordinated debt other than agreed exceptions. The agreed exceptions will be for non-material changes that do not have any financial impact on the debtor.

Ranking claims against professional advisers

10.27   Because the various due diligence reports commissioned as part of the due diligence process will be addressed to each of the acquisition financiers (with the exception of high yield bond holders, where it is not customary), the sponsor and newco, all of those parties may have claims against the professional advisers if any of the reports turn out to be flawed and the parties have suffered a loss as a result of relying on the reports.

To a certain degree the claims of the various parties against the professional advisers will compete for settlement. For this reason it is common practice for the intercreditor agreement to include a provision establishing a procedure for the proving of such claims and ultimately an order of priority for application of the proceeds of all such claims.

What many versions of this clause acknowledge is that newco, as the acquisition vehicle, has the primary loss for a flawed due diligence report and that the claims of its financiers are derivative of any loss by newco. Such clauses provide that the parties should allow newco to make its claim and that the proceeds are applied in rectifying whatever matter it is that gives rise to the claim.[31]

The clause will go on to provide, however, that the proceeds of a claim being an asset of newco, should be subject to the same prioritised rights of recourse for the acquisition financiers in a default scenario. This may to some extent be achieved by the taking of security over such claims[32] but also by prioritising the rights of recourse of the parties in the intercreditor agreement. In other words, the right to receive the proceeds of such a claim will be prioritised in accordance with the agreed order of ranking of the various investments.

One point of detail to note for the acquisition financiers is the precise identity of the parties to whom the reports are addressed. In the case of the deal sponsor (equity house) this may not be the same entity as the actual equity investors[33] and the acquisition financiers should ensure that all potential claimants have agreed to the provision ranking the claims of the parties. Newco must always be a recipient of the reports as its potential claims are at the core of the provision.

In relation to the rights of equity investors to make claims against professionals, a coordinated approach has been attempted between the main accounting

---

31 For instance, it might be environmental contamination that was negligently overlooked in an environmental report, or flawed accounts that the financial due diligence failed to spot. In each case, the business will have a financial liability or shortfall to cover.

32 The secured financiers will invariably wish to take security over proceeds of claims as part of their overall security package.

33 Instead it may be the corporate entity that acts as fund manager or investment adviser of the actual investor(s).

firms – who as providers of financial due diligence reports are potentially subject to claims more frequently than other professional advisers – and the British Venture Capital Association ('BVCA') as representative of the private equity industry. In particular, in 1998, the BVCA entered into a Memorandum of Understanding with the (then) Big Six accountancy firms in respect of a number of matters relating to the liability of those accountancy firms in respect of financial due diligence reports. In addition to providing a framework[34] on matters relating to the limitation of liability for the accountancy firms – and, in particular, the use of liability caps and the applicability of a proportionality principle where there is more than one negligent party – the Memorandum included a statement relating to the allocation of liability claims between multiple addressees. Specifically it referred to an agreement between the banking market and the BVCA that *'there will be no pre-agreed allocation of proceeds of any claim under due diligence reports, nor will there be any allocation in any subsequent documentation between the bank and BVCA member.'*

If this approach is adopted in a buy-out transaction the relevant provision to be included in the intercreditor agreement should be limited to undertakings by the group with regard to the conduct of claims against professionals and the use of proceeds in the rectification of the relevant defect, and not any order of ranking of claims against professionals and turn-over provisions. Ultimately, any secured creditors will have a prior right over the assets of the group – including the proceeds of any claim – in an enforcement scenario through their security. However, there would be no restriction on the subordinated creditors making a claim against the relevant professionals in their own name. In any event, this approach is not adopted in practice as frequently as it once was and the equity investors are accustomed to giving priority – and turn-over rights – to the acquisition financiers.

Miscellaneous standard provisions

Restrictions on transfers

10.28   A standard intercreditor agreement will include a provision to the effect that transfers of any subordinated debt are only permitted on the condition that the transferee has adhered to the intercreditor agreement so that it is legally bound as a subordinated creditor. There will typically be a form of deed of adherence scheduled to the agreement.

Guarantee and security release mechanism

10.29   This is one of the most important provisions for prior ranking creditors in a buy-out. The clause provides that the claims of all subordinated creditors against members of the group are automatically or mandatorily released to enable the prior ranking creditor to enforce its security and sell the business free from the claims of the subordinated creditors. This must include releases of guarantees and security given by any company in the group that is sold as part of a going concern sale of the business and releases of security over assets being sold as part of an asset enforcement sale.

---

34 The Memorandum is not legally binding but, given the BVCA's important role in the UK private equity industry, it was intended to have significant influence in practice.

Since the subordinated creditor only receives the excess of the enforcement proceeds that are not applied in satisfying the prior ranking claims, it is in their interest to ensure that the enforcement proceeds are maximised. For this reason, subordinated creditors that are subject to these release mechanisms will often seek some contractual protection against disposals of companies or assets by the prior ranking secured creditor at too low a price. This may be in the form of a condition to the releases that the disposal proceeds are received in cash and represent the fair market value of the company or assets disposed of. The provision may include a requirement that a third-party, such as an investment bank, determines what the fair market value is, although there is some concern as to the workability in practice of a mechanism requiring a fair value opinion, given the potential reluctance of investment banks to provide them in enforcement situations.

Senior creditors, on the other hand, will not wish to be fettered in their ability to enforce security any more than they have to and will argue that they have, in most jurisdictions, obligations under the law generally to conduct a reasonable sale process and get a fair price. Some jurisdictions, for instance, stipulate that a public auction must be held of any assets being disposed of by a secured creditor. Others rely on more general principles. Under English law, the formulation is broadly that the secured creditor must get the 'best price reasonably obtainable in the circumstances'. However, whether or not a subordinated creditor has the right to rely on the applicable principles of law in any given scenario (in addition to the debtor) is jurisdiction-specific and ultimately may only be determined at the time the security is being enforced. By including an express provision in the intercreditor agreement, the subordinated creditor has greater certainty that the agreed principles will offer protection at the time of any enforcement.

Automatic release provisions are vital where the acquisition financiers are enforcing share security and disposing of a business as a going concern. If the subordinated creditors have claims under guarantees against group companies that are not released on a disposal of the target group as a whole the value of the business on disposal is effectively diminished by the amount of the subordinated claims, in practice giving the subordinated creditors a right of veto over any such disposal.[35]

This will be of particular concern in a multi-jurisdiction transaction – where hard asset security is less likely – and the acquisition financiers must ensure that the automatic release mechanism is legally enforceable in all relevant jurisdictions.

Similarly, where on a disposal of the entire group, or even a part of it, the shares being sold are owned by a guarantor rather than the principal borrower the guarantor must waive, surrender or transfer to the acquisition financiers any right

---

35 Enforcing against assets directly will often be less of a concern since the secured creditor should be able to 'overreach' the junior ranking secured claims and dispose of the assets free of those claims. In fact, where (as is common in UK buy-outs) there is a single layer of security for all secured creditors held under a trust (or other legal mechanism), the junior creditors will merely have a claim under the terms of the trust (or other mechanism) as set out in the intercreditor agreement for their share of the excess disposal proceeds after satisfaction of the prior ranking claims. They will not have their own secured claim on the assets themselves. This should make enforcement directly against the assets cleaner still for the senior creditors. However, to effect a sale of an entire business as a going concern by enforcing against the individual assets of the business would be extremely time consuming, complex and ultimately costly. Consequently, in practice such a sale would be effected by a share sale at the top of the group, in which case all the junior claims on the group would need to be released.

of subrogation it has against the borrowers in the group disposed of.[36] If it doesn't do this, the group, as before, will be subject to surviving claims. The enforceability of such waivers, surrenders or transfers must be assessed by the acquisition financiers' lawyers at the outset.

Security trust

10.30 All of the secured acquisition financiers should be party to the intercreditor agreement as senior or junior creditors. This makes it the ideal document in which such parties can appoint the security trustee and establish the terms of the security trust.

The security trust will include a payment cascade under which the proceeds of enforcement of the security will be applied to the various secured liabilities in the agreed order of ranking.

First in line will be the costs of the security trustee, followed by the senior debt liabilities, then any second lien debt liabilities, and after that the mezzanine debt or possibly secured high yield debt liabilities and then perhaps even PIK note debt liabilities.[37]

At the end of the cascade the surplus (if any) of the proceeds of enforcement will be turned over to the debtors and will be available for application to meet unsecured claims.[38]

In a multi-jurisdictional buy-out there may be jurisdictions that do not recognise the concept of a security trust and a 'security agent' may be required to act on behalf of the secured parties in a different capacity. In a number of other European jurisdictions a 'parallel debt' mechanism is commonly used to ensure that the security is granted for the benefit of all the secured acquisition financiers without the need for them all to execute each security document.[39]

Instructing creditor concept

10.31 An important issue, that relates to the role of the security trustee, is who the security trustee take instructions from in performing its role. This is generally dealt with in the intercreditor agreement through the concept of the 'instructing creditor'. In most situations the instructing creditor will be the most senior ranking creditors acting through their facility agent. This will be the senior debt facility agent until the senior debt has been repaid in full and then the second lien facility agent or mezzanine facility agent depending on the precise funding structure. The role will only apply to layers of finance that are secured under the same security trust, which will generally exclude high yield debt and PIK notes.

36 This may be relevant for instance in a typical buy-out structure where the senior lenders enforce their share security over the borrower itself by enforcing on the guarantee given by its immediate holding company and the security over the borrowers shares.

37 In practice, high yield debt and PIK note debt may not be secured or, if they are, they may be secured under a seperate layer of security outside the main security trust established under the intercreditor agreement. See also para **10.82** and **Chapter 8** generally in relation to high yield debt and para **10.102** and **Chapter 9** generally in relation to PIK notes.

38 In fact, in the case of English companies some of the proceeds of floating charge security enforcement must be allocated to certain classes of preferential creditor and a certain amount for unsecured creditors ahead of the floating charge secured creditors. See Insolvency Act 1986, ss 175 and 176A and Sch 6.

39 Having each acquisition financier sign every security document is extremely impracticable in jurisdictions where security documents are required to be notarised and given that the acquisition financiers will be a changing class of investors as the debt is syndicated and otherwise traded.

The role is of key importance, theoretically at least, in the context of enforcement standstills. If at the end of an enforcement standstill the senior lenders have not instructed the security trustee to enforce the security and the relevant junior debt default still exists, the junior creditors subject to the standstill can then step into the shoes of the senior lenders and instruct the security trustee to enforce the security. In practice, however, the senior lenders are highly unlikely to yield control of the enforcement process to the junior creditors and in such circumstances they will almost certainly themselves instruct the security trustee to enforce, and so remain as instructing creditors. The junior creditors will at least have achieved their main aim, however, in ensuring that the enforcement process had begun.

Discharge date concept

10.32   As mentioned in the preceding paragraph, at the point at which the senior debt is repaid in full the role of instructing creditor will pass from the senior lenders to the second lien or mezzanine lenders. There will be a number of additional implications of one layer of finance (usually the highest ranking) being repaid in full. These principally relate to the lifting of restrictions applicable to the next highest ranking layer. In essence that layer then becomes the most senior ranking without all of the restrictions that applied to it as a subordinated layer. With this in mind, it is common for an intercreditor agreement to have a concept of 'senior discharge date', which is used to mean the date at which the senior debt is repaid in full. Similarly there will be a second lien discharge date, a mezzanine discharge date and so on.

Pro rata sharing

10.33   One of the principles of syndicated finance is that each investor in a particular layer of finance is treated equally. This means that no one investor can receive any greater return on the investment than any other on a *pro rata* basis by reference to the amount of the investment made by each. For this purpose the intercreditor agreement will typically include a provision that ensures that as between all investors in a layer of finance, no one investor can make and retain any recovery from the debtors other than in accordance with its *pro rata* entitlement. The provision is often also called the 'loss-sharing' clause because its principal purpose is to ensure that where there are insufficient borrower funds to repay the entire layer of finance each investor in that layer must share the loss equally (on a pro rata basis). Any receipt by an investor in excess of its pro rata entitlement must be shared with the other investors on the agreed basis. Certain layers of finance will include different instruments. For instance, the senior debt layer will generally include the senior acquisition finance facilities and also the hedging contract in respect of the senior debt. This means that the hedging counterparty and the senior lenders will share losses between themselves.

Definitions of senior debt, junior debt, subordinated debt etc

10.34   The definitions relating to the layers of finance must be carefully drafted to ensure that they perfectly delineate the scope of those layers for ranking purposes. They need to pick up permitted increases in amounts of prior ranking debt for instance and include *all* liabilities owing to the respective creditors.

'Senior debt' will, for instance, usually include the liabilities of the debtors to the hedging bank under the interest rate swap or other hedging arrangement. However, where, as is often the case, the hedging contract is in respect of junior debt in addition to senior debt the parties may consider ranking that part of the hedging that is in respect of the junior debt *pari pasu* with the junior debt hedged. In other words, the senior debt definition would only include hedging in respect of senior debt. Hedging in respect of junior debt would itself fall within the junior debt definition. That said, this approach will often not be acceptable to the hedging bank where, as is common, a single institution is hedging both the senior and junior debt.

Who should be a party?

10.35   All classes of creditor should be a party to the intercreditor agreement to acknowledge the terms on which their respective investments are ranked and to agree to turn-over provisions in case payments are made to them in breach of the agreed ranking. This should include the institutional equity investors[40] subscribing for subordinated loan capital and each member of the group in its capacity as a creditor in respect of group inter-company debt. Institutional equity investors sometimes argue that they need not be party on the basis that cash that might otherwise escape the group – to them – can be trapped at topco level by having topco party to the intercreditor agreement. This argument ignores the fact, however, that topco is a pass-through vehicle and not the end-recipient of any cash. It is the institutional equity investors that the prior creditors would prefer to have direct turn-over rights against in case of any dispute over payment rights.[41]

Each member of the group that is a debtor in respect of any category of debt regulated by the agreement should be a party, including guarantors of any category of regulated debt. The subordination on insolvency provisions, for instance, are particularly relevant to these companies.

There is often debate as to whether the equity investors in topco need to be party to the agreement, given that share capital is automatically subordinated by operation of law in an insolvency proceeding. Whilst this is true, the intercreditor agreement also ensures that the ranking of the parties' investment is preserved and regulated outside of any insolvency event. That said, controlling the payment of dividends and redemptions of share capital can be achieved by having topco – rather than the equity investors themselves – agree (in the intercreditor agreement) not to make any such payment and then including an acquisition finance override provision in the topco articles. This way the shareholders in topco will be formally on notice of the prohibition on such payments. Whilst the prior ranking creditor might not have a direct contractual turn-over claim against the shareholders if payments are made in breach of the prohibition they are likely to have an actionable claim against the shareholders either in tort or in equity.[42]

In practice it is common not to require each member of the management team to be party to intercreditor agreement if their only investment is in share capital.

---

40 This means the sponsor and each entity that is investing equity managed by the sponsor. Quite often this will mean the general partner of one or more funds managed by the sponsor.

41 In practice, acquisition financiers appear to be conceding this point to deal sponsors with increasing frequency.

42 The claim could, theoretically at least (but in practice with difficulty), be in tort for procuring breach of contract (by topco) or they might be deemed constructive trustees for money received which they knew to be in breach of contract.

If they are taking subordinated loan capital they should be made parties to the agreement as subordinated creditors. The institutional equity investors, which will in any event be taking subordinated loan capital, can be party in their capacities as shareholders too and thereby ensure that the acquisition financiers have a direct contractual turn-over right against them in all capacities.

Legal concerns in multi-jurisdictional deals

10.36   With multi-jurisdictional deals, one of the major concerns of the senior creditors – along with the enforceability of the guarantee and security package[43] – will be that the various contractual subordination and intercreditor provisions are legally enforceable. This will be of particular concern in relation to the provisions dealing with subordination, permanent enforcement standstill, automatic guarantee release and other waivers of creditor rights. In a number of jurisdictions, especially non-common law countries, perhaps where the provisions have not been tested fully in court, this cannot be taken for granted and the senior lenders will wish to obtain clear advice as to the position in each jurisdiction. The most efficient method of ascertaining the enforceability of the various provisions is for the acquisition financiers to ask for legal opinions from their lawyers. It is common practice for the legal opinions to include a detailed litany of 'qualifications' to their opinions and it is these qualifications that generally detail the extent to which the senior lenders can rely on the documentary provisions. As far as English law and the United Kingdom are concerned, the major provisions are enforceable and the courts have provided relatively recent judicial support on many of the key issues.[44]

SUBORDINATING THE VARIOUS TYPES OF FINANCE

10.37   The following sections outline how the various types of finance are typically subordinated in a UK buy-out through the application of the subordination techniques considered elsewhere.

Senior debt

Ranking generally

10.38   Senior debt ranks at the top of the capital structure and is not subordinated to any other layer of finance. All of the facilities that make up the senior acquisition finance package, together with the interest rate hedging arrangements, will be ranked together as 'senior debt' on a pari passu basis. In structures with second lien debt – at least where the second lien is structured as a form of stretched senior debt[45] – it is common for the core senior debt to be referred to as the 'priority senior debt' in the intercreditor agreement and for there to be a wider category of 'senior debt', including the second lien debt. There are really

---

43 See **Chapter 13** in particular.

44 See, for example, *Re SSSL Realisations (2002) Ltd* [2006] EWCA Civ 7 CA (Civ Div) in relation to contractual subordination and turn-over clauses.

45 In some structures the second lien is used as core junior debt in place of mezzanine or high yield. See **Chapter 6** generally.

two reasons for this. First, it is common for there to be a single class of 'senior' debt for decision-making purposes, including the second lien strip.[46] Secondly, when the second lien market was first developing there was a concern that the second lien should not appear to be true 'subordinated' debt so it was structured as far as possible to have the features of 'senior' debt.[47]

Structural status and security

10.39   The senior debt will be borrowed directly by the acquisition vehicle so that it is as proximate to the operating assets as possible.[48] Working capital facilities and loans to refinance the target's existing debt will generally be made available directly to the target group companies. In support of the debt provided, the senior lenders will benefit from guarantees from the target group so that the debt is not structurally subordinated to the trade creditors. They will also take the benefit of a full first priority security package from all borrowers and guarantors so that in an insolvency or enforcement scenario their claims rank ahead of all other creditors' claims including those of the trade creditors'.[49]

In diagrammatic form the senior debt structure can be shown as follows:

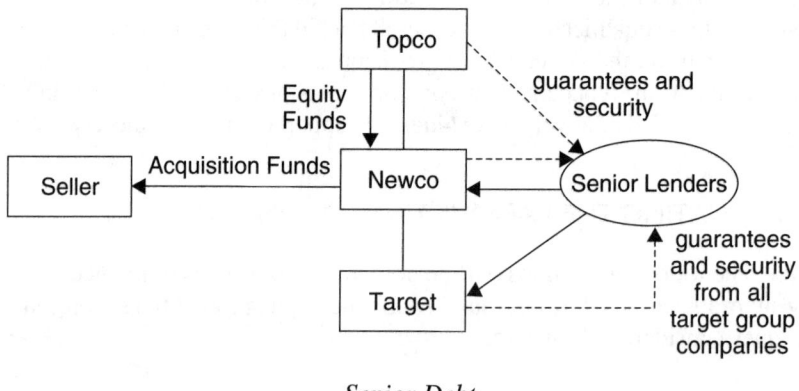

Senior Debt

Contractual subordination

10.40   The senior creditors will be party to the intercreditor agreement and most of the provisions in it will be for their benefit. The senior creditors will also

---

46   The voting rights of second lien creditors are considered further in para **10.56** and in **Chapter 6** generally.

47   This was so that it could be sold to investors that were familar with US second lien paper with its very limited level of subordination (see paras **6.2** and **6.15**). In fact, in Europe, second lien is more deeply subordinated than in the United States, so the categorisation of second lien as a form of 'senior debt' is really only cosmetic. See also para **10.52** et seq and **Chapter 6** generally.

48   In fact, in multi-jurisdictional buy-outs the senior debt may be pushed down into the target group itself in order to achieve deductibility of interest costs against operating profits for tax purposes. See **Chapter 13**.

49   In practice the availability of full guarantees and security may be limited by a number of factors. They may not be available from the target group in a multi-jurisdictional buy-out. See **Chapter 13**. UK security will also be subject to certain limitations. See **Chapter 5**.

have certain obligations in favour of the junior ranking creditors. The following paragraphs briefly consider the most pertinent provisions from the perspective of the senior creditors.

Subordination on insolvency

10.41   The senior debt will not be subordinated to any other layer of finance. The subordination on insolvency provision will be drafted for the benefit of the senior creditors who will rely on the clause to preserve their priority position in any winding-up of any of the debtors.

Permitted payments and payment blocks

10.42   All payments under the senior debt documentation will be permitted without condition. There will be no payment blockage mechanism applicable to the senior debt.

Acceleration and enforcement rights

10.43   Similarly, there will be no restriction on the ability of the senior creditors to accelerate the senior debt and take enforcement action in a default scenario.[50]

Permitted amendments to the senior debt

10.44   The intercreditor agreement will include certain restrictions on the ability of the senior creditors to amend the terms of the senior debt. These essentially relate to amendments which have a financial impact on the business or which are adverse to the junior debt. Typically they will include a cap on the amount by which the senior debt pricing can be increased.[51] There will also usually be a restriction on extending the maturity of the senior debt by a certain period.[52] In addition it is common to restrict any other amendments that render the covenants and other controls in the senior facilities agreement materially more onerous on the borrower, including changes that tighten financial covenants.[53]

Additional senior debt

10.45   There will also be limits on the amount of additional senior debt that can be put into the structure after initial funding. What that limit is in practice depends on the types of junior creditor – and junior debt – there are in the struc-

---

50   In fact, there will be an exception for this in relation to hedging liabilities, where the hedging counter-party will be restricted in any acceleration and enforcement action that it can take. See para **10.49**.

51   This might be in the region of, say, 1% on the margin and 50 basis points on non-utilisation fees. Sometimes no headroom is allowed at all.

52   For example, there might be a limit on extending any scheduled repayment date by more than one year or there might simply be a prohibition on extending the final maturity date beyond the date on which any junior debt is repayable/redeemable. The issue here is that because the junior debt cannot, as a general principle, be repaid/redeemed prior to any of the senior debt, by pushing back the senior debt repayment date the junior debt repayment dates may also automatically be pushed back.

53   The rationale for this very broadly is that by tightening covenants and the like the borrower is more likely to default, which will jeopardise the more junior debt to a greater degree than the senior debt.

ture behind the senior debt. For instance, in some structures second lien lenders have only limited rights of veto on additional senior debt by comparison with typical mezzanine lender rights. High yield bondholders will have relatively looser controls too and the rights of PIK noteholders are often negotiable on a deal by deal basis. The rights of these various categories of creditor are considered in the sections below relating to the respective forms of junior debt.

Claims against professionals

10.46   The rights of the senior lenders to make claims against professional advisers in respect of defective advice and due diligence reports will be effectively unfettered. In addition, the intercreditor agreement will usually include a provision that gives priority to those rights over the rights of the subordinated creditors.[54]

Automatic release of guarantees and security

10.47   The senior lenders will insist that the intercreditor agreement incorporates a standard automatic release mechanism to ensure that in an enforcement situation the security trustee is able to dispose of group companies, assets or the group itself free from the claims of all subordinated creditors. The same clause may also be used to facilitate permitted disposals of secured assets in the ordinary course.

Legal concerns in multi-jurisdictional deals

10.48   With multi-jurisdictional deals, the senior creditors will need to satisfy themselves of the extent to which they can rely on the various provisions in the intercreditor agreement. The principal way in which they will do this will be through the taking of detailed legal advice and the obtaining of legal opinions on the validity of the agreement and its enforceability in all relevant jurisdictions (including the locations of all obligors).[55]

Hedging Debt

10.49   One of the standard requirements of the senior lenders will be that the borrower enters into interest rate, and possibly currency exchange rate, hedging in relation to all or a material portion of the senior debt. The idea is to ensure that material movements in interest rates or foreign exchange rates do not leave the borrower unable to meet the payments due to the senior lenders. Most hedging works by indirectly changing the basis of the payments due by the borrower under the underlying debt document. The most common form of hedging used is an interest rate swap whereby the borrower swaps the floating rate of interest payable by it for a fixed rate. This is achieved by entering into an agreement with a hedging counterparty that agrees to meet the borrower's floating rate obligation (by paying that amount to the borrower) in return for receiving the fixed rate

---

54 The typical intercreditor provision is considered in more detail in para **10.27**.
55 See also para **10.36**.

from the borrower. Depending on where the underlying interest rates move to, a net payment will either be due to the borrower or to the counterparty. The borrower has certainty, however, that it will never have to pay more (or less) than the fixed rate agreed with the counterparty.

In entering into this agreement the counterparty will be taking credit risk on the borrower in respect of the net payments due to the hedging counterparty under the hedging agreement. As a result the hedging counterparty will insist on sharing in the benefit of the guarantee and security package that the core acquisition financiers receive so that it is not in effect subordinated behind all of the acquisition finance. In practice, essentially because of this, the hedging counterparty role will be taken by one of the senior lenders and usually the mandated lead arranger of the senior debt. It is possible for the hedging counterparty role to be taken by a third-party financial institution but this is rare in practice not least because the MLA will be extremely keen to take on the role. Provided the MLA can offer a market competitive quote for the hedging the borrower will usually be happy enough for it to be mandated in the additional role. This will have the benefit of reducing the number of parties involved in completing the finance. This is particularly relevant when it comes to the intercreditor implications of the hedging.

As indicated above, the hedging arrangements will be reflected in the intercreditor agreement. For starters, the exposure of the borrower under the hedging agreement will be included as a separate class of debt. Meaning that the 'hedging debt' will be expressed to constitute 'senior debt' and rank pari passu with the core senior debt.[56] In this way, the hedging counterparty can take the benefit of the senior debt guarantee and security package through the security trust and enforcement proceeds sharing mechanism that will be included in the intercreditor agreement.[57] It follows that the hedging counterparty will be required to be party to the intercreditor in that additional capacity. Not only will this enable it to take the benefit of those provisions but in return it will be required to agree to certain obligations relating to the hedging. The purpose of these obligations is essentially the same as those that apply to junior ranking debt. In particular, the right of the hedging counterparty to terminate the hedging agreement or to take enforcement action against the borrower will be fettered so as not to be inconsistent with, or to pre-empt the rights of, the core senior lenders. On top of this, the core senior lenders will wish to know that the terms on which the hedging has been arranged reflect standard market norms. So there will be a requirement that the hedging agreement is documented under a standard ISDA Master Agreement[58] and that the preferred elections contemplated under that agreement are made in relation to payments and early termination. As with other types of debt regulated by the intercreditor agreement there will also be restrictions on the ability of the hedging counterparty to amend the terms of the hedging agreement. In practice, all of these intercreditor provisions have become standardised and require little negotiation.

---

56 Certainly to the extent that the hedging is in respect of senior debt this will be the case. But to the extent that the hedging is in respect of say mezzanine debt the intercreditor might rank the mezzanine hedging alongside the mezzanine debt and not the senior debt.

57 See para **10.30**.

58 See the standard suite of documents produced by the International Swaps and Derivatives Association and the 1992 and 2002 master documents in particular.

Second lien debt

10.50   This section on second lien debt is mostly concerned with second lien in its 'stretched senior' form, where it is documented in the senior facilities agreement, usually as the D tranche of 'senior debt'. Alternatively, where (eg, in a leveraged corporate deal) the second lien is documented as a stand alone layer of quasi-mezzanine, with its own credit agreement, it might in practice be subordinated as if it were mezzanine debt although at the time of writing there was little precedent for this approach.

Ranking generally

10.51   Second lien creditors enjoy the second highest ranking in the capital structure with only the core senior creditors[59] ahead of them.

Structural status and credit support

10.52   Second lien debt will typically benefit from the same structural status as the core senior debt. That is, the borrower will be the same entity that borrows the core senior debt. In addition, the same credit support that is given for the core senior debt will also be for the benefit of the second lien debt, but on a second priority basis. In other words the second lien debt will be guaranteed by the same group companies as the core senior debt and the second lien borrower and each guarantor will grant second priority security to the second lien creditors over the same assts. In practice, a single layer of first priority security will be granted in favour of a security trustee who will hold that security on trust for all secured creditors in the funding structure. However, the right to receive the proceeds of enforcement of this security will be prioritised in accordance with the agreed order of ranking. Thus the second lien creditors will only benefit from the security granted by the borrowers and guarantors if the value of the assets given as security are greater than the amount of the core senior debt outstanding at the time of enforcement (plus the costs of enforcement).

A buy-out structure including priority senior and second lien debt can be shown in diagrammatic form as follows:

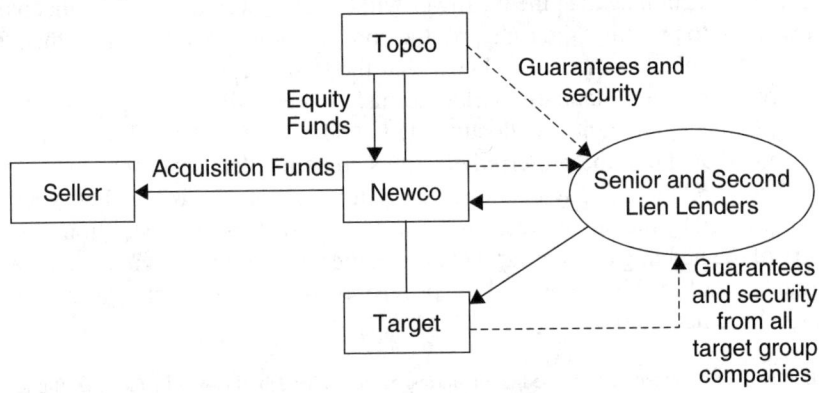

Senior and Second Lien Debt

---

59   Where the second lien debt is used as a form of stretched senior debt it will form part of a wider category of 'senior debt' for the purposes of the intercreditor agreement, with the core senior debt usually defined as the 'priority senior debt' (see also para **10.38**).

The structure shown on the previous page assumes that the second lien debt is in the form of a loan rather than notes, with both priority senior and second lien debt being borrowed by the same SPV, newco. Second lien notes would most likely be issued by a separate SPV, which would be granted the same structural status through the use of a structural guarantee from newco and otherwise the same guarantee and security package as that granted to the senior lenders.[60]

Contractual subordination

10.53 Each of the second lien creditors will be party to the intercreditor agreement. They will take the benefit of most of the provisions for the purposes of ranking ahead of more junior creditors but will also be subject to the provisions that are for the benefit of the prior ranking senior creditors.

Subordination on insolvency

10.54 Unlike its US counterpart (which fundamentally has no payment subordination and only 'lien' subordination), European second lien debt might be subordinated upon insolvency. In practice, although early variants of European second lien did include full contractual subordination, this feature was not replicated in several transactions in the second half of the 2000s. However, unless the core senior debt is undersecured such that upon enforcement of security the proceeds of enforcement do not satisfy the outstanding senior debt in full, there are no practical implications for the second lien creditors. If the senior debt is paid out in full from the security the second lien creditor will be the most senior ranking creditor in the capital structure for the purposes of claiming in the winding-up of the relevant group companies. If on the other hand the core senior debt is undersecured then the unsecured claims of the senior creditors would, by full contractual of the subordination (if applicable), rank ahead of the second lien creditors' claims in any winding-up of group companies.[61]

The position is less favourable with regard to the trade creditors of the group companies if there are insolvency proceedings at operating company level. This is because the trade creditors are not subject to the subordination arrangements in the intercreditor agreement. Thus, to the extent the second lien debt is undersecured, because the security package does not cover the entire amount of the second lien debt in addition to the senior debt, the unsecured claims of the second lien creditors against the operating companies will only rank pari passu with the unsecured trade creditors of the business. If part of the senior debt is unsecured it may also rank pari passu with the trade credit for the unsecured element although it might benefit from a turn-over right against the second lien debt in respect of any recovery made by the second lien creditors. In practice, however, it is rare in Europe for the intercreditor issues to play out at the operating company level. More often the senior ranking creditor will 'enforce' security at the holding company level in order to sell the business as a going concern.

---

60 See **Chapter 6** generally in respect of second lien debt, including second lien notes, and **Chapter 3** as regards structuring of the layers of finance.

61 In the United States (and possibly now also in Europe) the principle is that if the core senior debt is undersecured the senior creditors rank pari passu with the second lien creditors for their unsecured claim.

Permitted payments and payment blocks

10.55   Since second lien principal is not repayable until after all of the core senior debt[62] the only payments on the second lien debt that will be permitted during the life of the core senior facilities will be interest and certain miscellaneous fees, indemnities and similar payments.[63]

There are not usually any conditions applicable to payment of the up-front fees since they are paid right at the outset of the funding on completion of the acquisition. There will, however, be conditions applicable to the payment of interest and other permitted payments.

Typical payment conditions would be:

- no outstanding payment default in respect of the core senior debt; and

- no outstanding declared default[64] under the senior facilities agreement.

Both of these conditions will effect an automatic payment block that will endure for so long as the payment or declared default is outstanding.

In the case of second lien notes – where the payment block mechanism is more likely to mirror the equivalent provision for high yield debt – or a separately documented and usually larger tranche of second lien loans – where the payment block mechanism is more likely to mirror the equivalent position for mezzanine debt – and in certain cases of D tranche second lien debt,[65] there may be additional payment conditions that operate through a manual payment block mechanism. These might include:

- no outstanding financial covenant breach under the senior facilities agreement,[66] including failure to deliver the requisite financial information; and

- no other outstanding event of default in respect of the core senior debt.[67]

In order to stop a second lien interest payment being made in those circumstances the core senior lenders would be required to serve a payment blockage notice on the second lien borrower and lenders. This would block any second lien payment falling due for a pre-agreed period stipulated in the intercreditor

---

62   In theory, the prepayment mechanics in the senior facilities agreement might allow for some application of prepayment proceeds to a 'D' tranche of second lien debt in certain limited circumstances permitted by the core senior lenders, but this will be rare.

63   These will include the up-front fees payable at completion, amounts under the increased costs, tax gross-up and miscellaneous indemnity clauses, costs and expenses and an agency fee if one is payable.

64   A declared default generally means that an event of default has occurred and the lenders have declared the default and taken some action in respect of the default, which may include acceleration and security enforcement.

65   In practice, with second lien debt structured as part of the wider senior debt package (usually as the D tranche), whether or not there is a manual payment block mechanism operating off financial covenant or other general defaults appears to be deal specific and in some cases the payment block mechanism does not include such defaults.

66   It is common for the documentation to specify whether or not subsequent compliance with a financial covenant that was previously in breach acts to cure the prior breach, so that the permitted payment condition is then satisfied as of the subsequent financial covenant test date (or, more precisely, once the relevant financial information has been received demonstrating compliance).

67   This might be limited to 'financial' or 'material' events of default including insolvency related events. With second lien notes, as with high yield, any event of default may be sufficient.

agreement. If a manual payment block mechanism is included, the applicable period will probably be in the region of 90 or 120 days or 180 days for second lien notes.[68]

After the expiry of any payment block – that is, once the relevant default is remedied or any applicable payment block period expires – the second lien borrower would be at liberty again to resume payments of interest to the second lien creditors, including the catch-up of blocked payments, provided that the permitted payment conditions could then be met.

With all manual payment block mechanisms it is usual for the agreement to stipulate that in order to be able to serve a further payment blockage notice a further breach would need to have occurred with different underlying circumstances.[69] There may, but usually only in the case of an issue of second lien notes,[70] be a provision that states that there can be no more than one payment blockage notice served in any period of 365 consecutive days.

Importantly, if a payment blockage notice is issued and a payment is blocked, a payment event of default will arise in respect of the second lien debt. This will be a default trigger that will, subject to any applicable restriction on the acceleration and enforcement rights of the second lien creditors,[71] entitle the second lien creditors to exercise whatever rights they have following an event of default.

By contrast with mezzanine debt and high yield debt, there would not usually be any restriction on the frequency of the permitted interest payments. Thus the borrower will be free to select the duration of interest periods in the usual way.

Acceleration and enforcement rights

10.56 There will typically be extensive restrictions on the rights of the second lien creditors to accelerate the debt and to take action to enforce the guarantees and security given by the group companies.

Where, as is common with buy-outs, the second lien debt is documented as a tranche of debt within the senior facility agreement it is likely that there will be no separate rights for the second lien lenders to declare a default and accelerate the second lien tranche other than in a limited number of exceptional circumstances.[72] Rather than having a separate class vote for such purposes, the second lien lenders simply vote as part of the wider senior debt syndicate. Given that second lien tranches in buy-outs are often only a small portion of the entire senior debt package[73], the second lien lenders will only carry a small minority vote in their own right and not enough to block a majority lender decision by the

---

68 Provided that if an enforcement standstill period commences during the blockage period the blockage period will end on the expiry of the enforcement standstill period.

69 There may also be a time limit following notice of default within which a payment blockage notice must be issued if at all.

70 Reflecting the equivalent position in a typical high yield bond issue.

71 As to which see para **10.56**.

72 Only where there is a separate second lien facility agreement (which is rare in European buy-outs, but common in the United States) would the second lien lenders have their own full set of default triggers (covenants and events of default) and their own decision-making process and voting rights to determine whether, subject to the intercreditor agreement, they wish to take acceleration and enforcement action.

73 See also para **10.50** and **Chapter 6** generally.

entire senior lender syndicate.[74] In fact, because the A tranche of core senior debt amortises over a number of years there may come a time when the amount of second lien debt represents more than 33⅓% of the entire amount of outstanding senior debt. However, where that is a possibility the senior debt market has on occasion taken steps to ensure that even if the amount of the second lien debt does excess 33⅓% of the outstanding senior debt, the second lien lenders do not have a blocking vote and their voting rights may be expressly limited to a minority percentage below 33⅓%. In practice, therefore, in many buy-out structures the second lien lenders are generally left without a separate voice on acceleration and enforcement matters. If there were no exceptions to this position the second lien debt would be described as 'silent' second lien debt. Where there are limited exceptions it is described as 'quiet' second lien debt.

Most second lien debt in UK buy-outs is 'quiet' rather than 'silent' and the second lien lenders do have a separate voting right on certain issues.[75] These typically comprise the following:

- If there is a payment default in respect of the second lien debt, subject to a 60-day enforcement standstill.

  In other words, upon a payment default occurring under the second lien debt – perhaps as a result of a payment block occurring – the second lien lenders as a separate class would be permitted to decide (usually through a 66⅔% majority) to accelerate the second lien debt and, following the expiry of a 60-day standstill period, to enforce the guarantees and security given in support of the second lien debt.[76]

- Cross-acceleration, where the core senior debt has been accelerated.

  This exception typically permits the second lien lenders to decide, as a class, to accelerate the second lien debt if the core senior debt has been accelerated. However, it is unlikely that exception will also entitle them to enforce the guarantees and security for the second lien debt. That right will remain with the wider senior lender syndicate.

- Insolvency event in respect of the second lien borrower or a guarantor.[77]

  In these circumstances the rights of the second lien lenders to take enforcement action will be relatively unfettered. In practice, though, the core senior lenders will control any security enforcement action by virtue of being the instructing creditors for the purposes of giving instructions to the security trustee.[78]

---

74 For example, they may only hold 15–20% or less of the wider senior debt package provided and lenders need more than 33⅓ of the debt to block majority decisions. They are said to be 'swamped' by the core senior lenders.

75 Although second lien notes will often take the silent form.

76 In practice they will instruct the security trustee to enforce the security on their behalf unless the priority senior creditors stepped ahead of them in such circumstances, which would be likely.

77 The insolvency of a non-material guarantor may not be sufficient for these purposes and the requirement may be expressed to apply to a material guarantor subject to an insolvency event or even to the guarantors as a whole.

78 See para **10.31**.

- Where the core senior lenders have instructed the security trustee to enforce the security.

  Again, the second lien lenders will be able to accelerate the second lien debt, call on the guarantees and commence recovery action subject to the prior rights of the core senior lenders including in respect of the security package.

- Where the mezzanine or other junior creditors are taking permitted enforcement action.

  Similarly, if creditors who are subordinated to the second lien lenders are permitted to take enforcement action the second lien lenders will be permitted to.

Given these limited exceptions, second lien lenders in many buy-outs will actually enjoy fewer rights on default than mezzanine lenders. Mezzanine lenders will have their own set of default triggers – that is, separate events of default in a stand alone agreement – and decision making powers (voting rights) and, other than in respect of payment defaults, are subject to a less restrictive enforcement standstill mechanism.

As indicated earlier, however, where the second lien debt is of a sufficiently large size and is documented in a stand alone credit agreement – which is not common in buy-outs – the second lien lenders are likely to have a full raft of discrete default triggers (events of default). In that case the default triggers are likely to be subject to the same standstill provisions as mezzanine (or possibly high yield) debt.[79]

Similarly, where there are second lien notes that are *not* silent, the noteholders would expect to benefit from the same types of default triggers that are present in high yield bond documentation, which are notably less than for mezzanine debt.[80] For example, covenants will be of the incurrence rather than maintenance type, there may be a 30-day grace period for interest payment defaults and the enforcement standstill may be 179 days rather than the 90/120/150 days applicable under mezzanine debt. And if the high yield model is used, only 25% by value of the second lien notes would be required to accelerate the notes and take any enforcement action. Hybrid varietals of second lien notes are also possible where the notes have covenants and events of default of the kind used in loan documentation. This might occur where the second lien debt is structured with loans *and* notes and parity between the instruments is required.

Protections in respect of prior ranking debt

10.57   The protections that the second lien creditors have as regards amendments to the senior debt are to a large extent dependent on whether the second lien debt is documented with the core senior debt or not. If that is the case then

---

79 See the sections on mezzanine and high yield debt below.
80 See para **10.81** et seq and **Chapter 8** generally.

any protection afforded to the second lien lenders will often be set in the context of the provisions in the senior facilities agreement itself that detail the circumstances in which that agreement can be amended and whose consent is required. In practice, this may well mean that the second lien lenders cannot separately block any increase in the amount of the prior ranking senior debt or other amendments to its terms, unless a specific veto right is included in the document. If, on the other hand, there is a separate second lien credit agreement or note documentation, any protections would need to be provided in the intercreditor agreement.

Restricting additional prior ranking debt

10.58   As mentioned in the preceding paragraph, where the second lien is a tranche within the core senior facilities agreement, that document is likely to dictate the circumstances, if any, in which the second lien lenders can veto an increase to the core senior debt.

If there is a separate second lien facility agreement this will reflect the fact that the second lien debt is a significant part of the overall funding structure. In such circumstances the second lien lenders can expect to get similar protections to those that a mezzanine lender would get. There is likely to be a limit on additional prior ranking senior debt in particular.[81]

If there are second lien notes, the restriction on additional senior debt (if any) may be in the same form as for high yield debt, where the amount of permitted new senior ranking debt is principally limited to a financial ratio, such as a multiple of earnings (EBITDA), at the time the debt is incurred.

Restricting amendment to the terms of the prior ranking debt

10.59   Similarly, the level of protection against amendments to the terms of the core senior debt will most likely flow from the nature of the second lien debt. Where it is a tranche in the core senior facilities agreement the regime applicable to amendments to that document will apply. This may mean that the second lien lenders can only veto changes that would require a unanimous vote of all lenders. Typically this would not include increasing the pricing of the core senior debt, which a junior ranking creditor would usually wish to limit. At the time of writing no uniform approach had been adopted for dealing with this issue. Where it is a separately documented loan or issue of notes the protections can expect to be similar to those applicable to mezzanine debt or high yield debt respectively.[82]

Option to acquire prior ranking debt

10.60   The purpose of a provision enabling a subordinated creditor to buy out the prior ranking debt claims is to enable a junior creditor to take control of the intercreditor arrangements in a default scenario. This may be for the purpose of

---

81 Probably set at approximately 10% of the original amount of core senior debt (possibly less amortised amounts), as for mezzanine.

82 Each of which is considered in the following sections. Although second lien notes may not necessarily in practice have the same level of rights as high yield.

effecting a debt restructuring on terms more favourable to the junior creditor than those being imposed by the existing senior creditors. Or it may be to take control of the security enforcement process in order to maximise the recovery for the junior creditors.

Second lien lenders may or may not be granted such an option, as, say, a mezzanine lender would expect. In practice the right appears to be negotiable on a deal-by-deal basis. Where the second lien debt is a relatively large and discrete element of the funding structure, usually where it is documented as a separate layer of finance, the second lien lenders are likely to require an option to acquire the prior ranking debt given their greater proportionate exposure.

In the case of second lien notes, if they were to follow high yield convention, an option to acquire the senior debt would not be included.

Permitted amendments to the second lien debt

10.61   As with amendments to the terms of the prior ranking debt, where the second lien debt is documented in the senior facilities agreement, that document will dictate the circumstance in which the terms of the second lien debt can be amended with or without the consent of the core senior lenders. In addition, the intercreditor agreement will give the mezzanine lenders a level of protection against amendments that are adverse to their position in the capital structure.[83] This will most likely be achieved by a provision that restricts amendments to the wider senior debt package, including the second lien tranche.

If there is a separately documented tranche of second lien loan debt then a standard clause restricting amendments to its terms would need to be included in the intercreditor agreement for the benefit of both the senior lenders and the more junior ranking creditors, if any.[84]

In the case of second lien notes the restriction would in most cases follow the approach adopted for high yield bonds (or be even more restrictive).[85]

Claims against professionals

10.62   Where the second lien debt is structured as part of the wider senior debt package, the second lien lenders may have no separate class right to pursue claims against professionals beyond those of the wider senior debt syndicate. If they do, however, then the rights of the second lien lenders to take action against professional advisers in respect of defective advice and due diligence reports would most probably be subordinated to the equivalent rights of the prior ranking creditors in the same way that mezzanine lenders' rights would. There are relatively standard intercreditor provisions dealing with the prioritisation of such rights.[86] Second lien noteholders, by contrast, may not have the benefit of the due diligence reports in the first place given the different due diligence process for note issuances.

---

83   By contrast, high yield investors would typically not get this level of protection.
84   See paras **10.24** and **10.26**.
85   See para **10.95**.
86   The typical intercreditor provisions is considered in more detail in para **10.27**.

Automatic release of guarantees and security

10.63   The senior lenders will insist that the intercreditor agreement incorporates a standard automatic release mechanism to ensure that in an enforcement situation the security trustee is able to dispose of group companies, assets or the group itself free from the claims of all subordinated creditors.[87] The same clause may also be used to facilitate permitted disposals of secured assets in the ordinary course.

Legal concerns in multi-jurisdictional deals

10.64   With multi-jurisdictional deals, the second lien creditors will wish to satisfy themselves of the extent to which they can rely on the various provisions in the intercreditor agreement as against more junior ranking creditors. The principal way in which they will do this will be through the taking of detailed legal advice and the obtaining of legal opinions on the validity of the agreement and its enforceability in all relevant jurisdictions (including the locations of all obligors).[88]

Mezzanine debt

Ranking generally

10.65   Mezzanine debt ranks immediately behind the senior and any second lien debt in the funding structure for a buy-out. It ranks ahead of any PIK note debt and all equity investor debt.

Structural status and credit support

10.66   Other than in exceptional circumstances, mezzanine debt will benefit from the same structural status as the senior debt and any second lien debt. That is, the borrower will be the same entity that borrows the senior and second lien debt. An exception to this approach might be made where the borrower is incorporated in a jurisdiction that does not recognise contractual subordination or where it has not been tested in court, so that the senior lenders require the mezzanine debt to be structurally subordinated. That said, given that mezzanine debt is generally guaranteed and secured by the same entities as the senior debt, where that is the case, merely structurally subordinating the claims in respect of the borrowers would not achieve full structural subordination in any event.

In addition to enjoying the same structural status at borrower level, mezzanine debt will typically benefit from the same credit support that is given for the senior and second lien debt but on a second or, if there is second lien debt, third priority basis. In other words, the mezzanine debt will get the same guarantee and security package as the senior and second lien debt subject to the claims of the prior ranking debt to be repaid first from any enforcement action.

A typical structure including mezzanine debt could be shown in diagrammatic form as follows:

---

87   See para **10.29** above for a more detailed consideration of these provisions.
88   See also para **10.36** above.

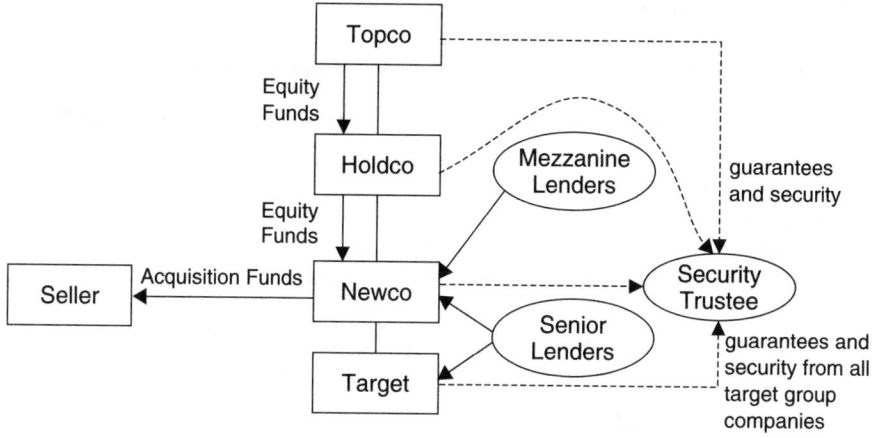

Senior and Mezzanine Debt

Contractual subordination

10.67   Each of the mezzanine lenders will be party to the intercreditor agreement. They will be subject to the various provisions in favour of the senior and second lien creditors but will also take the benefit of the provisions as against more junior creditors, such as PIK note holders and the institutional equity investors.

Subordination on insolvency

10.68   The claims of the mezzanine lenders against the borrower and guarantors will be expressly subordinated to the claims of the senior and second lien creditors in the event of a winding-up of any borrower or guarantor.

Permitted payments and payment blocks

10.69   The principal amount of the mezzanine debt will not be repayable until after the final repayment dates of the senior and second lien debt.[89] Therefore the only payments that will be permitted until the senior and second lien debt have been repaid in full will be interest and certain miscellaneous fees, indemnities and similar payments.[90]

There are not usually any conditions applicable to payment of the up-front fees since they are paid right at the outset of the funding on completion of the acquisition. There will, however, be conditions applicable to the payment of interest and other permitted payments.

---

89 In theory, there may be very limited circumstances where a prepayment of mezzanine debt is permitted by the senior and second lien lenders before all of the senior and second lien debt has been repaid but this would be very rare.

90 These will include the up-front fees payable at completion, amounts under the increased costs, tax gross-up and miscellaneous indemnity clauses, costs and expenses and the mezzanine agency fee.

Typical payment conditions would be:

- no outstanding payment default in respect of the core senior debt; and

- no outstanding declared default[91] under the senior facilities agreement.

Both of these conditions will effect an automatic payment block that will endure for so long as the payment or declared default is outstanding.

In addition there will be payment conditions that operate through a manual payment block mechanism. These will usually include:

- no outstanding financial covenant breach under the senior facilities agreement,[92] including failure to deliver the requisite financial information; and

- no other outstanding 'financial' or 'material' event of default under the senior facilities agreement.[93]

In order to stop a mezzanine interest payment being made in those circumstances the senior lenders would be required to serve a payment blockage notice on the mezzanine borrower and lenders. This would block any mezzanine payment falling due during a pre-agreed period stipulated in the intercreditor agreement. Typically the applicable period will be in the region of 120 or 150 days.[94]

After the expiry of the payment block period – or, if earlier, the date that the relevant default is remedied – the mezzanine borrower would be at liberty again to resume payments of interest to the mezzanine lenders, including the catch-up of blocked payments, provided that the permitted payment conditions could then be met.

It is common for the agreement to stipulate that in order to be able to serve a further payment blockage notice a new breach would need to have occurred so that a second payment blockage notice cannot be issued in respect of the same default, or underlying circumstances. In addition, it is common for there to be a time limit of say, six months following notice of default, within which a payment blockage notice may be served in reliance on such default. These provisions are intended to limit the scope for the senior lenders to use non-payment defaults to perpetually block interest payments on the junior debt. Unlike with high yield debt, there is not normally a restriction on the number of payment blockage notices that may be issued in any given period.

---

91 A declared default generally means that an event of default has occurred and the lenders have declared the default and taken some action in respect of the default (which may include acceleration and security enforcement).

92 It is common for the documentation to specify whether or not subsequent compliance with a financial covenant that was previously in breach acts to cure the prior breach, so that the permitted payment condition is then satisfied as of the subsequent financial covenant test date (or, more precisely, once the relevant financial information has been received demonstrating compliance).

93 In this category will fall insolvency-related events of default and other material events of default, usually of a financial nature that can be justified as a reason to block a mezzanine payment.

94 Provided that if an enforcement standstill period commences during the blockage period the blockage period will end on the expiry of the enforcement standstill period.

Importantly, if a payment blockage notice is issued and a payment is blocked, a payment event of default will arise in respect of the mezzanine debt. This will be a default trigger that will, subject to any applicable restriction on the acceleration and enforcement rights of the mezzanine lenders, entitle the mezzanine lenders to exercise whatever rights they have following an event of default.

In order to most proximately link the condition that there is no outstanding financial covenant breach to the payment of mezzanine interest it is common practice for the senior lenders to insist that the mezzanine interest payment dates are set at fixed dates that coincide with the testing of the financial covenants. So, for example, interest may be permitted to be paid only on six-monthly intervals each just following a testing date, which are usually each quarter. If this approach is taken, in practice, payment dates will be set to fall a few days after the date on which the borrower provides the financial statements and covenant compliance certificate for the purposes of testing the financial covenants and not the actual accounting date by reference to which the covenants are tested. This enables the senior lenders to receive the financial information and assess whether a breach has occurred before deciding whether to issue a payment blockage notice or not.

Junior mezzanine

10.70   In large buy-outs the mezzanine debt may be split into two tranches, a senior tranche and a junior tranche. The junior tranche will be subordinated to the senior mezzanine tranche (and also all senior and second lien debt). The extent of its subordination will usually be very similar to the extant that mezzanine debt is subordinated to senior debt. Thus senior mezzanine interest payments will be payable in priority to junior mezzanine interest payments. In particular, cash interest payments on the junior tranche may be stopped prior to interest payments on the senior mezzanine tranche.

In some structures the junior tranche is structured as 'pay-if-you-can' mezzanine (PIYC). Usually, this means that payment of cash interest on the junior mezzanine is subject to an automatic payment block if the financial covenants set out in the senior facilities agreement are not met or the borrower cannot demonstrate that they would be met, taking into account the payment of junior mezzanine interest then due. There may even be a requirement for enhanced covenant compliance. That is, the senior financial covenants are for this purpose deemed to require a higher level of financial performance.[95] The overall effect of the PIYC mechanics is that any cash interest payment that would otherwise be payable at a time when the financial health of the business is not sufficiently strong is no longer payable in cash. Instead it becomes payable in kind as part of the PIK element of the interest. In addition to providing that the cash interest payment is automatically converted to PIK, the provision will usually stipulate that no pay-

---

95   For example, the cash cover ratio may be deemed to be greater than 1.0:1 or the leverage ratio may be deemed to be lower, for the purposes of compliance.

ment event of default will arise in respect of the junior mezzanine loan by virtue of the payment block.[96]

A further variant of junior mezzanine is 'pay-if-you-want' mezzanine (PIYW). With this form of debt the borrower can simply elect not to make a cash interest payment – perhaps if it determines that the business is not in sufficiently good financial health or otherwise to preserve cash in the business – again without triggering an immediate payment default. The deferred cash payment would again switch to PIK and with such facilities the ability of the borrower to elect to switch cash interest to PIK interest is sometimes called the PIK 'toggle'.

Acceleration and enforcement rights

10.71   The mezzanine facility agreement will substantially mirror the senior facility agreement. The default triggers (covenants and events of default) will be almost identical in both documents, although there are a small number of common exceptions. First, the financial covenants in the mezzanine facility agreement will often be set with greater tolerance to financial underperformance by the group. The additional 'headroom' allowed may be in the region of, say, 10%. This means that a financial covenant breach may occur under the senior facility agreement but not under the mezzanine facility agreement, leaving the senior lenders with a default trigger but not the mezzanine lenders. Secondly, it is common to exclude default under the senior facilities agreement from the cross-default event of default in the mezzanine facility agreement. This again prevents the mezzanine lenders from having a default trigger merely because the senior lenders have one. In practice, however, this is of limited relevance given the substantial overlap of default triggers in both facility agreements and as a result it is usually only necessary to exclude a cross-default arising from a breach of senior financial covenant (without which the additional covenant headroom would be pointless). In addition to these differences the threshold voting requirement for acceleration of the mezzanine debt following default may on occasion be set at 50.1% by value of the outstanding mezzanine principal rather than the more common 66⅔%, as is universally used in senior facilities agreements in the United Kingdom. Having said that the acceleration threshold is often set at 66⅔% even if other voting matters are reduced to a 50.1% level.

Enforcement standstill

10.72   Whatever default triggers the mezzanine lenders have, the intercreditor agreement will restrict the actions that the mezzanine lenders can take as a result of a default arising. It will do this principally through the use of enforcement standstills.

---

96 However, this additional element may only apply for an initial period from completion (say, two years) following which a blocked junior mezzanine payment would give rise to a junior mezzanine payment default.

The following enforcement standstills are almost invariably applied to mezzanine defaults:

- payment default will usually be subject to a 90-day standstill period;

- financial covenant default will usually be subject to a 120-day standstill period; and

- other events of default will usually be subject to a 120 or 150-day standstill period.

In each case the standstill period usually commences on the date the mezzanine lenders express their intention to take some action following the event of default, by serving notice on the senior lenders.

At the end of the standstill period the mezzanine lenders will be free to take whatever enforcement action they are entitled to take under the mezzanine facility agreement, even if another default has occurred and another standstill period commenced. If at this point the senior lenders have themselves not commenced any enforcement action, then the right to instruct the security trustee to enforce the security will pass to the mezzanine lenders.[97] In practice, in those circumstances the senior lenders will wish to retain control of the enforcement process and themselves instruct the security trustee to enforce the security.

Certain other default triggers are not subject to any enforcement standstill. In particular:

- insolvency events in respect of the mezzanine borrower or a guarantor will allow the mezzanine lenders to take enforcement action, although this may be limited to enforcement action only against the borrower or guarantor that is the subject of an insolvency event;

- if the senior debt has been accelerated,[98] the mezzanine lenders will be permitted to accelerate the mezzanine debt; and

- if the senior lenders have instructed the security trustee to enforce the security, the mezzanine lenders will be permitted to take enforcement action

Protections in respect of prior ranking debt

Restricting additional prior ranking debt

10.73   A cap will be imposed on the amount of additional senior or second lien debt that the group can incur without the consent of the mezzanine lenders. This is typically set at 10% of the amount of senior debt (and any second lien debt, if applicable) in the structure, either as at completion or as amortised over time.[99]

---

97 That is, they will become the 'instructing creditors'.

98 This may be couched in terms of an event of default having been declared and the senior lenders having taken some action in respect of the default rather than being limited to cross-acceleration.

99 In many cases the senior lenders will insist that the cap will be set as a percentage of the original amount of senior debt. However, junior lenders will sometimes argue that the additional prior ranking debt cap is set as a percentage of the reduced amount of senior debt as the existing senior debt is amortised by repayments.

Restricting amendments to the terms of the prior ranking debt

10.74   In addition, the mezzanine lenders will have a veto on certain amendments to the terms of the senior and second lien debt. These are usually limited to amendments that would have an adverse financial impact on the borrower or on the mezzanine debt.

In particular, there will be a limit on the amount by which the interest rate margin in respect of the senior or second lien debt can be increased.[100] This may be limited to increases of, say, 1% on an aggregate blended basis across all tranches, or no increase at all may be permitted without the consent of the mezzanine lenders. Similarly, the commitment fees payable on any revolving debt will be limited, perhaps to a 0.50% increase or no increase at all. In addition, there will be a prohibition on amendments that have the effect of reducing the amount of time that the borrower has to make payments of principal or interest or other amounts – for example by reducing the average life of the facilities – and amendments that change the basis on which interest and similar amounts are calculated or which impose any additional payment on the borrower. There will also be a prohibition on amendments that make the representations, covenants and events of default, or the agreement as a whole, materially more onerous on the borrower.

In addition, there will commonly be a restriction on amendments which have the effect of extending the repayment dates of the prior ranking debt. This is often expressed to permit the repayment dates to be pushed out by up to 12 months, but in any event not later than the maturity date for the mezzanine debt.[101]

Option to acquire the prior ranking debt

10.75   It is common practice for the intercreditor agreement to include a provision enabling the mezzanine lenders to acquire the entire prior ranking debt in full (and not part only) at par in certain circumstances. The option to purchase the senior and any second lien debt is usually only exercisable if a declared event of default has occurred under the senior facilities agreement and the senior lenders have commenced enforcement action. The principal purpose of such provisions is to enable the junior creditors to take control of the security enforcement process in order to maximise the recovery in respect of the mezzanine debt.

Permitted amendments to the mezzanine debt

10.76   There are generally two approaches to the clause limiting the amendments that can be made to the terms of the mezzanine debt. One approach is to simply mirror the provision restricting amendments to the senior debt. That is, the mezzanine lenders are free to make amendments to the mezzanine debt documents other than the same types of amendments that are prohibited for the senior lenders, such as changes to the pricing or method of calculating interest etc.

---

100   There will need to be an exception for any increase in pricing, or any other amendment, made in accordance with the market flex provisions applicable to the senior debt, if any. See para **11.104**.

101   Because payment of principal on the mezzanine debt is subordinated in full to senior principal, allowing the senior repayment dates to be pushed out beyond the mezzanine repayment date would have the effect of pushing back the mezzanine repayment date too. This is a change that the mezzanine lenders would insist on approving first.

The other, more restrictive, approach is where the mezzanine lenders are prohibited from making any amendments to the terms of the mezzanine debt documentation without the consent of the senior lenders, subject to certain relatively standard exceptions.[102] The exceptions usually include:

- amendments correcting typographical errors and inconsistencies;

- administrative amendments that do not alter payment dates, amounts and so on;

- amendments that mirror amendments made to the senior facilities agreement that do not alter payment details and which are not adverse to the senior lenders; and

- amendments to the mezzanine warrant instrument (for warranted mezzanine) that are not adverse to the senior lenders.

The mezzanine lenders are normally required to give prior notice to the senior lenders of any proposed amendment.

Claims against professionals

10.77   The rights of the mezzanine lenders to take action against professional advisers in respect of defective advice and due diligence reports will usually be subordinated to the equivalent rights of the prior ranking creditors. There are relatively standard intercreditor provisions dealing with the prioritisation of such rights.[103]

Automatic release of guarantees and security

10.78   The senior lenders will insist that the intercreditor agreement incorporates a standard automatic release mechanism to ensure that in an enforcement situation the security trustee is able to dispose of group companies, assets or the group itself free from the claims of all subordinated creditors.[104] The same clause may also be used to facilitate permitted disposals of secured assets in the ordinary course. Theoretically, once the senior discharge date has occurred the mezzanine lenders will rely on the same provision as regard more junior ranking secured debt.

Legal concerns in multi-jurisdictional deals

10.79   With multi-jurisdictional deals, the mezzanine lenders will need to satisfy themselves of the extent to which they can rely on the various provisions in the intercreditor agreement as against more junior creditors. The principal way in which they will do this will be through the taking of detailed legal advice and the obtaining of legal opinions in all jurisdictions in which there are obligors.[105]

---

102 See also para **10.26**, where the clause gives rights to both prior ranking creditors and more subordinated creditors. In that case, the first (less restrictive) approach specified is more likely to apply.

103 The typical intercreditor provision is considered in more detail in para **10.27**.

104 See para **10.29** above for a more detailed consideration of these provisions.

105 See also para **10.36**.

Junior mezzanine debt

10.80   If, as may be the case with larger transactions and tranches of mezzanine debt, the mezzanine debt is split into two tranches, one ranking senior to the other, further subordination is required between the two tranches. In these circumstances the senior mezzanine tranche will generally be granted prior rights to receive payments, including in default and insolvency circumstances. The junior mezzanine tranche will generally, however, have higher pricing to compensate the junior mezzanine lenders for the consequent greater risk they face in realising the investment and return.[106]

For the purposes of the intercreditor agreement, the subordination and other provisions that are applied to mezzanine debt to subordinate it to the senior debt may also be applied to the junior mezzanine debt so that it is subordinated to the prior ranking debt, including the senior mezzanine debt.

As mentioned above, this will include a subordinate right to receive interest payments. This may be on a pay-if-you-can or even pay-if-you-want (PIK toggle) basis.[107] As for the other intercreditor terms applicable to junior mezzanine debt, these are likely to be the same as or very similar to those applicable to single tranche mezzanine debt. There may be a longer enforcement standstill period, perhaps of 179 days for all types of junior mezzanine default, rather than the standard 90, 120, 150 approach for mezzanine debt. In addition, the default triggers themselves may be more limited, with only a material or financial event of default under the junior mezzanine tranche capable of being used as a trigger for an enforcement standstill.

Generally junior mezzanine tranches are separately documented from the senior mezzanine tranche but this is not necessary per se.

High yield debt

Ranking generally

10.81   High yield debt ranks behind the senior debt and any second lien debt in the funding structure for a buy-out.[108] It ranks ahead of any PIK note debt and all equity investor debt.

Structural status and credit support

10.82   The structural status of high yield debt has been one of the defining debates of the European buy-out market. Certainly it has been the defining feature of the relationship between the senior banks and the high yield market. When high yield debt first hit the European buy-out market in the second half of the 1990s it was invariably structurally subordinated to the senior debt. This was a requirement imposed by the dominant senior bank market. The major concern of the senior banks at the time – with high yield debt – was with the potential composi-

---

106   They may also receive warrants that the senior mezzanine lenders do not receive.
107   See para **10.70**.
108   High yield is an alternative to mezzanine debt for larger buy-outs and will not be used in the same structure as mezzanine debt.

tion of the bondholder syndicate and the potential behaviour of that syndicate in work-out or restructuring negotiations with the banks, should that become necessary. In particular, given the relatively low threshold of bondholders required to accelerate the bonds (25%), and at that time the lack of a 'behavioural track record' of high yield investors in the European buy-out market, the senior banks were concerned that a relatively small group of activist bondholders[109] could hijack the bond syndicate and impose unreasonable conditions on any restructuring negotiations, perhaps without any real interest in the long term future of the underlying business. This – it was perceived by some at the time – was to be contrasted with the more predictable and supportive approach to be expected from the mezzanine market whose participants had been and would remain long term market players with relationships and reputations to protect.[110] Structural subordination was used to isolate potential bondholder claims in a default scenario.

This meant having the bonds issued by an SPV (often called 'bondco' or 'finco') further up the SPV group structure than the senior debt borrower, or as a sister company to the senior debt borrower with no ownership interest in the target business at all. In either situation bondco's ability to access target group cashflows can be blocked in a default scenario by the senior lenders' intervention at a lower level in the group structure.

These structures can be shown in diagrammatic form as follows:

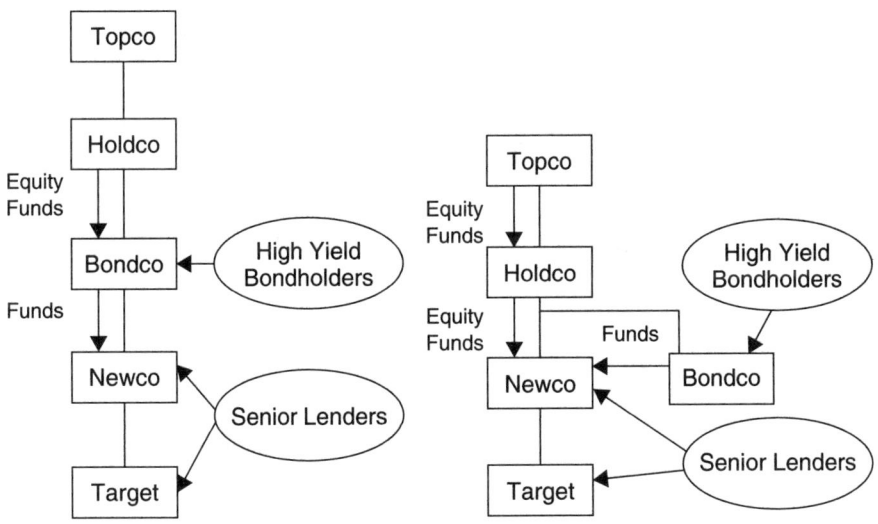

Senior and High Yield Debt

In a default scenario the only action that the bondholders could take would be to accelerate the bonds and sue bondco for redemption of the bonds. But that of itself gives them no means of accessing the assets and cashflows of the target business to meet the outstanding debt. In actual fact, by suing bondco and ulti-

---

109 Such as 'vulture funds' and the distressed debt desks of the big investment banks and hedge funds.
110 This was all long before the appearance of hedge funds as major buyers of mezzanine paper and other junior debt in Europe and although there is no direct evidence to the contrary, some commentators have questioned whether all hedge funds would be as supportive in restructuring negoations.

mately causing it to be wound up and its assets liquidated, the bondholders do have an indirect means of circumventing their structural subordination to a degree. This is through bondco accelerating and suing for payment under the funding loan that bondco makes to newco for the purposes of downstreaming the proceeds of the bond issue to fund the acquisition. By causing bondco to seek repayment of the funding loan the bondholders will force the hand of the senior lenders who will not simply be able to stand-by as bondco seeks repayment of the full amount of the funding loan from the senior debt borrower. For this reason, and this issue is still relevant in today's market, the senior lenders must ensure that the funding loan is itself subject to contractual subordination provisions.

In order to enhance their structural superiority the senior lenders would also take security over the shares in newco, and over the funding loan from bondco to newco. This enables the senior lenders to completely isolate bondco in a default scenario, leaving bondco – and thus the bondholders – with a residual interest in any excess enforcement proceeds but no other claims or assets.[111]

A structure that includes isolating security can be shown in diagrammatic form as follows:

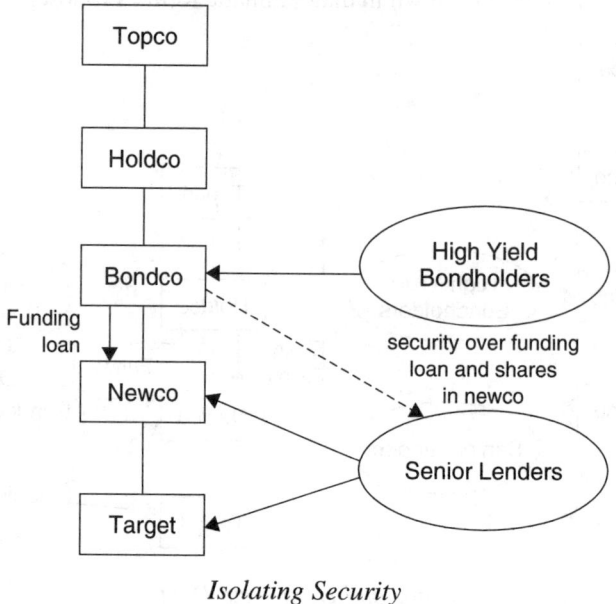

Isolating Security

All of this contrasted very unfavourably with the US market, which to date had been the only real precedent for most high yield bond investors. In the United States, bondholders would have structural parity with the senior lenders,

---

111 At one time, even more aggressive structures were proposed by the senior banks, including with 'golden shares' that could be used to block any insolvency actions instigated by the bondholders.

with the bonds issued by the same vehicle that borrows the senior debt and the senior lenders happy to rely on contractual subordination provisions only.

In any event, the sort of European structures described above proved to be the high watermark for the structural superiority of the senior banks and from the early 2000s there were a number of moves towards structurally enhancing the position of the bondholders rather than the senior banks.

One of the first developments was to provide the bondholders with a subordinated guarantee from the senior debt borrower.[112] This gives the bondholders a claim at the same level as the senior lenders, albeit on a contractually subordinated basis. This allows the bondholders to sue newco directly for redemption of the bonds in a default scenario, rather than indirectly through bondco and the funding loan. The guarantee does not create an unfettered claim, however, and the rights of the bondholders under the guarantee are subordinated to the claims of the senior lenders and made subject to payment block and enforcement standstill mechanisms. But once any payment block and enforcement standstills have expired the bondholders will be in a position to sue the senior debt borrower directly for redemption of the bonds. This at least gives the bondholders a 'seat at the table' and ultimately the ability to force the senior lenders to accelerate the senior debt and enforce the security package. To achieve this without the subordinated guarantee from newco would involve a longer and more indirect process, necessitating the liquidation of bondco before causing any action to be taken against newco. Subordinated structural guarantees from the senior debt borrower are now a standard feature of high yield debt in European buy-outs.

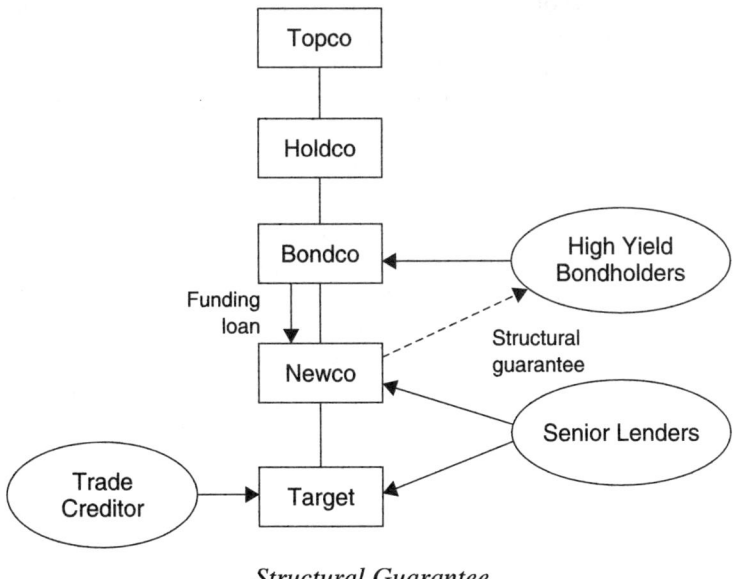

Structural Guarantee

---

112 Such guarantees are often called 'structural guarantees'. They do not provide any substantive credit support as would be the case with guarantees and security from the target group.

However, this still leaves the bonds structurally subordinated at operating company level, not only to the senior lenders but also to the trade creditors of the business. This was one further example of how the early European high yield market compared unfavourably with the US market, where upstream guarantees from operating companies are common and provide the high yield bondholders with pari passu status with the trade creditors. It was as a result of this perceived deficiency that, during the first half of the 2000s, the high yield debt market began demanding further structural support.

The senior debt market was originally hostile to upstream credit support for high yield debt, representing as it did a significant shift in the status quo in favour of the bondholders. However, following a sustained period of lobbying by the high yield market – including what amounted to an investor 'strike' at one point – the move did eventually come. Initially the senior debt market used the granting of upstream credit support for the bonds to create a new form of instrument called mezzanine notes. Mezzanine notes were a hybrid form of instrument carrying certain features of mezzanine debt that the senior lenders and sponsor wanted included – in return for conceding upstream credit support to the note holders – in addition to the general features and documentary style of a high yield debt issuance. Most importantly, the notes, at the bond holders' request, were granted second ranking guarantees from the operating companies in the group, a position traditionally reserved for mezzanine debt. In return, the bondholder voting threshold for requiring acceleration and enforcement action was increased from bondholders with 25% of the outstanding principal, as is the case for traditional high yield debt, to 66⅔% as is used in mezzanine debt. This development addressed one of the major concerns of the senior debt market, that a relatively small number of activist bondholder institutions could hijack negotiations in a restructuring scenario by threatening acceleration and enforcement of the bonds. In addition to these features the mezzanine notes also had limited call protection more akin to that found in mezzanine debt rather than high yield, principally for the benefit of the sponsor.

In fact, there were very few issuances of mezzanine notes per se following their first use in 2003 but in any event, it wasn't too long before the senior banks had conceded the debate on upstream credit support entirely. Consequently, the senior debt market began accepting subordinated guarantees from the operating companies with increasing frequency and since the mid-2000s they have become a standard feature of European high yield debt structures.[113] Hard security from the target group, on the other hand, remains very rare for high yield debt in Europe.

---

113 As with any upstream guarantees, however, the subordinated guarantees given to bondholders may be of limited practical value in a multi-jurisdictional buy-out given the laws of many European jurisdictions relating to corporate benefit, financial assistance and the like. See **Chapter 13** generally. On a related note, because high yield bonds are rated by the credit rating agencies there will often be a financial benefit for the issuer if the bonds have upstream credit support. The stronger the upstream credit support for the bonds, the better the rating should be (within the parameters of the ratings available) and thus the better (lower) the pricing of the bonds might be. See also **Chapter 8** generally in relation to the typical guarantee and security package enjoyed by high yield bondholders.

In actual fact, the bondholders will typically receive *some* security in addition to guarantees from newco and the target group. This will be in the form of structural security over the shares in newco and over the bond funding loan from the issuer to newco. Typically this is second ranking security, with the senior debt taking first ranking charges, although the security over the funding loan may on occasion be first ranking or exclusive to the bondholders. The purpose of structural security is to provide the bondholders with a means of stepping ahead of the equity investors in a default scenario that sees the senior lenders repaid in full but a shortfall on the bonds.

In the United States, fully secured senior ranking high yield notes can be found – 'senior secured notes' – where the notes in effect replace conventional senior secured bank debt but this is also relatively rare. In Europe senior secured notes can also be found but at the time of writing they were very rare.

A typical structure incorporating high yield debt can be shown in diagrammatic form as follows:

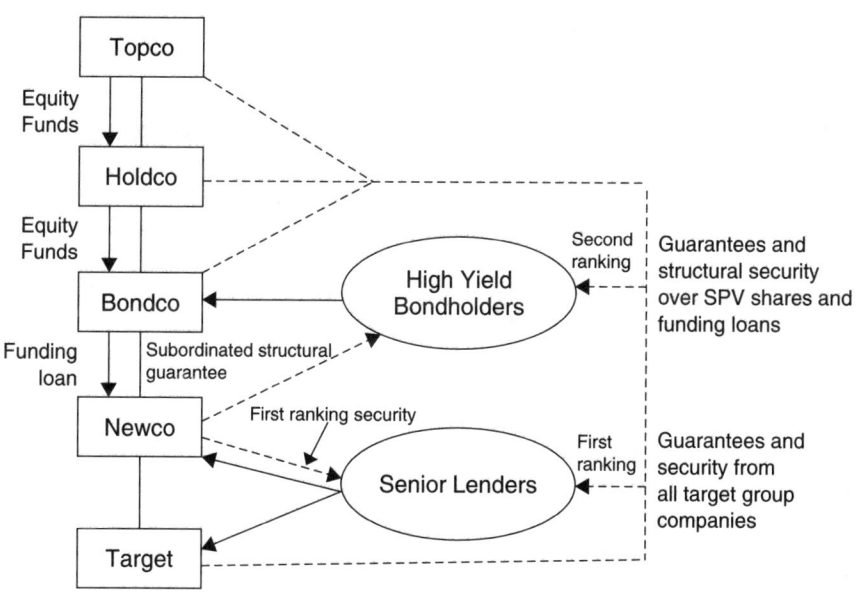

Senior and High Yield Debt

Despite the structural enhancements that have been given to high yield bondholders – and in particular, the granting of target group subordinated guarantees – the senior debt and high yield markets can genuinely reflect on whether this makes a significant difference in practice. This is because the target group guarantees are structured so as to be subject to an automatic release mechanism which takes effect on enforcement by the senior lenders. In Europe, by comparison with the United States, the preferred enforcement mechanism is a sale of the business as a going concern rather than a liquidation sale of the assets of each company.[114] This will generally be effected by an enforcement sale of the shares in the target holding company or in newco. In such circumstances, the guarantees given to the high yield bondholders – and to any other acquisition financiers – by the companies being sold must be released at the point of sale. A mechanism is included in the intercreditor agreement to ensure that this happens automatically. This is necessary from the perspective of the enforcing senior lenders because, absent the releases, the group companies cannot be sold free from the claims of the bondholders, which would deprive the sale of commercially viability. In most cases in practice therefore, the high yield investors do not obtain any real benefit from the upstream guarantees. They are only of assistance if there are competing claims with the trade creditors in a liquidation of the operating companies themselves.

One typical aspect of the automatic release mechanism that *does* provide some benefit for the high yield bondholders, however, is a requirement that any enforcement sale must be for cash consideration and at fair market value, perhaps as determined by a third-party investment bank or, possibly, following a public auction.[115]

Contractual subordination

10.83   The bond trustee will be party to the intercreditor agreement on behalf of the bondholders and individual bondholders will be deemed to agree to its terms by accepting the bonds issued. They will be subject to the various provisions in favour of the senior and any second lien creditors but will also take the benefit of the provisions as against more junior creditors, such as PIK note holders and the institutional equity investors.

In practice, given that the bonds will generally be structured so that the issuer itself is in a structurally inferior position to that of the senior and second lien debt borrower, claims under the bonds themselves may not *need* to be subject to all of the provisions of the intercreditor agreement. This is on the basis that the bond funding loan from the high yield bond issuer to the senior debt borrower and the structural guarantee from the senior debt borrower will be subordinated and subject to all the terms of the intercreditor agreement. This should amount to a sufficient level of subordination for the senior debt providers because cash cannot be paid to the bondholders under the bonds without first having been paid to the issuer (bondco) through repayment of principal or payment of interest under the bond funding loan. The only other route for cash to be paid directly to the bondholders is under the structural guarantee, which as indicated is also subordinated. In practice, however, the claims under the bonds themselves may in any event be included within the subordination provisions – for completeness and because

---

114 A major reason for this is that it is much more difficult to get security from operating subsidiaries in most jurisdictions in Europe than it is in the United States, given financial assistance and corporate benefit restrictions in particular. This means that in many transactions the senior lenders would be forced to sell the business or sections of the business through share sales rather than asset liquidations. This generally means leaving the trade creditors in place and a general need for their compliance.

115 See also para **10.29** on automatic release mechanisms generally.

even claims against bondco will potentially compete with senior debt claims, such as under a guarantee of the senior debt given by bondco.[116]

Subordination on insolvency

10.84   The claims of the bondholders under the structural guarantee, any target group guarantees and possibly under the bonds themselves[117] and the claims of the bond issuer under the bond funding loan will be expressly subordinated to the claims of the senior and second lien creditors in the event of a winding-up of any borrower or guarantor.

Permitted payments

10.85   The stated maturity of the high yield bonds will, in the vast majority of cases (possibly with the exception of refinancings involving existing bonds), be after the final repayment dates of the senior and second lien debt and the principal amount of the bonds will not be redeemable prior to this without the consent of the senior and second lien creditors. The only payments that will be permitted until the senior and second lien debt have been repaid in full will be interest, certain indemnity payments and fees.

As noted above, permitted payments under the bonds will primarily be controlled by applying the payment conditions and restrictions to the bond funding loan between bondco and newco.[118] This is the mechanism through which cash will be upstreamed to bondco to meet payments due under the bonds. The same controls may or may not also be applied to the bonds themselves. In any event, payments under the bond funding loan (interest in particular) will only be permitted shortly before the equivalent payment is due under the bonds.

Payment blocks

10.86   The making of permitted payments will be subject to a payment blockage mechanism. This has two limbs. First, a payment block will operate automatically and co-terminously whilst a payment default is outstanding under the senior or second lien debt, including where the senior and second lien debt has been accelerated. In addition, if any other default arises under the senior and second lien debt the senior lenders may manually issue a payment blockage notice on the bond trustee and bondco and on newco as borrower under the bond funding loan.[119]

---

116 That said, it may be possible for distinctions to be drawn between the subordination on insolvency provision and the payment block and enforcement standstill provisions, with the latter provisions, at least, often not applied to the bonds themselves.
117 See para **10.83**.
118 Payments under the structural and subsidiary guarantees will also be restricted but this is through the enforcement standstill rather than the payment block mechanism per se (because there should be no payments under the guarantees other than in an enforcement scenario).
119 Note that the typical position for mezzanine debt is different since only a material or financial default may be used as the basis for the service of a payment blockage notice. See para **10.69**.

As indicated above, the payment block mechanism does not usually *need* to be applied to the bonds themselves, although it may in practice. At the very least, payments under the bond funding loan must be subject to the payment block mechanism.

It is common for there to be a requirement to issue a manual payment blockage notice, if at all, within a period of, say, 45, 60 or 75 days of the senior lenders receiving notice of the relevant default. The duration of a manual payment block will usually be a period of 179 days from the date of issue of the notice. However, it will expire earlier if the relevant breach is then cured or the blockage notice withdrawn. A manual payment blockage period will also come to an end if any existing enforcement standstill expires during the period. At the end of the period payments may be resumed, unless another breach arises causing the permitted payment conditions not to be satisfied, and assuming that no automatic payment block has arisen by virtue of a payment being outstanding under the prior ranking debt. Usually the agreement will specify that the breach must be a new breach and not the one that resulted in the payment blockage notice being issued. Further, the provision will typically prohibit the issue of more than one notice in any one period of 360 or 365 days and also require that any interest blocked by a prior blockage notice is paid up before any further notice is served. These provisions are designed to prevent perpetual payment blockages unless there is an actual payment default under the senior or second lien debt.

It is worth noting that a payment block of itself will not necessarily prevent the bondholders from pursuing any remedies they may have against bondco or any guarantors for outstanding debts (if any[120]), including the taking of bankruptcy proceeding actions against bondco or any guarantors. For this a full enforcement standstill provision would be required. This is of particular significance in the case of bonds that are subject to US securities laws, given that the US Trust Indenture Act 1939 prohibits the inclusion of standstill provisions in the terms of the bonds.[121]

Acceleration and enforcement rights

10.87   The default triggers available to the high yield bondholders and bond trustee will be quite different to those available to the senior and mezzanine lenders. This reflects the different style of documentation used and, in particular, the nature of the restrictions imposed by the bond indenture or trust deed. Bond documents are designed to have more flexible terms than leveraged loan documents. This is because of the greater difficulty in obtaining waivers and amendments from bondholders than from lenders. Bonds are much more actively traded than leveraged loans and will generally be held by a wider group of financial institutions than leveraged loans. This is largely a result of the buy-to-hold

---

120 The existence of a payment block might, however, operate to mean that amounts are not actually outstanding and due to the bondholders at the relevant time, which could indirectly rule out enforcement remedies. However, note the different position for US bonds as a result of the US Trust Indenture Act 1939, which has the effect of granting the bondholder an inalienable right to sue for missed payments under the bonds. See also para **10.89**.

121 See also para **10.89**.

mentality of many leveraged loan investors but may also be due to the more restrictive transfer provisions commonly found in leveraged loan documentation. Given the relative difficulty in obtaining waivers and amendments and, indeed, given market norms generally, bond documents are drafted with a greater tolerance to 'default' than leveraged loan documents. Most noticeably the covenants that they include are less extensive[122] and with much greater headroom and exceptions. The negative covenants are of an 'incurrence' style rather than 'maintenance' style[123] and there will typically be no financial ratio covenants that are the key default triggers for financial underperformance with leveraged loan documentation.

If the terms of the bonds are breached or an event of default otherwise occurs, the bond trustee or bondholders with at least 25% of the principal amount of the bonds may accelerate all amounts due under the bond documents.[124]

Enforcement standstill

10.88   As for other forms of junior debt, the intercreditor agreement will restrict the actions that the bond trustee can take on behalf of the bondholders in respect of any event of default that occurs under the bonds. It will do this principally through the application of an enforcement standstill period following notice from the bond trustee to the senior facility agent that an event of default has occurred and that a standstill period is to commence. By convention, the duration of a high yield standstill period is a fixed period of between 120 and 180 days.[125] This, unlike mezzanine debt, where the length of the standstill period depends on the type of event of default which gave rise to the standstill period,[126] is regardless of the underlying event of default.

During a standstill period the bonds (if applicable[127]) and the bond funding loan may not be accelerated and no enforcement action may be taken under the bonds, the bond funding loan or under any guarantee of the bonds including the structural guarantee. The principal exception to this is where the senior debt has been accelerated or other enforcement action taken by the senior lenders, in which case the bond trustee can take action against the senior debt borrower or any guarantor against which the senior lenders have taken action and which have given guarantees of the high yield bonds. The provision will often provide that the bond trustee or holders will only be permitted to take the same action that the

---

122 See **Chapter 8** generally.

123 Meaning that they are only required to be complied with at the time of entry into of the relevant restricted transaction (eg, at the time of 'incurrence' of additional debt) and compliance is not required to be 'maintained' thereafter.

124 On very rare occasions – perhaps where the bonds are 'senior secured notes' that benefit from some shared security with conventional senior debt – the relevant threshold has been increased to 50.1% or, as with 'mezzanine notes', $66^2/_3$%. See also para **10.82** in relation to mezzanine notes.

125 It is quite often set at 179 days. This should not be confused with a 179-day payment block period, however. The two types of period are quite different.

126 See para **10.72**.

127 The bonds themselves are not always made subject to the standstill provision. It is not always necessary to do this to achieve the requisite level of subordination (see para **10.83**) and in the case of bonds that are subject to the US Trust Indenture Act 1939 this would be contrary to statute (see para **10.89**).

senior lenders have taken. The other common exception is where an insolvency event has occurred in respect of bondco or a guarantor, in which case the bond trustee or bondholders can normally only take action against bondco or the relevant guarantor that is insolvent.

US bond issues

10.89　A key distinction must be drawn for bonds that are issued in the United States or, more particularly, bonds that are subject to US securities laws. Broadly, this means bonds that are to be registered with the US Securities and Exchange Commission (the SEC) under the US Securities Act 1933, whether immediately or in due course pursuant to a registration rights agreement.[128] The reason for the distinction is that SEC registered bonds must comply with the US Trust Indenture Act 1939. This statute provides (among other things) that individual bondholders must have the right to sue for payment under the bonds if a payment is missed and that they cannot contract out of the Act. In other words, registered US bond issues cannot be subject to an enforcement standstill provision since this would contravene the Trust Indenture Act. In practice, the prohibition also applies to subsidiary guarantees – the terms of which are incorporated into the bond indenture – as much as to the bonds themselves.

Given that the Trust Indenture Act only applies to SEC registered bonds, it will not catch bonds that are exempted from the registration requirements of the Securities Act. In particular, this should mean that the Trust Indenture Act does not apply to bonds issued under Rule 144A of the Securities Act (private placements to 'qualifying institutional investors') or bonds issued under Regulation S of that Act (issues sold outside the United States). In fact, US practice dictates that bonds issued under Rule 144A are often drafted to conform with the Trust Indenture Act (ie, without an enforcement standstill) even in circumstances where they are intended to remain exempt from the SEC registration requirements 'for life'.

The fact that US bond issues do not include enforcement standstill provisions appears to give rise to an anomaly when one considers that the same bond issues do generally include payment blockage provisions (which, by contrast, are assumed *not* to be prohibited under the Trust Indenture Act). Thus, even though the bondholders might not be contractually entitled to receive a payment by virtue of a valid payment block, they could still sue for the payment and ultimately force the issuer into bankruptcy. That said, this does not occur in practice, not least because it would inevitably involve intense legal debate and the logistical hassle of corralling sufficient bondholder support to take this action potentially means that it would take as long as a quasi-standstill period in any event. Further, the taking of such action by the bondholders is not guaranteed to advance their cause. Often it would merely get them a 'seat at the table', which they should have in any event under US bankruptcy laws.[129]

128　See para **8.8**.
129　See in particular Chapter 11, Title 11, United States Code.

The fact that US issues do not include standstill provisions is not the only difference between US and European high yield practice. It is also worth noting that the issuer of US bonds will be a senior debt borrower rather than a dedicated issuer-SPV. This means that the senior lenders are entirely reliant on contractual subordination to subordinate the bonds. There is no structural protection in the SPV group. In addition, the terms of the subordination are incorporated into the terms of the bonds themselves rather than a separate intercreditor agreement, as is the case with European high yield.

Protections in respect of prior ranking debt

10.90   Given the difficulty in getting waivers from high yield bondholders, any restriction affecting the prior ranking debt will necessarily need to be relatively loosely drawn. This is reflected in the relatively limited intercreditor protections afforded to high yield bondholders by contrast with mezzanine lenders.

Restricting additional prior ranking debt

10.91   The principal mechanism by which high yield bonds are protected against increases to the amount of prior ranking debt is set out under the terms of the bonds themselves in the form of the limitation on the incurrence of indebtedness. The covenant will be relatively loose by leveraged loan agreement standards and in addition to a raft of specific exceptions for existing indebtedness, other agreed categories of permitted indebtedness such as intra-group indebtedness, and relatively large catch-all baskets, there will generally be an overriding exception for debt incurred at a time when a specified financial ratio test is met. The financial ratio will generally be any of leverage (debt to earnings), fixed charge cover (operating cashflow to fixed charges/debt service) or interest cover (earnings to interest expense), usually as tested for the most recent period of four complete accounting quarters. Provided that the test is met when the additional indebtedness to be incurred is taken into account in the relevant financial ratio (on a pro forma basis), additional senior ranking indebtedness can be incurred without any specific monetary cap. Because the covenant is of an incurrence nature there is no need for the relevant financial ratio to be maintained on an ongoing basis. In practice the high yield bondholders may also seek to get a direct right against the senior lenders in respect of additional senior debt incurred in excess of the agreed amount. This is often done by including a provision in the intercreditor agreement deeming that any additional senior debt incurred in excess of the amount allowed by the terms of the bonds only ranks pari passu with the high yield debt.

The high yield documents, and intercreditor agreement, will usually permit the senior debt to be refinanced entirely without any requirement for bondholder consent. Any increase in the senior debt amount pursuant to the refinancing would need to comply with the debt incurrence test, however. Ideally the intercreditor agreement will, in addition, include a provision entitling the senior lenders to require that the bondholders, or the trustee on their behalf, confirm that any restated senior debt documents and security in particular continue to rank ahead of the high yield debt documents.

Anti-layering

10.92   The bond indenture or trust deed will often, in addition to a general limitation on indebtedness, contain an anti-layering covenant. This will restrict the incurrence of senior ranking indebtedness that does not rank pari passu with the core senior debt. This might, therefore, preclude a refinancing of senior debt with senior and second lien debt.[130]

Restricting amendments to the terms of the prior ranking debt

10.93   As indicated above the intercreditor protections available to the high yield bondholders are often relatively weak by comparison to those available to other junior debt providers such as mezzanine lenders. This is often particularly true in respect of restrictions and amendments that may be made to the terms of the senior debt documents. In practice there may be no restriction at all on amendments that may be made to the senior debt terms without bondholder consent.

Right to acquire the prior ranking debt

10.94   An option for the bondholders to acquire the senior ranking debt in an enforcement situation would theoretically be possible but is not provided for in practice. Given the difficulty in marshalling bondholders, exercising such a right would be practically very difficult.

Permitted amendments to the high yield debt

10.95   The bond trustee and bondholders will typically be prohibited from making any amendments to the terms of the bond documentation, without the consent of the senior and second lien lenders, to the extent that the amendment would be adverse to the interests of the senior and second lien lenders.

In practice, instead of, or in addition to, a general prohibition on amendments that are adverse to the senior lenders, there will often be one or more specified types of amendments that are prohibited. These may include amendments granting greater credit support for the bonds, changing the interest rate or other payment terms under the bonds, tightening restrictions, widening the events of default and other similar types of amendments.

Claims against professionals

10.96   High yield bondholders do not have rights against the providers of the due diligence reports commissioned in a buy-out. The reports will generally not be addressed to them. Instead the due diligence exercise for the bondholders focuses principally on the disclosures in the offering memorandum. Consequently, there are no claims against professionals shared with the other financiers that are required to be subordinated as there are with, say, mezzanine debt.

---

130 See para **10.23** above for further consideration of the nature of anti-layering clauses.

Automatic release of guarantees and security

10.97   As previously indicated, the senior lenders will insist that the intercreditor agreement incorporates a standard automatic release mechanism to ensure that in an enforcement situation the security trustee is able to dispose of group companies, assets or the group itself free from the claims of all subordinated creditors. [131] The same clause may also be used to facilitate permitted disposals of secured assets in the ordinary course.

Legal concerns in multi-jurisdictional deals

10.98   With multi-jurisdictional deals, the high yield bond trustee will need to satisfy itself (as will individual noteholders) of the extent to which they can rely on the various provisions in the intercreditor agreement as against more junior creditors. The principal way in which they will do this will be through the taking of detailed legal advice and the obtaining of legal opinions on the validity of the agreement and its enforceability in all relevant jurisdictions (including the locations of all obligors). [132]

High yield bridge facilities

10.99   In European buy-outs, high yield bonds are not issued at the same time that the senior debt is borrowed. Principally this is a consequence of the longer and less flexible timetable for arranging and distributing a high yield issue. [133]

Consequently, at closing of the buy-out bridging finance is put in place in respect of that part of the funding requirement that will be provided by the bond proceeds. The bridge finance is then, if all goes to plan, refinanced by the proceeds of the bond issue in due course. In an ideal world this would be within, say, three months of closing.

From a subordination perspective, the prior ranking acquisition financiers will wish to ensure that the bridge finance is satisfactorily subordinated to their interests, not least because there is no certainty that the high yield bonds themselves will subsequently be issued. It is usual to structure the bridge so that it converts into longer term finance if the bond issue is not successfully completed within an agreed time frame. Subordination of the bridge is therefore as important as any other type of junior debt.

As a practical matter, the intercreditor agreement in a transaction with high yield debt will need to contemplate the high yield bridge finance as a form of subordinated debt until such time as it is taken out by the bonds. Typically, the extent of such subordination largely mirrors the proposed subordination of the high yield bonds themselves; although the subordination of the bridge finance may include some mezzanine-style subordination features such as standstill

---

131   See para **10.29** above for a more detailed consideration of these provisions.
132   See also para **10.36**.
133   See **Chapter 8** generally.

periods of varying duration depending on the default that triggers the standstill. When the bonds are issued in due course the intercreditor agreement should, with relatively little (if any) amendment, automatically provide for the required level of subordination of the high yield bonds. And in the meantime the bridge finance is subordinated in the same manner and to the same extent.

PIK note debt

Public PIK and private PIK

10.100   As considered in detail elsewhere,[134] PIK notes may be used in buy-outs in two forms: public PIK and private PIK. In practice both are relatively rare and are more likely to be used in times of excess liequity in the debt markets. Public PIK notes are documented for issue into the public debt markets and are really a form of high yield bonds that have a non-cash interest coupon.[135] They tend to be used in refinancings of mature – and very large – buy-outs and in particular to fund dividend recaps. Private PIK is also a non-cash pay instrument, as the name suggests, but is documented in the form of privately held subordinated loan capital or a straight loan.

A defining feature of public PIK issuances is that the issuer is an SPV at the top of, or above, the credit group to which most the acquisition financiers have recourse. The PIK note holders have no recourse to that group (unless the issuer itself is part of that group). Where public PIK is being used to finance a dividend recap in an existing structure, the PIK issuer will necessarily be above the existing credit group so that the restrictions in the acquisition finance documentation are not breached.[136] PIK notes issued in these circumstances are generally called 'holdco PIKs'. It follows that holdco PIKs and other public PIKs will be fully structurally subordinated to all of the acquisition finance. Where the proceeds are used to finance a dividend to the equity holders, there isn't even a downstream funding loan for the acquisition financiers to be concerned about. Public PIK holders therefore need not become party to the intercreditor agreement and it follows that this chapter is less concerned with public PIK than with private PIK.

Private PIK notes are more common in European buy-out structures and can be viewed as a discrete form of finance from public PIK. In the remainder of this section references to PIK notes generally means private PIK but it specifically does not encompass PIK notes invested by the sponsor as part of the equity package. In the more complex structures PIK notes may well form one layer of the overall equity package but the key consideration for intercreditor purposes is whether they are to be held by the equity investors that ultimately control the group or by a third-party investor. If held by the controlling shareholders, many of the intercreditor provisions that a third-party investor would wish to see

---

134 See in particular **Chapter 9**.
135 In fact public PIK may also be structured as a loan. See **Chapter 9**.
136 It is still possible, however, that a 'change of control' event might occur. See also para **9.37** and **Chapter 9** generally in relation to PIK notes.

included will not be necessary. In particular, controlling shareholders can veto additional prior ranking debt or amendments to the terms of the prior ranking debt by exercising management control. A third-party investor has no such control and in order to protect the position of the PIK note debt invested by it in the capital structure a third-party PIK note holder must rely on appropriate provisions in the intercreditor agreement.

Whether third-party PIK notes are deemed to be a senior layer of equity or a junior layer of debt is in some ways irrelevant for intercreditor purposes; the key issue, as mentioned, being who is subscribing for it. In either case it will lay sandwiched between all of the core senior and junior debt and the core equity investments. However, its designation as senior equity or junior debt, particularly in the eyes of the core acquisition financiers, may influence the extent of its subordination to the core acquisition finance. This is considered further in the following sections.

A further general comment must also be made. PIK note debt is arguably the least commoditised form of acquisition finance used in Europe. As a result, it is more difficult to generalise about its form including the terms of its subordination. With this in mind the following sections should be read as indicative rather than determinative.

Ranking generally

10.101 PIK note debt ranks behind all other layers of acquisition finance. Because it is often (but not exclusively) used in relatively small amounts in structures with a larger tranche of core junior debt this will often mean it ranks behind senior, second lien and either mezzanine or high yield debt. It will rank ahead of the main equity package.

Structural status and credit support

10.102 As a general rule PIK note debt will be structurally subordinated to the other layers of acquisition finance. It will be issued by an SPV higher up the group than the borrowers and issuers of the prior ranking debt in order to structurally enhance and protect the claims of the prior ranking creditors against the claims of the PIK note holders. This will be particularly important in jurisdictions that do not necesarily recognise contractual subordination (or where it has not been tested in court). But even in jurisdictions that do, the core acquisition financiers will wish to structurally separate the PIK note issuer from the rest of the group to ensure the maximum flexibility for their claims in a default scenario.

As mentioned above, PIK notes come in two main varietals, public PIK and private PIK. Public PIK, which will almost certainly be fully structurally subordinated to all of the core acquisition finance, is often used to finance a dividend recap and a structure incorporating 'holdco PIK' of this kind can be shown in the following diagram. The structure shown assumed a pre-existing structure of senior, second lien and high yield debt, with the PIK being issued above the existing 'group'.

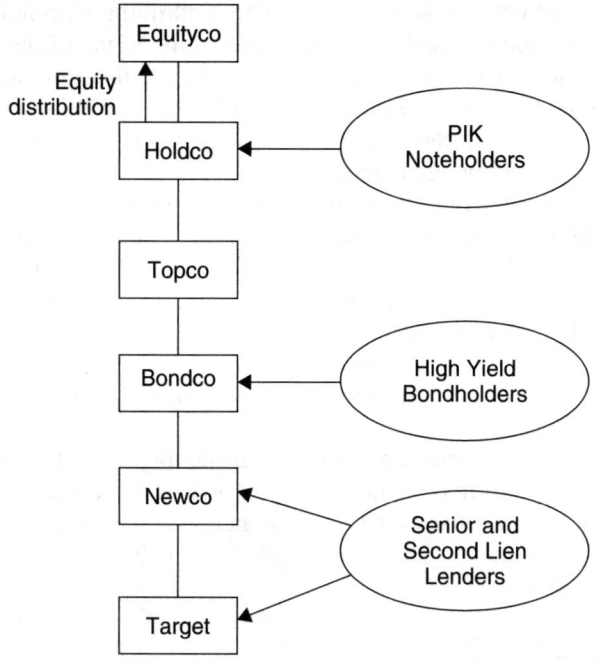

Holdco PIK financing dividend recap

Private PIK notes can be used with any combination of acquisition finance either as part of the initial acquisition financing structure or in a refinancing. In practice they are most likely to be used in a highly leveraged structure sitting behind senior, possibly second lien debt, and a tranche of either high yield or mezzanine debt. The structure shown below is not uncommon.

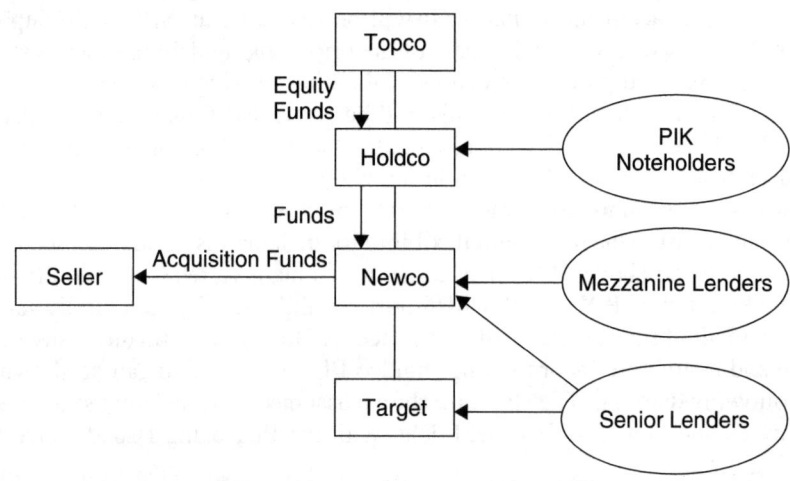

Senior, mezzanine and PIK note debt

Without any guarantees the PIK noteholders remain structurally subordinated to the other acquisition financiers.[137] Similarly, to the extent that the subordinated loan capital invested by the equity providers is issued by a higher SPV – topco in the structure shown above – the PIK noteholders will be in a structurally superior position to the equity investors. This will be a requirement of the PIK noteholders and reflects the higher ranking nature of PIK notes by comparison with any part of the equity package. In order for the various financiers to be able to crystallise their superior structural status in a default scenario – and without having to wait for the SPVs to be liquidated – it is necessary for each class of acquisition financier to take share security[138] within the SPV group. In a default scenario the secured financiers have the option of enforcing the share security in order to cut-off, or threaten to cut-off, those creditors that are in structurally inferior positions higher up the group.[139] The PIK noteholders are no different from more senior ranking financiers in this regard and should insist on share security in the SPV group at a level that enables them to step ahead of the institutional equity investors. For instance, in the structure above, the PIK noteholders would take a share charge from topco over the shares in the PIK note issuer holdco or possibly – although the senior and mezzanine lenders would probably not permit this, given their security requirements – over the shares in newco. In doing so the noteholders can, subject to the prior claims of the prior ranking creditors below them, cut off (or threaten to cut off) the equity investors from the assets of the business. Where structural security is taken from an SPV that is not the PIK note issuer the chargor will typically give a guarantee of the PIK notes and secure its own guarantee rather than granting true 'third-party' security. In any event, any structural guarantee and share security taken by the PIK noteholders will be contractually subordinated to the equivalent guarantee and security taken by the core acquisition financiers. The following diagram demonstrates the use of structural security for the PIK noteholders.

---

137 Note that the acquisition financiers would still need to contractually subordinate the funding loan from the PIK note issuer (holdco) to the acquisition vehicle (newco) in order to fully subordinate the PIK notes and avoid indirect competing claims from their main borrower.

138 The security will also include an assignment of shareholder loans owing to the chargor. In particular this will include an assignment of any funding loan made by the chargor.

139 Such security is often described as structural security. It does not provide any substantive credit support as would be the case with guarantees and security from the target group.

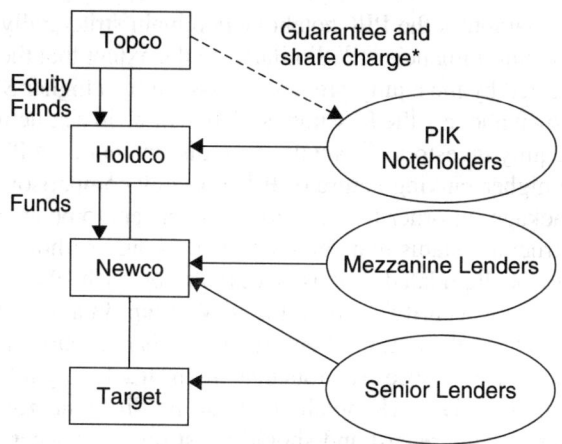

* the share charge would necessarily incorporate an assignment
of all shareholders loans, including the equity funding loan

Structural security for PIK note debt

The question of whether the PIK notes have the benefit of target group credit support is a much more complicated issue, at least in the case of private PIK (public PIK is unlikely to be given target group credit support). That is to say, it is generally a deal-specific matter requiring negotiation with the other financiers, who may be fundamentally opposed to the idea. There are four common issues. First, allowing target group credit support for the PIK note debt removes its structural subordination; and whilst contractual subordination may be acceptable to the core acquisition financiers it will be much less preferable for them. This is especially true where there are obligors in jurisdictions where there is no legal certainty as to the enforceability of contractual subordination provisions.[140] Secondly, the core acquisition financiers might take the view that by permitting the PIK noteholders to have target group credit support the PIK note debt will be viewed by the market as part of the overall acquisition finance debt package. If this is not how the debt has been packaged it might adversely affect syndication of the various layers of debt. For instance, the market might view the deal as being more leveraged than intended. In many cases this will be a matter of perception rather than substance and may not be an absolute reason to refuse security for the PIK note debt. The PIK noteholders will argue that, provided any guarantees and security granted to the PIK noteholders are effectively subordinated to the core acquisition finance,[141] the acquisition financiers should not be concerned that the PIK note debt is also guaranteed and secured on a subordinated basis. In practice there may be some nuisance value to subordinated guarantees and security in favour of PIK noteholders, even if it is the subject of extremely limited enforcement rights and automatic release mechanics, and the

---

140 The core acquisition financiers will not simply rely on the goodwill of subordinated creditors to adhere to contractual subordination, turn-over and other intercreditor provisions. They will generally seek legal comfort as to the enforceability of such provisions.

141 Probably to the extent that there are no independently exercisable default triggers and enforcement rights and certainly to the extent that any guarantees and security are subject to an automatic release mechanism.

core acquisition financiers will often argue forcefully that PIK note debt should remain unsecured by the target group. In jurisdictions where subordination, permanent enforcement standstills, automatic release mechanisms and other waivers of creditor rights are open to question legally the core acquisition financiers will be extremely reluctant to concede the position.

Another reason often given is that the other financiers will be sensitive to having too much secured debt and too many classes of creditor ranking ahead of the trade creditors. In a work-out situation the trade creditors are less likely to be supportive once they become aware of the increased number of layers of finance ahead of them. Finally, in a structure that includes high yield debt that is not secured, the PIK note debt must remain unsecured so as not to rank ahead of the high yield.

Contractual subordination

10.103 Each of the PIK note holders should be party to the intercreditor agreement. They will be subject to the various provisions in favour of the senior, second lien and mezzanine or high yield creditors but will also take the benefit of the provisions as against more junior creditors, including in particular the institutional equity investors and intra-group creditors.

Subordination on insolvency

10.104 The claims of the PIK note holders will be expressly subordinated to the claims of the senior and any second lien, mezzanine or high yield creditors in the event of a winding-up of any borrower or guarantor.

Permitted payments

10.105 The very nature of PIK notes is that there is no cash interest payable until the principal is repayable/redeemable at maturity of the notes. This will be after all of the prior ranking debt has been repaid in full. Consequently, the concept of a permitted payment is necessarily limited. Essentially the only payments that will be permitted until the senior and any second lien, mezzanine or high yield debt have been repaid in full will be the up-front fee and possibly an annual PIK note agency fee. Payment of the up-front fee should not be subject to any conditions as it will be payable at initial funding. Payment of other PIK note fees, such as agency fees, will usually be subject to the conditions that at the time of the payment there is no event of default under the core acquisition finance documentation. This will probably be policed by an automatic payment block. There may be a catch-up mechanic, however, to allow for blocked payments to be made once the relevant event of default is remedied.

Payment blocks

10.106 As mentioned above, a full payment block mechanism is not usually required for PIK note debt given that the only permitted payments are fees, which will usually be subject to an automatic payment block upon an event of default.

Acceleration and enforcement rights

10.107 PIK note debt is a less commoditised form of acquisition finance than senior, second lien, mezzanine or high yield debt. This is reflected in the nature and scope of PIK note documentation, which may be similar to a mezzanine style credit agreement or it may be more akin to equity level subordinated loan capital perhaps in the form of deep discount bonds. Public PIK will typically take the form of a high yield issue.[142] The documentation style used will almost certainly influence the extent of the default triggers available to the PIK noteholders. Credit agreements tend to have more extensive covenants and events of default than loan capital instruments and bond indentures and trust deeds. Theoretically the PIK noteholders will wish to have the same kinds of default triggers as the senior and core junior lenders, which will apply when the prior ranking debt has been repaid, thus releasing the intercreditor restrictions otherwise applicable to the PIK note debt. This is an unlikely circumstance in practice, however, and the core lenders will expect to see a reduced covenant package and limited events of default in the PIK note documents. In particular, they will not expect to see financial covenants. Where the PIK notes are sitting behind an issue of high yield bonds it will be important that the PIK noteholders do not have any default triggers that the bondholders themselves do not have. This would be inconsistent with the order of ranking. Whatever default triggers are included in the PIK note documents, the intercreditor agreement will essentially disapply them until the prior ranking debt is repaid in full. This will reflect the deeper subordination of the PIK notes by comparison with other forms of junior debt, where reduced default triggers will still apply and be exercisable after a standstill period. The default triggers for the PIK notes will be dissapplied entirely by a provision restricting acceleration and enforcement to a small number of exceptional circumstances. Consequently, there is not usually any need for any enforcement standstill mechanics. Bearing in mind that PIK notes have no cash payments of principal or interest until all the prior ranking debt has been repaid there is arguably no need for an active payment default trigger event, although one will generally be included.

Where the PIK notes benefit from target group guarantees and security it will be more important for the prior ranking lenders that the default triggers and enforcement rights are more limited. They should not accept that the PIK noteholders can trigger security enforcement in circumstances where they themselves do not support that approach. Where the PIK note debt is supported only by structural security at a level above the senior borrower and any mezzanine or high yield borrower or issuer then the concern is reduced to some extent. That said, it is likely that at the time of any enforcement of structural security and cutting-off of the equity by the PIK noteholders, the prior ranking creditors would be in an enforcement situation themselves. In practice it is the threat of enforcement by the PIK noteholders that would be in discussion and it is clearly preferable for the core acquisition financiers that the threat only be available to the PIK noteholders in the most limited circumstances.

With all this in mind the acceleration and enforcement rights that the PIK noteholders are left with in practice may be limited to circumstances where the prior ranking creditors have accelerated or taken other enforcement action or where an

---

142 In fact, several 'public PIK' issuances have been issued in the form of a loan. See **Chapter 9**.

insolvency event arises in respect of the PIK note issuer or guarantor. In both instances the PIK noteholders' enforcement actions will be limited to those taken by the prior ranking creditors or to action against the PIK note issuer or guarantor.

Protections in respect of prior ranking debt

10.108 Consistent with the deeply subordinated nature of PIK notes, the inter-creditor protections afforded to them are arguably both more important and harder to obtain from the prior ranking creditors. The starting point for PIK note-holders will often be to try and obtain similar protections to those that mezzanine lenders would obtain and the senior and mezzanine lenders may largely be willing to accept this.

Generally, given the deal specific nature of PIK note debt, more negotiation can often be expected in these areas than is the case with, say, mezzanine debt.

Restricting additional prior ranking debt

10.109 Given that the PIK notes sit behind all other layers of acquisition finance, the PIK noteholders will need to impose some limit on the amount of additional debt that can be incurred ahead of the PIK in the capital structure. From their perspective a limit of, say, 10% of the original amount of core senior debt would be the most favourable position. The sponsor and core acquisition financiers on the other hand may want more flexibility.

Restricting amendments to the terms of the prior ranking debt

10.110 In addition, the PIK noteholders will also wish to have a veto on certain amendments to the terms of the prior ranking debt. From the PIK noteholders' perspective these should mirror the controls that a mezzanine lender would seek. These are usually limited to amendments that would have an adverse financial impact on the borrower. In practice this may mean that the PIK noteholders are given the same veto rights over amendments to the terms of the senior and second lien debt that the mezzanine lenders have, and a similar level of veto rights over amendments to the terms of the mezzanine debt.

Right to acquire the prior ranking debt

10.111 Whether or not the intercreditor agreement includes a provision enabling the PIK noteholders to acquire the entire prior ranking debt in an enforcement scenario is negotiable on a deal-by-deal basis. The controlling equity investor may oppose this on the grounds that it potentially gives a purchaser of the PIK notes the opportunity to acquire all of the debt and, in a default scenario, potentially to control the group. Whilst this may be acceptable for larger tranches of junior debt and, in particular, mezzanine debt, to potentially cede control to a small tranche of deeply subordinated debt may not be acceptable.

Permitted amendments to the PIK note debt

10.112 The PIK noteholders will be prohibited from making any amendments to the terms of the PIK note debt documentation without the consent of the prior ranking creditors, subject to certain relatively standard exceptions. The exceptions are often expressed in general language permitting amendments that are not adverse to the interests of the prior ranking creditors, possibly with specific examples given. These would include changing the terms of payments due in respect of the PIK notes or affecting their subordination. There might also be specified exceptions allowing for amendments to cover typographical errors and amendments of an administrative nature that reflect similar amendments to the terms of the prior ranking debt. Generally, the restriction on amendments will be tighter than for core acquisition finance tranches.

Claims against professionals

10.113 The rights of the PIK noteholders to take action against professional advisers in respect of defective advice and due diligence reports would be expected to be subordinated to the rights of the prior ranking creditors and the senior lenders in particular. There are relatively standard intercreditor provisions dealing with the prioritisation of such rights.[143]

Automatic release of guarantees and security

10.114 As with other forms of finance, where the PIK notes benefit from upstream credit support from the target group, the senior lenders will wish to ensure that the intercreditor agreement incorporates a standard automatic release mechanism to ensure that in an enforcement situation the security trustee is able to dispose of group companies, assets or the group itself free from the claims of all subordinated creditors.[144] The same clause may also be used to facilitate permitted disposals of secured assets in the ordinary course.

Legal concerns in multi-jurisdictional deals

10.115 With multi-jurisdictional deals, the PIK noteholders will theoretically wish to satisfy themselves of the extent to which they can rely on the various provisions in the intercreditor agreement as against more junior creditors, principally the equity investor debt. The principal way in which they will do this will be through the taking of detailed legal advice and the obtaining of legal opinions on the validity of the agreement and its enforceability in all relevant jurisdictions (including the locations of all obligors). In practice, the PIK noteholders may rely on the more senior ranking creditors (and their lawyers) to ensure that the best legal position is achieved under the documentation.[145]

Equity investor debt

10.116 The principal form of finance within this category is the institutional subordinated loan capital that makes up the bulk of the core equity package.

---

143 The typical intercreditor provisions are considered in more detail in para **10.27**.
144 See para **10.29** for a more detailed consideration of these provisions.
145 See also para **10.36**.

There may also be management subordinated loan capital and, subject to one important exception, it would typically be subordinated on the same terms. The exception is for permitted payments. Whilst cash yield payments in respect of institutional loan capital are sometimes permitted the same is not true for management loan capital and it is unlikely that there would be a concept of 'permitted payments' in respect of the management loan capital. Consequently, all but the permitted payments section of the following sections can in general apply to both institutional loan capital and management loan capital.

Ranking generally

10.117 Equity investor debt ranks behind all other third-party finance in the funding structure of a buy-out. It may be expressed to rank ahead of intercompany liabilities owing between members of the group but this is not a prerequisite of the acquisition financiers. Often the intercreditor agreement will simply state that, as between equity investor debt and intercompany debt, there is no order of priorities. The institutional equity investors as creditors of the bulk of the equity investor debt and who also control the group (including all intercompany debtors and creditors) will not normally be too concerned with this approach.

Structural status and credit support

10.118 In most instances the acquisition financiers will prefer to structurally subordinate the equity investor debt by having it borrowed by an SPV high up the group structure and away from the main borrowing vehicles. In a pure UK deal this is not strictly required since the courts will enforce contractual subordination agreements. Even so there are other reasons for having multiple SPVs in a structure[146] and the acquisition financiers will take the opportunity to include an element of structural subordination and thereby enhance their structural status at the same time. At this level of structuring the parties will wish to consider if there are any adverse tax consequences for the group, in particular, as to the deductibility of interest accruing in respect of the equity investor debt.[147] In all but exceptional circumstances, however, it will be acceptable to structurally subordinate the equity investor debt in this way. With non-UK deals where the local laws relating to contractual subordination may be less certain, structural subordination will be even more important.

As far as credit support is concerned the standard position is that the equity investor debt does not benefit from guarantees and security at all. Exceptions are occasionally made, usually on an institution-by-institution basis, and the following factors should be considered by the acquisition financiers.

In a UK transaction the enforceability of subordination arrangements and the operation of standard intercreditor provisions do enable the acquisition

---

146 See para **11.23** generally.

147 For example, the UK tax regime which was substantially revised in March 2005 in relation to private equity shareholder debt (the transitional arrangements for which expired on 31 March 2007) may dictate that DDBs may be less tax efficient than interest bearing PIK notes or that the most beneficial tax position is to list shareholder debt on the Channel Islands Stock Exchange (CISX). As ever, detailed tax advice should be taken at the time in relation to every transaction and its funding structure.

financiers to concede third or fourth ranking guarantees and security to the institutional equity investors if the sponsor insists on it. However, it does increase the
complexity of the documentation process arguably for very little, if any, practical benefit for the institutional equity investor. Given the preference of acquisition financiers in Europe for enforcement sales of businesses as going concerns,
where the institutional guarantees and security would be automatically released,
and the fact that the institutional security ranks behind all of the acquisition
finance and thus in all probability with very little if any security coverage, the
circumstances where institutional guarantees and security are actually used are
very unlikely to arise in practice. Some acquisition financiers also point to the
fact that by securing even the equity element of the funding structure the parties
risk losing the support of the unsecured trade creditors in a distressed situation.
This could precipitate a full meltdown in such a circumstance and certainly hinder restructuring negotiations.

Upstream credit support for the equity investor debt will not be an option
where there is prior ranking but unsecured acquisition finance such as high yield
debt or PIK note debt. This would invert the ranking.

Where the equity investor debt *is* to be granted upstream credit support, the
acquisition financiers will wish to ensure that it is fully subordinated to the prior
ranking guarantees and security of the acquisition financiers and this can generally be achieved through the intercreditor agreement. It would be usual to duplicate the guarantee and security package granted to the acquisition financiers with
consequential amendments to reflect the subordinated status of the equity investor
debt. The security trustee for the acquisition financiers will often refuse to act as
agent and trustee for secured institutional equity investors, however, in the way
that it would typically act on behalf of senior, second lien and mezzanine lenders.

The following buy-out structure shows the standard structural status of equity
investor debt. It might alternatively be invested into topco along with the true
equity.

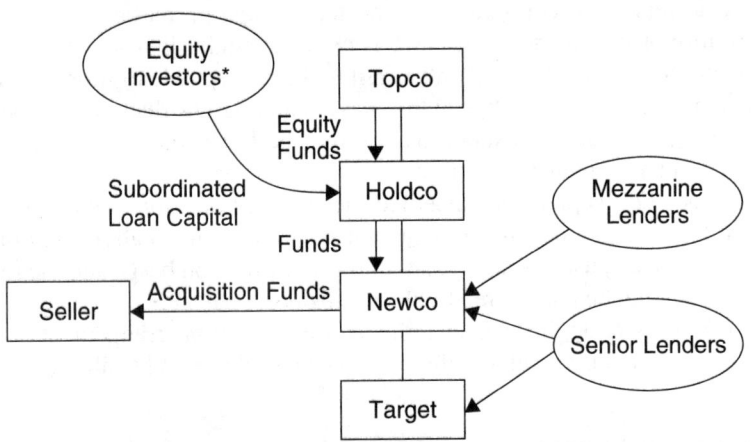

* Subordinated loan capital will be provided by the sponsor (the institutional equity
investor) and in certain structures, including many secondaries, the management team

Senior, mezzanine and equity investor debt

Contractual subordination

10.119 The institutional equity investor will normally be party to the intercreditor agreement.[148] It (or they) will be subject to the various subordination and other provisions in favour of the various acquisition financiers and will have very few rights under the agreement. The intercreditor agreement may even state on its face that it is not intended to confer any benefit on the institutional equity investors.

Subordination on insolvency

10.120 The claims of the institutional equity investor against the equity investor debt borrower (and any guarantor, if applicable) will be expressly subordinated to the claims of the acquisition financiers in the event of a winding-up of the borrower (or guarantor).

Permitted payments and payment blocks

10.121 The typical permitted payments on equity investor debt fall into three categories. There are upfront fees payable to the sponsor for arranging the equity package and possibly as a deal success fee. There are ongoing monitoring, management or director fees that are typically payable to the sponsor on an annual basis throughout the life of the transaction. Finally, in some deals, but this is a minority, there are periodic cash payments of yield on the equity investor debt. In any event, redemptions or repayments of the principal amount of equity investor debt would not be permitted payments.

Different conditions will apply to the making of different types of permitted payment. Thus, it is quite usual for the payment of transaction fees at the closing of the deal to be permitted without any intercreditor conditionality or to have very minimal conditionality in the intercreditor agreement. For instance, there might simply be a condition that there is no event of default outstanding under the acquisition finance.

Payment of annual and other on-going fees to the sponsor will typically be made subject to maximum annual amounts and a condition that at the time of payment there is no outstanding default or event of default but it is a matter for negotiation how tightly the condition is drawn. Payment of yield in the form of cash interest, on the other hand, will normally be subject to more extensive conditionality.

The typical conditions for payment of yield would include:

● no outstanding payment default under the acquisition finance facilities; and

● no outstanding declared default[149] under the acquisition finance facilities.

---

148 In practice the institutional equity will usually be provided by one or more funds managed by the sponsor. The acquisition financiers will wish to have all such funds join as parties and not just the sponsor, which will usually mean execution of the agreement by the general partners of the funds. See also para **10.35** above generally in this regard.

149 A declared default generally means that an event of default has occurred and the lenders have declared the default and taken some action in respect of the default (which may include acceleration and security enforcement).

Both of these conditions will effect an automatic payment block that will endure for so long as the payment or declared default is outstanding.

In addition there will be other conditions that may operate either through an automatic block mechanism or through a manual payment block mechanism, where the acquisition financiers are required to serve a blockage notice in order to effect the payment block. The latter is preferable from the sponsor's perspective for reasons given elsewhere.[150] The payment conditions will include any or all of the following and possibly other deal specific conditions.

- no outstanding event of default under the acquisition finance documents. The sponsor may seek to restrict this to material or financial events of default and this is a matter for negotiation;

- no outstanding financial covenant breach under the senior or mezzanine finance documents including on a pro forma basis, assuming that the relevant permitted payment had been made and included within the covenant calculations;

- look-forward financial covenant compliance for the next 6 or 12 months following the payment. In practice, this means that the company is required to produce a certificate containing a set of financial covenant forecasts for the financial covenants that are to be tested at the next two or four quarter-end dates following the proposed payment, in each case showing that no breach will occur. Again the proposed payment is included in the calculations on a pro forma basis; and

- enhanced financial performance tests. Conditions are sometimes included that require a level of financial performance by the group that exceeds that required by the financial covenants. The required level might mean performance in line with the business plan[151] or there might be other financial targets. Such tests might be on the basis of a minimum earnings level, a reduced leverage ratio or some other concept of financial performance on an enhanced basis. Such conditions are deal-specific.

In order to test compliance with those conditions that are determined by reference to the group's actual financial performance or a forecast of financial performance, it is common to tie the permitted payment dates to the delivery of financial information under the acquisition finance documents. Typically this will mean the relevant financial information delivered at each financial quarter-end for the purposes of testing the financial covenants. In practice this usually means setting the permitted payment dates approximately 45 to 60 days after the relevant financial quarter-end. This allows the company 30 to 45 days to produce the financial statements and necessary forecast certificates for the acquisition financiers and leaves a period of up to 15 days for the acquisition financiers to analyse the information and react accordingly by serving a payment blockage notice (or not as the case may be).

---

150 See para **10.16**.

151 The financial covenants themselves will not require performance to the absolute level of the business plan (in this context called the 'base case'). There will be an amount of headroom to allow for a certain degree of underperformance before a breach of financial covenant occurs.

The catch-up of blocked payments is usually permitted once the payment conditions can be satisfied again. However, it would be unusual to allow default interest to accrue on blocked equity investor debt yield.

As previously mentioned,[152] certain subordinated creditors that are fund managers have specific concerns with automatic payment blocks where the proceeds of permitted payments received are to be distributed to the investors in their funds. Where it transpires subsequently that the payment should not have been made the turn-over or claw-back clause will oblige the fund manager to return the money paid in error. The payment, however, may already have been distributed to the third-party fund investors that are not party to the intercreditor agreement and thus not subject to any claw-back clause.

Two compromises are often considered. With the first, the fund manager is entitled to give notice to the company and the acquisition financiers of the pending permitted payment and, in effect, a reminder that this is subject to conditions. If no payment blockage notice is then issued in respect of the payment the amount can be paid and distributed to the third-party fund investors without any obligation to claw-back if in fact the relevant conditions were not met. The other is to apply an amount equal to the amount that would otherwise be required to be clawed back as a deduction against the next permitted payment.

The concern of the acquisition financiers with a manual payment block mechanism is that they may not have all of the necessary information to hand at the time they need to serve a payment blockage notice. Or the information – particularly financial statements – they are relying on might subsequently prove to be inaccurate. With this in mind, the second of the two compromises, whilst not as favourable as an automatic payment block with unfettered claw-back right, is preferred.

Acceleration and enforcement rights

10.122 Given the subordinated nature of equity investor debt and the fact that a majority of it is typically held by the group's controlling shareholders, it is not appropriate to give the sponsor discrete default triggers.

In practice, this means that despite the fact that the equity investor debt documentation will often include events of default, the intercreditor agreement will override them and the sponsor will not be permitted to take any acceleration or enforcement action in respect of the equity investor debt. There are two possible exceptions to this general principle where the sponsor will be permitted to accelerate the equity investor debt and take enforcement action against the equity investor debt obligors. These are, where:

- the borrower (or a guarantor, if applicable) of the equity investor debt becomes subject to insolvency proceedings; or

- the acquisition financiers have accelerated the acquisition finance and taken enforcement action.

---

152 See para **10.16**.

In either case the scope for taking any enforcement action will be limited to action that the acquisition financiers have themselves taken, and usually to taking action against the equity investor debt borrower only.

It would be extremely uncommon for the equity investor debt to have other default triggers, even if subject to a standstill provision. Indeed it is not uncommon for *all* enforcement action to be prohibited in relation to equity investor debt.[153]

Protections in respect of prior ranking debt

Restricting additional acquisition finance and amendments to the terms of the existing debt

10.123 The sponsor is almost invariably the controlling shareholder of the group. As such it can control the incurrence of additional debt or amendments to the terms of the existing prior ranking debt through management control. Consequently, the intercreditor agreement will not include a separate right.

Right to acquire prior ranking debt

10.124 It would be unusual for investors in the institutional loan capital to be granted a right to acquire prior ranking debt.

Permitted amendments to the equity investor debt

10.125 It is not uncommon for the intercreditor agreement to prohibit any amendment to the equity investor debt documents without the prior consent of the acquisition financiers. Equally, common exceptions include amendments to correct typographical errors, amendments of an administrative nature that reflect similar amendments to the terms of the acquisition finance and, possibly, any other amendment that is not adverse to the interests of the acquisition financiers and in any event not being an amendment to the equity investor debt payment terms or affecting the subordination of the equity investor debt.

Deemed override

10.126 A deemed override clause is a relatively standard intercreditor provision applicable to equity investor debt. Broadly, it provides that any consent or waiver given in respect of any terms of the acquisition finance documents is deemed given in respect of the equivalent provision of the equity investor debt documents. This gives the acquisition financiers comfort that the group cannot be held to ransom over a required waiver or consent by the sponsor.

In practice, since the sponsor is generally the controlling shareholder of the group its interests will, in any event, be aligned with those of the company seeking the consent or waiver. For this reason the clause should be uncontroversial.

---

153 Note that enforcement action in this context includes the exercise of any remedies including declaring debt due and payable early (acceleration).

Claims against professionals

10.127 The rights of the sponsor to take action against professional advisers in respect of defective advice and due diligence reports will usually be subordinated to the equivalent rights of the prior ranking creditors.

This will be an important provision for the acquisition financiers, and even in situations where the institutional equity investors do not become a direct party to the intercreditor agreement – for reasons detailed elsewhere[154] – the acquisition financiers should insist on a side letter whereby the sponsor (and any other institutional equity investor) agrees to turn-over the proceeds of professional claims either to the borrower group to rectify the relevant underlying defect that gave rise to the claim or, where an event of default exists and the banks insist, directly to the acquisition financiers to pay down debt. There are relatively standard intercreditor provisions dealing with the prioritisation of such rights.[155]

Automatic release of guarantees and security

10.128 As with other forms of finance, where the equity investor debt benefits from upstream credit support from the target group, the senior lenders will wish to ensure that the intercreditor agreement incorporates a standard automatic release mechanism to ensure that in an enforcement situation the security trustee is able to dispose of group companies, assets or the group itself free from the claims of all subordinated creditors.[156] The same clause may also be used to facilitate permitted disposals of secured assets in the ordinary course.

Share capital

Should the shareholders be party to the intercreditor agreement?

10.129 At one level there is no need to include share capital as a form of subordinated finance within the intercreditor agreement. It is inherently subordinated to debt in an insolvency situation. That said, intercreditor agreements are not only concerned with post-insolvency situations. They also seek to restrict payments on instruments, such as yield payments, outside of insolvency. With this in mind the acquisition financiers will wish to ensure that shareholders in the group – that is, shareholders in the equity vehicle, topco – cannot receive payments that are not expressly permitted by the acquisition financiers. They will also wish to ensure that the shareholders are subject to turn-over provisions in respect of payments that are received in breach of the agreement, that they cannot amend the constitutional documents of topco in a manner adverse to the interests of the acquisition financiers and that they take no action against the group companies that is inconsistent with the intercreditor agreement and acquisition finance documents generally.

---

154 See para **10.35**.
155 The typical intercreditor provision is considered in more detail in para **10.27**.
156 See para **10.29** above for a more detailed consideration of these provisions.

In practice, given that the shareholders in topco will generally be parties to the intercreditor agreement in any event, as holders of equity investor debt, many intercreditors do not separately attempt to bind the shareholders in topco in that capacity. In any given situation, the question must be asked as to what issues, relating to the shareholders and share capital in topco, does the intercreditor agreement *need* to separately provide for? Many issues may already be dealt with through the controls in the agreement on the equity investors generally or in respect of equity investor debt. Some issues may be dealt with in any event through the main acquisition finance documentation, such as restrictions on distributions and redemptions of share capital. The key issue for the acquisition financiers will often be ensuring that they have a proprietary right to claw back any amounts paid to the shareholders in breach of the finance documents or in error. This will ideally mean binding the institutional equity investors directly in some capacity. But, as indicated below, English law does provide other remedies to claw back funds paid in breach of contract.

Share capital in topco will normally also be held by certain members of the top management of the group. These individuals may not also be investors in subordinated loan capital and thus not otherwise party to the intercreditor agreement. Consequently there must also be an assessment as to whether such individual shareholders need to be party to the intercreditor agreement. Where, as is almost always the case, the share capital is non-yielding during the life of the acquisition finance facilities, the 'commercial' approach is to exclude the individuals from the requirement to be party to the agreement. This analysis might change if there were a significant proportion of the shares held by an individual but even then the only material area of concern relates to the situation where a payment is made to the shareholder in breach of the intercreditor agreement and the acquisition finance documents and a direct turn-over right did not exist against the shareholder. In fact, as a matter of English law at least, a right to sue the shareholders for return of funds wrongfully received will almost certainly exist in any event. The receiving shareholder will in all probability be held to be a constructive trustee of the funds received leaving the acquisition financers a right *in rem* to the return of the funds.[157]

Equity structure

10.130   The following diagram shows how the true equity, in the form of share capital, is commonly invested into a funding structure. The quasi-equity – the equity investor debt – may be invested through the equity vehicle or into a lower SPV as shown below. Management may or may not provide quasi-equity along with the sponsor.[158]

---

157 See also para **10.35**.
158 See also **Chapters 3** and **4** generally.

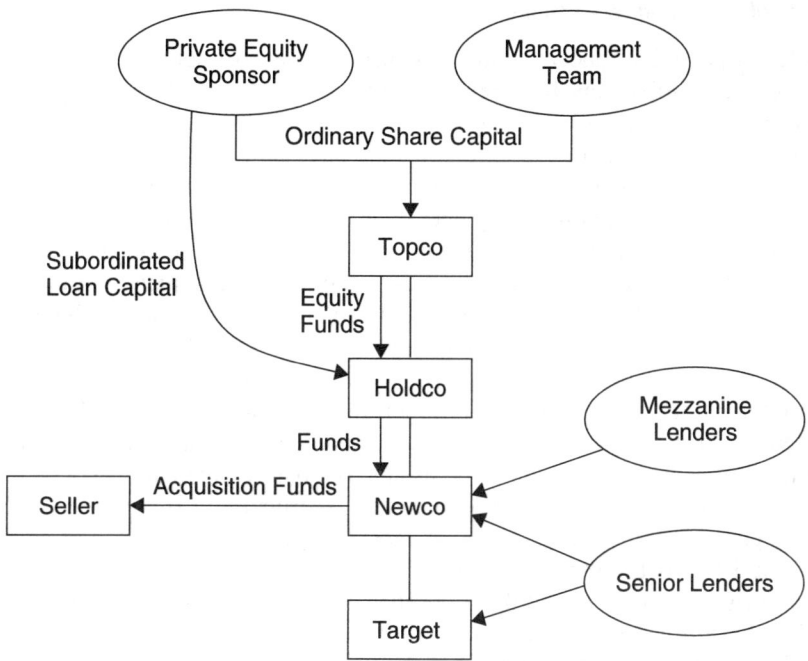

Senior, mezzanine and equity

Seller loan capital

Seller notes

10.131   Seller loan capital, or as it is often called, a seller 'note' or 'vendor note' is a form of deferred consideration structured as debt.[159] The subordination of seller loan capital should on its face be treated in the same way as other deeply subordinated loan capital such as equity investor debt. In actual fact, its treatment typically requires a much more deal-specific approach. There are a number of factors to be considered.

Ranking generally

10.132   As to ranking, seller loan capital does not easily fall into any particular place in a typical capital structure. Often it is repayable *before* the core acquisition finance if certain financial performance targets are met. On the other hand it would usually be subordinated to the acquisition finance on an insolvency.

---

159 Seller notes are occasionally used in buy-out structures to bridge the gap between the seller's expectations as to target group value and what the buyer is willing to pay. See also paras **3.23** and **4.12**.

Structural status and credit support

10.133 A potential concern with the structural status of seller loan capital is often that the seller may be a relatively unknown quantity to the acquisition financiers. It will generally have no ongoing interest in the transaction other than the repayment of its loan capital and it may have no practical concerns about maintaining a good relationship with the acquisition financiers. In short, whereas financial institutions that regularly operate in the acquisition finance market can to some extent be expected to behave in line with agreed market-standard intercreditor positions – irrespective of how the issues are documented – for the sake of maintaining relationships, for instance, this may not be the case with a third-party seller. For this reason the acquisition financiers need to ensure that the intercreditor position with the seller is as certain as possible.

In jurisdictions where contractual subordination is legally watertight a more relaxed approach to the structural status of the seller loan capital may be taken. In jurisdictions where this is not the case the acquisition financiers may be well advised to require that the seller loan capital is structurally subordinated. This may be easier said than done, however, as most seller loan capital is invested at the same level as the senior debt; that is, in newco as the acquisition vehicle. Unless it is separately agreed that the seller invests the seller loan capital in an SPV higher up the SPV group structure it will be the buyer that becomes the seller's obligor. If a higher vehicle is to be the seller's obligor then the proceeds of the note will need to be downstreamed to newco before being applied by newco, on paper at least, in meeting the full acquisition price owing to the seller. The downstreaming of these funds would ideally be effected by way of a capital injection in newco rather than a loan to newco. This would enhance the structural subordination of the seller note and avoid the need to contractually subordinate the downstream loan.

Irrespective of which vehicle borrows the seller loan capital it would be rare for there to be credit support in the form of guarantees or security from other parts of the group, especially the target group. Acquisition financiers would generally not accept the competing claims of the seller, even if fully contractually subordinated, at target group level. The most common structures including seller loan capital could be shown in diagrammatic form as follows:

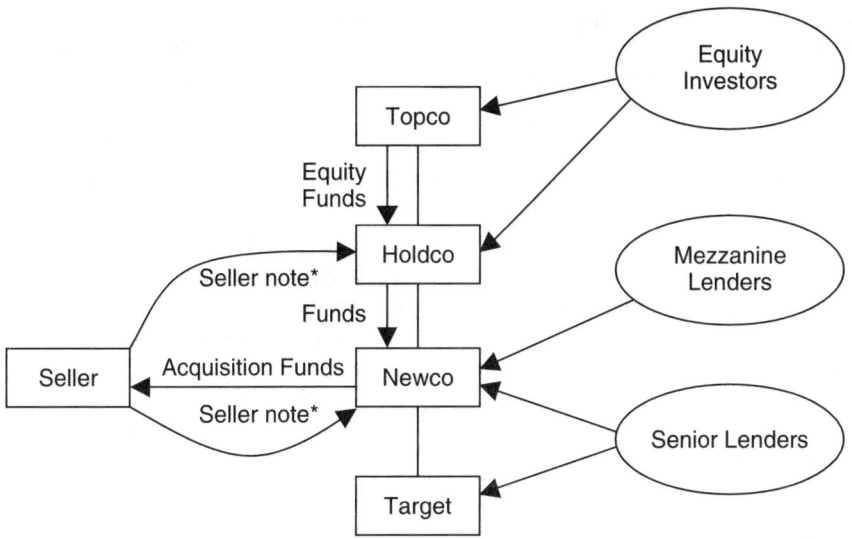

* In this diagram alternative structures for the seller note are shown. One structurally
subordinated to the acquisition finance and one pari passu, in newco.

Seller notes

Contractual subordination

10.134 It is, in theory, possible for a purely structural subordination arrangement to be created whereby the seller note is invested in holdco and the proceeds downstreamed to newco by way of capital injection rather than loan. This structure would isolate the seller's claim sufficiently in an insolvency situation. If, however, the seller note is invested in newco or there is a funding loan of the proceeds from holdco to newco then some level of contractual subordination is required. This could be limited to contractual subordination of the funding loan if the note is invested in holdco, which would also abrogate the need for the seller itself to sign up to the contractual subordination arrangements. That would not be a perfect structure from the acquisition financiers' perspective, however, since there would be no prohibition on the seller enforcing its claim against holdco and as a result disrupting the group or causing some adverse legal repercussions within the SPV group. It is better to get the seller to sign up to, and formally acknowledge, the subordination arrangements. In doing so the acquisition financiers can get the seller's direct contractual agreement on a number of intercreditor provisions including subordination on insolvency. Where newco is the seller's borrower – and there is no structural subordination – this is critical.

In practice getting the seller to sign up to the subordination arrangements is not always straightforward. Many are reluctant out of principle to review and sign 50 or 100-page intercreditor agreements, which other 'professional' subordinated creditors will generally be much more familiar with. In some transactions the deal sponsor may make the mistake of keeping the seller and the acquisition financiers at arms length for too long. In doing so it may overlook the different expectations that the seller and the acquisition financiers may have as regards the subordination of the seller note. Bringing the parties together at the last minute to agree the subordination arrangements is often problematic.

Best practice probably dictates agreeing a subordination term sheet for the seller note with both seller and acquisition financiers at the outset. This should include the terms of the note itself: amount, issuer vehicle, when payable, payment conditions, extent of contractual subordination and so on.

When it comes to actually documenting the subordination arrangements it is often better to have a stand-alone subordination agreement in respect of the seller note rather than incorporating the provisions into the general intercreditor agreement. This will make it more palatable for the seller and only the essential elements relevant to the seller note need be included.

This also has the added benefit of allowing subsequent amendments to the main intercreditor agreement to be made without needing the seller's involvement, which may be difficult to get once the deal has closed.

Subordination on insolvency

10.135 The claims of the seller against newco, or the claims of holdco against newco under any funding loan should be expressly subordinated to the claims of the acquisition financiers in the event of any winding-up of newco. If the seller note is invested in holdco it would be preferable to have the seller's claims against holdco subordinated in the same way.

Permitted payments and payment blocks

10.136 There are very few, if any, market standards for the terms on which payments in respect of a seller note may be made. This reflects the fact that many sellers are not in the 'market' and many are doing one-off deals. One or two observations may be made, however. Most seller notes mature prior to the final maturity of the acquisition finance. Consequently, the payment conditions will relate to payments of principle and not merely interest or yield as with other forms of subordinated capital. In most cases the terms on which the principal can be repaid are the precise payment conditions that the acquisition financiers will rely on. In other words, they are often financial performance targets that need to be achieved for the payment to be made rather than the mere passage of time.

Whether or not the acquisition financiers can impose further conditions, such as financial covenant compliance under the senior facilities agreement, or that no event of default is outstanding, is deal-specific and potentially controversial with sellers. For example, the seller may believe that it has done a straightforward deal with the buyer (sponsor) to the effect that the full amount of the note is repayable upon hitting pre-agreed financial targets. But this may be at odds with the more stringent conditions that the acquisition financiers would wish to impose.

The treatment of interest until repayment will need special consideration. Is it to be payable in cash, and, if so, what are the conditions to payment? Should there be a payment block mechanism? Alternatively, is all interest to be capitalised?

In most respects the principles applicable to the delivery of financial information showing compliance with the relevant tests or financial targets, the mechanics for payment blocks and the timing of payments and so on that apply to other forms of subordinated capital can be applied to seller notes.

Acceleration and enforcement rights

10.137 This is another area where a deal-specific approach is required. However, as a starting point, the acquisition financiers will wish to limit the default triggers on the seller note as much as possible. As with equity investor debt it may be possible to override them altogether. In most cases the seller's right to accelerate and enforce should be limited to the circumstance of insolvency of the seller note borrower and cross-acceleration and enforcement with the acquisition finance. There should arguably be a non-payment default trigger, but only for payments that are permitted and absolutely not for those that are legitimately blocked under the intercreditor arrangements.

Protections in respect of prior-ranking debt

10.138 This is an area where much depends on the seller's bargaining position. Where the seller note is a relatively small element of the capital structure it would be unusual to grant the seller any significant rights to veto matters relating to the capital structure going forward. Thus, there should be no right to veto amendments to the terms of the acquisition finance. Equally, it would be extremely rare for the seller to be granted a right to purchase the prior-ranking debt in an enforcement scenario, not least because if there has been financial underperformance the seller note should carry the least rights. It is usually an 'over-performance' instrument. In most cases a right to block additional prior-ranking debt would also be unpalatable to the company and the acquisition financiers even though from the seller's perspective it might be a key area of concern.

Permitted amendments to the seller note

10.139 Generally the acquisition financiers should expect to include an absolute prohibition on amendments to the terms of the seller note without their prior consent.

Automatic release of guarantees and security

10.140 As with other forms of finance, on the rare occasions where the seller loan capital benefits from upstream credit support from the target group, the senior lenders will wish to ensure that the intercreditor agreement incorporates a standard automatic release mechanism to ensure that in an enforcement situation the security trustee is able to dispose of group companies, assets or the group itself free from the claims of all subordinated creditors. [160]

---

160 See para **10.29** above for a more detailed consideration of these provisions.

Intercompany debt

10.141   For completeness it is worth mentioning intercompany debt. Standard intercreditor agreements also include the debts owing between group companies within the intercreditor arrangements. This is done for two principal reasons.

First, through the use of a permitted payment mechanism, the acquisitions financiers are able to exercise some degree of control over the flow of funds around the group. This is not for the purposes of stifling the normal cash management of the business, but it ensures, in particular, that excess cashflow is not upstreamed to companies in the group above the senior debt borrower other than to meet permitted payments in respect of junior debt or to meet the pre-agreed ongoing fees and expenses of the investors or the SPVs themselves. Typically, permitted payments under intercompany loans will be subject to a payment blockage mechanism whereby they are automatically blocked, or blocked following notice from the acquisition financiers, after the occurrence of some level of default under the acquisition finance documentation. The 'ring-fencing' provisions in the senior and mezzanine facility agreements will provide a certain level of control on payments to try to ensure that cash and other valuable assets remain within the guarantee and security net rather than leaking out to non-obligors but those provisions do not generally regulate the flow of funds between obligor companies – that is, payments *within* the ring-fencing.

The second reason is to facilitate any enforcement action that may be taken by the acquisition financiers. This is achieved by having intercompany creditors agree to subordinate their claims in the winding-up of any group company or, if directed by the acquisition financiers, to claim in such a winding-up and turnover the proceeds of any such claims to the acquisition financiers. There will also be a general prohibition on the intercompany creditors taking any enforcement action in respect of the intercompany debt unless instructed to do so by the acquisition financiers.

In order to effect these subordination arrangements, members of the group are required to enter into the intercreditor agreement as intercompany creditors and debtors. This would normally be limited to: (a) those members of the group that are obligors under the acquisition finance documents – that is, borrowers and guarantors – since these are the companies with claims that may compete with the claims of the acquisition financiers; and (b) non-obligor that are creditors to obligors.

Pension liabilities

10.142   As considered in more detail elsewhere in this book, pensions – and in particular, defined benefit schemes[161] – have become a major area of concern in the UK buy-out market.[162] The impact of new legislation in particular has been to

---

161   Defined benefit schemes include final salary schemes and career average schemes.
162   See para **11.112** in particular.

strengthen the hand of pension scheme trustees in buy-out negotiations with what can in some cases amount to a veto right over the deal or the deal structure at least.

The trustees' powers arise in a combination of ways. Trustees have sole control over the investment strategy of the pension scheme. The investment strategy directly affects the actuarial deficit in the scheme, which is reflected on the company's balance sheet under current accounting rules and is a key factor in the level of future contributions required to be paid to the scheme. In addition, the new legislation gives trustees complete or partial control over the level of contributions to be paid to the scheme (depending on the scheme's existing provisions). Further, the Pensions Regulator has power to impose funding or guarantee obligations on group companies in respect of the scheme. Protection from such obligations can be obtained by seeking the support of the trustees through a clearance process. Trustees have considerable leverage from their ability to withhold support for a clearance application.

The impact on the acquisition finance market specifically, of these powers, is essentially two-fold. On the one hand a scheme trustee might be able to insist on greater scheme contributions by the target company following completion of the deal, which in turn means that less cashflow is available to service debt, the effect of which will most likely be to reduce the amount of leverage that may be made available in the first place. Then in addition to this, the trustees may be able to require that future pension scheme liabilities – representing the claims of the scheme against the company for any deficit in funding – are granted protection similar to that granted to the acquisition finance itself, such as guarantees and security from the target group. It is this second point that is relevant from a ranking and intercreditor perspective.

What tends to happen in practice – with defined benefit schemes – is that an agreed amount of pension scheme liabilities are granted pari passu status with the senior debt and possibly a further amount is granted intermediate status immediately below the junior debt but above the equity investor debt, intercompany debt and unsecured debt. Thus the scheme trustee will become a party to the intercreditor agreement in order to be able to represent a discrete class of 'pension liabilities'. The key negotiation tends to concern the amount of the pension liabilities that benefit from that status and thus, from a pension trustee's perspective, how much will potentially rank behind the senior debt and the junior debt respectively.

In other cases agreement may be reached with the trustees on the basis of some acceleration of funding, either directly into the scheme or via a reserve fund.

CHAPTER 11

Deal Execution

INTRODUCTION

11.1   This chapter considers how a buy-out transaction is actually executed. It assumes that a basic commercial deal has been struck between buyer and seller and between buyer and financiers. As with other chapters the deal process is analysed principally from the perspective of the acquisition financiers rather than the financial sponsor, management team or seller. Emphasis is placed on the legal, documentation and due diligence processes that the parties will instigate and follow with the help of their legal and other advisers. No consideration is given to the internal procedures that the acquisition financiers or other parties will go through to approve the buy-out.[1]

The chapter is split into four main parts, respectively dealing with the appointment of advisers, the transaction structuring process, the due diligence process and the legal and documentation process. There is also a brief section dealing with syndication of the debt facilities, a section that considers what the overall timetable for a UK buy-out might be and then a final section offering some practical advice on dealing with some frequently arising issues.

APPOINTMENT OF ADVISERS

11.2   As soon as a basic commercial deal has been agreed, the principal parties will appoint their advisers. The advisers will include lawyers to advise on the transaction structure, to carry out legal due diligence and to document the commercial deal, accountants to provide tax structuring advice and to carry out the principal financial due diligence exercise, and other consultants to carry out specific commercial due diligence exercises. The sponsor may also engage an investment bank or corporate finance house to provide advisory services. Broad 'buy-side' mandates are much less common in private buy-outs than they are in public-to-privates, where there is a clear need for the bidder to have a financial adviser. In private buy-outs, the need for corporate finance advice is more deal- and sponsor-specific. For example, 'debt advisory' mandates started to become

---

1   Such as the credit or investment approval processes that the respective financiers will necessarily need to follow.

quite common during the 2000s and many of the accountancy firms and corporate finance boutiques in particular have developed teams to provide advice of this type to sponsors. The following paragraphs consider a number of practical matters relating to these various appointments. The matters referred to are generally considered from the perspective of the acquisition financiers.

Lawyers

Acquisition financiers' lawyers

11.3   It is important that the precise terms on which the acquisition financiers' lawyers are appointed are clear to both client and law firm.

The principal tasks to be carried out (and specified) are advising on structure, documenting the commercially agreed terms of the acquisition finance, reviewing and commenting on the acquisition and equity documentation, reviewing and commenting on certain of the due diligence reports, providing legal opinions on the finance documentation and project managing the transaction for the acquisition financiers, which will include coordinating all formalities for the execution and completion of the deal.

The acquisition financiers' lawyers will not usually be expected to carry out a general legal due diligence review themselves since this exercise will be undertaken by lawyers representing the deal sponsor or in some cases the seller. To duplicate the process would be costly and time-consuming. This is not usually an issue except in certain cases with seller due diligence, where the seller's lawyers and other advisors may initially be reluctant to extend legal reliance to the buyer and its financiers. That approach is generally not acceptable in the acquisition finance market. If the seller's advisers cannot agree to extend reliance to the buyer and its financiers, further reports would need to be commissioned on which reliance can be placed. In any event, the task for the acquisition financiers' lawyers should be limited to checking that the legal due diligence report and such other reports that they have agreed to review are satisfactory.

An exception to this general approach is that it is not uncommon for the acquisition financiers' lawyers to report specifically to the acquisition financiers on the target companies' legal title to their properties.[2]

The terms of engagement between the acquisition financiers and their lawyers should specify the scope of all of these matters. Additionally it will usually include an estimate of the adviser's fees and, if required by the sponsor, a cap on the fees that can be charged.

Separate lawyers for senior and junior creditors?

11.4   Where, as is usually the case, the acquisition finance includes junior debt there may or may not be a separate firm of lawyers appointed to advise the junior creditors. In the United Kingdom, a single firm is likely to be appointed to advise all of the acquisition financiers, other than where there is high yield debt in the structure. In the US market a 'one-stop shop' approach, where the same firm of lawyers advise all of the acquisition financiers, applies even where there

2   See para **11.63**.

is high yield. However, this has not been universally adopted in the UK market, at least at the time of writing. One reason for this, historically, is that not all law firms in the acquisition finance market have had adequate experience in both fields, with high yield expertise, in particular, concentrated in a small number of (mostly US) firms. A more fundamental reason dating back to the origins of the high yield market is that the intercreditor issues between the senior lenders and the high yield bondholders were not settled for many years, leaving a very real conflict of interest for a firm in acting for both sets of creditors.[3] The position with respect to second lien debt and mezzanine debt has traditionally been more flexible, with the same law firm often advising the respective creditors. As for PIK note debt, much hangs on who is underwriting the PIK notes. If it is a third-party then they may well use their own counsel but if it is the main acquisition finance arranger and underwriter then that institution will probably use the same lawyers to advise in respect of the PIK note too.

In practice, even if there are separate lawyers for the junior creditors, the senior lenders' lawyers will take a lead role for *all* the acquisition financiers on a number of matters. These would normally include review and commentary on the acquisition and equity documents and agreeing the forms of the condition precedent documents relating to the finance documents. The junior lenders' lawyers will review and have an opportunity to comment on these documents, but will usually pass their comments to the sponsor through the lawyers acting for the senior lenders. The junior creditors' lawyers will, however, be responsible for directly negotiating the documents relating to the junior debt with newco's lawyers (albeit that these are likely to be based substantially on the senior documents). Ultimately, the senior lender's lawyers will take a lead role in the overall management of the transaction from the perspective of the acquisition financiers.

If the same firm of lawyers *is* to act for both sets of creditors then steps will need to be taken to mitigate potential conflicts of interest. First, separate individual lawyers should be appointed to advise the respective principals, in respect of matters where a conflict of interest could arise.[4] Secondly, information barriers should be put in place to avoid information that is confidential to one class of creditor being passed to another class of creditor.

Sponsor's and management team's lawyers

11.5   The sponsor and the management team will each appoint legal advisers, each having a different role. One firm of lawyers, usually those acting for the sponsor, will take the lead in advising the acquisition vehicle and main borrower, newco.[5] That firm of lawyers will also be appointed to carry out the legal due diligence exercise.[6]

---

3   In practice, that issue no longer holds. See also **Chapter 8** and **Chapter 10**.
4   This will usually be limited to the terms of the intercreditor arrangements between the respective acquisition financiers.
5   In a true MBO the management team's lawyers will lead for newco.
6   The appointment of lawyers to carry out due diligence is principally done on behalf of newco rather than the sponsor, as newco is the direct buyer, and the acquisition financiers should ensure this is reflected in the terms of engagement relating to the due diligence. This is principally because they will be relying upon newco having a claim against any provider of a defective due diligence report in addition to any independent claim that they might have. See also para **11.70**.

The acquisition financiers are not particularly concerned with the terms of engagement of the lawyers acting for the sponsor or the management team. An exception to this relates to the scope of the legal due diligence. First, they will wish to ensure that the legal due diligence report will be addressed to and can be legally relied upon by the acquisition financiers. One potentially contentious area in this regard is the imposition of limitations on liability by the lawyers producing the legal due diligence in connection with that exercise.[7] Secondly, they will need to know that it will cover all areas which they would expect to be covered. Ideally a separate due diligence scope will be agreed by all parties.

Seller's lawyers

11.6   The acquisition financiers are generally not concerned with the terms of engagement of the seller's lawyers. However, if they are to rely on a seller commissioned due diligence report[8] they will, as with sponsor commissioned due diligence, be concerned that it is addressed to and can be legally relied upon by the acquisition financiers without any quantum limitation on liability, and that it covers all requisite areas.

Accountants

Due diligence

11.7   The reporting accountants retained to carry out the financial due diligence exercise will be selected by the deal sponsor. As with the legal due diligence, it is common practice – and from the acquisition financiers' perspective preferable – for the reporting accountants to be formally engaged by newco to produce the financial due diligence report. The report should be addressed to newco, the sponsor and the acquisition financiers on the basis that it can be legally relied upon by each of them.[9]

The terms of engagement with the reporting accountants will usually be in the form of a relatively standard letter, although over time the standard forms have evolved to be more favourable to the accountants. The acquisition financiers will need to approve the precise scope of the financial due diligence so that it covers all aspects they have in mind. They will also need to ensure that if the due diligence report is flawed to a material extent and they or newco suffer a loss as a result, they (or newco) will have a satisfactory right of recourse against the accountants.

Recourse against accountants

11.8   A right of recourse against the accountants in the event that their due diligence is flawed, is important if the parties are to place reliance on the due

---

7   This has traditionally been unacceptable to a sponsor, even though the accountants routinely and systematically cap their due diligence liabilities. In fact, at the time of writing most leading law firms were moving towards incorporating liability caps wherever possible. In practice, this has become entirely standard with seller due diligence (see para **11.71**) and increasingly common with buy-side due diligence.

8   This is increasingly common with seller initiated buy-outs, including secondaries, and most auctioned disposals.

9   It is not usually addressed to the management team, given that the amount of funding they will invest into the deal will be relatively small and because the financial due diligence may, to some extent, be in respect of historic financial information and a prospective business plan that they themselves are responsible for.

diligence. Much debate has followed the efforts of the accountancy firms to limit the extent of their liability in respect of a flawed due diligence report.

A key factor behind these efforts is the fact that, during the second half of the 20th century, English common law extended the scope for a professional advisor to be sued by a party which had relied upon certain work products of the adviser, even where no direct contract existed between them, through the concept of negligent mis-statement. With a buy-out, this potentially means that not only can newco – as contracting party – sue the accountants for a flawed report, but, in theory, any party to which reliance on the accountants' report is extended could also claim damages for loss arising as a result of the flawed report. In practice, this means extending liability to the sponsor and the acquisition financiers.

To deal with their concerns about potential liability, accountancy firms, led by what are now known as the 'Big Four' firms, developed two initiatives in particular. First, they introduced a cap on the quantum of their total liability and, secondly, they proposed contracting out of the principal of joint and several liability for damages and introducing in its place a principle of proportionality. The proportionality principle is based on their objection to the fact that even where the negligence of the accountants in providing a flawed due diligence report was less culpable than the contributory negligence of another party – such as the management team, but this could also be another firm of professional advisers – they could be liable for the entire loss incurred. On the 'deeper pocket' principle they are more likely to bear the vast majority of the damages for any such claim. To avoid this, a proportionality provision would be included in the terms of engagement and reliance. The provision would apportion damages for any claim between all negligent parties according to the respective degrees of negligence of such parties.

BVCA – Big Six Memorandum of Understanding

11.9   In 1996 the (then) 'Big Six' accountancy firms signed a Memorandum of Agreement concerning the limitation of liability in private equity transactions. They lodged it with the Office of Fair Trading (OFT) for registration under the Restrictive Trade Practices Act[10]. In response, the British Venture Capital Association (BVCA), on behalf of its members in the UK private equity industry, submitted objections and dialogue between the sides ensued. The result was the agreement of a Memorandum of Understanding (MoU) between the BVCA (on behalf of its members) and the Big Six firms.

The MoU contains a framework and set of guidelines, which are intended to be adopted by equity houses and the accountants in private equity transactions. Under the guidelines, there are three separate sets of rules summarised as follows:

- For small transactions (under £10 million deal size) – liability may be capped at the deal size but there may be no proportionality provision (leaving the common law to determine the respective liabilities of joint defendants to an action for damages).

- For mid-market transactions (£10 million to £55 million deal size) [11] – liability may be capped at £10 million plus one-third of the amount by which

10 See now the Competition Act 1998.
11 Note how since 1998 what is perceived to be a mid-market private equity transaction has changed materially. Now the mid-market is perceived by many commentators to extend up as far as £500 million.

the deal size exceeds £10 million (up to a maximum of £25 million), but again there may be no proportionality provision.

- For large transactions (above £55 million deal size) – liability will generally be capped at £25 million, but if there are unusually high or low risks involved (unrelated to the size of the transaction) this may be altered. A specific clause providing for proportionality may be negotiated in the context of the deal.

The MoU has no legal status. But, as it states on its face, 'Given that this Memorandum of Understanding has been mutually agreed, it is expected to gain widespread acceptance in the private equity market.' It goes on to say, however, that 'Specific engagement terms can still be contracted between the parties on each transaction.'

On the related question of ranking the rights of the various addressees to receive the proceeds of any successful claim, the MoU went on to state that as between the equity sponsors and the banks there should be no pre-agreed order of allocation between the parties. In practice, this suggestion is generally not followed and the equity investors are accustomed to giving priority – and turn-over rights – to the acquisition finance banks.[12]

Despite the material increase in average deal sizes, the MoU does still exist, although in practice it is not followed slavishly as perhaps it might have initially been intended by the accountants.

Reliance wording

11.10   To ensure that the relevant parties can rely on the accountants' due diligence report, appropriate reliance wording would ideally be included in the report itself.[13] In practice, however, the accountancy firm will have a separate standard form reliance letter dealing with who can rely on the report and on what basis. Those placing reliance on the report will be required to countersign this letter to acknowledge the terms, and, in particular, limitations, on which reliance is extended to them. Typically, the accountants will wish to limit reliance on the report only to the initial deal parties at closing of the acquisition. The acquisition finance MLAs, however, will need to ensue that banks and institutions that acquire the debt during primary syndication are included and can also rely on the due diligence. In practice, it is common for this to be agreed in principle at the time the accountants are engaged and for a separate form of reliance letter, watering down the scope of reliance, to be used to enable such parties – upon signature of the letter during the syndication process – to subsequently rely on the financial due diligence report.

The terms of the reliance letter should be reviewed to ensure that in signing it the acquisition financiers are not taking on any reciprocal obligations or liabilities to the accountants, and for general reasonableness. In practice, although intended to be in relatively standard form, the terms of such letters do change from time to time and also vary from accountancy firm to firm. Where possible these should be negotiated early – usually between lawyers for the acquisition financiers and the relevant accountants – to avoid last minute disagreements and misunderstandings about the extent of reliance and liability.

---

12 See para **10.27** in particular.
13 See paras **11.16** to **11.18**.

Financial assistance whitewash

11.11   Newco will also engage a firm of accountants in relation to the white-washing of financial assistance given by the target and its subsidiaries in connection with the acquisition.[14] This is necessary because one of the requisite components of the whitewash procedure is a report by the auditors of the relevant company giving the financial assistance, in the required form, which is annexed to the directors' statutory declaration to be filed at Companies House. Additionally, it is standard practice for the auditors to provide a further – non-statutory – letter in a market standard form to the acquisition financiers in support of the required statutory declaration and statutory report confirming that the company giving the financial assistance has net assets.[15]

A specific engagement letter will be agreed between newco and the accountants who will carry out the financial assistance whitewash exercise. It is common for the accountants to incorporate a liability cap into the letter – either of a separate, fixed amount[16] or possibly (but less common) by reference to the cap applicable to the due diligence. Although this is far from ideal from the acquisition financiers' perspective, on the basis that if the whitewash procedure is not correctly followed, the acquisition financiers' security package may be invalidated, caps are common in practice.

The group's auditors post-completion

11.12   The acquisition financiers will also be concerned with one further role for the accountants; namely as the group's auditors following completion of the buy-out.[17] In particular, they will wish to ensure not only that the annual audit is reliable, but also that the financial covenant compliance report prepared by the management team in relation to the year-end financial covenant test has been accurately produced and they will expect the auditors to report directly to them on this matter.[18] Separate engagement letters may be used for each of these matters.

---

14 In fact, the requirement for a private company to go through the financial assistance whitewash (as set out in Companies Act 1985, ss 151 et seq) is to be repealed on 1 October 2008, pursuant to changes brought about by the Companies Act 2006. However, at the time of writing, some commentators were suggesting that the acquisition finance banking market would replace the statutory requirements with their own similar (non-statutory) requirements. See also para **11.101**.

15 The reason for this is that it is a requirement of the Companies Act that a company giving financial assistance that is being whitewashed either has net assets which are not thereby reduced or, to the extent they are reduced, the financial assistance is given out of distributable profits. Unlike the statutory report, the Companies Act does not require the auditors to confirm the net asset position but the acquisition finance market by convention does. This non-statutory letter is consequently often referred to as the net asset letter since it confirms that the relevant company has net assets. It is also referred to as the FRAG 26 letter – with reference to Technical Release FRAG (Financial Reporting and Auditing Group) 26/94 issued by the Council of the Institute of Chartered Accountants in England & Wales in September 1994 on the considerations involved in reporting to banks in connection with the effect on net assets of giving financial assistance by a private company for the acquisition of its shares.

16 A cap of £1 million is common.

17 The deal sponsor will usually put the audit appointment out to tender but in practice the firm that carries out the due diligence and whitewash tasks will often be appointed.

18 See also paras **5.52** et seq and **Chapter 5** generally in relation to financial covenants and their testing.

Audit

11.13   The terms of engagement for an audit will be relatively standard and will include certain provisions limiting the scope of the auditors' liability for a negligent audit. It is extremely uncommon for the auditors to agree expressly to extend their liability beyond the company the subject of the audit to other parties who may wish to rely on their audit of the company's annual accounts, such as acquisition financiers. Whether or not, in practice, a third-party can in any event rely on an audit and have recourse to the auditor – under negligent mis-statement – has been the subject of considerable legal debate and judicial dicta and the established position is that absent a clear nexus a third-party will not be able to rely on an audit.

The position is likely to change significantly as of 6 April 2008, when Ch 6 of Pt 16 of the Companies Act 2006 is brought into force. These provisions will make it possible for the first time for a company's auditors to limit their liability to the company by agreement with the company; through a 'liability limitation agreement', provided that the agreement is fair and reasonable and subject to annual shareholder approval.[19]

Covenant compliance report

11.14   Ideally, the auditors would directly agree with the acquisition financiers to provide them with the annual financial covenant compliance report, on which they could rely without any limit on liability. In practice, however, the engagement of the auditors to produce this report is often only done after the deal has completed, without the involvement of the acquisition financiers (and consequently without any express right of reliance). In such circumstances, the acquisition financiers will rely on the contractual obligation on the borrower contained in the acquisition finance documents to procure the provision of a satisfactory form of report.

Other professional consultants

11.15   The due diligence process will cover a number of other key areas in addition to the core elements of legal and financial due diligence carried out by lawyers and accountants. Typically, these include any or all of environmental, insurance, market/commercial, pensions, real estate and tax. Some of these areas may be covered, to some extent, in the legal or financial due diligence reports rather than in a stand-alone report. If not, consultants in the relevant areas will be engaged to produce due diligence reports in the same manner as the lawyers and reporting accountants.

The terms of engagement of the consultants should be reviewed in the same manner as those for the reporting accountants. For instance, it is not uncommon with many of these reports for a monetary cap on liability to be imposed by the report provider. The relationship of the deal sponsor and acquisition financiers with the relevant consultants together with the specific circumstances relating to the scope of due diligence to be carried out by them in the context of the deal will dictate whether such a cap is acceptable or not.

19   At the time of writing, the Financial Reporting Council had announced that it was establishing a working group to produce guidance on liability limitation agreements.

It is important with, for instance, insurance, pensions, real estate and tax reports, that the terms of engagement do not relieve the consultants of any liability for their negligence, since the potential for material loss following negligence in these areas is quite high, whereas environmental liabilities, although significant, are more remote occurrences other than with particularly environmentally sensitive businesses.

Standard due diligence reliance language

11.16 In each case, in order to ensure that the acquisition financiers and other principal parties can rely on the reports, acceptable reliance wording should be included in each of the due diligence reports or in an accompanying reliance letter. The following is an example of standard form reliance language that may be used with all but the accountants' reports.[20]

Addressee wording

11.17 The professional reports should be addressed in the following (or an equivalent) manner:

'To: [*topco*]

To: [newco] (ie, the buyer)

To: [sponsor] in its capacity as manager of, adviser to, and/or sub adviser to various limited partnerships or other funds managed and/or advised by them or by other entities owned directly or indirectly by [sponsor].

To: [*bank*] and the other Secured Parties[21] as defined in a senior facilities agreement dated on or about the date of this [letter/report] and made between: (1) [*topco*] as Topco, (2) certain of its subsidiaries as Original Borrowers, (3) Topco and certain of its subsidiaries as Original Guarantors, (4) [*bank*] as Arranger, (5) the financial institutions listed therein as Original Lenders, (6) [*bank*] as Agent and (7) [*bank*] as Security Trustee (as amended, varied, novated or restated from time to time, the 'Senior Facilities Agreement') and, in each case, their respective successors, assigns and transferees

[22][To: [*bank*] and the other Secured Parties as defined in a mezzanine facility agreement dated on or about the date of this [letter/report] and made between: (1) [*topco*] as Topco, (2) certain of its subsidiaries as Original Borrowers, (3) Topco and certain of its subsidiaries as Original Guarantors, (4) [*bank*] as Arranger, (5) the financial institutions listed therein as Original Lenders, (6)

---

20 As previously mentioned, the forms of reliance that the accountants will accept have developed quite separately. See para **11.8**.
21 This term would pick up any lender from time to time, including those that become lenders in secondary syndication. In practice, however, it is quite common for advisers to limit reliance on their report to the original lenders and those that become lenders in primary syndication only.
22 Include if there is mezzanine debt. In principle, the language should extend to *any* provider of junior debt that is to rely on the reports. See **Chapter 10** generally in this regard.

[*bank*] as Agent and (7) [*bank*] as Security Trustee (as amended, varied, novated or restated from time to time, the 'Mezzanine Facility Agreement') and, in each case, their respective successors, assigns and transferees]'

Confirmation of reliance

11.18　The reports or reliance letters should also include the following confirmations to the parties:

'This/the report is addressed to and shall be capable of being relied upon by [topco], [newco] and [sponsor] and [bank] in its various capacities under the Senior Facilities Agreement [and the Mezzanine Facility Agreement] and each other person which accedes to the terms of the Senior Facilities Agreement [and/or to the terms of the Mezzanine Facility Agreement] pursuant to the primary syndication process[23] and pursuant to such accession has a commitment under the terms of the Senior Facilities Agreement [or, as applicable, Mezzanine Facility Agreement].

We understand that you may wish to disclose our report to other financial institutions that are considering whether to accede to the terms of the Senior Facilities Agreement [or to the terms of the Mezzanine Facility Agreement] (each a 'Potential Syndicate Member'). We confirm that [bank] may provide a copy of this report for information purposes only to a Potential Syndicate Member subject to the provision by it of a confidentiality undertaking.'

Tax structuring advice

11.19　In addition to the appointment of advisers to document the transaction and to carry out due diligence, one of the most important professional adviser appointments, certainly in multi-jurisdictional buy-outs but also in many UK buy-outs, will be to commission tax structuring advice. Usually the advice is provided by the same firm of accountants that is engaged to carry out the financial due diligence exercise. Less often, a firm of lawyers may provide the advice.

Ultimately, in any transaction, one of the most important aspects of the due diligence process is verification (as far as possible) of the assumptions underlying the base case model. This should include the assumed tax rate. In a domestic UK buy-out, the financial due diligence should, in particular, specify the extent to which interest on the equity investor debt is deductible for tax purposes. But the due diligence aspect is only part of the overall tax review. In addition, the tax advisers may be tasked with providing prescriptive advice on how best to structure the transaction and its financing in order to optimise the groups's tax position following completion. This is where the tax structuring advice extends beyond the due diligence exercise. Given its importance, tax structuring is considered in further detail in a separate section below.

As with all other appointments, the acquisition financiers and deal sponsor should ensure that the terms of engagement set out in detail the scope of the advice required.

23　The most common view is that only those lenders that come into the syndicate as part of the primary syndication process should be able to rely on the reports. See also fn **21**.

Corporate finance advice

11.20 A sponsor can obtain corporate finance advice in respect of a number of potential areas. It can include sector specific advice that is fed into the due diligence exercise (although not usually through a dedicated report on which the parties will rely), financial modelling and valuation advice, debt advisory services (considered briefly below) and general transaction management. In private buy-outs 'buy-side' corporate finance mandates are awarded on a deal and sponsor-specific basis. Meaning that if the sponsor feels that it does not have sufficient internal resource to analyse and execute a specific transaction it will utilize an investment bank or corporate finance house to assist. This may happen because the sponsor is stretched for resource at the time or because the transaction is particularly complex or involves a sector which it is not familiar with. It may also be possible that the deal idea was brought to the sponsor by an investment bank or corporate finance house in the first place, in which case it would be usual for some form of mandate to follow from the introduction.[24] In practice, most private buy-outs are executed by the sponsor without it awarding a general corporate finance mandate. Specific debt advisory mandates, however, are quite often awarded by sponsors although again this tends to be sponsor and deal-specific. A debt advisory mandate essentially involves the appointment of corporate finance advisers to run the process of selecting the acquisition finance arranger and underwriters. The idea is that they will be able to leverage their knowledge of the debt markets to get the best available deal for the sponsor. They may also then assist the lawyers in the negotiation of the debt documentation and related matters.

With public-to-privates an investment bank or corporate finance house will inevitably be engaged by the sponsor, as 'financial adviser'. This is necessary given the regulatory nature of these deals and the need for the bidder to have a financial adviser to interface with the target and the Panel.[25]

When engaging an investment bank or corporate finance house the proposed terms will require a detailed review by the sponsor and its lawyers. Fees in particular will generally be very deal specific and in many cases they may be success based, meaning that the fees are only payable if the buy-out is successfully completed. There may also be debate around the sharing of any break fees payable by the seller if the deal is not successful. The acquisition financiers will not usually have any specific interest in the terms of engagement save that the fees payable are properly reflected in the base case model and sources and uses analysis for the deal.

TRANSACTION STRUCTURING

11.21 Once a commercial deal has been agreed between buyer and seller – and usually at this stage the buyer will have done at least initial due diligence – the

---

24 This should be contrasted with the very common situation where an investment bank or corporate finance house is executing a 'sell-side' mandate for a seller by introducing the opportunity to a number of potential buyers.

25 Public-to-privates are considered in **Chapter 12**.

parties will focus further on the structure of the transaction.[26] Essentially, this means establishing a corporate structure to effect the acquisition and then determining how the various elements of the financing package for the buy-out will be interposed in the corporate structure.

A key aspect of the structuring process will involve the establishing of one or more bankruptcy-remote special purpose vehicle companies (SPVs). Most buy-outs will involve at least two such SPVs and together they will form an SPV group, usually established one above the other in a vertical ownership structure. The SPV group is used both to effect the acquisition and to provide a structural framework for the various layers of finance.

Acquisition vehicle structure

11.22   Depending on the nature of the target business and the financial instruments comprising the funding structure, there may be as few as one or as many as six or more SPVs established to fund and effect the acquisition.

As far as the acquisition itself is concerned, most buy-outs will have a single SPV established in the same jurisdiction as the target that makes the acquisition. Where there is more than one direct target company and they are incorporated in different jurisdictions an SPV will often be established in each of these jurisdictions to make the acquisitions of the target companies located there. It would be usual in that situation to have each acquisition vehicle owned by a common holding company vehicle. Where assets are being acquired, in addition to or instead of shares, further consideration will be required of the necessary acquiring SPV structure. In a domestic UK buy-out a single SPV usually suffices to acquire all of the target assets and business.[27]

Funding vehicle structure

11.23   Whereas only one SPV is typically required to effect the acquisition, the funding structure will normally demand that there be at least two and often several more.

Single SPV vs double SPV structure

11.24   Most acquisition financiers and deal sponsors will automatically assume that there will be at least one additional funding vehicle in addition to the acquisition vehicle. That second SPV will act as the holding company for the acquisition vehicle and, in addition, will have some of the funding invested in it. Strictly speaking, where there is no requirement for structural subordination

---

26 In practice, even before a basic deal is agreed, the parties and their advisors will most likely have spent some time considering a likely structure for the deal. In an auctioned deal, in particular, much of the structuring work may have been done by the time the winning mandate is awarded.

27 In practice, however, the acquisition financiers will almost certainly insist on at least a double SPV structure for the reasons mentioned in the following paragraphs, but only one SPV is actually *required* to fund and effect the acquisition.

within the funding structure and the acquisition is of shares rather than assets, the SPV established to make the acquisition can also be the sole investment vehicle for the purposes of the funding structure. This single SPV structure was for a number of years in the 1990s the standard model for a UK buy-out and it is still used in some of the more simple buy-outs. However, that structure has largely been superseded by a double SPV structure as the basic model for a UK buy-out. In the double SPV structure the SPV that makes the acquisition is 100% owned by a further SPV, often called 'topco' or the 'parent'. Topco is the vehicle into which the equity and quasi-equity is invested and the acquisition vehicle, newco, borrows the acquisition finance. Since newco needs the equity and quasi-equity funding to complete the acquisition, the proceeds of those investments are down-streamed by topco into newco, usually by way of an intercompany loan but possibly by a subscription for share capital or a combination of both.[28]

The purpose of having a double SPV structure is essentially two-fold. First, even though this is not strictly required in the United Kingdom, given the robustness of contractual subordination arrangements under English law, the acquisition financiers will take some comfort from having all of the private equity investments made in topco and the acquisition finance lent to newco, because of the structural subordination of the private equity that this creates. Secondly, such a structure will allow the acquisition financiers to take security over the shares in newco – without requiring direct recourse to the equity investors – and so enabling them to sell the shares in newco upon enforcement in a default scenario. The ability to sell newco (and with it the target), rather than just the target (by enforcing share security granted by newco over the shares in the target), has a number of potential advantages for the secured acquisition financiers. First, any available tax losses that newco has can be sold with the target business. In addition, newco's rights under the acquisition documentation can be transferred as part of the sale if newco is sold as part of the enforcement process.[29] This may be legally and practically less problematic than taking and enforcing security directly over those rights. Finally, future group reorganisations, including in anticipation of a flotation or sale of the group at exit, may be facilitated with a double SPV structure already in place.

Further SPVs

11.25   Certain transactions, particularly in upper mid-market and larger deals, will require further SPVs to reflect the funding structure in a manner acceptable to the acquisition financiers. The principal reason for this is to create structural subordination between the senior debt, certain forms of junior debt and the equity and quasi-equity packages.

---

28 At the time of writing UK legislation did not require that the capital structure of a company have a minimum amount of share capital (other than the share capital required for it to be properly incorporated under the Companies Act 1985 as superseded by the Companies Act 2006) but in some jurisdictions thin capitalisation regulations may dictate that each of the SPVs would need to have a minimum amount of share capital, often as a proportion of its total capital base (including long term loan capital).

29 Newco's rights under the acquisition documents will include potential warranty and indemnity claims against the seller.

The 'group'

11.26   At the top of the SPV structure a single holding company vehicle – topco – will be established as the parent company of the entire group. It will act as the holding company for the group for accounting purposes, so that all financial information required by the investors and financiers to measure the ongoing financial performance of the target business will be consolidated in the accounts of this company. Typically, this company also acts as the key management vehicle for the entire group. It will also be the entity into which the true equity is invested and which will issue any warrants to the financiers as required.

Topco and all of its subsidiaries, which will include each other SPV and each member of the target group, will comprise the 'group'. This term will have particular significance for the investors and financiers because the controls that they put in place to protect their investments will typically be binding on some or all of the members of the group.

Structural subordination requirements

11.27   Structural subordination is one of the key tools used by acquisition financiers to establish the agreed order of ranking between the various layers of finance used in a buy-out. Not all subordinated debt will be structurally subordinated, however, and in many cases contractual subordination alone will be adopted. The standard position for each of the different types of finance is considered in the following paragraphs.[30]

Senior debt

11.28   The senior debt will invariably be in the optimum position in a structure. It will be borrowed closest to the cash generative part of the group, the target business itself. Thus, the lowest SPV in the structure will generally be the senior debt borrower. Since that SPV will also be the acquisition vehicle the senior debt will be in the optimum place to fund the acquisition directly. Where there is more than one acquisition vehicle, each will borrow some debt to fund the respective acquisitions. In addition, working capital and capital expenditure facilities and that part of the core acquisition debt that is to be used to refinance existing target group debt may be borrowed directly by target group companies and there are usually advantages for the acquisition financiers in requiring this.[31] To enhance this structurally superior position for the senior lenders the senior debt will benefit from target group credit support in the form of guarantees and security from target group companies and structural guarantees and security from all other SPVs in the structure.

Second lien debt

11.29   By definition, second lien debt shares the same guarantee and security package as the core senior debt, albeit on a second ranking basis. Given this fact,

---

30 See also **Chapter 10** as regards the subordination of the various types of finance (other than senior debt) generally.

31 In particular, in public-to-private and in multi-jurisdictional deals. See **Chapters 12** and **13** respectively. See also para **11.36**.

a second lien loan will be afforded equal structural status with the core senior debt generally, with the same borrower as the core senior debt. There is no requirement for a further funding vehicle. Second lien notes on the other hand may be issued by a separate vehicle in the structure. They will, in any event, still benefit from the same structural status, however, and the senior debt borrower will provide a structural guarantee for the benefit of the noteholders to achieve this.

Mezzanine debt

11.30   The senior lenders will not usually require the mezzanine debt to be structurally subordinated to the senior debt. There are two reasons for this. First, contractual, rather than structural, subordination of mezzanine debt has been the standard approach in the UK market since the early 1990s. Secondly, as is the case with second lien debt, since UK mezzanine debt typically benefits from the same guarantee and security package as the senior debt – albeit on a second or third ranking basis – there can be no effective structural subordination in any event merely by having the mezzanine debt located in a different borrower. Structural superiority is already conceded by the senior lenders through the guarantee and security package.[32]

High yield debt

11.31   One of the most significant developments in the acquisition finance market during the 2000s centred around the structural status of high yield debt. For a long time, the senior banking market insisted on the structural subordination of high yield debt and the bonds would be issued by a structurally inferior SPV without the benefit of upstream credit support or even structural guarantees. However, since the early to mid-2000s, European high yield debt can expect to have structural parity with the senior debt. By convention the high yield issuer will still be an SPV one level or more removed from the senior debt borrower but it will take a structural guarantee of the high yield debt from the senior debt borrower in addition to guarantees from the same companies in the target group. Each of the high yield guarantees will then be contractually subordinated to the senior debt equivalents.

PIK note debt

11.32   The senior lenders and core junior creditors will almost certainly require any PIK note debt to be structurally subordinated to the acquisition finance provided by them. Given the legally robust nature of contractual subordination under English law this may not strictly be necessary in order to preserve their position higher up the order of ranking. However, isolating the core acquisition finance borrower from the PIK noteholders will provide a certain level of comfort in a default scenario. Naturally, in jurisdictions where the position with

---

32   In some multi-jurisdictional buy-outs there may still be some merit in effecting some level of structural subordination. See para **13.16** in particular.

contractual subordination is less clear, structural subordination will be more important. If the PIK note debt benefits from upstream credit support from the target group then contractual subordination will in any event be required, but even in that situation separating the issuer of the PIK note debt from the borrower of the senior and core junior debt will, optically at least, be of some comfort to the core acquisition finance providers. In addition, because the PIK note debt (private PIK, at least) will usually benefit from structural share security whether or not it gets target group guarantees and security – for the purposes of being able to step ahead of the equity investors in a default situation – it is preferable from the core acquisition financiers' perspective for that security to be taken at a level above the principal borrower. In doing so, the effect of enforcing that security would not include taking direct ownership of the principal borrower, a right that the senior lenders would reserve for themselves.

To accommodate the structural subordination of PIK note debt means having a further funding vehicle as an intermediate holding company above the main borrower. This company is the PIK note issuer. The structural share security granted for the PIK note debt should come from topco over the shares in the PIK note issuer. See also **Chapters 9** and **10** as regards the structural subordination of public 'holdco' PIK.

Equity investor debt

11.33   The acquisition financiers will invariably prefer to have the subordinated loan capital provided by the equity investors structurally subordinated to the acquisition finance. A further SPV, between topco and the acquisition finance borrowers/issuers will be used. In the more complex transactions, there may be more than one class of equity investor loan capital and the sponsor may structurally subordinate one class to another.

Seller notes

11.34   The structural status of seller notes is generally negotiated on a deal-by-deal basis. The acquisition financiers will usually insist on robust subordination of seller loan capital, at least in insolvency. Individual sellers, unlike junior debt providers, are not acquisition finance market participants and their behaviour in a default scenario is less predictable. Given also that sellers are often loath to sign up to extensive intercreditor agreements, the core acquisition financiers may use structural subordination as a further device to protect their borrower(s) from the potential claims of the seller.

This will be even more important in jurisdictions where contractual subordination provisions have not been tried and successfully tested in the courts. Where structural subordination *is* required, the seller note may be invested into one of the existing vehicles, perhaps alongside the equity investor debt or in an entirely new vehicle. Much depends on how sensitive the seller is to its structural status. Of course, where there are to be target group guarantees and security for the seller note, the debate will be largely moot. Further, the seller may insist on structural parity with the core acquisition finance as a condition of doing the deal.

Institutional and management equity

11.35 The SPV that issues the ordinary share capital comprising the true equity will be the top SPV in the structure.[33] Topco may or may not also be the issuer of the equity investor debt so a further vehicle may be required.

In some multi-jurisdictional buy-outs a further investment vehicle – above topco – is used by the institutional equity investors in order to enhance the status of their equity investments for tax purposes, particularly with regard to exit. In that case, that investment vehicle effectively acts as *the* institutional equity investor for structuring purposes and does not form part of the SPV group per se.[34]

Target group structures

11.36 Deal sponsors generally have little or no choice as to the target group structure at the time of making the acquisition. Most sellers are unwilling to undertake a target group reorganisation for the benefit of the buyer, not least because of the risk that the reorganisation occurs and then the acquisition does not happen for whatever reason. This is not invariably the case, however, and if the buyer can demonstrate to the seller that some of the benefit of the reorganisation – perhaps a reduction in tax arising as a result of the acquisition – can be passed on to the seller, particularly in respect of purchase price and costs then the seller may be willing to assist.

This is not limited to corporate restructurings and reorganisations. Where the target business has material existing borrowings the parties can chose to deal with these in either of two ways. Either the seller pays off the borrowings at the point of sale – using the sale proceeds – and thus sells the target business free of debt at a certain price, or it sells the target business with the borrowings in place for a commensurately reduced purchase price. Each solution has the same economic effect for both buyer and seller, but the buyer, and in particular its financiers, will often obtain substantial benefits from the latter route by acquiring the target business with its existing debt in place.

The reason for this is that, rather than advancing all of the acquisition finance to newco to effect the acquisition at the higher headline price, some of the debt can be borrowed directly by those target group companies that have the existing debt to repay that debt. By having some of the acquisition finance borrowed by the target group itself a number of benefits will often accrue to the financiers. Essentially, this is a form of 'debt push-down' that is often particularly desirable in multi-jurisdictional transactions but is also of significant benefit in pure UK public-to-privates.

The refinancing of target group debt in this manner will be equally advantageous where the existing target group debt comprises external bank borrowings

---

33 Hence, it is often called 'topco' or the 'parent'

34 Luxembourg incorporated companies (luxcos) are often used in European multi-jurisdictional buy-outs for such purposes.

or where the debt comprises intercompany balances owing by members of the target group to another part of the seller group.

Sometimes a target group reorganisation at or before completion of the acquisition will be an essential element of the acquisition. This may be true where the target business does not comprise one or more discrete corporate entities within the seller business or group so that a seller hive-down or hive-up is required.[35] Similarly, where the target company has subsidiaries that are not intended to be part of the sale, those companies will need to be transferred out of the target group prior to the sale.

Particular issues arise with acquisitions of a division of a seller business group where certain centralised functions such as sales and marketing, IT, accounting, human resources and management operations are carried out by seller group companies for the benefit of the entire group. If the seller has an ongoing need for such centralised services, and is to retain the companies that perform them, then the buyer will need to make alternative arrangements for the short and long term. What often happens is that the seller and buyer enter into a transitional services agreement pursuant to which the seller retains the relevant functions and subcontracts with the buyer to perform the services for a period until the buyer has established its own equivalent functions.

Tax structuring

Tax structuring advice

11.37   One of the most important aspects of the general structuring process of a buy-out will be the obtaining of advice on the optimum tax structure for the group post-completion. To this end the deal sponsor will engage a firm of accountants and/or lawyers to provide the advice and ultimately a tax structuring report or memorandum on which all of the principal parties will rely.

Deductibility of interest costs

11.38   As far as the target business is concerned one of the greatest single expenses it will face during the life of a buy-out will be the cost of servicing the acquisition finance debt and, in particular, meeting the interest payments due on the senior and junior debt packages. The extent to which such interest expense is deductible against the operating income of the target business for tax purposes is therefore of material significance to the target business and indirectly its financial backers. In fact, the base case model upon which the agreed funding structure is predicated will assume a certain level of taxation. If this assumption is not met in practice the viability of the base case model, and thus the funding structure itself, may be materially compromised. Since the principal aim of the tax structuring exercise will be to optimise the overall tax cost to the group, the deal sponsor will wish to have as much of the interest cost as possible deducted against the group's operating profits.

---

35   See para **2.11** and **Chapter 2** generally.

Domestic UK buy-outs

11.39   Ensuring that the interest costs are deductible from group operating profits will usually be a much more straightforward task with a pure domestic UK buy-out than with a multi-jurisdictional buy-out. The availability of group relief across a single consolidated UK group will generally allow for the deduction of the interest costs incurred by the borrower – including an SPV in the group that has no profits of its own – against target group operating profits. That is not to say, however, that interest on all of the interest bearing instruments in the funding structure will necessarily be tax deductible. The Inland Revenue rules as to deductibility of interest on shareholder loans, other equity investor debt and certain junior debt instruments must be carefully analysed and applied to any particular scenario to determine if a deduction will be allowed. In a pure UK buy-out this analysis will be one of the key areas for the tax advisers to focus on.

The tax advisers' advice as to what is or is not tax deductible should be reflected in the base case model. Or, more specifically, the base case model should not assume that interest accruing on all of the debt instruments – and equity investor debt in particular – is tax deductible unless the tax advisers provide sufficient reliable advice to such effect in their tax report.

Multi-jurisdictional buy-outs

11.40   With a multi-jurisdictional buy-out the tax advisors will look closely at two aspects of the transaction structure. First, they will consider the corporate structure of the group following completion. Because there is unlikely to be a single consolidated tax group, the advisors will try to ascertain if sub-groups exist for tax consolidation purposes or whether, by having the group structured in a particular way, a tax benefit (eg, a deduction for finance costs) can be obtained in more than one jurisdiction.[36] In certain cases, the tax structuring advice will propose a group reorganisation to be undertaken in the target group. It may be that this can be done following completion or the tax rules may require it to be effected prior to completion. In the latter case, the co-operation of the seller will be required. This may not be forthcoming if it puts the seller to material time or financial expense.

The second aspect that the tax advisors will focus on involves analysing ways in which the acquisition finance can most efficiently be structured within the group to achieve the lowest overall level of tax for the group. Because the group will comprise companies in a number of jurisdictions, with different tax regimes, there is unlikely to be a single 'group' for tax purposes whereby interest costs and operating profits within that group can be consolidated, and netted off. The tax advisers will therefore consider ways to achieve as much deduction of interest costs as possible. They will also consider the impact, if any, of withholding taxes on cross-border payments, particularly of interest and whether a structuring solution is available.[36a]

---

36 So called 'double-dipping'.
36a See also para **13.15**.

Debt push downs

11.41 The most common approach to increasing the level of interest expense deduction will involve trying to get as much debt as possible borrowed by the operating companies in the target group. The process of doing this is often loosely described as a 'debt push down'. The term is generic, however, and is variously used to describe the simple step of having the acquisition financiers directly refinance existing target group debt, or more complicated procedures such as post-completion mergers, or the formation of consolidated tax groups, between acquiring vehicles and target operating companies and wholesale group reorganisations.

In proposing any solution that results in a debt push down the tax advisers will need the input of lawyers in the various jurisdictions to confirm that none of the steps proposed contravenes the law. Concerns about financial assistance laws, in particular, will inevitably need addressing since the effect of many debt push down solutions is often to achieve what in a broad sense many financial assistance regimes aim to prohibit, namely the saddling of acquisition debt onto acquired companies.

Acquisition financier concerns

11.42 The acquisition financiers will carefully shadow the structuring advice being proposed by the tax advisors for two principal reasons. First, they will independently be concerned that the proposals achieve the stated aim of tax deduction where stipulated without contravening any laws. Secondly, they will be sensitive to the impact of the proposals on their guarantee and security package, particularly in respect of the target group. In the first case, the level of comfort to be derived will be dependent on the extent to which the tax advisors are willing and able to stand behind their advice and confirm that their proposals will result in the tax efficiencies suggested. In particular, they should be required to confirm that the effective tax rate assumed in the base case model is correct. The extent to which they can or cannot confirm this is of key importance to the acquisition financiers.

On the second issue, the acquisition financiers' lawyers should advise on the impact of the proposed structure on the ability of the financiers to take guarantees and security from target group companies. The major concern in multi-jurisdictional transactions is that the structure that is most beneficial for the target group from a tax perspective might not allow for the best guarantee and security package for the acquisition financiers. For instance, having large portions of the debt located in jurisdictions where there are significant amounts of target group assets and favourable regimes for granting security may provide the best security package for the lenders but may not result in as many tax savings as an alternative structure. On the other hand locating much of the debt in countries with the highest tax rates may produce a more tax efficient structure but, perhaps because of an unfavourable legal regime for upstream guarantees and security, may leave the acquisition financiers with an insufficient guarantee or security package.

That all said, in reality, where the steps taken to achieve tax deductibility of interest include pushing debt directly into the target group, the availability of target group credit support will often be increased. Finding a balance that achieves the acquisition financiers' aim of a strong guarantee and security package and the deal sponsor's aim of reducing the tax burden as much as possible should be feasible.

As a practical matter, the evolving legal and taxation regimes across Europe mean that whilst in most transactions tried and tested structures can be used in deal after deal, the lawyers and accountants will need to be involved in the structuring process for each transaction to ensure that the structure favoured by the principals is viable in practice.

In addition to advice in relation to tax deductibility of interest, the firm that is providing the tax advice will also be asked to confirm that cash that is generated in the operating companies can be upstreamed to the acquisition finance borrowers, including those in the SPV group, both lawfully and without any adverse tax consequences. This will involve an analysis of the applicable legal, accounting and tax regimes throughout the group. Legal, because the upstreaming of cash from a target company to an acquiring company will frequently breach financial assistance or corporate benefit laws if structured as a loan. Dividends may be the only lawful method. Accounting, because even though an operating company may be cash generative, it may not necessarily have an equivalent amount of profit available for distribution. Consequently, a dividend of the full amount of available cash may not lawfully be possible. Finally, tax, because a withholding tax may be levied on certain payments such as interest or dividends paid by a company in one tax jurisdiction to a company in another. Where operating cashflow cannot for any reason be upstreamed to a borrower, it is often designated as 'trapped'. One of the transaction structuring aims will inevitably be to avoid having much if any trapped cash in the target group.

Complete transaction structures

11.43   At completion of the acquisition the SPV group and the target group form a complete corporate structure for the transaction. It is common to describe transaction structures in diagrammatic form indicating not only the individual companies but also the various investments comprising the funding structure and, commonly, the guarantee and security package to be provided to the financiers.

Example transaction structures

11.44   Set out below are some transaction structures that are commonly used in UK buy-outs.

Simple MBO

11.45

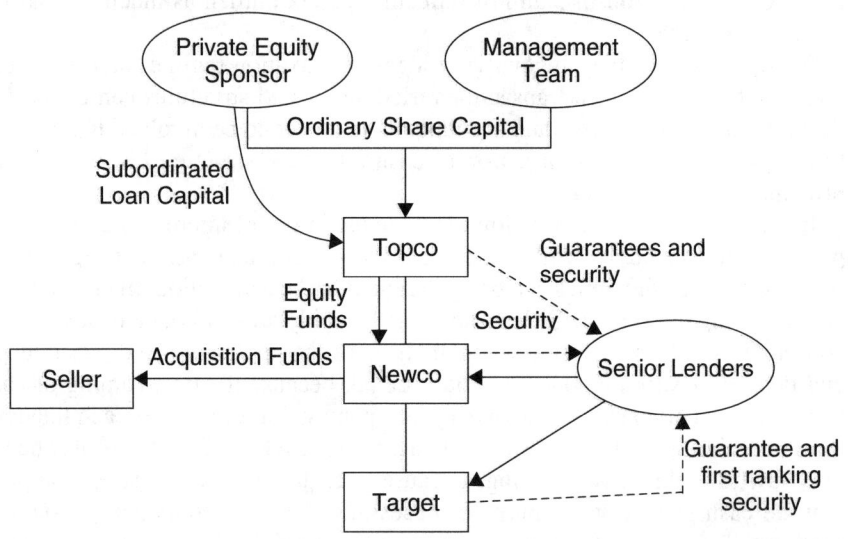

Mid-market LBO

11.46

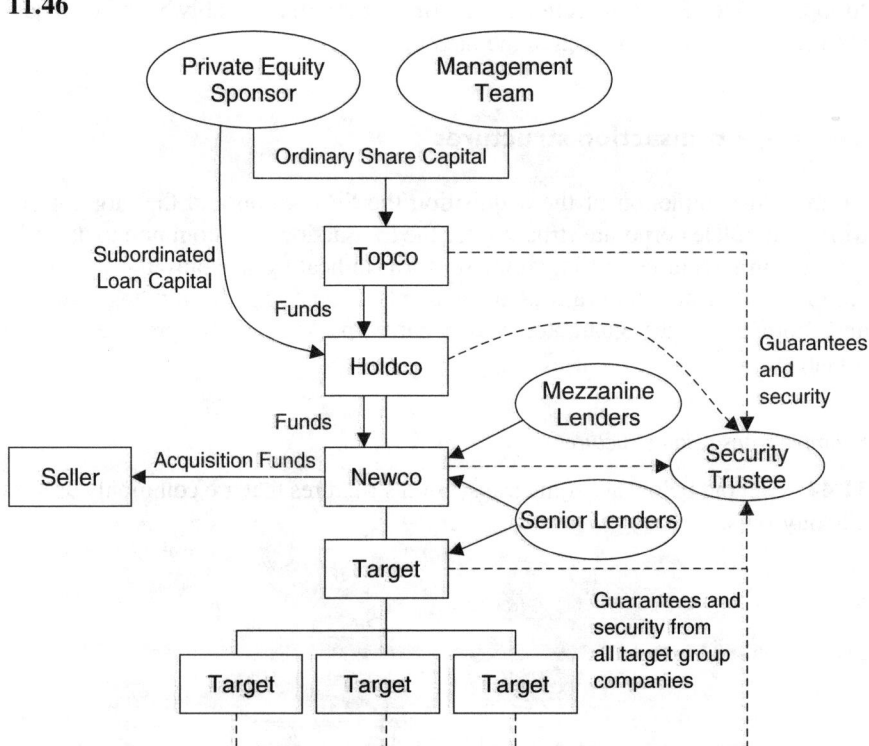

Large cap LBO

11.47

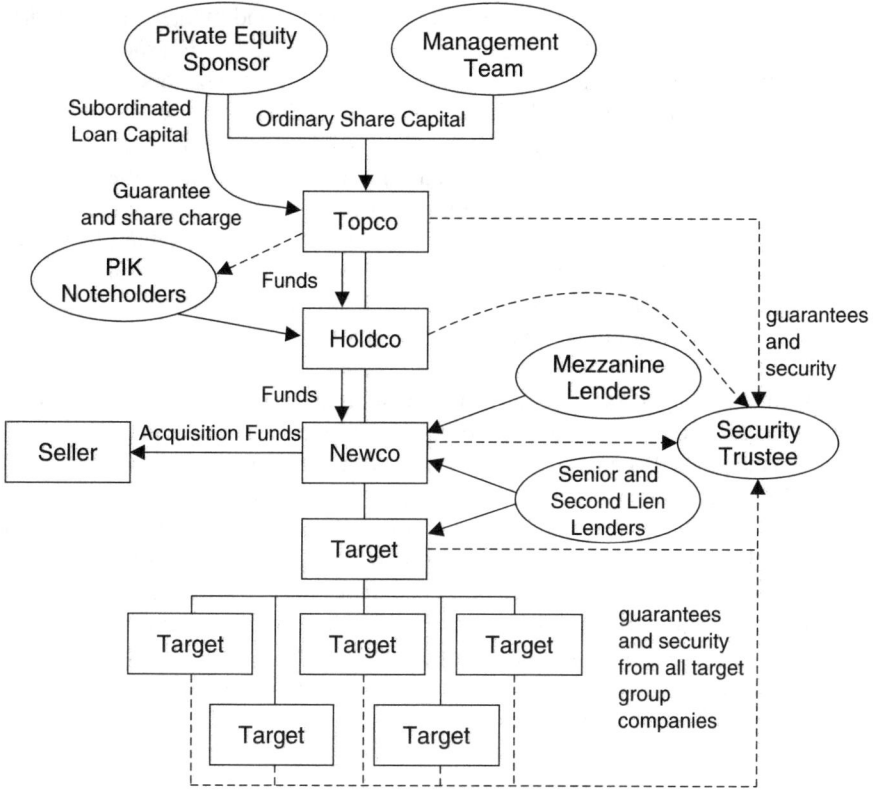

DUE DILIGENCE PROCESS

11.48   The aim of this section is to consider the broad parameters of the due diligence phase of deal execution. It is beyond the scope of this book to cover in great detail the scope of the due diligence exercise that will be undertaken in a buy-out as much of it will involve the application of specialist know-how and skills by dedicated professional advisers. The following paragraphs outline the areas of investigation undertaken by these advisers, in addition to the due diligence performed by the principal parties themselves. It also looks at the various ways that the parties can deal with issues of concern that are thrown up by the due diligence exercise.

The areas covered by due diligence

11.49   The due diligence process usually involves a comprehensive analysis of a number of key aspects of the target business. Areas covered include all aspects of the financial, accounting and tax history and current status of the business, the legal status of each member of the target group and all legal aspects of its business, including for example title to all real estate and intellectual property used in the business, the position of the business within its industry and markets, the key drivers of the industry and markets and any forecast changes to any aspect of them, whether the business plan is feasible in the light of all of these factors and whether the identified management team will be capable of delivering the key elements of the business plan. In addition, specific attention will be paid to a number of potentially significant areas of concern such as the environmental status of the business, its insurance cover, the status of its employee pension provisions, the condition of any real estate owned or used by the business and possibly the value of the real estate. Where the business includes technical processes or operations or uses mechanical or scientific equipment, a technical audit of the working condition and useful life of such equipment and the ability of such processes and equipment to deliver the level of performance set out in the business plan may be carried out.

Few financial sponsors retain sufficient internal expertise in many of these areas to be able to carry out the due diligence in-house. In any event, the acquisition financiers will generally insist that third-party advisers are appointed in many of the key areas so that both newco and the acquisition financiers receive the benefit of independent analysis in those areas and, ultimately, the right to seek some level of recourse against a third-party if a problem subsequently arises that was not uncovered by the due diligence undertaken.[37] That is not to say that the principal parties will completely hand over responsibility for due diligence to third-party advisers, however, and in addition to the reports the sponsor and acquisition financiers will carry out a certain amount of due diligence directly themselves. This is considered first.

Due diligence by the principal parties

11.50   As indicated above the sponsor and acquisition financiers will not rely solely on due diligence reports commissioned from third-party advisers to complete the due diligence exercise. There is much that they will do directly themselves. For starters, long before they commission any due diligence reports to be produced they will examine in some detail all available information that they have on the target business. Often this will have been packaged into an information memorandum either by the seller itself or by its financial advisers. If there is no formal information memorandum, the sponsor will only start looking at a potential buy-out target with any real commitment once it has received basic financial information on the business. A detailed review of this information will be at the heart of its initial assessment of the opportunity and decision to proceed further (or not). Similarly, the acquisition financiers will take whatever information they are provided with by the sponsor and make an initial assessment of their appetite for the transaction based largely on this information. Provided that they

37   In practice, the level of recourse will be quite limited in many cases as it is now customary for professional advisers to limit the extent to which they can be sued for producing a flawed due diligence report, often by reference to a monetary cap that might be relatively low in the scheme of things.

remain interested in pursuing the opportunity following their initial analysis of the financial information, both sets of parties will wish to take a more detailed look at the target business, including meeting with its management. This generally means visiting the headquarters and each of the other main locations where the business operates from. The following paragraphs consider these aspects of the due diligence process in a little more detail.

Financial analysis

11.51 The seller's information memorandum will usually be the chief source of information on the target business that the parties receive before the formal due diligence process is commenced and external advisers appointed. At its core it should include a summary of the historic financial performance of the target business.[38] Usually this will mean inclusion of the main data from the financial statements for the last three or more complete financial years. The actual accounts for those years, all of which (possibly with the exception of the most recent) should have been audited, will also be provided at some point and the reporting accountants will analyse these as per the scope of their due diligence engagement. In addition to the annual audited accounts, the information provided should also include the highlights of the current year to date financial position, as extracted from the monthly management accounts.

The historic and year to date financial information provided will be carefully analysed by the parties to obtain as clear as possible an insight into the finances of the business, including their assessment of any trends in performance, any areas of weakness, the scope for improvement and so on. This level of analysis will also be vital to their understanding of the more detailed financial due diligence report when it is produced. The financial statements for the most recent full financial year will be particularly important as these numbers are often used by the sponsor to value the business and by the acquisition financiers to determine the amount of debt, in broad terms, they are willing to make available.

In addition to historic and current financial information, the prospective investors will need trading projections for the business. Typically, these are provided by the senior management of the target business. Where the management team are closely involved in the buy-out they will prepare a business plan incorporating the projections. A business plan might also be prepared by external managers in preparation for a management buy-in (an MBI). However, the most important projections will be those provided by the existing management or perhaps the seller itself. As with the historic financial information, the sponsor and acquisition financiers will review the projections themselves in detail. Moreover, it is these projections that, as a starting point at least, will be used as the basic trading assumptions in the financial models used by the parties during the structuring process. The prospective investors will therefore be extremely keen to establish the viability of such projections. The experience of the individual professionals and industry or sector specialists employed by the sponsor and acqui-

---

38 In a true MBO, where there may not be a seller information memorandum, this information may be included in the management team's business plan or they may simply provide copies of the historic financial statements.

sition financiers will be vital in analysing the projections prior to engaging third-party specialists. On a detailed analysis they may not be as bullish as the management team that prepared the projections, for instance, and as a result each of the management team, the sponsor and the acquisition financiers will often end up using a slightly different financial model for their own analytical purposes.[39] When accountants are subsequently appointed to carry out financial due diligence the parties will generally wish to see some commentary from them on the achievability of the projections in the financial model.

The historic, current and forward looking performance of the target business taken from the financial information provided to the sponsor and the acquisition financiers will be at the core of the submissions by the parties to their respective investment and credit committees. The investment and credit approval processes of many firms and banks will require at least the initial submissions to occur before external advisers are appointed and the formal due diligence process that follows will to some extent be 'confirmatory' in nature. The initial analysis by the parties themselves will therefore be of fundamental importance.

Site visits

11.52   As part of the initial sale process, prospective buyers and financiers will generally be invited by the seller to visit the principal manufacturing or operating sites of the target business, including the headquarters. Such trips are important for two reasons. First, this is probably the initial opportunity that the parties will get to meet the management of the target. In the case of a buy-out where the incumbent management of the target business are to either take part in the buy-out or at least remain as managers after completion of the buy-out, there will usually be an opportunity to discuss the target business with the management in some detail. In most buy-outs, the management of the business will be fundamental to the success of the investment and the sponsor and acquisition financiers will be keen to assess their capabilities early on. This may be the first opportunity to begin that process of assessment. Moreover, it is the incumbent management that will have the most valuable insights into the financial history, current trading and potential going forward for the business, and the parties will use the opportunity to ask detailed questions to further enhance their own initial assessment and understanding of the business. In the case of an MBI the new management team should, where possible,[40] accompany the parties on their site visits and they will have important insights of their own into the target business that the principal parties will be keen to share.

In addition to meeting management, the parties will use such visits to assess at first hand how the target business operates but also to carry out some basic due diligence into the efficiency and performance of the business. Much depends on the

---

39   The various models employed by the parties may be referred to as the 'management team case', the 'sponsor's case' and the 'bank case'. The bank's model will often be more conservative that the other parties' reflecting its lower appetite for risk. Ultimately, one 'base case' will be agreed as the basis on which performance of the business is measured after completion of the deal, including for the purposes of the debt financiers' financial covenants (see **Chapter 5**).

40   This may be an extremely sensitive issue if there is de facto competition between the incumbent and proposed new management teams.

experience of the individuals attending the site visits but, potentially, comparisons may be made with other businesses visited in respect of previous transactions and so on. Where the business involves specialist mechanical or scientific processes the parties themselves may not be able to assess in any real depth the relative quality of the processes but in those cases it would be common for the sponsor to appoint technical advisers as part of the formal due diligence process.

One key area, which the sponsor and acquisition financiers will be keen to explore, is the extent to which the target business is reliant on the seller entity, especially where the seller is a larger group divesting itself of a division. For instance, to what extent is the target reliant on the seller for finance, accounting, marketing, IT, human resources, research and development or technical support? In any situation where the acquisition is not of the entire undertaking of a seller, one of the material issues for the buyer and its financiers will be replacement of any centralised functions such as those mentioned above that are not to be part of the sale. There may be both a personnel requirement and a capital requirement. What may be required is a transitional services arrangement whereby the seller agrees to continue to provide many of these functions for a transitional period of, say, six or twelve months after completion, during which time the purchase will establish its own replacement functions. The cost of taking over the relevant functions will be a major concern which will need to have been accurately factored into the business plan and financial model. In addition, the parties will need to obtain significant detail about any trading or similar relationships between those parts of the business that are being sold and those that are to be retained. They will be acutely concerned that the real value of the business is being captured in the part that is to be acquired. For example, it may not be obvious at first sight which part of the business is the real profit generator or the extent to which the different parts share profits. A red flag will be raised where the separate parts of the business do not have individual audited accounts, making it more difficult to make an accurate assessment of these concerns. Similarly, the parties will need to understand the terms which have governed the relationship between the different parts of the business, whether they were truly on arm's length terms or not. This would be particularly acute in the rare circumstances where a customer or supplier relationship is to remain with the seller entity after the acquisition.

Assessment of the management team

11.53 In all but the largest buy-outs, one of if not *the* most important factor in the success of the investment will be the quality and abilities of the management team. With this in mind, the prospective investors and financiers will wish to assess their capabilities from the outset of the process. They will do this in a number of ways, including by reputation, references and curricula vitae, by track record, in particular with respect to the recent performance of the business and ultimately on the basis of numerous personal meetings.

The sponsor, in particular, will carry out significant due diligence into the management team. The acquisition financiers will be less close to the management but equally concerned that they are capable of delivering the business plan. As indicated above, of key relevance will be the previous experience which individuals have in the relevant industry sector, both with the target business itself and other businesses. The sponsor will generally take detailed references on the management teams which they back. In addition to professional references, the sponsor will usually commission background checks into the credit history, criminal records and professional conduct records of the management team and any other reputational issues that may be uncovered. In many jurisdictions there are mandatory 'know-your-customer' regulations to be adhered to. These will generally extend to the equity investments to be made by the management team, for anti-money laundering and related purposes. It is not uncommon for the sponsor to require medical references too. This may be because key-man insurance cover is to be taken out for the most important members of the management team, which, certainly in true MBOs, will often be a requirement imposed by the acquisition financiers.

The acquisition financiers will seek to benefit from the management due diligence initiated by the sponsor by obtaining copies of background checks, references, curricula vitae and so on in addition to having their own meetings with the management. Ultimately, a detailed commentary on the individual members of the management team will be included in the submissions to the relevant investment or credit committees of the sponsor and acquisition financiers.

Third-party due diligence

11.54   At a certain point in the process the sponsor will be in a position to commission third-party due diligence. This is an important stage because it means that the sponsor will begin incurring significant costs. With that in mind sponsors will be reluctant to move to this stage without some certainty that a deal can be done with the seller. In deed a seller is unlikely to enable the due diligence process to begin unless it believes that a deal can be done with the sponsor.[41] Ideally this means signing up to heads of terms[42] incorporating a period of exclusivity for the sponsor to conduct its due diligence and submit a formal binding offer for the business. Whilst this may be possible in deals that are being privately negotiated between sponsor and seller,[43] in competitive sale processes exclusivity may only be awarded – if at all – quite late in the process after at least one round of bidding and at a point at which the seller will expect much of the due diligence to have been carried out. The approach to third-party due diligence will thus be different for proprietary deals and for auctioned deals.

As indicated, with proprietary deals the sponsor will commission the third-party due diligence once it has decided that a deal is in principle doable with the seller, usually upon signing of heads of terms with the seller and ideally with a period of exclusivity to complete its due diligence without concern that another competing buyer will step in. At this point the sponsor will also have completed some level of internal approval process, whether formal investment committee approval or an informal understanding to move to the next stage.

41 Not least for confidentiality purposes, since opening up the business to a full third party due diligence exercise will amount to a 'warts and all' disclosure of the inner workings of the business.

42 This might be in the form of a memorandum of understanding or letter of intent signed by sponsor and seller.

43 Such deals are sometimes described as 'proprietary deals'.

With auctioned deals the sponsor is also likely to have completed some internal approval process during the bidding stages but it will be reluctant to commission full due diligence until it has more visibility on the chances of success in the process. This is one of the main reasons why, in practice, sellers commission their own third-party due diligence to be carried out in advance of the auction process. Prospective sponsors will be able to take some level of comfort from the contents of the due diligence reports provided by the seller in progressing through the various stages of the process without necessarily having their own advisers engaged. At a certain point in the process it is likely that the competing sponsors will be required to submit a binding offer that is not conditional upon any further due diligence.[44] This will force the sponsors either to accept the seller's due diligence or to commission their own in advance of the final binding offer being submitted. Reliance on seller due diligence may not be an acceptable alternative in certain cases either because the scope is not sufficient to deal with all the concerns that the sponsor has or because the providers of the reports are unwilling to extend formal reliance on the reports to the prospective buyer and its financiers.[45] In those cases confirmatory due diligence will be required to be carried out by the sponsor's own advisers.

The following sections consider the common types of due diligence that can be commissioned from third-party advisers as well as the procedure that the parties will follow to complete the exercise.

Due diligence reports

11.55 This section briefly considers those aspects of a target business that are most commonly the subject of third-party due diligence reports. In some cases (insurance, pensions and real estate, in particular), the accountants' report or legal report may cover the relevant area and a separate report may not be commissioned.

Accountants' report

11.56 This is generally the most important report. It is intended to verify the financial status and health of the target business. More particularly it is used to identify unusual or non-recurring income and expenditure items in order to verify the reliability of the underlying earnings and cash flow of the business as represented in the base case model. It may separately cover pensions and tax or there may be separate reports on these items. It may also look at the target's IT systems and, in particular, any financial reporting and management information systems. It should also address the viability of the projections in the business plan and base case model from a financial perspective, although such an analysis may be heavily caveated.

Environmental report

11.57 Depending on the nature of the target business and the properties it owns or occupies, environmental consultants may be instructed to undertake an

---

44 Alternatively, the seller may select a winning bidder and then award a period of exclusivity to complete confirmatory due diligence in parallel with the legal documentation phase.
45 See also para **11.71**.

environmental audit of real estate owned or occupied by the target. Usually it is a simple desktop survey of the historic and current use of the relevant sites and the likely environmental risks if any. This is often called a Phase I survey. A Phase II survey, which is rare unless there are known material concerns, would involve the taking of soil samples and scientific analysis.

Insurance report

11.58   There may be a full report by an independent broker of the insurance that is in place, its adequacy for the target business and what further cover might be advisable and at what cost. Alternatively, and more likely in practice, there will be a letter from the target's insurance broker confirming the extent of the insurance policies in place and (ideally) stating that the target group is insured in accordance with a prudent policy for businesses of that type.

Legal report

11.59   There will invariably be a legal due diligence report. Unless there are deal specific reasons that reduce the scope, the legal due diligence report should normally cover the following areas:

- corporate structure and full details of all companies in the group (including all company books);
- financial liabilities including all borrowings, guarantees, finance leases and banking facilities;
- security granted;
- business arrangements including supply and sales contracts;
- other material contracts (such as acquisition and disposal agreements);
- employees and employment matters;
- pensions and benefit plans;
- environmental, planning and health and safety at work;
- plant and machinery owned or used;
- real estate owned or used (although there may be separate reports on title and/or valuation reports);
- intellectual property owned or used;
- insurance policies;
- historic and current litigation and other disputes;
- regulatory approvals required and status;
- possibly, taxation; and
- miscellaneous items.

The legal report may be given on a full analysis basis – where all documents in the data room (together with the results of public searches) are reviewed and reported on – or on a 'by exception' basis, where the documents are all reviewed but the report only details material matters of concern or specific interest.

Market report

11.60 Management or market consultants will often be commissioned to comment on the commercial environment within which the target business operates. In particular, it may detail the target's actual and potential competitors and the target's market share. The market report should also cover trends in the relevant business sectors and, ideally, specifically comment on the commercial and market-orientated assumptions underlying the business plan and confirm whether they are achievable. Some private equity houses retain a certain amount of sector expertise in-house and in certain cases they may choose not to commission a third-party report on a sector that they know well or can fully diligence themselves. That said, the acquisition financiers may still insist on a third party report for syndication purposes.

Pensions report

11.61 There may be a separate dedicated pensions or actuarial report or alternatively pensions issues may be covered in the accountants' and legal reports. The former approach is more likely where the target group sponsors a defined benefit scheme[46] for its employees, as material issues of concern for the buyer and its financiers will often arise where that is the case. In fact, during the 2000s pensions generally, and defined benefit schemes in particular, have become a major area of inquiry and concern for prospective buyers and their financiers. This is mostly because of the increased powers and activism of pension scheme trustees that have resulted from the Pensions Act 2004 and related regulation and guidance from the Pensions Regulator.[47] It is also a result of the fact that so many defined benefit schemes are, or have been, underfunded.

Where a dedicated pensions report is required, it should include confirmation of the actuarial funding level of the target's pension scheme and any other pension schemes to which it is potentially liable to contribute, on both an ongoing basis and a termination basis, and what the ongoing funding requirements will be. There should also be an analysis of where the balance of power lies between the scheme trustees on the one hand and the employer on the other under the constitutional terms of the scheme.

Property valuation/condition report

11.62 Depending on what properties are owned by the target group and whether they are material assets of the group, the sponsor may commission a property valuation report from professional valuers or perhaps structural survey reports. In practice, this is relatively rare in a buy-out.

---

46 Defined benefit schemes include final salary schemes and career average schemes.
47 See para **11.114** for more detail.

Property reports on title

11.63   The legal report will typically include a section setting out the headline details of all real estate owned or used by the target group, including the nature of the title, freehold, leasehold etc and title details, location and so on. This will often satisfy the property due diligence requirements of the sponsor and the acquisition financiers. However, where real estate forms an important part of the target business, there may also be discrete reports or certificates on title produced by the target's lawyers (certificates) or newco's lawyers (reports) and establishing the title of the target to each of the properties owned by it.[48]

Tax

11.64   Tax can be considered on two levels, tax due diligence and tax structuring. The two exercises serve different purposes.

Tax due diligence

11.65   Depending on the nature of the target business and the complexity of its tax arrangements, there may be a stand-alone tax due diligence report or the accountants may include a section on tax in the main financial due diligence report. Wherever it is reported, the tax due diligence will focus the target's historic tax status and its compliance with all applicable tax laws and regulations. The parties will wish to know that all applicable taxes have been paid correctly and up to date and that there are no hidden tax liabilities in the target group.

There is also transaction-specific due diligence – namely an analysis of the tax effects of the acquisition and its funding – but this will often be covered in a separate tax structure memorandum. The key item of tax-transaction due diligence will be verification of the assumed tax rate and payments set out in the base case model. Particular concern exists around the deductability of interest on equity investor debt, although the model may not necessarily assume this in any event.

Tax structuring memorandum

11.66   As indicated above, the parties will be concerned with the tax treatment of the target group following completion of the buy-out and in particular the assumed rates and amounts of tax set out in the base case model for the business going forward. This aspect of the tax analysis has been of increasing importance in UK buy-outs during the 2000s principally because of the complicated legislation that affects the treatment of interest on shareholder debt for tax purposes.[49] As a result, it is now common – even in some pure UK buy-outs – for there to be a separate tax structuring paper. Whereas with a domestic UK buy-out the analysis may be limited to confirmation (under UK tax rules) of the deductability of interest on the various layers of debt and, particularly, equity investor debt (and possibly some exit planning matters for the sponsor), with multi-jurisdictional buy-outs the analysis will be much more extensive. For starters the analysis will

---

48   See also para **11.74** as regards real estate due diligence.

49   In particular, this directly relates to any interest or other yield accruing on the loan capital subscribed by the sponsor or the management team as part of the overall equity package.

necessarily cover the tax rules applicable in each jurisdiction in which the target has material revenues. Furthermore, in addition to interest deductability, the analysis will cover the tax implications of moving cash from operating subsidiaries to acquisition finance borrowers.

In either case, but particularly with multi-jurisdictional buy-outs, the tax structuring paper will often make recommendations as to the preferred corporate and funding structures to be adopted for the buy-out.[50]

Technical report

11.67   With businesses that operate in highly technical areas or that involve specialist or scientific processes, a technical adviser may be appointed to report on the quality and reliability of those processes. This may mean benchmarking against industry standards. The technical adviser will also be asked to comment on the capacity of the business to deliver any performance improvements such as capacity increases or efficiency or productivity enhancements assumed in the business plan.

Even in relatively low-tech businesses where the output is largely dependant on plant and machinery it is good practice to have the state of the plant and machinery diligenced, in particular to asses its useful working life and ability to deliver the productivity assumed in the business plan.

The process

11.68   Once the selected advisers have been engaged to carry out due diligence into the various aspects of the target business they will need a certain amount of access, both to information held by the target and management. As with most acquisitions, the seller or its advisers will establish a data room (perhaps a 'virtual' date room on a web-based platform) at the start of the sale process, ideally containing all written information relating to the target business. The sponsor and its financiers and advisers will be granted access to the data room in order to carry out their due diligence using the information provided. This is where much of the due diligence will be carried out for most of the advisers. It is good practice, however, at the start of the process for each of the advisers to have an opportunity to meet the management of the target and to raise any initial questions that will help them carry out their due diligence more effectively. Ideally the management will make a presentation to the principal parties and their advisers and this will often be followed by a tour of relevant sites. Technical advisers will generally need much more physical access to the target business and they will often need to spend extensive periods with the operational management of the business. The same may be true for insurance advisers and environmental consultants, at least in the case of a Phase II environmental study given that a Phase I study is essentially a desk-top exercise.

As the due diligence progresses, the various advisers may require follow up meetings with management to clarify issues that have arisen, ask follow-up questions and so on. Establishing a good rapport in the first place is therefore impor-

---

50 See also paras **11.37** to **11.42** generally in relation to tax structuring.

tant. Depending on what is agreed at the outset of the process, at a certain point the advisers will come back with initial findings. This may be through a first draft report, a presentation, or it may be less formal. Highlighting material issues and potential 'deal breakers' early – without waiting to input into a written report – is key given the significant transaction costs that are incurred on a daily basis. In any event, this is an important stage in the process since it gives the parties the opportunity to request further clarifications and to focus the diligence onto certain aspects that may be of more concern than others. It may also become apparent at this stage that certain matters cannot satisfactorily be dealt with by including further information and analysis in the reports. If not, it may be that the legal documentation can be amended to deal with any material matters revealed, for example, by obtaining a specific indemnity from the seller.[51] Throughout the process, which can usually be expected to last between two and eight weeks depending on the nature, size and complexity of the business, some of the reports may go through a number of drafts before being finalised. Ultimately, a final set of due diligence reports will be produced. Their provision and the acquisition financiers' satisfaction with them will be set out in the finance documents as conditions precedent to the provision of the debt.

The acquisition financiers may or may not require their lawyers to review any of the due diligence reports. It is good practice for them to have the legal report reviewed, given its subject matter, although such reports are generally produced on the assumption that they will principally be read by non-lawyers. Where matters of concern are raised in the report but the actual or potential financial exposure of the group in respect of the issue is not quantified or insufficient detail is provided, the acquisition financiers' lawyers should request that further detail and, as appropriate, a quantification of the financial exposure of the group, should be included. For these purposes, the lawyers should also have agreed in advance with the financiers what level of financial exposure is to be regarded as 'material'.

It is not uncommon for a seller to deliberately make certain final disclosures to the buyer towards the end of the process and it is possible that these issues will be brought to the attention of the acquisition financiers and their lawyers for the first time in the very late stages of the legal due diligence exercise. Since the effect of disclosure by the seller is usually to render ineffective any warranty comfort given by the seller in the acquisition agreement in respect of the matter disclosed, any such disclosure should be fully diligenced and reported on to the acquisition financiers before any sign-off can be given on the final form of the due diligence report.

As far as the financial and commercial due diligence reports are concerned, given the non-legal nature of most of the contents of these reports, the lawyers will not usually be requested to conduct a review of them and the acquisition financiers themselves will carry out a detailed review. Exceptions may be made for environmental, pensions and tax reports, however. These aspects of the due diligence exercise are subject to considerable statutory regulation and the input of lawyers may be required to interpret references to regulations and potential statutory liabilities. Occasionally, the acquisition financier's lawyers may also be

---

51 See paras **11.75** to **11.81** for further consideration of how issues raised in due diligence may be dealt with.

requested to carry out due diligence into certain items of particular concern to their clients, even if this means duplicating work carried out by the sponsor's lawyers. This might include a review of certain material contracts that the target is party to, for example, or confirmation that a specific regulatory approval is in place.

Seller due diligence

11.69 With the increasing competition for deals that has arisen through the 2000s, resulting in auctions becoming commonplace, sellers have looked at various ways to make the process more efficient. Alongside stapled offers of finance,[52] sponsor drafted term sheets[53] and interim loan facilities,[54] sophisticated sellers commission due diligence themselves in order to pre-empt the requirements of prospective buyers. There are a number of advantages in this initiative. Thus, pre-emptive due diligence can highlight potential problems early in the process, enabling the seller to rectify the issues or at least factor them into the price on its own terms. The process of finding a buyer is also improved because more buyers should be tempted to express an interest knowing that a minimum level of investigation has already been carried out without their needing to commission their own costly due diligence. Prospective buyers can also take comfort from the level playing field effect of having the same information made available to all potential buyers. In addition, the target business itself should suffer less disruption than would occur with multiple teams from interested buyers carrying out investigations and asking detailed questions of management. This also enables the sale process to remain secret for longer.

Despite some concerns over potential conflicts of interest for the reporting professionals carrying out the due diligence – in being commissioned by the seller but ultimately producing a report for the benefit of a buyer – the leading accountancy and law firms in particular do regularly accept these engagements. Some debate remains, more in the case of law firms, as to whether formal legal reliance is extended to the ultimate buyer, but this has largely been accepted now by the leading firms, although often subject to a liability cap. Where reliance is not extended, the sponsor is really left with no choice but to commission its own due diligence, which to some extent defeats the purpose of seller due diligence.[55] That said, sponsors will often look to update or supplement seller due diligence that may have been completed some time prior to the deal's ultimate completion, as a matter of course, and this will generally entail commissioning their own reports.

Reliance on the due diligence reports

Buyer due diligence

11.70 All of the sponsor commissioned due diligence reports should be addressed to newco and the acquisition financiers in addition to the deal sponsor

---

52 See para **1.57**.
53 See para **5.14**.
54 See para **5.15**.
55 See paras **11.70** and **11.71** on reliance generally.

(in its capacity as equity investor). Each report itself, or a separate reliance letter, should explicitly state that the addressees can formally rely on the report.[56] Newco, as buyer of the target business, is the entity which has the most direct interest in the due diligence and it should be the party that formally engages the relevant consultants. This will ensure that it has a direct contractual relationship with the report providers and ultimately a right to sue for breach of contract if the resultant reports are flawed. The acquisition financiers will generally insist on this approach in any event, given that newco's rights in respect of the due diligence reports will fall within their security package, whereas the deal sponsor's would not. The acquisition financiers or their lawyers should always review the terms of engagement and reliance relating to the various reports to ensure that they conform to their requirements as to both scope and their ability to rely on them. This should be done early – directly by the lawyers advising the acquisition financiers – to avoid last minute issues on the extent of the reliance and liability.

Seller due diligence

11.71 Although it is now usually possible for a buyer and its financiers to formally rely on seller commissioned due diligence, the seller must address this when commissioning the due diligence, by ensuring that the report providers extend formal legal reliance to the buyer and its financiers. In any event, there are material implications for the buy-side parties if they intend to place reliance on seller commissioned due diligence – even if formal legal reliance is extended – especially if it is as an alternative to sponsor commissioned due diligence. In particular, it is unlikely that the financiers (or the sponsor) will be given an opportunity to input into the scope of the due diligence or indeed to have any dialogue with the diligence providers with respect to issues that arise in the process. In many cases, the seller due diligence process may be completed and reports prepared before the sponsor and its financiers become involved in the deal. Further, and as a direct result of their lack of involvement in the scoping of the due diligence, the formal reliance that the parties are able to place on the due diligence will often be substantially more limited than with sponsor commissioned due diligence. Indeed, as indicated above, the providers of seller commissioned due diligence may even be unwilling to extend formal reliance to prospective buyers and their financiers, citing the different requirements that any given buyer might have for the exercise than the seller. Ultimately, if the buy-side parties are unable to obtain formal legal reliance on the seller due diligence, they may be forced to commission their own reports in order to obtain sufficient comfort from the process.

Additional legal due diligence

11.72 Along with financial due diligence, legal due diligence is one of the two key areas of investigation for the buyer and its financiers, certainly as regards risk management. It is the means by which the parties will discover if there are material liabilities potentially hidden in the target group. In practice, most of the legal due diligence is carried out by the sponsor's lawyers and the lawyers advising the

---

56 Sample reliance wording is set out in para **11.17**.

acquisition financiers will generally have a secondary role. Often they will shadow the work carried out by their counterparts advising the sponsor, in which case their role will mainly comprise reviewing the legal report, discussing it with their clients, and to the extent necessary, feeding back comments to the lawyers who produced it. In addition, by convention, the acquisition financiers' lawyers will be directly responsible for carrying out company searches in respect of the target group companies and reporting directly to the acquisition financiers on their findings. They may also perform some real estate due diligence directly. These two areas of additional legal due diligence are considered in the following paragraphs.

Company searches

11.73   Company searches are carried out for a number of purposes. In particular, they are used to verify and support the corporate authority and financial assistance documentation that the acquisition financiers rely on in support of the main finance documents.[57] This will include ensuring that the guarantees and security to be given in respect of the acquisition finance are within the corporate powers of the relevant companies and have been validly approved and whitewashed[58] and whether any provisions of the constitutional documents of the companies would hinder enforcement of such security. Confirmation of these matters, following 'clean' company searches, is necessary to enable the acquisition financiers' lawyers to issue the legal opinions that the acquisition financiers will require to be addressed to them in respect of the main finance documents. The searches will also be used to discover what, if any, security each company has already granted over its assets and whether any insolvency related filings have been made against the companies.

Company searches will be carried out in respect of each of the target group companies, possibly with the exception of dormant companies[59]. Searches in respect of the SPVs may also be carried out.[60] Law firms have standard lists of matters to cover as part of the searches. These include the corporate powers of the company, its corporate governance rules, the existence of security interests registered against the company and the like. If there are defects or issues raised by the company searches – such as the existence of security over target group assets that was not anticipated – either the seller should be required to remedy the matter prior to completion or more likely newco should be obliged to remedy the matter as a condition of completion. This will typically mean including specific conditions precedent in the finance documents. In the case of unanticipated security interests the remedial conditions should include delivery of evidence of releases of the security interests. Where the constitutional documents of a target group company include a 'defect', the remedy will involve ensuring that the corporate authorities of the target group company required as conditions precedent authorise and resolve to effect the requisite amendment of the memorandum or

---

57   See para **11.96**.

58   In fact, the financial assistance whitewash procedure applicable to private companies is to be repealed on 1 October 2008. See para **11.101**.

59   Dormant companies may be exempted but only on the basis that their status is the subject of a representation in the finance documents.

60   The SPVs may occasionally be exempted on the basis that they are newly formed 'off the shelf' companies whose clean status will be the subject of detailed representations in the finance documents and the fact that new constitutional documents for these companies will be adopted as part of the deal.

articles of association. Alternatively, but this is rare, if the matter is not capable of remedy an indemnity or other form of comfort may be sought from the seller.

Real estate due diligence

11.74   In relation to properties owned or used by the members of the target group it is common for the legal report to include a section outlining some basic information on real estate including tenure (leasehold or freehold), use and location of the properties. Where there is valuable freehold or long leasehold property, the legal report will ideally be supported by a certificate of title in respect of each property from the target group's solicitors. The certificates should be addressed in the same manner as the due diligence report, that is, to newco, the sponsor and the acquisition financiers. Alternatively, if certificates of title are not available for any reason, newco's lawyers (the sponsor's lawyers, in practice) should be required to provide a formal report on title on the relevant properties. Again, this should be addressed to newco, the sponsor and the acquisition financiers.

The principal purpose of a certificate of title or a report on title is to provide third-party legal confirmation that the relevant target group companies have good legal title to the relevant properties. It should also confirm that there is nothing arising from the title or out of enquiries and searches made by the lawyers which may materially and adversely affect the marketability, use or value of such property, that has not been taken into account in any valuation of the properties or that would prevent the acquisition financiers from enforcing their security or from realising that value.

If a certificate of title or report on title discloses any matters which are material the acquisition financiers will need to assess the impact of such disclosures in relation to the effectiveness of such property as security. As with the due diligence report the certificate of title or report on title should be a self-contained document which does not require any other supporting documentation in order to be readable and to enable an accurate assessment to be made of the materiality of any disclosure made. Standard forms of certificate of title and reports on title have been widely adopted by most major firms of lawyers in England and Wales.

Where there are a very large number of properties (such as with a retail or pub chain) the main legal report should still detail all of the properties in the outline terms referred to above. However, the certificate of title or report on title is unlikely to cover every single property. Instead, to save time and costs, it may be limited to a number of key properties or be carried out on a random sample basis or some other agreed basis.[61]

Dealing with issues raised in the due diligence process

11.75   Where the due diligence process throws up a material issue a number of options are available to newco and its financial backers. If the due diligence has

---

61 Further comfort may also be obtained from the fact that the seller will often, in any event, be required to give warranties in respect of the title of the target group companies (or itself) to the properties in the acquisition agreement.

been carried out to greatest effect, the materiality of the issue raised should already have been reduced to a potential financial exposure to the group. If not, the parties will wish to quantify the matter before determining how to deal with it. Matters with a potential exposure below a certain level will be viewed as immaterial. However, a distinction will be drawn between actual liabilities and potential liabilities. An actual liability is far more likely to be dealt with by way of a request for further seller comfort.

The main options are set out in the following paragraphs.

Taking a view

11.76 The parties may take the view that the relevant issue is only a remote possibility and does not justify any of the other options being taken. This will often reflect their own commercial judgment in the context of the transaction. Such an approach may contrast with that of an independent, third-party consultant, who will often be motivated by a desire to be as conservative as possible in order to ensure that every issue that could give rise to a liability (above a *de minimis* threshold) is brought to the attention of the parties, and ultimately to avoid any scope for liability on their part by failing to point out a material issue. The report providers are not paid to take the final decision of whether or not an issue is sufficiently material and adverse; only the principal parties can do this. Consequently, they will generally include certain matters in their reports that the principals will simply take a view on.

Further due diligence

11.77 Where the due diligence suggests that a material issue may exist but is not definitive, the most sensible step may be to require a more in depth analysis of the issue. This may happen naturally as the relevant consultant focuses in on potential issues. However, it may – for instance in the context of an environmental audit – require a further, more detailed, analysis to be carried out.

Seller warranties, indemnities, and undertakings

11.78 There is some doubt as to whether a party will be allowed to rely on a warranty in respect of a circumstance which it knows to be untrue at the time the warranty is given, and certainly no claim will succeed where the party giving the warranty has made adequate disclosure against the warranty. Consequently, where the buyer uncovers a material matter in due diligence, even if direct disclosure has not actually been made by the seller, it will not in practice be able to obtain comfort in respect of the issue just because it has a warranty from the seller apparently covering the issue. Warranties may, however, be useful to provide comfort that other related issues do not exist. In other words, by obtaining a warranty from the seller which is not disclosed against, the buyer should feel comfortable that the relevant matters so warranted are 'clean'.

An indemnity, rather than a warranty, is the remedy which a party should seek in order to obtain comfort from the seller in respect of a known actual or potential liability.

An indemnity is usually expressed as a direct contractual right to compensation if the circumstances specified by the indemnity arise. In the context of a buyout, newco could seek indemnities from the seller to obtain comfort on any specific material issues which are raised by the due diligence. An indemnity is particularly suited to a known liability which cannot be quantified and so cannot be dealt with by a price reduction or retention. It is a matter of negotiation of course, as to whether the seller will give any indemnity sought. Indeed, since an indemnity amounts to a contingent liability of the seller that will survive completion, perhaps for a period of two years or so, it will detract from the clean break which sellers prefer when making disposals. Private equity sellers in secondary buy-outs, in particular, will be reluctant to provide such comfort.[62]

In addition to known but unquantifiable liabilities, indemnities are also often sought in relation to unknown but potentially significant sources of liability, or hidden liabilities that may lay dormant for a long period. A common example here would be environmental liabilities, and with particularly environmentally sensitive businesses it is not uncommon for the buyer to obtain a specific environmental indemnity undertaking from the seller. Into this category will also fall specific tax indemnities since Her Majesty's Revenue and Customs may pursue a company up to six years after the end of the financial year in which a tax liability first arose.[63]

Ultimately, whether an indemnity will be given or not is a question of allocation of risk of the potential liability actually arising between buyer and seller. The more certain the liability, and the greater the potential quantum, the stronger the case there will be for having the seller give a specific indemnity. As an alternative to a pure monetary indemnity, the seller may be willing to undertake specific remedial action to put right a problem after completion and this may be more acceptable to the seller.

Purchase price reduction

11.79   When the issue on which comfort is sought is an actual liability or other real – rather than contingent – issue which can have a quantifiable adverse effect on the value of the target business, the sponsor may seek a price reduction from the seller. For the buy-out parties this will usually be the best solution, as it provides certainty and there is no exposure to the seller's creditworthiness through an indemnity or warranty protection.

It is not just liabilities or other specific circumstance-driven matters that may lead a buyer to seek a price reduction, however. In fact, the most common reason is that the financial or commercial due diligence identifies a previously unidentified weakness in the current or projected financial position of the target business, usually one that challenges the basis on which the business was valued. For example, the sponsor may determine, based on the due diligence, that the historic EBITDA on which the price is ultimately based is not completely sustainable going forward. Alternatively, the projected EBITDA or cash generation in the

---

62 See also para **2.37**, as regards seller comfort in secondary buy-outs.
63 See also **Chapter 2** in relation to specific indemnity undertakings for environmental and tax liabilities.

business plan may not be deemed achievable, although, depending on the valuation basis, the seller may not accept this as grounds for a price reduction.[64]

Retention of purchase price

11.80 Where the creditworthiness of the seller is in question, any seller comfort obtained in the form of warranties or indemnities may be of limited value at the time any claim is made.[65] In such circumstances, the sponsor should seek to agree a purchase price retention mechanism with the seller. The amount to be retained should in theory reflect the maximum potential liability of the seller to the buyer under all the warranties and indemnities, or it may be limited to a specific indemnity. The period of the retention should similarly reflect the time frame within which any claim may be made under the warranties and indemnities or any specific indemnity for which the retention is made. There will be a time limit on the making of most warranty and indemnity claims of no more than two years, although for certain specific indemnities (including for tax and environmental liabilities) this may be extended.[66]

Where an amount of the purchase price is to be retained in this way, an escrow account may be used. An escrow account in this context is a blocked deposit account, usually with a third-party escrow bank/agent, into which newco pays the retained consideration. The purpose of having an escrow account is to avoid either party (buyer or seller) having to take a view on the creditworthiness of the other for the retention period and gives each the comfort that the money is under the control of a third-party. The money sits in the escrow account (accruing interest) pending release to the seller after a fixed period of time if no claim is made by that time, or release to newco to satisfy the relevant liability if a claim is made.

Deferred consideration

11.81 Deferred consideration is a form of contingent price retention that may be used where the buyer and seller disagree on the value of the target business at completion but are willing to defer final resolution of the issue pending, usually, subsequent evidence of a certain level of financial performance by the target business. This may mean payment of the deferred amount over a period of between six months and a number of years following completion upon achieve-

---

64 One of the most common methods of valuing a business – certainly a mature business – is to apply a multiple to the historic, current (usually last 12 months) or prospective (for no more than the next 12 months normally) EBITDA or earnings of the business, or to a combination of current/prospective EBITDA/earnings. In the case of a business for which the historic or current performance may not be a true indicator of the real 'value' of the business – perhaps because it has not reached maturity or is on a particularly steep growth curve – a common alternative valuation methodology is to analyse the future cash generating potential of the business, using a discounted cash flow (DCF) method.
65 In particular, where the seller is a holding company vehicle with no real assets of its own, further comfort will be required. This will inevitably be the case where the seller is a private equity vehicle, and the sale proceeds will be distributed by the relevant vehicle to the ultimate investors sitting behind it. Where the seller is not willing to provide one, an alternative to a purchase price retention mechanism, that is often used in practice, is a guarantee of the seller's warranty and indemnity obligations, either from a bank or from another company related to the seller that is of sufficient financial substance. See **Chapter 2**.
66 See **Chapter 2** generally.

ment of certain pre-agreed financial performance criteria, such as annual EBITDA targets.

In practical terms, deferred consideration is usually structured as a seller note. That is, the higher headline purchase price is in theory paid to the seller but the seller immediately re-invests the deferred consideration amount into newco or another SPV as a loan. The loan (or 'note') will be repayable if the relevant financial performance criteria are met in due course, by reference to the financial statements of the target business.[67]

LEGAL AND DOCUMENTATION PROCESS

Giving legal effect to the overall transaction structure

11.82   Once a final transaction structure has been agreed on paper the buy-out parties will – usually in parallel with the due diligence phase – turn to their legal advisers give the structure legal effect. To this end the appropriate legal documentation will be drafted, negotiated, finalised and signed. In addition, SPVs will be established to receive the finance and to make the acquisition. Finally, the funds will be advanced and the acquisition completed. These different aspects of the process are considered in the following sections.

Establishing SPVs

11.83   At some stage during the legal and documentation process one or more special purpose vehicle (SPV) companies will be established to take up the roles of the various SPVs in the acquisition and funding structure. Each will be a recently formed legal entity that has not traded before and thus has no assets or more importantly liabilities, making it 'bankruptcy-remote'. The top SPV (topco) will be the true equity vehicle and it will also act as the group holding company. A further SPV may be formed above topco to make the equity investment on behalf of the institutional equity investors, particularly in multi-jurisdictional deals, where there may be tax benefits in using an SPV in a favourable tax jurisdiction such as Luxembourg. Equity vehicles such as these, however, do not form part of the 'group' for purposes of the acquisition financiers' analysis of the structure.

In a domestic UK deal each SPV will be a newly-formed limited liability company incorporated in England and Wales,[68] probably acquired 'off the shelf' so that although it will be a clean company it will already have been incorporated and registered with the Registrar of Companies. English SPVs might also be used in a multi-jurisdictional buy-out depending on the nature of the target business, where it operates and what the acquisition and tax structuring advice dictates. Outside the United Kingdom – in a multi-jurisdictional buy-out – the lawyers and accountants advising the sponsor on the acquisition and funding structure will advise as

---

67   See **Chapter 2** for further detail on deferred consideration and seller notes.
68   Or possibly Scotland or Northern Ireland.

to the appropriate types of entity to be the respective acquisition and funding vehicles within the SPV group. Their advice may be predicated on the assumption that one or more reorganisation steps are to occur after completion, such as a debt push-down merger, in order to complete the tax structuring necessary to achieve the assumed rates and quanta of tax underlying the base case model.[69]

Legal documentation

11.84   The documentation process will usually commence a little after the due diligence process but the two processes will generally run concurrently up to completion.[70]

The following paragraphs describe the typical package of legal documentation required to complete a UK buy-out including a public-to-private. Detailed consideration is given to the terms and substance of the principal documentation in other parts of this book and the emphasis in this section is on process. In particular, it examines who the parties are, who drafts and negotiates the documentation and when the documentation is signed. To simplify the analysis it is useful to consider the documentation as falling into four categories. First, there are the terms of the acquisition of the target business.[71] Secondly, there are the terms on which the equity investments are made and the agreements between the various shareholders in topco. Thirdly, there is the documentation setting out the terms of the acquisition finance and governing the relationship between the respective parties in the funding structure and how their respective investments inter-relate. Finally, there are the ancillary conditions precedent documents that the financiers will need to receive before agreeing to fund.

Acquisition documentation

Private buy-out

11.85

Document	Parties	Comments	Procedure to agree
Acquisition agreement[72]	Newco and seller and possibly a guarantor of the seller	If the seller is not particularly creditworthy, perhaps because its only asset is the target business, a guarantee may be required from a creditworthy affiliate in respect of its warranty and indemnity obligations. Alternatively a purchase price retention mechanism might be used. See **Chapter 2** generally.	Newco's lawyers draft and seller and newco negotiate, although in an auction process will often be drafted by seller's lawyers. Acquisition financiers' lawyers will feed in comments through newco's lawyers but will rarely be involved in the negotiations.

69 See paras **11.37** to **11.42** as to tax structuring generally
70 Since the early 2000s, sellers generally have taken a more aggressive stance on deal execution than was previously the case. One of the results of this has been an increase in seller initiated due diligence and a general requirement that the buyer signs off on due diligence earlier in the process. This may mean completion of the due diligence exercise some time before completion of the legal and documentation exercise.
71 Including offer or scheme documentation for a public-to-private.
72 This is often called an SPA for share purchase agreement or sale and purchase agreement.

Document	Parties	Comments	Procedure to agree
Disclosure letter	Seller to newco	This is used to qualify the seller's warranties.	Seller will produce and update as the due diligence and disclosure process is completed.
Tax covenant	Seller in favour of newco and possibly target	Occasionally an environmental indemnity undertaking is also required by newco, but only in an environmentally sensitive industrial sector.	Seller's lawyers produce and negotiate with newco's lawyers. Acquisition financier's lawyers will review and monitor negotiations.

Public-to-private by takeover offer

11.86

Document	Parties	Comments	Procedure to agree
Press announcement (also known as a Rule 2.5 announcement)	Bidder's financial adviser or bidder itself. See **Chapter 12**.	This document will contain the main terms of the offer itself and the offer document will replicate large parts of the final form of press announcement. See **Chapter 12**.	Bidder (its lawyers with input from its financial adviser) will draft and then negotiate with the target (its advisors) unless the bid is un-solicited. The acquisition financiers will also approve the final form.
Offer document	Bidder and possibly its financial adviser	The target shareholders accept the offer by executing and returning the form of acceptance appended or through CREST.	As with press announcement.

Public-to-private by scheme of arrangement

11.87

Document	Parties	Comments	Procedure to agree
Press announcement (also known as a Rule 2.5 announcement)	Target and bidder's financial advisor or bidder itself. See **Chapter 12**.	The document will contain the main terms of the scheme itself and the scheme document/circular will replicate large parts of the final form of press announcement.	Bidder (its lawyers will input from its financial advisors) will draft and then negotiate with the target (its advisors).
Scheme circular	Target and its financial advisor	The scheme document will explain the scheme and contain all of the terms of the scheme. It will also contain the notices to shareholders convening the requisite shareholder meetings.	Usually drafted by the target's lawyers with significant input from bidder and its advisers.
Transaction or implementation agreement	Target and bidder	This agreement has not always been used but is increasingly common and sets out the ground rules for the target's progression of the scheme.	Bidder will draft and negotiate with the target.
Court documents	Target	Since a scheme of arrangement is a court approved process there are court hearings which will require the preparation and submission of various court papers.	Target will draft and agree with bidder. Counsel will be retained by target to finalise the papers and to present them in court.

Equity documentation

11.88

Document	Parties	Comments	Procedure to agree
Investment agreement[73]	Topco, institutional equity investors and management team	This contains a number of important provisions agreed among topco's shareholders, including management. See **Chapter 4**.	Drafted by the lawyers advising topco (ie, the sponsor's lawyers) and negotiated with the lawyers representing the other equity investors (ie, management team). Acquisition financiers' lawyers will review and comment.
Topco articles of association	Topco	When topco is first established it will have standard shelf-company articles. These will be replaced by the new articles at signing through a special reduction approved by topco's shareholders.	Drafted by the lawyers advising topco (ie, the sponsor's lawyers) and in respect of provisions that differentiate the rights of different classes of shareholder will be negotiated with lawyer's for the other shareholders (ie, the management team). Will be commented on by the acquisition financiers' lawyers.
Loan capital instrument(s)	Topco or other SPV(s)	The equity investor debt may comprise more than one type of subordinated loan capital, each constituted by a separate instrument. Each may be invested in a different SPV. There may also be seller loan capital.	Drafted by the lawyers advising topco (ie, the sponsor's lawyers) and will be commented on by lawyers representing the management team and the acquisition financiers respectively.
Loan capital security documents[74]	Relevant group companies and the security agent for the institutional equity investors or in respect of secured seller loan capital the seller.	These are generally not required. It is rare for the acquisition financiers to permit any equity investor debt to be secured.	Drafted by the lawyers advising topco (ie, the sponsor's lawyers) and will be commented on by lawyers representing the acquisition financiers.

Acquisition finance documentation

Senior debt

11.89

Document	Parties	Comments	Procedure to agree
Senior facilities agreement	Topco, borrowers, guarantors[75] and the senior lenders	See **Chapter 5**.	Usually drafted by the senior lender's lawyers and negotiated with the sponsor's lawyers on behalf of topco, the borrowers and the guarantors. In some competitive deals, if the fees of the acquisition financiers' lawyers are not then underwritten, the sponsor's lawyers may produce the first draft.

73 May be described as the subscription and shareholders agreement.
74 These are only rarely required as equity investor debt is not usually secured. See **Chapter 4**.
75 This assumes that the guarantee is incorporated into the facilities agreement (which is common) rather than being contained in the security agreement or a stand alone guarantee document.

Document	Parties	Comments	Procedure to agree
Ancillary facilities letter	Working capital borrowers and ancillary facilities lender	This document houses the commercial banking facilities, if any, such as the overdraft terms.	Drafted by the senior lender's lawyers and negotiated with the sponsor's lawyers on behalf of the borrowers.
Fee letters	Topco and lead senior lender (as agent and arranger)	These will detail the up-front arrangement fee and the annual agency/monitoring fee. They are documented outside the main facility documentation by convention so as not to be disclosed to all syndicate lenders.	Drafted by the senior lender's lawyers and negotiated with the sponsor's lawyers on behalf of topco.
Hedging documents	Hedging bank and borrowers	A single document will usually cover the hedging for the senior and any floating rate junior debt (second lien or mezzanine).	Usually drafted in-house by the hedging bank. Will need to comply with the requirements set out in the intercreditor agreement.

Second lien debt[76]

11.90

Document	Parties	Comments	Procedure to agree
Facilities agreement (see comments)	As for the senior facilities agreement unless a separate second lien facility agreement is used[77]	See **Chapter 6**. In the case of second lien loans, unless the tranche of second lien debt is particularly large (which is rare in buy-outs) it is likely to be documented as the senior 'D' tranche in the senior facilities agreement. If a separate second lien facility agreement is used it will substantially mirror the senior facilities agreement. Second lien debt may also take the form of an issue of notes[78]	As for the senior facilities agreement, unless a separate second lien facility agreement is used (see comments), in which case the procedure will follow that for the mezzanine facility agreement.
Fee letter		It is common for the second lien debt to be arranged by the senior debt arranger, in which case a separate arrangement/underwriting fee letter will not be necessary. Similarly, unless there is a discrete second lien syndicate with separate voting rights (ie, a separate document) there is unlikely to be a separate second lien agency fee letter.	

76 The table assumes that the second lien debt is in the form of a loan. If it is to be structured as an issue of notes the documentation will generally follow the form used for high yield debt.

77 As to which see **Chapter 6**.

78 See fn **76**.

Mezzanine debt

11.91

Document	Parties	Comments	Procedure to agree
Mezzanine facility agreement	Topco, borrower, guarantors[79] and the mezzanine lenders	See **Chapter 7**. The form of this agreement will substantially mirror the senior facilities agreement.	Drafted by the mezzanine lender's lawyers[80] and negotiated with the sponsor's lawyers on behalf of topco, the borrower and the guarantors once the senior facilities agreement is largely agreed.
Fee letters	Topco and lead mezzanine lender (as agent and arranger)	These will detail the up-front arrangement fee and the annual agency/monitoring fee.	Drafted by the mezzanine lender's lawyers and negotiated with the sponsor's lawyers on behalf of topco.
Warrant Instrument[81]	Topco	This instrument is typically in the form of a deed poll with topco as the only 'party'	Drafted by the lead mezzanine lender's lawyers and negotiated with the lawyers representing the sponsors on behalf of topco.

High yield debt

11.92

Document	Parties	Comments	Procedure to agree
Offering memorandum	Bondco as issuer	See **Chapter 8**. Sets out the terms and structure of the high yield issue together with detailed business and financial information on the issuer and the target group.	The drafting will be split with the description of the notes drafted by the lead manager's[82] lawyers and the parts of the memorandum that relate to the status, condition and history of the issuer drafted by its lawyers. A final draft – known as the 'red herring' – excluding pricing and possibly size of issue will be used to market the issue. Will also be reviewed by senior lenders and their lawyers in particular in relation to intercreditor aspects of the bonds.
Trust indenture or trust deed	Bondco and trustee	Constitutes the bonds themselves. A US indenture may contain the intercreditor provisions but a European trust deed will not and a separate intercreditor agreement will be used.	Drafted by lead manager's lawyers and negotiated with bondco's lawyers. Will be reviewed and approved by senior lenders and their lawyers.
Purchase agreement	Bondco and the initial purchasers (the underwriters of the issue)	The underwriters of the issue will acquire the notes – conventionally at a discount representing the underwriting fee – and then sell into the desired market/private placement.	Drafted by lead manager's lawyers and negotiated with bondco's lawyers.

79 This assumes that the guarantee is incorporated into the facility agreement (which is common) rather than being contained in the security agreement or a stand-alone guarantee document.

80 This will typically be the same lawyers that are advising the senior lenders.

81 True or warranted mezzanine is less common than it used to be and a warrant instrument may not be required.

82 The lead manager might also be described as the underwriter.

Document	Parties	Comments	Procedure to agree
Paying agency agreement	Bondco and the paying agents, transfer agent and registrar	Purely mechanical document setting out the appointment and duties of the paying agents, transfer agents and registrar. It also usually details the delivery of the notes to the relevant depositaries.	Drafted by lead manager's lawyers.
Registration rights agreement	Bondco, guarantors and initial purchaser (for all noteholders)	Used if a full US public offering is to be undertaken.	Drafted by lead manager's lawyers and negotiated with bondco's lawyers.

PIK note debt[83]

11.93

Document	Parties	Comments	Procedure to agree
PIK note instrument	PIK note issuer[84]	See **Chapter 9**. The instrument will be drafted as a deed poll rather than an inter-partes agreement.	Drafted by the lawyers representing the PIK note arranger and negotiated with the sponsor's lawyers on behalf of the issuer. It will be reviewed and commented on by lawyers representing the other acquisition financiers.
PIK note subscription agreement	PIK note issuer and the initial note holders as subscribers	This document contains the agreement to subscribe for the notes at completion and the initial representations given by the issuer.	Drafted by the lawyers representing the PIK note arranger and negotiated with the sponsor's lawyers on behalf of the issuer. It will be reviewed and commented on by lawyers representing the other acquisition financiers.
PIK note warrant instrument	Topco	If the structure includes warranted mezzanine debt, the form of the PIK note warrant instrument should be substantially the same as that used for the mezzanine warrants.	Drafted by the lawyers representing the PIK note arranger and negotiated with the sponsor's lawyers on behalf of topco. It will be reviewed and commented on by lawyers representing the other acquisition financiers.

83 The table assumes that the PIK note debt is in the form of loan capital rather than a loan or a capital markets bond issue. If it is to take the form of a loan the documentation will often be similar to that used for mezzanine debt. If it is to take the form of a public issue of bonds it will be broadly similar to that used for high yield debt. See **Chapter 9** generally as to the various forms of PIK note debt.

84 This will generally be an intermediate SPV in the SPV group, below topco but above newco.

Intercreditor

11.94

Document	Parties	Comments	Procedure to agree
Intercreditor agreement	Topco, obligors, senior lenders, second lien lenders, mezzanine lenders or high yield bond holders, PIK note holders, equity investor creditors, inter-company creditors and security trustees	See **Chapter 10**. It is usual to have a single agreement ranking all of the lawyers of finance perhaps with the exception of seller loan capital.	Drafted by the senior lender's lawyers and negotiated with the lawyers representing each discrete class of creditor.
Seller subordination agreement	Seller loan capital issuer and any guarantors, seller and security trustee (on behalf of the acquisition financiers)	Sellers are often reluctant to sign up to the main intercreditor agreement so a separate document is used. This also facilitates subsequent amendments to either document.	Drafted by the senior lender's lawyers and negotiated with the seller's lawyers.

Security

11.95

Document	Parties	Comments	Procedure to agree
Security agreement	Each borrower and guarantor with assets in the UK and the security trustee	It is usual for a single composite 'debenture' to be used for all UK companies.[85] If the guarantee is not incorporated into the facility agreements, either a stand-alone guarantee must be used or a guarantee included in the security agreement.	Drafted by senior lender's lawyers and negotiated with the sponsor's lawyers on behalf of the group. If there are multiple layers of debt secured under the same document, comments from lawyers representing them should be obtained.
Non-UK security documents	Each borrower and guarantor with assets outside the UK and the security trustee	Local counsel will advise of the documentation requirements.	As for the UK security agreement.

Conditions precedent[86]

11.96   Subject to certain minor differences, the providers of each type of acquisition finance will generally require the same CPs to be satisfied as a condition to funding. The CPs will take the form of documentary CPs (which must be received in satisfactory form) and other non-documentary conditions which must be satisfactorily complied with. Note that in the table below 'topco' refers to the ultimate holding company in the acquisition financiers' credit group.

---

85 Companies in Scotland and Northern Ireland may, however, need to execute separate security documents in addition, in respect of real estate.

86 'CP' for short.

Document	Parties	Comments	Procedure to agree
Obligor corporate documents:	Each obligor	These documents are required principally to give the acquisition financiers comfort about the due execution and enforceability of all relevant finance documents. They will largely mirror the documents required for the senior lender's lawyers to issue a legal opinion to that effect. They are commonly attached to a director's/secretarial certificate certifying their accuracy and that up to date.	Topco's lawyers will draft and send to the acquisition financiers' lawyers for comments and final sign-off.
Constitutional documents	Each obligor	Acquisition financiers' lawyers will obtain these in advance from company searches. Formal CP versions will be delivered and certified by the company at completion.	See above.
Board resolutions	Each obligor	Approving execution and performance of all transaction documents. To include specified signing authorities.	See above.
Specimen signatures of authorised signatories	Each obligor	Will be incorporated into the director's/secretarial certificate that accompanies the corporate documents.	See above.
Shareholder resolutions	Target (and possibly other obligors)	A special resolution of the target will be required for the financial assistance whitewash if the target is not wholly owned by a single seller entity.[87] It is also good practice for corporate benefit purposes to have a resolution of the shareholders of the target approving the giving of upstream guarantees and security by the target and its subsidiaries.[88]	See above. Note that the provision of security and related financial assistance and corporate authority documentation may on occasion be required only as conditions subsequent (rather than as CPs), in which case they will be required within perhaps 30, 60 or 90 days of completion.
Financial assistance whitewash documents[89]	*Each obligor that is giving financial assistance or approving a subsidiary's financial assistance*	*Will include statutory declarations by the directors, auditor's report, net asset letter and copies of the registers of the directors and shareholders of each company.*	*See above.*
Director's or secretarial certificate	Each obligor[90]	Should confirm that each corporate document is correct, complete, current and has not been amended.	See above.

87 Until 1 October 2008, see s 155 (4) of the Companies Act 1985. Thereafter there is no statutory requirement, but see also para **11.101** below.
88 Where the shareholder is a corporate entity, a board resolution of that company should be obtained approving the shareholder resolution.
89 But see para **11.101**, concerning the repeal of the prohibition applicable to private companies on 1 October 2008 and what secured financiers may insist on seeing in place of whitewash documentation.
90 It is quite common for a single 'global' certificate to be produced in respect of *all* obligors, which they each sign.

Document	Parties	Comments	Procedure to agree
Additional equivalent documentation for companies incorporated outside the UK	Each obligor	These documents will largely mirror the UK equivalents, with emphasis on what is required to enable local counsel to issue their legal opinions.	Local counsel for topco will draft and agree with local counsel for the senior lenders.
Topco director's or secretarial completion certificate	Topco	Should confirm: (i) that no borrowing, guarantee or security limits would be exceeded by any obligor (ii) that all CPs have been duly satisfied – perhaps referring specifically to certain non-documentary CPs, such as satisfaction of acquisition conditions without waiver (iii) which companies in the target group are dormant.	The senior lender's lawyers will often draft this. Agreed form may be a schedule to the main facilities agreements.
Lawyer undertaking to file UK financial assistance documentation with Registrar of Companies[91]	*Topco's lawyers*	*Filing this documentation is a statutory requirement. Obtaining the undertaking is therefore good practice.*	*See above.*
Acquisition (offer/scheme) documents	See earlier section	See earlier section.	See earlier section.
Equity documents	See earlier section	See earlier section.	See earlier section.
Senior debt documents	See earlier section	See earlier section.	See earlier section.
Second lien debt documents	See earlier section	See earlier section.	See earlier section.
Mezzanine debt documents	See earlier section	See earlier section.	See earlier section.
High yield debt documents	See earlier section	See earlier section.	See earlier section.
PIK note debt documents	See earlier section	See earlier section.	See earlier section.
Intercreditor documents	See earlier section	See earlier section.	See earlier section.
Other transaction documents:			
Hedging strategy letter	Topco and the lead senior lender	This will stipulate how much debt is to be hedged (swapped) and for how long.	The senior lender's lawyers will produce a draft to be agreed with topco and its lawyers.
Syndication strategy letter	Topco and the lead senior and junior lenders	This will typically stipulate how much of the debt is to be syndicated and which prospective lenders are to be approached. It may include market flex language.[92]	The senior lender's lawyers will produce a draft to be agreed with topco and its lawyers.

91 See fn **89** above.
92 See para **11.104**.

Document	Parties	Comments	Procedure to agree
Management team service contracts	Management team and usually topco	Acquisition financiers are not usually too interested unless the deal is heavily management lead. In a true MBO full management CVs, references, criminal and credit searches and medicals may be required.	May be prepared by the management team's lawyers with input from the sponsor and its lawyers. Should be copied to acquisition financiers.
Downstream funding loan agreements[93]	Topco and other SPVs	A funding loan will be required to downstream funds received in SPVs other than newco to newco for acquisition purposes. The acquisition financiers will take security over them.	Sponsor's lawyers will draft and agree with lawyers representing the acquisition financiers.
Upstream intra-group loan agreement	Target group companies and newco	This agreement is used to upstream cash from the operating companies to newco. *It must be whitewashed at completion and be in a form that satisfies the financial assistance legislation.*[94]	Sponsor's lawyers will draft and agree with lawyers representing the acquisition financiers.
Security Documents	See earlier section	See earlier section.	See earlier section.
Real estate security documents:			
Satisfactory Land Registry and Land Charges searches		This has two purposes: to check for prior charges and to establish priority against subsequent charges.	Usually carried out by topco's lawyers, with results produced to the acquisition financier's lawyers.
Prior security discharges	Prior security parties/each relevant obligator	Discussions with the prior security holder should begin as soon as possible in the process.	Topco's lawyers should control and keep the acquisition financiers' lawyers updated.
Notices of charges and registration fee	Each relevant obligor to each relevant landlord or other third-party	This is often carried out by topco's solicitors under the solicitor's undertaking referred to below.	Topco's lawyers will draft and agree with security trustee's lawyers.
All title documents and related security documents	Each obligor	Title deeds are rarely sent to the security trustee in practice. Usually they are retained by topco's solicitors on undertaking to hold to the security trustee's order.	A schedule should be agreed between the lawyers representing topco and the security trustee respectively.
Solicitor's undertaking to register the charges at the Land Registry	Solicitors for topco	Where the new security is accompanied by an asset transfer, solicitors for topco usually register both the transfer and the security agreement at the Land Registry (the security trustee's solicitors will also register the security agreement at Companies House). If there is no asset transfer, the security trustee's solicitors will often deal with registration of the security agreement at both the Land Registry and Companies House, in which case no undertaking will be required from topco's solicitors.	Agreed between the lawyers representing topco and the security trustee respectively.

93 See para **4.25** in respect of the downstreaming of equity proceeds. Would also be required for high yield and PIK note debt.

94 But see fn **89** above and para **11.101**.

Document	Parties	Comments	Procedure to agree
Landlord consents to leasehold security	Landlords in favour of the relevant obligors and the security trustee	This requirement may be deferred to a condition subsequent for certain properties. If so, a further security agreement must be executed when the consent is obtained.	The forms of consent will be agreed between the lawyers advising topco, landlords and the security trustee respectively.
Share security documents:			
Share certificates and other title documents	Each obligor granting share security	Any shares that are de-materialised may be materialised and new certificates issued and delivered to the security trustee. See below in respect of target shares.	Topco should deliver at completion.
Blank executed stock transfer forms	Each obligor granting share security in favour of the security trustee	Enables the security trustee to perfect the security by transferring to itself or its nominee upon enforcement without any court procedure or further recourse to any obligor.	Standard form documents which topco will deliver at completion.
Copies of share registers	Each company whose shares are the subject of security	The target's share register will only be updated once the transfer to newco is stamped by the stamp office.	Topco will deliver at completion.
Undertaking in respect of target's shares	Topco's lawyers, newco and the target in favour of the security trustee	Because the transfer of target's shares to newco will need to be stamped, the security trustee should obtain an undertaking that the stamping will be carried out, the old share certificates (and stock transfer forms) presented to the target for cancellation and re-registration in the name of newco, new share certificates issued to topco and these certificates plus blank executed stock transfer forms delivered to the security trustee.	May be drafted by topco's lawyers or the security trustee's and agreed between them.
Other security documents:			
Notices to third parties in respect of certain security including in respect of bank accounts with third-party banks, insurances, the acquisition documents, certain material contracts and leases of real estate	Each relevant obligor to relevant third parties	This achieves a level of security perfection. In particular, third parties on notice of security in respect of assets (including contracts) in which they have an interest have more limited rights against the security trustee in respect of the asset/contract once they are on notice of the security.	Form to be agreed between lawyers representing topco and the security trustee respectively. Agreed form may be scheduled to the security agreement. Should be dispatched by topco on completion.
Acknowledgements of third-party notices	Each third-party in favour of the security trustee	Certain acknowledgements may be difficult to obtain. As a matter of English law, they will in most cases be desirable – as evidence of receipt of notice and in order to obtain direct undertakings from the third-party – rather than necessary to perfect the security.	The forms will be agreed with the forms of notice (see above). Topco should deliver the acknowledgements at completion or as a condition subsequent within a number of days if not practicable at completion.

Document	Parties	Comments	Procedure to agree
Insurance documents:			
Insurance broker adequacy letter	The group's insurance broker in favour of the security trustee	It should confirm that the group will be insured in accordance with the requirements of the finance documents (which will usually mean prudent insurance in accordance with sector norms) and that all premiums are up to date.	The brokers will propose a draft and agree it with the security trustee's lawyers.
Copies of insurance policies (including key-man insurance)	Insurer and group companies or topco as group policy holder	This request may be waived by the financiers.	Topco will deliver at completion.
Evidence that the security trustee is named as loss payee	N/A	The insurance broker should confirm this in the adequacy letter separately.	Topco should arrange.
Legal opinions:	Lawyers advising the senior lenders or possibly the obligors in favour of the finance parties	An opinion will be required for each jurisdiction in which an obligor is established and each jurisdiction, the laws of which govern any finance document.	The relevant lawyers will draft and send to the acquisition financiers for internal approval. Opinions produced by the obligors' counsel will be reviewed and negotiated/approved by counsel for the acquisition financiers.
Other documents and evidence:			
Evidence of appointment of agents for service of process	Each non-UK obligor and the agent appointed by them	The finance documents will specify the appointment. The process agent must confirm irrevocable acceptance of the appointment.	Topco will deliver a letter at completion.
Evidence of payment of all fees due to the financiers	N/A	These will normally be deducted from the proceeds of first drawdown by the initial lenders and retained.	Newco should include an instruction in its drawdown requests to deduct the fees from the initial drawdowns.
Group structure chart	N/A	It should show the group post-completion, with sufficient detail on shareholdings, status of companies (dormant/trading) and confirming the material companies, obligors etc.	Topco will deliver at completion.
Budget for the next 12 months	Topco	Delivery of an annual budget is a standard requirement in the finance documents. This will be the first one.	Topco will deliver on completion. It will have been pre-agreed between the sponsor, management team and acquisition financiers.
Due diligence reports and reliance letters	Each advisor in favour of the SPV and finance parties[95]	See earlier section.[96]	The forms of engagement letter and reliance language will need to be pre-agreed with the acquisition financiers' lawyers, who will often produce the required reliance language.

95 See paras **11.17** and **11.18** for appropriate reliance language.
96 See paras **11.48** et seq.

Document	Parties	Comments	Procedure to agree
Accountants engagement letters	Accountants	They should cover all applicable engagements including due diligence, *whitewash*, covenant compliance certificates, tax structuring and possibly audit.	The accountants will produce and circulate to the lawyers for topco and the acquisition financiers to agree.
Tax structuring memorandum	Tax advisor in favour of the SPV and finance parties	This paper will evolve during the structuring phase. It should be completed well before signing (but often is not!). See earlier section.[97]	Tax advisors produce and take in comments from all principal parties and their lawyers.
Last three years audited accounts for the target business	N/A	Three years is normal but may be less.	Topco will deliver at completion but they will have been received and reviewed well in advance as part of the due diligence exercise.
Year-to-date (YTD) management accounts for the target business	N/A	The financiers will be acutely interested in the 'current trading' of the target business.[98]	Topco will deliver at completion but, as above, should be reviewed well in advance of signing and completion.
Opening balance sheet of the group	N/A	May be updated as part of completion account audit and used as the basis of a purchase price adjustment (PPA) if a PPA mechanism is used in the acquisition agreement. See **Chapter 2**.	Determined as part of the base case model.
Funds flow statement	N/A	Should include details of all payments to be made at completion including bank account details. Will itemise all transaction costs.	Either produced by topco (or its advisors) or the acquisition financiers (or their advisors) and then agreed with the other principal parties.
Evidence that the acquisition agreement has become unconditional	N/A	This is normally satisfied by a topco completion certificate. It should confirm that topco is not aware of any breach of warranty or otherwise – and that no provision has been waived or varied.	See earlier section 'Obligor corporate documents.'
Evidence that the equity documents have become unconditional	N/A	As above.	As above.
Evidence that the equity investments have been made	N/A	There will usually be a closing account into which the funds have been received. The closing account holder should confirm receipt. Topco should also certify that the investments have been made in the completion certificate.	As above.
Evidence that the acquisition finance documents have become unconditional (apart from advance of funds)	N/A	The various acquisition financiers will usually swap letters confirming satisfaction of the CPs.	The acquisition financiers lawyers will draft.

97 See paras **11.37** to **11.42** and **11.66**.
98 Current trading is sometimes colloquially referred to as the 'run rate'.

Document	Parties	Comments	Procedure to agree
Evidence that the acquisition finance has been drawn down	N/A	Typically, the parties will be in a completion meeting at which the financiers will give the instructions to fund.	Forms of drawdown request will have been pre-agreed between the lawyers for topco and the financiers which will be submitted by topco to formalise the drawdown.
Evidence that the obligors have opened all necessary accounts with the lead bank	Each relevant obligor	In order to satisfy this CP the bank's know-your-customer compliance procedures must have been followed. This process should be started early as it involves detailed paperwork (see below). Accounts for the target group companies will be moved over to the new banks after completion.	The bank will provide standard account opening forms for the new directors of topco and newco to sign.
Know-your-customer checks	N/A	Will usually involve the production of passports, utility bills etc and may include criminal and credit searches.	Each finance party will need to have the obligors cleared in advance of funding. This involves compliance checks on the directors of the group.
Evidence of appointment of auditors for the group	Auditors and topco	This may be deferred to a condition subsequent as the sponsor will often run a competitive mandate process. This document will ideally include confirmation that the auditors will provide the correct compliance reports in a form agreed with the acquisition financier.s[99]	A letter of engagement signed by the auditors and topco will be produced in standard form and agreed between the parties. The acquisition financiers should request a review of the document.
Regulatory consents	N/A	If the target business is in a regulated sector such as financial services the parties may be required to get regulatory consent before completion (but not necessarily signing if obtaining the consent is a condition to completion only).	Topco's lawyers will take the lead and keep the acquisition financiers informed of progress.
Merger authority clearance	N/A	If a merger authority clearance is required, it must be obtained before completion, but as above not necessarily before signing. Some clearances may not be absolute conditions to funding in which case the acquisition financiers should obtain confirmation that the failure to obtain the clearances will not have a material adverse effect.	As above.
Any other authorisation or opinion or document that the lead lender considers to be necessary or prudent	N/A	This CP may be removed from the final draft.	Topco should request detail from the acquisition financiers well in advance of signing.
Post-closing undertaking	Topco in favour of the acquisition financiers	This document itemises matters that could not be completed by completion and which the acquisition financiers have agreed to waive for a specific time period	The senior lender's lawyers will produce a standard form

99 See para **11.14**.

Signing and completion

Signing and completion

11.97 There are two discrete stages to the formal completion of a buy-out. Signing is the process whereby the agreed transaction documents are executed by the various parties.[100] Completion means the stage following signing when each of the conditions precedent in the main acquisition, equity and finance documents have been satisfied or waived, at which point the funding is drawn down and the acquisition completed.

Given that the acquisition cannot occur without funding, and that funding is only being provided for the purposes of financing the acquisition, completion of the acquisition and provision of the funding must be interconditional. This either means that signing and completion occur simultaneously or that completion under each of the core acquisition, equity and acquisition finance documents is expressed to be conditional upon the simultaneous completion of each other core document.

A common reason for signing and completion not being simultaneous is that a regulatory clearance is required for the acquisition and it can only be applied for at signing.[101] Another common situation is where the deal timetable is extremely short and the parties agree to sign the deal as early as possible and then complete formalities in full a short period thereafter.

In circumstances where there is split signing and completion each of the financiers will need to ensure that it is not required to fund until all other aspects of the transaction that it requires to be in place are in place. In the case of the senior facilities agreement, for instance, there will be CPs that the equity has been subscribed in newco, that any junior debt has been provided and that the acquisition agreement is unconditional except for payment of the purchase price.

Certain funds

11.98 When sellers first started dealing with private equity sponsors in the early stages of the buy-out market, they would of course be aware of the fact that the buyer was reliant on third-party funding to complete the deal. The buyer's financing was acknowledged as a key part of getting the deal done and one of the key skills for the private equity deal doer therefore, was getting the bank funding – in addition to the private equity funding – onto the table at the point at which buyer and seller were ready to complete the deal. This would be made more complicated whenever signing and completion were not simultaneous, but in order to create sufficient certainty that completion could only occur once all the elements of the deal were in place, the buy-out industry developed a 'subject to financing' condition that was to be included in the acquisition agreement. This condition – also known as a 'financing out' – enables the buyer to pull out of the deal if the acquisition finance is ultimately not forthcoming. Sellers, although initially hostile to these conditions, accepted that they would not be used lightly in practice

---

100 This stage is sometimes referred to as 'exchange' because the buyer and seller exchange executed copies of the acquisition agreement.
101 Such as merger authority clearance or a statutory employment consultation period or where the target is a regulated company such as a financial institution.

and for a time they became a standard feature of the market. This proved to be the high watermark of the buyer's market, however, and since the beginning of the 2000s with more and more private equity buyers vying for assets, sellers have been increasingly resistant to such clauses. The general approach of sellers now is that they should not be required to make concessions to a financial buyer that they would not need to make to a trade buyer with cash. In particular, the seller will not wish to be exposed to the buyer's sources of funding. Indeed one approach of sellers now is to require buyers to give 'reverse warranties' as to the status and availability of the buyer's funding.

The difficulty this approach poses for sponsors stems from the fact that the acquisition financiers will have their own set of conditions to be satisfied before providing funding and not all of these conditions may be capable of being satisfied when buyer and seller are ready to exchange on the acquisition agreement. In addition, where signing and completion are split by any length of time the financiers will wish to retain the right not to fund if some unforeseen event occurs before completion that prejudices their view of the transaction. Without a financing out the buyer will in practice be left with a mismatch in conditionality between the acquisition agreement and the finance documents and, ultimately, an unconditional obligation to buy, but conditional funding. The issue therefore lies in the conditionality in the finance documents.

Finance documents really contain two types of funding condition, documentary CPs and drawstop events based on the events of default. Whereas it is usually possible to satisfy all of the main documentary CPs by the time the acquisition agreement is ready to sign, the drawstop events will continue to apply during the period between signing and completion. Included within the drawstop events will be matters relating to the target group including, usually, a material adverse change (MAC) clause, which is designed to be triggered upon severe negative circumstances occurring which affect the target business, particularly in an economic or financial sense.[102] In certain cases the buyer may be able to insist that some conditionality remains in the acquisition agreement (after signing and until completion), to reflect the main drawstop events in the finance documents, such as target business MAC. This at least gives it an out in circumstances when the funding is most likely to be pulled. But the scope for achieving this in practice has diminished significantly during the 2000s, in what has been a clear seller's market.

The solution that sponsors have come up with is the concept of 'certain funds', which effectively reallocates the risk of adverse events arising during the period between signing and completion from the buyer to its financiers. In very broad terms, this is achieved by requiring the acquisition financiers to satisfy all of their conditions at signing and disapplying the drawstop events until after completion has occurred, subject to whatever exceptions the buyer is able to negotiate and mirror in the acquisition agreement. Buyers are, in effect, seeking to have unconditional funding available from signing.

---

102 This is called a 'business MAC'. Some banks may also wish to include a 'market MAC' which is triggered if there is a material adverse change in the financial markets that would adversely impact the ability of the bank to fund the deal or perhaps to syndicate it. In practice, other than in some emerging market buy-outs, most sponsors will insist that the underwriting bank takes the market risk for the period between signing and completion.

As a concept, certain funds was already a mandatory feature of the public-to-private market, where the provisions of the Takeover Code include a requirement that the bidder has unconditional funding available at the date the offer or scheme is launched, and the term 'certain funds' itself comes from the public-to-private arena.[103] In extending the concept to private buy-outs, however, buyers and sellers have made the requirement even stricter than the regulatory version. In particular, with public-to-privates, the market has developed relatively standard exceptions to the base requirement that private sellers and buyers will often not accept. For example, offer and scheme documents often include conditions relating to the solvency and general financial health of the target that the financiers can indirectly rely on in the finance documents. Many private sellers, however, do not permit any equivalent conditionality.

A key factor that should be in the parties' minds when considering how to approach certain funds is the length of the period between signing and completion. For long periods of, say, three months or more, the absence of a MAC clause at least is likely to be an issue for financiers. Sellers will argue that the financiers must assume that they are on risk from signing and the only reason that completion has not occurred is because of the buyer's own conditionality, usually merger clearance. But acquisition financiers are extremely averse to funding transactions that are immediately in default – because an event of default has occurred that is not a drawstop event – even if theoretically at least they were willing to fund at an earlier date (signing). A key issue will be the impact that this would have on syndication of the debt. It is more difficult for underwriting banks to syndicate an unfunded deal than a funded one, meaning that until completion they may not have syndicated the debt at all. Funding into a default scenario would certainly rule out syndication, leaving them with the entire amount of debt on their balance sheets and a borrower in default.

Equity commitments

11.99 Since the advent of certain funds in private buy-outs, and on the back of a roaring market, sellers have taken the concept to even greater levels in the latter half of the 2000s. One notable development has been the rise of so-called 'equity commitments'. The most aggressive form of equity commitment is a direct obligation by the sponsor in favour of the seller to invest the equity component of the funding at the point at which the acquisition agreement becomes unconditional. It is effectively a guarantee by the sponsor of the equity funding portion of the purchase price. This commitment is usually coupled with an obligation on the sponsor to take various steps to ensure that the debt portion of the funding is also available at completion, including ensuring that newco enforces its rights under the finance documents, satisfies conditions precedent and so on.

Reverse break fees

11.100 Sellers in a few deals have taken equity commitments to a yet further level by introducing reverse break fees into negotiations. The idea is that if the

---

103 See **Chapter 12.**

sponsor pulls out of a deal because of lack of funding it will pay a pre-agreed break fee to the seller. To date this has only been used in a small number of mega buy-outs, principally in the United States, but as a matter of principle it is a natural corollary of having a true certain funds requirement; the funds are supposed to be unconditionally available at signing of the deal. That said, on one level, reverse break fees – and equity commitments – do appear to transgress the basic principle that a private equity fund will not grant any third-party direct financial recourse to the fund. In practice, at the time of writing, reverse break fees were rare and may prove to have been the high watermark of the seller's market.

Financial assistance whitewash

11.101 In 2006 it was announced that the UK's financial assistance laws were being overhauled. In particular, the prohibition on the granting of financial assistance by private companies contained in Companies Act 1985, ss 151 et seq was to be repealed.[104] In doing so the UK legislature signalled the end of the financial assistance 'whitewash' procedure, which has for years been a fundamental feature of the vast majority of UK buy-outs. The repeal of the private company prohibition will come into effect on 1 October 2008 (with the updated provisions applicable to public companies coming into effect on 1 October 2009) and until that time the whitewash will remain an integral part of most buy-outs. The following paragraphs briefly outline the basic financial assistance prohibition and the related relaxation procedure (the whitewash).

Financial assistance arises under Companies Act 1985, s151 (and, for public companies, from 1 October 2009, Companies Act 2006, Pt 18, Ch2), where a target company or any of its subsidiaries provides 'financial assistance' for the purposes of the acquisition of shares in that target company. The prohibited assistance can occur at the time of the acquisition or, in certain circumstances, at a later stage following the acquisition. Financial assistance is defined broadly and includes the provision of a loan or credit support by target group companies to an acquiring company such as newco. In the context of a buy-out this means, in particular, that any loan from a target group company to newco to enable it to repay or service acquisition finance would be prohibited. Similarly, guarantees and security from the target group in favour of the acquisition financiers would also be prohibited. The whitewash is a procedure that enables the prohibition to be relaxed for private companies. For any public company or any subsidiary of a public company the prohibition on the giving of financial assistance is absolute (ie, the whitewash is not available to relax the prohibition). This has particular relevance, therefore, for public-to-privates and means that upstream loans or

104 The changes are to be effected under the Companies Act 2006, which replaces the Companies Act 1985 in stages between 2006 and 2009. Importantly, the new provisions do not remove the prohibition on the granting of financial assistance by a public company, or its subsidiaries, which means that financial assistance will remain a key issue in public-to-privates (see **Chapter 12**). However, note that further changes may be made in this area to deal with implementation of European Union Directive 2006/68/EC amending the Second Company Law Directive on Capital Maintenance and Share Capital. This Directive is required to be implemented in Member States of the European Union by 15 April 2008 and provides an option for Member States to relax the prohibition on public companies giving financial assistance, subject to certain conditions being satisfied.

credit support from the target group cannot be obtained until the target is acquired and re-registered as a private company, which, in practice, will only occur after the acquisition finance has been advanced (and, in the case of a takeover offer, some time after funding). Since this aspect of the prohibition is not being repealed by the recent legislative reforms, practitioners still need to heed the relevant statutory provisions.[105]

Under the pre-existing terms of the Companies Act 1985, as applicable until 1 October 2008, failure to comply with the whitewash requirements would invalidate the loan or credit support obtained in breach of the financial assistance prohibition. In theory, it also gives rise to a criminal offence for directors of companies in breach of the provisions. In any event, the mere fact that failure to follow the procedure could result in the guarantee and security package for the acquisition financiers being invalidated means that the provisions are treated extremely seriously.

In brief, the principal conditions of the whitewash procedure are that:

- the company giving the financial assistance has net assets which are not reduced by the giving of the financial assistance (or are only reduced to the extent of its distributable profits);[106]

- where the company giving the financial assistance is not a wholly-owned subsidiary of another company, the members of the company pass a special resolution approving the giving of the financial assistance;[107]

- all the directors of the company giving the financial assistance make a statuary declaration[108] confirming that in their opinion, as at the time immediately after the financial assistance is given, the company could not be found to be unable to pay its debts and that it will be able to pay its debts as they fall due during the next 12 months;[109] and

- the director's statuary declaration has annexed to it a report of the company's auditors stating that, having enquired into the company's affairs, they are not aware of anything that would indicate the directors' opinion in the statuary declaration to be unreasonable in the circumstances.[110]

---

105 See **Chapter 12** for the impact of the financial assistance laws on public-to-privates. See also fn **104** as regards the potential for further reform of the financial assistance laws as regards public companies.
106 See Companies Act 1985, s 155(2).
107 See Companies Act 1985, s 155(4). Where the financial assistance is to be given by a company in respect of an acquisition of shares in a holding company of that company a special resolution must also be passed by the members of that holding company and any intermediate holding company between it and the company giving the financial assistance; in each case, except where it is a wholly-owned company (see Companies Act 1985, s155 (5)).
108 In a particular form, in front of an independent solicitor.
109 See Companies Act 1985, s 155(6). Where the shares acquired or to be acquired are shares in a holding company of the company giving the financial assistance, all the directors of that holding company and of any intermediate holding company between it and the relevant company shall also be required to make such statuary declarations. There is a further alternative to this formulation (that the company must be able to meet its debts as they fall due etc) (see Companies Act 1985, s 156(2)(a)).
110 See Companies Act 1985, s 156(4).

In light of the scheduled removal of the whitewash process from UK buy-out and acquisition finance practice, debate has begun as to whether the acquisition finance banks would replace the statutory requirements with their own contractual requirements and what these might comprise.

Completion outside banking hours

11.102   Where completion is set to occur outside banking hours, the acquisition financiers will be unable to fund precisely at the time completion occurs. Instead, they will need to pre-fund the completion by raising the debt and placing it in an account pending completion. It is common practice for the account used to be the client account of the sponsor's lawyers and for the funds credited to it to be held by that law firm to the order of the acquisition financiers (or their lawyers) only to be released to newco, and thus the seller, when completion actually occurs. If completion does not subsequently occur after the funds have been placed with the sponsor's lawyers, the financiers will wish to recover interest on the amount re-funded, usually at the agreed margin over cost of funds (LIBOR/EURIBOR or an alternative funding rate such as EONIA[111]). In addition, the financiers may incur broken funding costs.[112] With this in mind, if the main finance documents have not been signed (so that the indemnity in those documents would not apply) the acquisition financiers should obtain a funding indemnity to cover all such amounts either from newco or, if the equity funding has not yet been advanced to newco, the sponsor.

SYNDICATION OF THE ACQUISITION FINANCE

The need for syndication

11.103   With loan facilities of a certain size – say, above £50 million – the underwriting bank will wish to syndicate the facility so that it lays-off some of the credit risk to that individual business. The amount that individual banks and financiers are willing to hold on their balance sheets in respect of particular businesses depends on a number of factors. These include the creditworthiness of the borrower, the sector and jurisdictions in which it operates, the currency of the debt and the ability of that bank or financier to carry debt at all, given the size of its balance sheet and how much of it is available. Some underwriting banks, particularly investment banks, tend not to have the same balance sheet capacity as others, particularly the large commercial banks, and they traditionally arrange and underwrite debt facilities with a very aggressive syndication strategy in mind

---

111   Euro Overnight Index Average. This is the weighted average of overnight EURIBOR rates.

112   Broken funding costs are the costs that the lenders incur by virtue of having taken out a matching loan in the London or European interbank market for the loan made to the borrower and then discharging the interbank loan early (before expiry of the relevant period for which the loan was taken out). Notionally at least it reflects any reduction in LIBOR or EURIBOR that occurs between the date the loan was taken out and the date it was repaid.

so that they do not retain large amounts of debt on their own balance sheets. They are said to be very 'distribution' driven. For those institutions, the fee income from arranging and underwriting transactions is much more important than the returns to be made from interest revenue. Commercial banks by contrast, tend to be less distribution driven. They typically have bigger balance sheets and a greater appetite for interest income rather than, or in addition to, fee income. That is not to say that commercial banks will not actively syndicate the debt they underwrite. They, like investment banks, must keep their balance sheets free to underwrite other deals and ultimately they also prefer to spread their exposure to individual borrowers, sectors, jurisdictions and currencies.

Syndication is therefore a vitally important aspect of the arranging and underwriting of acquisition finance facilities and the larger the deal the more important it becomes.

In order to successfully syndicate a transaction, the arranging and underwriting bank or financial institution (often called the 'MLA', for mandated lead arranger) will seek to ensure that the deal structure – and its funding structure in particular – falls within market acceptable parameters and norms. This largely explains why senior debt structuring has developed in the way it has in the United Kingdom, with relatively uniform pricing and maturity models. This also partly explains the evolution of standardised documentation such as the LMA precedent documents.[113] Similarly, during the negotiation stage of the finance documentation, certain borrower proposals that do not conform to market norms may be rejected by the MLA on the grounds of 'syndication risk'. The idea being that if the proposed amendment were made, it would jeopardise syndication of the debt by being off-market. However, the strength of this argument will largely depend on the strength of the debt markets at the time, including available liquidity in particular – so that in a very liquid market where the supply of debt is great (such as through the mid 2000s) the argument will not be as compelling.

Market flex

11.104 One key development from the late 1990s that has had a significant impact on the syndication of acquisition finance facilities is 'market flex'. Market flex was developed by underwriting banks in the US market in response to the Japanese banking crisis of 1997. This event had an adverse impact on the ability of MLAs to syndicate debt packages because, in simple terms, there were fewer banks to sell down to. As a result, the MLAs found that they were being forced to retain more of the debt themselves. A market flex provision is designed to mitigate the risk of this happening by allowing the MLA to increase the pricing of the debt, and otherwise change the structure and terms, if, by doing so, it is able to syndicate the debt to the level it had intended. By increasing the pricing in particular, the theory is that more banks and financiers will buy the debt in syndication.

---

113 In particular, the London Loan Market Association has developed market standard forms of senior facilities agreement for use in leveraged buy-outs.

This approach was very quickly adopted in the UK market and after that the rest of Europe and market flex provisions have been a standard feature of the European acquisition finance market ever since. Only in times of super-liquidity are sponsors able to resist them. Typically, the market flex provision is included in the MLA's fee letter or in a syndication strategy letter, in each case so that the precise terms remain private between the MLA and the sponsor; although in practice market flex provisions often follow a relatively standard form. The provision typically stipulates that if the MLA has not successfully syndicated the debt within three to six months of completion, it will be entitled to increase the pricing up to a certain limit or, in the more aggressive versions, to otherwise change the structure or terms of the debt.

'Successful syndication' is normally defined by reference to the MLA's targeted final hold position – that is, the amount of debt to be held by the MLA following primary syndication – or by reference to a percentage of the total debt package that must have been sold. The pricing element of the flex will normally be capped at a certain level blended across all of the facilities including fees. So, for example, the MLA might be permitted to increase the fees and interest rate margin on any or all of the facilities so that, on a blended basis, the overall cost increase to the borrower is not more than say 25 or 50 basis points per annum on the total amount of debt. In practice, the cap on the pricing increase is negotiable although market conditions and dynamics will largely dictate what is acceptable. Distinctions may be drawn between the pricing increases that may be made to senior facilities and those that might be made to second lien or mezzanine facilities. The more heavily negotiated flex provisions may also oblige the MLA to allocate more of the upfront fee to the syndicate lenders before resorting to an increase of the debt pricing.

As a matter of pure English law, anything other than a simple pricing flex provision is arguably unenforceable in court. A borrower would have a strong argument that a structural flex provision is a mere 'agreement to agree' and thus void for uncertainty of its terms. In any event, this is largely moot since market flex provisions are given teeth by virtue of being included in a 'finance document', as defined in the senior and mezzanine facility agreements. Breach of a finance document will be stipulated as an event of default entitling acceleration and enforcement of the debt. This is why the flex provisions are included in fee letters or syndication strategy letters, rather than, say, commitment letters or term sheets as the latter are not usually defined as 'finance documents' in the core facility agreements.

A market flex clause should also include a consequential amendments provision that contemplates any necessary changes to be made to the facility agreements to reflect any changes to the pricing or structure of the debt. For example, where the pricing of the debt is increased it may be necessary to re-set the financial covenant levels to preserve the pre-agreed headroom in light of the increased interest payments that will be due.

Reverse flex

11.105 In response to the increased liquidity in the debt markets in the mid-2000s, sponsors began reciprocating MLA-driven market flex provisions by pushing for reverse flex arrangements. Reverse flex works by reducing the pricing of the acquisition finance in circumstances where syndication of the debt is oversubscribed. A reverse flex provision usually provides that the interest rate margin on the facilities – but not typically the up-front fees of the MLA – will be reduced by a certain amount if, in doing so, syndication is not adversely affected; that is, 'successful syndication' can still be achieved. If enough prospective syndicate lenders would drop out following the margin reduction, the reverse flex cannot be enforced by the sponsor. This will be implemented by the MLA testing the market prior to the syndication date and gauging the response. As with upward flex, whether or not a price reduction can be effected will largely reflect how close to the prevailing market conditions the debt has been structured and priced. The cap on the amount of the reduction may be tighter than with an upward flex provision and 25 basis points is not uncommon. In some cases the sponsor may offer a monetary incentive to the MLA to deliver reduced pricing through the successful activation of a reverse flex provision, although such arrangements are necessarily deal specific. In some cases the sponsor may even push for reverse structuring flex where debt is moved from, say, a more expensive mezzanine tranche to a cheaper second lien tranche.

Syndication practicalities

11.106 In order to successfully syndicate the debt underwritten by it, the MLA will need to ensure that the prospective syndicate banks and lenders have sufficient information to assess the creditworthiness of the underlying business and the attractiveness of the transaction as a whole. With this in mind, the MLA will produce an information memorandum. This is, in effect, a selling prospectus that details the investment case for lenders, the target's historic performance, the business plan going forward, sector dynamics, the transaction structure and terms of the facilities and so on. The information memorandum, although put together by the MLA will be expressed to be issued by or on behalf of the borrower, and the borrower will be required to give a representation in the document – which will also be included in the acquisition finance documentation – that in broad terms all of the factual information in the information memorandum is correct and that the projections made are based on reasonable assumptions.

Together with the information memorandum, the MLA will compile a complete information package that will also include all of the due diligence reports. This information package, together with the transaction documents, will then be sent to all prospective syndicate lenders to be used as the basis for their review of the proposal. As with most documents issued during a syndication process this is usually done through an on-line document exchange platform. Before any syndicate lender receives or gains access to the information package, however, it will first need to have signed a confidentiality agreement with the MLA and possibly topco, which requires it to keep all of the information provided confidential and usually to return or destroy the information if the proposal is declined.

Some of the due diligence reports may be expressed to be available only to financiers that agree in writing to the terms on which they are then disclosed. In particular, formal reliance on the reports will be limited to the extent previously agreed by the report providers with the MLA. Consequently, the MLA will need the requisite letters relating to the extent of reliance to be signed up by prospective lenders before releasing those reports. The main purpose of these reliance letters is to ensure that recipients have expressly agreed to the terms on which reliance is extended to them before actually relying on the reports. For instance, there will often be a monetary cap on the amount of any claims that may be made against the authors of a report if it turns out to be flawed.

On the syndication date, the syndicate lenders will enter into novation agreements with the MLA whereby they legally acquire an interest in the debt facilities. Standard form novation agreements (typically referred to as 'transfer certificates') will be included in schedules or exhibits to the main facility agreements. Because the transfer of debt on the syndication date effectively involves the underwriting bank breaking its notional matched deposit in the banking market through which it has funded the debt,[114] it and the sponsor will want to ensure that the syndication date is also an interest period roll-over date. This will avoid the MLA incurring broken funding costs, which ultimately will be passed on to and borne by the borrower. With this in mind, it is common for the MLA and borrower to agree in the finance documents that until the syndication is completed, the borrower will only select interest periods of one month in duration. This enables the MLA to schedule syndication to occur on a roll-over date. Given the need for the syndicate lenders to review and become satisfied with all of the information provided and the terms of the transaction documentation before completion of the syndication process, and to enable syndication to be legally effected on a roll-over date, a practical approach to timing is required.[115]

TRANSACTION TIMETABLE

11.107 This section considers what a typical timetable might be for a buy-out of a private company in the United Kingdom. It focuses on a fully negotiated deal rather than an auctioned disposal where the timetable often has less in common with buy-outs and more to do with general M&A practice and processes.

One effect of the proliferation of auction processes in the 2000s has been the truncation of the documentation phase once the winning bid is awarded. In extreme cases, from the time a winning bidder is announced, the parties may only be given a number of days to put the necessary finance documentation in place. This has led, for instance, to the use of temporary bridge documentation (also known as interim loan or funding agreements) as the means to sign up deals, with full documentation being finalised in the period immediately after signing.[116] Seller due diligence is similarly used to shorten the overall timetable of the deal.[117]

---

114 This will be the London interbank market for UK deals other than for euro-denominated loans, where the European interbank market applies. See also fn **112**.
115 Having a realistic timetable assists syndication.
116 See para **11.116** for more information on interim loan documentation.
117 See para **11.69**.

Legal and documentation timetable

11.108 The following paragraphs consider a specific aspect of the overall deal timetable, that is, the timetable for the legal and documentary processes. They outline a generic timetable for a typical UK buy-out from the point at which the basic commercial deal is agreed, with the parties in a position to appoint legal and other advisers to give the prospective transaction legal effect, until the point at which the finance is made available and the acquisition completed. By its nature such a timetable is indicative only and deal-specific circumstances will invariably operate to lengthen or shorten some or all of the various elements. The timetable applicable to a public-to-private will be quite different and is considered separately in **Chapter 12**. The timetable for a multi-jurisdictional buy-out is also less likely to follow the indicative model suggested below and such a deal may take longer to complete given the extra complexity typically involved. **Chapter 13** considers some of these additional complexities.

From the perspective of the lawyers acting for the acquisition financiers, the legal aspects of a UK buy-out can be expected to take anywhere from three to six weeks from the initial instruction to begin work until signing and completion. However, as mentioned above, deal timetables have undergone a certain amount of truncation in the mid-2000s, especially on larger deals, where the sale process is likely to follow an M&A auction timetable and the documentation process is often compressed into just one or two weeks. One of the major reasons for this is the prevalence of competitive bidding processes (auctions and even contract races) that force parties to accelerate the process. This may include pre-agreeing as many terms as possible before commencing the legal and documentation process proper. One noticeable feature of the procedure for agreeing the finance documents since the mid-2000s has been the development by sponsors of their own debt term sheets. Rather than being drafted and provided by the banks, as was the convention for many years, a sponsor provides what is usually a very extensive term sheet (perhaps running to more than 70 pages), which it then distributes to prospective MLAs. This is designed to have two effects – first, the sponsor is more likely to get debt finance on the terms it wants, and secondly, the process of agreeing the finance documentation is in theory speeded up since all of the main documentary provisions are agreed up-front, before the lawyers begin negotiating the full documents. The trend of shortening the documentation timetable has also been aided by the standardisation of acquisition finance documentation, which has occurred as the market has evolved.

The documentation process is yet further shortened by the use of interim loan documents. Rather than negotiating a full facilities agreement the parties will put in place a shorter form document, with substantially reduced representations, covenants and events of default, and use this to fund the acquisition. In the period of, say, 14 days following signing the parties will then replace the interim documents with the full standard documentation. From the MLA's perspective, it is preferable for completion and funding itself to occur under the full documentation rather than the interim documentation.

Legal and documentation timetable summary

11.109 In summary form the timetable for the legal and documentation aspects of a private UK buy-out might be as set out below.[118]

Timing	Action
Week 1	• appointment of all legal advisers
	• legal due diligence commenced, if not already as part of the initial buy-out process
	• initial drafts of senior debt[119] and acquisition and equity documents produced and distributed to all except the seller (which will generally be concerned with acquisition agreements only[120])
	• if there is warranted mezzanine debt, the warrant instrument will be drafted and distributed but the mezzanine facility agreement will usually only be produced at a later stage on the basis that the negotiated senior facilities agreement will be the template
	• if the funding structure includes high yield debt, a bridging facility will be put in place at completion and the bond issued subsequently.[121] The bridging facility documents will be produced and distributed over the same period as the senior debt documents
	• if there is PIK note debt, the principal documentation for that will be produced and distributed
Week 2	• review of acquisition, equity and finance documents by relevant parties
	• comments on the documents fed into the lawyers responsible for drafting them
	• first draft legal due diligence report produced and distributed to the acquisition financiers, equity providers and their respective lawyers[122]
Weeks 2–3	• negotiation and further drafts of the acquisition, equity and finance documents
	• drafting and distribution of corporate authorities, financial assistance (whitewash) documentation[123] and any other ancillary condition precedent documents by newco's lawyers for review by the acquisition financiers' lawyers
	• further draft legal due diligence report produced and distributed
	• when the senior facilities agreement is in relatively final form a mezzanine facility agreement (if relevant) or possibly a second lien facility agreement[124] will be created using the senior facilities agreement as a template
	• final or near-final drafts of the acquisition, equity and finance documents produced and distributed

118 As indicated above this process could be substantially different for an auctioned deal.

119 In a buy-out with second lien debt, this will often also be documented in the senior debt document. If not, a separate second lien facility agreement will usually only be produced once the senior debt document is largely agreed, as with mezzanine. See also **Chapter 6**.

120 But see para **11.98** in respect of 'certain funds'.

121 See **Chapter 8** generally.

122 The point at which the legal report is made available depends on when the overall due diligence process was begun. More often than not since the early to mid 2000s, when auction processes became the norm for most mid-market and larger deals, the due diligence will be begun very early in the process with the legal report possibly being completed very early in the overall legal and documentation stage. Seller due diligence in particular will be available prior to the legal and documentary stages. See also para **11.69**.

123 In fact, the prohibition on the giving of financial assistance by private companies, together with the whitewash procedure, will be repealed as of 1 October 2008. See para **11.101** generally.

124 See **Chapter 6**. Second lien debt is often documented as the 'D tranche' of senior debt in the senior facilities agreement.

Timing	Action
Week 3 – 4	• final comments and negotiation of outstanding points on all documents resulting in production of execution drafts • final draft legal due diligence report produced and distributed • final run through of condition precedent documents • signing of equity and finance documents • exchange of acquisition agreement
Week 3 or 4[125]	• delivery of all conditions precedent at signing and exchange or, if completion is to be delayed, as many as possible as can be delivered and satisfied[126] • funding and completion

Overall buy-out timetable

11.110 The following diagrams provide examples of the overall timetable for a typical private buy-out. Since all deals involve variable factors that can impact the timing of various stages, the timetables shown are necessarily illustrative. For example, it might be possible to compress the whole process into a much shorter timeframe if all necessary decisions are made quickly, the due diligence and documentation processes expedited, and no time critical obstacles, such as regulatory clearances, encountered.

Two example timetables are given. The first illustrates a full auction process including seller due diligence and the second a buy-out where the sponsor is awarded exclusivity earlier in the process (an 'exclusive deal').

---

125 In some cases completion will occur on the same day as or shortly after signing and exchange. However, in larger or more complex deals there may be a scheduled delay between signing and completion perhaps where a regulatory clearance is required, such as competition clearance, or, in a multi-jurisdictional deal, to put in place the security package, although more often than not now completion will not wait for the full security package and the security is put in place as a condition subsequent.
126 See para **11.98** in respect of the 'certain funds' principle.

Auction process

11.111

1 week	2 weeks	3 weeks	4 weeks	5 weeks	6 weeks	7 weeks	8 weeks	9 weeks	10 weeks	11 weeks	12 weeks	13 weeks	14 weeks	15 weeks

Advisors appointed and sale strategy finalised

Seller and advisers finalise information memorandum and prepare data room

Seller's advisers prepare seller due diligence reports (including as a minimum financial and legal)

Seller may obtain stapled offer of finance

Potential buyers identified

Distribution of information memorandum and seller due diligence reports

Seller's lawyers prepare acquisition documents

Buyers obtain indicative offers of funding from financiers

First round bids submitted by interested buyers

Selected potential buyers and their financiers granted access to data room to undertake due diligence, and may be given access to management

Buyers' funding arrangements advanced

Acquisition documents distributed to buyers

Second round bids submitted (incorporating mark-up of acquisition documents)

Seller awards exclusivity chosen buyer

Buyer's funding arrangements finalised including documentation

Acquisition documentation negotiated and finalised

Satisfaction of outstanding (post-signing) conditions if any (including permanent loan documentation)

Signing (and possibly Completion)

Completion (if not at Signing)

Exclusive deal

11.112

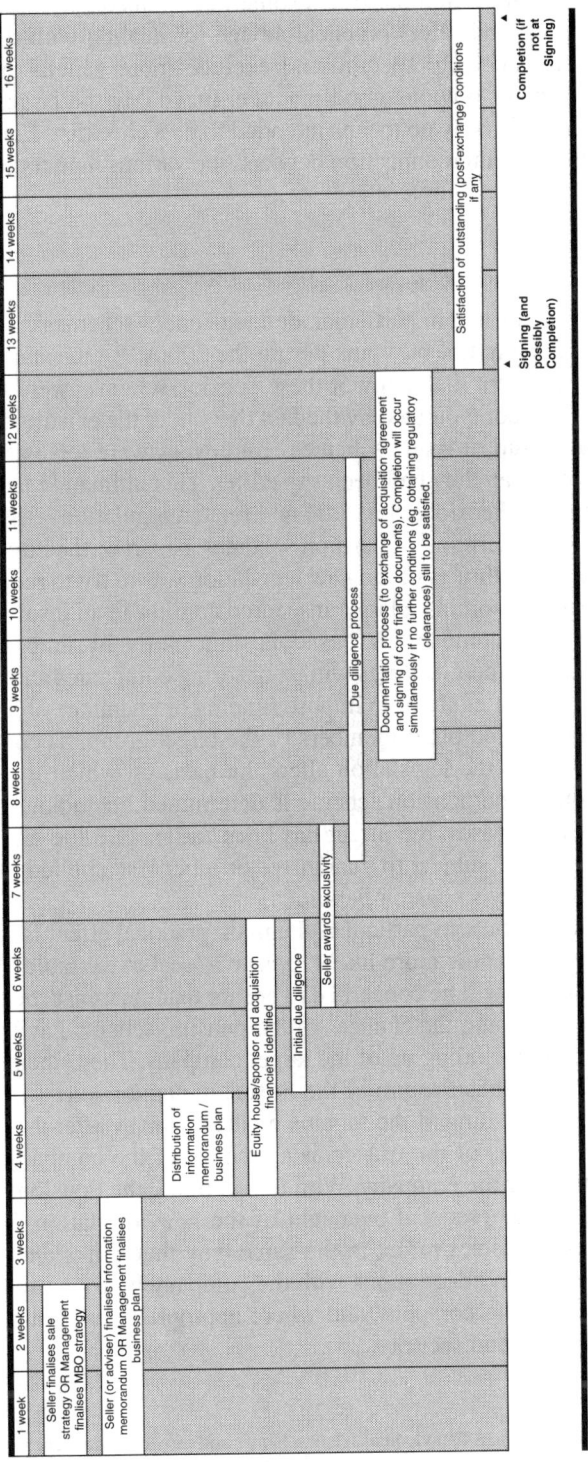

PRACTICAL ADVICE ON SOME COMMONLY ARISING ISSUES

11.113 This final section considers some miscellaneous issues that frequently arise in buy-outs and offers practical advice for dealing with them. The issues considered are relatively specific and exclude more general matters that fall within the scope of obvious good practice. Inevitably the issues raised are not exhaustive and this is by no means intended to be a checklist. Equally there is no particular order or interconnection between the various matters set out.

Pensions

11.114 Pensions – and in particular, defined benefit schemes[127] – have become a major issue in many UK buy-outs during the 2000s. By the start of the 2000s it had become apparent that many of these pension schemes were under-funded, a concern that was compounded by the fact that under the existing legislation, on a solvent winding-up of many schemes, employees were left with pensions that were much less than they had been expecting. This ultimately led to a change of law – through the Pensions Act 2004 and related regulation – that itself has further increased the scrutiny of pension schemes as part of the buy-out process.

One of the main thrusts of the new legislation was to try to reduce the risk of a pension scheme becoming a large unsecured creditor in an insolvent winding-up of its sponsoring company. It has done this partly by empowering pension scheme trustees in their dealings with sponsoring companies and by giving powers to the Pensions Regulator to impose funding or guarantee obligations on both the buyer's group and other members of the target group, as considered further below. In addition, the legislation alters the basis on which the liability of the company to fund the pension scheme is determined, including in a winding up situation. In most cases, the effect has been to increase the amounts paid into pension schemes or subject to guarantees or otherwise applied to provide security for the company's pension liabilities.

Looking at buy-outs in particular, the main practical effect is that the pension scheme trustees are now more likely to have a 'seat at the table' during negotiations at which they will be concerned to ensure that the transaction does not have the effect of increasing the chances of the pension scheme having a large unsecured claim in the winding up of the target company. The principal way this can be achieved – and thus the aim of the trustee in negotiations – is by strengthening the on-going funding of the scheme by the company after the buy-out and by preserving the status of the trustee as a creditor of the company, including the creditworthiness of the company. With this in mind, the Pensions Regulator, the office that provides practical oversight of the new legislation, has encouraged pension scheme trustees to act in the same way that banks and other financial institutions would in negotiations with the company by trying to limit the scope for insolvency of the company and where appropriate to obtain credit support such as guarantees and security.

---

127 Defined benefit schemes include final salary schemes and career average schemes.

The trustees' powers in negotiations are ultimately rooted in regulation. The Pensions Regulator has powers to impose funding or guarantee obligations on the buyer's group and other members of the target group that otherwise have no obligations to the pension scheme. It may exercise these powers, in particular, when it considers that a transaction has the effect of increasing the chances of the pension scheme having a large unsecured claim in the winding up of the target company. Protection from the risk of such obligations being imposed may be obtained by seeking the approval of the Pensions Regulator, for which the support of the trustees is generally required.

In practical terms, the impact on buy-out deal dynamics is really three-fold. First, as a general matter, understanding any scheme that the target group has in place has become more important than ever. Irrespective of any general powers of the Pensions Regulator, it is vital that the buyer and its financiers become comfortable with the actual and contingent liabilities that a company has under the scheme and with the rights of the scheme trustee under the constitutional terms of the scheme. Appropriately detailed due diligence is therefore key. The second practical effect is that the pension scheme trustee may be able to insist that the company's contributions to the fund, whether on a one-off basis or on an ongoing basis, must be increased, perhaps materially. This may therefore have a material effect on the business plan and base case model and consequently the projected returns of the equity investors. It may also impact the viability of the financial structure as a whole by reducing the amount of available cashflow for debt service purposes. Finally, the trustee might have requirements in relation to the financial structure of the buy-out for the purposes of protecting the claims of the scheme against the company, ultimately in an insolvent winding-up of the company. In particular, the trustee might require that the scheme be granted pari passu status with the acquisition financiers in relation to any funding liability to the scheme that arises in due course. This may also have a material impact on the viability of the financial structure as a whole since the acquisition financiers may not accept pari passu ranking of the pension liabilities or they might not agree the amount of pension liabilities that benefit from this ranking.

As a result of these potential issues, detailed negotiations with pension scheme trustees have now become a relatively common deal feature in the UK and they are not always resolved to the satisfaction of all parties, with a number of prospective buy-outs having been aborted as a result. It follows that the sponsor and the acquisition financiers should prioritise an analysis of the target's pension schemes – and defined benefit schemes in particular – from the outset of the transaction. From the perspective of the acquisition financiers there may be an additional and material intercreditor concern to deal with if, as is not uncommon, the scheme trustees insist on scheme claims against the company being accorded intercreditor type rights within the overall financial structure of the buy-out.[128]

Auctions

11.115 As the buy-out market has matured, with private equity playing an increasingly prominent role in mergers and acquisitions activity generally in the

---

128 See also para **10.142** for more detail on the intercreditor aspect.

developed economies, sellers have become more sophisticated in their approach to doing deals with sponsors. One of the most obvious indicators of this trend has been the increasing use of competitive sale processes – auctions. Rather than negotiating a deal with a single buyer, sellers are increasingly likely to have more than one prospective buyer compete for the target business. In most cases they can safely assume that this is more likely to provide them with the fullest market price available and to more than make up for the additional cost of hiring an investment bank or corporate finance team to run the process. On the other side, for sponsors that are seeking to acquire assets that are auctioned, are there particular techniques or strategies that can improve the chances of success?

Although every deal is different and generalisations may have no particular relevance to the case in hand, a buyer should certainly approach an auction process differently from an exclusively negotiated deal and certain general strategies might indeed improve the chances of success.

One obvious strategy to improving the chances of success for a buyer is to reduce the conditionality of its bid. Usually this will happen naturally as the auction process passes through various stages, including, in particular, due diligence and documentation, but if the sponsor can demonstrate to the seller at each stage a greater level of commitment to the deal than other bidders, most sellers will view that sponsor's ultimate bid that much more strongly. This approach can be encapsulated in the idea that a buyer should front-end as much work on the investment case as possible so that it is able to form the view that it definitely wants the target business as early as possible in the process. Once it has passed that point much of the effort can be directed towards winning the bid and in particular by removing obstacles to completion. Winning an auction will almost certainly involve the sponsor pursuing the opportunity that much more aggressively than with an exclusively negotiated deal. Thus, in the acquisition documentation it is likely to have to concede issues to the seller that it might not need to concede in an exclusive deal. Acknowledging this fact early on in the process and perhaps volunteering certain concessions may mark a particular buyer's bid out at an early stage. In actual fact, some sponsors have taken this principle to the logical extreme by making an unconditional and fully underwritten bid at the very start of the process and thus pre-emptively gazumping the other bidders.

From the debt finance perspective, reducing the conditionality of the debt offer in an auction situation is also vital. There are various levels of commitment that can be obtained from lenders, ranging from the indicative commitment to make finance available to the fully underwritten and documented offer of funds. The best position for a sponsor is where it can demonstrate that it has unconditional debt available on a 'certain funds' basis.[129] Achieving this as early as possible in the process – usually by no later than the date final round bids are submitted – requires very supportive lenders and sponsors will often run their own competitive process for the debt finance mandate in order to improve their position with the lenders. Some sponsors might go further than this even and bid on the basis that they will bridge the debt element of the funding structure themselves whatever happens. Such an approach does of course have an additional element of risk if there is any scope that

---

129 See para **11.98**.

the deal or its structure is not bankable to the extent assumed by the sponsor, so even if a sponsor is willing to bridge the deal entirely itself it should still have lenders lined up to provide the finance. With most auctioned deals, given the full price generally required to win the asset, the finance structure will need to be finely tuned, with the optimum amount of debt built in. Consequently, any failure to secure the requisite amount of debt at the assumed pricing and structure is likely to materially detract from the projected returns of the equity investors.

The ability to actually demonstrate that funds are available to satisfy a prospective buyer's bid will also be a key element of most successful bid strategies. With sponsors that manage third-party funds, showing available drawn funds in a bank account will be the ultimate in proof of funds. Not all sponsors will be in this position, however, and other approaches may be required. One increasingly common mechanism used by sponsors is to take out an equity bridge facility with a bank so that the sponsor can provide the equity component of its bid in advance of drawing more cash from its fund investors.

As far as documentation is concerned, auction processes generally require that at least some level of negotiation of the acquisition agreement occurs before a winning bidder is announced and ultimately a deal signed. Consequently, as indicated above, a buyer is likely to have to concede matters to the seller that it would not necessarily concede in a fully negotiated exclusive deal. Probably the most important area of interest for the seller will be the completion conditions. It will wish to see the minimum amount of conditionality. The extent of the warranty and indemnity cover will also be important, including the provisions limiting the ability of the buyer to make claims. A seller can allocate a tangible value to the cap on the total amount of claims that may be made, for example. This all said, it is difficult to generalise on the approach to documentation for any given situation and by comparison with the actual price bid, documentation may be relatively unimportant. On the other hand, buyers should not assume that price is the *only* consideration that a seller will take into account in selecting the winning bidder.

On a less formal level, where members of the incumbent management team of the target business are reasonably involved in the sale process or where the management are otherwise close to the seller, a buyer is likely to benefit from having the management team as on-side as possible to its bid. This might be achieved by offering particularly attractive post-deal terms to the management team – although there may be no way for a buyer to know what other bidders are contemplating in this regard – or a sponsor might achieve just as much simply by establishing a good rapport with the management team through the deal process.

The use of interim loan documents and short term facilities

11.116 One of the features of auctions that has had a major impact on the acquisition finance market has been the strict timing constraints imposed on the documentation process. Sellers expect to finalise all necessary documentation and then complete the sale as quickly as possible after a preferred or winning bidder emerges. In practice, this generally means that the period within which the parties document the acquisition finance is materially shorter than for an exclusively negotiated deal. It might be one week or two weeks in total. This is largely imposed by sellers, who with a number of bidding parties can afford to demand a shorter timetable as part of the competitive process. In some cases bidders may move to documentation of the acquisition finance before being awarded preferred bidder status in order to demonstrate their readiness to complete the deal or perhaps because the sellers demand it themselves. But in doing so, they risk incurring additional costs without certainty that they will win the auction. The alternative is simply to truncate the documentation as much as possible, which often puts enormous pressure on the sponsor and the acquisition financiers and their advisers in particular to meet the necessary timeframe.

Acquisition financiers have responded to this situation by developing the use of short term facilities under interim loan or funding agreements. A short term facility is an acquisition bridge facility made available by the MLA that enables the acquisition to be signed and in theory funded and completed in the shorter timeframe required to win the deal. Typically, the interim documentation is required to be replaced with the final full documentation within 14-30 days of signing, which usually still means pre-funding, although not necessarily and some deals have been funded under an interim loan agreement. Since the facility is documented in short form[130] it can be agreed and signed in a much shorter time frame than the permanent facilities. Given the short term nature of the facility there is no practical need to negotiate detailed representations, covenants and events of default in respect of the target group. The document will, however, usually include representations, covenants and events of default in respect of the SPV group, which are much more straight forward to agree, given that those companies are all pure holding companies. The short tenor of the facility incentivises the parties to replace it with the full facility documentation as soon as possible. Typically the only security given for the short form facility will be from newco, which will include the shares of the target company. No target group security is given until full documentation is in place for the permanent facilities – and thus no financial assistance whitewash is required until that time[131] – which (in circumstances where this occurs after funding) is a major departure from standard acquisition finance practice.[132]

Due diligence

11.117 When carrying out due diligence it is quite easy for the buyer and its financiers to simply rely on third-party consultants and advisers to highlight material matters. In practice, the scope of the exercise will be agreed in advance with the consultants and advisers – often based on relatively standard templates – who then go off and perform the exercise with relatively little additional input from the principals until a first (and possibly final) draft of their report is available. There are two relatively straightforward approaches that can enhance this process materially. The first goes to the scope itself and is discussed in further detail in the following paragraphs. The second, which does not really need much

---

130 Perhaps only 25 pages or so by contrast with the 150 pages or more that might be required for the permanent facilities.

131 See para **11.101** on financial assistance and the whitewash procedure generally, including the fact that the whitewash is to be repealed on 1 October 2008.

132 See also para **5.15** in relation to interim loan documents generally.

further explanation, is that the consultants and advisers should be instructed to report back on material matters promptly before they issue their initial report so that the parties have as much time as possible to react. There is nothing more frustrating or resource wasting than for a deal to abort late in the process because of something that comes up in due diligence. Deal breakers should be uncovered as early as possible; and potentially having the matter raised early may leave room for a mitigating solution to be negotiated.

As for the scope of the due diligence, time should be taken in preparing the engagements to ensure that the available resources are focused on the areas of most relevance to the deal. With this in mind the parties should identify the key features of the deal and ensure that the due diligence teams understand what these are too. Similarly, it is generally worth establishing with the due diligence teams right at the outset the level of financial impact on the target business at which a matter becomes 'material' in the context of the deal as a whole. This is particularly important with due diligence reports that are produced on a 'by exception' basis.[133] So, for example, the parties may determine that a liability that exceeds say £250,000 is material. More information can then be sought and reported on these matters and indeed the buyer is more likely to seek seller comfort on these matters generally.

Main drivers of the target business

11.118 Arguably the most important aspect of any due diligence process is an assessment of the achievability of the business plan by the target and its management team. Understanding the key drivers of the business is therefore vital and precisely how the target generates profit may give particular cause for concern. For example, where a target business has only a very small number of revenue sources, such as a small number of customers, the due diligence should focus on the quality of those relationships. This will include analysing the legal status of the relationships – are there long term contracts in place, do those contracts require the customer to purchase a fixed number of products per year, is the price fixed, are those contracts 'tripped' by a change of control and so on? The due diligence should also cover the financial value of each of those contracts and the history of dealings between the parties and also how each customer views the target – and in effect how reliant they are on the target for supply. Ultimately, the value of such a business is closely linked to the value of those contracts or relationships; they are a key driver of the business. With other businesses there will be other drivers that are key to the delivery of the business plan and by identifying what they are early on and focusing on those aspects the parties and their advisers can take a more educated call on the key issue of achievability of the business plan.

Unusual deal features

11.119 Right at the outset of the process the sponsor and its advisers should try and identify any particularly unusual features of the transaction so that any consequent additional work can be factored in early on. What might fall into this cat-

---

133 See paras **11.54** and **11.68** on due diligence generally.

egory is necessarily not an exhaustive list but some examples are given in the following paragraph.

Where the target business is in a regulated industry, such as financial services, education, healthcare or utilities, the nature of the regulatory regime and any approval required from the regulatory body will need to be factored into the deal viability and timetable. In some transactions the target group might include a company that is constitutionally unusual, that is, it might not simply be a limited liability private company. For example, companies limited by guarantee or companies that are created by private act of parliament may need special attention as part of the documentation process. Another example of a relatively unusual deal feature is where the target business is merely a division of a large business that the seller is not selling. In this circumstance, the seller might not be transferring the target business together with all necessary centralised functions, such as accounting, IT, human resources and so on. Consequently, the buyer may need to agree with the seller the provision of these functions on a transitional basis for say six months until the buyer can establish its own equivalent functions for the target.

Third-party consents

11.120   In some buy-outs, more than just the principal parties – buyer, seller and financiers – will need to be involved in order to complete the deal. For example, where the target business has contractual relationships that would be breached or terminated by the change of control occurring in the buy-out, the buyer or its financiers will generally insist that the requisite waiver or consent to the change of control is obtained from each other party to the contracts as a condition of completion and funding.[134] Often such third parties will have no incentive to provide their consent within the timeframe envisaged by the principal deal parties and they may also prove unpredictable in their approach to the request for consent. Therefore approaching these parties within plenty of time before completion – subject to any necessary confidentiality constraints – is generally prudent.

Seller notes

11.121   Seller notes often present a specific area of practical concern for the parties.[135] Because sellers and financiers rarely need to interact directly in a buy-out, it is often overlooked that, when the seller becomes a financier itself, by taking a seller note, intercreditor issues arise as between the acquisition financiers and the seller. If these issues are not addressed early in the process the sponsor may be storing up material problems for the later stages. Particular concerns arise when the seller's expectations of the terms on which the note is repayable and its structural status – in particular which entity is the issuer and whether the note is to be secured at all – do not match those of the acquisition financiers. In reality, differ-

---

134   This might include consents under leases, material supplier or customer contracts and loan agreements.
135   See also para **4.12** with regard to seller notes generally.

ent expectations in this context are quite likely to arise. A seller will often treat the seller note as pure deferred consideration that is payable in due course irrespective of the issuer's arrangements with its financiers. By contrast, the acquisition financiers will generally treat the seller note as subordinated debt that should be unsecured and structurally, or at a minimum contractually, subordinated to the acquisition finance and possibly subject to extensive payment conditions such as enhanced financial performance or the like.

To avoid the risk of these different expectations remaining unsettled until late in the deal process, when they might even become a deal breaker for one party or another, the sponsor should at the minimum agree a term sheet for the seller note with the financiers and then the seller as early as possible in the process.

Multi-jurisdictional buy-outs: target group security

11.122 This paragraph briefly raises two related aspects of multi-jurisdictional deals that it is easy to overlook until relatively late in the process, by which point they can become more material. They should both be addressed early in the process. First, the management team of the target must agree to the required level of target group credit support for the acquisition finance. The concern here is that the granting of upstream guarantees and security by companies incorporated in many jurisdictions involves the exercise of corporate power by the directors of those companies that can in certain circumstances be challenged at a later date, particularly by a liquidator or bankruptcy official if there is an insolvency event. Such a challenge might in certain jurisdictions and circumstances result in personal liability for the directors. With this in mind, directors of target group companies often take a more conservative approach to the granting of upstream credit support than say the sponsor, which means that negotiating the guarantee and security package with the sponsor alone may not be sufficient.

The second point also relates to target group credit support and the legal limitations on its enforceability. Most acquisition finance houses and sponsors – and their advisers – have over the years completed several multi-jurisdictional buy-outs across many different jurisdictions. They will therefore be reasonably familiar with commonly occurring legal issues, such as the extent to which target group guarantees and security are available for the acquisition finance. However, where new jurisdictions are involved or, with any jurisdiction, simply because their expectations in this regard may no longer reflect current law in that jurisdiction, it cannot be taken for granted that the requisite target group guarantee and security package will be available in any given transaction (even if the target group directors are happy to approve it). With this in mind, it is good practice for the acquisition financiers to insist on the delivery of draft legal opinions – or at least the qualifications that will be made against the opinions – early in the process. This should identify where there are any legal limits to the value of the required security package in good time to enable any consequent structural or even pricing adjustments to be made before signing and completion.

CHAPTER 12

Public-to-privates

INTRODUCTION

What is a public-to-private?

12.1 This chapter is concerned with buy-outs of public companies or, perhaps more accurately, companies to which the City Code on Takeovers and Mergers[1] applies. In most cases the target will be a company that is listed on the Official List and traded on the Main Market of the London Stock Exchange or whose shares are traded on AIM (or PLUS[2]). In fact, the Code has broader applicability and encompasses all *public* companies resident in the UK, Channel Islands and Isle of Man, whether listed or not.[3] Generally this chapter assumes the target to be a public company that is traded on the Main Market or on AIM but for ease of reference they are simply referred to as public companies.

Buy-outs of public companies are different from buy-outs of private companies in a number of respects. Many of the differences simply result from the applicability of the Code – and other regulations – to public bids. Others stem directly from the fact that public companies tend to have multiple 'owners' so a standard negotiated sale and purchase approach is not feasible. Instead the acquisition must be effected in an altogether different manner, either through a takeover offer under the Code or through a court sanctioned scheme of arrangement under the Companies Act[4].

---

1 Usually just called the 'Takeover Code' or the 'Code' for short or sometimes the 'blue book'. See also para **12.5**.
2 The chapter does not specifically deal with companies whose shares are quoted on London's PLUS market (previously known as OFEX).
3 The Code also applies to certain private companies. See also para **12.9** for a more detailed consideration of the types of companies and transactions that are covered by the Code. As a more general matter, note that it is not an absolute requirement that a company must be a public company in order to issue securities to the public (see Section 81 Companies Act 1985 and its successor provision in Chapter 1 of Part 20 of the Companies Act 2006, which is to be brought into force on 6 April 2008).
4 See Section 425 Companies Act 1985 and the successor provision in Part 26 Companies Act 2006 (which is to be brought into force on 6 April 2008).

Terminology: 'public-to-privates', 'offers', 'schemes', 'takeovers' and 'bids' etc

12.2   The sponsor's main aim in acquiring a public company is normally to acquire a sufficient stake so that it can re-register it as a private company (and take it off the relevant stock market). For this reason buy-outs of public companies are generally referred to as 'public-to-private' transactions.

Until the 2000s, the vast majority of public-to-private deals were effected through 'takeover offers' under the Code. Practice evolved during the 2000s, however, and a large proportion – if not the majority – of public-to-privates are now effected by way of a 'scheme of arrangement' under the Companies Act.[5] Prospective public-to-privates of both kinds are generally referred to as 'bids' or indeed 'takeovers' and the acquisition finance used for bids may also be referred to as 'bid finance' or 'takeover finance'. The acquirer in a public-to-private is often referred to as the 'bidder' or – using the Code terminology – the 'offeror'. The term 'bidco' is also used because the actual bid vehicle is usually an SPV.

Throughout this chapter the terms 'bidder' and 'bid' are preferred in the context of both offers and schemes.

Takeover offers and schemes of arrangement

12.3   As indicated above, public-to-privates can be effected through two different procedures: traditional takeover offers, and court sanctioned schemes of arrangement under the Companies Act. There are advantages and disadvantages to each and both mechanisms are used in practice. In fact, whereas offers were once much more common than schemes, the second half of the 2000s saw a reversal of this trend for recommended bids. This may, in large part, be a result of growing confidence in the successful use of schemes for takeovers as evidenced by a number of high profile scheme takeovers in 2006 and 2007. That is not to say that the traditional offer strategy is no longer used, and indeed a common strategy now is for a bid to be launched initially in the form of a scheme but with a traditional offer procedure reserved as a fallback if the scheme runs into difficulty.[6] Subsequent sections of this chapter consider both offers and schemes in some detail including the key differences between the two procedures.

THE REGULATION OF PUBLIC-TO-PRIVATES

Applicable regulations

12.4   Public-to-privates are subject to a number of regulations that don't apply to private buy-outs. First, and most significantly, is the Takeover Code. The

---

5   See fn **4**.
6   Usually because a competing bid arises and the target board then refuses to recommend the initial offer. In fact, it is also possible to switch from an offer to a scheme. See also para **12.39**.

main provisions of the Code are summarised briefly below. The second major piece of regulation is the Companies Act. At the time of writing the Companies Act 1985 was in the process of being replaced by the Companies Act 2006 and wherever possible reference has been made to the relevant section of the incoming legislation and the date when it is to become effective.[7] The Companies Act is generally applicable to both private and public companies and is therefore also relevant for private buy-outs, but certain provisions apply to public-to-private transactions in particular. The main provisions of the Companies Act that apply to public-to-privates are also considered separately below. Finally, there are a number of other important pieces of legislation and regulation that will apply in a bid situation and these are briefly considered at the end of this section.

The Takeover Code

12.5 The Takeover Code is at the core of the UK regulatory regime for public-to-privates. It applies to *all* takeover bids for public companies however effected, including both traditional takeover offers *and* schemes of arrangement. Its applicability to schemes of arrangement is not as complete as with offers and certain modifications apply to reflect the statutory procedure and court timetable applicable to schemes.[8] An important development occurred in May 2006 with the adoption into UK law of the EU Directive on Takeover Bids,[9] which for the first time gave the Code a statutory basis (to the extent it is derived from that directive[10]). The Code is published and enforced by the Panel on Takeovers and Mergers.

The Panel on Takeovers and Mergers

12.6 The Takeover Panel is an independent body that was established in 1968. It is comprised of up to 34 members drawn from major financial and business institutions. The Chairman, Deputy Chairman and up to 20 independent members are appointed upon the recommendation of the Panel's own nomination committee, with the remaining members nominated by certain professional bodies such as the Confederation of British Industry, the London Investment Banking Association and the National Association of Pension Funds. Its day-to-day operations are handled through its 'executive', a professional staff headed by the Director General. The Takeover Panel existed as a non-statutory body until the implementation of the EU Directive on Takeover Bids[11] in May 2006, which gave the Panel statutory powers.[12] The main job of the Panel is to oversee and

---

7 The new provisions are being brought into force in stages between 2006 and 2009.

8 See also para **12.11** below.

9 Directive 2004/25/EC.

10 It is beyond the scope of this chapter to consider all of the changes to the Code that resulted from the Takeover Directive but many of the key provisions of the Code generally are considered.

11 Directive 2004/25/EC.

12 The Panel's Takeover Directive functions are set out in Chap 1 of Pt 28 of the Companies Act 2006.

enforce the Code and to ensure its application to specific takeover transactions. As a practical matter the Panel will expect to be consulted both before and during a bid. This is particularly important with buy-outs, which tend to raise more issues under the Code than other takeover offers.[13]

Status of the Code

12.7   As indicated above, the Takeover Directive that gave the Panel statutory powers also gave the Takeover Code – to the extent it is now derived from that directive – a statutory basis for the first time. Prior to this the Code did in practice have quasi-statutory effect but for the most part only through convention and practical necessity. In particular, any institution or professional firm that was involved in takeovers had a *de facto* statutory obligation to adhere to the Code and to refuse to act in an advisery capacity for any person that it had reason to believe was not complying or would not comply with the Code, or else face being shut out of the market.[14] But the Code did not have statutory force. In any event, notwithstanding that the Code now has a statutory foundation, the Code is not like most statutes in the way it is framed. The introduction itself makes it clear that the General Principles and specific Rules that collectively make up the Code are not expressed in technical language and are to be interpreted so as to achieve their underlying purpose. Their spirit must be observed as well as their letter. In practical terms, the Panel encourages companies and their advisers to consult with the Panel before and during takeover transactions about how the Code should be applied in particular circumstances, rather than adopting a technical, legalistic approach to its interpretation.

In terms of enforcement, the Panel may give any direction that it deems necessary to prevent a person from acting in breach of the Code or otherwise to ensure compliance with the Code. Ultimately, it has power to seek enforcement through the UK courts. Where it deems that disciplinary action is appropriate, the Panel has power to issue public or private statements of censure, to report the offender's conduct to a UK or overseas regulatory authority or professional body for disciplinary or enforcement action or to publish a Panel Statement that the relevant person is someone not likely to comply with the Code, which – as was also the case prior to the granting of statutory status to the Code and powers to the Panel[15] – can result in the application of 'coldshouldering' rules by the FSA and certain professional bodies and render the person shut out of the market. This is of particular significance to advisers.

Code framework and purpose

12.8   The Code is comprised of six general principles – which reflect the general principles set out in Article 3 of the Takeover Directive – and 38 specific rules, which in turn have explanatory notes. From time to time amendments to the Code are published by the Panel following a consultation process.

---

13 Note that the Code applies to takeovers by corporate sponsors just as much as takeovers by financial sponsors (private equity houses).
14 In fact, this principle ultimately became reflected in the 'cold-shouldering' provisions of the Financial Services and Markets Act 2000.
15 See paras **12.5** and **12.6** above.

The Panel also publishes Practice Statements from time to time which indicate how they expect to apply the General Principles and the Rules to particular circumstances. However, the Panel has warned against using such Statements too rigidly – such as in the manner of legal precedents – and the Panel inevitably reserves its rights to consider every referral to it on its circumstance-specific merits.

Ultimately, the principal purposes of the Code are:

* to ensure fair and equal treatment of all shareholders in the target;

* to provide an orderly framework for the conduct of takeover bids; and

* to enable shareholders to make an informed decision on the merits of a bid.

Companies and transactions to which the Code applies

12.9   The nature of the target and not the bidder determines if the Code applies. Principally, the Code applies to two categories of company.[16] It applies to any company that has its registered office in the UK, the Channel Islands or the Isle of Man and which has securities listed on a regulated market. This could include a company whose shares are listed on the Official List and traded on the Main Market of the London Stock Exchange but not one whose shares are traded on AIM or PLUS (unless it has other securities listed on a regulated market). Additionally, the Code applies to all public companies that are deemed resident[17] in the UK, the Channel Islands or the Isle of Man, whether listed or not. The Code also applies to certain private companies, notably those – in very broad terms – whose shares have in the past been listed or quoted to the public.[18] AIM and PLUS traded companies can therefore also be subject to the Code under one of the other categories. Finally, the Code also applies to certain companies – again in broad terms – where either the company is registered in the UK and its shares are traded on a regulated market in other European Economic Area jurisdictions or it is registered in another such jurisdiction and its shares are traded on a regulated market in the UK.

The Code applies to all takeover and merger transactions involving these companies including public-to-privates structured as offers or schemes and, in any case, whether or not the transaction has been announced.[19]

Key provisions

12.10   The following are among the most important and relevant provisions of the Code.

* the timetable for making and completing a bid;

* offer mechanics, including when an offer can be declared unconditional;[20]

---

16 See Para 3(a) of the Introduction to the Code.
17 For these purposes, a company that is incorporated and has its place of central management in a jurisdiction will normally be deemed resident there.
18 See the Introduction to the Code.
19 See Para 3(a) of the Introduction to the Code.
20 Note that scheme mechanics are not set out in the Code; rather they are found in Section 425 Companies Act 1985, which is to be replaced by Part 26 Companies Act 2006 with effect from 6 April 2008.

- rules concerning the dissemination of information by the target to competing bidders;

- the concept of parties 'acting in concert';[21]

- restrictions on dealing in the target shares and related disclosure requirements;

- mandatory offer requirement when 30% of the share capital is acquired (a 'Rule 9' offer)

- rules relating to the minimum price that must be offered to shareholders by reference to the price paid for any other shares in the target either during or for a period before the bid

- requirement for cash bids to be supported by a confirmation of available funds

Applicability of the Code to schemes of arrangement

12.11   The Code applies to takeovers effected by way of a scheme of arrangement as well as traditional takeover offers. Certain modifications to the provisions of the Code apply for the purposes of schemes, in particular to reflect the statutory requirements applicable to schemes under the Companies Act and the court timetable for hearing and approving a scheme of arrangement application. Until relatively recently the Panel interpreted the Code so as to apply to schemes and their different mechanics but there was no separate codification of the necessary modifications. Then in November 2007, following a detailed consultation process, the Panel published a new Appendix to the Code codifying the position by detailing how the Code is to apply to a scheme, including a list of the provisions of the Code that are disapplied for a scheme.[22]

---

21 The 'concert party' concept has important implications for the conduct of a bid. In particular, the actions of parties that are 'acting in concert' in connection with a bid may be aggregated for the purposes of certain provisions in the Code (e.g. Rules 6, 9 and 11). The Code defines persons acting in concert as "persons who, pursuant to an agreement or understanding (whether formal or informal), co-operate to obtain or consolidate control of a company or to frustrate the successful outcome of an offer for a company." Control for such purposes is defined as meaning an interest, or interests, in shares carrying 30% or more of the voting rights of the company. In the case of a public-to-private buy-out, the bidder, any member of the management team that is participating in the bid and the sponsor are all likely to be treated as acting in concert. Rule 8 – relating to the disclosure of dealings in relevant securities by the bidder, the target and their associates – should also be considered in this context as the concept of 'associate' and 'concert party' overlap. Outside of the Code there are other implications for parties that are related to the bidder. In particular, shares held by the bidder and associates of the bidder – including concert parties – at the date of an offer do not count as 'shares to which the offer relates' for the purposes of the statutory squeeze-out procedure under the Companies Act 2006 (see para **12.15**).

22 See Appendix 7 to the Code (the Scheme Appendix), which will apply to all transactions announced after 14 January 2008. See also RS 2007/1 issued by the Panel on 29 November 2007, which contains the Panel's statement following the consultation process and the form of the Scheme Appendix.

Companies Act

12.12 The Companies Act[23], although of general applicability to private and public companies, is of particular relevance to public-to-privates in three aspects.

Financial assistance

12.13 Although the prohibition on the giving of financial assistance by a target company is to be repealed for private companies,[24] this does not affect the applicability of the prohibition to public companies.[25] This means that in a public-to-private, until such time as the target company is re-registered as a private company, the target company and all of its subsidiaries are subject to the restrictions set out in s 151 of the 1985 Act, which will be replaced by Ch 2 of Pt 18 of the 2006 Act on 1 October 2009. Furthermore, the whitewash provisions in ss 155–158 of the 1985 Act – which are not being retained in the 2006 Act – do not apply to public companies, so the prohibition is absolute.

The implications for a public-to-private are particularly relevant to acquisition financiers, since one of the major effects of the prohibition is to rule out upstream credit support – particularly loans, guarantees and security from target group companies – for the acquisition finance. In practice this means that the acquisition financiers can only take guarantees and security from the target group for acquisition debt once the target has been re-registered as a private company (and, until 1 October 2008, the whitewash procedure has been completed). Given the fact that the funding necessary to complete a public-to-private will be provided before this stage is completed the acquisition financiers are left unsecured in respect of the acquisition debt for a certain period after funding.[26] This all means that actually being able to re-register the target as a private company has great significance for the acquisition financiers.

Its not just target group guarantees and security that are affected. A further implication of the prohibition is that cash sitting on the balance sheets of target group companies would not be able to be lent up to the bidder until after the target has been re-registered as a private company (and, until 1 October 2008, the whitewash procedure has been completed).[27] This may also have implications for the funding of the transaction.

---

23 Although many of the provisions of the Companies Act 1985 remain in force at the time of writing, that Act is to be superseded by the Companies Act 2006. The provisions of the new Act are being brought into force in stages between 2006 and 2009.

24 See also para **11.101** generally and paras **12.134** et seq.

25 Note, however, that further changes may be made to this area to deal with implementation of EU Directive 2006/68/EC amending the Second Company Law Directive on Capital Maintenance and Share Capital. The Directive is required to be implemented in Member States of the EU by 15 April 2008 and provides an option for Member States to relax the prohibition on public companies giving financial assistance, subject to certain conditions being satisfied.

26 But see para **12.93** in relation to schemes.

27 It could, however, be distributed by way of dividend provided that sufficient distributable reserves are available because lawful dividends paid by target group companies do not amount to financial assistance.

Schemes of arrangement

12.14   A scheme of arrangement is a statutory procedure established by Companies Act 1985, s 425 and its successor provision in Pt 26 of the Companies Act 2006 Act (from 6 April 2008). These provisions set out the basis on which a company can make an arrangement with its members (or creditors), including for the purposes of a takeover bid, and the detailed statutory requirements must be followed in each case. Whilst the Code does apply to the manner in which a scheme bid is launched and many other aspects of its prosecution, the actual mechanism by which the scheme becomes legally effective and binds the shareholders of the target is set out in the Companies Act.

Squeezing-out minorities

12.15   Chapter 3 of Pt 28 of the 2006 Act (which replaced Pt XIIIA of the 1985 Act) contains the provisions that enable the bidder under a traditional takeover offer to squeeze-out minority shareholders once a 90% threshold of acceptances is achieved.[28] This is the mechanism that the bidder will invoke to achieve 100% ownership of the target. It is not applicable to schemes but nor is it required since the scheme legislation has the same effect (of achieving 100% ownership of the target).

Other regulations

12.16   In addition to the Code and the Companies Act, the parties to a bid must comply with the Listing Rules and the Disclosure and Transparency Rules ('DTR') of the Financial Services Authority. For example, under the DTR any person that acquires 3% of the voting share capital of a company whose shares are admitted to trading on a regulated market or prescribed market (eg, AIM) must inform the company and the FSA within two trading days. The company must then pass that information on to the market. The target and its directors should also have regard to the Model Code on Directors' Dealings. All the parties will also need to be aware of their potential liability under the Financial Services and Markets Act 2000, in particular the potential criminal liability for making misleading statements in certain circumstances.[29] There are also restrictions on dealing and communicating price sensitive information under the 'Market Abuse' regime established by that Act for which there are financial penalties, public censure powers and injunctive relief and restitution remedies. Furthermore, Pt V of the Criminal Justice Act 1993 establishes insider dealing as a criminal offence.

28 See paras **12.69** to **12.73** for more detail.
29 See FSMA 2000, s 397.

STRUCTURING THE BID

Takeover offer or scheme of arrangement?

12.17   This section considers the two alternative structures that can be used to effect the acquisition of a public company, namely takeover offers and schemes of arrangement. There are advantages and disadvantages to each and although historically takeover offers were much more common, this trend had reversed in the second half of the 2000s with schemes becoming more common, for recommend bids at least.[30] The following paragraphs briefly describe the most important features of offers and schemes and the factors that a bidder will consider in determining which procedure to use.

Takeover offers

12.18   A takeover offer is the traditional method of acquiring a public company in the UK. Offers are essentially a regulatory creation and the Code determines how they may be made and completed as well as dictating many of their terms.

What is a takeover offer?

12.19   A takeover offer is a contractual offer made by a bidder directly to the shareholders of the target company to acquire their shares. The offer is made in an offering circular – usually just called the offer document – that is posted directly to the shareholders and which sets out all of the terms and conditions of the offer. Shareholders then have the option of accepting the offer (or not) by completing a form of acceptance incorporated into the offer document or in the case of shares held in CREST[31] by accepting the offer through the CREST system. If sufficient shareholders accept the offer – which means such number as gives the bidder (including shares it already had) more than 50% of the voting share capital of the target – it can be declared unconditional and the takeover will go ahead. In fact, merely obtaining a controlling stake of more than 50% will not normally be sufficient to guarantee the success of a public-to-private. In particular, the acquisition financiers will insist that the bidder obtains a much greater number of acceptances so that no minority shareholders remain in the target to potentially block the granting of loans, guarantees and security by the target group as credit support for the acquisition finance debt. In order to ensure that this is the case the offer must be accepted by 90% or more of the shareholders. If this level of acceptances is achieved the bidder can invoke the compulsory purchase provisions of the Companies Act 2006[32] to 'squeeze-out' the remaining minority and thereby acquire 100% of the target.

---

30 Schemes can only be used in recommended bids because the statutory requirements are implemented by the target board rather than the bidder.
31 See the **Glossary**.
32 See Chap 3 of Pt 28 of the Companies Act 2006, which replaced Pt XIIIA of the Companies Act 1985.

Schemes of arrangement

12.20   As indicated previously, having not been used with any frequency for this purpose for many years, in the second half of the 2000s schemes of arrangement became the preferred method of effecting a recommended takeover of a UK public company.

What is a scheme of arrangement?

12.21   A scheme of arrangement is a statutory procedure set out in s 425 of the Companies Act 1985 (which is to be replaced by Pt 26 of the Companies Act 2006 on 6 April 2008). The purpose of schemes is that they enable a company to make an arrangement with its shareholders or creditors or a class of shareholders or creditors. The scope of the arrangements that can be made is wide and includes the restructuring of debts, reorganising capital and effecting a transfer of share capital. Schemes can therefore be used to effect a change of control – a takeover. In order to be effective the arrangement must be sanctioned by the court but once sanctioned it will be binding on *all* the shareholders (or creditors) or all of the relevant class of shareholders (or creditors) and upon the target itself.

There are three main requirements of a scheme of arrangement. First, the scheme must be approved by not less than 75% of the members of the target at a special meeting convened at the direction of the court, which means applying to the court for leave to convene the scheme approval meeting. The scheme approval meeting is sometimes called the 'court meeting' to distinguish it from a further general meeting of the company – the 'general meeting' – held after the court meeting to approve related matters. The 75% threshold is determined by reference to those that attend (including by proxy) and vote at the meeting. Shares held by the bidder and persons connected with the bidder cannot be voted. This means that there is less incentive for the bidder to make market purchases. If the target has more than one class of shares – a 'class' for this purpose effectively meaning each group of shareholders with a special interest, even if not technically a separate class – each class must be treated separately and vote in favour of the scheme.

Secondly, after the scheme has been approved by the members, it must be sanctioned by the court. Although the court has discretion to approve a scheme or not, the judge would normally be reluctant to override the shareholder vote unless there were compelling circumstances to do so such as material conflicts of interest, failures in disclosures or new developments. The court order sanctioning the scheme is then filed with the Registrar of Companies and the scheme will become effective and bind all shareholders (even those that voted against it). In practice, where the scheme is a reduction scheme[33] the terms of the scheme may provide that it only becomes effective once the court order confirming the reduction of capital has also been registered.

The third statutory requirement of a scheme is that the circular sent to shareholders with the notice convening the court meeting includes a statement

---

33 See para **12.22**.

explaining the effect of the scheme and, disclosing any material interests of the target's directors and the effect of the scheme on those interests (if different from the effect on similar interests of other shareholders). The explanatory statement must be fair and give all information reasonably necessary to enable the recipient to decide how to vote.

Unlike offers, schemes of arrangement are proposed by the target itself rather than the bidder and it is the board of the target rather than the bidder that circulates the scheme document, including the explanatory statement, to the shareholders and is otherwise responsible for implementing the scheme in accordance with the statute. With this in mind, schemes are essentially only appropriate for fully negotiated deals that the target board is willing to recommend to the shareholders. Furthermore, since the on-going co-operation of the target is required throughout the process, schemes can be susceptible to competing bids. In order to mitigate execution risk and, to some extent, competing bid risk the sponsor will usually require the target to sign up to a 'transaction agreement'[34] with the bidder at the start of the process. The agreement will provide a procedural framework for completing the scheme process and may include some bidder protection in the form of break fees, work fees and a non-solicitation undertaking.[35]

Transfer schemes and reduction schemes

12.22 There are two main types of scheme, transfer schemes and reduction schemes. With a transfer scheme the existing share capital of the target is transferred from the existing shareholders to the bidder. With a reduction scheme, the bidder is issued new share capital and the existing share capital, held by the existing shareholders, is cancelled by a reduction of capital. With a reduction scheme there is no transfer of shares so the stamp duty that would be payable on a transfer is not payable. This generally means that reduction schemes are used more frequently than transfer schemes. The reduction of capital required by a reduction scheme must be approved in a general meeting of the target and this is normally convened immediately after the court convened meeting to approve the scheme. This also requires a 75% majority of those present and voting at the meeting. The consideration payable by the bidder to the shareholders is either in return for the shares transferred by them in the case of a transfer scheme or in return for the cancellation of their shares in the case of a reduction scheme.

Comparing offers and schemes

12.23 As noted above, for a long time the vast majority of public-to-privates were effected by way of takeover offers, with schemes remaining extremely rare. One reason for this was the perception that schemes of arrangement were unwieldy – requiring court processes and full shareholder meetings – and more

---

34 These are also sometimes called 'cooperation' or 'implementation' agreements.
35 See paras **12.49** (non-solicitation undertakings), **12.50** (break fees), **12.51** (work fees), and **12.25** (transaction agreements generally).

time consuming, with resultant additional cost. There was also the issue of competing bid risk upsetting the essential requirement of a supportive target board. In actual fact, schemes of arrangement have one fundamental advantage over offers that can increase – rather than decrease – the likelihood of success of the public-to-private. That is, the fact that the bidder only needs the support of 75% of the target's shareholders in order to take ownership of 100% of the target's shares. That compares with 90% for offers. Moreover, it is 75% of those shareholders that *attend and vote* at the relevant shareholders meeting (whether in person or by proxy). This means that apathetic shareholders do not get to register as 'no' votes simply by virtue of not voting 'yes' and a sponsor that has mobilised a sufficient number of supportive shareholders can have a reasonable amount of visibility on reaching the 75% level. Once the scheme has been approved by the shareholders of the target – and sanctioned by the court – it will bind all shareholders, irrespective of whether they voted in favour.

The lower threshold of support required for full ownership to be achieved under a scheme reduces the opportunity for minority shareholders to hold a bid to ransom[36] and since the early 2000s sponsors have been increasingly attracted to this feature and schemes generally, especially when used in conjunction with a fallback offer.[37] Indeed, this is not the only attractive feature of schemes, by comparison with offers. For example, where there are a material number of US shareholders in the target a scheme will necessarily avoid the need to comply with the US tender offer regulations whereas an offer might not.[38] In addition, with a reduction scheme the stamp duty cost arising on a transfer of shares is eliminated, which may reduce bid costs significantly, especially with a large deal.

Takeover offers are still used in certain circumstances, however. Ultimately, offers are less reliant on the goodwill of the target's board and the bidder can address its offer directly to the shareholders. Offers may also be more appropriate where the bidder already owns or controls a significant stake in the target, since shares held by the bidder and connected persons cannot be voted in the general meeting to approve the scheme.

The following paragraphs explore in further detail the main differences between offers and schemes and the factors to consider when choosing between an offer and a scheme.

Main differences between offers and schemes

12.24   The following paragraphs set out the main differences between offers and schemes.

36 So-called 'greenmailing'; a tactic that certain opportunistic investors can employ to drive up the price of a bid and turn a quick profit.
37 See para **12.39**.
38 See para **12.34**.

Approval percentages

12.25 A scheme must be approved by a *majority in number* of the shareholders *who vote*, representing at least 75% *in value* of the shares *voted* at the scheme approval meeting convened by the court. Votes attaching to shares controlled by the bidder and connected persons can normally *not* be voted. Since only those shareholders who *vote* count toward the majorities needed to approve a scheme[39], active support and opposition are both magnified. In practice, where there is little organised opposition and a number of shareholders simply do not respond (or are untraceable), a scheme may succeed more easily than an offer. On the other hand, active opponents will be able to vote above their weight and even if they fail the court hearing provides a public forum for continued opposition.

In the case of an offer, the bidder can declare the offer unconditional once it has received acceptances that give it control of more than 50% by value of the voting shares, whether through the offer or otherwise.[40] Therefore, if it already owns a sizeable stake a relatively low level of acceptance is all that is needed to achieve control. This level of acceptance alone will usually be insufficient for a public-to-private, however, as the financiers will often insist that the bidder reaches the squeeze-out threshold in order to eliminate minorities.

Reaching 100% ownership

12.26 Once a scheme has been declared effective all shareholders are bound irrespective of whether they voted for the scheme. Therefore successful schemes always result in 100% ownership. In the case of an offer, by contrast, in order to obtain 100% ownership the bidder must satisfy a much higher level of support. Specifically, it must acquire at least 90% (by both value and voting rights[41]) of the 'shares to which the offer relates' in order to invoke the compulsory acquisition procedures under Companies Act 2006, s 979 to 'squeeze out' non-accepting shareholders and obtain ownership of 100% of the target. Note that shares already acquired by the bidder or its associates (before the offer is made[42]) do not count as 'shares to which the offer relates'.

A further consideration with target companies that are particularly widely held by the public – such as privatised companies – is the impact of lost or untraceable shareholders. In the context of an offer, untraceable shareholders might make the 90% level more difficult to achieve since no account can be taken of untraceable shareholders without the consent of the court. With a scheme, untraceable – like abstaining – shareholders are less likely to have an impact because the required majorities are calculated by reference to shareholders who actually vote.

---

39 If the level of voting is unusually low, the court might still consider that a factor in deciding whether or not to approve the scheme.
40 Thus, unlike schemes, shares held by the bidder do count.
41 See Companies Act 2006, s 979(2).
42 For such purposes, the offer is not made until the posting of the offer document to shareholders, not at the time of the public announcement of the offer.

Market purchases[43]

12.27   Since shares held by the bidder and connected persons do *not* get to be voted in the scheme approval meeting, market purchases can not assist the bidder to reach the requisite approval threshold for a scheme. This is irrespective of when the shares are acquired. In fact, market purchase could even be counter-productive to a scheme since the shares acquired would not be able to be voted in favour. That all said, it is possible that market purchases could be used to dissuade a competing bidder. In the case of an offer the position is more complicated. As regards the acceptance condition, shares held by the bidder and connected persons *will* count towards the threshold irrespective of when they are acquired (before or after the bid is launched). Thus market purchases can assist the bidder in reaching the over 50% level required to gain control of the target. However, as regards the 90% squeeze-out threshold only shares acquired *once an offer has been made* will count towards the 90%. Shares already acquired by the bidder (and its associates) before the offer is made[44] do not count as they are not 'shares to which the offer relates' for the purposes of the statute.[45]

Ultimately, an offer can provide more tactical flexibility to the sponsor if it uses market purchases, perhaps to dissuade a potential competing bidder from making a counter offer or to gain control of the target below the 90% squeeze-out threshold.

In practical terms, to accept an offer, shareholders must submit share certificates or transfer shares into escrow in the CREST system. With a scheme, target shareholders may normally continue trading until just before the scheme effective date.

Stamp duty saving

12.28   With an offer, stamp duty (or stamp duty reserve tax for uncertificated shares) is payable by the bidder at the rate of (approximately) 0.5% of the amount paid for the target shares. Schemes normally take the form of reduction schemes, where the target shares are cancelled and reissued, rather than transferred, in which case there will be no stamp duty.[46]

Deal costs

12.29   The stamp duty saved on a reduction scheme may be offset a little by the higher level of advisory costs that are generally incurred with a scheme. In particular, the need to instruct counsel in relation to the court aspects of a scheme adds to the deal costs.

---

43 See also paras **12.55** and **12.56** in relation to market purchases and dealings in target shares.
44 For such purposes, the offer is not made until the posting of the offer document to shareholders, not at the time of the public announcement of the offer.
45 See paras **12.69** to **12.73** for more detail on the squeeze-out generally.
46 Note, however, that where the scheme proposal includes a loan note alternative the loan notes taken up may involve a transfer of shares in exchange for the notes, so some stamp duty may be payable.

Control of the bid process

12.30   An offer is typically bidder-led, whereas a scheme must be progressed by the target. In practice, either side may take the lead in driving the deal forward, but there is inevitably some shift of control to the target in a scheme.

Timing

12.31   The timetable for a scheme varies, depending upon court schedules and other factors, but in an uncontested situation it would be reasonable to expect a scheme to take around four to six weeks longer from announcement to its effective date than a recommended offer would to the earliest date it could be declared wholly unconditional. However, with an offer it takes another six weeks from the time the 90% test is satisfied to complete the compulsory acquisition of non-accepting shares. Thus a scheme is likely to get the sponsor to 100% ownership more quickly, but take somewhat longer than an offer to achieve day-to-day control.

'Irrevocables'

12.32   Until the mid-2000s, it was standard practice for the counsel (barristers) who present schemes to the court to advise sponsors *not* to obtain undertakings from shareholders to vote in favour. The concern was that the court might regard such shareholders as in effect a separate class. Instead the usual practice had been to rely on non-binding public 'statements of intent'. This contrasts with the practice for offers, where it has long been common for the bidder to obtain undertakings (to accept the offer) from target directors and where possible major shareholders.[47]

Practice in this area is evolving, however, and it is now common for the bidder to obtain voting undertakings at least from target directors in respect of their shares if not from third party shareholders. In any event, there remains a concern that a court might not approve a scheme if the requisite shareholder votes would not have been obtained but for voting undertakings obtained in advance in this manner.

Competing bids

12.33   In broad terms, schemes are less well suited to competitive bid situations than offers. The fact that the scheme is sponsored by the target board means that a reversal of their support for the bid could be fatal to the scheme. Furthermore, other than a simple increase in the bid price, it is usually more difficult to amend a scheme than an offer and the court process is less flexible. With this in mind, if a competitive situation emerges the sponsor may find it necessary or convenient to switch to an offer, perhaps even if the target board stands by its recommendation and there have been several cases of bids which started as schemes being successfully completed as offers.[48] That said, there have also been examples of where the bidder has not switched to an offer in the face of a

---

47 See also para **12.54** in relation to 'irrevocables'.
48 See also para **12.39** in relation to scheme-bid combinations.

competing bid and as the market evolves, with advisers, the Panel and the courts becoming more accustomed to dealing with competitive situations involving schemes, this trend is likely to increase. There has even been at least one instance of a scheme being proposed in competition with an existing scheme. In any event, ultimately retaining or reinstating the target board's support for a scheme remains vital since it is practically impossible to implement a scheme with a hostile target board.

Overseas shareholders

12.34   A conflict of laws may arise when a takeover bid is made in respect of a target that is also subject to non-UK takeover rules. This can happen, for instance, where a large block of shareholders are from a particular jurisdiction. If the laws or regulations of another jurisdiction arise the bidder may be faced with having to comply with inconsistent rules. This is the case, for example, with certain requirements of the US federal tender offer regime, which are inconsistent with normal practice under the Code.[49] In particular, the minimum offer period is longer and rights to withdraw acceptances are more extensive. There is an exemption from most of these regulations where the target is a 'foreign private issuer' and US persons own less than 10% of its shares, provided certain minimal procedural requirements are followed, but above that level many of the US tender offer regulations would have to be complied with in order to extend an offer into the United States. A scheme, however, unlike an offer, is exempt from the US tender offer regulations. Inevitably the position must be checked individually with appropriate advisers in relevant jurisdictions, particularly those where there are large concentrations of shareholders.

Employee share schemes

12.35   Although many employee share schemes, especially those drafted more recently, contain takeover provisions which contemplate a scheme as well as an offer, there are sometimes more difficult technical issues with a scheme.

Bids involving offers of securities: exchange offers

12.36   When a bid includes shares or other securities as an alternative to or in addition to cash the bidder would need to prepare a prospectus in addition to all of the other documents. The FSA has confirmed, however, that an issue of securities pursuant to a scheme – provided the securities are not to be listed on a regulated market – does not involve an 'offer' of the securities and thus no prospectus is required.

Acquisition financier concerns

12.37   With an offer, the taking of upstream credit support from the target will normally only be practicable after compulsory acquisition of non-accepting

---

49 It is beyond the scope of this chapter to consider non-UK laws or regulations and (in addition to US federal laws) US state securities laws or the laws of any other jurisdiction might also be relevant.

shares, ie, at the end of six weeks from the date of the squeeze-out notices. It is only after this point that the re-registration of the target as a private company can occur without any concern for minority shareholder objections, which in turn means that it is at this point that the financial assistance prohibition on upstream credit support from the target group can be overcome. If the 90% test is not met then theoretically that essential step could be blocked.[50] A scheme, by contrast, will provide certainty to the acquisition financiers that the bidder will acquire 100% of the target shares immediately upon the scheme becoming effective. Furthermore, with a scheme, the whitewash procedure can be carried out very shortly after the scheme effective date.[51]

Summary of key differences

12.38   The following table summarises very briefly the significant differences between a takeover by means of an offer and a scheme.

Offer	Scheme
Acceptance levels	
The bidder only requires more than 50% voting control to declare offer unconditional and take control of target. This can include any shares held by the bidder (and connected persons) including market purchases after the offer date. But at this level minorities remain and the acquisition financiers will typically insist on the bidder reaching the 90% squeeze-out threshold.	Scheme requires approval by a majority in number of shareholders voting, representing at least 75% in value of shares voted. Any shares held by bidder (and connected persons) are excluded from the vote.
Reaching 100%	
Compulsory acquisition of non-accepting shares is only possible if achieve 90% acceptance of the offer. Shares already held by the bidder (and associates) before the offer is made are disregarded from both sides of the 90% calculation. However shares acquired after the offer date may be counted.	If the scheme is approved, all shareholders will be bound and the bidder will obtain 100% ownership on the effective date.
Untraceable shareholders	
Untraceable shareholders effectively count as non-acceptances when calculating the 90% level unless court decides otherwise.	In practice, untraceable shareholders are unlikely to be relevant as the requisite majority is calculated by reference to shareholders who actually vote.

50 See also paras **12.13**, **12.90**, **12.91** and **12.136** generally.
51 See also paras **12.13** and **12.93** in practice.

Offer	Scheme

Irrevocables

Offer	Scheme
Common practice to obtain these to enhance acceptances once offer launched.	Historically not taken as risk of excluding the shares from the vote. Now may be obtained from target directors.

Stamp duty

Offer	Scheme
Stamp duty is payable by the bidder on the transferred shares at (approximately) 0.5% of the consideration.	No stamp duty is payable if a reduction scheme is used.

Market purchases

Offer	Scheme
Before offer date: (a) Acceptance condition: purchases *will* count towards the acceptance condition. (b) Compulsory purchase: purchases *will not* count in determining the 90% test. After offer date: (a) Acceptance condition: purchases *will* count towards the acceptance condition. (b) Compulsory purchase: purchases *will* count towards the 90% test.	Market purchases of relatively little benefit since all shares held by the bidder and its associates are excluded from the vote at the scheme approval meeting. May even be counterproductive as shares acquired might otherwise have been voted in favour of scheme. That said market purchases could in theory be used to exclude competing bidders.

Deal Costs

Offer	Scheme
Typically the costs of the advisers will be less than with a scheme as the process is less complex. However, note the stamp duty costs above.	The fact that counsel (barristers) will be instructed to handle the court hearings will add to the cost.

Process and Timetable

Offer	Scheme
The mechanics of an offer differ from those of a scheme and, in particular, the bidder inevitably drives the process of an offer whereas a scheme requires more active involvement of the target board. No court approval is required for an offer as it is with a scheme. The timetable is potentially shorter for an offer, at least until time bid becomes unconditional, although squeeze-out process will add a further 6 weeks or more. See later section on process and the summary timetable for detail.[52]	The scheme mechanics include the approval of the court, at its discretion. Risk that the court hearing provides a forum for opposing minorities, causing delay or disruption. The court would usually be reluctant to reject a scheme approved by the required majorities, absent compelling circumstances; such as material conflicts of interest, failures in disclosure or new developments. The scheme may take 4-6 weeks longer to reach the effective date but there is no subsequent squeeze-out period necessary. See later section on process and the summary timetable.[53]

52 See paras **12.40** et seq.
53 See paras **12.40** et seq.

Offer	Scheme
Target board recommendation	
An offer can proceed even if not recommended but acquisition financiers rarely support bids that are not recommended from the outset (hostile). So in practice all public-to-private offers must at least start as recommended.	Scheme can only be completed if recommended by target board. Even if initially recommended, risk that board may withdraw recommendation. Bidder must then consider withdrawing or switching to offer or possibly trying to increase bid and continue with scheme (see below).
Flexibility on a contested bid	
Relatively easy to change terms of offer, subject to limitations imposed by the Code.	More complicated to change terms materially during scheme process (other than simple increase in bid price), without restarting timetable, so a scheme is usually seen as less suitable if risk of a competing bid is significant. It is possible, however, to switch from a scheme to a bid mid-process with the Panel's consent and contested schemes are becoming more common generally. There has even been at least one instance of a scheme being proposed in competition with an existing scheme.
US shareholders	
If less than 10% of the target shares are owned by US persons, cash offer can be made into US pursuant to Tier I exemption thus avoiding US SEC registration requirements. If between 10% and 40% held by US persons, then under Tier II more SEC requirements apply.	A scheme is exempt from US tender offer rules.
State securities laws must still be considered.	State securities laws must still be considered.
Employee share scheme	
Employee share schemes need careful consideration to ensure the offer contemplates and deals with them properly.	Dealing with exercise of share schemes often more complex with schemes.
Exchange offers	
When a bid includes shares or other securities as an alternative to or in addition to cash the bidder would need to prepare a prospectus (to be approved by the FSA) in addition to all of the other documents.	The FSA has confirmed that an issue of securities pursuant to a scheme – provided the securities are not to be listed on a regulated market – does not involve an 'offer' of the securities and thus no prospectus is required.

Offer	Scheme
Acquisition finance	
Statutory financial assistance hurdle (by re-registering target as a private company) can only be carried out with certainty after 90% acceptance test for compulsory acquisition of non-accepting shares has been met and a further 6 weeks have expired.	Scheme provides certainty that the re-registration process can be achieved as soon as scheme effective date occurs.

Combining offers and schemes

12.39   A strategy for public-to-privates that is increasingly common is to combine an offer with a scheme. This does not mean that both an offer and a scheme are actually launched. Rather, the sponsor will initially plan on utilising a scheme of arrangement – and thus take advantage of the lower threshold required for full ownership to be achieved – but also retain the option of switching to an offer should the scheme route no longer be a viable option, usually because a competing bid appears and the target's board are unwilling to propose the scheme to the shareholders in view of the competing offer. Although it is not necessary for the bidder to formally reserve its right to switch to an offer (in the announcement or scheme document), the consent of the Panel is required for a switch to be made. In considering whether to give consent the Panel will primarily have regard to the effect of the switch on the interests of the shareholders and if the effect of the switch is to reduce the likelihood of the bid being successful this is unlikely to be in the interests of the shareholders. In assessing the impact of the switch on the shareholders the Panel is likely to pay heed to the views of the target board and its Rule 3 adviser. On the basis that the effect of a switch will usually be to increase the chances of the bid being successful and that such an increase will not normally be detrimental to the shareholders, the Panel will often be in a position to give the consent. The Panel is likely to be sympathetic in particular where the switch is being made as a result of actions taken by the target board that make implementing the scheme practically impossible.

It is also possible to convert an offer to the scheme but this is less common. Again the Panel's consent would be required and it would consider whether the switch would be more likely to offer an exit opportunity for target shareholders as well as taking into account the target board's views.

BID PROCESS AND TIMETABLE

Overview

12.40   This section is concerned with the practical execution of a takeover bid, whether by way of offer or by scheme of arrangement. In considering these practical aspects it addresses many of the key differentiating features of public-to-privates from other buy-outs. In particular, in pursuing a public-to-private, a sponsor, its bidding vehicle and the management team of the target (assuming some members are participating in the sponsor's bid) must have regard to the strict regulatory requirements applicable to takeovers of either kind. These requirements include detailed procedural steps and a relatively rigid timetable. The principal source of this regulation is the Takeover Code, which applies to both offers and schemes. Various provisions of the Companies Act[54] also apply.

Perhaps surprisingly, given that the two alternative procedures originate from quite separate regulatory origins, the procedures for executing a public-to-private via an offer or a scheme are – or have become – very similar. With this in mind, the following paragraphs have been arranged so that steps and processes that are common to both procedures are considered once in respect of both procedures rather than separately for each. Necessarily there will be instances where there are different nuances or perhaps more pronounced divergences applicable, depending on whether an offer or a scheme is being followed and an attempt has been made to highlight the major differences.

The entire process has been broken down into the following subsections:

- matters prior to launch;

- launch of the bid;

- bid mechanics; and

- matters following bid effective date.

It is actually only in the bid mechanics itself where there are material differences between offers and schemes and in that subsection they are considered separately. Indeed, it may be helpful generally when considering public-to-privates not to focus too heavily on whether an offer or a bid procedure is to be used and to consider that as a discrete issue in the context of the transaction as a whole. The section concludes with separate summary timetables for the two processes. Throughout the following paragraphs the terms 'takeover' and 'bid' are each used to mean an offer or a scheme.

Matters prior to launch

Identification of target

12.41   Much of the work required to successfully achieve a takeover is carried out in advance of the launch of the bid and any of the steps set out in the Code or the Companies Act. For starters, actually identifying a target in the first place will require the sponsor to have carried out an extensive desktop analysis of the target company and its suitability for a takeover. In some cases the idea for a takeover may have been generated by an investment bank, many of which routinely analyse public companies as potential targets for public-to-privates before presenting possible deal ideas to private equity sponsors and corporate acquirers. The investment bank will usually have carried out a certain amount of analysis

---

54 Companies Act 1985 as superseded by the Companies Act 2006.

of the target, such as its share price performance, fundamental value, growth potential, strategic options and value to an acquirer, how the bid could be financed and so on before bringing the idea to a sponsor. Where the deal idea is generated internally by the sponsor it will either carry out the analysis itself or more commonly engage an investment bank to assist. Not surprisingly, much more information is usually readily available to sponsors about listed public companies than it is about private companies. In particular, this is through the quarterly, semi-annual and annual filings that are required under the FSA's Disclosure and Transparency Rules or under the AIM Rules, all of which are publicly available. In addition, the research and equity analysis departments of investment banks and other corporate finance houses produce significant amounts of collateral information on public companies. All of this information, plus whatever additional sector and target specific analysis the sponsor can perform, should mean that – aside from the very detailed confidential information that relates to a specific target company – a relatively detailed investment case can be made for a specific target without any approach ever having been made to the target. Indeed true hostile takeovers will often be based on this information alone as the target company may be unwilling to provide any additional confidential data.

Hostile takeovers

12.42   Hostile and other non-recommended takeovers are very rare within the private equity arena. There are really two related reasons for this. First, the execution risk with a hostile or non-recommended takeover bid is significant. In a hostile bid scenario, the fact that the target board rejects the approach and signifies to shareholders that they should reject it creates a significant obstacle to the likelihood of success of the bid. Even with a non-recommended but not out-and-out hostile offer, the lack of a recommendation from the board is usually enough to cause most private equity buyers to stay away. The costs that will be incurred in launching a public takeover are usually very significant and will act as a material disincentive to any speculative bid. With a scheme the lack of target board support is effectively fatal since it is the target board and not the bidder that is required to execute the scheme process. Secondly, acquisition financiers have traditionally proven even more conservative when it comes to financing non-recommended bids than sponsors have been in launching them. In order to launch a bid all of the financing must be in place so that the certain funds requirements of the Code can be satisfied.[55] Meaning that the acquisition financiers must have completed all of the work they would have to do for a full buy-out, with no certainty that the funds will ever be utilised and, unless they have a special arrangement as to fees, without any certainty that any arrangement and underwriting fees will be payable to them for their efforts.[56] So even if a speculative bid did appear viable to the sponsor they might still struggle to raise acquisition finance.

   Assuming that a target has been identified and the sponsor has determined that a viable investment case exists (that can be financed), it will then approach the target.

---

55 See para **12.155**.
56 Up-front fees payable to acquisition financiers are generally only payable if the buy-out completes and the funds are drawn down.

Approach to target

12.43 A sponsor will often approach the target directly or it might do so through its financial adviser. At the core of its approach the bidder will propose the main terms of its bid, the price in particular. It will also wish to demonstrate to the target that it has finance lined up, so that its bid is credible. This may be evidenced by a 'highly confident' letter issued by its financial adviser or bankers. At this stage the sponsor is unlikely to have had any real contact with the management of the target and the terms of any management deal will typically be addressed separately. In any event, the involvement of target directors in a public-to-private raises particular issues given the inherent conflict of interest that arises from potentially being on two sides of the transaction.

Conflicts of interest for target directors

12.44 Where a target director is to be involved in a public-to-private buy-out on the acquirer side he or she will inevitably have a conflict of interest. This arises principally because of a director's duty to avoid conflicts of interest and as a result of his or her duty to act in the way he/she considers, in good faith, would be likely to promote the success of the target for the benefit of its members as a whole on the one hand, while at the same time participating in a bid to acquire the target. Even where a target director is not invited to participate in the equity of the bidder, the fact that he or she is to continue in a role with the target after the buy-out constitutes a sufficient conflict of interest. The same conflicts of interest do also arise in private buy-outs (in particular, where the target's directors are participating in newco) but they are often more acute in a public deal where the shareholders are more reliant on the target board for direction as to the best approach to the proposed takeover.

To protect shareholders against these inherent conflicts of interest, the Code establishes two specific principles that must be adhered to.

Independent advisers

12.45 For *any* takeover bid the board of the target must obtain competent independent advice on the bid and the substance of that advice must be made known to its shareholders.[57] Target's financial adviser in a takeover situation is often referred to as the 'Rule 3 adviser', referring to the relevant part of the Code which requires its appointment. As indicated above, the independent advice will be particularly important where the bid is a public-to-private involving any of the directors or other management of the target and the board should appoint an independent adviser as soon as it becomes aware that a prospective public-to-private bid may be made. If the target's usual financial adviser is particularly close to any participating member of the management team the financial adviser should consult with the Panel as to whether it is sufficiently independent to advise the target in respect of the transaction.

---

57 See Rule 3.1 of the Code.

Where the target's usual financial adviser is part of a larger group of companies that includes affiliated entities otherwise involved in the transaction – such as the sponsor, its financiers or any adviser to the sponsor – it should decline to act in that capacity where it would otherwise have a conflict of interest, including at the wider group level.[58]

The Institutional Shareholders Committee, an influential voluntary body that represents a number of associations of leading institutional investors in public companies, has adopted a position that goes further than the strict requirements of the Code. It has stated that the bidder should not appoint advisers previously employed by the target unless the independent board of the target established in respect of the bid approves the appointment.[59]

Independent committee to consider bid

12.46 The Code also provides that any director of the target that has a conflict of interest must be excluded from board level consideration of the bid and any statements on behalf of the company in respect of the bid.[60] Any director who is to have a continuing role if the bid is successful will be regarded as having a conflict of interest,[61] including both executive and non-executive directors. In practice this all means that as soon as it becomes aware that a bid may be made for the company, the board of the target should appoint a committee of the independent directors and delegate to it full authority to consider the terms of the bid and to make appropriate recommendations to shareholders. It is this committee which represents the interests of the target's shareholders and which determines whether to recommend the bid to shareholders. The committee also has the power to determine whether it is in the best interests of shareholders to permit the management team to spend time on the bid whilst remaining as employees and officers of the company, and if so a carve-out from their obligations under their service agreements will normally need to be agreed.

The directors who comprise the independent committee of the board should have no continuing role with either the target or the bidder once the bid is successful and with a recommended bid it is customary for the letter of recommendation from the independent directors, which will be included in the bid document, to state that the committee members will resign from the board if the bid goes through.

In circumstances where a separate committee cannot be formed, because all of the directors are conflicted, any recommendation to the shareholders on behalf of the target should come from the independent adviser. Again the Institutional Shareholders Committee has gone further than the strict requirements of the Code and custom, stating that a bid by a private equity sponsor backing the existing management is unlikely to be 'favourably received' unless there had for 'some time' been a strong, independent non-executive presence on the board of

---

58 See Rule 3.3 of the Code.
59 Guidance on management buy-outs issued by the Institutional Shareholders Committee in December 1989.
60 See Note 3 to Rule 25.1.
61 See Note 4 to Rule 25.1.

the target and those independent directors recommend the bid.[62] Whilst this is not a regulatory requirement, given the influence of that body, most sponsors and target boards will in practice treat it as such.

The nature of any conflicts of interest arising for target's directors must be explained to the shareholders in the first circular sent to them in relation to the bid.

The problem of 'special deals' for roll-over managers

12.47   A fundamental principal applicable to all takeover bids is that the bidder must treat all shareholders of the target of the same class equally.[63] This raises a particular issue for public-to-privates where any member of the existing management team (or indeed any other shareholder) is participating in the bid and is also a selling shareholder in the target – a roll-over manager. The bidder will in effect not be treating that shareholder in the same way as other shareholders; the roll-over manager will receive cash for his or her shareholding in target but also be granted an equity interest in the bidder. There are two exemptions to the equal treatment rule set out in Rule 16 of the Code.[64]

The first is for *bona fide* 'joint bidders', where the bid is a consortium bid. The Panel has stated that a genuine bidder is a person that, alone or with others, seeks to obtain control of the target and that, following the acquisition of control, can expect to exert a significant influence over the target, to participate in distributions of profits and surplus capital and to benefit from any increase in the value of the target, while at the same time bearing the risk of a fall in its value resulting from the poor performance of the target's business or adverse market conditions. The Code itself does not define 'joint offeror' (to use the Code's terminology) but the Panel has published a list of non-exhaustive criteria which it uses in making a determination in this regard.[65]

The second exemption is specifically for special deals for target management. The criteria that need to be met under the management exemption are set out in Note 4 to Rule 16 of the Code and include – in addition to the Panel's consent – a requirement that the roll-over managers bear the risks as well as the rewards of equity ownership in the bidder, that the Rule 3 adviser publicly states that the arrangements with the managers are fair and reasonable (this has been extended to include other incentivisation arrangements and not just equity interests) and that the approval (on a poll) of the independent shareholders of the target is required at a general meeting. The Panel's consent is obtained through the bidder's financial adviser writing to the Panel setting out full details of the proposed arrangements.

In practical terms, the roll-over managers will either structure their roll-over as a share swap – in the simplest example, receiving shares in the bidder in return for their shares in target – or as a cash transaction followed by a fresh subscrip-

---

62 See fn **59** above
63 General Principle 1 of the Code as supported by Rules 14 to 16 of the Code.
64 See in particular the Notes to Rule 16 of the Code.
65 See Panel Statement 2003/25.

tion in the bidder. The former route may be preferred in order to defer the capital gains tax arising on the disposal of shares in target.[66]

Arrangements with the target

Target board recommendation

12.48   As indicated above,[67] most financial sponsors – and even more so, most acquisition financiers – would not entertain launching a bid for a target where the target board was not willing to recommend the bid to the shareholders. This reflects the fact that significant costs and time are required to launch a takeover bid and without the support of a recommendation from the target's board the execution risk is high. With this in mind, the sponsor will make obtaining the recommendation of the target's board a key priority of its strategy.

As already mentioned, only the independent committee will be permitted to consider the bid on behalf of the target and, given their statutory duty to promote the success of the target, they must be free to consider competing bids which they receive both before and after the sponsor's bid has been announced. If a competing bid is received and the independent directors form the view – taking into account the advice of their financial adviser – that the terms of the competing bid are more likely to benefit the members of the target as a whole than those offered by the sponsor, they will be duty bound to recommend the competing bid even if this means withdrawing their earlier recommendation of the sponsor's prior bid. So even a bid that starts out recommended may lose that recommendation during the bid process if a competing bid emerges. This is why bid secrecy is often vital to the success of a takeover bid. If the sponsor can get to the formal launch date without alerting potentially competing bidders there may be insufficient time for rival bids to be launched.

In the case of a scheme of arrangement, the buy-in of the target board is even more important. Indeed it is fundamental because without the support of the target board a successful scheme is practically impossible to execute given the fact that it is the target and not the bidder that proposes and executes the procedure. Therefore, as with a recommended offer, the sponsor and the target board must agree the terms and conditions of the bid in advance of the scheme being launched. While it is not usual for a formal agreement to be signed between a bidder and the target in the case of an offer – except perhaps to record related matters such as break fees or non-solicitation agreements – in the case of a scheme there is often a 'transaction agreement' covering the implementation of the deal. The purpose of this agreement is to bind the target into the process from the beginning. Whilst it will not go as far as to rule out the possibility of the target board considering a potentially competing bid, it will provide a measure of comfort against the execution risk inherent with a public bid by binding the

---

66   However, the currently proposed abolition of taper relief means that in some circumstances a share swap will be unattractive. Some management teams involved in transactions prior to April 2008 will prefer to make a disposal of shares for cash, triggering capital gains tax at an effective rate of (potentially) 10% and then to reinvest the proceeds.

67   See para **12.42**.

target into a clear process for the scheme. The transaction agreement will usually also include any deal on non-solicitation, break fees and work fees.

Non-solicitation arrangements

12.49 Exclusivity arrangements of the kind that are routinely granted by sellers to prospective buyers in private buy-outs[68] are not typically available in public-to-privates. In practical terms, there is no single seller per se that can grant exclusivity pending completion of due diligence and documentation. Furthermore, the directors of the target – meaning both the independent committee as regards any formal decisions on behalf of the target but also as a general matter those directors that are participating in the buy-out – are under a duty to act to promote the success of the company for the benefit of its members as a whole and this duty will not necessarily be served by simply agreeing to exclusive talks and negotiations with one prospective buyer to the exclusion of others. However, this all said, where a particular entity is the most viable buyer for the target and most likely to deliver maximum value to shareholders, perhaps because it is unlikely that there is another interested buyer at the proposed bid price, there may be grounds for the target to agree to some form of non-solicitation agreement and this will normally be raised by the prospective bidder at the time of the initial approach.

Break fees

12.50 It is increasingly common for prospective bidders to seek an agreement from the target that the bidder will be paid a fee if the bid is launched but subsequently fails in certain agreed circumstances; usually where the target board's recommendation is subsequently withdrawn, where a higher third party bid is received that is not matched by the first bidder or perhaps where the bid fails for other reasons. The fee agreement is made by the target as an inducement to the bidder to launch its bid and to incur the significant costs and time commitments inherent in a public bid. Absent an agreement on fees, prospective bidders – and financial sponsors in particular – will often be reluctant to enter into bid talks or to launch a bid and this may not serve the interests of the members of the target. Such fees are typically referred to as break fees or inducement fees.

An agreement by target to pay a break fee raises issues under a number of heads. First of all, the Code lays down certain requirements in relation to 'inducement fees'.[69] In particular, any fee must be *de minimis* and not normally more than 1% of the offer value[70], both the independent target board and the Rule 3 adviser must confirm to the Panel in writing that they believe the fee to be in the best interests of shareholders, all the arrangements must be fully disclosed in the press announcement and the bid document and the fee agreement must be put on display in accordance with Rule 26 of the Code. Furthermore the Panel must be consulted on the fee at the earliest opportunity.

68 See para **1.55**.
69 See Rule 21.2 of the Code.
70 The 1% maximum should be calculated on the fully diluted equity share capital of the target, including the exercise of any warrants and options, and it should be inclusive of any unrecoverable VAT. See Panel Practice Statements 4 and 15.

Aside from the target board's obligations to comply with the Code, in agreeing to any break fees each target director (ie, those on the independent board) must also have regard to his or her duties as such. Thus the independent directors should only approve the fee if they determine that it is likely to promote the success of the target for the benefit of its members as a whole. In forming such view the directors should also satisfy themselves that it is not being agreed to for a collateral purpose; for example, in order to discourage another, less welcome, bidder. The quantum of such fee will also need to be scrutinised and approved in this regard, although given the Code position that 1% should normally be the maximum amount, for all practical purposes there is a market standard ceiling in effect.

Break fees also require consideration of the UK's financial assistance legislation.[71] In the past, the perceived wisdom was that a break fee *can* be financial assistance even though a person is only *proposing to* acquire shares in the target and indeed the fee will only be payable if that person does *not* actually acquire those shares. However, the current view is that a properly documented break fee[72] should *not* amount to unlawful financial assistance if it does not amount to a material reduction of target's net assets.[73] This is why 1% of the value of the bid is generally viewed as the upper threshold for break fees. This book does not deal with the necessary legal detail and, in practice, the target's legal advisers will need to carry out a detailed analysis of the proposed break fee to determine if it would constitute financial assistance.

Finally, care also needs to be taken that the proposed arrangement does not constitute a Class 1 transaction for the purposes of the Listing Rules of the UK Listing Authority – and thus require a circular to shareholders and their approval at general meeting – either because of its size or because it constitutes a restricted indemnity under paragraph 10.2.7 of the Listing Rules. This is unlikely, given the financial assistance concerns discussed above, but the issue might arise, for example, in the case of a target with low profitability in relation to its assets.

Work fees

12.51   Break fees provide comfort to the bidder for the period following the launch of the bid, since they are given as an inducement for the bid being made. They do not necessarily cover the bidder for costs incurred prior to launch, particularly if the bid is not ultimately launched. Increasingly, financial sponsors are also seeking cost coverage for this period in the form of 'work fees'. The issues applicable to break fees also require consideration in relation to work fees.

---

71 Currently in Companies Act 1985, s 151 et seq, but to be repealed for private companies on 1 October 2008 and superseded by Chap 2 of Pt 18 of the Companies Act 2006 for public companies as of 1 October 2009.

72 It should not appear to be a gift or indemnity, which would amount to unlawful financial assistance, and should be structured as an inducement to the potential bidder.

73 This is not a strict accounting test of net assets but is a reasonable and informed estimate by the directors of the target of the market value of the target's assets (including goodwill) less liabilities.

Due diligence

12.52   Although there will be more publicly available information on a listed public company than a private company, the buyer will have less opportunity to conduct specific due diligence on the target in a public-to-private than in a conventional private buy-out. In particular, although most public-to-privates are recommended by the board of the target, the independent directors of the target will usually impose strict limits on the information which the target may make available to the bidder and its financiers. The main reason for this is the 'equality of information' requirements under the Code.[74] In particular, the Code provides – in broad terms – that any information that is made available by the target to one potential bidder must also be made available to other, potentially competing, *bona fide* bidders.[75] The concern for a target company is that by furnishing confidential information to the bidder, it might subsequently be required to make available the same information to a less welcome bidder or potential bidder, which might even include a trade competitor of the target. In fact, for most public-to-privates the disclosure requirement is not as open ended as this might seem. Specifically, in the case of a 'management buy-out or similar transaction' (which would include a public-to-private as the term is used in this chapter) the Code goes on to provide that the information that the target board is required to give to competing bidders is that information that is generated by the target (including target's management) which is passed to the bidder's equity or debt providers.[76]

The obligation under Rule 20.2 referred to above is an obligation of the target but in the case of a management buy-out it is supported by a further obligation that applies to the bidder. Rule 20.3 of the Code provides that any information that is passed by the bidder to the providers of equity and debt finance for the bid must on request also be furnished to the target's independent board. This would then form the basis for any required disclosure by the target under Rule 20.2. An important but subtle distinction must be drawn between the two rules, however. Rule 20.2 (in the case of a management buy-out) is concerned with information generated by the target (including the target's management in such capacity) whereas Rule 20.3 is concerned with information issued by the bidder. In practice, considerable care needs to be taken by the management team and its advisers to ensure that only information that truly emanates from the target is required to be disclosed to competing bidders and not, say, financial models, business plans and projections generated in respect of the bid itself by the bidder.

There is of course a related conflict of interest point here for target directors that are participating in the buy-out. Even though they may not be part of the independent committee they do continue to have fiduciary duties to the target and cannot release non-public proprietary information concerning the target to the bidder or its equity and debt providers. To do so they would need the consent of the target, meaning the independent committee.

---

74 See Rule 20 of the Code.
75 See Rule 20.2 of the Code.
76 See Note 3 to Rule 20.2 of the Code.

As a pure due diligence matter, even though the amount of information made available is likely to be substantially less than with a private buy-out, some comfort may be taken from the fact that the target will already have been the subject of a significant due diligence process when it was initially floated, depending of course on how long ago that was. It is also noteworthy, given the reduced information made available by targets in public-to-privates, that virtually all public deals do involve the participation of the incumbent management team rather than a pure buy-in team. Existing management's knowledge and understanding of the target will generally be more reliable and therefore attractive to potential private equity sponsors and their financiers than the limited knowledge of an entirely new team.

Acquisition finance and equity finance

12.53   The key differences in the raising of acquisition finance for public deals by contrast with private deals are considered in more detail later in this chapter.[77] In terms of process, however, it is worth noting here that all of the finance for the acquisition (debt and equity) must be in place at the outset of the bid. This is a result of the absolute requirement under the Code that a third party acceptable to the Panel – by custom the bidder's financial adviser – must provide confirmation both in the press announcement and the bid document that sufficient cash resources are available to the bidder to enable it to satisfy acceptance in full of the bid.[78] Accordingly the finance must be in place from the date of announcement.

The implications of this requirement cannot be overstated. In practice, it means that all conditionality under the acquisition finance documentation will need to have been satisfied by the date the bid is announced; subject to certain exceptions that the market deems acceptable.[79]

Irrevocable commitments from target shareholders

12.54   Not content with getting the recommendation of the target's independent committee, most potential bidders will also canvass the main shareholders of the target before launching a bid. At the least they will wish to test the water for their likely bid price – and the point at which shareholders are sellers – but they may also use the opportunity to try and tie in certain shareholders to their bid in advance of it being made. That is, the sponsor will aim to elicit from certain shareholders – ideally those with relatively large stakes – an irrevocable undertaking in respect of its up-coming bid.

In broad terms an 'irrevocable undertaking' is an agreement by a shareholder in favour of the bidder that it will accept the bid when made. In practice they can take two forms, each bringing a different degree of certainty to the bid process for the bidder. A 'hard' undertaking means that the relevant shareholder agrees

---

77 See paras **12.126** et seq.
78 See Rules 2.5(c) and 24.7 of the Code.
79 See paras **12.128** et seq.

that it will accept the proposed bid even if a higher competing bid is made by a third party. If hard irrevocables are received in respect of sufficient target shares, the bidder may be able to 'shut-out' any competing bidders by ensuring that no other bidder can get to the necessary 50.1% threshold necessary to declare an offer unconditional (or indeed get the requisite 75% necessary for a scheme to go through). A 'soft' irrevocable is an undertaking that the shareholder will accept the bidder's bid, provided that a subsequent higher bid (or a higher bid above a certain amount) is not made, perhaps within a period of, say, 21 days of the bidder's bid being made. In practice, many institutional shareholders are constitutionally unable to give hard irrevocables, or at least have a policy of not giving them, so a reduced level of comfort is often the most that a bidder can expect. Hard irrevocables will, however, often be available from roll-over managers; that is, members of the target's senior management that are participating in the buy-out and who own shares in the target.

The strategy of seeking irrevocables is not without risk, of course, given the overriding strategic aim of keeping the bid secret until the very last minute[80], but by using its financial adviser a sponsor may be able to conduct its research on a no-names basis (initially at least). Note also that the consent of the Panel is required before a bidder can approach any private individuals or small corporate shareholders with a view to seeking an irrevocable undertaking.[81] The Code also requires that details of any irrevocable undertakings received before a bid is launched – including whether they are hard or soft – must be disclosed in both the press announcement and in the bid document itself.[82]

Market purchases

12.55 A further tactic for increasing the chances of success of an offer (but perhaps less so with a scheme[83]) is for the sponsor to build a pre-emptive stake in the target by acquiring target shares directly from the market before it launches its offer. In doing so the sponsor moves its starting point nearer to the threshold for successful completion of the offer. In fact, whilst pre-launch market purchases would count towards the acceptance condition, they would not count towards the 90% compulsory purchase threshold required by statute[84] because they would not be 'shares to which the offer relates'.[85] By contrast, shares acquired after the offer is posted can count towards the 90% threshold (as well as to the acceptance condition). In any event, a pre-bid stake building strategy is not without risk. One of the major concerns, especially with a target in which the shares are not that actively traded, is that the stake-building will result in a leak of the proposed offer; although this may be mitigated by using a reputable broker to acquire the stock. By buying in the market before a bid is launched the sponsor would also

---

80 See para **12.57**.
81 See Rule 4.3 of the Code.
82 See Rules 2.5(b) and 24.2(d)(x) of the Code respectively.
83 As considered further below.
84 See Chap 3 of Pt 28 of the Companies Act 2006.
85 See para **12.69** generally in relation to the statutory squeeze-out mechanism.

be taking a commercial risk on the success of its bid. If the bid is not subsequently successful the sponsor may be left holding shares in the target that may not even be worth what the sponsor paid for them. It may, however, take an alternative view and assume that the only way its bid would not be successful would be if a higher competing bid were successful, in which case the sponsor will have hedged its downside by buying shares that are subsequently sold on at a profit. In any event, because of the commercial risk inherent with market purchases, a financial sponsor is unlikely to be able to fund the market purchases through a conventional acquisition finance facility although dedicated 'market purchase' facilities are very occasionally made available by banks as part of the overall acquisition finance package. Alternatively a sponsor might be able to utilise a discrete 'margin' facility to raise some of the finance for the market purchases.[86] Failing that it will need to use its own cash resources.

As regards schemes of arrangement, stake building through market purchases – whether before or after the launch of the bid – does not directly enhance the bidder's position. This follows from the fact that shares held by the bidder and its associates cannot be voted in the general meeting to approve the scheme. Indeed, the fact that any shares acquired are no longer able to be voted could even be counterproductive for the bidder's scheme. On the other hand market purchases can be used to dissuade a potentially competing bidder from making a bid and to provide possible momentum to the bid generally – and they are quite often made in practice. In any event, where a bid is to be launched as a scheme, the bidder may still need to bear in mind the implications of any market purchases that it does make on the squeeze-out procedure because many schemes now reserve for the bidder an option of switching to an offer at a later stage if the scheme is abandoned for any reason.[87]

Regulatory implications of market purchases

12.56 Ultimately, there are regulatory implications of making market purchases (in addition to the Companies Act 2006 (squeeze-out threshold) implications mentioned above). Specifically, certain provisions of statute, the Code and the FSA Disclosure and Transparency Rules are triggered when a person acquires a certain number of shares.

Thus, before an approach has been made to the target, where the stake-building leads to rumour and speculation in the market or an untoward movement in the share price (irrespective of the number of shares acquired) and there are reasonable grounds for concluding that it is the potential bidder's actions that have lead to the situation, the Code requires that a preliminary announcement is made by the bidder.[88] Any such announcement is likely to be untimely from the sponsor's perspective.

---

86 A margin facility or account allows a person to acquire liquid stock such as public equities on the basis that the stock is given as collateral with the borrower required at all times to ensure that the amount of the loan is no greater than an agreed percentage of the market value of the stock.
87 See also para **12.39**.
88 See Rule 2.2(d) of the Code and para **12.58** below generally regarding preliminary announcements.

Similarly, under the FSA Disclosure and Transparency Rules any person that acquires 3% of the voting share capital of a company whose shares are admitted to trading on a regulated market or a prescribed market (eg, AIM) must inform the company and the FSA within two trading days. The company must then pass that information on to the market.

Ultimately, the Code requires a person that acquires 30% of the target's issued share capital (even by acquiring just one share that when added to an existing holding takes it to 30%) must launch an offer for all of the shares – a 'Rule 9' mandatory offer, referring to the relevant part of the Code. Shares held by persons 'acting in concert' with the bidder[89] will also count towards the 30%. A Rule 9 mandatory offer must not include any conditions other than the acceptance and competition clearance conditions dictated by the Code itself.[90] The acceptance condition must be set at its lowest possible threshold such that the bidder will be obliged to declare the offer unconditional once it acquires more than 50% of the target's voting rights.[91] Rule 9 is also triggered where a shareholder that already owns between 30% and 50% of the issued share capital of the target acquires any more shares at all.

Also under the Code, once a bid has been launched any dealings by the bidder in the target must be disclosed to the Panel, and any dealings (including derivatives dealings) by shareholders of the target who own or control 1% or more of any class of shares must also be disclosed.[92]

Another serious concern with all market purchases and for all persons involved in or aware of a pending bid is the need to comply with the relevant provisions of Part V (Insider Dealing) of the Criminal Justice Act 1993 and to ensure that their conduct does not constitute 'market abuse' within s 118 of the Financial Services and Markets Act 2000.

Finally, there may even be non-UK regulatory implications of market purchases. For example, in broad terms, buying shares during an offer period is prohibited under US securities laws and where there are significant US shareholders those laws may come into play. There are exemptions depending on how many shares are held by US shareholders and whether or not these are available will require careful consideration and professional advice. Schemes are less likely to be caught by the US tender offer rules but appropriate advice should still be taken nonetheless.

Confidentiality

12.57 Confidentiality at all preliminary stages of a bid is vital to the success of the bid. If news that a bid is imminent is leaked the share price of the target is quite likely to rise sharply. Whilst this might not take the price above the intended bid price it will reduce the apparent bid premium when the bid is made. It will also make market purchases more costly. From the perspective of the target and its shareholders the effects of a leak may also be unwelcome largely

---

89 See fn **21**.
90 See Rules 10 and 12.1 of the Code and paras **12.116** to **12.119** below generally.
91 See Rule 9 of the Code generally as to mandatory offers.
92 See Rule 8.3 of the Code

given the uncertainty that is created. With all this in mind the Code includes provisions intended to reduce the chances of a leak occurring.

First, there is a basic requirement that a prospective bid must be kept confidential and that all persons privy to confidential information must conduct themselves so as to minimise the chances of an accidental leak of information.[93] In addition, in order to encourage bidders and target companies to keep those in the know to an absolute minimum, the Code imposes an obligation on the bidder or, if it is already in talks with the target, the target to make an announcement when negotiations or discussions are about to be extended to include more than a very restricted number of people (outside those who need to know in the companies concerned and their immediate advisers).[94] Also, a bidder wishing to approach a wider group, for example to arrange equity or debt financing for the bid, should consult the Panel.[95] In practice, the Panel must always be consulted prior to more than six external parties being approached. Like any other person privy to confidential price-sensitive information concerning a bid, the external parties approached must keep the bid discussions secret and such parties should not themselves approach additional third parties without consulting the Panel.[96]

There is another side to confidentiality and that is not using the knowledge of the bid for insider trading purposes. Dealing in the target's shares by an 'insider' or communication of a prospective bid to another may also constitute a criminal offence of insider dealing[97] or contravening the restrictions on market abuse[98]. There are defences (ie, the so-called 'market information' defence or safe harbour) under both regimes where the only relevant knowledge is that the bidder is proposing to make the bid. But if the bidder has access to other inside information, for example as a result of its due diligence, it will not fall inside the safe harbour.

Preliminary announcements

12.58   Rule 2.2 of the Code sets out all of the circumstances when an announcement must be made by the target company or a prospective bidder in relation to a pending bid. From the bidder's perspective it is clearly preferable for the first announcement to be the press release announcing that the bidder has a firm intention to make an offer. This will mean that details of the offer are not out into the market before the bid is ready to be launched. However, the Code also legislates for circumstances when the bidder or the target is required to make a preliminary announcement, before the press announcement.

Thus, as indicated above, an announcement might be required just before the bid talks are extended beyond the immediate 'need to know' circle.[99] In addition, where, following an initial approach to the target by the bidder, the target is the

---

93 See Rule 2.1 of the Code
94 See Rule 2.2(e) of the Code.
95 See Rule 2.2 (e) of the Code.
96 Panel Statement 2003/15 – 2003 Annual Report.
97 Criminal Justice Act 1993, ss 52-64.
98 Financial Services and Markets Act 2000, s 118.
99 See Rule 2.2(e) of the Code.

subject of rumour and speculation or there is an untoward movement in its share price, the target will normally be required to make a preliminary announcement that it has been approached.[100] Even before an approach, if the target is the subject of rumour and speculation or there is an untoward movement in its share price, the bidder will usually be required to make a preliminary announcement if there are reasonable grounds for concluding that its actions have led to the situation.[101] In both cases, the question of what is 'untoward' is for the Panel to determine and must be considered in the light of all relevant facts and not solely by reference to the absolute percentage movements in price. In any event, the Panel should be consulted – and, if the target is so directed, a statement made – if there has been a movement of 10% or more above the lowest share price since the approach was received or an abrupt price rise of a smaller percentage which could be regarded as untoward. The Code requirements for any preliminary statement will normally be satisfied by a brief announcement that talks are taking place or that a potential bidder is considering making a bid.[102] Just as with an informal leak into the market, any formal statement that a target company is 'in play' will generally cause a sharp rise in the share price. It may also alert competing bidders and allow them more time to consider a move for the target themselves. Consequently, bidders will usually take considerable care to ensure that they or the target are not forced to make a preliminary announcement.

Target companies that find themselves the subject of bid speculation that results in or follows a preliminary announcement are protected from a prolonged siege through a specific provision of the Code. This takes the form of a 'put up or shut up' right. Specifically, once a preliminary announcement of a possible offer has been made, the target board is entitled to request the Panel to impose a time limit on the bidder for it to clarify its intentions.[103] Within the period specified the bidder must either 'put up' by announcing a firm intention to make an offer under Rule 2.5 or else 'shut up' and announce that it has no intention of making an offer under Rule 2.8. Once it has made a no intention to bid announcement the bidder will in most circumstances be locked out from launching another bid for six months.[104]

Launch of the bid

Press announcement

12.59   The first formal stage of any takeover bid – as required by the Code[105] – is the announcement by the bidder that it is has a firm intention of making a bid for the target. It is often simply referred to as the press announcement. As considered above, preliminary statements may on occasion be required prior to this point but the announcement of a firm intention is the step that officially launches

---

100 See Rule 2.2(c) of the Code.
101 See Rule 2.2(d) of the Code.
102 See Rule 2.4(a) of the Code.
103 See Rule 2.4(b) of the Code.
104 See Rule 2.8 of the Code.
105 See Rule 2 of the Code.

a bid. Under the terms of the Code the bidder has 28 days following the press announcement within which to make the bid but it is extremely rare for the bidder to use all of this period. Tactically the bidder will wish to follow the press announcement almost immediately with the offer or scheme itself so as not to give potentially rival bidders much time to assemble their bids. In fact, in the case of a scheme, the period between the press announcement and posting of the scheme document will necessarily need to accommodate the process of having the scheme document approved by, and the notice convening the scheme approval meeting issued by, the court. This may take approximately one week.

The substance of the announcement is also governed by the Code[106] and in broad terms it will include substantially all the terms of the bid itself.

Given that the bidder is de facto bound to make the bid once it has issued the press announcement – because the Panel will only excuse the bidder from following it up with the offer or scheme in exceptional circumstances of if a precondition is not satisfied[107] – and indeed since it is required under the Code to include a cash confirmation in the announcement,[108] it will need to have all of its finance in place at this time.

Posting of the bid document

12.60   As indicated above, once the firm intention announcement has been issued, the formal proposal to the target's shareholders must normally follow within 28 days.[109]

In the case of an offer this means the posting of an offering circular – the 'offer document' to each of the shareholders of the target, usually identified by the most recent register of members available. Historically the offer would be made by the bidder's financial adviser on its behalf but it is now more common – at least in the case of offers for companies whose shares are traded on a regulated exchange such as the main market of the London Stock Exchange (and thus the subject of the EU Takeover Directive[110]) – for the bidder to make the offer itself.

In the case of a scheme the formal proposal to shareholders is documented in the form of a scheme circular – the 'scheme document' – that is very similar to and effectively replaces the offer document (and target circular) used for an offer. Unlike an offer, however, it is posted by the target.

Bid document contents

12.61   The Code stipulates the minimum requirements that an offer document must contain[111] and many of these requirements are considered later in this chapter.[112] A form of acceptance will be included with the offer document and shareholders that decide to accept the offer complete the form of acceptance and

---

106 See Rule 2.5 of the Code.
107 See Rule 2.7 of the Code.
108 See Rule 2.5(c) of the Code.
109 See Rule 30.1 and para **12.59**.
110 Directive 2004/25/EC. There is a concern that financial advisers themselves could become criminally liable for the contents of the offer document.
111 See, in particular, Rules 10, 12, 13, 24 and 25.
112 See paras **12.109** et seq.

then send that together with any share certificates that they hold for their shares[113] to the 'receiving agent' appointed by the bidder to handle the administrative task of collecting and accounting for acceptances. Alternatively, in the case of shares held in CREST, they will transfer their shares within the CREST system. The target's recommendation of an offer is set out in a circular addressed to all shareholders that is included with the offer document.

The scheme document, as with an offer document, must contain all the information required by the Code.[114] In addition, it must satisfy the requirements of the Companies Act,[115] including notice of the requisite target shareholder meeting(s). The scheme document is posted by the target but only once the court's permission has been obtained and the scheme approval meeting convened for a date in due course. Because of this additional procedural step scheme documents cannot easily be posted immediately following the press announcement as often occurs with offers.

Bid conditions

12.62   Voluntary offers – which are to be contrasted with mandatory offers under Rule 9 of the Code, which must be unconditional except for the two mandatory conditions[116] – are made by the bidder making a conditional offer to each of the shareholders of the target. The key condition (which is also required with a Rule 9 offer) will be that the bidder has acquired or agreed to acquire (through the offer or otherwise, thus including shares held prior to the launch of the bid) more than 50% of the voting share capital of the target, effectively so that it obtains control. This is called the 'acceptance condition'. In practice, the acquisition financiers are likely to insist that the acceptance condition is set at a higher level (75% in total or 90% of the shares the subject of the offer) for reasons considered elsewhere.[117]

The other mandatory condition that the Code requires the bid to contain (whether a bid is voluntary or mandatory under Rule 9) is a condition that the bid will lapse if it is referred to either the UK or European Commission competition authorities before the first closing date or the date on which it is declared unconditional as to acceptances, whichever is later.

Other typical conditions that a voluntary bid may contain – each of which will be negotiated with the target (unless the bid is hostile) – will relate to the financial position of the target; in particular that it is not insolvent and usually that there has been no material adverse change in the financial position of the target since the date of its most recent audited (or perhaps other non-audited) accounts.[118] With multinational targets, the bidder might also include obtaining additional competition clearances as conditions, in addition to the mandatory UK and EC clearances.

---

113 In the case of dematerialised shares, the form of acceptance alone is sufficient although an offer can also be accepted completely through CREST alone.

114 See in particular Rules 10, 12, 13, 24 and 25 of the Code and paras **12.109** et seq.

115 See Companies Act 1985, s 426 (to be replaced by Companies Act 2006, s 897 with effect from 6 April 2008).

116 The 'acceptance' and 'competition clearance' conditions, which are discussed in paras **12.116** to **12.119**.

117 See para **12.75**.

118 But see also para **12.121** as to the 'enforceability' of 'MAC' conditions.

The Code effectively requires that none of the conditions are subjective; that is, that the bid must not normally be subject to conditions or pre-conditions which depend solely on subjective judgments by the directors of the bidder or the target or the fulfilment of which is in their hands.[119] In addition, the Panel will not permit the bidder to invoke a condition (or pre-condition) unless the circumstances giving rise to the right to invoke the condition (or pre-condition) are of material significance to the bidder in the context of the bid.[120] These rules prevent the bidder from abusing conditionality in the bid to effectively create an option over the target shares.

The conditions to a scheme will be the same as those for an offer, save that the acceptance condition will be different to reflect the statutory requirements for approval of a scheme as opposed to the contractual acceptance condition for an offer.

Bid mechanics

12.63   In this section the procedures applicable to offers and schemes are inherently different and require separate consideration.

Takeover offers

Contractual basis of takeover offers

12.64   The principle behind takeover offers is that the bidder seeks to make a contract with the individual shareholders to buy the target's shares held by them. The terms of the contract are set out in the offer document and the bidder's offer must be formally accepted by shareholders for the contract to form. Acceptance is also provided for in the offer document and shareholders agree to the terms by executing the form of acceptance annexed to the offer or, in the case of shares held in CREST, by accepting the offer through the CREST system. As previously outlined, the bidder is not free to include whatever conditions it wishes, as the Code dictates certain minimum conditions that must be included as well as rules relating to any other conditions that might be included.[121] The Code also imposes certain procedural requirements on the manner in which these contracts are formed including a structured timetable with backstop dates. The following paragraphs outline these procedural requirements in further detail.

Closing dates

12.65   When an offer is made it will stipulate when the first closing date is. This is tactical and is designed to prompt shareholders to accept the offer before it closes. The first closing date can not be less than 21 days after the offer date.[122]

---

119 See Rule 13.1 of the Code.
120 See Rule 13.4(a) of the Code and paras **12.120** and **12.121** generally for further consideration of this principle.
121 See para **12.62**.
122 See Rule 31.1 of the Code.

This means that all shareholders get at least 21 days to deliberate and, if they so wish, to accept the offer. Depending on the response to the offer by that date the bidder may then extend the offer for a further period and stipulate the next closing date.[123]

Offer declared unconditional

12.66 The ultimate aim of any offer is for it to be declared unconditional. This by definition means that the offer has been successful. In fact there are two levels of unconditionality; an offer may be 'unconditional as to acceptances' and it may be 'unconditional in all respects'. An offer can be declared unconditional *as to acceptances* only once the acceptance condition is satisfied. It can be declared unconditional *in all respects* when all conditions including the acceptance condition have been satisfied or waived (as permitted by the Code[124]). The 'unconditional date' is the date on which the offer is declared unconditional in all respects and it is this date that crystallises the takeover and the obligation on the bidder to pay for acceptances.[125] In many cases the acceptance condition will be the last condition to be satisfied so that an offer will be declared unconditional as to acceptances and in all respects at the same time. An exception to this might be where a competition clearance or other regulatory consent is required – as a condition to the offer – that is not obtained by the time the offer is declared unconditional as to acceptances.

The Code stipulates that an offer must be declared unconditional as to acceptances within 60 days of the date of the offer or else it will automatically lapse.[126] Once it has been declared unconditional as to acceptances an offer must then become unconditional in all respects within a further 21 days – from the date it was declared unconditional as to acceptances or the first closing date whichever is the later – or else it must lapse.[127] This means that the backstop date for an offer to go unconditional is 81 days after the date of the offer (usually referred to as D+81).

If a competing offer emerges during the offer period then the timetable for the existing offer is re-set and automatically moves to the same timetable as the new offer so that they run in parallel. The other possible interrupting factor in the timetable is where the transaction is referred to either the UK or EU competition authorities, in which case the offer must lapse.[128]

Shareholders' right of withdrawal

12.67 Unless an offer has been declared unconditional as to acceptances by the date falling 21 days after the first closing date (which is usually 21 days after the

---

123 See Rule 31.2 of the Code.
124 See paras **12.120** and **12.121**.
125 Under Rule 31.8 of the Code the bidder must pay for any acceptances received as at the unconditional date within 14 days of that date. In addition, until the offer if closed (if at all), the bidder must pay for any subsequently received acceptances within 14 days of their receipt.
126 See Rule 31.6 of the Code.
127 See Rule 31.7 of the Code.
128 See Rule 12.1 of the Code and para **12.119**.

offer date[129]), a shareholder that has tendered its shares into the offer can withdraw its acceptance at any time thereafter until the offer is declared unconditional as to acceptances.[130]

Drawdown of funds

12.68   Once an offer has been declared unconditional in all respects the bidder is bound to make the payments due to accepting shareholders. Although the Code gives the bidder 14 days to make such payments – either by telegraphic transfer to the accounts stipulated by the shareholders in their forms of acceptance or through settlement in the CREST system – it is common for the bidder to effect such payments on the 12th or 13th day after the unconditional date so as to allow for some administrative glitches and bank holidays. The payment date will be the first date that the acquisition finance funds are drawn down. Since it is highly unlikely that 100% of the shareholders will have accepted the offer – at least by this point – there will usually be at least one more subsequent drawdown when the relevant minorities are squeezed-out.[131] Note that at the date of the first drawdown, the target group companies may not yet be in a position to give guarantees and security to the financiers because of the financial assistance prohibition applicable to public companies and their subsidiaries.[132]

Squeezing-out minority shareholdings

12.69   It would be extremely rare for an offer to be accepted by 100% of the shareholders of a target company. Individual shareholders may simply forget to complete the requisite form of acceptance and indeed individuals may not even get notice of the offer if they have moved from their registered address. Other shareholders may just hold out and not accept the offer even if the majority do accept it, hoping that it will not in any event be declared unconditional. There is also an increasing trend among institutional shareholders to view private equity sponsored bids as an opportunity to benefit from the value addition techniques of the private equity market and thus to remain in the target until the sponsor subsequently exits with a higher level of return. The sponsor on the other hand will much prefer to have no minorities remain in the target, no matter the reason for them being there. For one thing, minority shareholders have the benefit of both statutory and common law rights that might impede the sponsor's ultimate control of the target. Moreover the existence of minority shareholdings in the target has a dilutive effect on the absolute return that the sponsor can make from its investment in the bidder and the target business.

In addition to the sponsor's desire to have no minorities remaining in the target's equity, the acquisition financiers themselves have one major issue with rogue minorities; that is, the possibility that minorities could block the granting of target group credit support in the form of loans, guarantees and security for the

---

129 See para **12.65**.
130 See Rule 34 of the Code.
131 See para **12.69**.
132 See para **12.13**.

acquisition finance. In particular, minority shareholders with sufficiently large holdings possess certain statutory rights that can be used in certain circumstances to object to the re-registration of the target as a private company, which (because of the financial assistance prohibition applicable to public companies and their subsidiaries[133]) is a pre-requisite to the granting of target group credit support for the acquisition finance. A similar but separate right of objection also exists in relation to the whitewashing of any financial assistance given by private companies that (at the time of writing) necessarily follows the re-registration process.[134]

Recognising a successful bidder's need to be able to take ownership of the target free from rogue minorities, the Companies Act 2006 legislates for a compulsory purchase mechanism to enable a bidder to 'squeeze-out' residual minority shareholders in certain circumstances.[135] This is the mechanism by which a bidder can obtain 100% ownership of the target.

In order for a bidder to be in a position to invoke the compulsory purchase legislation two main conditions must be satisfied. First, the offer made by it must satisfy the statutory definition of a 'takeover offer' and secondly that offer must be accepted by shareholders holding not less than 90% in value and of the voting rights of the 'shares to which the offer relates' within the statutory period. These two requirements are considered below.

Applies to 'takeover offers'

12.70   For an offer to qualify as a 'takeover offer' for the purposes of the squeeze-out legislation it must satisfy two conditions. First, the offer must relate to *all* of the issued share capital of the target (or, if there is more than one class of shares, all of the shares of one class) excluding any shares held by the bidder (or its associates[136]) at the date of the offer.[137] Secondly, the offer must be on the same terms for all the shares to which the offer relates. One exception to this is where a shareholder is resident in a country that has securities laws that make requirements on the form of the offer. In these circumstances the terms of the offer to overseas shareholders can be varied to the extent necessary to enable the overseas shareholders to receive alternative consideration of 'substantially equivalent value'.[138] Similarly, in some jurisdictions it may be unlawful for the offer to be made by posting the offering circular to shareholders resident there, such as the United States and Japan. In those circumstances the bidder will be entitled to consider alternative ways of making the offer for it still to qualify, such as advertising the offer in the *London Gazette*.[139]

---

133 See para **12.13**.
134 See also paras **12.13** and **12.134** et seq.
135 See Chap 3 of Pt 28 of the Companies Act 2006 (which replaced Pt XIIIA of the 1985 Act).
136 This would include its nominees, any member of the bidder's group and persons 'acting in concert' with it (see also fn **21**).
137 See para **12.71** below in relation to shares that the bidder has contracted to acquire before the date of the offer.
138 See Companies Act 2006, s 976(3).
139 See Companies Act 2006, s 978.

The 90% threshold

12.71   In order to invoke the compulsory purchase provisions the bidder must have acquired or contracted to acquire (mainly through acceptances of the offer) not less than 90% in value and of the voting rights of the 'shares to which the offer relates'.[140] Furthermore, the 90% threshold must be reached within the statutory period. More particularly, no notice to invoke the compulsory purchase provisions may be served after the end of three months from the last day on which the offer can be accepted or, where the offer is *not* an offer for a company with its shares admitted to trading on a regulated market (ie, it is an offer for an AIM company), before the expiry of six months from the date of the offer if that period ends earlier.

Target shares acquired in the market (ie, outside the offer per se) *after the offer date* can count towards the 90% threshold provided that either: (a) the price paid for those shares does not exceed the offer price; or (b) if it does, the offer price is revised upwards to be at least equal to that price.[141] But shares acquired by the bidder *before the offer date* do not count towards the 90% calculation (on either side of the equation) since they are not shares to which the offer relates. For these purposes, any shares which the bidder has *contracted to acquire before the date of the offer* shall be deemed to have been held by the bidder at the date of the offer (and thus do not count towards (or against) the 90% calculation). However, shares which are the subject of an irrevocable undertaking to accept the offer when it is made will *not* count as shares which the bidder has contracted to buy (and thus they *would* count as 'shares to which the offer relates' and towards the 90% calculation) provided that the undertaking is given either: (a) by deed and for no consideration; or (b) for consideration of negligible value; or (c) for no consideration other than a promise by the bidder to make the offer.[142]

Where there is more than one class of shares the subject of the offer the right to squeeze-out minorities within any class is reliant on the 90% threshold having been achieved for that class.

Procedure for effecting the squeeze-out

12.72   Once the 90% threshold has been achieved – provided it is within the requisite time period[143] – the bidder may give notice to any shareholder that has not accepted the offer that it wishes to acquire its shares. The form of the notice is prescribed by statute and will stipulate that the shares will be acquired compulsorily six weeks later. It must be copied to the target together with a statutory declaration of a director of the bidder stating that all conditions for the giving of such notices have been satisfied. On the date falling six weeks after the date of the notices the bidder is bound to acquire the shares and for such purposes it must

---

140 See Companies Act 2006, ss 979 and 980.
141 In fact, if the bidder or any person acting in concert with it acquired shares during the offer period at a price higher than the offer price, the Code would in any event require the terms of the offer to be revised upwards to be not less than the highest price paid by the bidder or any of its associates for those shares. See Rule 6.2 of the Code.
142 See Companies Act 2006, s 975.
143 See para **12.71** above.

pay the consideration for all the outstanding shares to *the target*. The target must then pay the consideration into a separate bank account where it will be held on trust for the relevant shareholders until such time as they claim it.[144] If unclaimed after 12 years it will be paid into court.

In certain circumstances the bidder can apply to court for an order that it may serve the requisite compulsory purchase notices even though it has not reached the 90% threshold. This applies where a number of shareholders necessary to get to the 90% threshold cannot be traced. A court will only grant the order if the bidder has made reasonable enquiries to locate the shareholders and the consideration offered is fair and reasonable. In addition the court must be satisfied that it would be 'just and equitable to grant the order having regard, in particular, to the number of shareholders who have been traced but who have not accepted the offer'.[145]

Right to object

12.73 Any shareholder that receives a compulsory purchase notice can, prior to the expiry of the six week period, apply to the court for an order blocking the purchase of its shares or specifying that the terms of the acquisition should be different to the terms of the offer. If such an application is made, the compulsory purchase of that shareholder's shares is put on hold pending the court hearing on the application.[146] A court is likely to uphold an objection only in exceptional circumstances.

What if the 90% threshold is not achieved?

12.74 If the bidder fails to achieve the 90% threshold within the requisite time period, it still has certain options to acquire the minority shareholdings.

First, it could make a new offer to the minority shareholders and hope to get acceptances from 90% of those shareholders by value and of voting rights of shares held. In order to do this at a higher price it would need to wait for six months after the date on which the initial offer was closed.[147]

Secondly, the bidder could have the target propose a scheme of arrangement to the minority shareholders. This would then need the approval of a majority in number holding not less than 75% in value of shares of those shareholders (that attend and vote at the relevant shareholder meeting) and the sanction of the court. Again, if the terms of the scheme were better than the prior offer the bidder and target would need to wait for six months from closure of the offer.

In either case, the success of the arrangement is likely to be dependent on improving the offer somehow, in which case the bidder will need to wait for at least another six months.

---

144 The target is obliged to make reasonable efforts periodically to locate any missing shareholders.

145 See Companies Act 2006, s 986(9) and (10).

146 See Companies Act 2006, s 986(1) and (2).

147 See Rule 35.3 of the Code. This would mean formally closing the initial offer.

Complete ownership of the target

12.75   Once the compulsory purchase of the minority shares has been effected the bidder will own 100% of the target. This removes any concerns about rogue minorities and their minority shareholder rights. It means that the target can be de-listed and re-registered as a private company without any objection. This in turn will allow the granting of financial assistance by the target group for the acquisition finance. From the perspective of the acquisition financiers, enabling the target group to give financial assistance in the form of loans, guarantees and security, is of fundamental importance. Absent this credit support, the acquisition financiers would be left unsecured by the target group. With this in mind, it is entirely standard practice for the acquisition financiers to insist that the acceptance condition of the offer is set at the 90% threshold. That way the acquisition financiers can be sure that if the offer goes through they will obtain the credit support they need.

However, that is not to say that the offer will not actually be declared unconditional at a lower level. What often happens in practice is that the bidder's financial adviser, who will both be tracking acceptances and speaking with target shareholders, will advise the bidder to declare the acceptance condition satisfied at a lower level *in order to get to 90% acceptance*. The logic with this is that certain institutional shareholders may not accept the offer until it has been declared unconditional, so that the offer must be declared unconditional in order to reach the higher level of acceptances. This waiving down of the acceptance condition will require the consent of both the bidder and the acquisition financiers, who will have undertakings relating to the conduct of the offer in the finance documentation. Because this happens relatively frequently, bidders often seek to pre-agree this approach with the acquisition financiers, perhaps in a side letter. In such circumstances it is not uncommon for the consent of the acquisition financiers to be expressed to be conditional upon there being visibility at the relevant time of the route to 90%, using statements to be provided by the bidder's financial adviser based on their discussions with shareholders and so on. More often it will just be left open with no pre-agreed basis on which the consent is to be granted.

In any event, even where they are willing to waive the acceptance condition down below 90%, it would be relatively rare for the acquisition financiers to permit the offer to be declared unconditional below 75% (counting *all* shares held by the bidder[148]). This is the minimum level of ownership necessary to implement the re-registration of the target as a private company and to carry out the financial assistance whitewash. At 75%, although minorities can in theory still object to the re-registration or financial assistance resolutions, this is unlikely to be a real impediment in practice.

---

148 Note that this threshold is determined differently than the 90% threshold. It is concerned with how many voting shares the bidder controls – so that it can pass special resolutions – not how it acquired them for the statutory squeeze-out test.

Closure or lapse of the offer

12.76 As indicated previously, for tactical reasons offers are generally open for acceptance for limited periods only and the bidder stipulates a closing date in advance.[149] If the offer is not extended on a particular closing date because the acceptance condition is not satisfied then there is no obligation to extend the offer.[150] An offer will also lapse automatically if there is a UK or EU merger authority referral, as it is a requirement of all offers that they contain a condition that the offer will lapse in these circumstances.[151]

An offer will invariably contain other conditions that on their face must be satisfied, in addition to the acceptance and no-UK or EU merger referral conditions, in order for the offer to be declared unconditional in all respects but, unlike the acceptance and merger referral conditions, the bidder does not have total discretion to invoke them as a reason not to declare an offer unconditional or to allow it to lapse on a closing date. In order to invoke a condition as a ground for not closing the offer (other than the acceptance and merger referral conditions) the bidder must in effect obtain the permission of the Panel. This is because the Code stipulates that the circumstances giving rise to the right to invoke a condition must be of material significance to the bidder in the context of the offer.[152]

In practice, although the bidder could finally close the offer once the unconditional date has occurred by giving 14 days' notice in accordance with Rule 31.4 of the Code, it is likely to leave it open for a while, at least for subsequent minorities to accept it, even where the 90% threshold has been achieved and the squeeze-out procedure has become available.

Share option arrangements

12.77 A bidder will be concerned that its takeover proposals contemplate and capture any shares that might be issued or issuable under any share option scheme established by the target. Indeed a bidder is obliged under the Code to make appropriate arrangements to safeguard the interests of option holders.[153] Most share option schemes will be triggered by the change of control that occurs when an offer is declared unconditional; that is, the option holders will have the right to exercise their options and subscribe for shares in the target. The option scheme may also contemplate that the option holders will be able to accept the offer in respect of their option shares. At all stages the bidder will need to consider whether any option shares would count as 'shares to which the offer relates' for the purposes of the squeeze-out legislation. This may depend on how the offer itself is drafted. As a practical matter where possible the bidder should also seek the co-operation of the target in ensuring that option shares are swept up.

---

149 See para **12.65**.
150 See Rule 31.1 of the Code.
151 See Rule 12 of the Code.
152 See Rules 13.1 and 13.4 of the Code and paras **12.62** and **12.121** generally in respect of conditionality.
153 See Rule 15 of the Code.

Schemes of arrangement

Statutory basis of schemes of arrangement

12.78   A scheme of arrangement is a statutory procedure and in order to implement one the detailed provisions of the statute must be followed to the letter.[154] The three main requirements for a scheme are:[155]

- a statement explaining the effects of the scheme and other matters must be circulated to shareholders;[156]

- it must be approved by the shareholders of the target;[157] and

- it must be sanctioned by a court order.[158]

Importantly, the statutory provisions are framed from the perspective of the target company; that is, the right to propose a scheme of arrangement and the responsibility for executing it in accordance with the statute rest with the target and not the bidder. From a bidder's perspective this means that the target board's cooperation is vital and schemes cannot be used in hostile situations.[159]

Explanatory statement

12.79   The scheme document posted to shareholders is required to include a statement – usually expressed to be from the target's independent board and the Rule 3 adviser jointly – explaining the effects of the scheme to the shareholders. Ultimately, the court will only sanction a scheme if it is satisfied with the substance of the explanatory statement and in making its determination it will consider whether the statement was fair and gave all information reasonably necessary to enable the recipient to decide how to vote on the scheme. In addition to explaining the effects of the scheme, the statement must disclose any material interests of the target's directors and the effect of the scheme on those interests (if different from the effect on similar interests of other shareholders). If the director's interests subsequently change in any material respect following the posting of the scheme document and before the scheme approval meeting, then those changes must be notified to the shareholders.

Shareholder approval

'Court' meeting

12.80   The key substantive requirement of a scheme is the approval of the target's shareholders. This is obtained at a special meeting of the shareholders convened by the court (the 'court meeting'). In order to convene the court meeting the

---

154 See s 425 of the Companies Act 1985 and its successor provisions in Pt 26 of the Companies Act 2006, which come into force on 6 April 2008.

155 See also paras **12.21** and **12.22** in relation to schemes generally.

156 Companies Act 1985, s 426, as superseded by Companies Act 2006, s 897 from 6 April 2008.

157 Companies Act 1985, s 425, as superseded by Companies Act 2006, s 899 from 6 April 2008.

158 Companies Act 1985, s 425, as superseded by Companies Act 2006, s 899 from 6 April 2008.

159 They have, however, been used in competitive situations.

target applies to the Companies Court using a claim form together with a support-ing witness statement setting out the background to the application. The 'claim' includes the court's ultimate sanction of the scheme in addition to the convening of the court meeting. The court order will usually appoint a chairman of the court meeting (one of the target's senior independent directors) and direct the chairman to advertise notice of the meeting and in due course to report the results of the vote to the court. Once the court order is obtained the target will advertise the notice of the meeting and post the scheme document (including notice of the meeting) to the shareholders. The shareholder meeting must normally be convened for a date which is at least 21 days after the date of the scheme circular.[160]

75% approval

12.81 At the court meeting a *majority in number* of target shareholders *who vote*, representing at least *75% in value* of the shares *voted*, must vote in favour of the scheme for it to be approved. Shares held by the bidder and its associates are not permitted to be voted, however, which is why market purchases are less common with schemes than with offers.[161]

Following the vote and the closing of the meeting the chairman of the meeting is required to report the result to the court. For this purposes he or she will pre-pare a report of the meeting including a statement of the result and various other details and lodge this with the court pending the final court hearing to sanction the scheme.

Reduction meeting

12.82 It is common for a takeover scheme to be structured as a reduction scheme, whereby the bidder is issued new share capital and the existing share capital held by the existing shareholders is cancelled by a reduction of capital. The main benefit of a reduction scheme is that there is no transfer of shares so the stamp duty that would be payable on a transfer does not arise.

Procedurally, because the reduction of capital inherent in a reduction scheme must be approved in a general meeting of the target, a further general meeting of the shareholders is required in addition to the court meeting.[162] Usually this is convened – also by a notice in the scheme document[163] – immediately after the court meeting. To distinguish this meeting from the court meeting it is often referred to as the 'general meeting' or the 'reduction meeting'. The resolution to approve the reduction of capital at this meeting also requires a 75% majority of those present and voting at the meeting.

---

160 See para 3 of Appendix 7 to the Code.
161 See para **12.55**.
162 See Companies Act 1985, ss 135 et seq and the successor provisions in Ch 10 of Pt 17 of the Companies Act 2006 which are to be brought into force on 1 October 2009.
163 In giving notice of this meeting the target must have regard to its articles of association, which apply generally to shareholders' meetings of the target (but not to the court meeting for a scheme), and the statutory requirements for reductions of capital. Indeed at the court hearing to sanction the reduction of capital the target will need to produce evidence that the notice was duly given.

Since a reduction of capital also requires the sanction of the court,[164] following the general meeting to approve the reduction, the target must apply to court for directions including to fix the date for the court hearing to sanction the reduction.

Court sanction

12.83 Once the scheme has been approved by the members, it must be sanctioned by the court. This is sought at a final court hearing. In determining whether to sanction the scheme or not the court must be satisfied that:[165]

- the statutory provisions were properly complied with – in particular, that the court meeting was duly convened with proper notice, that the explanatory statement was satisfactory and that the shareholder approval was properly passed by the requisite majority;

- the relevant class of shareholders was fairly represented at the meeting and the majority voting in favour was bona fide; and

- the approval of the scheme is reasonable.

Shareholders do have a right to attend and speak at the final court hearing and thus to raise objections and in practice these would need to demonstrate a failure to satisfy the criteria set out above. Although the court has some discretion whether to sanction the scheme or not, the judge is unlikely to reject a scheme duly approved by shareholders unless there were compelling circumstances. An uncontested hearing normally takes only about half an hour.

Although a scheme is prosecuted by the target and not the bidder, at the final court hearing to sanction the scheme the bidder will appear and be represented by counsel for the purposes of undertaking to be bound by the scheme and to do whatever is necessary to give effect to the scheme.

Reduction of capital hearing

12.84 As indicated above, a resolution to reduce the share capital of a company must also be sanctioned by the court. It is common for the application for the court's sanction to be heard at a separate court hearing say two days after the scheme sanction hearing so that as many shares as possible can be included within the reduction of capital. In particular, shares issued pursuant to options that are exercisable when the court sanctions the scheme can be captured. This approach will mean holding the two court hearings and registering the respective court orders in sequence over a few days.

Effective date

12.85 Following the final court hearing the court order sanctioning the scheme is then filed with the Registrar of Companies and once filed the scheme will become effective and bind all shareholders (even those that voted against it).

---

164 See Companies Act 1985, s 137 and from 1 October 2009 Ch 10 of Pt 17 of the Companies Act 2006.

165 See *Re Anglo – Continental Supply Co Ltd* [1922] 2 Ch 723 *per* Astbury J.

Alternatively, with a reduction scheme the terms of the scheme may provide that it only becomes effective once the court order confirming the reduction of capital has also been registered.

On the effective date the target becomes a wholly-owned subsidiary of the bidder.

Drawdown of funds

12.86 Consideration due to the shareholders must be posted within 14 days of the effective date.

Share option arrangements

12.87 As with an offer a scheme bidder is obliged under the Code to make appropriate arrangements to safeguard the interests of option holders.[166] Share option schemes will usually contemplate a takeover scheme, as they would a takeover offer. In many cases the options will be expressed to be exercisable during a fixed period following the court order sanctioning the scheme of arrangement. This may mean that the option shares are issued after the scheme record date and consequently that they are *not* subject to the scheme. In the case of reduction schemes the splitting of the court hearings to sanction the scheme and the reduction of capital respectively by two or more days should enable option shares to be swept into the scheme before it is effective. Otherwise it might be possible to acquire the option shares that are issued after the scheme record date through the use of a compulsory transfer provision that is inserted into the target's articles and approved in a general meeting held on the same date as the court meeting. In any event, detailed advice will need to be taken on a transaction specific basis to ensue that any option shares are dealt with appropriately.

Applicability of the Code to the scheme

12.88 Provided that the target company falls within the scope of the Code,[167] the Code will apply to a scheme transaction almost to the same extent that it does to an offer, including as to certain timetable requirements, except for the provisions that inherently relate to the offer process rather than the scheme process. Although the Code was not originally conceived to contemplate schemes, whenever a scheme has been used as a takeover mechanism the Panel has interpreted the Code as if it were intended to cover the scheme. With the rise in popularity of takeover schemes in the 2000s, this has culminated in certain amendments being made to the Code so that it expressly contemplates schemes as well as offers. In particular, in November 2007, following a detailed consultation process, the Panel published a new Appendix to the Code codifying the position by detailing how the Code is to apply to a scheme, including a list of the provisions of the Code that are disapplied for a scheme.[168] The Scheme Appendix should be

---

166 See Rule 15 of the Code.

167 See Para 3(a) of the Introduction to the Code and para **12.9**.

168 Appendix 7 to the Code (the Scheme Appendix), which will apply to all transactions announced after 14 January 2008. See also RS 2007/1 issued by the Panel on 29 November 2007, which contains the Panel's statement following the consultation process and the form of the Scheme Appendix.

referred to in detail for the purposes of assessing how the Code is applied to a scheme.

Matters following bid effective date

De-listing of target

12.89   As soon as it can following the offer unconditional date or scheme effective date the bidder will wish to de-list the target; that is, to take it off the Main Market of the London Stock Exchange or to remove it from trading on AIM. In practical terms this is part of the take-private process that also sees the target re-registered as a private company. Irrespective of the bidder's own intentions, the acquisition financiers will also insist on this step.[169] De-listing will have the effect of removing the market for trading in the shares and also removes the requirement for compliance with the Listing Rules of the UK Listing Authority or the AIM Rules, as applicable. Subject to exceptions, these rules grant the minority shareholders (if any) certain limited rights of veto that can inhibit transactions between the target and the bidder that are outside the ordinary course of business. This could theoretically rule out certain post-closing restructurings and other arrangements contemplated in the overall buy-out strategy. De-listing is therefore an important step that the bidder will need to take as soon as possible after the unconditional date.

In order to de-list, the directors of target must first pass a board resolution to that effect. In exercising their powers to do so, the directors must act in the way they consider, in good faith, would be most likely to promote the success of the company for the benefit of its members as a whole. They should also act in a manner that is not unfairly prejudicial to the minority shareholders under s 994 of the Companies Act 2006.[170] In practice, these concerns would only apply in the case of an offer as the effect of a scheme is to remove all minorities and leave the bidder as the sole shareholder of the target. Even in the case of an offer these principles are unlikely to be of material concern in practice where the offer has been accepted by a significant majority of the shareholders, as the fact that such a majority had acquiesced to the takeover would present a major hurdle to overcome for any objecting minority. In any event, in the case of an offer, it is common for the de-listing procedure to be commenced as soon as the bidder has reached the 90% threshold necessary to carry out the squeeze-out procedure and thus has the right to remove minorities. In such circumstances a minority shareholder would not have any sustainable right to object to the de-listing. Below 90% a minority might technically be able to claim that de-listing was unfairly

---

169   Note that technically the de-listing is not a necessary step to enable the target to give financial assistance; the re-registration of target as a private company is the key step. In practice, however, both steps are carried out as soon as possible after the unconditional date/scheme effective as part of the take-private process.

170   This is the successor provision to Companies Act 1985, s 459.

prejudicial to them as a minority but in practice, since the ultimate remedy for breach of their rights would be to be bought out at market value, accepting the offer itself would be their most likely final position. Therefore any claim that the de-listing was unfairly prejudicial is unlikely to yield any additional rights or remedies for the minority. As a matter of pure authority, the UK Listing Authority cannot require a company to maintain its listing if it decides to de-list and it is highly unlikely a court would make an order to that effect.

The procedure for de-listing following an offer is different for companies whose shares are traded on the Main Market of the London Stock Exchange and those whose shares are traded on AIM. In the case of a company traded on the Main Market that wishes to de-list, the Listing Rules normally require the company to send a circular to shareholders, which has been pre-approved by the FSA, and obtain, at a general meeting, the prior approval for the cancellation by a resolution from a majority of not less than 75% of the shareholders. The circular must include an anticipated date of cancellation of not less than 20 business days from the date of the cancellation resolution.[171]

In the case of a takeover offer, however, these requirements do not need to be met when the bidder has acquired or agreed to acquire 75% of the voting share capital of the target company and has stated in the offering circular or other circular that a notice period of not less than 20 business days prior to cancellation of the listing will commence either on the date the bidder acquires 75% of the target share capital or on the date of issue of the 'squeeze-out' notices.[172] The target must also notify the London Stock Exchange not later than 20 business days before the date it intends trading in its shares to be discontinued.[173] At the end of the 20 business day notice period the target is removed from the list of the market.

In the case of AIM companies the truncated procedure under the Listing Rules as applicable to takeover offers (as referred to in the paragraph above) is not available. With AIM companies, save where the London Stock Exchange otherwise agrees, the shareholders of the target must pass a special resolution approving the de-listing.[174] The shareholders are entitled to not less than 14 days' notice of the general meeting unless short notice can be called – which will require 95%[175] of the shareholders to agree – or unless the target's articles of association specify a longer period. The target must also give AIM not less than 20 business days notice of its de-listing from AIM.

In the case of a scheme the target can be de-listed immediately following the effective date when the bidder is the sole 100% shareholder. This will require the

---

171 See Listing Rule 5.2.5.
172 See Listing Rule 5.2.10. The target must also notify the shareholders that the required 75% has been reached and the notice period has commenced and the anticipated date of cancellation – see Listing Rule 5.2.11.
173 See Rule 3.17 of the Admission and Disclosure Standards of the London Stock Exchange.
174 See AIM Rule 41. At the time the general meeting is held the bidder should be able to cast the necessary 75% votes.
175 The requirement for private companies is 90%. See Companies Act 2006, s 307.

assistance of the target (usually given) to send out the necessary notifications to the London Stock Exchange or AIM as applicable, and if necessary a written resolution by the bidder.

Re-registration of target as private company

12.90   An entirely separate procedure must be followed to re-register the target as a private company. This step is carried out with two principle issues in mind. First, UK legislation, and the Companies Act in particular, imposes obligations on public companies that do not apply to private companies and the lower levels of compliance that follow from being private are usually attractive to owner-managers. Secondly, given the requirement inevitably imposed by the acquisition financiers that the target group companies provide upstream credit support in respect of the acquisition finance, the target must be taken private so that it (and its subsidiaries) can bypass the prohibition on the granting of financial assistance for the acquisition of its shares set out in the Companies Act.[176]

The procedure for re-registering a public company involves the passing of a special resolution by the shareholders of the company at a general meeting.

In the case of an offer it follows that for the bidder to invoke this procedure it must have received acceptances sufficient to take its holding to not less than 75% of the entire voting share capital of the target. In actual fact, this may still not guarantee that the re-registration can be effected. In particular, a minority or minorities holding not less than 5% of the share capital of the target or 50 or more members of the target can formally object to the passing of a resolution to approve a take-private and apply for its cancellation.[177] When a special resolution to re-register a public company as a private company is passed there is a 28-day waiting period within which an objection may be lodged by qualifying minority shareholders to cancel the resolution. In practice, it is thought that the minority shareholders of a company that has been taken over using a Code offer would find it difficult to sustain an objection of this nature. The bidder can point to the fact that by definition a majority of shareholders in the target had accepted the takeover offer and that a transaction of this nature would inherently involve the company being taken private. The objection of the minority would most likely be based on some concept of minority protection – similar to the unfair prejudice concept in the Companies Act[178] – but even if an objection could be sustained, the remedy for such an action would most likely be to be bought out at market value and not the blocking of the re-registration. Indeed, given the market value benchmark established by the acceptance of the offer by a significant majority of the shareholders, the most likely 'remedy' would be for such shareholders to be bought out through the offer.

---

176   See Companies Act 1985, s 151 and the successor provisions in Ch 2 of Pt 18 of the Companies Act 2006, which come into force on 1 October 2009. See also paras **12.13** and **12.134** et seq.
177   See Companies Act 1985, s 54 and the successor provision in Companies Act 2006, s 98, which comes into force on 1 October 2009.
178   See Companies Act 2006, s 994.

In any event, even though the success of a minority action to cancel the special resolution might be a relatively unlikely outcome, the acquisition financiers will almost invariably insist – at least for the purposes of setting the acceptance condition in the offer document[179] – that the offer can only be declared unconditional at the 90% threshold thus ensuring that any minority shareholders can be squeezed-out under the statutory procedure.[180] As indicated above, the need to take what amounts to financial assistance from the target group companies inevitably requires the re-registration to occur. The sponsor will usually be sympathetic to the requirement for a 90% acceptance condition in any event since it will wish to obtain 100% of the target for its own reasons.

In order to pass a special resolution to re-register the target, certain procedural formalities must be followed. First, the bidder must have been registered as the shareholder in respect of shares for which acceptances have been received (together with any market purchases totalling not less than 75% of all the voting shares). This will enable the bidder to pass the resolution. The directors of the target must also have resolved that the re-registration is likely to promote the success of the target for the benefit of its members as a whole as it is they who instigate the special resolution procedure. The board will need to give not less than 14 days' notice to all shareholders of the general meeting.[181]

At the general meeting shareholders with not less than 75% of the voting share capital present at the meeting and voting must vote in favour of the resolutions to take the target private. Resolutions will also be passed altering the target's memorandum and articles of association to be consistent with its new status as a private company. In the case of an AIM-listed company, the meeting will usually also be used to approve the de-listing of the target.

Once the 28-day waiting period has elapsed, the target can apply to the Registrar of Companies to be re-registered as a private company. There is a prescribed form for this application that must be signed by a director or the secretary of the target and this must be accompanied by the amended memorandum and articles of association. Assuming that no minority shareholder objection was lodged, the Registrar will issue the target with a certificate of incorporation as a private company, potentially on the same day as the application using the 'same day' service.

Once the target has been registered as a private company the directors of the target can make the necessary statutory declarations to complete the financial assistance whitewash procedure.[182]

---

179 They might agree to waive it down subsequently in order to allow the offer to be declared unconditional at a lower level on the basis that other shareholders would then accept the now unconditional offer and thereby push acceptances above 90%. This is a tactic that is sometimes used with offers where institutional shareholders hold out to see if a bid will go through before committing their shares.

180 See para **12.69**.

181 The articles of association may dictate a longer period than 14 days. In theory shareholders holding not less than 95% of the shares of the target can agree to hold the general meeting at shorter notice. See Companies Act 2006, s 307.

182 But see para **12.13** concerning the repeal of the financial assistance whitewash (and prohibition applicable to private companies) and paras **12.134** et seq generally.

All of the above analysis applies to the take-private steps to be taken following a successful offer. In the case of a scheme the procedure is much simpler. Following the scheme effective date, when the bidder is the sole 100% shareholder of the target, it can pass a written resolution approving the re-registration without the need to call a general meeting or to give minorities a 28-day period to object (there being no minorities). The resolution is then lodged with the Registrar of Companies for the re-registration to take effect.

Target group credit support

12.91   Subject to certain exceptions usually only applicable to non-UK companies,[183] the acquisition financiers in a buy-out will insist on receiving guarantees and security for the acquisition debt from the target group companies. It is one of the core requirements of the acquisition financiers in all buy-outs. This applies to public-to-privates as much as it does to other buy-outs except that the procedure and timing to obtain the guarantees and security must reflect the public-to-private process and timetable. In addition to guarantees and security, the target group companies will also be required (again, in common with any buy-out) to enter into loan agreements with the bidder to enable them to upstream cash to the bidder so that it can service the acquisition finance. Each of the upstream loans, guarantees and security – collectively, upstream 'credit support' – constitutes financial assistance under the Companies Act[184] and will be unlawful unless the target has been re-registered as a private company and, at least until the repeal of this procedure on 1 October 2008, completed the whitewash procedure.[185]

Not all guarantees and security given in respect of the acquisition finance facilities will be financial assistance, however. Credit support given for working capital debt and for refinancing debt may not amount to financial assistance, even where granted by target group companies. The financial assistance laws only prohibit guarantees and security granted 'directly or indirectly for the purposes of the acquisition'.[186] True working capital debt that cannot be used to service acquisition debt should not be caught by the provision. Similarly, debt borrowed by a target group company to refinance its existing debt should be outside the scope of the legislation, although debt that is in effect voluntarily refinanced at the time of the acquisition – rather than being required to be refinanced by virtue of restrictive covenants and change of control provisions in the existing debt documentation – might be caught. A legal analysis should be carried out at the time. Credit support that is not caught by the financial assistance laws can be granted by target group companies as soon as the bidder takes control of the target. In practice this level of credit support will be put in place when funds are first drawn down following the unconditional date. Target group credit support in respect of acquisition debt is necessarily provided much later only once the financial assistance hurdle can be overcome. The fact that target group security is taken some time after initial funding is a key feature of takeover offers from the perspective of acquisition financiers.

---

183 See **Chapter 13** generally.
184 See also paras **11.101, 12.13** and **12.134** et seq.
185 See also paras **11.101, 12.13** and **12.134** et seq.
186 See Companies Act 1985, s 151(1) and, from 1 October 2009, the successor provision in Companies Act 2006, s 678(1).

Security given by the bidder itself does not amount to financial assistance – its shares are not being acquired in the buy-out – and it can grant security at the outset, when the acquisition finance documents are signed at the launch of the offer. There are therefore three types of security given at three different times. At signing and launch the bidder gives security; at initial drawdown the target group companies give security for non-financial assistance debt; and then following the take-private (and possibly whitewash) the target group companies give security for financial assistance debt.

Minority shareholder rights

12.92 Until the repeal of the financial assistance whitewash procedure on 1 October 2008[187], residual minority shareholders in the target have a statutory right to object to the granting of financial assistance by target group companies. It is similar in many ways to the right to object to the re-registration special resolution referred to above.[188] The Companies Act 1985[189] permits shareholders that together hold 10% or more of the share capital of the target to challenge a special resolution passed pursuant to the whitewash procedure[190] for the purposes of approving the granting of financial assistance. A similar logic applies as before, however, that to sustain a challenge the minority shareholders would need to establish some sort of unfair prejudice, which would be difficult in the context of a takeover that had been accepted by a large majority. In any event, this is just one more technical reason to justify squeezing out minorities in a public-to-private buy-out.

Schemes of arrangement

12.93 In the case of a scheme, because the bidder should obtain 100% ownership of the target on the effective date it can proceed with the whitewash almost immediately and as soon as the target is re-registered as a private company. There is no need for a shareholder resolution, for example, since that requirement only applies to companies that are not wholly-owned.[191] Since the bidder has 14 days following the scheme effective date to despatch the consideration to the shareholders it would theoretically be possible to time the completion of the whitewash procedure with the funding of the acquisition finance and thus have all of the target group credit support in place from the time that the acquisition financiers first advance funds. This would be a material advantage for the debt providers by comparison with offers where the squeeze-out procedure must first be completed to go through these steps. In practice, however, it may not necessarily be feasible to complete the whitewash procedure within that 14-day period, given the need (as part of that process) for the auditors of the target group to assess the financial position of the target group companies giving the financial assistance[192] and the fact

---

187 See para **12.13**.
188 See para **12.90**.
189 See Companies Act 1985, s 157 which is being repealed as of 1 October 2008.
190 See Companies Act 1985, s 155(4) which is being repealed as of 1 October 2008. See also para **12.136** generally.
191 See Companies Act 1985, s 155(4) (until 1 October 2008).
192 See para **11.101**.

that they may not have sufficient access to the target group prior to the scheme effective date. In any event, once the whitewash procedure is repealed on 1 October 2008, matters should be simplified sufficiently such that the target group credit support *should* – as a strict matter of law[193] – be available immediately upon the re-registration, which certainly should be before the acquisition debt is provided.

Failed offers and follow-on offers

12.94　For the sake of completeness, it is worth noting that when an offer fails, the Code protects the target from the uncertainties of a further offer by the same bidder or any person who acted (or is acting) in concert with it.[194] For the period of 12 months from the date on which the offer is withdrawn or lapses, except with the consent of the Panel, neither the bidder nor any persons acting in concert may, *inter alia*:

- announce a bid or possible bid for the target;

- acquire any interest in shares in the target if the bidder and persons acting in concert with it would thereby be required to make a mandatory offer under Rule 9 of the Code; or

- acquire any interest in, or procure irrevocables over, shares in the target if the bidder and the persons acting in concert with it would be interested in shares which carry over 30 per cent. but not more than 50%. of the voting rights of the target.

In certain circumstances, the Panel will normally grant a dispensation from Rule 35, in particular, where an offer has lapsed following a competition authority reference but has subsequently been cleared, if a new offer is recommended or where a competing bid has been announced.

Failed schemes

12.95　The Code rules applicable to failed offers, as considered above, also apply to failed schemes.

Note, as an incidental matter, that if the scheme fails because of a withdrawal of target board support *before* the general meeting to approve the scheme it may be possible to switch to an offer.[195] If the scheme fails because of a lack of shareholder support, however, it is unlikely that the sponsor would choose or indeed have the option of switching to an offer given the higher threshold of shareholder support usually required to successfully complete an offer that is financed with debt.[196]

193　Although this will be the legal position, many commentators have suggested that the acquisition finance market itself will replace the statutory whitewash process (and the financial rigour that this contemplates) with a quasi-whitewash requirement of its own.

194　See Rule 35 of the Code.

195　See para **12.39**.

196　See for example, para **12.75**.

SUMMARY TIMETABLES

12.96 The previous paragraphs of this section outline the various procedural elements of both takeover offers and schemes of arrangement. In both cases most of the relevant steps must be completed within a particular timeframe dictated by either the Code or the Companies Act. Set out below are summaries of the over-all timetables applicable to offers and schemes respectively and, separately, the matters to be completed after the offer unconditional date or scheme effective date. The timetables are necessarily indicative and include backstop dates for certain steps set out in the Code or the Companies Act. In other respects they assume timely completion of procedural steps.

Offer timetable

12.97

D-?	Initial approach to the target; appointment of 'Rule 3' independent adviser to target board; appointment of independent committee of target board; period of due diligence into target; arrangements for funding/investment in the bidder. Secrecy vital.
D-28	Earliest date for issue of press announcement of a firm intention to make an offer is released. In practice the period between the announcement and the posting of the offer is likely to be much less than 28 days and may be as short as a day or so. Committed funds should be in place before the firm announcement is made.
D	The offer document must be posted within 28 days of the firm announcement.[197] In practice, it is often posted only a few days after the press announcement if not immediately after.
D+14	The target's response is due. The independent committee must circulate its views of the offer, whether there are alternative offers and what the advice of the independent adviser is. In a recommended offer this information will be included in the offer document itself.
D+21	First closing date for acceptances The offer must be open for at least 21 days following posting of the offer document.[198]
D+22	First day after the closing date. Announcement of acceptance levels and (if appropriate) extension of the offer.
D+35	An offer must remain open for 14 days after it becomes unconditional as to acceptances so if it is declared unconditional as to acceptances at the first closing date this will be the final date for acceptances.[199]
D+39	This is the last day target can release new information, such as trading results and dividend proposals etc.[200]

197 See Rule 30.1 of the Code.
198 See Rule 31.1 of the Code.
199 See Rule 31.4 of the Code.
200 See Rule 31.9 of the Code.

D+42	Right of withdrawal arises. Unless the offer has become or been declared unconditional as to acceptances, shareholders can withdraw their acceptances. The right to withdraw lapses once the offer has become or been declared unconditional as to acceptances.[201]
D+46	Last date on which revisions can be made to the offer (ie, 14 days before final closing date), giving shareholders at least 14 days within which to accept the revised offer.[202]
D+60	Final closing date for acceptances. An offer may not become or be declared unconditional as to acceptances after this date.[203]
D+74	Earliest date on which offer can close assuming offer became or is declared unconditional as to acceptances on day 60;[204] in practice, the bidder may leave the offer open to pick up further acceptances, particularly if it has not reached the 90% threshold necessary to exercise the compulsory acquisition procedure.
D+81	Final date on which offer can become or be declared unconditional in all respects (ie, 21 days after the last date on which the offer could be declared unconditional as to acceptances). All conditions must be fulfilled or waived within 21 days of the later of the first closing date and the date on which the offer becomes, or is, declared unconditional as to acceptances.[205] If the offer is not declared unconditional by this date then it must lapse.
UD[206]+14 (D+95[207])	Final date for despatch of consideration. Consideration for acceptances received on or before the date on which the offer becomes or is declared unconditional in all respects is required to be posted within 14 days of the later of the first closing date and the unconditional date. Payment in respect of an acceptance received after the unconditional date must be posted within 14 days of receipt of the relevant acceptance.[208]

If a competing offer is made, the offer timetable above is reset by reference to the posting of the competitor's offer document.[209]

Squeeze-out

12.98   In the case of a bid for a target whose shares are admitted to trading on the Main Market of the London Stock Exchange (or any other regulated market), the squeeze-out procedure must be commenced within three months of the last date on which the offer can be accepted.[210]

In the case of a bid for a target whose shares are traded on AIM (or otherwise

---

201 See Rule 34 of the Code.
202 See Rule 32.1 of the Code.
203 See Rule 31.6(a) of the Code.
204 See Rule 31.4 of the Code.
205 See Rule 31.7.
206 The date the offer is declared unconditional in all respects.
207 Assuming the unconditional date is on D+81. In practice it may well be sooner (and as early as D+21 in theory).
208 See Rule 31.8 of the Code.
209 See Rule 31.6(a)(i) of the Code.
210 See Companies Act 2006, s 980(2)(a). See also Rules 31.4, 31.6 and 31.7 of the Code.

not admitted to trading on a regulated market), the squeeze-out procedure must be commenced within three months of the last date on which the offer can be accepted[211] and by no later than the date falling six months after D, if that date occurs within the three month period referred to.[212]

UD+1 (D+82)   Bidder issues compulsory purchase notices to all remaining minority shareholders (provided 90% threshold reached) and sends a copy of the notices plus a statutory declaration that the compulsory purchase requirements have been met to the target.

UD+43[213] (D+124[214]) Bidder pays the consideration due to the minority shareholders to an account with the target. Target maintains this amount in a segregated account until claimed.

Scheme timetable

12.99

D-?   Initial approach to the target; appointment of 'Rule 3' independent adviser to target board; appointment of independent committee of target board; period of due diligence into target; arrangements for funding/investment in the bidder. Transaction agreement executed if applicable. Secrecy vital

D-28   Earliest date for issue of press announcement of a firm intention to make bid is released. In practice, the period is much shorter although since the process must go through the court it is usual to budget on about a week minimum between announcement and posting. Committed funds should be in place before the firm announcement is made.

D-9   'Claim form' seeking leave to convene the target shareholder meeting issued by the target. This must normally be no less than seven days before the hearing of the 'claim' (ie, for the court hearing to approve the scheme circular and to convene the shareholder meeting).

D-4   Evidence in support of the claim is lodged with the court, including the final draft scheme circular (and proxy form) substantially in final form. Normally this must occur no less than two business days before the hearing of the claim. From this time no further changes may be made to the scheme document except with the court's approval.

D-2   Hearing for leave to post scheme document and convene shareholders' meeting – and court order granted. This should be no less than seven days after the claim form is issued by the target and no less than two business days after the supporting evidence is lodged.

---

211 See Rules 31.4, 31.6 and 31.7 of the Code.
212 See Companies Act 2006, s 980 (2)(b) and (3). Technically the distinction is between Takeover Directive regulated transactions (ie, takeover bids for companies with shares admitted to trading on a regulated market) and non-Takeover Directive regulated transactions.
213 This is the date falling six weeks after the date of the notices. See Companies Act 2006, s 981.
214 This is about the earliest it would be in practice assuming the unconditional date is on D+81. In practice the unconditional date may be sooner; and as early as D+21 in theory.

D	Scheme document (and forms of proxy) dispatched to the target's shareholders by the target board, including notice of meetings. This must be no less than 21 clear days before the target shareholder meeting.
D+24	Court convened shareholder meeting to approve scheme. If the scheme is a reduction scheme a separate general meeting may be held following the 'court meeting' to approve (inter alia) a reduction of the target's capital.
D+25	'Application notice' in relation to the court directions (to fix date, give notice etc.) in relation to final court hearing is lodged with the court with supporting evidence. This must be no less than seven business days before the court hearing for directions.
D+34	Hearing for directions from the court. This must be no less than seven business days after the application is made.
D+35	Newspaper advertisement of notice of the final court hearing published as directed. This must be no less than seven business days before the final hearing.
D+44	Latest time by which any conditions can be invoked and all competition and antitrust clearances obtained. No condition (except the grant and registration of the final court order) can remain outstanding at time of final court hearing.
D+44[215]	Final court hearing. The court order is granted assuming there are no objections by shareholders made at the hearing. If there are objections there would be a delay for the court to consider them. The date of the final court hearing must be no less than seven business days after advertisement/notice of the hearing. With a reduction scheme the hearing to sanction the reduction of capital may be held, say, two days later in order to capture option shares.[216]
Effective Date (D+45)	Court order(s) sanctioning the scheme and confirming the reduction of capital (if applicable[217]) registered at Companies House in Cardiff, Wales. This is the 'effective date' and the bidder now owns 100% of the target.
ED+2 (D+47)	Advertise notice of reduction of capital as directed by the court.
ED + 14 (D+59)	Last date for dispatch of consideration to the target's former shareholders. This must be no more than 14 days after the effective date unless otherwise agreed with the Panel.

Note that all court hearing dates will require agreement with the court clerk and should be provisionally booked with the court as soon as a timetable has been agreed. Note in particular that hearings for certain purposes can only be held on specific days of the week. Petitions and summonses cannot be issued, and evidence

---

215 Depending on the nature of the target's option schemes and the chosen treatment of those options it may be necessary to split the court hearings approving the scheme and the reduction of capital (where applicable) respectively into two hearings a few days apart. See also para **12.87**.
216 See para **12.87**.
217 See paras **12.84** and **12.87**.

cannot be lodged, on public holidays or weekends, or on any dates on which court offices are closed. The court operates on a very restricted schedule during August and September, in particular. The indicative timetable above assumes no court holidays or scheduling difficulties to intervene and extend the timetable.

Matters following the bid effective date

12.100 The following procedures and related timetables apply to offers and schemes but note the important differences in terms of timing for the de-listing and re-registration steps following a scheme.

De-listing

12.101 With an offer it is common for this step to be undertaken once the 90% threshold has been reached so that minority shareholders cannot sustain any objection. The following assumes that the unconditional date occurs at the 90% level and not a lower level.

UD+1	Bidder procures that the new directors of target pass a resolution to de-list the target from Main Market of the London Stock Exchange or from AIM.

Main Market

UD+1	For a Main Market listed target, pre-emptive notice (of at least 20 business days) of the proposed de-listing is given to target shareholders in the offering circular (and separately to the London Stock Exchange).[218] In the squeeze-out notice issued on day UD+1 the bidder notifies the shareholders that the 20 business days period has started.[219]
UD+1+20BD	De-listing from Main Market of London Stock Exchange takes effect.

AIM

UD+1	For an AIM target, bidder must call a general meeting of the target's shareholders to pass a special resolution approving the de-listing. Bidder procures the target to give 20 business days notice of the de-listing to AIM conditional upon the special resolution.
UD+15[220]	At the general meeting, bidder, as shareholder with at least 75% of the voting shares, passes special resolution.
UD+20BD	De-listing from AIM takes effect.

In the case of a scheme, by contrast, the de-listing can be effected immediately on the day following the scheme effective date by the target (which will usually assist) sending out notifications to the London Stock Exchange or AIM as applicable, and if necessary a written resolution by the bidder.

---

218 See para **12.89**.
219 See Listing Rule 5.2.11. See also para **12.89**.
220 This assumes 14 days notice of the general meeting. The articles of association of the target may specify a longer period, however. In any case, it is possible to call the meeting at shorter notice with 95% shareholder approval (see Companies Act 2006, s 307).

Re-registration as private company

12.102

S[221]	Bidder procures the target to call a general meeting to pass a special resolution re-registering target as a private company and making appropriate amendments to its memorandum and articles of association.
S+15[222]	At the general meeting, the bidder, as shareholder with at least 75% of the voting shares, passes special resolution.
S+44[223]	Target makes application in prescribed form to Registrar of Companies for re-registration as private company and to register amended constitutional documents. If no application to cancel the special resolution is made – which a court would then determine first – the certificate of incorporation as private company can be issued on same day.

In the case of a scheme, as with the de-listing, the process is much simpler and quicker. Since the bidder should be the only shareholder of the target upon the scheme effective date occurring it can pass a written resolution approving the re-registration immediately following the scheme effective date and then immediately file the resolution with the Registrar of Companies without needing to wait for the 28-day period for minorities to object to expire (ie, there would be no minorities).[224]

Target group credit support

12.103 From the perspective of the acquisition financiers, the main point of the squeeze-out, de-listing and take-private is to enable them to take upstream credit support from the target group, in the form of loans, guarantees and security. This can only occur once the target has been taken private. The following steps assume that the whitewash procedure is also to be completed. In fact, from 1 October 2008 this procedure is being abolished along with the financial assistance prohibition for private companies.[225] From that date, target group credit support will be permitted as soon as the target is re-registered as a private company.[226]

---

221 S is the date – as soon as practicable following the unconditional date – on which the bidder is registered as the shareholder of at least 75% of the voting share capital of the target.

222 This assumes 14 days notice of the general meeting. The articles of association of the target may specify a longer period, however. In any case, it is possible to call the meeting at shorter notice with 95% shareholder approval (see Companies Act 2006), s 307.

223 That is, 28 days after the special resolution, being the statutory waiting period for minorities to apply to court to cancel it. See Companies Act 1985, s 54 and the successor provision in Companies Act 2006, s 98, which comes into force on 1 October 2009. See also para **12.90** generally.

224 See also para **12.90**.

225 See para **11.101** for further discussion of the financial assistance laws and their revision under the Companies Act 2006. See also paras **12.13** and **12.134** et seq generally.

226 See also para **12.91** generally. Note that some commentators have speculated that the acquisition finance market may develop its own (non-statutory) form of 'whitewash' to replace the statutory version and the financial healthcheck that this involves.

S+45[227]	*Bidder procures target directors to make statutory declaration, with auditors report annexed to it*[228] *and to call a general meeting to pass a special resolution approving the giving of financial assistance.*[229]
S+59[230]	*At the general meeting, the bidder, as shareholder with at least 75% of the voting shares, passes special resolution.*
S+89	*Financial assistance can be granted not less than 28 days later.*[231]

In the case of a scheme, again the process is more straightforward. Since the bidder will be the only shareholder of the target upon the scheme effective date occurring, no shareholder resolution is required as part of the whitewash and the whitewash can be carried out as soon as the re-registration of target as a private company is effective.

DOCUMENTATION

12.104 This section is concerned with the documentation of public-to-privates. More specifically, it is concerned with the documentation of the bid itself. The equity and debt finance documents are not considered in this section and the general principles and detailed provisions considered in the earlier chapters will, in broad terms, apply as much to a public-to-private as they would to a private buy-out. In addition, a later section of this chapter specifically considers the key areas of an acquisition finance facilities agreement that would require tailoring to a public-to-private.

Takeover offers

Principal documents

12.105 The principal documents which will need to be issued in connection with a takeover offer (as required by the Code) are listed below.

Press announcement

12.106 The press release constituting the bidder's announcement of a firm intention to make an offer is a Code requirement[232] and its contents must also satisfy the requirements of the Code.[233] In particular, it must contain all of the terms and conditions of the offer. In addition to this it should include details of the

---

227 That is, immediately following the re-registration of target as a private company. See para **12.102**.
228 See Companies Act 1985, s 156(4) (until 1 October 2008). But see also paras **11.101** and **12.13** generally on the repeal of the financial assistance laws for private companies and the white-wash procedure.
229 See Companies Act 1985, s 155(4) (until 1 October 2008).
230 This assumes that general meetings of the target can be brought on 14 days notice. See also fn **222**.
231 This affords shareholders the statutory period to apply to cancel the special resolution. See Companies Act 1985, s 157 (until 1 October 2008).
232 See Rule 2.2(a) of the Code.
233 See Rule 2.5(b) and (c) of the Code.

interests that each of the parties has in the bid vehicle and the target, all relevant arrangements related to the offer (including, for example, break fees) as well as a cash confirmation statement.[234]

The press announcement will be prepared on behalf of the bidder by its professional advisers (in particular its lawyers and financial adviser). With a recommended bid it will also be approved by the target's independent board and professional advisers.

Offering circular

12.107   The formal offer document (an offering circular) is issued by the bidder to the shareholders following the press announcement.[235] It contains the contractual offer to acquire the target's issued share capital and sets out the terms and conditions on which the offer is made. It also includes the form of acceptance which shareholders can complete and send back to the receiving agent[236] by way of acceptance of the offer. Alternatively, for uncertificated shares held in CREST, accepting shareholders can complete the acceptance through the CREST system. The offer document must also comply with the content requirements of the Code.[237]

As both the press announcement and the offer document contain all of the terms and conditions of the offer they are almost identical in most places. There is therefore considerable overlap in preparation. As with the press announcement the sponsor's advisers will take the lead in drafting and – assuming the bid is recommended – they will solicit and receive comments from the target and its advisers.

Circular from the board of the target

12.108   With a recommended offer, the form of the offer document will include a letter (or circular) the target board's letter from the target's board setting out its views on the offer and the substance of any advice it has received from the independent Rule 3 adviser. It will include information about the target and its directors and other matters set out in the Code.[238] Ultimately (with a recommended offer) the target board's letter will recommend to shareholders that they accept the offer. In the case of a public-to-private in which some of the existing directors of the target are to participate, the independent directors will take sole responsibility for the board's recommendation and any associated opinions set out in its letter, although all the target directors will be required to accept responsibility for information about the target that is included in the letter.

---

234 See para **12.111**.
235 Historically the offer document would be issued by the bidder's financial adviser on behalf of the bidder. This practice has changed with the implementation into UK law of the EU Takeover Directive (Directive 2004/25/EC), however, with financial institutions now concerned about potential criminal liability arising in respect of the contents of any offer document issued by them.
236 The receiving agent is the person, usually a financial institution appointed the bidder, that is responsible for performing a number of important administrative tasks in relation to the offer including collecting shareholder acceptances.
237 See in particular Rules 10, 12, 13, 24 and 25 of the Code and paras **12.109** et seq.
238 See Rule 25 of the Code.

With a recommended offer, the target board's circular is incorporated into the circular prepared by the bidder and posted together as a single offer document.

In the case of an offer that is not recommended, the offer document posted by the bidder will not include the letter from the target's board. In this situation the target will write separately to the shareholders with their views on the offer and presumably recommending that the shareholders reject the offer and/or wait for a better offer.

Code requirements

12.109 The following paragraphs briefly consider the main requirements of the Code as regards the contents of the offer documents.

Terms and conditions of the offer

12.110 The terms and conditions of the offer itself are the subject of various Code requirements. These include prescriptive provisions that dictate certain minimum requirements to be included in any offer and provisions of more general application that limit the use of certain types of condition. A number of the key requirements relating to the terms and conditions of the offer are considered separately in later paragraphs.[239]

Cash confirmation

12.111 When an offer is made in cash, or partly in cash and partly in shares, the offer document must include a confirmation from an appropriate third party – usually the bidder's financial adviser or bank – that the cash resources available to the bidder are sufficient to satisfy full acceptance of the offer.[240]

A similar confirmation is required in the press announcement[241] and an announcement of a firm intention to make an offer must only be made when the bidder has every reason to believe that it can and will continue to be able to implement the offer.[242] Responsibility in this regard also rests with the bidder's financial adviser.

As a result of the cash confirmation requirements of the Code and the fact that an offer must, other than in exceptional circumstances, follow an announcement, the bidder must have all of the debt and equity funding for the offer available from the date on which the announcement is made. Furthermore, it must be unconditionally available, without any of the usual raft of conditions precedent that are normally incorporated into the finance documents for a buy-out. In practice, this does not mean that the finance documents are without any conditions precedent; rather, it means that all such conditions – other than certain 'fundamental' ones – must have been satisfied or waived as at the date of the press announcement. This is commonly called the 'certain funds' requirement of the Code and the confirmation that the bidder's financial adviser must give is usually called the 'cash confirmation'.

---

239 See paras **12.116** to **12.121**.
240 See Rule 24.7 of the Code.
241 See Rules 2.5(c) of the Code.
242 See General Principle 5 and Rule 2.5(a) of the Code.

With a public-to-private, given the heavy reliance that the bidder typically has on third party finance and debt in particular, the certain funds requirement has particular importance. It is considered in more detail later on.[243]

Financial information

12.112   The offer document must contain certain financial information relating to the bidder.[244] Where the bidder is not the ultimate acquirer of substance and in particular where it is merely a vehicle company – which is typical in a public-to-private – the Panel will look through the bidding vehicle to the ultimate sponsor and require the relevant financial information to be provided in respect of that company.[245]

With a private equity sponsored bid, a strict application of the Code would require the information to be given in respect of the ultimate parent company of the sponsor's group. In practice, however, this is a matter which should be discussed with the Panel's Executive and, generally speaking, the Panel will draw a distinction between a financial sponsor that is investing third party funds and one that is investing proprietary funds. In the former case the Panel is likely to focus on the fund and possibly its investors. In the latter case the sponsor itself or its group will be the subject of the requirement. Typically, the level of satisfaction that the Panel will require from sponsors will have been agreed over time through precedent.

Disclosure of source of financing and other material contracts[246]

12.113   The Code also requires the offer document to contain a summary of the principal contents of each material contract (not being a contract entered into in the ordinary course of business) entered into by any member of the bidder's group during the period of two years before the commencement of the offer period.[247] In addition, there is an overriding disclosure requirement that the offer document satisfies the highest standards of accuracy and the information given is adequately and fairly presented.[248]

Whilst the Code does not provide a definition of 'material contract', as a rule of thumb, any contract which may reasonably be considered as likely to influence the target's shareholders in deciding whether to accept the offer may potentially be disclosable. A contract is likely to be material where it is significant or important in relation to the conduct of the business of the bidder or its group (including the target group following completion of the offer) or its future conduct or prospects.

The Code specifically requires that the offer document contains a description of how the offer is to be financed, including the names of the principal lenders.[249]

---

243 See paras **12.127** to **12.133**.
244 See Rule 24.2 of the Code.
245 See Note 1 to Rule 24.2 of the Code.
246 See Rules 24.2(a)(xi), 24.2(f) and 26 of the Code.
247 See Rule 24.2(a)(xi) of the Code.
248 See Rule 19.1 of the Code.
249 See Rule 24.2(f) of the Code.

Furthermore, the material contracts and documents relating to the financing will need to be made available for inspection.[250] Consequently, all the material terms of the debt and equity financing arrangements will be in the public domain and it will not be possible for the sponsor or the acquisition financiers to keep these matters confidential, as one would expect with a wholly private deal.

Special arrangements with management[251]

12.114 The arrangements which the bidder has made with any members of the target's management team that are participating in the offer – principally as regards their equity stake in the bidder and any new service contracts they enter into – will also need to be summarised in the offer document.

Responsibility statements

12.115 It is a requirement of the Code that each document issued to shareholders and any advertisement published in connection with the offer must state that the directors of the bidder and/or where appropriate the target accept responsibility for the information contained in the relevant document or advertisement and that, to the best of their knowledge and belief (having taken all reasonable care to ensure that this is the case), the information contained in the document or advertisement is in accordance with the facts and does not omit anything likely to affect the import of such information.[252]

Where the bidder is controlled directly or indirectly by another person or group, the Panel will normally require additional persons, such as the directors of its ultimate parent company, to take responsibility for the documents or advertisements.[253] In the case of private equity sponsored bids the Panel's standing position is that the sponsor's directors will need to accept responsibility, although it has been willing in certain circumstances to limit the additional individuals required to give the responsibility statements to members of the sponsor's investment committee. This is another matter which should be discussed in advance with the Panel on a case by case basis.

Ultimately, by making a responsibility statement in an offer document or advertisement, the persons making that statement assume personal liability for those parts of the document or advertisement for which they have accepted responsibility.

The responsibility statements which appear in the offer document will usually divide responsibility between the directors of the bidder (including any additional persons required to accept responsibility) and the directors of the target as follows:

- the directors of the bidder (and appropriate directors of the sponsor) will accept responsibility for all the information contained in the offer document, other than that relating to the target, its directors and any persons con-

---

250 See Rule 26 (k) of the Code.
251 See Rule 24.5 of the Code.
252 See Rule 19.2 of the Code.
253 See Note 5 to Rule 19.2 of the Code.

nected with them and the recommendation of the independent directors and their associated opinions;

- the directors of the target (ie, both the members of the management team (if any) involved in the offer and the independent directors) will accept responsibility for the information appearing in the offer document relating to the target, themselves and persons connected with them, but not for the recommendation of the independent directors and their associated opinions; and

- the independent directors alone will accept responsibility for their recommendation of the offer and the associated opinions set out in their letter to the target's shareholders.

Terms and conditions of the offer

12.116 Both the press announcement and the offer document will set out the terms of the offer itself.[254] Typically these are set out in Appendix 1 of the offer document or press announcement. The main terms will include the price being offered per target share, whether there is a loan note alternative and possibly, although this would be extremely unlikely in a private equity sponsored bid, whether the shareholders can accept shares in the bidder as an alternative.

In addition to these headline terms, an offer – other than a mandatory offer under Rule 9 of the Code[255] – will be expressed to be subject to the satisfaction of a number of conditions, each of which must be satisfied or waived for the offer to succeed. As mentioned above, the bidder is not free to include whatever conditions it wishes, however, and the Code imposes certain minimum requirements and limitations on the offer conditions and the ability of the bidder to invoke them.

First, the Code requires that every offer must include two specific provisions – a condition that a minimum number of acceptances are received (the 'acceptance condition') and a condition that the offer will lapse if it is referred to the UK or EU competition authorities (the 'competition referral condition'). Both of these conditions are considered below. Secondly, any and all other conditions of the offer, and any pre-conditions to an offer being made that are included in the press announcement, must satisfy the requirements of Rule 13 of the Code. Rule 13 and its practical implications are also considered below.[256]

The acceptance condition

Importance of the acceptance condition

12.117 The most important condition of any offer – and one that the Code requires in any offer[257] – is that a sufficient number of shareholders accept the offer such that the bidder has acquired or agreed to acquire (pursuant to the offer or otherwise) over 50% of the voting share capital of the target. This is called the

---

254 See Rules 2.5(b)(i) and 24.2(d)(v) of the Code.
255 See para **12.56**.
256 See paras **12.120** and **12.121**.
257 See Rule 10 of the Code.

'acceptance condition' and its purpose is to ensure that the bidder must at least gain control of the target for an offer to go through. Once this condition is satisfied an offer may be declared 'unconditional as to acceptances'. This term is used throughout the Code and has a number of implications.

Even though the Code requirement is that the bidder acquires more than 50% of the target's voting share capital, the ultimate aim of a takeover offer is normally to acquire 100% of the target or if not 100% a substantial majority. This is particularly true in the case of a public-to-private, where the act of taking the target company private requires a high level of acceptances and, in theory at least, no active and dissenting minority. Accordingly, it is usual to see the acceptance condition initially set at a 90% level of acceptances for each class of share. If this level of acceptances is achieved then the bidder can be certain of acquiring the remaining shares through the use of the statutory squeeze-out procedure that is considered elsewhere in this chapter.[258] In practical terms, the acceptance condition will usually be worded to permit the bidder, in its absolute discretion, to reduce the level of acceptances required below 90% provided the bidder still satisfies the minimum acceptances requirement by gaining control of the target.

In between the 50% threshold required by the Code and the 90% threshold required to instigate the squeeze-out, there is a further key threshold – at 75%. This is of key importance in a public-to-private since a special resolution of the shareholders requiring 75% of the voting share capital is necessary to re-register the target as a private company. This itself is necessary to enable the target and its subsidiaries to give upstream credit support for the acquisition finance, which will be a core condition of the finance being made available.[259] The ability to pass a special resolution will also enable the bidder to change the constitutional documents of the target company, which may or may not be necessary to implement its own strategic management goals.

In practice, the acceptance condition, although set at 90% at the outset, may be reduced to a lower level during the offer period. The following paragraphs consider when and why that might happen.

Variation of acceptance condition

12.118 With any public-to-private involving acquisition finance, the debt providers will be concerned to ensure that the offer is not declared unconditional as to acceptances before they are satisfied that there is a high likelihood (if not certainty) that the bidder will be able to acquire 100% of the target. As previously indicated, this is so that they can be sure that the target will ultimately be in a position to give upstream credit support for the debt.

With this in mind, the financiers will require a specific undertaking from the bidder not to reduce the acceptance condition without their prior consent. In doing so, the financiers can ensure that they will not be required to provide the

---

258 See paras **12.69** et seq.
259 See paras **12.91** and **12.92** for more detail. Not only is a special resolution required to take a company private, it is also required to complete the financial assistance whitewash process for a company that is not wholly-owned, although note that the whitewash procedure is to be repealed on 1 October 2008. See also paras **12.13** and **12.134** et seq.

financing other than where they are confident that the bidder will acquire the entire issued share capital of the target. By contrast, the sponsor will prefer to retain the widest possible discretion and to be free to declare the offer unconditional at a lower level than 90% in order to at least gain control of the target. Such broad discretion is very rarely afforded to the sponsor, however. If the financiers *do* agree in a particular transaction to a lower level of acceptances than 90% – and it would be extremely rare for the permission to extend below the 75% threshold – this agreement is likely to be subject to an important caveat. That is, that the bidder will only be permitted to declare the offer unconditional as to acceptances at the lower level if no circumstances have arisen which indicate that the 90% level might not be reached – eg, the appearance of a competing bidder with a potentially blocking stake – *and* that there are strong indications that the 90% threshold *will* be reached in due course. Importantly, details of any such agreement would need to be disclosed in the offer document[260] and although it was once common to provide side letters setting out this agreement, it is now relatively uncommon for the financiers to agree in advance the circumstances when they would agree to waive the acceptance condition down below 90%.

Competition referral condition

12.119 In addition to the acceptance condition, an offer must include a provision that it will lapse if the proposed takeover is referred to the UK or EU competition authorities before the later of the first closing date and the date the offer is declared unconditional as to acceptances.[261]

Other conditions

12.120 Other – non-mandatory – conditions that will commonly be incorporated into an offer may include the following:

- no government or other relevant authority having taken or threatened to take any proceedings or other measures which might adversely affect the making or implementation of the offer or have an adverse effect on the ability of the target to carry on its business or affect its profits or prospects, etc, or which would require or prevent the sale of any part of the target's business;

- all necessary consents, approvals and permissions, etc required to carry on the target's business having been obtained and being in full force and effect;

- relating to the financial condition of the target generally, including insolvency events etc; and

- other than as publicly disclosed or disclosed to the bidder before the offer is made, there having been no material adverse change in the target's business, etc.

---

260 See Rule 24.2(d)(ix) of the Code.
261 See Rule 12.1 of the Code.

Although the offer will invariably be made subject to extensive conditions (including those mentioned above), the bidder's ability to include any particular condition in the offer or to invoke a condition in order to withdraw the offer or allow it to lapse is significantly curtailed by the Code. In particular, an offer cannot be subject to a condition or pre-condition that depends solely on subjective judgments by the directors of the bidder or the target or the fulfilment of which is in their hands.[262] Furthermore, a bidder must not invoke a condition so as to cause an offer not to proceed, to lapse or to be withdrawn unless the circumstances which give rise to the right to invoke the condition are of material significance to the bidder in the context of the offer.[263] The Panel is the ultimate arbiter of whether a matter is sufficiently material to permit the bidder to withdraw. The Code goes on to require the bidder to use all reasonable efforts to ensure the satisfaction of any conditions or pre-conditions to which the offer is subject.[264]

Unless the Panel otherwise consents, all conditions must be fulfilled (or waived) within 21 days of the first closing date (typically 21 days after the date of the offer document) or the date on which the offer becomes or is declared unconditional as to acceptances, whichever is later, failing which the offer must lapse.[265]

'Material adverse change' conditions

12.121 In late 2001, a bidder sought to withdraw from an announced offer by invoking a 'material adverse change' clause. The bidder argued that there had been a material and adverse change in the prospects of the target and sought to invoke the condition in the offer document which entitled it to withdraw the offer in the event that a material adverse change in the financial condition of the target had occurred. Such a clause, the precise form of which may differ slightly from transaction to transaction, is often referred to as the 'MAC clause'. In that particular case, the Panel ruled that the event on which the bidder sought to rely was not sufficiently material to permit the bidder to withdraw.[266] The Panel's ruling provides valuable guidance as to the circumstances in which a bidder could expect to be able to rely on a MAC clause (or indeed any other condition other than the acceptance condition and the competition clearance condition) to withdraw from an announced offer. In its ruling, the Panel stated that for a material adverse change to have occurred the bidder would need to show 'an adverse change of very considerable significance striking at the heart of the purpose of the transaction in question, analogous to something that would justify frustration of a legal contract'. This set an extremely high hurdle for a person seeking to invoke an express condition of an offer.

From this ruling it appeared that unless truly exceptional circumstances occur, which relate to the particular target involved, a bidder is very unlikely to be able to rely upon a MAC clause to withdraw from an announced offer.

---

262 See Rule 13.1 of the Code.
263 See Rule 13.4(a) of the Code.
264 See Rule 13.4(b) of the Code.
265 See Rule 31.7 of the Code. See also para **12.62** generally in relation to bid conditions.
266 See *WPP/Tempus* ruling by Panel as reported in Panel Statement 2001/15, 6 November 2001

Subsequently, in Panel Practice Statement No 5 the Panel's position was clarified further. It stated that:

> 'The Executive is aware that certain practitioners have interpreted Panel Statement 2001/15 to mean that an offeror would need to demonstrate legal frustration in order to be able to invoke a condition to its offer (other than the acceptance condition or any UK or EC competition condition). The Executive does not consider this interpretation to be correct.
>
> In applying Note 2 on Rule 13 in the light of the Panel's decision set out in Panel Statement 2001/15, the Executive's practice is as follows:
>
> • as set out in the Note, the appropriate test for the invocation of a condition under Rule 13 is whether the relevant circumstances upon which the offeror is seeking to rely are of material significance to it in the context of the offer – which must be judged by reference to the facts of each case at the time the relevant circumstances arise;
>
> • in the case of a MAC, or similar, condition, whether the above test is satisfied will depend on the offeror demonstrating that the relevant circumstances are of very considerable significance striking at the heart of the purpose of the transaction; and
>
> • whilst the standard required to invoke such a condition is therefore a high one, the test does not require the offeror to demonstrate frustration in the legal sense.
>
> The Executive should be consulted in cases of doubt.'

Thus, whilst legal frustration is not the requisite benchmark the standard is still a high one. Following *WPP/Tempus*,[267] advisers have considered other steps which a bidder might take to assist its case in the event that it wishes to withdraw its offer. Possibilities considered include:

● the bidder and the target expressly agreeing that the offer will lapse in the event that certain specified events occur and that the occurrence of such events would constitute a material adverse change.

● the bidder highlighting in the offer document (ideally as a specific condition to the offer) its expectations concerning the target which are fundamental to the bidder and to the offer. In this way, if an event concerning the target did occur during the offer period which meant that those expectations could not be met it should be easier to establish that such event is of material significance to the bidder.

In each case, the inclusion of such provisions in the offer document would need to be discussed with the Panel. However, even if the Panel agrees to their inclusion, should the bidder subsequently wish to invoke the provisions to lapse the offer, the Panel would consider any representation made by the target and could still apply the Panel's stringent materiality test and prevent the bidder from relying on such provisions.

---

267 See fn **266**.

Schemes of arrangement

Principal documentation

12.122 The principal documents which will need to be issued in connection with a scheme of arrangement are very similar to those used for an offer. There is the initial press release containing the bidder's announcement of a firm intention to make a bid (in this case through a scheme of arrangement) and this is followed by a scheme document, which takes the place of both the offer document (including the target board's circular). In addition to these core documents there are various court papers associated with the statutory requirement that the scheme be sanctioned by the court. Lastly, in many cases, there will also be a 'transaction agreement' or 'implementation agreement'.

Press announcement and scheme document

12.123 The form of the press announcement is essentially the same as that used for an offer, with consequential references to a proposed scheme of arrangement as opposed to an offer. Broadly speaking, the document must comply with the same content requirements of the Code as apply to offers, including a cash confirmation.[268] Likewise the scheme document is very similar to an offer document except that it describes a scheme of arrangement as the mechanism by which the target will be acquired. As mentioned above, it also incorporates the target board's circular since the scheme document is itself (by contrast with an offer document which is issued by the bidder) issued by the target. As with the press announcement, the content requirements of the Code also apply to the scheme document.[269]

Before being posted to shareholders the scheme document must be approved by the court. This will usually take approximately one week to organise so that, unlike with an offer, the posting of the scheme document can not follow immediately after the press announcement. From the court's perspective it will be particularly concerned with two aspects of the scheme document. First, it must include notice of the shareholder meeting at which the scheme is to be considered. In fact, technically speaking it is the court that convenes this meeting. Secondly, the scheme document must include a statement issued jointly by the target's independent board and its Rule 3 adviser explaining to shareholders the effect of the scheme. The court's satisfaction with this explanatory statement is ultimately one of the statutory requirements for a scheme of arrangement.[270]

Court papers

12.124 Court papers are required at various stages of the scheme process.[271] This stems from the fact that a scheme of arrangement must be approved by the High Court for it to become effective and that various aspects of the process involve applications to court. These will be prepared by counsel for the target company

268 See paras **12.106**, **12.111** and **12.116**.
269 See paras **12.109** to **12.121**.
270 See also para **12.79** in relation to scheme explanatory statements.
271 See in particular the scheme timetable in para **12.99**.

but in practice also approved by the bidder. The court's involvement in the scheme process and the related documentation are considered briefly in earlier sections.[272]

Transaction agreement

12.125 The bidder will typically wish to conclude a transaction agreement with the target before launching a scheme. They are required because the scheme document itself is a target company document and the bidder therefore looks for contractual comfort from the target that the production of the scheme document (and indeed the whole scheme process) will be handled in an efficient and timely manner. In addition, the transaction agreement will normally also include provisions dealing with break fees, work fees, any non-solicitation arrangements and any other areas where the bidder would like to receive the co-operation of the target – eg, in relation to antitrust/competition clearance applications, assistance to enable the necessary whitewash procedures to be completed in a timely fashion following the scheme effective date, help in relation to refinancing target group debt and assistance in dealing with the trustees of any pension schemes within the target group.[273]

ISSUES FOR ACQUISITION FINANCIERS

12.126 The purpose of this section is to consider those aspects of a public-to-private buy-out that are of specific concern or interest to acquisition financiers.

Certain funds

The principle

12.127 For any bid (offer or scheme) that is made wholly or partly for cash, it is a requirement of the Code that both the press announcement[274] and the offer or scheme document[275] includes a confirmation by an appropriate third party (usually the bidder's bank or financial adviser) that the bidder has sufficient funds available to it to satisfy full acceptance of the offer or completion of the scheme (as the case may be). This is called the 'cash confirmation' and the principle it reflects is the 'certain funds' principle. The relevant provisions of the Code go on to provide that the third party giving the confirmation will not be expected to make up for any shortfall if in giving the confirmation it acted reasonably and took all reasonable steps to assure itself that the cash was available.

In practical terms, the certain funds principle means that the bidder must have available to it cash or committed funding sources in an aggregate amount equal to the total amount payable under the offer if it is accepted by all of the target's

---

272 See paras **12.83**, **12.84** and **12.99**.
273 Transaction agreements are also considered briefly in paras **12.21** and **12.48**.
274 See Rule 2.5(c) of the Code.
275 See Rule 24.7 of the Code.

shareholders or to meet the full consideration due under the scheme if it is successful. Not only must the funding be fully committed, it must be unconditionally committed with all conditions precedent satisfied or waived and no further drawdown conditions outstanding or required to be satisfied before the time it needs to be drawn down. In the case of the acquisition finance, this is a significant departure from the standard position, where the facilities will be subject to extensive conditions precedent and drawdown conditions right up to the point the funds are actually borrowed. With a public-to-private, these conditions must be fully satisfied right at the outset of the bid and well in advance of any borrowing being made if and when the bid is successful.

It is worth noting that the Code itself merely requires the cash confirmation to be provided by a suitable third party. It does not dictate the precise manner in which the cash confirmation is backed up by 'certain funds'. The certain funds requirements have evolved over time and are 'enforced' by the financial advisers and banks (and their legal advisers) that give the cash confirmations.Thus, the market has developed a number of exceptions to the basic certain funds principle and these are set out below.

Exceptions

12.128 The common exceptions to the strict certain funds principle – where a condition to drawdown of the acquisition finance can be retained – fall into four broad categories.

Matters that are within the control of the bidder

12.129 To the extent that compliance with a condition of the debt finance documents is absolutely within the control of the bidder, such that compliance or assistance from a third party is not required and the financiers have no remaining discretion to exercise, the financial adviser will normally allow that condition to remain unsatisfied at the date of the cash confirmation. The following types of conditions may fall within this category.

First, there are one-off conditions precedent that for practical reasons cannot be satisfied at the time the debt documentation is signed up but which the financier must have satisfied before advancing funds. This would include, for instance, the provision to the senior debt lenders of the share certificates in respect of the target shares acquired, as part of the security package, which can only be provided once the offer goes unconditional or the scheme becomes effective. At the unconditional/effective date those shares will by definition be under the control of the bidder and consequently delivery of such share certificates should always be within the control of the bidder at the time the condition is required to be satisfied. That condition can therefore remain a condition outside the scope of the certain funds principle. In practice, most of the one-off, deliverable conditions precedent that the financiers typically require in an acquisition financing will be capable of being satisfied at the date of signing of the financing agreements, but there will inevitably be a number that cannot. Those that cannot must be capable of falling within the 'bidder's control' category in order for the financial adviser to give the necessary confirmation.

A second sub-category of conditions that fall within the control of the bidder, includes certain general covenants and undertakings that all acquisition finance facility agreements contain, such as a negative pledge. To the extent that the bidder alone can clearly control compliance with such conditions, the financial adviser may permit them to fall outside the strict certain funds principle. In practice, the exception for most of these covenants will only apply to the bidder's own obligations under the finance documents and not covenants that apply to the target, even though the target will fall under the legal control of the bidder on or soon after the unconditional date.[276]

A further discrete category of obligations under the control of the bidder that the financial adviser will often permit to be excepted from the strict certain funds requirement are the specific conditions relating to the conduct of the bid by the bidder. These are obligations imposed on the bidder by the financiers that are usually of significant importance to the financiers, such as a condition not to trigger a Rule 9 offer,[277] or to waive down the acceptance condition or otherwise amend any material term of the bid.[278]

The final item under this category is a condition that there has been no change of control in respect of the bidder. The acquisition financiers will typically include this as a mandatory prepayment event or default in the finance documents that is triggered if the bidder ceases to be under the control of the sponsor. Although this may not appear to be a matter within the control of the bidder, since the bidder will be under the direct control of the sponsor (which is effectively the real bidder) and because the matter is of fundamental importance to the financiers, market practice generally accepts this as an exception.

Fundamental matters relating to the bidder's status

12.130 The conditions covered in this category are those relating to insolvency events and other fundamental status conditions, such as due incorporation, and perhaps fundamental business related conditions, such as maintenance of a requisite business authorisation.

Fundamental matters relating to the finance documents

12.131 Included in this category are the standard conditions that require the debt finance documentation to be legally binding and enforceable and not repudiated by the bidder.

---

276 The Panel would be extremely unlikely to allow the funding for an offer to be pulled based on a breach of condition imposed on the target by the financiers. Indeed, with *any* condition that could result in the funding not being available and the bid pulled, the Panel will apply the principles set out in Rule 13 of the Code, which may exclude the possibility of the condition being invoked in practice. See paras **12.120** and **12.121** in particular and also para **12.132**.

277 A Rule 9 offer is a mandatory offer that a person is obliged to launch if it acquires 30% or more of the share capital of the target. See also para **12.56**.

278 Conditions of this nature relating to the bidder's conduct of the bid are considered briefly in para **12.144**.

Fundamental matters relating to the target group

12.132 In all buy-outs the fundamental credit risk taken by the financiers is on the target group and so the creditworthiness of the target group is of utmost importance to the financiers. With that in mind, the allocation of the risk for an adverse change in the creditworthiness of the target group is arguably the area of greatest concern for financiers when assessing the implications of the certain funds principle in a public-to-private.

The sponsor itself will attempt to mitigate the risk of an adverse change in the creditworthiness of the target by including conditions in the bid that no member of the target group (usually excluding non-material subsidiaries) is insolvent or subject to any insolvency event or procedure and that no other material adverse change has occurred to the business of the target group.[279]

The financiers will wish to mirror these conditions in the finance documents and it is accepted market practice that they can be an exception to the certain funds requirement, at least to the extent that the Panel does not prevent the bidder from invoking such conditions in order not to declare the offer unconditional (or, in the case of the scheme, to prevent the scheme from becoming effective).[280] Thus, if a circumstance arises that the bidder is willing to close over but the financiers are not, the financiers can invoke the condition indirectly (provided that the Panel accepts it as material etc[281]).

Documenting the certain fund principle and exceptions

12.133 The certain funds principle requires that the normal conditionality of the debt finance is limited in a number of ways. In particular, the conditions precedent that are normally required to be satisfied as of funding must in fact be satisfied at signing, subject to a small number of exceptions agreed with the financial adviser (and considered above). This means that it is common for the schedule of conditions precedent to be split into separate parts to distinguish between those that are required to be satisfied at the announcement date (the vast majority) and those (the smaller list) that must be satisfied at funding. Separately, the circumstances where the financiers can refuse to actually advance the finance are limited to defined categories of default which are also pre-agreed with the financial adviser. It is common for these pre-agreed defaults to be defined in the documents as 'major defaults' or 'drawstop defaults' or 'specified defaults' or some other such term. Similarly, once the finance has been drawn down there are usually limits placed on the ability of the financiers to declare an event of default and demand repayment of the finance. Again, it is common for the 'specified defaults' to be the only circumstances where this can occur. The practical impact of the certain funds principle therefore is that only a 'specified default' will be a ground for not funding or for accelerating the debt.

---

279 MAC clauses, and the ability of the bidder to invoke them, are considered in para **12.121**. See also para **12.120** as to conditions generally.
280 As to which, see para **12.120**. See also fn **276**.
281 See fn **280**.

It is important to note, however, that not all of the debt facilities being made available will necessarily be subject to the certain funds principle. Rules 2.5(c) and 24.7 of the Code are only concerned with finance that is being used to satisfy acceptances of the offer or to meet consideration due under the scheme. They are not concerned with working capital debt, capital expenditure facilities or even finance that is to be used to repay the target's existing debt at completion of the acquisition. With this in mind it is quite common for the acquisition facilities to be defined as 'certain funds facilities' to differentiate them from facilities that are not subject to the principle. In drawing this distinction, however, many sponsors are able to argue that debt that is to be used to refinance target debt should also be included within the certain funds facilities on the grounds that without that debt the deal itself would no longer be viable.

Consideration is normally also given to the period for which the certain funds principle is to apply. Applying Rules 2.5(c) and 24.7 literally, the certain funds principle should apply for so long as the offer is capable of being accepted by a shareholder or to meet payments due under the scheme. With this in mind the 'certain funds period' may be defined as the period from the date of the finance agreement until the last date on which consideration might be required to be posted to an accepting shareholder or any shareholder whose shares are subject to a scheme. More often a fixed backstop date is given, usually taking the maximum amount of time that is allowed under the Code for an offer or scheme to be completed plus some leeway. On occasion there is debate as to whether debt that is to be advanced to finance squeeze-out payments should fall within the certain funds period or not. In practice, this is technically moot (or should be) because with most offers the bidder will leave the offer open for minority shareholders to accept even following the unconditional date. In any event, market practice usually dictates that with a bid structured as an offer the certain funds period *does* extend to include the squeeze-out. On this basis, it will usually be assumed that the bidder will despatch the compulsory purchase notices promptly upon reaching the 90% threshold, and that consequently the length of the certain funds period may be set at 180 days (or thereabouts) from the date of the finance agreement. This will usually provide enough time for the squeeze-out process to be completed even if the offer takes the maximum amount of time allowed under the Code.

As indicated above, the same certain funds issues arise generally whether the bid is being effected by means of a takeover offer or a scheme of arrangement. Indeed, even despite the different timetables applicable to offers and schemes, it is conventional to set the certain funds period for a scheme at around 180 days from the date of the finance agreement, a similar period to that used for offers. Where an option to switch from a scheme to an offer is included in the finance agreements, it is common for the certain funds provisions in the finance agreement to be revisited at the time of the switch – when a cash confirmation statement will in any event need to be repeated – rather than trying to fix, upfront, what could be a rather open-ended period given there is at that stage no certainty as to if or when such a switch might be made.

Finally, the acquisition financiers should generally acknowledge that pulling the finance for a bid in *any* circumstances once a cash confirmation has been given is likely to result in considerable concerns for the Panel and the bidder's financial adviser or bank that gave the cash confirmation, should the circumstances be such that the Panel would not permit the bid to be pulled.[282] This may be one benefit to having the acquisition finance underwritten by the bidder's financial adviser (and the party giving the cash confirmation).

Financial assistance

12.134 The financial assistance laws have for many years raised important legal issues for all types of buy-out including public-to-privates. In fact, they take on even greater significance with public-to-privates given that the laws are more onerous for public companies than they are for private companies. This distinction is to become complete in October 2008 when the financial assistance prohibition applicable to private companies will be abolished (but retained for public companies). For public-to-privates therefore, financial assistance will continue to be an important legal issue to factor in to the process.[283] The following paragraphs consider the particular relevance of the financial assistance laws to acquisition finance in public-to-privates.[284]

Target group guarantees and security

Financial assistance prohibition

12.135 At the time the financing documentation is entered into – ie, immediately before the issue of the press release announcing a firm intention to make the bid – the only asset security available to the debt providers will be a charge from the bidder over the shares of the target to be subsequently acquired by it.[285] This does not provide direct access to the assets and cashflows of the target group, however, and when the bidder acquires the target the financiers will be structurally subordinated to the creditors of the target group. Therefore, when the target comes under the control of the bidder following the unconditional date, the financiers will look to substantially enhance their security position by taking guarantees and security from the target group. It is this additional level of credit support that raises the financial assistance issue. In brief, the granting of guarantees or security by the target or any of its subsidiaries in support of debt that is used to acquire the target may be unlawful financial assistance.[286]

Until 1 October 2008 the financial assistance laws apply to *any* company that is subject to the Companies Act, including both public companies and private

---

282 See paras **12.120** and fn **276** and Rule 13 of the Code.
283 But see para **12.13** and fn **25** in particular.
284 See also paras **11.101** and **12.13** generally, including the changes being effected by the Companies Act 2006.
285 In a public-to-private, the bidder will be an SPV formed for the purpose of making the bid.
286 See Companies Act 1985, s 151 and from 1 October 2009 Ch 2 of Pt 18 of the Companies Act 2006. Note, however, that financial assistance is not the only legal impediment to the taking of upstream credit support from the target group. For example, the corporate benefit principle must also be satisfied in respect of each company providing the credit support.

companies. In the case of a *private* company or its subsidiaries, however, the giving of financial assistance *may* be permitted, provided that it does not reduce the net assets of the company giving the assistance or is provided out of distributable profits and provided further that the statutory relaxation procedure (the 'whitewash') is complied with.[287] With effect from 1 October 2008, however, the prohibition applicable to private companies will be removed completely and there will be no need to go through a statutory whitewash procedure (and the whitewash procedure will be abolished). The absolute prohibition applicable to public companies and their subsidiaries is to remain, however, meaning that until the target is re-registered as a private company neither the target nor any of its subsidiaries will be able to give upstream credit support for the acquisition debt.[288]

Minority shareholder concerns

12.136   The taking of financial assistance in the context of a takeover offer gives rise to a series of theoretical legal concerns for the acquisition financiers whenever there are residual minority shareholders in the target following the unconditional date.[289] These concerns all relate to minority shareholder protection rights. The first relates to the take-private step that is necessary before any member of the target group can give financial assistance. In order to re-register a public company as a private company and thus take advantage of the relaxed financial assistance regime applicable to private companies,[290] a special resolution of shareholders is required, as prescribed by the Companies Act.[291] The same part of the Act then goes on to give certain minority shareholders a right to lodge an objection to the passing of the resolution.[292] This means that whilst there are any potentially dissenting shareholders with a sufficiently large minority stake in the target, the acquisition financiers cannot be certain of being in a position to re-register the target as a private company and thus take guarantees and security from the target group. Although it would be difficult for any minority shareholder to sustain an objection to the re-registration in the context of a successful

---

287   See Companies Act 1985, ss 155-158. The main requirements of these sections are that all the directors of the target and each relevant subsidiary of the target will be required to make a statutory declaration (in the requisite form) that relates to the solvency of the relevant company and these declarations will need to be supported by a report from the target's auditors confirming the reasonableness of the matters contained in the declarations. Note also, that the whitewash procedure is only available to companies whose net assets are not reduced by the giving of the financial assistance or where any such reduction is made out of distributable profits, although the giving of guarantees and/or security does not normally amount to a reduction of net assets. See also para **11.101** in relation to financial assistance and the whitewash generally.

288   But see para **12.13** and fn **25** in particular.

289   With a scheme there should be no minority shareholders after the scheme effective date. See for example para **12.85**.

290   In fact, from 1 October 2008, the prohibition applicable to private companies will be abolished altogether. See para **12.135**.

291   Companies Act 1985, s 53 and, from 1 October 2009, Companies Act 2006, s 97. See also para **12.90**.

292   Companies Act 1985, s 54 and, from 1 October 2009, Companies Act 2006, s 98. This provides that the holders of 5% in nominal value of a company's share capital of any class or not less than 50 of its members may apply to the court to object to any special resolution passed by the company under s 53 of the 1985 Act (or s 97 of the 2006 Act). See also para **12.90**.

takeover,[293] the fact that it could potentially do so and thereby leave the acquisition financiers with only share security at the bidder level and structurally subordinated to the creditors of the target group means it is not simply disregarded by the acquisition financiers.

Furthermore, the right to object to a re-registration resolution is not the only minority protection right that can be invoked in this context. Until 1 October 2008, minority shareholders can also lodge an objection against the special resolution required under the whitewash procedure for any company that is not wholly-owned.[294] As with the re-registration objection, it would be difficult to make the case against the backdrop of a successful takeover offer[295] but this is a further theoretical cause for concern for the acquisition financiers if a sufficient minority stake remains outstanding in the target.

In fact, there is one further legal issue of this nature to consider. *Any* minority shareholder in the target may, under provisions in the Companies Act for the protection of minority shareholders generally, be entitled to challenge actions taken by the target if it can show that the board of the target (as constituted following the change of ownership) is conducting the target's affairs in a manner which is unfairly prejudicial to the interests of the minority shareholder.[296]

In practice, none of these minority protection actions are likely to be upheld and to prevent the taking of upstream credit support following a successful offer that has been accepted by a majority of the target's shareholders. Even if the action in question were upheld, it is thought that a court would identify the relevant remedy for any such action as a right for the minority to be bought out at fair market value rather than to enable it to block actions of the majority. In an offer situation this would effectively mean accepting the offer, the market value having been set quite literally by the market to the extent represented by the majority shareholders that accepted the offer. Nonetheless, taking the most conservative approach, the acquisition financiers will generally not wish to leave such an important issue to the courts alone to decide.

Importance of acceptance condition threshold

12.137 It is with the concerns considered in the preceding paragraphs in mind that – in the case of an offer[297] – the acquisition financiers will make it a condition of the finance that the bidder acquires 100% of the target shares and does not

---

293 In fact, there is very little precedent or academic commentary on what an objecting shareholder would be required to demonstrate to set aside a resolution to re-register a public company as a private company, in the context of a takeover offer. In the absence of evidence of unfair prejudice, which may be difficult to show where a majority of shareholders have accepted the terms of the takeover offer, such an objection may be very hard to substantiate in practice.

294 See Companies Act 1985, ss 154(4), (5) and 157(2). Here the qualifying requirement is 10% or more of the target's shares. Since the whitewash is being abolished, these provisions are not being re-enacted under the Companies Act 2006.

295 As with re-registration objections there is little in the form of precedent and it is thought that the background of a successful takeover offer would be fatal to any claim for the resolution to be set aside in practice. See also fn **293**.

296 See Companies Act 2006, s 994. Similar problems exist for this type of claim as for the other minority shareholder actions, in the context of a successful takeover.

297 These concerns are not relevant to a scheme, where the bidder will inevitably acquire 100% if the scheme is effective.

leave any minorities outstanding. To do this, the offer needs to be accepted by only 90% of the shareholders (by value), at which point the bidder can invoke the statutory squeeze-out mechanism.[298] For acquisition financiers in an offer the 90% threshold is therefore of great significance and in practice they will always insist that the acceptance condition in the offer is set at 90% and that they have a veto over any reduction or waiver down below that level.[299]

Three stage approach to security

12.138 As mentioned in an earlier section of this chapter,[300] the actual taking of guarantees and security by the acquisition financiers will in practice happen in three stages. Stage one is at signing of the finance documents on or before the announcement date when the bidder grants security over its present and future assets, including in due course the target shares. Stage two is when, following the unconditional date, members of the target group give guarantees and security that do not amount to unlawful financial assistance, ie, where they secure working capital debt and possibly refinancing debt. Stage three is when the main target group security package is granted, including guarantees and security for the acquisition debt. This occurs following the take-private and – at least until its repeal on 1 October 2008 – the whitewash.

Debt service

12.139 The financial assistance provisions of the Companies Act impact not only the granting of guarantees and security by the target group but also direct credit support to the bidder in the form of loans. This is important because the bidder is wholly reliant on cash from the target group in order to service the debt that it incurs to finance the acquisition of target's shares. There are two principal ways in which the bidder can access the target group cashflows for this purpose.

Dividends

12.140 First, the bidder can extract dividends from the target group, assuming that there are profits available for distribution and cash resources to meet such dividends. There are three material concerns (and one advantage) with relying on dividends to service the debt incurred by the bidder. First, even if the target group generates cash, it may not generate distributable profits in equivalent amounts. Secondly, the declaration and payment of dividends is unwieldy in practice and the timing requirements of the finance documents (with variable interest periods and semi-annual repayment dates) are not well suited to servicing the debt purely from dividends. Finally, to the extent that there are minority shareholders in the target, they will participate rateably in any such dividend resulting in cash leak-

---

298 See paras **12.69** et seq.
299 See also paras **12.117** and **12.118** in relation to the acceptance condition generally.
300 See also para **12.91** generally.

age to third parties. The advantage of dividends is that they are excluded from the financial assistance provisions in the Companies Act.[301]

Loans

12.141 In practice, target group cashflows are upstreamed to the bidder by way of loans. Loans are more flexible than dividends since there is no requirement for the lender to have distributable profits and no procedural restriction as to when and how often a loan may be made. Furthermore, minority shareholders do not have a right to 'participate' in any loan so there is no cash leakage. The concern with such upstream loans is financial assistance. The making of a loan by a target group company to the bidder to enable it to service acquisition debt is financial assistance that is absolutely prohibited for a public company and which would need to be whitewashed for a private company. In this respect the same analysis in terms of timing and availability that applies to guarantees and security (as set out above) also applies to this form of credit support. In fact, it was once assumed by legal practitioners that each time a loan was made by a target group company to the bidder to service acquisition debt the loan would need to be whitewashed; because the making of each loan was financial assistance for the purposes of assisting the bidder acquire the shares in target. However, the majority opinion reflecting current conventional wisdom is that, provided a committed and effectively unconditional loan agreement[302] is put in place at the outset (between the target group companies as lenders and the bidder as borrower), only the loan agreement needs to be whitewashed and not each loan made under it. This can – and in practice is – done at the same time as the whitewash of the target group guarantees and security.

Finance documentation issues

12.142 In broad terms the finance documentation used in a public-to-private transaction is essentially the same as that for a private buy-out.[303] The principal differences stem from the slightly different acquisition mechanics of a public-to-private, the certain funds principle and the fact that the taking of guarantees and security from the target group is more difficult and is done in stages. The following paragraphs outline the most significant differences in the finance documents applicable to public-to-privates.

---

301 See Companies Act 1985, s 153(3)(a) and, from 1 October 2009 in respect of public companies, Companies Act 2006, s 681(2)(a).
302 The form of such loan agreements has become relatively standardised. Typically the amount made available to the bidder under the loan agreement will be the full principal amount of all acquisition debt owing by the bidder to the acquisition financiers. That amount will be available for the full term of such acquisition facilities and the only condition to lending will be that in making the loans the relevant target group company will not render itself insolvent (on the basis of not having sufficient cash resources to pay its debts as they fall due or otherwise). All cash generative companies in the group will be parties (as lenders) and the bidder will be the borrower.
303 See the earlier chapters of this book as regards the standard forms of finance documentation used.

Certain funds

12.143 Certain funds and the manner in which the principle impacts the finance documentation in a public-to-private is considered above.[304]

Controlling the conduct of the bid

12.144 The acquisition financiers will wish to impose a number of restrictions on the bidder's conduct of the bid. These will take the form of a discrete set of positive and negative undertakings. Breach of most of those undertakings should constitute a 'specified default' for certain funds purposes allowing the financiers to refuse to advance further funds or to accelerate funds already advanced.[305]

The following undertakings are common examples of those required by the financiers:

- issue of the relevant press announcement within one or two days of signing the facilities agreement;

- issuing the offer document – or, in the case of a scheme, procuring the issue of the scheme document – within a number of days of the issue of the press announcement;

- procuring compliance with the Code and other relevant legislation;

- no waiver or amendment of the terms and conditions of the bid without the financiers' consent;[306]

- no action that would result in the bidder being required to make a mandatory offer pursuant to Rule 9 of the Code;

- keeping the financiers informed as to the progress of the bid and supplying them with copies of all documentation and announcements issued in the context of the bid;

- de-listing the target from the Main Market or AIM as soon as practicable after the unconditional date or scheme effective date;

- re-registering the target as a private company as soon as practicable after being entitled to do so; and

- in the case of an offer, effecting the squeeze-out process in a timely fashion.

Interim loan agreements and funded commitment papers

12.145 Given the short time frames often used in public-to-privates, some public bids have been launched off the back of short form finance documentation – often referred to as 'interim loan agreements' – put in place at very short notice. In some cases these can amount to little more than commitment papers. In

---

304 See paras **12.127** et seq.
305 See para **12.133** for further consideration of the 'specified default' concept.
306 This condition is usually expressed to be subject to the overriding directions of the Panel and to Rule 13 of the Code. See also paras **12.129** and **12.132** and fn **276** in particular.

practice, this is also common in other forms of buy-out which are executed on shorter than normal time frames, as is often the case with auctioned transactions.[307] In both types of deal the interim documentation tends to be replaced by full documentation as soon as possible after signing and generally, although not necessarily, before funding. With a public-to-private, the certain funds principle means that even though the documents are in short form they must still satisfy the requirements of the Code and, more particularly, provide sufficient comfort as to certain funds to the third party that is giving the cash confirmation.[308]

Loan note guarantee facilities

12.146 Most bids offer the target shareholders a loan note alternative to cash. The purpose of a loan note alternative is to enable accepting shareholders to defer cashing out their shares until a date in the future when they cash in the loan notes. They replace their shares with a loan note issued by the bidder. In doing so, they can take advantage of the tax benefit of deferring part of the capital gain that would otherwise arise by cashing out the shares straightaway.[309] In the vast majority of instances – and certainly in a public-to-private buy-out, where the bidder will be a new SPV – the loan notes will need to be guaranteed by an acceptable bank. Absent this they would not be a viable alternative to the cash offer and would therefore add nothing to it. In practice, the loan notes will be backed by a bank guarantee given as part of the acquisition finance facilities. There are very standard documentary mechanics that require relatively simple changes to the finance documents in order for the acquisition facilities to accommodate this approach. Thus the loan note guarantee will be made available within, and on the same terms as, the principle tranche of senior acquisition debt. Depending on whether shareholders accept cash or a loan note, the bidder can borrow cash to cash out the shareholders or add the principal amount of the loan note to the guarantee given by the acquisition finance banks. And when the loan note is subsequently cashed in, the guaranteed amount can then be replaced by a drawing of cash.

PUBLIC-TO-PRIVATES VS PRIVATE BUY-OUTS

12.147 The following paragraphs briefly summarise the main differences between public-to-privates and buy-outs of private companies. Previous sections of this chapter deal with many of the highlighted features of public-to-privates in more detail.

---

307 See paras **11.115** and **11.116** for example.
308 See paras **12.127** et seq generally in relation to the certain fund principle and the cash confirmation requirements of the Code.
309 The capital gain in respect of the target shares is postponed until a disposal (including by way of redemption) of the loan notes. Prior to the abolition of taper relief (proposed to take effect from 6 April 2008) non-qualifying corporate bonds may prove useful as a means of enabling target shareholders to accrue further taper relief in the meantime.

Regulatory regime

12.148   A public-to-private is more heavily regulated than a private acquisition. The sponsor, the bidder and the target will all need to comply with the Code in relation to the conduct of the transaction, including conduct before the bid is actually launched. The sponsor and the management team will also need to ensure that they do not contravene the provisions of the Financial Services and Markets Act 2000 relating to price sensitive information and market abuse and avoid breaching any of the insider dealing provisions of the Criminal Justice Act 1993. On top of this the target and its directors are subject to the Disclosure and Transparency Rules and the Model Code on Directors' Dealings. The Companies Act is also applicable to public-to-privates in ways that it is not for a private buy-out, in particular to schemes of arrangement but also in relation to takeover offers (particularly the squeeze-out of minority shareholders).

Process

12.149   A public-to-private is effected either by way of a takeover offer under the Code or by way of a scheme of arrangement under the Companies Act and the Code. In both cases the procedure is codified and the relevant regulatory provisions will dictate much of the process.

Execution risk

12.150   The execution risk with a public-to-private is much higher than with a negotiated private buy-out. There are two reasons for this. First, there is no guarantee that shareholders will accept the offer or approve the scheme of arrangement. Secondly, whenever a takeover is launched there is always a risk that a competing bidder will emerge and ultimately make a higher bid. This is a major reason why acquisition financiers would vary rarely support a hostile bid and nearly always insist that any bid must be recommended by the target's board. Parties do not like deals with high execution risk because of the time spent and costs incurred in deals that abort at a late stage and perhaps after the vast majority of the work has been done, ie, once the bid is launched with all the funds in place. That all said, the increase in the use of auctions in the 2000s means that even with private buy-outs the sponsor may face considerable uncertainty and execution risk when it enters into a transaction process.

Timetable

12.151   The Code lays down a fixed timetable for the making and completion of a takeover offer. A further fixed timetable is set out in the Companies Act for the minority compulsory acquisition procedure (the squeeze-out). As far as schemes are concerned the Companies Act legislates for a specific procedure involving court hearings and shareholder meetings that inevitably dictates a certain timetable. Parts of the Code timetable are also applicable to schemes. In any case, whichever procedure is used, completion of a public-to-private is likely to take considerably longer than a conventional private buy-out.

Acquisition structure

12.152 The acquisition of a private company is effected through an acquisition agreement negotiated between the buyer and the seller. The parties are more or less free to negotiate whatever terms they want. With a public-to-private the acquisition is structured quite differently. For starters, there will be no single 'seller' to negotiate with and thus no single acquisition agreement. Some negotiations may be had with large block shareholders as regards the terms on which they might be willing to pre-agree to consent to the takeover, but by and large the only negotiations will be between the bidder and the target. Instead of a negotiated acquisition agreement, the buyer will either launch an offer, by posting an offer document to all shareholders for acceptance, or it will presume that the target proposes a scheme of arrangement to shareholders through the posting of a scheme document.

Acquisition recourse: warranties and indemnities

12.153 In a public-to-private there will not, generally speaking, be an acquisition agreement with a single seller containing seller warranties and indemnities relating to the target, leaving the bidder without any effective recourse in the event there are defects in the target group that it was unaware of. A possible exception to this is where the buyer is able to get some warranty and indemnity cover from a large shareholder but this would be subject to deal specific negotiation and is rare in practice. In addition, some warranties may be obtained from those members of the management team that are participating in the buy-out but these will be limited by comparison with standard seller warranties and indemnities.

Comfort as to the condition of the target can only be obtained, in most cases, through due diligence which will be much more limited in a public-to-private (see below).

Documentation

12.154 As previously indicated, there will be no single negotiated acquisition agreement with a public-to-private. A takeover offer is launched with a press announcement followed up by the posting of an offer document to shareholders. The shareholders can accept the offer by completing the form of acceptance included within the offer document or by accepting the offer through the CREST system or reject it by doing nothing.

A scheme of arrangement is also launched by a press announcement. This is then followed up by a scheme document that is first approved by the court and then circulated to shareholders. In addition to the scheme document various court forms are required to ensure that the correct court procedure is followed in order to have the court sanction the scheme. In many cases a 'transaction' or 'implementation' agreement is also negotiated between the bidder and the target for the purposes of giving certainty and structure to the process and to document such matters as break fees.

Certain funds

12.155 One of the most important provisions of the Code from an acquisition financier's perspective is set out in Rules 2.5(c) and 24.7. This provision requires a statement to be given in both the press announcement and the bid document by an acceptable third party – either the bidder's bank or financial adviser – that the bidder has sufficient cash resources available to it to satisfy the full acceptance of the offer or to meet all payments due under the scheme if it becomes effective. This is the so-called 'cash confirmation' which establishes the 'certain funds' principle for public-to-privates. Having given the cash confirmation, if the offer is subsequently declared unconditional or the scheme declared effective but the bidder does not have the requisite finance to pay for the shares, the Panel might require the bank or financial adviser that gave the cash confirmation to put up the shortfall itself. It will only escape this liability if it can demonstrate that it acted responsibly in giving the confirmation and took all reasonable steps to assure itself that the cash would be available.

The implications of this requirement for the terms of the acquisition finance are profound. In broad terms it means that the acquisition finance must be unconditionally available from the time that the cash confirmation is required at the launch of the bid until payment of the last amount due to shareholders. The financial adviser or bank will insist on this as a condition of it giving the cash confirmation. In practice, the public-to-private market has developed exceptions to the rule, which allow some conditionality in the terms of the acquisition finance.

The same requirement of unconditional funds also applies to the equity component of the funding structure.

Due diligence

12.156 The extent of the due diligence that the bidder and its financial backers can carry out in a public-to-private will be extremely limited by comparison with a buy-out of a private company. The main reason for this will be that, aside from publicly available information, access to information concerning the target will be carefully controlled by the independent directors of the target. They will be particularly aware of the provisions in Rule 20 of the Code that mean that, in broad terms, information that is made available to the bidder must also be available to any other – and perhaps less welcome – bidders (including potentially a trade competitor).

CHAPTER 13

Multi-Jurisdictional Buy-outs

MULTI-JURISDICTIONAL BUY-OUTS

13.1   This chapter is concerned with buy-outs of target businesses which have significant operations in more than one country. A true cross-border or multi-jurisdictional buy-out will involve a target business with substantial parts of its cash generating business in several countries. A buy-out of a target which has the majority of its business in one country – say, the United Kingdom – and one or two relatively small subsidiaries operating elsewhere is not really a multi-jurisdictional deal as many of the issues which distinguish such a deal from a domestic buy-out will not arise. The purpose of this chapter is to highlight specific issues that are often relevant in a multi-jurisdictional buy-out, but which don't generally arise in a domestic UK buy-out. It does not, however, consider the law or practice of any jurisdiction in particular as this is beyond the intended scope of this book.

The most significant differences between a multi-jurisdictional buy-out and a purely domestic buy-out will arise in the structuring process. In particular, the need to balance the competing interests of the sponsor and the acquisition financiers will require detailed consideration of the legal and taxation regimes of each of the countries involved.

Differences from pure UK buy-outs

13.2   A number of legal and structural principles, which are taken for granted in the context of domestic UK buy-outs, cannot be assumed in the context of a multi-jurisdictional buy-out. Multi-jurisdictional deals tend to be more complex than UK equivalents and generally take longer to structure and complete.

The principal reason for this is that the laws that underpin the various aspects of a buy-out vary from jurisdiction to jurisdiction. To some extent the parties can select which laws they wish to govern the various contractual relationships that are established in a buy-out, but there are legal and practical limits to this. For instance, it is usually necessary for any transfer of assets – including shares in companies – in a particular jurisdiction to be effected by an agreement governed by the law of that jurisdiction. Failure to do so may render the transfer ineffective and unenforceable in court. In the context of an acquisition financing this means that the taking of security over assets in a particular jurisdiction will generally need to be effected by an agreement governed by the law of that jurisdiction. The same principle also usually applies to the transfer of shares or assets that is at the core of the acquisition itself. As a result, multi-jurisdictional deals invariably involve an analysis of the laws of a number of jurisdictions.

In addition to a pure legal analysis, the deal sponsor will instigate a detailed analysis of the tax regime applicable in each jurisdiction in which the target business has material taxable revenues. Unlike the legal analysis referred to above, which will be undertaken by lawyers advising the deal sponsor and the acquisition financiers, the tax analysis is usually undertaken by an international firm of accountants. The product of their analysis will be a tax structuring memorandum which will usually make certain structuring recommendations. The results of both this analysis and the legal analysis referred to above will often have a fundamental influence on how the acquisition and its financing are structured.

Although each multi-jurisdictional deal will be different, it is possible to identify a number of key issues that arise frequently, no matter which jurisdictions are involved. It is these issues that are often the focus of the legal and tax analyses referred to above and generally have the greatest impact on the structuring of a multi-jurisdictional buy-out.

They include:

- the nature of the acquisition itself;

- the availability of upstream credit support for the acquisition finance from target companies;

- the availability of target group cashflows to service the acquisition finance;

- the ability to set acquisition finance interest costs against target group profits for tax purposes;

- concerns with withholding tax;

- concerns about the enforceability of subordination provisions;

- the need for 'local' working capital banking requirements; and

- concerns with currency exchange rate exposure.

Each of these concerns is dealt with in more detail in the following paragraphs.

Nature of the acquisition

13.3   It is relatively common with a multi-jurisdictional buy-out for the acquisition to include more than one sub-acquisition, each of a discrete part of the business, usually in different countries. This may be required in order to create a post-completion group structure that is more tax efficient than the pre-completion structure in light of the increased amount of debt that the group will take on. In certain cases this might, in effect, amount to a full reorganisation of the target group. In some jurisdictions, buying assets rather than shares may be preferable. That is, the laws, taxation rates and local business practices and customs of certain jurisdictions may naturally mitigate in favour of an asset purchase rather than a share purchase and one or more of the acquisitions at the heart of the relevant multi-jurisdictional buy-out may need to be structured accordingly.

Upstream credit support

13.4 A fundamental characteristic of senior debt, and certain categories of junior debt, is that it receives the benefit of upstream credit support from the target group. That is, it will be secured by guarantees from all non-dormant companies in the target group and on all or substantially all of the assets of the target group. In many countries outside the United Kingdom, including many on mainland Europe, this is unlikely to be legally or practically possible.

The reason for this is that, quite often, the legal system in which the guarantee or security is sought imposes a restriction that does not exist under English law or a higher legal hurdle than the equivalent under English law. There are three areas of law that provide the most commonly arising restrictions and hurdles.

First, financial assistance legislation, which exists in most European jurisdictions, including the United Kingdom,[1] *prima facie* prevents a company from giving financial assistance for the purchase of its shares or the shares of any of its holding companies. Financial assistance usually includes the giving of guarantees or security to banks financing the acquisition. In the United Kingdom, the basic prohibition against financial assistance can be relaxed for private companies which go through the so-called 'whitewash' procedure.[2] However, many other jurisdictions do not have an equivalent relaxation procedure, meaning that the financial assistance prohibition is absolute. There are steps that can be taken in the structuring of some deals to mitigate the effects of such prohibitions in certain countries but, as a general rule, the availability of upstream credit support in the form of guarantees and security from a target company outside the United Kingdom will be significantly more limited than in the United Kingdom.[3]

Secondly, rules concerning corporate benefit and the abuse of company assets[4] may hinder the giving of guarantees or third-party security[5] by non-borrowing members of the target group.

---

1 In actual fact, the English financial assistance laws are set to be substantially reformed pursuant to legislation to be enacted under the Companies Act 2006. In particular, the prohibition on the granting of financial assistance by private companies set out in the Companies Act 1985, s 151 – and with it the whitewash provisions in the Companies Act 1985, ss 155–158 – is to be repealed on 1 October 2008. The absolute prohibition on the granting of financial assistance by public companies is set to remain under Companies Act 2006, Pt 18, Ch 2 which will come into force on 1 October 2009.

2 See ss 155–158 of the Companies Act 1985. However, see fn **1** above.

3 It is interesting to note that the two countries of the developed Western economies that have had the most relaxed financial assistance laws – the UK and the US (the US does not have financial assistance laws per se, although it (the individual States) has a similar concept of 'fraudulent transfers/conveyances') – are the two where leveraged buy-outs have clearly flourished the most.

4 Broadly speaking these require that a transaction must be for the benefit of the company concerned and does not amount to an abuse of its assets.

5 Third-party security is where a company gives security for the debt of another company. This is to be contrasted with the normal method of giving security whereby the company grants a guarantee of another company's debt and then gives security for its *own* debt under the guarantee. In such circumstances it is the guarantee in particular that must survive the corporate benefit analysis.

Thirdly, a number of specific legal provisions in individual jurisdictions render the taking of security over certain categories of assets innately too costly,[6] impracticable or legally impossible.

Faced with these three commonly arising issues, acquisition financiers have developed certain mitigating tactics that are often used in the structuring or documentation processes. These are considered in the following paragraphs.

Target group borrowing and 'debt push-downs'

13.5   Financial assistance and corporate benefit laws – both or either – may mean that in many jurisdictions guarantees and security can not be obtained from target group companies or that security can only be given by a target group company in respect of its own borrowings. As discussed further below, one of the mitigants often employed is to structure the transaction so that as much debt as possible is provided at the operating company level – that is, borrowed directly by a target company – rather than at the SPV level. The granting of security by a company for its own borrowings will nearly always avoid problems with laws relating to corporate benefit and abuse of assets and depending on the precise nature of the borrowing, financial assistance concerns too.[7] It will not normally remove concerns relating to the cost of taking security, however, although this is often seen as a secondary concern, at least by the acquisition financiers.

With this in mind, the acquisition financiers will generally wish to have as much debt as possible borrowed in the target group so that target group borrowers can give security.

The most commonly used method of placing debt in the target group is to ensure that instead of acquiring the target group on a debt free basis – meaning that the seller would ensure the repayment of any existing debt at completion – the existing debt is left in the target group and refinanced directly by the acquisition financiers.[8] In some structures this might also generate tax efficiencies by allowing greater deductibility of interest costs against target group profits, which generally results from having the debt and the profits in the same companies. A detailed legal and tax analysis will invariably be required to assess the best option for both upstream credit support and tax deductibility. In practice, it is possible that these twin aims will suggest different structures, in which case the interests of the acquisition financiers and the tax paying companies themselves will not be wholly aligned.

As with the refinancing of existing debt of the target group, the lending of working capital debt directly into the target group can be used to enhance the

---

6   In particular, material taxes, stamp duties, registration fees, notarial fees or other fees and expenses are payable for the taking of security in certain jurisdictions. In addition, the lawyers' costs in documenting the security may vary materially from jurisdiction to jurisdiction.

7   A target group company cannot normally borrow funds that are indirectly used to finance its acquisition. This will fall foul of the financial assistance laws of most jurisdictions.

8   If a target is acquired with its debt in place and refinanced by the acquiring company (its banks) there is no increased funding requirement as the consideration attributable to the acquisition of the target's shares will be reduced by the amount of target group debt to be acquired and refinanced.

acquisition financiers' security position. Acquisition debt, which by its nature is used to acquire target companies, and which will form the bulk of the acquisition finance package, is more problematic. This is where so-called 'debt push-down' techniques may be required. The term debt push-down is used widely to mean any technique which results in debt being borrowed in the target group. Loosely it therefore includes the techniques mentioned above – with refinancing and working capital debt. The real benefit of a debt push-down, however, is where it results in acquisition debt being borrowed in the target group. This is far from easy to achieve in practice and, in any case, the issue is acutely jurisdiction- and deal-specific.

In certain jurisdictions the placing of debt at operating company level may be achieved by a merger of the acquiring newco and the target after completion or by leveraging the target companies after completion and using the proceeds to reduce newco's debt. Various methods of achieving a debt push down have been used but most rely on a form of merger of newco with one or more target companies or the refinancing of newco's debt with target group debt at some point after completion. Whether or not a debt push down mechanism can be used in any given transaction requires a detailed analysis of the target group structure and the laws of the jurisdictions concerned. Quite often the financial assistance laws in the jurisdiction of the relevant target group companies impose material restrictions on the feasibility of a merger or refinancing of newco debt by target companies. In practice, this rules out any debt push-down of acquisition debt in most countries that have financial assistance laws. The most reliable method of pushing acquisition debt into the target group is, as mentioned above, through the refinancing of existing target group debt, but this is necessarily limited to the amount of debt that exists in the target group at completion.

The problem of undersecured junior debt

13.6   As a result of the legal and practical impediments to the taking of upstream credit support outlined above, the security package available to the acquisition financiers in a multi-jurisdictional deal is frequently limited. However, the problem will often be significantly worse for secured junior creditors than it is for the senior lenders. This follows from the fact that the most commonly available mitigant – the refinancing of existing target debt – will only be a partial solution. Naturally the senior lenders will insist that it is senior debt that is used to refinance the existing debt and thus benefit from the enhanced security position. This is likely to leave any second lien or mezzanine debt without the benefit of the 'debt push-down'. Of course, a portion of the senior debt is also likely to be in the same position but not all of it, as would probably be the case with the junior debt. In addition, the senior lender may apply a further mitigant to the situation by insisting that the 'undersecured' newco debt is amortised before any of the secured target group debt.

Share security

13.7   Where asset security or guarantees are not available from the target group companies, security granted by newco over the direct target companies themselves,[9] that is, over the shares in the direct target(s), may be the only security available.[10] Such security would at least enable the acquisition financiers to sell the business as a going concern upon enforcement following default. However, without guarantees and asset security from the target group, the acquisition financiers are structurally subordinated to the liabilities of the target group and, in particular, to the trade creditors since they, unlike the acquisition financiers, would have direct recourse against the target group companies. An additional concern to note is that since the problems of financial assistance and corporate benefit/abuse of assets will in general apply to all target companies, in the situation where, as is common, the direct target is not the main operating company but merely a holding company, the acquisition financiers will not even get direct share security over the operating companies. The operating companies, as subsidiaries of the target holding company would be one layer removed. The target holding company is unlikely to be able to give share pledges over the operating companies because in doing so it would still have to give a guarantee of newco's acquisition debt, debt that was used to acquire it. The effect of this could be to leave the acquisition financiers with security limited to a share pledge from newco over the holding company's shares only.

In any event, such security does still allow the acquisition financiers to sell the operating companies indirectly, by enforcing the share pledge over the target holding company, and such security is a common feature of multi-jurisdictional deals.

By contrast with target group companies, newco will not be faced with financial assistance or corporate benefit problems in giving security. This is because newco's shares will not have been acquired – or at least not using the proceeds of the acquisition finance – so there is no financial assistance concern at the newco level. Newco is said to be 'above the line' for financial assistance purposes, where the notional line represents the level in a group structure separating acquired companies from their acquirer. As regards corporate benefit, newco will be giving security for its own debt, which rarely raises any corporate benefit concerns. Similarly, newco can also normally grant guarantees and security for the debt of its subsidiaries without raising corporate benefit concerns, because in doing so it is indirectly assisting itself. This is the distinction between a downstream guarantee and an upstream guarantee. An upstream guarantee is effectively for the benefit of a third-party, albeit a third-party that directly or indirectly owns shares in the guarantor. A downstream guarantee is given by a company in respect of its own subsidiary, its own asset. Cross-guarantees are akin to upstream guarantees since they are of sister companies or assets of a third-party parent company.

Documentary controls

13.8   In addition to taking share pledges and getting what guarantees and security they can from the target group, the acquisition financiers will also expect

---

9 That is, the companies whose shares are acquired directly by newco. Often there is only one direct target.
10 Share security is almost universally described as a share 'pledge'. This is the correct legal term in a number of jurisdictions, although it is not in the UK. The correct term to use for security over a UK company's shares would be a mortgage or charge, with mere charges more common than mortgages.

to put in place various controls (contained in the finance documentation) that are specifically designed to mitigate the absence of direct recourse against target group companies. These will include controls on the incurrence of non-trade liabilities and the granting of security to third parties together with so-called 'ringfencing' provisions. Ring-fencing provisions are designed to maintain as much value as possible within the key target group companies that are the subject of any guarantees or security by restricting the transfer of assets and the making of loans or investments outside such companies. Thus, transfers of assets, the lending of money or the granting of guarantees by companies which have provided a guarantee and/or security (obligors) to or for the benefit of non-obligors will be prohibited. The ring-fencing of the obligor group in this way is designed to prevent leakage of cash and assets – including indirectly as a result of the giving of guarantees – from the pool of assets against which recourse is available to the acquisition financiers. Ideally the ring-fencing operates to maintain value within those companies over which direct security is available, that is, from obligors that have given guarantees *and* asset security.

In addition, the banking documentation will often include an obligation on non-obligors to upstream cash not needed for working capital to obligors and, in particular, to borrowers and other companies which have given security over cash balances. Again this is in order to reinforce the value within the ring-fence. In drafting all of these controls there is a balance to be drawn between meeting the acquisition financiers' legitimate concerns regarding the preservation of assets within the obligor companies against whom they have direct recourse and allowing the group the freedom to run its business in the ordinary course.

Guarantee limitations

13.9   One of the most commonly used methods of mitigating the effects of the legal restrictions that apply to upstream guarantees and security is to limit the scope of the guarantees so that they fall within the relevant restrictions. In other words, rather than having an unenforceable guarantee that would otherwise breach financial assistance or corporate benefit laws or, more likely in practice, not taking a guarantee because it would cause such a breach, the parties will agree to limit the scope of the guarantee so that a breach would not arise. With guarantors from some jurisdictions this can be done quite simply by stating that the guarantee is limited to the extent required by the relevant laws in order to be fully enforceable. In others it might be necessary to expressly limit the value of the guarantee to, say, the distributable assets of the guarantor or some other financial measure that the relevant laws require. In jurisdictions where it is not absolutely certain how the courts would interpret the relevant laws in the specific circumstances, agreeing guarantee limitation language is often hotly negotiated by the acquisition financiers on the one side and the guarantors themselves on the other (or in practice by lawyers representing each).

One particularly sensitive area is director liabilities. In some jurisdictions the directors of a company that gives a guarantee in breach of corporate benefit/abuse of assets laws might be personally liable. The temptation for the directors therefore is to give extremely limited guarantees. This will be at odds with the position of the acquisition financiers. Their lawyers will often take a much more robust and less cautious view of the relevant laws and look for a less restrictive form of wording for the guarantee limitation language. Given the sensitivity of this area in particular, it is important to involve the directors of the guarantors (and their lawyers) at a very early stage in agreeing the form of the guarantees.

A further type of guarantee limitation language that is often used to reduce the cost to the group of the guarantee and security package – and thus make it more acceptable to the sponsor – involves artificially capping the amount of certain guarantees by reference to the value of the assets securing the guarantee. This method will be used where the guarantees are secured by security documents that attract *ad valorem* costs such as registration or notary fees that are assessed by reference to the amount secured, usually as a fixed percentage or a percentage on a sliding scale. For example, if the total amount of debt is €150 million but the assets of the guarantor are only €30 million, the parties might agree to limit the value of the guarantee to less than €150 million in circumstances where it costs a percentage of the amount secured to notarise the guarantee or security documents. It is usual to build in sufficient headroom to allow the value of the guarantor's assets to increase and remain as security for the guarantee. So in the example given, the guarantee might be capped at, say, €40 or €50 million.

In practice, as a result of the various legal and practical restrictions previously outlined, a key feature of multi-jurisdictional deals is that the acquisition financiers' security package will be more limited than that available in a domestic UK buy-out. It may be limited to share pledges over target group companies or a combination of share pledges and varying degrees of guarantees and security from target group companies in different countries. As a result, the contractual restrictions and protections in the finance documentation – and in particular, the ring-fencing provisions – will be important.

Agreeing principles to govern the taking of guarantees and security

13.10   In theory at least, each transaction will require a fresh analysis of the relevant laws of a number of jurisdictions in order to determine what guarantee and security package is available. This is potentially extremely time-consuming and often leads to inefficiencies as different approaches can be taken by different parties to the same issues. There may also be significant cost implications for the group in granting different guarantee and security packages and deal sponsors are very sensitive to the demands made by acquisition financiers for extensive credit support packages, the actual benefit of which they may see as disproportionate to the costs involved. For these reasons the leading banks and sponsors have taken steps to adopt a consistent approach to the taking of guarantees and security in multi-jurisdictional deals.

In particular, it is customary for the acquisition financiers and the deal sponsor to agree at the outset certain guiding principles that will apply to the taking of guarantees and security. The principles will apply not only to the guarantee and security package that will be taken at the outset of the transaction, at funding and completion of the acquisition, but also during the life of the deal as the underlying business develops and expands through acquisitions of other businesses or through organic growth.

These principles are normally documented in the form of two separate provisions, as set out below.

Guarantor coverage requirements

13.11 The first type of provision acknowledges that a requirement to obtain guarantees from every member of the target group will raise legal and practical hurdles that may not be overcome in every case. The provision is included in the principal acquisition finance documents (senior facilities agreement and mezzanine facilities agreement) and operates by allowing the borrowers to decide which companies in the target group are to give guarantees, provided that those companies account for a minimum level of financial strength. Typically the clause requires the guarantors together to represent not less than a specified percentage of the total revenues, profits (usually EBITDA) and assets of the entire target group. The percentage is normally set in the region of 75 to 90%. In setting the agreed percentage the borrower must be certain that it can actually comply with the requirement at the outset. If the effect of financial assistance or corporate benefit laws, for instance, is that a number of companies cannot give a guarantee at all, then the borrower may not be able to comply with, say, a 90% requirement. Other aspects of the provision are negotiable or will vary from deal to deal. For instance, the requirement may not apply to all of revenues, profits *and* assets, but, say, only profits and assets. Some provisions stipulate that any company that owns any 'material company' must become a guarantor irrespective of its own (unconsolidated) revenues, profits or assets. The purpose of this is to assist the taking of share pledges over material companies by having the pledgor grant security for its own obligations (as guarantor). Most provisions require that any company that is a 'material company' must become a guarantor irrespective of whether the overall guarantor coverage test is satisfied. Typically, although again this is negotiable, a material company is defined as a company that contributes not less than say 5% of the revenues, profits or assets of the entire group. In this formulation the alternative qualifier is used so that a company is material if it qualifies under revenues, profits *or* assets, whereas the total guarantor coverage requirement is typically cumulative (revenue, profits *and* assets).

Guarantor coverage provisions have the benefit of being dynamic. No matter how large the group becomes the borrower is under an ongoing obligation to maintain the same minimum level of guarantor coverage. They also have the benefit of allowing insignificant companies to fall outside the guarantor package and thus permitting simplification of the documentation process to a certain degree.

Agreed security principles

13.12 The second type of provision that is also usually included in the senior facilities agreement (and mezzanine facility agreement) is designed to further delineate the scope of the guarantee and security package. There are two forms of the provision, one short form and one long form.

The short form version typically provides that group companies are not required to comply with the obligation to provide a guarantee and security in certain specified circumstances, and is usually worded so that compliance is not required *to the extent that* the circumstances apply, so the provision is not of an absolute or binary effect.

The exceptions can be worded in a number of ways but the usual stated exceptions include where compliance would:

- be prohibited by statute or otherwise unlawful;

- be beyond the corporate powers of the company (but only if those powers cannot be modified);

- result in a material adverse tax consequence for the company or the group; or

- result in costs to the group that are disproportionately high in comparison with the benefits to the acquisition financiers of compliance.

The longer form version includes a more detailed and prescriptive set of principles that apply to the taking of guarantees and security. As with the short form versions the provision will acknowledge the legal and practical difficulties in obtaining full guarantees and security from group companies and provide for exceptions of the sort indicated above in respect of the short form version, but in greater detail.

In addition, the principles set out in the longer form version will consider the extent of the security to be granted over different categories of assets. So, for instance, the provision will commonly stipulate that security over bank accounts may be subject to the prior interests of the account bank, since to require otherwise will often have a material impact on the security provider's ability to operate the business. The principles will also specify when notice of the security may be given to third parties for security perfection purposes and whether an acknowledgement from the third-party is required. For most if not all categories of assets it will be a requirement that the security documents are drafted in such a way that it is clear that the company can continue to use those assets in the normal course of its business, at least until an event of default is declared.

Generally the longer form versions should operate to reduce the level of negotiation that is required in respect of individual security documents. At the same time the principles should prescribe a uniformity of approach across all relevant jurisdictions. This streamlines the documentation process but it also ensures that if the security documents are ever required to be invoked in an enforcement scenario there is consistency between the equivalent operative provisions in each of the documents.

Given the general applicability of the agreed security principles it is important that the parties agree them early in the documentation process and certainly in advance of negotiating individual security documents.

Accessing target group cashflows

13.13   It is of pivotal importance to a buy-out structure that the cash generated by the target business is available to the borrowers to enable them to service the debt borrowed by them. Given that the acquisition finance will largely, if not wholly, be borrowed by newco this will mean that the target group operating companies are required to upstream cash to newco. The three principal ways in which this can be achieved are dividends, intercompany loans or in satisfaction of management fees charged by newco to the target companies. In the United Kingdom, all of these options are available to varying degrees, although the most practical and effective, and thus the most commonly used, method is the making of upstream loans. As the law stands at the time of writing,[11] the making of upstream loans to service acquisition finance debt is unlawful financial assistance in the UK unless it is 'whitewashed' from the outset. In practice this means whitewashing the upstream loan documentation at the same time that any upstream guarantees and security are whitewashed, usually at completion of the acquisition.[12]

Under the laws of certain other European jurisdictions,[13] however, the granting of upstream loans to newco – to enable it to service its acquisition debt – by a company owned by newco would be unavoidably unlawful. In these circumstances cash generated by such a company would almost certainly need to be dividended to newco. In most jurisdictions, including the United Kingdom, however, dividends may only be made out of distributable profits. As a result, unless a company is both profitable and cash generative, the cash generated by that company may become 'trapped' in the target group. The charging of management fees is rarely of material assistance because corporate benefit/abuse of assets laws generally restrict the amount of any fee to an amount commensurate with the value of the management services provided (determined on a reasonable basis).

The difficulty of upstreaming cash to newco is one more reason why pushing the debt down into the operating companies is a great benefit in many multi-jurisdictional deals as the cash can then be used to meet the finance costs without the need to be upstreamed.

As mentioned further below, another implication of the need to upstream cash by way of dividend is the possibility that withholding tax may be levied on the divided payment if it is made to a company in another jurisdiction.

Whatever the solution in any given scenario, it is of key importance that the sponsor's advisers (both tax and legal) address the issues as early as possible in the structuring process. They should obtain the input of the acquisition financiers' advisers at an early stage too, since the acquisition financiers are as much concerned with the accessing of target group cash flows as the borrowers are themselves.

---

11 This is scheduled to change on 1 October 2008, however, when the legislation prohibiting financial assistance by private companies is to be repealed, pursuant to legislation to be enacted under the Companies Act 2006. See also para **13.4** and fn **1**.

12 Certain legal commentators take a more conservative view, whereby a whitewash must be carried out each time any cash is to be upstreamed. The scope of this book does not extend to rehearsing the legal arguments of either view.

13 It is beyond the intended scope of this book to summarise the financial assistance or other laws of other jurisdictions. Advice should invariably be taken of lawyers appropriately qualified in the relevant jurisdictions.

Tax deductibility of interest costs

13.14   A UK SPV can, in very broad terms, deduct the interest costs it incurs in respect of its third-party acquisition finance borrowings from its profits before tax. Although newco, as a non-operating company, has no profits of its own against which the interest cost can be deducted for tax purposes, where it and the target group constitute a 'group' for UK tax purposes, newco's interest costs can be deducted from the taxable profits of the target group.[14] However, where the target group includes entities in other jurisdictions, it may not be possible to consolidate their profits with newco's interest expenses for tax purposes. Inevitably, this will need careful consideration at the time of structuring the debt facilities.

This is the principal reason why, in a multi-jurisdictional buy-out, one of the first advisers to be appointed during the earliest stages of the process will be the deal sponsor's tax advisers. Their brief will be to devise a structure for the acquisition (incorporating the various elements of the funding structure) which provides the most favourable tax position for the group following completion. More particularly, this usually means devising a structure that has the lowest overall effective tax rate for the group. In addition, the sponsor may take the opportunity to create a structure that optimises the tax treatment of its investment upon exit.

In a multi-jurisdictional buy-out there will often be tax efficiencies to be gained by arranging the corporate structure of the group, and the allocation of debt across the group, in a particular way. This may be because by structuring the group or the debt in a certain way a tax benefit accrues in more than one jurisdiction or it may simply be that the tax laws of one or more jurisdictions mitigate towards a particular funding and corporate structure. As already indicated for example, it may be necessary to push debt down from the SPVs into the target group operating companies in order to achieve deductibility, for tax purposes, of the interest accruing on the acquisition debt against the operating profits of the group. Moreover, by pushing debt down into target group companies in those jurisdictions with the highest rates of tax it should be possible to achieve the highest tax savings. Pushing debt down into target group companies will in most instances have the added benefit of ensuring that security can be taken by the acquisition financiers over the assets of those companies. However, whilst the two aims may not wholly contradict each other, it is also possible that the structure that is the most tax efficient for the group may not be the structure that provides the best overall guarantee and security package for the acquisition financiers. With that in mind, the advisers to the acquisition financiers will need to shadow closely the tax structuring process to try to ensure that a balance is achieved between the interests of the sponsor in achieving the best tax structure for the group, or for the sponsor upon exit, and the interests of the acquisition financiers in getting good upstream credit support. In many cases, small changes to the structure that might have no adverse tax implications might significantly improve the acquisition financiers' position.

---

14 This assumes compliance with the UK Inland Revenue rules covering group relief.

Withholding tax

13.15   A multi-jurisdictional buy-out will generally involve cross-border payments. Certain payments and, in particular, interest payments on bank debt and dividends of profits may be the subject of a withholding tax by the taxation authority in the jurisdiction of the payer. In many cases the countries where the payer and the payee respectively are resident for tax purposes will have entered into a double-tax treaty which provides for the rate of withholding tax to be reduced (often to zero).[15] Where a double-tax treaty does *not* exist, or does not reduce the rate of the withholding to zero, the payment that is subject to the withholding will effectively be reduced and an amount will be payable to the taxing authority. In order to deal with the situation where a double-tax treaty does not exist or where it does not reduce the tax to zero, the acquisition finance documents generally include a provision whereby any payment subject to withholding tax is increased by such an amount that will, once the withholding is applied, leave the payee (a lender) with the same amount it would have received had no withholding been levied. Such provisions are call tax 'gross-up' clauses.

In practice, most gross-up clauses in respect of interest payments are only made available to lenders that are at the outset of the transaction entitled to receive interest gross. In other words, only a subsequent change of law resulting in a withholding would result in the gross-up applying.

In any event, the fact that a payment must be grossed up does not necessarily mean that the additional payment is a permanent cost for the borrower. Depending on the tax rules in the jurisdiction of the recipient lenders, a tax credit may be awarded to the lenders in respect of the tax withheld which the lenders may, to some extent, be able to reclaim or set against their profits in due course. Most tax gross-up provisions will contemplate this possibility and require the lender to pass any benefit obtained back to the borrower. These provisions may also, to varying degrees, oblige the lenders to claim the tax credit and maximise the use of it. Even in these circumstances, however, the process of the borrower grossing-up and the lender claiming a tax credit for the withheld tax and passing the benefit to the borrower does have a cash flow impact for the borrower.

In situations where interest payments may be subject to a withholding tax the parties may also look for a structuring solution to mitigate the risk of a gross-up being required. This is usually a problem with foreign banks lending otherwise than through a local branch to borrowers in jurisdictions which do not have many tax treaties which provide for nil withholding tax on interest payments to non-residents (eg, Italy). One structure that has been used successfully in several transactions is a so-called 'IBLOR' structure.[16] IBLOR structures operate by ensuring that the cross-border payment is not an interest payment that attracts withholding tax. The structure usually involves the syndicate banks that are to

---

15   Although, even where there is a treaty a number of procedural steps will still need to be taken in order to obtain the relief.

16   IBLOR structures were first used for Italian borrowers and the acronym originally stood for 'Italian bank lender of record'. Since they can also be used for other countries 'international bank lender of record' may also be used.

benefit from the structure depositing cash with a conduit bank either resident or lending through a branch in the jurisdiction of the borrower. That conduit bank lends to the borrower and receives interest from the borrower free of withholding tax. The conduit bank then makes payments to the syndicate banks without withholding tax through a combination of guarantee fees and interest on their deposit (on the basis that such interest often does not suffer withholding tax). This is not the only structure that has been successfully used, however, and up to date tax structuring advice should always be sought in practice.

Enforceability of subordination provisions

13.16   In the vast majority of buy-outs the funding structure will incorporate two or more layers of debt. As discussed in detail elsewhere, the various layers of finance are ranked to reflect the pre-agreed order of priority for realising both the capital invested and the yield on the respective investments.[17] In order to preserve the agreed order of priorities between the various investments, subordination principles are applied and various legal and contractual mechanisms are used. The senior debt will not itself be subject to any subordination but any junior debt, any equity investor debt and generally the intercompany debt owing between companies in the group itself, will all be required to be subordinated to the senior debt and, in each case amongst such instruments, any other higher ranking debt.

There are four primary means of achieving subordination, each considered in detail in **Chapter 10**:

- in most jurisdictions share capital is subordinated to debt as a matter of law;

- structural subordination of one layer of debt to another;

- unsecured debt ranks behind secured debt; and

- contractual subordination of one layer of debt to another.

In a UK buy-out all four of these concepts can be relied upon to be applied effectively in a buy-out. There are legal issues that need to be properly addressed but the legal principles underpinning the various types of subordination have all been successfully tested and enforced by the UK courts. This means that the parties have a high level of legal certainty that the pre-agreed order of priorities will be respected by the courts in any dispute or attack by third-party creditors or liquidators.

Such a high level of certainty does not exist in all jurisdictions. In a number of jurisdictions the most fundamental and practically important principle, that one creditor of a company can agree to subordinate its claims in the insolvency of that company to another creditor, has not been tested in court with a sufficient degree of certainty. This may mean that a senior debt provider is unable to rely, to a satisfactory degree, upon the contractual subordination provisions in an

---

17 See **Chapter 10** in particular.

intercreditor agreement in an insolvency situation. In theory this concern will be acute where, because of other legal restrictions,[18] only limited asset security is available to the acquisition financiers, meaning that they end up relying on unsecured claims rather than the security package.

In practice, however, in most of Europe at least, little reliance will be placed on the making of unsecured claims into the target group in any insolvency scenario. Instead the acquisition financiers will rely upon enforcing their share security over the target group in order to sell the target business as a going concern. As a result, the main concern shifts from the enforcement of contractual subordination of claims by competing creditors in the target group to another standard provision in the intercreditor agreement, the subordinated claim release mechanism.

A subordinated claim (or guarantee) release mechanism is used in intercreditor agreements to enable a prior ranking secured creditor to enforce its security without concern for the claims (usually subordinated guarantees) of any subordinated creditors. It generally works by automatically effecting a release of the subordinated claims. Sometimes there are conditions relating to the manner of enforcement by the prior ranking creditor that need to be satisfied, such as a requirement that the prior ranking creditor enforces its security and achieves fair market value from the proceeds of the enforcement or enforces through an open or public auction of the assets in issue.[19] But essentially the prior ranking creditor can rely on the release mechanism to ensure that it can effect a clean sale of the target business free from the claims of the junior ranking creditors. It follows that the guarantee release mechanism needs to be legally watertight in each relevant jurisdiction. This, as with contractual subordination, should not be taken for granted, and if the provision proves to be unenforceable the security package of the senior lenders will be materially compromised. In circumstances where there is insufficient legal certainty on the enforceability of this provision, as with the contractual subordination clause, the senior lenders might be well advised to consider applying strict structural subordination to all junior ranking debt.

There are other related legal principles that underpin the finance documentation used in buy-outs, the enforceability of which can largely be taken for granted in the United Kingdom, to which this same level of analysis must be applied. These include the enforceability of waivers of rights of subrogation by guarantors (particularly against subsidiary company borrowers that are disposed of in an enforcement scenario), the enforceability of second ranking security and the enforceability of 'turn-over' provisions,[20] to name just a few. In practice, the obtaining of legal opinions from lawyers in each relevant jurisdiction will assist in flushing out any issues during the documentation phase. It follows that it is good practice for the acquisition financiers to seek drafts of the opinions at the very outset of the process rather than towards the end, by which time it may be more difficult to take remedial steps in the structuring of the documentation.

---

18 Particularly, corporate benefit and financial assistance. See para **13.4**.
19 The laws of some jurisdictions require public auctions to be held for the disposal of assets by way of security enforcement.
20 Turn-over provisions are considered in **Chapter 10**.

Working capital requirements

13.17   In most buy-outs the target business will have an ongoing requirement for working capital finance. To some extent cash generated in the group may be distributed to those companies with a net working capital requirement. However, this rarely provides a total solution and a dedicated working capital facility will need to be made available to certain companies. This is traditionally provided by the senior lenders and forms part of the senior debt. Where the target group has operations in more than one jurisdiction there are likely to be working capital requirements in a number of these jurisdictions, often in the relevant local currency.

In practice, working capital requirements fall into three broad categories: cash loans, guarantees and letters of credit, and commercial banking facilities, including overdrafts. Commercial banking facilities will normally need to be made available by a bank in the jurisdiction of the company with the working capital requirement and they are often referred to as the 'local' working capital requirements. Cash loans and guarantees and letters of credit by contrast can generally be provided centrally through the senior debt syndicate.

In standard European buy-out loan documentation the commercial banking facilities fall into the category of 'ancillary facilities' and their documentation is considered further in **Chapter 5**. Ancillary facilities are generally structured so that they also fall within the senior debt package, in which case, provided that the senior debt syndicate includes banks with operations in all relevant jurisdictions, all of the working capital requirements of the group can be sourced through the senior debt syndicate.[21] However, in circumstances where this is not the case, alternative arrangements must be made to meet the local working capital requirements of the relevant members of the group.

One option is for the local facilities to be made available by a bank outside of the senior debt syndicate. This option may not always be available to the borrowers, however, as the acquisition financiers may not be willing to allow a third-party bank that is not subject to the collective voting and intercreditor arrangements set out in the acquisition finance documents to be a creditor of the group. There will at the very least be limits on the amount of working capital debt that can be financed this way.[22] In addition, it is most unlikely that the acquisition financiers would permit such a third-party bank to take security for the facilities made available by it as this reduces the security available to them in an enforcement scenario. This may in turn rule out the third-party bank, which may be reluctant to lend on an unsecured basis. In any event, where this arrangement is permitted and used and a bank that is not in the senior debt syndicate *does* provide local working capital facilities, it would be common practice for the available amount of the core working capital facility to be reduced by the amount of the local facilities since they would, by implication, no longer be required under the core facility.

---

21   There may be a timing issue with this given that syndication of the senior debt usually occurs after completion of the acquisition. This may mean having a transitional arrangement with the group's existing banks.

22   The acquisition finance documents limit such debt through negative undertakings.

An alternative approach is for a third-party local bank to provide the ancillary facilities but on the basis that it receives a guarantee issued under the core working capital facility made available by the senior debt syndicate. This should give the local bank comfort as to credit risk but it also means that the total amount of working capital made available to the group is no more than the total amount of the core working capital facility, since the guarantee will constitute a utilisation of that facility. This also generates a return for the senior lenders on the amount of the guarantee issued.[23]

Exchange rate exposure

13.18 In a multi-jurisdictional buy-out, the cash revenues of the target business may be in more than one currency. In that case, unless the acquisition finance debt is also outstanding in the same currencies – and in broadly the same proportions as the cash generated by the target business – a potential exchange rate exposure will arise for the target business. This is because movements in exchange rates might affect the extent to which the borrowers have enough cash in the right currencies to meet their payment obligations to the acquisition financiers. The position will be complicated further where there are multiple borrowers, each with its own currency exposures. Each borrower will need to hedge its exposure. In practice, to the extent that a particular borrower has access to the cashflows of the other group companies through loans or dividends, the position of that borrower may be mitigated to some extent.

The simplest mitigant to this potential problem is for the acquisition finance debt to be borrowed in currencies and proportions which match the cashflows of the target business.[24] This will often happen naturally to some extent by having the target group companies that have debt at completion refinance their existing debt directly from the new facilities, since that debt will often be denominated in currencies that already match the target group's cashflows. The same applies to the target group's working capital facilities provided by the senior debt providers, which will generally match the relevant target companies' cashflows. Having the debt denominated in currencies that match the group's cashflows is often called a 'natural hedge' and it is the most commonly used method of limiting exchange rate exposure. At the newco level, however, where the core acquisition debt is borrowed, a mis-match may occur. This is because the seller will generally wish to be paid the sale consideration as a fixed amount in a single specified currency; it will not be concerned as to the denomination and mix of the target's underlying cash flows. Therefore, to meet the seller's requirements and to have the acquisition finance debt match the underlying cash flows, newco will need to borrow the acquisition debt in the currencies it needs to match the underlying cashflows and then to immediately enter into a foreign exchange transac-

---

23 As a result, this alternative has a cost implication for the borrower, as it will be paying two lots of margin. The margin payable to the local bank should, however, be relatively small given the bank guarantee given in support of the local facilities.

24 Through the use of a multi-currency facility.

tion at completion. It will exchange the cash borrowed in other currencies into the currency required by the seller.[25]

An alternative to the natural hedge is for the group to enter into foreign exchange hedging arrangements in order to limit exposure to future exchange rate movements between the relevant currencies. This may or may not entail a cost for the borrowers.

25 In Europe the adoption of the euro across most of Europe's largest economies has reduced the impact of this concern in practice.

Index

[all references are to paragraph number]

A

Acceleration and enforcement rights
deemed consent, 10.20
default triggers, 10.18
equity investor debt, and, 10.122
high yield debt, and, 10.87
mezzanine debt, and, 10.71
override, 10.20
PIK note debt, and, 10.107
second lien debt, and, 10.56
seller loan capital, and, 10.136
senior debt, and, 10.43
standstills, 10.19

Acceptance condition
importance, 12.117
threshold, 12.137
variation, 12.118

Accountants
covenant compliance report, 11.14
due diligence, 11.7
financial assistance 'whitewash', 11.11
post-completion auditors, 11.12–11.13
recourse against, 11.8–11.9
reliance wording, 11.10

Accountants' report
due diligence, and, 11.56

Accounting due diligence
generally, 1.104

Acquisition agreements
assignability, 2.31
business continuity, 2.26
business transfer agreement, 2.18
commercial deal, 2.24
completion conditions, 2.25
introduction, 2.16
review
  business continuity, 2.26
  commercial deal, 2.24
  completion conditions, 2.25
  introduction, 2.23
  seller protection provisions, 2.29

Acquisition agreements – *contd*
review – *contd*
  seller status, 2.30
  seller warranties and indemnities, 2.28
  transitional services, 2.27
seller protection provisions
  de minimis amounts, 2.43
  disclosure, 2.46
  double recovery, 2.45
  generally, 2.40
  introduction, 2.29
  knowledge qualification, 2.44
  liability cap, 2.42
  time periods, 2.41
seller status
  bank guarantee, 2.48
  generally, 2.47
  introduction, 2.30
  parent company guarantee, 2.48
  purchase price retention, 2.49
seller warranties and indemnities
  due diligence, 2.33
  generally, 2.32
  insurance, 2.38
  introduction, 2.28
  management buy-outs, 2.36
  representations in finance documents, 2.39
  secondary buy-outs, 2.37
  short form summary, 2.35
  standard warranties, 2.34
share sale and purchase agreement, 2.17
transitional services, 2.27

Acquisition documentation
acquisition agreements
  assignability, 2.31
  business continuity, 2.26
  business transfer agreement, 2.18
  commercial deal, 2.24
  completion conditions, 2.25
  introduction, 2.16

68000 Machine Code Programming

David Barrow

COLLINS
8 Grafton Street, London W1

Collins Professional and Technical Books
William Collins Sons & Co. Ltd
8 Grafton Street, London W1X 3LA

First published in Great Britain by
Collins Professional and Technical Books 1985

Distributed in the United States of America
by Sheridan House, Inc.

British Library Cataloguing in Publication Data
Barrow, David
68000 machine code programming.
1. Motorola 68000 (Microprocessor)——Programming
2. Machine codes (Electronic computers)
I. Title
001.64′24   QA76.8.M67
ISBN 0–00–383163–9

Typeset by V & M Graphics Ltd, Aylesbury, Bucks
Printed and bound in Great Britain by
Mackays of Chatham, Kent

Contents